Date Due

10-26-70	6¢ Paid	
12-27-71		

Code 436-279, CLS-4, Broadman Supplies, Nashville, Tenn., Printed in U.S.A.

1200
NOTES QUOTES AND ANECDOTES

1200
NOTES QUOTES
AND ANECDOTES

A. NAISMITH, M.A.

1449

MOODY PRESS

CHICAGO

This edition is issued by
special arrangement with
PICKERING & INGLIS LTD.
the British publishers

Made and Printed in Great Britain

PREFACE

FOR the last forty-five years I have been collecting the quotations and illustrations which I now publish in the hope that they may prove useful to many who, like myself, are engaged in the ministry of the good Word of God. The notebook in which these 'notes, quotes and anecdotes' were written or pasted, under alphabetically-arranged subject titles, by bulging and breaking its binding, has been urging me for some time to put them into a more permanent form and make them available to a larger number of people. Indeed, to myself it will be a great advantage to have a printed book with selected illustrations and quotations to carry around instead of the dilapidated notebook in which they were brought together.

Often a quotation or an illustration gives permanence to an important point in a message from God that would otherwise be missed or soon forgotten. Some of the illustrations have been used in our Telugu Conventions in Andhra Pradesh, India, to convey vital truth to the large number of God's people there in a way they can better understand. Again and again, after giving a message in English, I have had requests for copies of poems quoted in the address.

Without windows, a house, however carefully planned and solidly constructed, will be very dull and drab, very hard and bleak. Likewise a sermon without quotes or anecdotes, however sound and instructive, may lack the essential element of interest. With too many windows, on the other hand, the structure develops into something like a glass house at which every naughty person wants to throw stones. It lacks body and solidity. When the preacher arrives at his 'anecdotage', it is an indication that the swing of the pendulum has reached this other extreme.

In a chapter on the structure of a sermon, Alfred P. Gibbs recommends the use of an illustration, or story, that will serve to throw light on the text itself, or some incident in one's own experience, in which the text figures prominently. Recognizing the wisdom of this counsel, I have given, after most of the quotations and illustrations, several Scriptural references on which they may have some bearing. In preaching to the Jews the apostles made frequent quotations from their Scriptures, and Paul, when proclaiming the Gospel to the Gentile Athenians, quoted from their own poets. In his book on 'Public Speaking', Dale Carnegie suggests that an appropriate verse of poetry will add beauty, individuality and dignity to the close of an address.

This volume is just a collection of 1,200 items that the author has found useful in his own oral ministry. They are arranged alphabetically. The index of Scripture texts will, it is hoped, prove useful to some who may be searching for an apt quotation or illustration for the subject or text they have chosen. The index of subjects may assist in the location of a poetical or prose quotation, or a story already partly known. Wherever possible, the name of the author or originator of an item has been given.

Very gratefully indeed do I acknowledge my indebtedness to my friend, James Hislop, M.A., B.Sc., Rector of Grove Academy, Broughty Ferry, for his careful and painstaking perusal and correction of my typescript, and for his encouraging 'Foreword' to this volume of 'Notes, quotes and anecdotes'.

FOREWORD

MORE than forty years of Christian experience as teacher, headmaster, preacher and missionary in this country and, more particularly, in India have surely given the author of this book the right to be heard in a sphere wherein he has excelled.

The tens of thousands, who have been privileged to hear his oral ministry, will agree that in Mr. Naismith we have an artist in words, one who has always been a lover of the 'mot juste,' the apt quotation and the graphic illustration. Here and there, as a main theme is being pursued, it almost seems as if 'handfuls of purpose' are being dropped, so fruitful are the 'notes' in his asides. Something hard to be understood, darkness to the mind and heart, is suddenly lit up becoming warm in the process as some 'anecdote' is quietly introduced. And few messages are ever really complete without his peroration being rounded off with a 'quote'.

> '*Can you count me the leaves on the forest trees*
> *Or the sand on the sea-washed shore?——*'

is just one of those many striking quotations which, for me, spells out Archie Naismith of India.

Preachers, young and old, will find herein such material as will bring sparkle, warmth and life to their messages. Ordinary believers will not fail to be refreshed in quiet meditation on what is written in this book. Many will find comfort, fresh hope and new courage to hold on in the Christian way.

Mr. Naismith has arranged his material with great care choosing with delicacy what is of spiritual value, and has given us a veritable treasury wherewith to enrich the soul.

J. HISLOP

1. **Abraham.** Is thrice called the 'friend of God' (2 Chron. 20. 7; James 2. 23). His outstanding faith is the theme of Romans Chapter 4—verse 11 the sign or seal of faith, that made his faith Prospective: verse 12 his steps of faith, showing that his faith was Progressive: verse 16 the seed of faith, which proves that faith is Productive: verse 20 the strength of his faith, for it was also Persuasive.

Abraham's was the faith that justifies (Gen. 15. 6), that testifies (Gen. 12. 7, 8), that verifies (Gen. 12. 8), that multiplies (Gen. 13. 16; 15. 5) and the faith of enterprise (Heb. 11. 8).

'The annals of adventure have few tales to match the courage and daring of the man who, at the call of God in the Twentieth century B.C., left Mesopotamia and struck out across the desert with no compass but the stars and no guide but God. Abraham's secret was, of course, faith, but we should note that, while it was faith that made a Moses and a Muller and marked them out among their fellows, it is this very quality of faith which levels them all and proves that they were not supermen but men of like passions to ourselves. It is the fact of their faith that brings their glorious exploits within the range of possibility in our own puny lives.'

2. **Abundance.** Three similar expressions with almost identical meaning — huperperisseuō, huperperissōs, huper ek perissou—are used in the New Testament to signify 'abundance'. They are applied to—the grace of God (Rom. 5. 20), which Bishop Moule described as superabounding 'with that mighty overflow of the bright ocean of love', and to the energy of God on His people's behalf (Eph. 3. 20): while the Christian abounds in astonishment at the miraculous healing power of the Lord (Mark 7. 37), in joy (2 Cor. 7. 4) and in prayer (1 Thess. 3. 10).

Other Scriptures teach that the believer has abundance of grace (2 Cor. 9. 8), of life (John 10. 10), of hope (Rom. 15. 13), of love (Phil. 1. 9), of joy (Phil. 1. 26), of work (1 Cor. 15. 58) and of consolation (2 Cor. 1. 5).

3. **Access.** At the entrance to an Abbey in Yorkshire there are three steps near the chancel door, one of black marble—type of sin; one of red marble—picture of the blood of Jesus; and one of white marble—indicating cleansing by that precious blood.

1 John 1. 7; Heb. 10. 19)

4. **Adornment.** It is said that one of the early Christian fathers, seeing a woman of loose morals arrayed in rich apparel, was moved to tears and confessed that he had never taken such pains to adorn his soul with faith and godliness as she had taken to adorn her body to please the world.

(1 Tim. 2. 9, 10; 1 Pet. 3. 3.)

5. **Adversity—Blessings of.**
Ill that God blesses is our good:
    All unblest good is ill;
And all is right that seems most wrong
    If it be His blest will.
(Gen. 50. 20; Heb. 12. 11)

6. **Adversity—Brings out the best in the believer.** Just as torches burn most brightly when swung to and fro; just as the juniper plant smells sweetest when flung into the flames; so the richest qualities of a Christian often come out under the north wind of suffering and adversity. Bruised hearts often emit the fragrance God loves to smell.

—Selected

(Song of Songs 4. 16; 2 Cor. 4. 8-10; Heb. 12. 11)

7. **Adversity—For our Good.** Sir James Thornhill, a famous mosaic painter, was on one occasion painting in St. Paul's Cathedral, high up on a narrow scaffolding. Every now and then, engrossed in his work, he would step back for a better view. His servant, seeing his danger, hurled a pot of paint at the mosaic. Thornhill was at first very angry but realised that, by spoiling his painting, his servant had saved his life.

(Job 33. 14-24; Heb. 12. 11)

8. **Adversity—How to view.** 'Whenever I find myself in the cellar of affliction, I always look about for the wine,' said Samuel Rutherford. (Rom. 8. 28; Heb. 12. 11)

9. **Adversity—Misunderstood.**
Adversity misunderstood becomes a double curse:
Her chastening hand improves the good but
    makes the wicked worse.
Thus clay more obdurate becomes, to the fierce
    fire consign'd;
While gold in the red ordeal melts, but melts to
    be refined.

—C. C. Colton

(Heb. 3. 7-8, 15-16; 4. 7; 12. 5)

10. **Adversity—Sent in love.**
Is my gloom after all
Shade of His hand outstretched caressingly?

'Sometimes God sends His love letters in black-edged envelopes,' said Spurgeon. 'He allows us to taste the bitterness of want and the desolation of bereavement. If you have lived many years, you have passed through the narrows. We have all been there. It looks as if things have got out of hand, and somehow or other we have been forgotten. When there is no one at hand to say it to you, say it to yourself, "God is faithful, Who will not suffer the pain to exceed the measurement of my endurance".'

(1 Cor. 10. 13; Heb. 12. 6, 11)

11. Adversity—Uses of.

Sweet are the uses of adversity
Which, like the toad, ugly and venomous,
Wears yet a precious jewel in its head.
    —Shakespeare in *As You Like It*

(Eccl. 7. 14; Heb. 12. 11)

12. Adversity—Viewing it the right way.

It is not raining rain to me,
  It's raining daffodils;
In every dimpling drop I see
  Wild flowers upon the hills.
A cloud of grey engulfs the day
  And overwhelms the town,
It is not raining rain to me—
  It's raining roses down.

It is not raining rain to me,
  But fields of clover bloom,
Where any buccaneering bee
  Can find a home and room;
So a health to him that's happy
  And a fig for him that frets—
It is not raining rain to me,
  It's raining violets.

So when the cloud is o'er the day
  And everything seems wrong,
Just think of what I said to you
  And sing this little song;
God's love to me is just the same,
  And I must not forget
It is not raining rain to me,
  It's raining mignonette.

It is not raining rain to me,
  But waterfalls of flowers—
Before my inward sight's a sea
  Of green and shady bowers.
The wind and moisture sprays my face
  And sings among the trees:
It is not raining rain to me
  But hawthorn-scented leas.
    —Robert Loveman

(Gen. 9. 17; Heb. 12. 11)

13. Adversity—Wrong Way to view it.

The child sits at the window, looking out on the showers and flattening his nose against the pane, as he says:

'O you naughty little raindrops! How I wish
  you'd go away,
For you keep me in the schoolroom when I
  might be out at play.'

14. Advocate.

A lady received a summons to appear in court on a certain day at a certain hour to answer a charge brought against her. She knew she was guilty of the breach of law specified on the charge sheet, and knew also that it would be necessary to find a good lawyer to take up her case and defend her in court. One of her friends recommended an excellent advocate who, she was certain, could present the case for the defence so well that she would be acquitted. She decided to put her case into this lawyer's hands, took his address and put it carefully away. But days passed and she did nothing, thinking that 'tomorrow' would be all right. After weeks of procrastination, she realised that the date fixed for the hearing of her case was perilously near, and, finding the address of the advocate recommended to her, she went to his office. She gave him particulars of the case and a list of helpful witnesses, and asked him to be her advocate and conduct her defence. 'Madam,' he said, 'had you come last week, I should gladly have undertaken your defence, but only a day or two ago I was appointed judge, and shall have to sit in judgement on your case.' The Lord Jesus Christ, in virtue of His having paid sin's penalty on the cross, is the sinner's Advocate now. The day is drawing near when He will be the 'Judge of the quick and the dead'. (1 John 2. 1; Rom. 2. 16; 2 Tim. 4. 1; 2 Cor. 6. 2)

15. Afflictions.

The trials come, sore disappointments vex,
Life oft appals, and reason will perplex;
Friends change, forsake; misunderstandings rise;
The foolish ride in triumph o'er the wise.
Yet faith looks onward, mists will pass away;
The afterward will come, of perfect day.

So hard the sorrow, weariness and pain,
The sighs escape, the tears will flow again;
What murmuring, what weakness, what distress;
And doubts arise, grim fears the spirit press;
Then faith lays hold of promises so bright.
The afterward will come, morn follows night.
    —A. Gardner

16. Afflictions—Reward of.

Let thy gold be cast in the furnace,
  Thy red gold, precious and bright:
Do not fear the hungry fire, with
  Its caverns of burning light.
And thy gold shall return more precious,
  Free from every spot and stain:
For gold must be tried by fire, as
  A heart is tried by pain.

In the cruel fire of sorrow
  Cast thy heart—do not faint or wail:
Let thy hand be firm and steady,
  Do not let thy spirit quail.
But wait till the trial is over,
  And take thy heart again,
For as gold is tried with fire, so
  A heart must be tried by pain.

I shall know by the gleam and glitter
  Of the golden chain you wear,
By your heart's calm strength in loving,
  Of the fire you have had to bear,
Beat on, true heart, for ever:
  Shine bright, strong golden chain,
And bless the cleansing fire, and
  The furnace of living pain.
    —Selected

(Job 23. 10; Heb. 12. 11; 1 Pet. 1. 6, 7)

17. Afflictions—Reward of.

John Taylor Smith, who became the well-known Bishop Taylor Smith, when a student, had planned to attend the meetings of the Mildmay Conference, then at the height of its influence.

Just before the time, however, he injured his knee and had to go to bed. He felt led to turn to the Epistles as he lay in bed, and he began to read through the Epistle to the Romans. He received such a blessing at that time that he prayed in the simplicity of faith, 'Lord, if this be the result of a bruised knee, please give me a broken leg.'
(Ps. 119. 67)

18. **Agnostic—Challenged.** At a meeting once, where Col. Robert Ingersoll and Henry Ward Beecher were present, the noted agnostic, Col. Ingersoll, had spoken at some length and put forth brilliantly his agnostic views. It was expected by those present that Beecher would have replied to those attacks and defended Christianity, but the old man said not a word. At last Col. Ingersoll remarked, 'Mr. Beecher, have you nothing to say on this question?' The old man slowly lifted himself and replied:

'Nothing: in fact, if you will excuse me for changing the conversation, I will say that while you gentlemen were talking, my mind was bent on a most deplorable spectacle which I witnessed today.'

'What was it?' at once inquired Col. Ingersoll who, notwithstanding his peculiar views of the hereafter, was noted for his kindness of heart.

'Why,' said Mr. Beecher, 'as I was walking down town today I saw a poor lame man with crutches, slowly and carefully picking his way through a cesspool of mud in the endeavour to cross the street. He had just reached the middle of the filth, when a big, burly ruffian, himself all bespattered, rushed up to him, jerked the crutches from under the unfortunate man, and left him sprawling and helpless in the mud.'

'What a brute he was,' said the Colonel. 'What a brute!' they all echoed.

'Yes,' said the old man, rising from his chair and brushing back his long white hair, while his eyes glittered with their old-time fire as he bent them on Ingersoll. 'Yes, Colonel Ingersoll, and you are the man. The human soul is lame, but Christianity gives it crutches to enable it to pass along the highway of life. It is your teaching that knocks these crutches from under it and leaves it a helpless and rudderless wreck in the slough of despond.

'If robbing the human soul of its only support on earth be your profession, why, ply it to your heart's content. It requires an architect to erect a building: an incendiary may reduce it to ashes.'

The old man sat down, and silence brooded over the scene. Col. Ingersoll said nothing, and the company took their hats and departed.

19. **Agnostic—Challenged.** Dr. H. A. Ironside was once walking up Market Street in San Francisco on a Sunday, and the Salvation Army was holding a meeting at the junction of Market Street and Grant Avenue. The captain, recognizing Dr. Ironside, asked him to give a message, and he gladly agreed. After the address a well-dressed gentleman stepped up to Dr. Ironside and handed him a card on which he had been writing. On one side was his name, Arthur Morrow Lewis, the well-known agnostic lecturer. On the other side he had written: 'Sir, I challenge you to debate with me the question, "Agnosticism versus Christianity", in the Academy of Sciences Hall next Sunday afternoon at 4 p.m. I will pay all expenses.'

Dr. Ironside read the card aloud and replied, 'Mr. Lewis, I already have an engagement for next Sunday at 3 o'clock, but, if necessary, I think I could cancel it. I am disposed to accept your challenge and will if it is really worthwhile. But in order to prove that you have something worth debating, I accept on these conditions: First, that you promise to bring with you to the platform next Sunday one man who was once an outcast, a slave to sinful habits, but who on some occasion heard you or some other infidel lecture on agnosticism, and was so helped by it that he cast away his sins, became a new man, and is today a respected member of society, all because of unbelief. Second, that you will also agree to bring with you one woman who was once lost to all purity and goodness, an abandoned female sunk in the depths of depravity, but who can now testify that agnosticism came to her while deep down in sin and implanted a new hatred of impurity in her poor heart, putting a new power into her life and delivering her from her base desires, and making her now a clean, chaste woman, all through disbelieving in God and the Bible. Now, sir, if you will agree to these conditions, I will promise to be there with one hundred men and women who were once just such lost souls as I have described but who heard the precious gospel of the grace of God, who believed it and ever since have hated sin and loved righteousness and have found new life and joy in Christ Jesus, the Saviour Whom you deny. Will you accept my terms?'

He shook his head and turned away while the crowd applauded. They knew that in all the annals of agnosticism no one ever heard of unbelief making bad people good, but the Bible has demonstrated its power in untold myriads of cases to turn men from sin to righteousness, from darkness to light and from the power of Satan to God.
(Acts 26. 18)

20. **Agnostic—Converted.** George Muller of Bristol went one day to preach in the Free Assembly Hall, Edinburgh, and the place was packed to overflowing. A well-known agnostic, inspired by curiosity, pressed his way into the hall. Just when the preacher began to deliver his address, a young mother attempted to leave the building because her baby began to cry rather loudly, but the crowd was so great that exit was impossible. Mr. Muller came at once to the troubled mother's help by saying: 'Will that dear mother sit down, and we shall ask Jesus to put baby to sleep.'

The mother quietly took her seat, and the

great assembly reverently bowed their heads while Mr. Muller prayed as follows: 'Blessed Lord Jesus Christ, be pleased to put this baby to sleep.' Immediately the child went to sleep, to the evident astonishment of the audience. The agnostic was startled beyond measure and said to himself, 'If that man has a God like that, it is time for me to seek Him': and under the power of the Holy Spirit he sought and found George Muller's God. He became a true Christian and an earnest advocate of the faith he so long tried to destroy, and God used him in winning many souls to Christ. When his work was finished, he fell asleep in Jesus in a hospital in Edinburgh.
(1 Thess. 1. 9; 1 John 4. 8)

21. **Alexander the Great.** Alexander, when he had taken Gaza, made haste to go up to Jerusalem; and Jaddua the high priest, when he heard that, was in an agony—not knowing how he should meet the Macedonians, since the king was displeased at his foregoing disobedience. . . .

Alexander, when he saw the multitude at a distance, in white garments, while the priests stood clothed with fine linen, and the high priest in purple and scarlet clothing, with his mitre on his head, having the golden plate whereon the name of God was engraved, approached by himself and adored that name, and first saluted the high priest. The Jews also did altogether, with one voice, salute Alexander . . .

And when the book of Daniel was shown him, wherein Daniel declared that one of the Greeks should destroy the empire of the Persians, he supposed that himself was the person intended; and as he was then glad he dismissed the multitude for the present, but the next day he called them to him, and bade them ask what favours they pleased of him.
—Josephus—Antiquities of the Jews. Book XI, Ch. 8: Sections 4, 5.
(Dan. 7. 6; 8. 3-8, 20, 21, 22; 11. 3)

22. **Alexander the Great—His Ambitions.** After his world-wide conquests Alexander wept because there were no more worlds to conquer. He died, after a short life of debauchery, at the age of 32.
'A tub was large enough for Dionysius: a world was too little for Alexander.'
(1 Tim. 6. 8; Heb. 13. 5)

23. **All.** 'All we like sheep have gone astray; we have turned every one to his own way; and the Lord hath laid on him the iniquity of us all.' (Isa. 53. 6)
'Go in at the first all and come out at the last all.'—D. L. Moody.

> All thy sins were laid upon Him,
>   Jesus bore them on the tree,
> God, who knew them, laid them on Him,
>   And, believing, thou art free.
>   —J. Denham Smith

(1 Peter 2. 24)

24. **Allurements—Resisting.** When Ulysses was passing in his ship the island of the Sirens (sea-nymphs) he filled the ears of his seamen with wax so that they would not hear their music, and had himself bound to the mast so that he would not be tempted to yield to their attractions.
(Heb. 11. 24-27)

25. **Allurements—Satan's.** Rowland Hill began a sermon. 'The other day I saw a drove of pigs following a man. This excited my curiosity so much that I determined to follow. To my surprise I saw them follow him to the slaughter-house, so I said to the man, "My friend, how did you induce those pigs to follow you here?" "I had a basket of beans," said the man. "I dropped a few as I came along, and so they followed me for the beans"?'
(1 John 5. 19; 2. 15, 16; 2 Tim. 2. 26)

26. **Ambassadors.** W. D. Dunn, the evangelist, was holding a campaign of gospel meetings in a large hall in the town of Motherwell, Lanarkshire, Scotland, an industrial town about 10 miles from Glasgow. During the campaign a friend of his, Mr. Carr of Carlisle, died, and he was invited to attend the funeral. Carlisle is some 90 miles south of Motherwell and about 100 miles from Glasgow. Consulting his Bradshaw Time Table, he found that he could travel by express train to Carlisle on the morning of the day of the funeral, attend the funeral, and catch a train from Carlisle to Motherwell, arriving back in good time for his evening meeting. He decided to do this, attended the funeral, but arrived in Carlisle station a few minutes after his train for Motherwell had left. His Bradshaw showed that there was only an express train to Glasgow, non-stop in about an hour, and a slow train that stopped at Motherwell, but would be much too late for his meeting.

Approaching the Stationmaster, he asked if the express train to Glasgow could be stopped for a minute or two at Motherwell to enable him to alight and be in time for a very important meeting there. The Stationmaster said it could not be done. Lifting up his heart in prayer, the evangelist was turning away when the Stationmaster added: 'But are you a Member of Parliament? I have authority to have the train stopped for an M.P.' 'No,' replied Dunn, 'I am not an M.P.; but I hold a much higher rank. I am an ambassador.' 'An Ambassador,' said the Stationmaster. 'All right, I shall have the train stopped at Motherwell for you.' Mr. Dunn walked off, thanking him, but on further consideration he felt he ought to clarify his position to the Stationmaster, and so, going to him again, he said, 'I told you I was an ambassador, and that is true. But I am not an ambassador of an earthly king. I am an ambassador of the King of kings, and have a message from Him for over 1,000 people who will gather in Motherwell to hear it. Now I have told you frankly my position. Will the train still stop at Motherwell?' 'Yes,' replied the Stationmaster, 'I have arranged that it shall stop and it will stop without fail.'

The compartment into which the evangelist entered and sat down had only two other travellers, a man and his wife. 'That's the last stop now till Glasgow,' said the man to his wife, as the train left Carlisle station.

'Pardon me,' said W. D. Dunn, 'but the train is going to stop at Motherwell.' 'Well!' said the man, 'I have travelled often on this train, and it has never yet stopped at Motherwell. Why should it stop at Motherwell to-day?' 'Because,' said the evangelist, 'there's an ambassador on the train and he is going to alight there.'

Curious to see this ambassador, the couple got into the corridor and stood looking through the window, straining their eyes to see who this person might be. Only one passenger alighted, their fellow-traveller carrying his little brief bag. The King of kings runs the trains and takes care of His ambassadors.

(2 Cor. 5. 20)

27. Ambassadors—Their Service.

Thou hast no tongue, O Christ, as once of old,
To tell the story of Thy love divine;
The story, still as strange, as sweet, as true;
But there's no tongue to tell it out but mine.

Thou hast no hands, O Christ, as once of old,
To feed the multitudes with bread and wine;
Thou hast the living bread enough for all,
But there's no hand to give it out but mine.

Thou hast no feet, O Christ, as once of old,
To go where Thy lost sheep in desert pine;
Thy love is still as deep, as strong, as kind,
But now Thou hast no feet to go but mine.

And shall I use these ransomed powers of mine
For things that only minister to me?
Lord, take my tongue, my hands, my feet, my all,
And let them live, and give, and go, for Thee!

(Isa. 6. 8, 9; 2 Cor. 5. 20)

28. Ambition—The Christian's.

The Greek 'philotimeomai', to be ambitious, or, literally, to covet the honour, occurs three times in the New Testament, and is not once translated 'be ambitious' in the Authorised Version. The ambitions a true Christian should have are: To get on quietly with his own business—translated 'study' (1 Thess. 4. 11). To be well-pleasing to the Lord—translated 'labour' (2 Cor. 5. 9). To preach the gospel in places where Christ is not known—translated 'strive' (Rom. 15. 20).

29. Ambition—A Conqueror's.

Cineas, when dissuading Pyrrhus from undertaking a war against the Romans, said, 'Sir, when you have conquered them, what will you do next?'

'Sicily is near at hand and easy to master,' replied Pyrrhus.

'And what when you have conquered Sicily?' 'Then we will pass on to Africa and take Carthage.'

'When these are conquered, what will be your next attempt?' asked Cineas.

'Then,' said Pyrrhus, 'we will fall upon Greece and Macedon and recover what we have lost there.'

'Well, when all are subdued, what fruit do you expect from all your victories?'

'Then,' said Pyrrhus, 'we will sit down and enjoy ourselves.'

'Sir!' said Cineas, 'may we not do it now? Have you not already a kingdom of your own? He that cannot enjoy himself with a kingdom cannot with a whole world.'

(1 Tim. 6. 8; Heb. 13. 5)

30. Ambition—Unworthy.

Cardinal Wolsey, dying, charged Cromwell:

'I charge thee, Cromwell, fling away ambition:
By that sin fell the angels: how can man, then,
The image of his Maker, hope to gain by't?'
            —Shakespeare in *Henry VIII*

(Jude 6; Jer. 45. 5)

31. Amen.

I do not know what I was playing,
Or what I was dreaming then,
But I struck one chord of music
Like the sound of a great Amen.
            —A. A. Procter

'Amen' is a Hebrew word usually transliterated but sometimes translated. So it is a word found in all languages. Its meaning is—'So be it!' or 'So it is!' or 'Steadfast!' It is an expression of finality, though it sometimes comes at the beginning of a sentence. It occurs more in John's writings than in the writings of any of the other inspired writers.

Our Lord used 'Amen' 99 times. 9 is the number of finality. The Gematria of 'Amen' is 99. In the Old Testament Scriptures it is—the solemn response of Israel to the curses on the lawbreaker on Mount Ebal, the ready response of Israel to the worship of Jehovah at the return of the ark, the joyful response of the returned exiles at the reading of the Law, the fitting response of the Psalmist David to the praise of Jehovah, the cheerful response of Jeremiah to God's promise to overthrow the oppressor and deliver His people from captivity.

In the Gospel of St. John there are 25 double 'Amens'—translated 'Verily, verily'. The first is in John 1. 51 and the last in John 21. 8. The 'Amens' in John's writings may be classified as follows: the Amen of gracious affirmation (50 times in John's Gospel), the Amen of grateful adoration (Rev. 1. 6-7), the Amen of glorious annunciation (Rev. 3. 14), and the Amen of glad anticipation (Rev. 22. 20).

32. Amplius.

Michael Angelo, entering the studio of his pupil Raffaello and finding his style too cramped, drew a chalk line across it and wrote at the foot of the canvas the word 'Amplius'—broader, fuller, wider. That is God's perpetual word to us in relation to the filling of the Holy Spirit. We can never have

enough to satisfy His yearning desire. When we have apprehended most, there are always unexpected supplies in store ready to be drawn on.
—F. B. Meyer
(2 Kings 6. 1, 2; Ps. 119. 32; Matt. 5. 6; 2 Cor. 6. 11-13; Eph. 5. 18)

33. Anger. The Emperor Julius Caesar, when provoked, used to repeat the whole Roman alphabet before he permitted himself to speak.
(Jonah 4. 4; Eph. 4. 26)

34. Apostles—The Twelve.
Matthias was chosen in Jerusalem by lot in place of Judas Iscariot (Acts 1. 26). His symbol was a Book and axe.

Their sins He bore, 'mid cruelty and railing,
And then He rose,
O'ercame His foes,
And to Heav'n's worship was received again.

He now appears in Heav'n to intercede,
With incense-laden censer in His hand;
And wearing priestly mitre He doth plead
Our cause on high,
Each tear, each sigh,
Of His loved church, His own in every land.

He will appear in God's appointed time
To consummate salvation's peerless plan,
E'en so, dear Lord,
Fulfil Thy word,

Name	Other Names	Native Place	Occupation	Symbol
Simon	Peter, Cephas	Bethsaida	Fisherman	Keys
Andrew		Bethsaida	Fisherman	Cross shaped X
James	Boanerges	Bethsaida	Fisherman	Pilgrim's staff
John	Boanerges	Bethsaida	Fisherman	Chalice with serpent
James	Son of Alphaeus			Carpenter's saw
Jude	Thaddaeus, Lebbaeus			Carpenter's square
Philip		Bethsaida		Two loaves
Bartholomew	Nathanael	Cana, Galilee		Knife on book
Matthew	Levi	Capernaum	Taxgatherer	Money bags
Thomas	Didymus	Galilee		Spear and square
Simon	Zelotes	Galilee		Fish on hook
Judas	Iscariot	Kerioth, Judaea		Yellow shield

35. Apostles—Their call.
They have seen Him, they have heard Him.
He has bid them follow Him
From the mists of Judaism,
From the dispensation dim.
Light above the midday brightness
Of the sun in cloudless skies
Breaks from Him Who stands unveiled
As Son of God before their eyes.
Glory of the great Messiah,
Meekness, truth and righteousness;
Glory of the grace of God
To ruined sinners in distress.
(John 1. 36-51; Matt. 4. 18-22; Mark 1. 16-20; 2. 14)

36. Appearing—Loving His. Two small lads were left by their parents to look after the house for an hour or so while the parents attended a meeting. Being sweet-toothed, the boys soon found out where the sweets and confectionery were kept and began to help themselves, sparingly and cautiously at first, but with increasing boldness each successive time. Suddenly their parents appeared on the scene and caught them in the act of helping themselves.

Those lads loved their parents but they did not just then love their appearing.
(2 Tim. 4. 8; 1 John 2. 28)

37. Appearings—Christ's three.
He once appeared, His brightest glory veiling,
In lowly guise, among the sons of men;

For Thy appearing we the skies would scan.
And reign in righteousness in every clime.
—J. R. Rollo
(Heb. 9. 24-28)

38. Appointments—with God. Dr. Billy Graham, the much-used evangelist, was invited to dine with the Queen of Great Britain, Queen Elizabeth. In Holland he was invited to dine with the Queen of Holland. Rather than risk being late for such important appointments, he was in the vicinity at least 45 minutes before the appointed hour. Let us keep our important appointments with the Lord Jesus Christ, the King of kings, regularly and punctually!
(Dan. 6. 10; Luke 22. 14)

39. Approval—of God. A new ticket-collector had been appointed at a suburban railway station and commenced his duties during a severe spell of wintry weather. Being very conscientious, he insisted on all season tickets being produced as passengers passed through the gate of the station. His predecessor had got to know most of the regular passengers and allowed them to pass without asking them to show their season-tickets. After a few days, as the new ticket-collector continued to insist on all season tickets being shown, one of the travellers said to him one evening, 'You're not at all popular with the travelling public, sir.'

Pointing to the Station-Master's Office, the ticket-collector replied, 'I don't mind that. It's the man in there with whom I want to be popular; it's his approval that I desire.'
(Rom. 16. 10; 2 Cor. 5. 9; 2 Tim. 2. 15)

40. Assembly—Prayer at Gatherings of the Lord's People.

Lord, once again assembled in Thy Name,
Who ever art and will be still the same,
Do Thou, within our midst, Thyself proclaim.

Lord, Thou hast met with us in times gone by,
Now in Thy love and glorious power draw nigh,
Grant us the hearing ear, the seeing eye.

That which we see not, do Thou teach us, Lord,
Lead us to where the honey sweet is stored,
And on each gathered be Thy blessing poured.

Break Thou Thyself, O Christ, the heavenly bread,
Appoint who shall distribute in Thy stead,
So shall the multitude be amply fed.

Give us hinds' feet that we may climb and stand
In the high places of Thy promised land;
Held ever only by Thy strong right hand.

And may we from this Mount of God descend
To meet the duties which each path attend,
Resolved to serve Thee only to the end.

None empty, Lord, but each one fully filled,
Each thirsting quenched, each eager longing stilled—
Each willing for that which Thy love hath willed.
(1 Cor. 14. 26; Matt. 18. 20; 1 Thess. 4. 9)

41. Assurance—Full.
The Greek word 'Plerophoria', translated 'full assurance' occurs 4 times in the New Testament:

1 Thess. 1. 5   Full assurance of the gospel.
Heb. 10. 22   Full assurance of faith.
Col. 2. 2   Full assurance of understanding.
Heb. 6. 11   Full assurance of hope.

Illustration—The need arises for a missionary to go to a city a few thousand miles from where he is, and to get there as quickly as possible. A friend sends him the fare to travel by plane, tells him what to do, how to book, and where to embark, and promises to meet him at the airport at the other end. That is good news, and his friend's letter gives him full assurance of it. Acting on instructions given, he purchases his ticket, takes the bus to the airport and boards the plane, believing that in due time he will reach his destination. That is full assurance of faith. He has never travelled by plane before, and knows little or nothing about the pilot, controls or route. Near him sits another passenger who has provided himself with a map of the route and knows a good deal about the plane. He is friendly, shares his map and binoculars with the missionary, and explains the details of the flight so simply that the missionary is able to take it in. That is full assurance of understanding. His friend tells him when they are approaching his destination and the plane is about to land. So the missionary passes the time, hopeful that soon they will be there, and his friend who paid his fare will be at the landing stage to meet him. That is full assurance of hope. This hypothetical narrative illustrates the 'full assurance' God's pilgrims may have on their journey homewards to Heaven.

42. Assurance—of Unwavering Confidence.
Michael Faraday, the distinguished scientist, was asked by some of his students as he neared death, 'What are your speculations now?' He immediately replied: 'Speculations I have none. I'm resting on certainties.' Then he repeated slowly and deliberately, 'For I know whom I have believed, and am persuaded that He is able to keep that which I have committed unto him against that day.'
(2 Tim. 1. 12)

43. Atheism—Arguments against.
Why I believe in God:
1. The Teleological reason—Every effect must have an adequate cause.
2. The Ontological reason—There is an intuitive desire after God among all nations and tribes.
3. The Experiential reason—God's presence is felt and realised by millions of people.
4. The Apocalyptic reason—God has revealed Himself in His Word, His works and His ways.
(Gen. 1. 1; Heb. 1. 1; Ps. 14. 1; 53. 1)

44. Atheism—Cannot alter facts.
A sceptic once came to Dr. Bonar and said, 'I do not believe there is a God.' It was 10 p.m. and there was no time for argument. Dr. Bonar silently prayed and looked up with a happy face. 'Are you laughing at me?' asked the atheist. 'No!' replied Dr. Bonar, 'but I was thinking that if all the grasshoppers on earth said there was no sun, it would not alter the matter.'
(Ps. 14. 1; 53. 1; Rom. 1. 20)

45. Atheism—Creation's answer to.
Kepler, the astronomer, was troubled by one of his friends who denied the existence of God and took the view of the universe which prevails in some circles today, namely, that it came into being of itself by mechanical methods. Kepler, in order to convince his friend, constructed a model of the sun with the planets circling round it. When his friend came into the Observatory and saw the beautiful model, he exclaimed with delight, 'How beautiful it is! Who made it?' And Kepler carelessly answered, 'No one made it: it made itself.' His friend looked at him and said, 'Nonsense, tell me who made it.' Kepler then replied, 'Friend, you say that this little toy could not make itself. It is but a very weak imitation of this great universe which, I understood, you believe did make itself.'
(Gen. 1. 1)

46. Atheism—Creation's answer to.
An American cutlery manufacturer wrote: 'It

takes a girl in our factory two days to learn to put the 17 parts of a meat chopper together. It may be that these millions of worlds, all balanced so wonderfully in space—it may be they just happened: it may be, by a million of years of tumbling about, they finally arranged themselves. I don't know. I am merely a plain manufacturer of cutlery. But this I do know that you can shake the 17 parts of a meat chopper around in a washtub for the next 17 millions of years, and you'll never make a meat chopper.'
(Gen. 1. 1; Col. 1. 16, 17; Heb. 1. 2)

47. Atheism—Man's Nobility an answer to. 'They that destroy God destroy man's nobility, for certainly man is kin to the beasts by his body, and if he is not kin to God by his spirit, he is a base and ignoble creature. It destroys likewise magnanimity and the raising of human nature. For, take an example of a dog and mark what a generosity and courage he will put on when maintained by a man who to him is instead of God. So man, when he resteth and assureth himself upon Divine protection and favour, gathereth a force and faith which human nature in itself could not obtain.' — Francis, Lord Bacon
(Gen. 1. 26-28; 2. 7; 9. 6; 1 Thess. 5. 23)

48. Atheism—Men in danger abandon. During a prayer meeting, many years ago, Captain Nickerson, an American, rose and said:
'I remember when I was a sailor on board the *Heroine*, of Darien, Georgia, we were east of the Barbados, running under single-reefed topsails. It was a dog-watch, and a sailor named George and myself were on the watch on the top-gallant forecastle in the forward part of the ship. I was talking with him of my early life, and of the lessons of piety I had learned at home. He ridiculed the whole, and declared that there was no God, and that all this talk was mere moonshine.
'Eight bells rang and the watch was changed, the men being called away to pump ship. George took a bucket to get some water to "fetch" the pump, and as he flung it over the side of the vessel it caught the water, and, as we were going quite fast, George was dragged overboard. Instantly the cry was raised, "Man overboard". We were on the larboard tack; the mate shouted, "Hard-a starboard the wheel!" and the vessel came round and stood on the starboard tack. We could hear George crying in the darkness, "Save me! Save me! Save me"!
'We immediately launched a boat and hastened to his rescue. The night was dark and the sea rough. We pulled into the darkness and followed the sounds as well as we could, until we reached poor George struggling with the waves a quarter of a mile from the vessel. Being a good swimmer, he had kept himself free from sinking and before long we had him safe in his bunk as comfortable as we could make him.

'The next morning I said to George, "Did you think that the ship was going to leave you and that you were lost?"
"Yes, I did," said he.
"Now, George, be honest, what did you do then?"
"I prayed to God."
"But I thought you did not believe there was a God," said I.
'George replied very seriously, "When a man is overboard in a dark night and the ship is going away from him and he expects to die, a man thinks differently, and talks different from what he does when he is on the top-gallant foremast spinning yarns in safety."
'We heard no more infidelity from George.'
(Jonah 2. 9, 10)

49. Atheism—Nature's answer to.
  'There is a God,' all nature cries.
  I see it painted on the skies;
  I see it in the flowering spring,
  I hear it when the birdlings sing.
  I see it in the flowing main,
  I see it on the fruitful plain,
  I see it stamped on hail and snow,
  I see it where the streamlets flow;
  I see it in the clouds that soar,
  I hear it when the thunders roar;
  I see it when the morning shines,
  I see it when the day declines;
  I see it on the mountain height,
  I see it in the smallest mite,
  I see it everywhere abroad:
    I feel—I know—there is a God.
(Gen. 1. 1-31; Ps. 14. 1)

50. Atheist—Grave of an. Gerald B. Winrod, who was Editor of an American magazine, *The Defender*, related a remarkable story about an atheist who had been very bold, blatant and outspoken against God and the Bible. He had defied God by saying, 'If there is a God, my grave will be infested with snakes.' At the funeral it was necessary to remove a snake from the grave before the coffin could be lowered, the sexton saying that he had killed four big snakes at one time, yet never saw a snake at any other grave.
Mr. Winrod's informant said he would ask a gentleman in Ohio to give him more details, and in due course he received a further word, together with a picture of the bronze monument of the atheist, Chester Beddell, who had died in 1908 at the age of 82. The letter said, 'Mr. Beddell said while living there was no God, and he never did believe in one. He did not hesitate to speak of these things. . . . He built the monument years before his death. His statue is of bronze, and in his uplifted right hand there is a scroll with this inscription, "Universal Mental Liberty". Under his left foot is a scroll representing the Bible, with the inscription, "Superstition". Before his death he made this remark: "If there is a God, or any truth in the Bible, let my body be infested with snakes". Since his burial the family lot has been full of snake holes around the curbing.

Snakes can be seen any day you visit the graveyard. Last year twenty of us went out on the 30th October, and saw three snakes. The neighbours there say the more they kill, the thicker they seem to be.'

Later the opportunity came to Mr. Winrod to make an observation of his own. While engaged in a Conference in Youngstown, he was taken by car to North Benton. He asked an old man if he could tell him where the Beddell grave was. 'Sure, everybody around here knows where Chet Beddell was buried,' said the old-timer. 'You can't miss it—big monument in the graveyard. Looking for snakes?' Later, another man said, 'Well, if Beddell did ask for snakes, he sure got 'em.'

He and his companions came to the place in question where they saw the monument, the uplifted scroll, the other scroll under his foot, the stern bronze countenance. They approached the grave, camera in hand. Was it a hoax, or was it true? One of his companions was the first to see a snake. 'Look there,' he shouted. Yes! there it was. They walked round the grave and counted six snakes. His companion killed one. He photographed one. They also took other photographs. The sexton told them that he killed four that morning—he had killed as many as twenty snakes in a single day. Finally he said, 'I don't know, maybe the Lord did have something to do with it.'

It is a remarkable story, and only one of the many others that could be related of the danger of putting God out of the life.

—E. Matheson in *Gathered Gems*

(Ps. 14. 1; 53. 1)

51. Atonement. A certain man on the Malabar Coast of Southern India had enquired of various devotees and priests how he might make atonement for his sins. He was directed to drive iron spikes, sufficiently blunted, through his sandals and on those to walk about 480 miles to a place of pilgrimage. He undertook the journey and walked a long way but found no peace. One day, halting under a large banyan tree, he heard a Christian missionary preach on 'The blood of Jesus Christ—cleanseth from all sin'. He arose, threw off the torturing sandals, and cried aloud, 'This is what I want!' and from that day became a living witness.

(1 John 1. 7; 2 Cor. 5. 21; 1 John 2. 2)

52. Authority—Different from Power. In the Greek, the word for 'authority' is 'exousia'; for 'power' 'dunamis'.

A Government surveyor one day brought his theodolite along to a farm, called on the farmer and asked permission to set it up in a field nearby to take readings. Seeing the farmer's unwillingness to let him enter the field, he produced his papers and explained that he had Government authority for entering the field and could, on the same authority, go anywhere in the country to take necessary readings. Reluctantly the farmer opened the

barred gate and allowed him to enter and set up his survey table, but went to the other end of the field and let in the fiercest of his bulls. The surveyor was greatly alarmed at seeing the bull approach, and the farmer from the other side of the gate shouted to him, 'Show him your credentials: show him your authority'. The surveyor had the authority to enter but had not the power to resist the bull. The God-sent evangelist has both authority and power to fulfil his commission.

(Matt. 28. 18; Rom. 1. 16)

53. Avarice. In the ruins of Pompeii there was found a petrified woman who, instead of trying to flee from the city, had spent her time in gathering up her jewels. In one of the houses was found the skeleton of a man who, for the sake of sixty coins, a small plate and a saucepan of silver, had remained in his house till the street was half-filled with volcanic matter, then was trying to escape from the window.

(1 Tim. 6. 9, 10; James 5. 1-3)

54. Avarice. One summer afternoon a steamer, crowded with passengers, many of them miners from California, suddenly struck a submerged wreck as it sped down the Mississippi. In a moment her deck was a wild confusion. The boats were able to take off only one-fourth of the passengers: the rest, divesting themselves of their garments, succeeded in swimming to shore. Immediately after the last had quitted the vessel, a man appeared on deck. Seizing a spar, he leapt into the river but instantly sank like a stone. When his body was recovered, it was found that, while the other passengers were escaping, he had been rifling the miners' trunks, and round his waist he had fastened bags of gold. In a quarter of an hour he had amassed more than most men do in a lifetime; but he lost himself in an instant. 'Thou fool, this night thy soul shall be required of thee.'

—*The Dawn*

(Luke 12. 20; 1 Tim. 6. 10)

55. Axe-head—the Lost. The Hebrew word used in 2 Kings 6 for 'axe-head' is 'Barzel' which means a piece of iron. Barzillai, the man who brought provisions to King David in his need at the time of his rejection, means 'the man of iron', or 'the man of the axe-head'. There are five sections in the story of the lost axe-head in 2 Kings 6. 1-7:

1. Vs. 1, 2—Enlargement—'The place . . . is too strait for us'.
2. V. 3   —Encouragement—'Go ye' and 'I will go'.
3. V. 4   —Employment—Felling and building.
4. V. 5   —Embarrassment—'Alas, master, for it was borrowed'.
5. V. 7   —Empowerment—'he put his hand in and took it'.

The late Mr. Harold St. John, well-known minister of the Word of God, referring to the sceptic's objection to iron floating and

swimming, described his arrival at South-
ampton Docks to embark for North Africa.
Before him was a colossal mass of iron, the
ship on which he had booked his passage, and
he embarked on it. Soon the iron that had been
floating in the docks began to swim and in due
course he landed at the port for which he was
bound. On his return, having to make the
journey very speedily, he went to the airfield
where he saw another tremendous mass of
metal. When he went aboard, he found that
the metal could fly.

56. **Babylon—Fall of.** The sound of revelry
and mirth is in the royal palace, for there, in
the magnificent hall, Belshazzar has made a
feast to a thousand of his lords. Hundreds of
lamps, fed with perfumed oil and suspended
by chains of gold, illuminate the glittering
scene. On the embroidered couches recline
many of the beauties of the Babylonian court,
gracing with the charm of loveliness, if not of
modesty, the festive scene. The mirth is
boisterous; the loud blasphemy or obscenity
provokes the louder laugh, and the king is the
merriest reveller of all.

Amidst the drunken approbation of his
guests, the monarch commands to be brought
the sacred vessels of gold and silver which had
been plundered from Jehovah's temple in
Jerusalem. The vessels are filled with sparkling
wine, and, while the unhallowed lips of the
king, his princes and his ladies, inhale the
draught, the song of praise rises from a
thousand voices to the helpless gods of gold,
silver and stone.

But what has suddenly arrested the
monarch's loud laugh and thrown an ashy
paleness across his lately-flushed cheeks? See
how he trembles as he clutches at the table
for support, how his white lips quiver, and
how his eyes are starting from their sockets as
they stare upon the wall beside him! The
uproar of the board is hushed and every face
is turned to the spot. There, upon the alabaster
wall, in the full glare of the great central lamp,
is seen a cloudy hand. Slowly those ghostly
fingers move along and trace upon the polished
slab, in the sight of the paralysed throng,
mysterious characters, every letter distinctly
visible and flashing with coruscations of
ghastly light.

All through Belshazzar's reign there had
been a war between Babylon and the advancing
power of the Medes and Persians. This ancient
and mighty city was the only one that now
held out against the victorious arms of Cyrus
the Persian. Two years the siege of Babylon
had lasted, but such was the strength of the
city, so high and massive the walls, so impregnable the fortifications, so innumerable
the warriors, so abundant the supply of all
kinds of provisions, that no hope seemed to
exist that Cyrus would be able to effect an
entrance. The city was provisioned for twenty
years.

At length stratagem succeeded where force
had failed. Having learnt that a great festival
was approaching in which the Babylonians
were accustomed to devote the whole night to
revelry, Cyrus determined to surprise them in
the midst of their debaucheries. One of the
great works of Nebuchadnezzar had been the
construction of an artificial lake above the city
to receive the superfluous waters of the
Euphrates in the annual floods. This lake was
square, 52 miles every way and 55 feet deep,
so that it was capable of holding an immense
volume of water. Into this lake Cyrus determined to draw off the water of the Euphrates
and enter the city through the bed of the river.
In the evening of the eventful day he sent a
party of men to cut the dam that separated the
river from the lake. Some hours elapsed before
the river was sufficiently shrunk to be fordable.
About midnight the soldiers were able to
march in the diminished stream and entered
the city. In the neglect and disorder of the
festival the brazen gates that led to the streets
from the river had been left open, so that the
armies met with no impediment but marched
up into the streets. At the royal palace they
surprised the half-intoxicated guards and soon
dispatched them.

The king, trembling under the judgement
just pronounced upon himself and his kingdom,
heard the noise from within and commanded
some to see what it meant. No sooner was the
great gate opened than the victorious Persians
rushed in and took the palace, and the wretched
monarch was put to the sword.

—P. H. Gosse in *Sacred Streams*

(Isa. 45. 1-3; Dan. 5. 1-9; 25-31)

57. **Baca—and Berachah.** Baca is a valley
mentioned in Ps. 84. 6. 'Emek-baca' in Hebrew
means 'Valley of tears' and is the title of a
book describing the persecutions of the Jewish
people. In Ps. 84. 6 the psalmist gives the
names of two valleys: Baca, Weeping: and
Berachah, Blessings. The last clause translated
in the A.V.—'the rain filleth the pools' can also
mean—'the rain also covers it with blessings'.
Thus, for the pilgrim to Zion, Baca has become
Berachah; the vale of tears is changed into the
valley of blessing.

(Ps. 84. 6; 2 Chron. 20. 1-4, 21-26)

58. **Baptism.** Baptism is a symbol of death,
burial and resurrection with Christ. Some
years ago a Brahmin believer in the Lord Jesus
Christ was baptised in the Meeting-room,
Broadway, Madras. He came to the ceremony
wearing, as all Brahmins do, the 'Yagnopavita'
or sacred thread, hanging round his neck.
Immediately after his baptism, as he came out
of the water, he snapped the thread and threw
it into the water in which he had been
immersed, thereby signifying that the old life
as a Brahmin had come to an end and that he
would thenceforth 'walk in newness of life'
in Christ.

(Rom. 6. 3-6; Col. 2. 12)

59. Baptized for the dead. Some years ago the late W. E. Vine wrote an article for the 'Indian Christian' giving an interpretation of this difficult phrase in 1 Cor. 15. 29. He said:

'I submit the following as a solution to the interpretation of this verse, making clear that the reference is to the subject of baptism as elsewhere taught in the New Testament. It is needful to bear in mind that the original was written with scarcely any punctuation marks. Further, that in an argumentative passage like this the verb "to be" is frequently omitted and has to be supplied in italics, in order to supply the meaning in translation, as for example, in vv. 11, 14 and frequently in the Greek text (e.g. vv. 14, 27, 32, etc.).

'Having regard, therefore, to these facts, the following is a legitimate translation: "Else what shall they do which are baptized? It is for the dead, if the dead are not raised at all. Why then are they baptized for them?" This involves the insertion of punctuation marks as they were probably to be understood. The first question mark comes after the word "baptized", and the meaning of the phrase "what shall they do" is the same as in the English versions. It means "What is the use of being baptised?" It is quite in keeping with the argumentative character of the passage to insert "it is" as already mentioned. That is to say, of what value is baptism if the dead have not been raised? It is on behalf of a dead Christ, and on behalf of, that is, in the interests of, others who have fallen asleep. There is no community of resurrection life as set forth in the rite of baptism, if the dead are not raised.'

(1 Cor. 15. 29)

60. Beauty—of Christ. Some years ago I went down the banks of the Severn to visit a poor girl dying of tuberculosis in a small cottage of two rooms on the river's bank. I found this river in flood, with the result that when I reached the cottage I found it surrounded by water, through which I waded, and when I opened the door I found the kitchen knee-deep in water. The girl I knew was dying alone upstairs, to which a strip wooden staircase gave access. She had no servant, but a poor woman came in each morning for an hour and 'did for her'.

Here, I felt, was a case that called for all my powers of cheer; and as I slowly mounted the bare wooden stairs I wondered how best I could comfort the sufferer. I needn't have troubled, for as my head appeared in the bedroom I looked toward the bed, and there lay the sufferer, eagerly looking at me, her rare visitor. With deep earnest eyes, and with a heavenly smile, she said, without the slightest greeting or preface, 'He is the chiefest among ten thousand, the Altogether Lovely.'

I found myself in the presence of one of God's holy priests, offering up her morning sacrifice of praise (Heb. 13. 15). It was I that was cheered, not her. She was not in that swamped cottage, but seated far away with her Lord in the heavenlies, and so she sang her song in the light.

—Dr. A. T. Schofield

(Song of Songs 5. 9, 10, 16; Eph. 2. 6; 2 Cor. 3. 18)

61. Beauty—of God's Word. There is on record a conversation between Daniel Webster and some of his illustrious compeers. Somebody raised the question as to the finest and most beautiful passage in the Bible. One argued for the Creation story, another for the Sermon on the Mount, a third for the description of the redeemed in Revelation. Webster slowly quoted the exquisite words: 'Although the fig tree shall not blossom, neither shall fruit be in the vines; the labour of the olive shall fail, and the fields shall yield no meat; the flock shall be cut off from the fold, and there shall be no herd in the stalls; yet I will rejoice in the Lord, I will joy in the God of my salvation'. (Hab. 3. 17, 18)

62. Beauty—of the Lord.

Hast thou heard Him, seen Him, known Him?
Is not thine a conquered heart?
Chiefest of the thousands own Him;
Joyful, choose the better part.

Idols once they won thee, charmed thee—
Lovely things of time and sense:
Gilded thus does sin disarm thee,
Honeyed, lest thou hie thee hence.

What has stripped the seeming beauty
From the idols of the earth?
Not a sense of right and duty
But a sight of peerless worth.

Not the crushing of the idols
With the bitter void and smart,
But the beaming of His beauty,
The unveiling of His heart.

Who extinguisheth the taper
Till he hails the rising sun?
Who discards the garb of winter
Till the summer has begun?

'Tis the look that melted Peter,
'Tis the face that Stephen saw,
'Tis the heart that wept with Mary
Can alone from idols draw;

Draw and win and fill completely
Till the cup o'erflows its brim.
What have we to do with idols
Who have companied with Him?

—Oran Rowan

(Song of Songs 5. 16; Ps. 90. 17; Hos. 14. 8; 2 Cor. 3. 18; 1 Thess. 1. 9, 10)

63. Belief. Dr. Thomas Chalmers who matriculated at the age of 12, was a Divinity student at 15, and was licensed to preach at 19, was called to the Parish of Kilmany in Scotland. Of himself at that time he wrote, 'I could expatiate only on the meanness of dishonesty, on the villainy of falsehood, on the despicable arts of calumny, in a word, upon all those deformities of character which awaken the natural indignation of the human heart.' Now and again he denounced the designs of Napoleon Buonaparte. In May 1811 Chalmers wrote in his journal, 'I am much taken with Walker's observation that we are *commanded* to believe on the Son of God.' Then he stepped from the treacherous ground of 'Do and Live' to place his feet on the firm foundation of 'Believe on the Lord Jesus Christ and thou shalt be saved.'

—Dr. F. W. Boreham

(John 3. 16, 36; 5. 24; Acts 16. 30, 31)

64. Belief—after Unbelief. Anthony Harrod, an old pensioner, was a slave to drink. He was persuaded to attend a gospel meeting where he was convicted of his sin. John Lawson, an earnest evangelist, hearing of Anthony's condition, visited him and tried to lead him to Christ. Taking his Bible from his pocket, John Lawson slowly read the words: 'God so loved the world that He gave His only-begotten Son, that whosoever believeth in Him'—he stopped, and looking Anthony in the face, said, 'and that means you'—'should not perish, but have everlasting life'—'and that means you'.

Anthony was amazed. He had no idea that God loved him—a drinking, swearing sinner. In fact, he believed it to be impossible that a holy God could love a wretch like him. Bringing his big fist down on the table, he exclaimed, 'I don't believe it.'

Lawson was a man of good judgement. Instead of blaming Anthony for discrediting the words of the Scripture, he inquired how long Anthony was in the army. 'Twenty-one years and fourteen days,' was Anthony's reply. Lawson struck the chair with his fist and said, 'I don't believe it.'

'Do you think I would tell a lie?' retorted the old man. 'It was twenty-one years and fourteen days.' 'I don't believe it,' said Lawson quietly.

'Bring me the parchment,' said Anthony to his wife. The document being produced, Lawson inquired, 'How can you expect me to believe you when you refuse to believe the Word of God?' And once more John Lawson read the life-giving words of John 3. 16, and added 'and that means you'.

The scales were removed from the old pensioner's eyes: the light of the Gospel of Christ streamed into his soul: and he exclaimed, 'I see it all. I believe it. Thank God!'

(John 3. 16; Rom. 10. 9, 10)

65. Best—Ours are not good enough for God. Bishop Taylor Smith, the evangelical stalwart, was one day sitting in a barber's shop having a shave. When he spoke to the barber about being right with God, the barber replied, 'I do my best, and that's good enough for me.' When the Bishop's shave was completed and the next man had taken his place, he asked, 'May I shave this customer?' 'Oh no!' replied the barber firmly. 'But I would do my best,' said the Bishop. 'So you might', replied the barber, 'but your best would not be good enough for this customer.' 'No, and neither is yours good enough for God,' was the Bishop's reply. You are saved by letting God do His best for you, and He did that at Calvary.

—Selwyn Hughes (abridged)

(Isa. 64. 6; Tit. 3. 8)

66. Bible—An Architect's view of. The Bible is like a magnificent palace constructed of precious oriental stone, comprising 66 stately chambers. Each one of these rooms is different from its fellows and is perfect in its individual beauty, while together they form an edifice incomparable, majestic, glorious and sublime.

In the book of Genesis we enter the vestibule where we are immediately introduced to the records of the mighty works of God in creation. This vestibule gives access to the Law Courts, passing through which we come to the Picture Gallery of the Historical Books. Here we find hung upon the walls scenes of battles, heroic deeds, and portraits of valiant men of God. Beyond the Picture Gallery we find the Philosopher's Chamber—the Book of Job— passing through which we enter the Music Room, the Book of Psalms, and here we linger, thrilled by the grandest harmonies that ever fell on human ears. Then we come to the Business Office—the Book of Proverbs—in the very centre of which stands the motto, 'Righteousness exalteth a nation, but sin is a reproach to any people'. Leaving the Business Office we pass into the Research Department— Ecclesiastes—and thence into the Conservatory —the Song of Solomon—where greet us the fragrant aroma of choicest fruits and flowers and the sweet singing of birds. We then reach the Observatory where the prophets with their powerful telescopes are looking for the appearing of the 'Bright and Morning Star', prior to the dawning of the Sun of Righteousness. Crossing the courtyard we come to the Audience Chamber of the King—the Gospels—where we find four life-like portraits of the King himself, revealing the perfections of His infinite beauty. Next we enter the workroom of the Holy Spirit—the Acts—and beyond that the Correspondence Room, the Epistles, where we see Paul, Peter, James, John and Jude busy at their tables under the personal direction of the Spirit of Truth. Finally we enter the Throne Room—the book of Revelation—where we are enraptured by the mighty volume of adoration and praise addressed to the enthroned King, which fills the vast chamber; while in the adjacent galleries and Judgement Hall there are portrayed solemn scenes of judgement and wondrous scenes of glory associated with the coming manifestation of the Son of God as King of kings and Lord of lords.

—Selected

(John 5. 39; Luke 24. 27, 44-45)

67. Bible—Authorship of. John Wesley said that the Bible must have been written by God, or good men, or bad men, or angels, or devils.

Bad men or devils would not write it because of the condemnation of sin and pronouncement of fearful judgement upon the sinner. Good men or angels would not deceive men by lying as to its authority and claiming that God was the writer. Therefore the Bible must have been written, as it claims to have been written, by God Who by His Spirit inspired men to record His words, using the human instrument to communicate it to man.

(2 Tim. 3. 16; 2 Pet. 1. 21)

68. Bible—Authorship of. The authorship of this book is wonderful. Here are words written by kings, by emperors, by princes, by poets, by sages, by philosophers, by fishermen, by statesmen, by men learned in the wisdom of Egypt, educated in the schools of Babylon, trained at the feet of Rabbis in Jerusalem.

It was written by men in exile, in the desert, in shepherds' tents, in green pastures and beside still waters.

Among its authors we find a taxgatherer, a herdsman, a gatherer of sycamore fruit; we find poor men, rich men, statesmen, preachers, captains, legislators, judges, exiles.

The Bible is a library filled with history, genealogy, ethnology, law, ethics, prophecy, poetry, eloquence, medicine, sanitary science, political economy, and perfect rules for personal and social life. Its diction declares its Divine Speaker.

—Hastings

(Exod. 34. 27, 28; 2 Sam. 23. 1; Prov. 1. 1; Eccles. 1. 1; Song of Songs 1. 1; Isa. 1. 1; Jer. 1. 1, 2; 36. 32; Hos. 1. 1; Joel 1. 1; Amos 7. 14, 15; Jonah 1. 1; Mic. 1. 1; Zeph. 1. 1; Hag. 1. 1; Zech. 1. 1; Mal. 1. 1; Luke 1. 1-4; Acts 1. 1; Rom. 1.1.; James 1. 1; 1 Pet. 1. 1; 2 Pet. 1. 1; Jude 1; Rev. 1. 4)

69. Bible—Christ's estimate of. I cannot conceive of a true disciple of Christ who belittles or disparages his Master's estimate of the Word of God. The Lord Jesus was accustomed to take the Old Testament in His hand and appeal to it on all occasions, and His word is 'The Scriptures cannot be broken'. If you and I are to be disciples of Jesus, then it behoves us to see to it that we rate the Bible as highly as He rated it.

—J. Russell Howden

(Matt. 5. 17, 18; Luke 4. 21; John 5. 39; 10. 35)

70. Bible—Comforting in hour of death. 'He (Sir Walter Scott) expressed a wish that I should read to him, and when I asked him from what book, he said, "Need you ask? There is but one." I chose the 14th chapter of St. John's Gospel; he listened with mild attention and said when I had done: "Well, this is a great comfort—I have followed you distinctly, and I feel as if I were yet to be myself again".'

—Lockhart, *Life of Sir Walter Scott*

(John 14. 1-6; Rom. 15. 4)

71. Bible—Books of the. One day, in company with some of the Directors of the Limerick and Waterford Railway Company, Mr. Joseph Robinson of Limerick and Moate had by arrangement waited on Mr. Gladstone, who was at the time Chancellor of the Exchequer of Great Britain and Ireland, with a view to obtain a loan for the completion of the railway. Mr. Gladstone received the deputation at Hawarden Castle.

After the business was concluded, Mr. Robinson stepped forward and asked Mr Gladstone if he would accept a tract, offering him one entitled *The Books of the Bible*. With characteristic promptness Mr. Gladstone took the tract and hurriedly read it through. Taking Mr. Robinson by the hand, he said:

'Mr. Robinson, this is remarkable. When you were at the door, Mrs. Gladstone and I were reading the Bible and she said to me: "Is it not strange that with all the tracts that are written, there is not one to tell me in short compass what the Bible is about. And here you come and put a tract on this very subject into my hands. It is most remarkable. I thank you most gratefully for this tract, and may I ask you for a copy for Mrs. Gladstone"?'

Mr. Robinson was as delighted to give Mr. Gladstone another copy as Mr. Gladstone was to receive it. The following comprised the contents of the tract:

Old Testament

In Genesis the world was made by God's creative hand;
In Exodus the Hebrews marched to gain the promised land;
Leviticus contains the Law, holy and just and good;
Numbers records the tribes enrolled—all sons of Abraham's blood.
Moses in Deuteronomy records God's mighty deeds.
Brave Joshua into Canaan's land the host of Israel leads.
In Judges their rebellion oft provoked the Lord to smite,
But Ruth records the faith of one well-pleasing in His sight.
In First and Second Samuel of Jesse's son we read:
Ten tribes in First and Second Kings revolted from his seed.
Next, First and Second Chronicles see Judah captive made,
But Ezra heads a remnant back by princely Cyrus' aid.
The city walls of Zion Nehemiah builds again;
While Esther saves her people from plots of wicked men.
In Job we read how faith will live beneath affliction's rod,
And in the Psalms are precious songs to every child of God.

The Proverbs, like a goodly string of choicest
    pearls, appear.
Ecclesiastes teaches man how vain are all things
    here.
The mystic Song of Solomon exalts sweet
    Sharon's Rose:
Whilst Christ the Saviour and the King the 'rapt
    Isaiah' shows.
The warning Jeremiah apostate Israel scorns;
His plaintive Lamentations their awful downfall
    mourns.
Ezekiel tells in wondrous words of dazzling
    mysteries;
And kings and empires yet to come, Daniel in
    vision sees.
Of judgement and of mercy Hosea loves to tell;
Joel describes the blessed days when God with
    man will dwell
Among Tekoa's herdsmen Amos received his call,
And Obadiah prophesies of Edom's final fall.
Jonah enshrines a wondrous type of Christ our
    risen Lord;
Micah pronounces Judah lost—lost, but again
    restored.
Nahum declared on Nineveh just judgement shall
    be poured.
A view of Chaldea's coming doom Habakkuk's
    visions give;
Next Zephaniah warns the Jews to turn, repent
    and live.
Haggai wrote to those who saw the temple built
    again,
And Zechariah prophesied of Christ's triumphant
    reign.
Malachi was the last who touched the high
    prophetic chord
Whose final notes sublimely show the coming of
    the Lord.

New Testament

Matthew and Mark and Luke and John the holy
    Gospels wrote,
Describing how the Saviour died—His life and
    what He taught.
Acts proves how God the Apostles owned with
    signs in every place.
St. Paul in Romans teaches us how man is saved
    by grace.
Th'Apostle in Corinthians instructs, exhorts,
    reproves:
Galatians shows that faith in Christ alone, the
    Father loves.
Ephesians and Philippians tell what Christians
    ought to be.
Colossians bids us live to God and for eternity,
In Thessalonians we are taught the Lord will
    come from heaven.
In Timothy and Titus a bishop's rule is given.
Philemon marks a Christian's love which only
    Christians know.
Hebrews reveals the Gospel as prefigured by the
    Law.
St. James insists that without works faith is but
    vain and dead;
And Peter points the narrow way in which the
    saints are led.
St. John in his epistles on love delights to dwell,

And Jude gives awful warning of judgement,
    wrath and hell.
The Revelation prophesies of that tremendous
    day
When Christ, and Christ alone, shall be the
    trembling sinner's stay.

72. Bible—Criticism of. A tourist looked nonchalantly round a Florence picture gallery and exclaimed, 'Are these your masterpieces? I certainly don't see much in them.' 'Sir!' said the curator, 'these pictures are not on their trial. It is the visitors who are on trial.'

So the Bible, though much criticised, is not on trial today: but it will come up in the Day of Judgement to try those who reject its testimony.

          —Selected

(John 12. 48)

73. Bible—Criticism of.

Last eve I passed beside the blacksmith's door
    And heard the anvil ring the vesper chime;
When looking down, I saw upon the floor
    Old hammers worn with use in former time.

'How many anvils have you used,' said I,
    'To wear and batter all these hammers so?'
'Just one!' said he, and then, with twinkling eye,
    'The anvil wears the hammers out, you know.'

Just so—I thought—the anvil of God's Word
    For ages sceptic blows have beat upon;
Yet, though the noise of falling blows was heard,
    The anvil is unharmed, the hammers gone.
          —Selected

(Mark 13. 31; Luke 21. 33; 1 Pet. 1. 24, 25)

74. Bible—Daily Reading of. General McArthur told an American Bible Society visitor: 'Never a day goes by, be I ever so tired, but I read the Bible before I go to bed.'
(John 5. 39; Acts 17. 11)

75. Bible—Evidence of truth of. A young Italian girl sat at her fruit stand intently absorbed in reading a small book. A gentleman, pausing to get some fruit, asked her what she was reading with so much interest. She replied, rather timidly, 'The Word of God, sir.' But he was one who called himself a sceptic. He said, 'Who told you the Bible was the Word of God?' With childish simplicity she replied, 'God told me Himself.' 'God told you? Impossible! How did He tell you? You have never seen Him nor talked with Him. How could He tell you?'

For a few moments the girl was confused and silent. Then looking up, she said respectfully, 'Sir, who told you there is a sun in the sky up there?' The gentleman replied, rather contemptuously, 'Who told me? Nobody; I don't need to be told. The sun tells this about itself. It warms me. I love its light.' And the young Italian girl earnestly answered, 'You have put it straight, sir, for the sun and the Bible. I read it. It warms my heart. It gives me light. I love its light and its warmth. None but

God could give the light and warmth I get from this Book.' And he turned away quietly, abashed by her simple faith.

—S. D. Gordon

(Ps. 19. 8; 119. 105)

76. Bible—a Fruitful garden. Our fathers read the Book when the blinds were drawn in the home, and they read it through tears. The tears hindered the physical vision, but they vivified the vision of the soul. Our fathers took that Book as their help when trade was bad, and the battle of bread waxed hot, and all around them was a dark, discouraging wilderness. But they heard the Bible say concerning itself what it represents God as saying, 'Have I been a wilderness unto you?' And they said, 'No, it has been a fruitful garden and well watered. It has been everything we needed.' Surely it is too late in the day to whittle down the infinite authority of this blessed Book!

—Dinsdale T. Young

(Prov. 6. 22-23; Ps. 19. 10; 119. 165; Job 23. 12)

77. Bible—Guide to man.
The Bible? That's the Book—the Book indeed,
The Book of books,
Of which who looks,
As he should do, aright, shall never need
Wish for a better light
To guide him in the night.

—George Herbert

(Ps. 119. 105; Prov. 6. 22, 23)

78. Bible—Hatred of. Man's hatred of the Bible has been of a most persistent, determined, relentless and bitter character. It has led to eighteen centuries of repeated attempt to undermine faith in the Bible, and to consign the Bible itself to oblivion. These attempts have utterly failed. Celsus tried it with the brilliance of his genius, and he failed. Porphyry tried it with the depth of subtlety of his philosophy, and he failed. Lucien tried it with the keenness of his satire, and he failed. Then other weapons were used. Diocletian, the mightiest ruler of the mightiest empire of the world, brought to bear against the Bible all the power of Rome. He issued edicts that every Bible should be burned, but that failed. Then he issued an edict that all who possessed a Bible should be put to death. But even that failed.

So for centuries the assault upon the Bible was continued. Every engine of destruction that human philosophy, human science, human reason, human art, human cunning, human force, and human brutality could bring to bear against a book has been brought to bear against this Book, and yet the Bible stands absolutely unshaken today. At times almost all the wise and great of the earth have been pitted against the Bible, and only an obscure few for it. Yet it has stood.

—Dr. R. Torrey

(Ps. 19. 9; 1 Pet. 1. 24, 25)

79. Bible—Knowledge of. I thoroughly believe in a university education for both men and women, but I believe a knowledge of the Bible without a college education is more valuable than a college education without the Bible.

—William Lyon Phelps of Yale University

(John 8. 32)

80. Bible—Knowledge of. The following illustrates three ways of reading the Bible, and only one way of reading it so that the reader may get to know it and derive benefit from it.

The late H. P. Barker, a master of illustration, described three things he saw in a garden among the plants and flowers. The first object was a butterfly that alighted on an attractive flower, sat for a second or two, then moved on to another, seeing and touching many lovely blossoms but deriving no benefit from them. Next came a botanist with a large notebook and a microscope. He spent some time over each flower and plant and made copious notes of each. But when he had finished, his knowledge was shut away in his notebook: very little of it remained in his mind. Then a busy bee came along, entering a flower here and there and spending some time in each, but emerging from each blossom laden with pollen. It went in empty and came out full.

There are those who read the Bible, going from one favourite passage to another, but getting little from their reading. Others really study and make notes, but do not really get to know the teachings of the Scriptures. Others, like the bee, spend time over the Word, read, mark and inwardly digest it; and it feeds their minds with wisdom and their lives with heavenly sweetness.

(Ps. 19. 10; John 7. 17; 2 Pet. 1. 2, 3)

81. Bible—Knowledge of.
I supposed I knew my Bible, reading piecemeal
hit or miss—
Now a bit of 'John' or 'Matthew', now a snatch
of 'Genesis',
Certain chapters of 'Isaiah', certain Psalms, the
twenty-third,
Twelfth of 'Romans', first of 'Proverbs'; Yes! I
thought I knew the Word.
But I found a thorough reading was a different
thing to do,
And the way was unfamiliar when I read the
Bible through.
Ye who treat the crown of writings as ye treat
no other book—
Just a paragraph disjointed, just a crude,
impatient look—
Try a worthier procedure, try a broad and
steadier view.
You will kneel in very rapture when you read
the Bible through.

—Selected

(John 5. 39; 1 Cor. 2. 13; 1 Tim. 4. 13)

82. Bible—in Literature. The Bible is a book of facts as well authenticated as any heathen history, a book of miracles incontestably avouched, a book of prophecy confirmed by past as well as present fulfilment, a book of poetry—pure, natural and elevated—a book of morals such as human wisdom never framed, for the perfection of human happiness. (Ps. 19. 9; John 17. 17)

83. Bible—in Literature.

Whence but from Heaven could men unskilled in arts,
In several ages born, in several parts,
Weave such agreeing truths? Or how, or why
Should all conspire to cheat us with a lie?
Unasked their pains, ungrateful their advice,
Starving their gains and martyrdom their price.
Then for the style, majestic and divine,
It speaks no less than God in every line—
Commanding words whose force is still the same
As the first fiat that produced their frame.
All faiths beside, they did by arms ascend,
Or sense indulged has made mankind their friend,
This doctrine only doth our lust oppose,
Unfed by nature's soil on which it grows.
(Exod. 20. 1; 2 Pet. 1. 21)

84. Bible—a Living Book.

There is a somewhat humorous poem with the refrain, 'And the barber kept on shaving.' It describes the visit of a young man to a barber's shop in which there were samples of a taxidermist's work—some stuffed birds, and among them an owl. The youth, priding himself in his knowledge of ornithology, commenced a tirade on the work of the taxidermist, pointing out the faults in the owl's wings, legs, and the angle of its head. He continued for a few minutes in this strain till the owl surprised its critics by turning its head and winking, thus making him feel more of an owl than he had ever felt. It was a live owl. Many people mistakenly put the Bible, the living Word of God, on a par with the dead literature everywhere around, imagining it to be mere man's handiwork when it is God's all the time. The young man in the poem vainly thought himself wise until one act of the living bird stultified all his babblings.
(Rom. 1. 21, 22; Heb. 4. 12)

85. Bible—a Living Book.

When Stanley started across the continent of Africa he had seventy-three books, but as the journey continued through the days and weeks he was obliged to throw away the books one by one until they were all gone but his Bible. It is said that he read it through three times on that remarkable trip. It is the one book that lives through the ages, having stood the test of time. A noted professor in the University of Edinburgh was asked by his librarian to go into the library and pick out all the books on his special subject that were no longer needed. His reply was, 'Take every book over ten years old and put it in the cellar.'
(Luke 21. 33; 1 Pet. 1. 25)

86. Bible—Power of.

Dr. Robert Moffat, in one of his lonely travels in Africa, came faint and hungry to a village, and the natives appeared anything but friendly. Soon a poor Bechuana woman came from one of the huts and spread before him meat, milk and fruit. She was about to slip away unobserved when Moffat called her and asked her the reason for her conduct. Taking out from her bosom an old and well-worn copy of the Bible in Dutch, she exclaimed, 'This is the fountain whence I drink. This is the oil that makes my lamp burn.'
(Heb. 4. 12; Ps. 119. 63)

87. Bible—Power of.

I was at a big Dutch trading house in Benguella, where thirty or forty Europeans—British, Dutch and German—had congregated for a commercial conference. A Dutchman at the head of the table greeted me, saying: 'The Bible is not believed in now. I know all about it.'

I replied, 'I shall be glad to prove to all of you that the Bible is true. Allow me to fetch mine.' I did so, sat down at the table, and asked the man to mention what portion was untrue.

'Oh,' said he, 'it is so long since I left home that I don't remember. You read, and I will tell you.' I began to read the first chapter of Romans, solemnly. By the time I had finished there were only six men left and the man at the head of the table drew his slouched hat from under his chair and, muttering that there was a nigger calling him, stole out. There was no one calling him; but that was the last of the discussion that was to prove the Bible untrue.

—F. S. Arnot in *Thirty Years a Missionary in Africa*

(Heb. 4. 12, 13)

88. Bible—Repository of Truth.

Man's dignity and freedom, the corner-stone of our structure of free government, have their source and substance in deeply-felt religion. In the highest sense the Bible is to us the unique repository of eternal spiritual truths. In the most tangible sense, it is the ultimate and indispensable source of inspiration for America's life in freedom. By enabling men to renew, in their minds and spirits, the religious concepts of equality, justice and mercy, the Pocket Testament League, and all others engaged in distributing the Bible, have dedicated themselves to a noble work.

—Dwight D. Eisenhower

(Ps. 138. 2; John 17. 17)

89. Bible—Repository of Wealth.

A young man heard with disgust that his wealthy old uncle had left him in his will a Bible. The will read thus: 'To my nephew I leave a copy of God's priceless Word which I trust he will use daily and find within its pages real treasure.'

The beneficiary threw the Bible into an old trunk in the attic, disgusted and disappointed with his share in his uncle's bequests. Years passed by, and one day, pressed beyond measure, he turned to the good Book for comfort. Between its pages he found bills worth many hundreds of thousands of dollars.

But, beyond the material wealth, he found also the exceeding riches of Christ, for the Bible led him to the Saviour.
(Ps. 19. 10; Eph. 1. 7; 2. 4; 3. 8, 16)

90. **Bible—Secret of Greatness.** An African chief wanted to know the secret of Britain's greatness. Queen Victoria, holding a Bible in her hand, said, 'Tell the chief that this book, the Bible, is the secret of our greatness.'
(Ps. 19. 9; Prov. 14. 34)

91. **Bible—Testimonies to.** Earl Baldwin said, 'The Bible is a high explosive. It works in strange ways, and no living man can tell or know how that Book in its journey through the world has startled the individual soul in ten thousand different places into a new life, a new belief, a new conception, a new faith.'

In a study of the life and work of Moses in his book of Essays, Sir Winston Churchill has this forthright passage concerning the historical accuracy of Holy Scripture. (Our quotation is condensed) 'We reject with scorn all these learned and laboured myths that Moses was but a legendary figure. We believe that the most scientific view, the most up-to-date and rationalistic conception, will find its fullest satisfaction in taking the Bible literally and in identifying one of the greatest human beings with the most decisive leap forward ever discernible in the human story. We may be sure that all these things happened just as they are set out according to Holy Writ. The impressions these people received were faithfully recorded and have been transmitted across the centuries with far more accuracy than many of the telegraphed accounts of goings-on today. In the words of a forgotten work of Mr. Gladstone, we rest with assurance upon "The impregnable rock of Holy Scripture". Let the men of science and learning expand their knowledge and pride and prove with their researches every detail of the records which have been preserved to us from those dim ages. All they will do is to fortify the grand simplicity and essential accuracy of the recorded truths which have lighted so far the pilgrimage of man.'

In one of his speeches Emperor Haile Selassie said, 'We in Ethiopia have one of the oldest versions of the Bible, but however old the version may be and in whatever language it might be written, the Word remains one and the same. It is eternal, and one of the most complete proofs of this can be found in the body of the Bible itself. Gamaliel, one learned in the law, warns Israel of their attitude to the apostles and their teaching. "Refrain," he says, "and let them alone, for if this counsel and this work be of men, it will come to naught but if it be of God you cannot overthrow it." No doubt you all remember reading in the Acts of the Apostles of how Philip baptised the Ethiopian official. He was the first Ethiopian on record to have accepted Christ; and from that day onward the Word of God continues to grow in the heart of Ethiopians. And I must say for myself that from early childhood I was taught to appreciate the Bible, and my love for it increases with the passage of time. All through my life I have found it a cause of unfailing comfort. Unless a man accepts with clear conscience the Bible and its great message he cannot hope for salvation. For myself I glory in the Bible.'
(Acts 2. 41; 8. 32-36)

92. **Bible—a Traveller.** The Bible is the greatest traveller in the world. It penetrates to every country, civilized and uncivilized. It is seen in the royal palace and in the humble cottage. It is the friend of Emperors and beggars. It is read by the light of the dim candle amid Arctic snows. It is read under the glare of the equatorial sun. It is read in city and country, amid the crowds and in solitude. Wherever its message is received, it frees the mind from bondage and fills the heart with gladness.

—Dr. A. T. Pierson

Amid the crowds of the court, or the forum, or the street, or the market-place where every thought of every soul seems to be set upon the excitements of ambition, or of business, or of pleasure, there too, even there, the still small voice of the Holy Bible will be heard, and the soul, aided by some blessed words, may find wings like a dove, may fly away and be at rest.

—William Ewart Gladstone

93. **Bible—Treasure Trove.** When one of our sons, a lad then of six or seven, attending school in Great Britain for the first time, came home saying he had to write a short essay on 'My greatest treasure', we wondered which of his treasured possessions he would choose to write about. When he showed us his completed composition, we were delighted to find that his first sentence was 'My greatest treasure is my Holy Bible.'

—A.N.

A Christian business gentleman, manager of a factory, used to find pleasure in visiting fellow-Christians in their homes for a time of fellowship in spiritual things. One day, being in a mining area, he called on a Christian friend who was a miner. It was late in the afternoon, and the miner, having returned from the pit, bathed and changed his clothes, was busy poring over his well-worn Bible. 'Well, Jamie, where are you gleaning today?' asked his visitor. 'In Romans 8,' was Jamie's reply. Several weeks later the factory manager again called at the miner's cottage and found him, as usual, studying his Bible, and still at Romans 8. 'Why, Jamie, you were digging into that chapter when I came to see you some weeks ago,' he said. The miner's reply was, 'Aye, sir, I'm sinking a shaft here.'
(Ps. 119. 162; Isa. 45. 3)

94. **Bible—Universality of.** Scripture, the Jewish Word, is the universal Book. The most cultivated nations bow before it, and learn as docile children from its inexhaustible pages; to

3

the rudest tribes light and love are brought from its simple and powerful declarations. While kings and philosophers find wisdom and counsel in this inspired volume, it is the companion of the artisan and the merchant, the comfort of the widow, and the instructor of the unlettered and uneducated. There is no age of man when it is not suitable. It gives milk to babes, guidance to the young, strength to men, and consolation to the aged.

—Adolph Saphir

(Ps. 19. 7-10; Rom. 3. 23; 10. 12)

95. Bible—Usefulness of. A sceptic in London recently, in speaking of the Bible, said that it was quite impossible in these days to believe in any book whose authority was unknown. A Christian asked if the compiler of the multiplication table was known. 'No!' he answered. 'Then, of course, you do not believe in it.' 'Oh yes,' was the sceptic's reply 'I believe in it because it works well.' 'So does the Bible,' was the rejoinder. The sceptic had no answer to that.

(Ps. 119. 105; 1 Tim. 3. 15, 16)

96. Bible—Usefulness of.

When I am tired, the Bible is my bed;
Or in the dark, the Bible is my light.
When I am hungry, it is living bread;
Or fearful, it is armour for the fight.
When I am sick, 'tis healing medicine,
Or lonely, throngs of friends I find therein.

If I would work, the Bible is my tool;
Or play, it is a harp of tuneful sound.
If I am ignorant, it is my school:
If I am sinking, it is solid ground.
If I am cold, the Bible is my fire,
And it gives wings if boldly I aspire.

Does gloom oppress? The Bible is a sun;
'Midst ugliness it is a garden fair.
Am I athirst? How cool its waters run!
Or stifled? What a vivifying air!
Since thus thou givest of thyself to me,
How I should give myself, great Book, to
thee!

(Ps. 12. 6; 19. 7; 119. 50; Eph. 5. 26; 6. 17; Col. 3. 16)

97. Bible—Variety of. There are no songs to be compared with the songs of Zion, no orations equal to those of the prophets, and no politics equal to those the Scriptures can teach us.

—John Milton

Written in the East, these characters live for ever in the West; written in one province, they pervade the world; penned in rude times, they are prized more and more as civilization advances; product of antiquity, they come home to the business and bosoms of men, women and children in modern days. Then is it an exaggeration to say that 'the characters of Scripture are a marvel of the mind'?

—R. L. Stevenson

98. Birth—The New. The much-used revival evangelist, George Whitefield, two centuries ago preached frequently from the text, 'Ye must be born again'. One day someone said to him, 'Mr. Whitefield, why do you preach so often about the new birth?' His immediate reply was, 'Because ye must be born again.' (John 3. 1-7)

99. Birth of Christ. Luke's account of the census at the birth of Jesus Christ says that Quirinius (Cyrenius) was Governor of Syria. Tertullian says that Saturnius was Governor. Which is right—Luke or Tertullian?

In 1912 Sir William Ramsay dug up at Antioch a slab whose inscription tells us, among other things, that Quirinius was in authority in Syria at the time of our Lord's birth. Fearing a rising, Quirinius went as Commissioner in charge of the forces and thus would take precedence of the civil governor while the province was under martial law. Hence both Luke and Tertullian were right. (Luke 2. 2)

100. Birthdays. Alexander the Great, Julius Caesar, Plato and Philip Melancton died on their birthdays. John Huss, the martyr, was burned at the stake on his birthday. Timoleon, a successful general, and Philip of Macedon gained their greatest victories on their birthdays. Charles Kingsley was at the seaside on one of his birthdays, and there on the beach he gave his heart to the Lord. His second birthday was thus on the same day as his first. Every year on his birthday David Livingstone repeated his covenant with his Master. The most tragic birthday party ever celebrated took place in the palace of Herod the king. (Matt. 14. 6; Mark 6. 21)

101. Birthday Presents. Dr. W. Graham Scroggie told a story of a boy who received on his birthday three gifts, a box of chocolates, a silver watch and a beautiful Bible. Asked some weeks later what had become of his birthday gifts, he replied: 'The box of chocolates—well! it's gone. The silver watch is going. But the Bible is the Word of the Lord and it endures for ever.' (1 Pet. 1. 25)

102. Birthday Presents. The late H. P. Barker used to relate an incident in connection with a birthday to illustrate the freeness of salvation. The son of a friend at whose home he was staying was named Harold. He was a lad of about 10 and enjoyed Mr. Barker's friendship and confidence. One day Harold came to him and said, 'Mr. Barker, tomorrow is our school Sports' Day. Would you like to come and see the sports?' Mr. Barker replied that he would be delighted, and accordingly Harold gave him a ticket for the sports and arranged to meet him at the entrance to the field and be his guide for the day. Soon after they entered the field Harold took his guest to a large case where the prizes for the various events were displayed under glass. Pointing to a lovely silver watch, Harold said, 'Mr. Barker, do you see that watch? That is the first prize for a race for which I have entered and it is going to be mine.' Mr. Barker, wishing him all the success he coveted in that particular event, waited eagerly to see the race. Alas! Harold was outstripped by others, and did not come in first, or even second, but had to be content with a third place. At the distribution of the prizes Harold's face fell when he saw the silver watch being presented to someone else. Nothing was said at the time, by either Mr. Barker or Harold.

A few days later Harold was again in conversation with Mr. Barker and said, 'Tomorrow is my birthday, and I shall get up early and come downstairs to see my birthday presents which will all be laid out on a table in the hall.' That day the boy was an early riser, but Mr. Barker had come downstairs before him and was waiting inside one of the rooms to see his young friend's joy and surprise as he opened the parcels containing his birthday gifts. When Harold appeared he brushed aside the larger packages and picked out a silver watch in the centre, which was his parents' gift to him. Putting it to his ear, he exclaimed joyfully, 'It's going.' Then Mr. Barker approached from his place of vantage and said, 'Harold, you wanted a silver watch and did your very utmost to earn one at your school sports, but you failed. Now what you could not earn by your own efforts you have received as a free gift. That is like God's gift of eternal life. It cannot be earned by our good works but must be accepted as the free gift of God.'
(Rom. 6. 23; Eph. 2. 8, 9)

103. Blinded Eyes.

Rugged Roman, thou that wieldest
Sword and sabre, spike and spear,
Iron-clad and iron-hearted,
Soul unmoved by mortal fear.

Ruler of an empire, glorying
In the light of peace imposed;
All thy fated foes securely
In a Caesar's grasp enclosed.

Seven hills on tawny Tiber
Vied with distant Ararat;
Sabine forests overwhelmed the
Valley of Jehoshaphat.

Though thine armies trample Zion,
Israel's King thou didst not see,
For thine eyes could ne'er envisage
Him from Whom thy heart would flee.

Vast the legions thou hast garnished,
Temples splendid, columns grand,
Lo! beneath a rod of iron
Broken, dashed, returned to sand.

Who shall stand when He appeareth?
Who may e'er abide His day?
Kiss the Son lest He be angry
And ye perish from the way.
—John Cochrane, Vancouver
(Ps. 2. 10-12; 2 Cor. 4. 3, 4; John 12. 40)

104. Blindness—A Monk's.

Sadhu Sundar Singh, the Sikh who was converted and became a follower of the Lord Jesus Christ, tells of a Buddhist monk he met in Tibet who had lived five or six years in a dark cave. When he went in his eyesight was good, but gradually in the darkness of the cave his eyes grew weaker till he was totally blind.
(Eph. 4. 17, 18)

105. Blindness—of Myopia.

Myopia is short-sightedness. Oculists say it is brought on by always looking at objects that are near, so it is good sometimes to go to the hilltop and take a long view of the landscape. The Greek word from which 'myopia' is derived, in its verbal form, occurs only once in the New Testament, and is translated 'cannot see afar off' (2 Pet. 1. 9).

In the World War from 1914-1918 oculists were kept busy on eye-tests for soldiers. Glasses were provided when required but many of them were thrown away. The men were so short-sighted and so accustomed to a blurred vision that they felt uncomfortable in a clear world. If a whole army were short-sighted and refused glasses, it would mean instant defeat.
(John 9. 40, 41; 2 Cor. 4. 3, 4; 2 Pet. 1. 9)

106. Blindness—of Prejudice.

Galileo with his lens made discoveries that threatened to upset all theories previously held, so Christendom opposed him. One bishop refused to look through his telescope and see what Galileo had seen. He was wilfully blind and did not want the light.
(Isa. 42. 18, 19; 56. 10; Matt. 23. 16, 24; John 9. 40)

107. Blindness—Uncomplainingly endured.

When I consider how my light is spent
Ere half my days in this dark world and wide,
And that one talent which is death to hide
Lodged with me useless, though my soul more
*   bent*
To serve therewith my Maker, and present
My true account, lest He returning chide,
'Doth God exact day-labour, light denied?'
I fondly ask. But Patience, to prevent
That murmur, soon replies, 'God hath not need
Either man's work or his own gifts. Who best
Bear His mild yoke, they serve Him best. His
*   state*
Is kingly: thousands at His bidding speed,
And post o'er land and ocean without rest:
They also serve who only stand and wait.'
—John Milton's *Sonnet*
(Prov. 8. 34; Isa. 42. 16-first clause)

108. Bliss—of Heaven.

One with Christ within the golden city—
*   Welcomed long ago,*
When for me He passed within the glory
*   From the depth below.*

Still the gladness of that blessed welcome,
*   Mystery of that kiss—*
Meeting of the Son and of the Father,
*   Floods my soul with bliss.*

That sweet welcome mine, yea, mine for ever
  That eternal home,
Whereunto when all these wanderings over,
  I shall surely come.

There my heart is resting and is joyful
  With a joy untold.
Earth's dark ways, lit up with that fair glory
  Gleam as streets of gold.
—C.P.C. in Hymns of Ter Stegen and others.
(Rom. 8. 18-21; 1 Cor. 6. 17; 2 Cor. 4. 17, 18)

109. Blood of Christ—Cleansing by. Captain Hedley Vicars, awaiting in November, 1851, in Canada the arrival of a brother-officer, sat in his room idly turning over the pages of his Bible. His eye alighted on the words, 'The blood of Jesus Christ His Son cleanseth us from all sin'. Closing the Book he said, 'If this is true for me, henceforth I will live, by the grace of God, as a man who has been washed in the blood of Christ.'
(1 Pet. 1. 17-20; 1 John 1. 7)

110. Blood of Christ—Entrance to Heaven through. Queen Victoria, as was her wont, often visited the humble and the poor. On one occasion she had been seeing a lonely cottager who was a happy believer in the Lord Jesus, and before leaving had enquired if she could do anything for her. 'I have all I want, thank your Majesty,' said the poor woman. 'But I should like to do something for you,' said the Queen. Again came the response, 'I have all I need, thank your Majesty, but if your Majesty would promise me one thing I would be very glad.' 'I shall do that if I can,' replied the Sovereign. 'Oh, your Majesty, if you would just promise to meet me in Heaven.' Softly and firmly came the Queen's reply, 'I shall do that in virtue of the blood of the Lord Jesus Christ.'
—Selected

(1 Pet. 1. 17-20; 1 John 1. 7)

111. Blood of Christ—Entrance to Heaven through. Martin Luther once visited a dying student and asked the young man what he would take to God in Whose presence he must shortly appear. The young man replied, 'Everything that's good, sir.' Luther, surprised, said, 'How so, seeing you are but a poor sinner?' The youth replied, 'I shall take to God in Heaven a penitent, humble heart sprinkled with the blood of Christ.'
(1 Pet. 1. 2; Rev. 7. 14)

112. Blood of Christ—Forgiveness by. A. Fallaize, for many years a missionary in North Africa, addressing a large audience at a missionary meeting, told of a lady missionary whose service in the Gospel led her to visit the tents of nomadic Arabs who passed, and camped near the town where she lived On one of her visits she came to a tent where a woman stood, engulfed in deep sorrow and anxiety. Entering, she saw lying on a mat on the floor an Arab lad, sick, emaciated and evidently dying of tuberculosis. She asked the mother,

'May I tell him a story?' Receiving a nodded assent, she knelt down beside the lad and began to tell the story of the Lord Jesus and his sufferings and death for sinners. She described how he was beaten, crowned with thorns, led out of the city of Jerusalem, nailed to a cross and left to die, and explained simply how He there bore our sins and now lived in Heaven to forgive the sins of those who came to Him. The lad lay with closed eyes, but toward the end of her narration he opened them and appeared to take some interest in the story. She left, to return the next day, when she told the same story, emphasizing the fact that the blood of Jesus Christ was shed on the cross for the forgiveness of the lad's sins if he would only come to Jesus. This time the sick boy showed a greater interest and his face seemed to lighten up toward the end of her narration. Next day, thinking it might be well to introduce something new into her message, she began to tell of the birth of Christ and was describing the place where He was born when the sick lad raised his hand and said, 'Not that! Not that! Tell me about the cross and the blood and the forgiveness of my sins.' And again the same moving and marvellous story was told.

When the lady missionary returned again she found the woman still sad and weeping bitterly: but there was no lad on the mat inside her tent. She asked the mother how he had died. The mother, when she saw he was dying, had called the Mohammedan priest who came with his copy of the Koran and began to read aloud to the dying lad. Then she described how he had feebly raised his thin hand and said, 'Not that! Tell me about the cross: about the blood and the forgiveness of sins.'
(Lev. 17. 11; Eph. 1. 7; Heb. 9. 22)

113. Blood of Christ—Sheltered by. During a cruel and bloody war, a commander took an oath in the presence of his troops that he would slaughter the entire population of a certain town, and in due course the bloodhounds of war were let loose on the defenceless people.

Now it so happened that a fugitive, seeking for a shelter, saw a sight which was indirectly the means of saving both his own life and the lives of others. He spied a number of soldiers as they broke into a house, the inmates of which they put to the sword. On leaving it, they fastened up the place again, and one of them, dipping a cloth in a pool of blood, splashed it on the door, as a token to any who might follow of what had taken place inside.

Quick as his feet could carry him, the poor fugitive sped away to a large house in the centre of the town where a number of his friends were concealed, and breathlessly told them what he had seen. At once it flashed upon them how to act. A goat was in the yard. It was immediately killed, and its blood splashed on the door. Scarcely could they close the door again when a band of soldiers rushed into the street and began to slay right and left. But when they came to the blood-marked door they made no attempt to enter.

The sword—so they thought—had already entered and performed its work in that house. Thus, while the many around were put to death, all inside the blood-sprinkled door were saved.

(Exod. 12. 13; 1 Cor. 5. 7)

114. Blood-transfusion. Many years ago the Nobel prize was awarded to the discoverer of a difference in the quality of human blood, which had hindered its use in transfusion. Until then transfusion had been a 'hit or miss' experiment. The donor of the blood might be in perfect health, all conditions might be favourable, but the patient would die. Now it is known that there are several blood groups. The largest is the most important, for blood from it will be accepted by most patients though to some it would be poison.

When the haemorrhage has been stopped after a successful operation, the patient, who has lost much blood, lies pale, listless, exhausted, and it seems that death is only a question of hours. But a suitable blood has been found, and a transfusion effected. The result is magical. Colour comes back to the lips, the pulse beats strongly, and the patient will live, for the patient has shared the life blood of the donor and literally received life from him.

Our Lord's statement as to the all-importance of eating His flesh and drinking His blood cannot refer to a sacrament not then instituted, nor could He mean what the Jews seemed to understand by His words, the actual eating of the Lord's real flesh and drinking His real blood. No! He meant that we must share His life, for 'the life of the flesh is in the blood'. We must receive Him as food, to the nourishment of our souls. He must be appropriated as a personal Saviour Who gave Himself for us and shed His blood for the forgiveness of our sins. The Son of God is the universal donor. His blood avails for all.

But usually the life-fluid for a blood transfusion is costly. And sometimes, even if the price can be paid, the patient may belong to a different blood-group from the donor: for there are no universal donors. The most costly thing in the universe is freely offered to sinners by God. It is the blood of Jesus Christ His Son Who gave His life that we might receive that eternal life through His death. It is priceless, yet is offered 'without money and without price'. And it is suited to all sinners, for Christ is the 'universal Donor'.

—Selected

(Lev. 17. 11; Matt. 26. 28; 1 Pet. 1. 18, 19)

115. Boasts. John Newton's boast was: 'I am not what I ought to be: I am not what I wish to be: I am not what I hope to be: but by the grace of God I am what I am.'

(1 Cor. 15. 10; 1 John 3. 2)

116. Bondage. Among the Rikuanian Franks in the early centuries A.D., a free woman who married a serf, disgracing herself thereby, was given a sword and a distaff. Choosing the one, she must strike the husband dead and remain free. Choosing the other, she adopted the symbol of slavery and became a slave for ever.

(Rom. 6. 13-16; 8. 13; Gal. 5. 24; Col. 3. 5)

117. Book of Life. Within the precincts of the ancient castle of Edinburgh, hidden from the sight on the storm-swept site by its grim masonry, lies Scotland's Memorial to her dead. It is perhaps the most wonderful building of its kind in modern times. It is vividly modern, yet lacks nothing in dignity. It seems as if it is the very expression of the heart of Scotland proudly mourning for her lost sons.

Round its walls is a pageant of weariness and suffering in bronze, and there, in the centre, the rugged old granite rock of the hilltop bursts through the polished granite of the floor. Upon the rock stands a rich green marble altar; upon the altar is a steel casket, and within the casket, hidden from all human eyes, lies a book which contains the name of every Scotsman who gave his life in the Great War of 1914-1918.

In the Book of Revelation written by the Apostle John as he laboured in the mines in Patmos as a slave, are the words: 'There shall in no wise enter into it anything that defileth . . .' but they which are written in the Lamb's book of life.'

The names of the sons of Scotland, written in Scotland's book of remembrance will endure well-nigh as long as this old earth endures; but the names which are written in the Lamb's book of life will endure to the furthest bounds of Eternity.

—Selected

(Mal. 3. 16; Luke 10. 20; Rev. 20. 15; 21. 27)

118. Book of Life.

Upon the golden seashore sand
I wrote my name one day;
The waves came in and when they left
My name had passed away.

Upon the shifting sands of time
Men write their names today,
But when eternal years roll in
Their names will pass away.

Upon the spotless Book of Life
God wrote my name one day;
Eternal years can never take
That God-penned name away.

My name is there for ever
Through all God's endless day;
For He Who died to write it there
Has put it there to stay.

—Fred Cowell

(Rev. 20. 15; 21. 27)

119. Borrowed.

They borrowed a bed to lay His head
When Christ the Lord came down:
They borrowed the ass in the mountain pass
For Him to ride to town.
But the crown that He wore
And the cross that He bore
Were His own—the Cross was His own.

He borrowed the bread when the crowd He fed
On the grassy mountain side;
He borrowed the dish of broken fish
With which He satisfied.
But the crown . . .

He borrowed a ship in which to sit
To teach the multitude;
He borrowed the nest in which to rest,
He had never a home so rude.
But the crown . . .

He borrowed a room on the way to the tomb
The Passover lamb to eat;
They borrowed a cave—for Him for a grave;
They borrowed the winding-sheet.
But the crown . . .

The thorns on His head were worn in my stead;
For me the Saviour died;
For the guilt of my sin the nails drove in
When Him they crucified.
So a crown I shall wear,
Since the cross now I bear;
But His own none other can share.

(Luke 2. 7; 5. 3; 9. 16, 58; 22. 11, 12; 23. 53;
John 19. 5, 17)

120. Bread of Life.

It is told of Sadhu Sundar Singh that many years ago he was distributing Gospels in the Central Provinces of India and he came to some non-Christians on the railway train and offered a man a copy of John's Gospel. The man took it, tore it in pieces in anger and threw the pieces out of the window. That seemed the end, but it so happened, in the Providence of God, there was a man anxiously seeking for truth walking along the line that very day, and he picked up as he walked along a little bit of paper and looked at it, and the words on it in his own language were 'the Bread of Life'. He did not know what it meant; but he enquired among his friends and one of them said: 'I can tell you; it is out of the Christian book. You must not read it or you will be defiled.' The man thought for a moment and then said: 'I want to read the book that contains that beautiful phrase': and he bought a copy of the New Testament. He was shown where the sentence occurred—our Lord's words 'I am the Bread of Life'; and as he studied the gospel, the light flooded into his heart, and he came to the knowledge of Jesus Christ, and he became a preacher of the gospel in the Central Provinces of India. That little bit of paper through God's Spirit was indeed the Bread of life to him, satisfying his deepest need.

                 —John A. Patten

(Ps. 78. 24, 25; John 6. 33, 35, 48)

121. Bridge—over the Gulf.

In his *Legend of the Eagles* George d'Espartes says that the most heroic piece of self-sacrifice known to history occurred in the building of a bridge. In the depth of winter the French army, pressed on all sides by the Cossacks, had to cross a river. The enemy had destroyed all the bridges and Napoleon was almost at his wit's end. Suddenly came the order that a bridge of some sort must be thrown across the river, and the men nearest the water were the first to carry out the almost impossible task. Several were swept away by the furious tide. Others, after a few minutes, sank through cold and exhaustion: but more came, and the work proceeded as fast as possible. At last the bridge was completed and the army reached the opposite bank in safety. Then followed the most dramatic scene, and one of the most touching, recorded in the annals of history. When the men who had built the bridge were called to leave the water, not one moved. Clinging to the pillars, they stood silent and motionless, frozen to death. Even Napoleon shed tears.

                 —F. W. Boreham

(1 Pet. 3. 18; Heb. 10. 19, 20)

122. Bridge—over the Gulf.

Between the righteousness of God
   And all that's best in man
There is a chasm deep and wide
   That only God can span.

If man was ever to be saved
   Across this chasm vast,
The wisdom and the power of God
   Were needed for the task.

But God so loved us erring ones,
   His creatures that were lost,
That Christ came down to bridge the gulf
   That all who would might cross't.

The Word of God declares the truth,
   There is no way but this
To get across the gulf of sin
   From earth to Heaven's bliss.
               —Jonathan Beansifter

(Eph. 2. 13; Col. 1. 20, 21)

123. Burden-bearing.

'Blessed be the Lord, who daily beareth our burden.' (Ps. 68. 19). That is the Revised Version translation.

Christ is the Sin-bearer in His propitiation—1 Pet. 2. 24, 25:

He is the Burden-bearer in His priestly ministry—1 Pet. 5. 7:

He will be the Glory-bearer in the day of His power—Zech. 6. 12-13.

'Thinkest thou canst sigh a sigh, and thy Maker
   is not nigh?
Thinkest thou canst shed a tear, and thy Maker
   is not near?'

In the course of a sermon an old Scottish preacher quoted three texts: 1 Pet. 2. 24—'Who His own self bare our sins in His own body on the tree', adding—'There's ma sins awa'; 1 Pet. 5. 7—'Casting all your care upon Him, for He careth for you', adding 'There's ma cares awa'; and John 14. 3—'I will come again and receive you unto myself'—and added 'There's masel' awa'.

(Heb. 4. 15)

124. Burden-bearing. 'The further the intrepid voyager proceeded up the great waterway (River Amazon), the finer became the physique of the natives. And at last, when I reached a point to which no white man had ever before penetrated, I discovered men and women, any of whom might have posed as models for Grecian sculptors,' wrote Alfred Russel Wallace in his *Travels on the Amazon.*

The reason is obvious. The savage knows nothing of the law of Christ. He will bear no other's burden. The sick must die, the wounded perish, the feeble go to the wall. Only the mightiest and most muscular survive.

—Dr. F. W. Boreham

(Rom. 15. 1; Gal. 6. 2)

125. Burden-bearing. I remember going down the High Street in Edinburgh early one morning and meeting a number of children coming up. One of them was borne on the shoulders of another, and, on my asking the reason, he said that the little fellow had burned his foot the night before, and he was carrying him to school. That could not have happened in any other school in Edinburgh.

—Dr. Thomas Guthrie

'Bear ye one another's burdens and so fulfil the law of Christ.' (Gal. 6. 2)

126. Call—of Abraham.

> He called him out: he knew not where,
> An unknown land to north and south
> And east and west:
> But He who called him also loved—
> Sure He knew best.
>
> He led him on o'er unknown land;
> He walked in hand and step with God,
> With Him as friend;
> What need to ask the why or where
> His callings end?
>
> And still He calls, and leads the way,
> And they who answer to His call
> Need have no fear.
> For He Who leads them also loves:
> This answers all.

—F. Howard Oakley (written during a night walk from the ruins of Abram's city to Ur Junction in Iraq)

(Gen. 12. 1-5; Hos. 11. 1; Mark 1. 20; 2 Tim. 1. 9)

127. Call—of Matthew.

> So Matthew left his golden gains
> At the great Master's call;
> His soul the love of Christ constrains
> Freely to give up all.

(Mark 2. 14; Luke 5. 27, 28)

128. Call—to Persia. Dr. Donald Carr of Persia was asked how he got the call to serve the Lord as a missionary in Persia. His reply was, 'I had no call to stay at home but I had the command to go.'

(Matt. 28. 18-20; Mark 16. 15)

129. Call—to Service. When I stood at the crossways in my early life to choose my career, I decided for the Bar. My father was making all the necessary arrangements for my being articled in a solicitor's office, but just when I was about to begin, an old Sunday School teacher of mine met me. I can perfectly remember where we met. It was on the North Bridge in the town of Halifax. He asked me what I was going to do with myself, and I told him I was going in for the Law. He quietly answered, 'I always hoped and prayed you would go into the ministry.' That was a momentous word. It threw all my life into confusion. I went exploring down another road, and I met the great Companion, Christ. In reverence I obeyed His call to follow. At the end of thirty-five years I have to say that I have never regretted my choice.

—Dr. J. H. Jowett

(Ps. 78. 70, 71; Acts 26. 16-18; 1 Cor. 1. 1; 1 Pet. 2. 21)

130. Call—to Service. Sometimes the Church welcomes home a man whose speaking may be more or less effective, but his impressiveness is not dependent upon eloquence of speech. If he made an appeal for volunteers he would doubtless have an abundant response, but he usually seems loath to do so. When the young men get hold of him and ask for help in this problem of recognising a call, he says such stiff things that he leaves his enquirers asking: 'Who then can be called?'

His answer to the young men is uncompromising. 'What constitutes a call?'

'It is the summons of God to your spirit, for a special and specific service.'

'How does the call reach a man?'

'He will not perceive it through the senses nor reason it through the mind, therefore it is intangible and indefinable.'

'When it comes, does one know it unmistakably?'

'It is the breath of God upon the spirit, and the spirit of man feels, understands, knows and responds.'

'Must the call always be a personal one?'

'Seeing the service is to be a personal one, the call to it must be personal also.'

'Is the general command "Go" not sufficient in itself?'

'For the commission to service, certainly, and a very inclusive command it is—preach the gospel to every creature—but the general call is followed by individual designation. Seeing that the field is the whole world, it is more needful that each man hears the order which tells him where his own appointed sphere may be.'

'Missionary life, as I hear it presented, has a romantic and appealing side which makes the certainty of the call more difficult to distinguish. When I hear a missionary speak about Africa, I think my call is there, yet when I hear one tell of India, or of China, I believe that to be the place to which I should go.'

At this the missionary sat in silence for a moment seeming loath to put into words what he had in mind. At last he said:

'I fear that the whole issue has been hopelessly confused by the men and women who have gone abroad uncommissioned by their Master. They have increased the staff, but weakened the army, and we should have done better without them.'

—Mildred Cable and Francesca French
(1 Cor. 1. 17; 9. 1, 16)

131. Capacity. During a time of great scarcity of food and poverty among the people, the Government of a certain country decided to open 'Soup-kitchens' where the poor could obtain a daily provision of nutritive vegetable soup free of cost. Many availed themselves of the free soup. One day at the beginning of the soup-kitchen arrangement, two women emerged from neighbouring houses, one carrying a very large vessel and the other a small jug. The latter said to the former, 'You don't think you'll get that filled, do you?' 'Well! I am taking this in hopes of having it filled', came the reply, 'but if they don't fill it to the brim, there's no harm in taking it.' Arrived at the kitchen, the woman with the small jug had first turn, and her jug was filled to the brim. Then she waited, and, to her surprise, her neighbour's very large vessel was also filled to the brim. Each obtained according to her capacity.—'Ask and ye shall receive,' said the Lord Jesus.
(Ps. 81. 10; Eph. 3. 19-21)

132. Captain. The Emperor Napoleon's last words in St. Helena were, 'Tête d'Armée,'— Head of the army. By his death France had lost a great and successful leader who failed when he lost his last battle, Waterloo. The Captain of our salvation is always Conqueror and is 'alive for evermore'. The Greek word translated once 'Captain' occurs four times in the New Testament, viz. Acts 3. 15; 5. 31; Heb. 2. 10; 12. 2.

133. Cards. A Christian evangelist, W. Romaine, was asked once to take a hand at cards. He immediately rose from his seat and uncovered his head. When the company asked him what he was going to do, he replied, 'I am going to ask God's blessing on the game.' 'But,' they immediately exclaimed, 'we never ask a blessing on such occasions.' 'Then', said he, 'I never engage in anything on which I cannot ask God's blessing.' That ended the game.

134. Cards. Travelling in a railway train with some men who were playing a game of cards, a Christian was asked to have a hand. 'I'm sorry,' he said, 'but I have not my hands with me.' 'What do you mean?' they asked, pointing to his hands. 'These are not mine,' he said, 'they belong to the Lord Jesus Christ. When they were mine I used to play cards. But since I yielded them to Christ, they are never employed in that way, for He has filled them for His service.'
(Lev. 8. 26, 27; Rom. 6. 13; 12. 1)

135. Care. On a parcel sent from Norway to England was affixed a label with the words— 'Glass with anxiety'—in large letters, to indicate the fragile nature of the contents and obtain for the parcel cautious handling. The sender, with a limited knowledge of English, evidently thought that 'anxiety' was a synonym for 'care'. The label would suit many Christians— 'Christians with anxiety'.
(Phil. 4. 6; 1 Pet. 5. 7)

136. Carefree. One of the Christian martyrs was named John Careless. While in prison just before his martyrdom, he wrote to a friend, 'Now my soul is turned to her old rest again and has taken a sweet nap on Christ's lap. I have cast my care upon the Lord and will be careless, according to my name.'
(Ps. 55. 22; 1 Pet. 5. 7)

137. Care of the Lord.

Without a glimpse of darkened skies
Our hearts would never realise
The beauty of the day.
Without the silver of the shower
No loveliness of leaf or flower
Would blossom on our way.

And so in life we value more
The joys unrealised before
With every hurt we bear.
It takes the daily cares we face
To prove our Saviour's tender grace
And realise His care.

(Isa. 43. 1, 2; 2 Cor. 12. 9)

138. Carpenter. 'Is not this the carpenter?' In Mark 6. 1-6 three questions are asked, first as to the source of His words, then as to the nature of His wisdom, and then as to the meaning of His works.

A story is told of the days of Diocletian, the persecuting Emperor of Rome, that a Christian bishop was brought before Caesar who, in mockery, asked him, 'And pray, what is your carpenter doing now?' The martyr replied, 'He is busy making a coffin for your Majesty and for your Empire.' The answer was true but it cost him his life

—H. St. John in *Analysis of Mark's Gospel*

139. Categories. There are five classes of people in the world in relation to God:
  1. The Atheist says, 'There is no God.'
  2. The Agnostic says, 'We don't know whether there is a God or not.'

3. The Materialist says, 'We don't need a God.'

4. The fool says, 'I wish there were no God.'

5. The believer says, 'There is a God and He has revealed Himself to me.'

(Ps. 14. 1; Heb. 1. 1)

140. Cedar Tree. The cedar tree is a wonderful type of the Christian. It grows by dying. As it develops, stately and beautiful, putting forth new boughs and leaves, the old ones drop off to give strength to the new ones. Likewise the saints live to die and die to live.

—Vernon Hart

(Rom. 6. 8-11; Gal. 2. 20)

141. Changes.

Change and decay in all around I see,
  O Thou Who changest not, abide with me.
    —H. Francis Lyte

The great world spins for ever
Down the ringing grooves of change.
    —Alfred, Lord Tennyson

(Heb. 1. 11, 12)

142. Changes. Man's history in the world has been full of changes, but God says, 'I am the Lord, I change not.' In relation to change, history might be summed up as follows:

The woeful change that sin has wrought,
The blessed change the blood has brought:
Changes with which man's life is fraught:
The Christ of God Who changes not.

(Heb. 1. 11, 12; 13. 8; 1 John 1. 7)

143. Channels.

We are not storerooms but channels;
We are not cisterns but springs,
Passing our benefits onward,
  Fitting our blessings with wings,
Letting the water flow outward
  To spread o'er the desert forlorn;
Sharing our bread with our brothers,
  Our comforts with those who mourn.

(Neh. 8. 10; John 7. 38)

144. Charity. What is charity?

It's silence when your words would hurt,
It's patience when your neighbour's curt,
It's deafness when the scandal flows,
And blindness for another's woes;
It's promptness when stern duty calls
And courage when misfortune falls.

(1 Cor. 13. 4-8; 1 Pet. 4. 8)

145. Chastening.

Aliens may escape the rod,
  Nursed in earthly, vain delight;
But a trueborn child of God
  Must not, would not if he might.

(Heb. 12. 6-7)

146. Choosing—aright. Rowland Hill, a preacher of renown, was one day preaching to a large crowd of people in a main highway. A magnificent chariot, in which sat a titled lady on her way to the royal palace, approached and the outrider walked ahead to clear the way. The preacher told him that, though it was the King's highway, he was for the time being occupying it in the name of the King of kings. The incident continues in verse—

Then, bending his gaze on the lady and marking
  her soft eye fall—
'And now, in His name, a sale I proclaim and
  bids for this fair lady call.
Who will purchase the whole, her body and soul,
  coronet, jewels and all?

'I see already three bidders; the World steps up
  as the first.
"I will give her my treasures and all the pleasures
  for which my votaries thirst.
She shall dance each day, more joyous and gay,
  with a quiet grave at the worst."

'But out speaks the Devil boldly: "The kingdoms
  of earth are mine.
Fair lady, thy name with an envied fame on their
  brightest tablets shall shine.
Only give me thy soul, and I give thee the whole,
  their glory and wealth to be thine."

'And pray, what hast Thou to offer, Thou Man
  of sorrows unknown?"
And He gently said, "My blood I have shed to
  purchase her for mine own.
To conquer the grave and her soul to save I trod
  the winepress alone.

'"I will give her my cross of suffering, my cup
  of sorrow to share,
But with endless love, in my home above, all will
  be righted there.
She shall walk in light in a robe of white, and a
  radiant crown shall wear."

'Thou hast heard the terms, fair lady, that each
  has offered to thee.
Which wilt thou choose and which wilt thou lose
  —this life or the life to be?
The fable is mine but the choice is yet thine.
  Fair lady, which of the three?'

She took from her hands the jewels and the
  coronet from her brow:
'Lord Jesus,' she said, as she bowed her head,
  'the highest bidder art Thou.
Thou gav'st for my sake Thy life, and I take
  Thine offer and take it now.'

'I know the world and its pleasures: at best they
  weary and cloy;
And the tempter is bold, but his honours and gold
  prove ever a fatal decoy.
I long for Thy rest—Thy bid is the best; Lord, I
  accept it with joy.'

(Josh. 24. 15; John 1. 12)

147. Choosing—Implications in. Portia, a beautiful lady of wealth, is the heroine of Shakespeare's *Merchant of Venice*. There were many suitors of noble birth and fame who wanted to marry her. But it had been decreed that her hand would be won by that suitor who chose the right casket of three in her possession. The winning casket was the one that contained her portrait. A silver casket had for its inscription—'Who chooseth me shall get as much as he deserves'—and the suitor who made that his choice found a fool's head inside. A golden casket bore the inscription—'Who chooseth me shall get what many men desire'—and contained a skull. The other casket was of lead, and bore the words—'Who chooseth me must give and hazard all he hath'. This was the choice of the successful suitor, Bassanio, who won Portia's hand. For those who, like Paul, desire to win Christ, there is the choice that involves the full renunciation of self and of all they possess.

(Luke 14. 33; Phil. 3. 8; Heb. 11. 24-26)

148. Choosing—Necessity of.

O lads, as ye stand at the break of day,
   As it were at the foot of the hill,
Will you halt and think 'ere you choose your way,
   For choose you must—not choose you may:
      Yes—choose you must, and will.

There are roads leading high to worldly fame,
   There are paths where pleasures devour,
There are prizes of glory and wealth and name,
   There are prizes of princely power.
There are rivers that flow with a mighty rush,
   There are lakes that mirror Heaven's calm;
There are bowers just bathed in a holy hush,
   There are rooms of odorous balm;
There are roads that are heavy and oft untrod,
   There are steps that are rough and bare;
There are pathways so narrow that only God
   And His pilgrimage knight may share.
There are altars which call for a sacrifice,
   There are crosses that promise pain;
There's a refuge of love which will e'er suffice,
   There's a loss that is but a gain.

Let us look once again, dear lads, right out,
   Right out to the top of the hill,
Since choose you must—not choose you may;
   Yes—choose you must and will.
      —F. Howard Oakley

(Josh. 24. 15; Heb. 11. 25, 26)

149. Choosing—once for all.

Once to every man and nation comes the moment
   to decide
In the strife of Truth and Falsehood for the
   good and evil side:
Some great cause, God's new Messiah, offering
   each the bloom or blight,
Parts the goats upon the left hand and the sheep
   upon the right;
And the choice goes by for ever 'twixt that
   darkness and that light.

Then to side with Truth is noble, when we share
   her wretched crust,
'Ere her cause bring fame and profit and 'tis
   prosperous to be just.
Then it is the brave man chooses while the
   coward turns aside,
Doubting in his abject spirit till his Lord be
   crucified;
And the multitude make virtue of the faith they
   had denied.
      —J. Russell Lowell

(Deut. 30. 19; 1 Chron. 12. 18; Matt. 26. 14, 15)

150. Choosing — wrongly.
R. Murray McCheyne, a godly Scottish minister, hearing that a friend of the family had said that she was determined to keep by the world, wrote the following lines on her melancholy decision:

She hath chosen the world and its paltry crowd;
She hath chosen the world and an endless shroud;
She hath chosen the world with its misnamed
   pleasures;
She hath chosen the world before heaven's own
   treasures.
She hath launched her boat on life's giddy sea,
And her all is afloat for eternity.
But Bethlehem's star is not in her view,
And her aim is far from the harbour true.

When the storm descends from the angry sky,
Ah! where from the winds shall the vessel fly?
When stars are concealed and rudder gone,
And heaven is sealed to the wandering one.
The whirlpool opes for the gallant prize,
And, with all her hopes, to the deep she hies!
But who may tell of the place of woe
Where the wicked dwell, where the worldlings go?

For the human heart can ne'er conceive
What joys are the part of them who believe,
Nor can justly think of the cup of death,
Which all must drink who despise the faith.
Away, then—oh, fly from the joys of earth!
Her smile is a lie—there's a sting in her mirth.
Come, leave the dreams of this transient night,
And bask in the beams of an endless light.

(Jer. 8. 20; Heb. 2. 3)

151. Christ—Attitude to.

'What think ye of Christ?' is the test
   To try both your state and your scheme.
You cannot be right in the rest
   Unless you think rightly of Him.

As Jesus appears in your view,
   As He is belovéd or not—
So God is disposéd toward you
   And mercy or wrath is your lot.

Some take Him a creature to be,
   A man, or an angel at most;
But they have not feelings like me,
   Nor know themselves helpless and lost.

So guilty, so helpless am I,
   I durst not confide in His blood,
Nor on His protection rely
   Unless I were sure He is God.

Some call Him a Saviour in word
   But mix their own works with His plan,
And hope He His help will afford
   When they have done all that they can.

If doings prove rather too light,
   (A little, they own, they may fail)
They purpose to make up full weight
   By casting His name in the scale.

Some style Him 'the Pearl of great price'
   And say, 'He's the Fountain of joys,'
Yet feed upon folly and vice
   And cleave to the world and its toys.

Like Judas, the Saviour they kiss
 And, while they salute Him, betray.
Of what will profession like this
 Avail in His terrible day?

If asked what of Jesus I think,
 Though still my best thoughts are but poor,
I say, 'He's my meat and my drink,
 My life and my strength and my store.

My Shepherd, my trust and my Friend,
 My Saviour from sin and from thrall,
My hope from beginning to end,
 My Portion, my Lord and my all.'
                              —John Newton

(Matt. 22. 42; 27. 22; John 1. 12; Song of Songs 5. 16)

152. Christ—Historical. It has been said that History is His story, and His story is History. Outside the Bible there are several secular writers who make mention of the Lord Jesus Christ.

Tacitus—in Book XV, Ch. 44—writing in A.D. 114, tells us that the founder of the Christian religion, Jesus Christ, was put to death by Pontius Pilate in the reign of the Roman Emperor, Tiberius.

Pliny the Younger wrote a letter to the Emperor Trajan on the subject of Christ and Christians (Book X—96).

Josephus, the Jewish historian, writing A.D. 90, has a short biographical note on Jesus Who is called Christ in his 'Antiquities'— Book XVIII, Ch. III, Section 3.

The *Babylonian Talmud* makes mention of Jesus Christ.

(Luke 1. 1)

153. Christ—Historical. In Book xviii of his *Antiquities* Josephus wrote:

'Now there was about this time Jesus, a wise man, if it be lawful to call him a man, for he was a doer of wonderful works—a teacher of such men as receive truth with pleasure. He drew over to him both many of the Jews and many of the Gentiles. He was (the) Christ; and when Pilate, at the suggestion of the principal men amongst us had condemned him to the cross, those that loved him at the first did not forsake him, for he appeared to them alive again the third day, as the divine prophets had foretold these and ten thousand other wonderful things concerning him; and the tribe of Christians, so named after him, are not extinct at this day.'

(John 7. 26; 1 Cor. 2. 8)

154. Christ—Historical. Tacitus, the Roman writer, has attested the existence of Jesus Christ, the reality of his personage, his public accusation and execution under the administration of Pontius Pilate, the temporary check this gave to the progress of His religion, its revival a short time after His death, and its progress over the land of Judaea and right to Rome itself.

                              —Dr. T. Chalmers

The discovery of a stone in 1961, with the name of Pontius Pilate inscribed on it, gives weight and interest to the mention of his administration by both Josephus and Tacitus. (John 4. 29; Luke 24. 46, 47)

155. Christ—Incomparable.

He is stronger than the strongest,
 He's far better than the best;
And His love has lasted longest—
 It has stood the hardest test.
And the sinfullest may trust Him
 And a welcome never doubt,
For He's pledged His word of promise
 That He will not cast them out.

He's the Lord of life and glory
 Now exalted far on high,
But we love to tell the story
 Of His coming down to die.
But He's coming, quickly coming,
 All His glories to display;
And we'll see Him and be like Him
 Through Heaven's everlasting day.

(Matt. 12. 5, 6, 41, 42; John 4. 10-14; 8. 53-58)

156. Christ—Incomparable. He came from the bosom of the Father to the bosom of a woman. He put on humanity that we might put on divinity. He became Son of Man that we might become sons of God.

He was born contrary to the laws of nature, lived in poverty, was reared in obscurity, and only once crossed the boundary of the land— in childhood. He had no wealth or influence, and had neither training nor education in the world's schools. His relatives were inconspicuous and uninfluential.

In infancy He startled a king; in boyhood He puzzled the learned doctors; in manhood He ruled the course of nature. He walked upon the billows and hushed the sea to sleep. He healed the multitudes without medicine and made no charge for His services. He never wrote a book, yet all the libraries of the country could not hold the books that have been written about Him. He never wrote a song, yet He has furnished the theme for more songs than all song writers together. He never founded a college yet all the schools together cannot boast of as many students as He has. He never practised medicine, and yet He healed more broken hearts than the doctors have healed broken bodies.

He is the Star of astronomy, the Rock of geology, the Lion and the Lamb of zoology, the Harmoniser of all discords and the Healer of all diseases. Great men have come and gone, yet He lives on. Herod could not kill Him: Satan could not seduce Him: death could not destroy Him: the grave could not hold Him.

He was rich yet for our sake became poor. How poor? Ask Mary. Ask the wise men. He slept in another's manger: He cruised the lake in another's boat: He rode on another man's ass: He was buried in another man's tomb. He is the ever perfect One, the Chiefest among ten thousand. He is altogether lovely.

—Selected and slightly abridged

(Song of Songs 5. 16; Isa. 9. 6; Mark 7. 37; John 4. 29; Col. 1. 18)

157. Christ—Incomparable. Leonardo da Vinci was a wonderful painter, and one of his masterpieces was 'The Last Supper', which has been called the most perfect composition in the history of painting in all ages. It was painted on a convent wall, and the artist put all his talent into it. Even the cup the Lord used was perfect, an ornate golden vessel richly set with jewels. When he completed the picture he admitted a few friends to see it. 'What a wonderful cup!' they exclaimed, 'How it sparkles! Such a cup was never painted before.' The genius immediately splashed some dark colour over the glittering chalice and made it look an ordinary cheap vessel. The glory of Christ, and not the beauty of the cup, must be the central object of his great work. In all things He must be pre-eminent.

(Col. 1. 18)

158. Christ—Perfections of. Two fellow-travellers were seated together in a railway compartment engaged in earnest conversation of a religious nature. One of them, a sceptic, was evidently trying to excuse his unbelief by expatiating on the various evils which afflict Christendom, detailing with pleasure the hypocrisy and the craft, and the covetousness and divisions, found in the professing Church, and then he pointed to some of the leaders as the most markedly corrupt of all.

In front of them sat a Christian who was compelled to hear all this. He knew the accusations to be true—too true to be concealed from the most charitable mind, so all he could do was to bow his head and bear the deserved reproach. Soon, however, the accuser, anxious to extend the circle of his audience, addressed this fellow-passenger in front of him.

'I see you are quick to detect evil,' said the Christian, 'and you read character pretty well. You have been uncovering here the abominable things that have turned Christendom into a wreck, and are fast ripening it for the judgement of God. You have spared none, but given all a good measure. Now, I am a Christian and love the Lord Jesus and His people. Not a word shall I offer in defence, but I solemnly challenge you to speak the first word against the Lord Jesus Christ Himself.'

The sceptic was surprised. He seemed almost frightened and sheepishly replied—'Well, no! I couldn't find fault with Him. He was perfect.'

'Just so!' said the Christian, 'and therefore was my heart attracted to Him, and the more I looked, the more I found I wasn't like Him at all, but only a poor, guilty, sinful man. All the evil which professed followers of His may

do cannot turn me away from Him My salvation hangs on what He has done, and not on what they are doing.'

—Dr. Horatius Bonar (abridged)

(Mark 7. 36, 37; Luke 23. 14, 41; 1 Pet. 2. 21-24)

159. Christ—Preciousness of.

As the bridegroom to his chosen, as the king unto
*   the realm,*
As the keep unto the castle, as the pilot to the
*   helm,*
So, O Lord, art Thou to me.

As the fountain in the garden, as the candle in
*   the dark,*
As the treasure in the coffer, as the manna in
*   the ark,*
So, O Lord, art Thou to me.

As the music at the banquet, as the stamp upon
*   the seal,*
As the medicine to the fainting, as the wine-cup
*   at the meal,*
So, O Lord, art Thou to me.

As the ruby in the setting, as the honey in the
*   comb,*
As the light within the lantern, as the father in
*   the home,*
So, O Lord, art Thou to me.

As the sunshine to the heavens, as the image to
*   the glass,*
As the fruit unto the fig-tree, as the dew upon
*   the grass,*
So, O Lord, art Thou to me.

—J. Tauler in *Hymns of Ter Stegen and others*

(Ps. 45. 2; Song of Songs 2. 3; Col. 2. 9)

160. Christ—Preciousness of. In the interesting life of A. McLay of Cardiff, the following is given as typical of his testimony.

'On one occasion the dining-room of a hotel was full of business men taking lunch, including a person well known as an inveterate blasphemer and specialist in all that is unsavoury. A. McLay was also of the company, and was silently partaking of his meal. Opportunity was taken by the foul-mouthed infidel to break forth into a prolonged harangue in which exceptionally vile things were said about the Lord Jesus Christ. The atmosphere became tense, whilst the effect was electrical. No one responded, and there was a dead silence. Presently, and probably to break the spell, some one said, "Mr. McLay, haven't you anything to say to all this?" The company almost breathlessly awaited the reply. It came gently and with restrained emotion. He said, "Well, gentlemen, with yourselves I have been obliged to listen to these blasphemous and scurrilous remarks, and I have been thinking of what I could say. May I put it in a few words this way? Many of you know me intimately; you know my wife. You know her worth and what I owe to her; you agree that I could not well exaggerate the felicity of our home life. You realise what my feelings would be, dared anyone utter scandal regarding her. Yet this man in his ignorance and blindness presumes to speak these untrue words against the One Who is infinitely more to me than the closest earthly friend, One Who has died for me, which no one else could have done. My reply is that I declare my heart's allegiance to my Lord Jesus Christ, crucified for sinners, now made both Lord and Christ at the right hand of the throne of God."

'There was such character behind those words and such grace, that the writer was informed by an eye-witness that, two excepted, these men rose as one man and with gusto shouted, "Hurrah, Mr. McLay!" Some one, under the spell of such a noble testimony, and without due time for thought, called for "three cheers for Jesus Christ!"'
(1 Pet. 2. 7; Rev. 5. 9, 10)

161. Christ—Radiance of.

> Marvel not that Christ in glory
>   All my inmost heart hath won;
> Not a star to cheer my darkness
>   But a light beyond the sun.
> All below lies dark and shadowed,
>   Nothing there to claim my heart,
> Save the lonely track of sorrow
>   Where of old He walked apart.
>
> I have seen the face of Jesus—
>   Tell me not of aught beside;
> I have heard the voice of Jesus—
>   All my soul is satisfied.
> In the radiance of the glory
>   First I saw His blessed face,
> And for ever shall that glory
>   Be my home, my dwelling-place.

—T.P. in *Hymns of Ter Stegen and others*
(Acts 22. 11; Eph. 1. 20, 21; Heb. 2. 9)

162. Christ—Rejection of.

> Why dost Thou pass unheeded, treading with
>   pierced feet
> The halls of the kingly palace, the busy street?
>
> Oh marvellous in Thy beauty, crowned with the
>   light of God,
> Why fall they not down to worship where Thou
>   hast trod?
>
> Why are Thy hands extended beseeching while
>   men pass by
> With their empty words and laughter, yet passing
>   on to die?
>
> Unseen, unknown, unregarded, calling and
>   waiting yet—
> They hear Thy knock and they tremble—they
>   hear, and they forget.
>
> And Thou in the midst art standing of old and
>   for ever the same—
> Thou hearest their songs and their jesting, but
>   not Thy Name.
>
> The thirty-three years forgotten of the weary
>   way Thou hast trod—
> Thou art but a Name unwelcome, O Saviour God.
>
> Yet amongst the highways and hedges, amongst
>   the lame and the blind,
> The poor and the maimed and the outcast, still
>   Thou dost seek and find.

> There by the wayside lying, the eyes of Thy love
>   can see
> The wounded, the naked, the dying, too helpless
>   to come to Thee.
>
> So art Thou watching and waiting till the wedding
>   is furnished with guests—
> And the last of the sorrowful singeth, and the
>   last of the weary rests.

—C.P.C. in *Hymns of Ter Stegen and others*
(Prov. 1. 24; Rev. 3. 20)

163. Christ—Sufficiency of. I heard Booth-Tucker say that he preached in Chicago one day, and out from the throng a burdened toiler came and said to him, before all the audience: 'Booth-Tucker, you can talk like that about how Christ is dear to you and helps you; but if your wife was dead, as my wife is, and you had some babies crying for their mother, who would never come back, you would not say what you are saying.'

Just a few days after, he lost his beautiful and nobly gifted wife in a railway wreck, and the body was brought to Chicago and carried to the Salvation Army barracks for the funeral service. Booth-Tucker at last stood up after the funeral service and he stood there by the casket, and looked down into the face of the silent wife and mother, and said: 'The other day when I was here, a man said I could not say Christ was sufficient if my wife were dead and my children were crying for their mother. If that man is here, I tell him that Christ is sufficient. My heart is all crushed. My heart is all bleeding. My heart is all broken, but there is a song in my heart, and Christ put it there; and if that man is here, I tell him that, though my wife is gone and my children are motherless, Christ speaks comfort to me today.'

That man was there, and down the aisle he came, and fell down beside the casket, and said 'Verily, if Christ can help us like that, I will surrender to Him.' He was saved there and then.

—Dr. John Wilson in *The Christian*
(2 Cor. 12. 9; Heb. 4. 15, 16)

164. Christ—Testimonies concerning.
Henry Morgenthau—'The greatest personality in human history is Jesus. We shall never escape from war but by following His teaching.
Horace Bushnell—'His character forbids possible classification with men.'
A Hindu Professor in S. India—'My study of modern history has shown me that there is a moral pivot, and that more and more the best life of the East is revolving round it. That pivot is Jesus Christ.'
A Brahmo-Samajist—'There is no one else seriously bidding for the heart of the world except Jesus Christ. There is no one else in the field.'
Benjamin Franklin—'Christ's system of morals and religion as He left them to us is the best the world has seen or is likely to see.'
Ernest Renan—'He is the incomparable Man to whom the universal conscience has decreed

the title of Son of God, and that with justice.'
(Renan was a French infidel, a philosopher and
historian acknowledged to be the first man of
letters of his day).

Daniel Webster—'I believe Jesus Christ to
be the Son of God. The miracles which He
wrought establish in my mind His personal
authority and render it proper for me to
believe what He asserts.'

Professor Simpson, M.D., D.Sc., President
of the Royal College of Physicians, said in his
final address to the College:

'I do not know in what mood of pessimism
I might have stood before you today had it not
been that, ere the dew of youth had dried from
off me, I made friends with the sinless Son of
Man Who is the well-Head of the stream that
vitalizes all advancing civilization and Who
claims to be the First and the Last, and the
Living One Who was dead and is alive for
evermore.'

(Matt. 27. 54; John 4. 42; Acts 2. 36; Heb. 13.
8; 1 John 1. 1-3)

165. Christian. A Christian man is 'Christ in
a man'. The word 'Christian' occurs three
times only in the Bible:

In Acts 11. 26 it is associated with their
separation from the two great races of the
world, Jews and Gentiles. They had been
regarded as merely a sect of the Jews, but the
Jews disowned them and thus they took the
place 'outside the camp' and were neither Jews
not Gentiles.

In Acts 26. 28 it is used with scorn by King
Agrippa, an adulterer, a tyrant and a slave to
sin. His use of the term is typical of the
world's attitude to those separated to Christ.

In 1 Pet. 4. 16 it is connected with suffering
that was the consequence of the reproach and
scorn heaped upon those who were separated
to the Lord.

166. Christians.

We are the Bibles the world is reading:
We are the creeds the world is needing:
We are the sermons the world is heeding.

—Dr. Billy Graham

(Eph. 4. 1; 1 Pet. 2. 12)

167. Christmas.

That glorious Form, that Light unsufferable,
And that far-beaming blaze of Majesty
Wherewith He wont at Heaven's high council-
table
To sit the midst of Trinal unity,
He laid aside; and here with us to be,
Forsook the courts of everlasting day
And chose with us a darksome house of mortal
clay.

—John Milton, *Ode on the morning of*
Christ's nativity

(John 1. 14; Gal. 4. 4-5; 1 Tim. 1. 15)

168. Christmas. E. C. Adams, missionary in
Chagallu, West Godavari District, India, told
of a loved and respected Indian brother, long
with the Lord, who years ago was asked to
give a Christmas message to the assembled
congregation. It was a message not to be
readily forgotten. He spoke of the preparations
that were made by many to observe the day—
the decorations to the houses, the coloured
paper streamers, the plants and flowers on the
verandahs and tables of their homes, the
presents given by one to another, the home-
coming of members of the family who had
been long absent, the invitations sent out to
friends to share in the rejoicings, the abundance
of food and dainties eaten with such relish, the
jovial singing and the happy talk that made
the day one long to be remembered. But,
said he, in the midst of all such delights, how
many thought of Him in Whose honour the
day was being observed? Many would be sated
with feasting, and some would be drunken;
but what place would the Lord have in it all?
What place has He in our hearts?

Then breaking off, the speaker sang a verse
of a Telugu hymn written by a saint of God
whose songs have enriched the hymnology of
the Church. The verse might thus be rendered
in English:

What would Heaven be without Him?
For Him alone my heart would pine:
If here and now I know Him with me,
Untold joy and Heaven are mine.

(Isa. 9. 6; Matt 2. 1, 2; Luke 2. 10, 11; 2 Tim.
2. 8)

169. Church. The early Church was distinguished by simplicity, purity and directness.
She possessed little silver or gold; she attached
little importance to external authority; her
organization was but slender; her social
prestige was negligible; but the Apostle Peter,
himself made a bold warrior by the coming
of the Holy Ghost, could say to a man who
thought that gold was as good as God, 'Thy
money perish with thee!' Whenever the early
Church sounded the trumpet, the walls of some
Jericho fell down.

—Life of Faith

(Acts 2. 42, 47; 9. 31; 16. 5; Eph. 2. 22)

170. Church—Glorious. The kingdoms of
this world are only the scaffolding God uses
for the building of His Church. When the
building is completed, the scaffolding will be
removed. It is necessary in the work of construction, but not all-important or permanent.

Dr. Culyer saw Cologne Cathedral in
process of construction. The picture was
disfigured by scaffolding. When he saw it
again, completed, years later, it was the most
magnificent view, he said, from the Alps to the
sea.

View the vast building: see it rise,
The work how great, the plan how wise!
O wondrous frabric! Power unknown
That rests it on the Living Stone.

(Matt. 16. 18; Eph. 2. 19-22; Rev. 21. 10, 11)

171. Church—Militant. Albert Enstein, the famous scientist, said:

'Being a lover of freedom, when the revolution came in Germany, I looked to the universities to defend it. But no! they immediately were silenced. Then I turned to the great editors who in days gone by proclaimed their love of freedom, but they too were silenced in a few weeks. Only the Church stood squarely across the path of Hitler's campaign for the suppression of truth. What I once despised— the Church—I now praise unreservedly.'

(Matt. 16. 18; Eph. 6. 13)

172. Church—Rich and increased in goods. Two church dignitaries were viewing a costly and ornate Cathedral. One said to the other, 'The day is gone when the church can say, as Peter said, "Silver and gold have I none".' 'Yes!' replied the other, 'and the day is gone when the church can say, as Peter said, "In the name of Jesus Christ of Nazareth, rise up and walk". The poverty has gone, and also the power.'

(Acts 3. 6; Rev. 3. 18, 19)

173. Church—Worldly.

The Church and the world walked far apart on
the changing shores of time:
The world was singing a giddy song, and the
Church a hymn sublime.
'Come, give me your hand,' cried the merry
world, 'and walk with me this way.'
But the good Church hid her snowy hand, and
solemnly answered—'Nay!'
'Nay, walk with me but a little space,' said the
world with a kindly air,
'The road I walk is a pleasant road, and the sun
shines always there.
My path, you see, is a broad, fair path, and my
gate is high and wide;
There is room enough for you and for me to
travel side by side,'
Half-shyly the Church approached the world and
gave him her hand of snow;
The old world grasped it and walked along, saying
in accents low:
'Your dress is too simple to suit my taste; I will
give you pearls to wear;
Rich velvet and silk for your graceful form and
diamonds to deck your hair.'
The Church looked down on her plain, white
robes and then at the dazzling world,
And blushed as she saw his handsome lip with a
smile contemptuous curled.
'I will change my dress for a costlier one,' said
the Church with a smile of grace;
Then her pure white garments drifted away, and
the world gave her in place
Beautiful satins and shining silks, and roses, and
gems and pearls;
And over her forehead her bright hair fell,
crisped in a thousand curls.
'Your house is too plain,' said the proud old
world, 'I'll build you one like mine;
Carpets of Brussels and curtains of lace, and
furniture ever so fine.'

And he bought her a costly and beautiful home—
splendid it was to behold;
Her sons and her beautiful daughters dwelt
there, gleaming in purple and gold.
And fairs and shows in the halls were held, and
the world and his children were there;
And laughter and music and feasts were heard
in the place that was meant for prayer.
The Angel of Mercy flew over the Church, and
whispered, 'I know thy sin.'
The Church looked back with a sigh and longed
to gather her children in.
'Your preachers are all too old and plain,' said
the gay old world with a sneer,
'They frighten my children with dreadful tales
which I like not for them to hear.
They talk of brimstone and fire and pain, and the
horrors of endless night;
They talk of a place that should never at all be
mentioned in ears polite.
I shall send you some of the better stamp,
brilliant and gay and fast,
Who will tell them that people may live as they
list and go to heaven at last.'
The sons of the world and the sons of the church
walked closely, hand and heart,
And only the Master Who knoweth all could tell
the two apart.
Then the church sat down at her ease and said, 'I
am rich and in goods increased;
I have need of nothing, have nought to do but to
laugh and dance and feast.'
The sly world heard her and laughed in his sleeve,
and mockingly said aside,
'The church is fallen, the beautiful church, and
her shame is her boast and pride.'

(John 17. 16; 2 Cor. 6. 17; Heb. 13. 13; Rev.
3. 17-19)

174. Circumstances—Fretting under. Napoleon Buonaparte, when intoxicated with success and at the height of his power, is reported to have said, 'I make circumstances.' Let Moscow, Elba, Waterloo, and St. Helena, that rocky island where he was incarcerated until he fretted his life away, testify to his utter helplessness in his humiliating fall.

(Gen. 42. 36; Job. 3. 23-24; Rom. 8. 23, 31, 35-37)

175. Circumstances—Superiority to. The water-spider lives in the water and is made for life in the water but it cannot live without air. It would drown in the water, so is constantly surrounded by an element deadly to it; yet it continues to live a happy life against odds. Over its body is a thick covering of hair. When it plunges into the water it carries with it an envelope of air which at once forms a bubble round it. It chooses its place, spins a silken dome attached to water-weed, and into this dome flicks the bubble of air. Then it rises and brings another until it fills its home with the air it needs.

(Rom. 8. 37; 2 Cor. 4. 8, 9)

176. Claim—on kindness. Dr. Barnardo, the great friend of friendless children, told a story of how a dirty ragged urchin hailed him in the street one day, with the request that he might be taken into one of Barnardo's Homes.

'I know nothing about you, my lad,' said the Doctor. 'What have you to recommend you?'

'I thought these would be enough,' said the little chap, pointing to his rags.

Dr. Barnardo gathered him up in his arms and took him in.

When I reach those pearly gates I'll then put in my plea—
I was a guilty sinner, but Jesus died for me.
(Rom. 5. 8; 1 Tim. 1. 15)

177. Cleansing. A soap manufacturer, who was an unbeliever, walked along the road one day with a preacher of the gospel. Said the soap manufacturer: 'The gospel you preach has not done much good, for there is still a lot of wickedness in the world and a lot of wicked people too.' The preacher made no reply until they passed a dirty little child, making mud pies in the gutter. Seizing his opportunity, the preacher said: 'Soap has not done much good in the world, I see; for there is still much dirt and many dirty people about.' 'Oh, well,' said the manufacturer, 'soap is only useful when it is applied.' 'Exactly!' said the preacher, 'so it is with the Gospel that we proclaim.'
(2 Kings 5. 14; Ps. 51. 7; 1 John 1. 7)

178. Collections.

Two spiders, so the story goes, upon a living bent,
Entered the meeting-house one day,
And hopefully were heard to say,
'Here we shall have at last fair play
With nothing to prevent'.

Each chose his place and went to work: the light web grew apace;
One on the sofa spun his thread,
But shortly came the sexton dread,
And swept him off, and so, half-dead,
He sought another place.

'I'll try the pulpit next,' said he, 'there surely is a prize;
The desk appears so neat and clean,
I'm sure no spider there has been;
Besides how often have I seen
The preacher brushing flies.'

He tried the pulpit, but alas! His hopes proved visionary.
With dusting brush the sexton came
And spoilt his geometric game,
Nor gave him time nor space to claim
The right of sanctuary.

At length, half-starved and weak and lean, he sought his former neighbour,
Who now had grown so sleek and round
He weighed the fraction of a pound,
And looked as if the art he'd found
Of living without labour.

'How is it, friend,' he asked, 'that I endured such thumps and knocks,
While you have grown so very gross?'
''Tis plain,' he answered, 'not a loss
I've met since first I spun across
The contribution box.'
(1 Cor. 16. 2; 2 Cor. 9. 5-7)

179. Comfort. Mrs. Charles Beer, for many years, with her husband, a missionary in Narsapur, India, sat on one side of the bed of her dying husband. Opposite her, on the other side, sat Mr. E. S. Bowden, their close associate in the Lord's work among the Telugus for many years. They watched his strength failing and looked on as the veteran worker passed into the presence of his Lord and Master Whom he had loved and served. As the heart ceased to beat and the last breath was drawn, Mr. Bowden looked across to the now widowed and sorrowing sister and said quietly, 'Gone in to see the King.' Mrs. Beer found in those words the comfort that her heart needed.
(Isa. 33. 17; Matt. 5. 8; 2 Cor. 5. 8; Phil. 1. 23)

180. Comfort—in Bereavement. John was a gardener to a Christian gentleman. He had lost his lovely little daughter and was bitter and rebellious against God for taking her from the home. One morning he found that a special rose he was training for the local Flower Show was gone. He was very angry and, turning to the maid, said, 'Who did this?' 'It was the master,' she replied. Just then the master himself came on the scene. 'John!' he said, 'these flowers belong to me. Have I not a right to pluck any of them as I please?'

John learnt the lesson. The darling daughter he had lost belonged to the Lord, and He had taken the lovely bud to blossom in His Paradise above. John was comforted.
(Job. 1. 21; 1 Thess. 4. 16-18)

181. Comfort—Meaning of. A missionary translator, labouring amongst a tribe in the mountains of Mexico, found it hard to get the right word for 'comfort'. One day his helper asked for a week's leave, and explained that his uncle had died and he wanted some days off to visit his bereaved aunt 'to help her heart around the corner'. That was just the expression the missionary needed.
(Ps. 23. 4; Isa. 66. 13; Eph. 6. 22; Col. 4. 8)

182. Coming of Christ—The Second.
When the flowers of earth are springing,
And the birds with gladness singing,
And the cloud-chased sunbeams touch me with a fervent glow and fleet,
Then there comes a sacred feeling
O'er my spirit strangely stealing,
As I think upon the rapture and the coming of His feet.

When the summer sun shines stronger,
And the days are warm and longer,
And a world of blended beauties on the smiling
*   landscape meet,*
Then my love-smit heart seems vying
With the zephyrs in their sighing
For the 'Altogether Lovely' and the coming of
*   His feet.*

When the year with harvest golden
In rich autumn's hand is holden,
And the leaves begin to wither and earth's
*   glories to retreat;*
When the dull days are returning,
Oft I feel a greedy yearning
For the rustling of His garments and the coming
*   of His feet.*

When the wintry winds are howling
And the heavens darkly scowling,
And the mariner is praying while the storms
*   against him beat,*
I can feel a deep emotion,
Like the wave that swells the ocean,
As I listen with impatience for the coming of
*   His feet.*

In the day of light and gladness,
In the night of gloom and sadness,
When my cup is running over or when favours I
*   entreat;*
At all times and in all places,
This sweet hope my spirit braces—
It is only till I see Him at the coming of His feet.

'He is coming! He is coming!'
Air and earth and sea are humming;
Restrained creation yearneth the King of peace
*   to greet;*
Victor crowned and glory bearing,
Everlasting honours wearing,
Yet for me, as ever, caring at the coming of His
*   feet.*

—William Blane

(John 14. 3; Tit. 2. 13; Rev. 22. 16, 20)

183. Coming of Christ—Glory of.

After the silence of ages,
*   After the waiting of years,*
He cometh—the answer to sages,
*   The vision foretold by the seers.*

Regal in splendour He cometh
*   Sceptre of iron to sway;*
Glorious, the King in His triumph
*   On His inaugural day.*

Comes for the help of His people,
*   Conqueror—Faithful and True,*
Calls from the parted blue heaven,
*   'Behold, I make all things new.'*

(Heb. 10. 37; Rev. 19. 11)

184. Coming of Christ—Hope of.
On many a
tombstone, after the name and description of
the deceased and under the details of age and
date of passing, three short words express the
hope of the believer who is buried there, during
the days of life on earth. The words are 'Till

He come'. Then 'the dead in Christ shall rise
first'.

When the weary ones we love
Enter on their rest above,
When their words of love and cheer
Fall no longer on our ear,
Hush! be every murmur dumb,
It is only 'Till He come!'

(1 Cor. 15. 51-55; 1 Thess. 4. 15-18)

185. Coming of Christ—Imminence of.
Dr.
Horatius Bonar, as he drew the curtains at
night and retired to rest, used to repeat to
himself the words, as if in prayer, and certainly
with expectancy, 'Perhaps tonight, Lord!' In
the morning, as he awoke and looked out on the
dawn of a new day, he would say, looking up
into the sky, 'Perhaps today, Lord!' He
expected the Lord to return at any moment.
(Tit. 2. 13; 1 John 2. 28; Rev. 22. 20)

186. Coming of Christ—Nearness of.
Many
years ago there was a father who had to leave
his home to go on a long journey. Just before
he left, his little three-year old son asked him,
'Daddy, when will you be coming back again?'

Now the father knew that he would not be
back till the end of September. However, he
realized that it was no use talking about dates
and times and seasons to his boy, for he would
not know the difference between them.

Sitting down beside him, the father said to
the boy, 'Now, listen; when you see the leaves
on the trees turning red and brown and
beginning to fall to the ground, then you can
be sure that Daddy is coming back very soon.'

The next day the father left home. During
the months of July and August the little boy
would go for walks with his nurse. On these
walks he used to talk about his absent daddy.
Slowly the weeks went by until it came early
September and then mid-September. Although
the boy did not notice it, the leaves on the trees
were changing colour.

Then one night there was a big wind storm
and millions of leaves came down, filling the
sidewalks and the gutters. The next morning
when the little fellow went out, he immediately
saw them. Letting go his nurse's hand, he went
amongst the leaves and began to kick them
sky-high. Then he began to shout, 'Hurrah!
Hurrah! Daddy's coming soon.'

Likewise all over the world there is an
expectation; the leaves are turning brown and
they are beginning to fall. Jesus said, 'When ye
see these things begin to come to pass'—be very
gloomy? No, chins up—'Lift up your heads.'
The great future of every child of God may be
dawning, for the coming of the Lord is drawing
near.

—Harold Wildish

(Luke 21. 28, 31; James 5. 7, 8)

187. Coming of Christ—Preaching the Second.
For nearly 20 years a spiritual enrichment has
come into my ministry, because I have realised
the great New Testament revelation of the

personal return of our Lord. Dr. Andrew Bonar told the story of a plain man in one of the Scottish Presbyterian churches who had learnt this precious doctrine. The man spent a Sunday in Edinburgh. When he returned to his village, the people asked how he liked the Edinburgh preachers. His reply was, 'They all fly on one wing. They all preach the first coming of Christ but not the second.'
— Dr. Dinsdale T. Young

(Acts 1. 11; 1 Thess. 1. 10; 4. 13-15)

188. **Coming of Christ—Preparation for.** John was the chauffeur of a Christian whom God had prospered and who was a faithful witness for Christ. Often he would have talks with John about his soul, the necessity of accepting Christ and being ready for what lay beyond this life. One day, telling his chauffeur of the blessed hope of the Lord's return, he said to him, 'John, when the Lord comes, you may have my cars'. This evoked from John a polite and very joyous expression of gratitude. 'And John,' he added, 'you and your wife can come and live in our nice large house.' Again John responded with a very fervent 'Thank you, sir!' His master also told him he could have all the money and property he possessed when the Lord Jesus came.

Overjoyed, John returned to his cottage and told his wife what his master had said. Both were elated at the prospect but had not considered the implications. John went to bed but could not sleep. In the middle of the night he made his way to his master's house and knocked loudly till his master came and asked who was there. 'It's me, John, your chauffeur' was the reply from the other side of the locked door. 'What's the matter, John? Why have you come at this time of night?' 'Oh sir,' said the chauffeur, 'I don't want your car.' 'Don't want my car, John? Why not?' asked his master. 'Nor your house, nor your money, nor your property,' added John. 'Well, John,' said his master, 'what is it that you do want?' 'I want to be saved—to be ready, like you, for the coming of the Lord.'

(Matt. 25. 10-13; 1 Thess. 5. 2)

189. **Coming of Christ—Promise of.**
There's a whisper from the glory of the coming of the Lord,
Oh the joy my heart is tasting as I rest upon His Word,
And what peace amid earth's tumult does this precious truth afford—
'Hold fast! I'm coming soon!'

In the glory of His promise I am living day by day,
And the light of heaven is dawning on earth's dreary, desert way,
While I wait that sweetest whisper, 'Up, my child and come away,'
The Lord is coming soon.

There's a glory on the mountains and a glory on the sea,
And the valleys now are glowing, and the desert way can be
Just a pilgrimage to glory, since He whispered this to me,
'Hold fast! I'm coming soon.'

(John 14. 3; 1 John 3. 2; Rev. 2. 25)

190. **Coming of Christ—Promise of.**
'Where is the promise?' the scoffers say,
'He said He would come—why this strange delay?
Don't all things continue unto this day?'—
But He will come.

Where is the promise? Let men deride:
Let scoffers and sceptics and all decide
The Blessed Hope has been misapplied—
Yet He will come.

Where is the promise? The signs all say
His coming again is not far away.
Rejoice, ye saints—He may come today!
He's bound to come.
— J. Danson Smith

(Tit. 2. 13; Heb. 10. 37; 2 Pet. 3. 4)

191. **Coming of Christ—The Rapture at.** As the chill blasts of winter approach the islands of the United Kingdom, the swallows take their flight to find a refuge in some warmer clime in Southern Spain or North Africa. No one sees them go, yet not one is left behind. They all go. When the swallows are gone, severe and wintry weather begins. So will it be at the rapture of the saints when the Lord Jesus comes to the air with a shout, with the archangel's voice and the trump of God. All believers will be caught up. 'We shall not all sleep but we shall all be changed.'

(1 Cor. 15. 51, 52; 1 Thess. 4. 16, 17)

192. **Coming of Christ—The Results of.**
We look for our Saviour, we look for His coming,
When living and sleeping shall meet in the skies,
When from every nation, with great jubilation,
The blood-bought unite at the wondrous assize.

We look for that season with Christ in the glory.
How wondrous 'twill be!—No mortal can tell.
When works now recorded shall then be rewarded
And, sharing His glory, with Him we shall dwell.

We look for that time when this earth, undistracted,
Shall cease from its wars and true peace shall enjoy,
With Christ's sceptre swaying and millions obeying
And Satan chain-bound; none shall hurt or destroy.
— J. Danson Smith

(Rom. 8. 19-23; Phil. 3. 20, 21; Tit. 2. 13; Heb. 10. 37)

193. **Coming of Christ—Suddenness of.** R. Murray McCheyne, the godly Scottish minister,

who went to be with Christ before he reached the age of 30, on one occasion asked some friends in his home, 'Do you think that Christ will come tonight?' Pausing before each, he waited for their reply. One and all answered, 'No, I think not.' Then he solemnly quoted the words of our Lord, 'In an hour when ye think not the Son of Man cometh.'

(Matt. 24. 42; 25. 13; Mark 13. 35; Luke 12. 40)

194. Coming of Christ—Suddenness of.

One moment here in this dark world of woe,
This weary vale where tears will ever flow:
The next—caught up to meet Him in the air
With but a moment between here and there.

The twinkling of an eye! O precious thought!
No time for moan or cry, up to Him caught
Away from all that drives us to despair
With but a twinkling between here and there.

Oh! pending weight of joy! Oh hope so bright—
Makes every moment fly on wings of light:
Each moment nearer, every hour more fair,
Perhaps today we shall be with Him there.

195. Commands.

Rabbi Simlai in the third century said that Moses gave us 365 prohibitions and 248 positive commands.

David in Psalm 15 reduced them to eleven: Isaiah—in 33. 14, 15—made them six: Micah 6. 8 binds them into three: and Habakkuk reduces them all to one, namely—'The just shall live by his faith'.

—H. St. John

(Exod. 35. 1; Hab. 2. 4)

196. Commendation.

In Paul's second letter to the Corinthians 'commendation' is used in two senses—self-commendation which is to be avoided, and the commendation of the Lord and of our lives and service which is to be coveted. The Greek word translated 'commend' occurs in 2 Cor. 3. 1; 4. 2; 5. 12; 6. 4; 10. 12, 18; and 12. 11.

On special occasions several important buildings in large cities are floodlit. Artificial light thrown from outside on such buildings lights up the exterior and gives the buildings a radiant appearance. This is done to attract people's attention to the exterior—an illustration of what self-commendation is.

But did anyone ever hear of a floodlit lighthouse? No, for flood-lighting is not required. The lighthouse, illuminated from within, gives out its own light for the benefit of mariners sailing the seas. Paul wrote, 'Ye shine as lights in the world.'

(Phil. 2. 15)

197. Communion.

Two friends stood in a large railway station and watched an express train with the most modern of engines go flying through. 'What a powerful engine!' remarked one of them to his friend, who was the Station-master of that station. 'Yes!' said the Station-master who was a Christian, 'On the rails. But off the rails it is the weakest thing in the world. And,' he added, 'how like the Christian! His power lies in communion with his Lord and Saviour, but when he leaves the path of communion he is the weakest person in the world.'

(Phil. 4. 13)

198. Communion.

The story is told of a certain minister who was disturbed to see a shabby old man go into his church at noon every day and come out again after a few minutes. What could he be doing? He informed the caretaker and bade him question the old man. After all the place contained valuable furnishings.

'I go to pray,' the old man said in reply to the caretaker's questioning.

'Come, come now,' said the other, 'you are never long enough in the church to pray.'

'Well, you see,' the shabby old man went on, 'I cannot pray a long prayer, but every day at twelve o'clock I just comes and says, "Jesus, it's Jim" and waits a minute and then comes away. It's just a little prayer, but I guess He hears me.'

When Jim was injured some time later and taken to hospital, he had a wonderful influence in the ward. Grumbling patients became cheerful and often the ward would ring with laughter.

'Well, Jim,' said the sister to him one day, 'the men say you are responsible for this change in the ward. They say you are always happy.'

'Aye, sister, that I am. I can't help being happy. You see, it's my Visitor. Every day He makes me happy.'

'Your visitor?' The sister was puzzled. She always noticed that Jim's chair was empty on visiting days, for he was a lonely old man, with no relations. 'Your visitor? But when does he come?'

'Every day,' Jim replied, the light in his eyes growing brighter. 'Yes, every day at twelve o'clock He comes and stands at the foot of my bed. I see Him and He smiles and says, "Jim, it's Jesus".'

—William Aitken

(Hos. 2. 14; Matt. 28. 20)

199. Companionship.

Sir Ernest Shackleton, when in the Antarctic with two companions, spoke of the tremendous loneliness and the feeling of severance from the world. But as they took some of their long treks over the ice, he said he realised the presence of a fourth Person with them, invisible yet real. The Lord Jesus Himself was their Companion.

(Dan. 3. 25; Matt. 28. 20; 2 Tim. 4. 17)

200. Companionship.

In 1896, Glasgow University conferred on Dr. David Livingstone the degree of Doctor of Laws. He rose to speak and was received in respectful silence. Gaunt, haggard as a result of hardships in tropical Africa, his left arm, crushed by a lion, hanging helplessly at his side, he announced his resolve to return to Africa, without misgiving and with great gladness. He added, 'Would you like me to tell you what supported me through all the years of exile among a people whose language I could not understand, and whose attitude toward me was always uncertain and often hostile? It was this, "Lo, I am with you alway, even unto the end of the world". On these words I staked everything, and they never failed.' He had the companionship of the Son of God.

—Dr. F. W. Boreham

(Matt. 28. 20)

201. Companionship—Everlasting.

Where no spot nor stain can enter nor the gold be dim,
In that holiness unsullied I shall walk with Him.
Meet companion then for Jesus, for Him, from Him made,
Glory of God's grace for ever there in me displayed.
He Who in the hour of sorrow bore the curse alone,
I who through the lonely desert trod where He had gone—
He and I in that bright glory one deep joy shall share,
Mine to be for ever with Him, His that I am there.

—P.G. in *Hymns of Ter Stegen and others*

(Rev. 3. 4; 21. 9)

202. Companionship—Now and for ever.

I'll walk beside you on the world's highway:
Your darkest night shall be as brightest day.
With my right hand to guide you, never fear,
For to thy Saviour's heart thou art most dear.

I'll stay beside you in the battle's strife:
'Tis I Who brought your soul from death to life.
In peace and quiet or amid the din,
Be guided by my still, small voice within.

I'll watch beside you when death's hour is near:
My constant presence shall dispel all fear.
Lean hard upon me, trusting in my love;
I'll bear thee upward to the realms above.

There'll come a happy time when wars shall cease
And nations dwell in harmony and peace.
We'll meet our loved ones: what a day 'twill be
When God Himself gives glorious liberty!

—Mrs. Henderson, formerly of Sankeshwar, India

(Exod. 3. 12; 2 Tim. 4. 17)

203. Concordances—History of.

The first Latin Bible Concordance was that of Cardinal Hugo in 1244, and the first printed Concordance in Latin was offered for sale in 1470. The first Hebrew Concordance of the Bible was completed by Rabbi Mordecai in 1523, and a year later the first German Concordance of the New Testament was produced. Nearly two centuries elapsed before the publication of the first Greek Concordance in two volumes in 1718.

When Thomas Matthews' Bible in the English language came out in print, John Warbeck of London had a desire to own one. Being far too poor to purchase such a book, he decided to borrow one from a friend and to copy it by hand. After proceeding with great care through the Pentateuch, he was turning his attention to Joshua when one day his task was interrupted by a visit from a friend named Turner.

'Tush!' quoth he, 'thou goest about a vain, tedious labour. But this were a profitable work for thee, to set out a Concordance in English.'

'A Concordance!' exclaimed Marbeck, 'what is that?'

'A book to find out any word in the whole Bible by the letter, and there is such a one in Latin already,' was Turner's reply.

'But I have no learning to go about such a thing,' objected Marbeck.

'Enough for that matter,' said his friend, 'for it requireth not so much learning as diligence. And seeing thou art so painstaking a man, and one that cannot be unoccupied, it were a good exercise for thee.'

In 1550—after a great struggle—appeared a folio volume, faulty and defective, but the first Concordance to the whole English Bible, John Marbeck's work.

Several Bible Concordances were published in the Eighteenth and the Nineneeth centuries—the first edition of Cruden's in 1737, a two-volume Concordance in German in 1750, Mark Wilk's Concordance to the French Bible in 1840, Young's Analytical in 1879, Walker's in 1894, and Strong's also in 1894. Prior to Young's and Walker's Concordances Wigram had published his Concordance of the Bible in the original languages, Hebrew, Chaldee and Greek, in three volumes, adapted to the use of English-speaking students. The scholarly work of W. E. Vine, published first in 1939—an *Expository Dictionary of New Testament words*—combines concordance, dictionary and careful exposition in one work.

(1 Cor. 2. 13)

204. Condemnation.

There is no condemnation, there is no hell for me,
The torment and the fire my eyes shall never see;
For me there is no sentence, for me has death no stings,
Because the Lord Who saved me shall shield me with His wings.

No angel, and no Heaven, no throne, nor power, nor might,
No love, no tribulation, nor anger, fear nor fight,
No height, no depth, no creature that has been or can be,
Can drive me from Thy bosom, can sever me from Thee.

—Paul Gerhardt

Romans Chapter 8 commences with 'No condemnation' and ends with 'No separation'.

(Rom. 8. 1, 38, 39)

205. Conformity. 'Predestinated to be conformed to the image of His Son.'

And is it so, I shall be like Thy Son?
Is this the grace which He for me has won?
Father of glory, thought beyond all thought,
In glory to Thine own blest likeness brought.

Oh Jesus Lord, who loved me like to Thee?
Fruit of Thy work, with Thee, too, there to see
Thy glory, Lord, while endless ages roll,
Myself the prize and travail of Thy soul.

Yet it must be, Thy love had not its rest
Were Thy redeemed not with Thee fully blest—
That love that gives not as the world, but shares
All it possesses with its loved co-heirs.

Nor I alone—Thy loved ones all, complete,
In glory round Thee there with joy shall meet,
All like Thee—for Thy glory like Thee, Lord,
Object supreme of all, by all adored.

—J. N. Darby

(Rom. 8. 29; Phil. 3. 20, 21; 2 Thess. 1. 10; 1 John 3. 2)

206. Conscience. In his book on 'Conscience', Thomas Baird deals with several kinds of conscience mentioned in the Word of God— the natural conscience (Rom. 2. 15), a defiled conscience (Tit. 1. 15), an evil conscience (Heb. 10. 22), a convicting conscience (John 8. 9), a purged conscience (Heb. 9. 14), a pacified conscience (Heb. 10. 2), a good conscience (1 Pet. 3. 16), an answering conscience (1 Pet. 3. 21), a pure conscience (2 Tim. 1. 3), a witnessing conscience (Rom. 9. 1), and a conscience void of offence (Acts 24. 16) among others. He quotes the following lines by a coloured poet, Paul Lawrence Dunbar:

I said good-by to my Conscience,
Good-by foraye and aye;
And I pushed her hands off harshly
And turned my face away.
And Conscience, sorely wounded,
Returned not from that day.

But the time came when my spirit
Grew weary of its pace;
And I said 'Come back' to Conscience,
'For I long to see thy face.'
But Conscience said, 'I cannot,
Remorse is in my place.'

207. Conscience—a Canker.
When ranting round in Pleasure's ring
Religion may be blinded:
Or if she gie a random sting,
It may be little minded.
But when on life we're tempest-driven,
A conscience but a canker,
A correspondence fixed in Heaven
Is sure a noble anchor.

—Robert Burns

(Acts 24. 16)

208. Conscience—Friend or Foe.
Oh, Conscience! Conscience! man's most faithful friend,
Him thou canst comfort, ease, relieve, defend;

But if he will thy friendly checks forego,
Thou art, oh! woe for me, his deadliest foe!
—Crabbe—*Struggles of Conscience*
(Rom. 2. 15)

209. Consecration. Mary's ointment was wasted when she broke the vase and poured it upon the Lord. Yes! but suppose she had kept the ointment in the unbroken vase, what remembrance would it then have had? She broke the vase and poured it out, lost it, sacrificed it, and now the perfume fills the earth. We may keep our life, if we will, carefully preserve it from waste, but we shall have no reward, no honour from it at last. But if we empty it out in loving service, we shall make it a lasting blessing to the world and we shall be remembered for ever.

—Selected

(Mark 8. 35; John 12. 3; Rom. 12. 1; Phil. 1. 21)

210. Consecration. In a garden near Gloucester Cathedral, England, on a sundial, may be read the inscription:

'*Give God thy heart, thy service and thy gold;*
The day wears on and time is waxing old.'
(1 Chron. 29. 5; Rom. 6. 13; 2 Cor. 8. 1-5)

211. Consecration. Lady Huntingdon was on her way to a brilliant assembly when there darted into her soul the words, 'Man's chief end is to glorify God and to enjoy Him for ever.' These words she had long before committed to memory. From then on she consecrated herself and all she had to the Lord.

(Ps. 50. 23; Matt. 5. 16; 1 Cor. 6. 19, 20; 1 Pet. 4. 16)

212. Consecration. Baron von Welz renounced his title, estates and revenues and went as a missionary to British Guiana where he fills a lonely grave. Renouncing his title, he said, 'What is to me the title "Wellborn" when I am born again to Christ? What is to me the title "Lord" when I desire to be the servant of Christ? What is it to be called "Your Grace" when I have need of God's grace? All these vanities I will away with and all else I will lay at the feet of my dear Lord Jesus.'

(Rom. 12. 1, 2; 2 Cor. 12. 15; Heb. 11. 24, 25)

213. Consecration. 'Give me thine ordinances,' says the god of Pharisaism: 'give me thy personality,' said the god of Hegel: 'give me thy reason,' says the god of Kant. It remains for the God and Father of our Lord Jesus Christ to say, 'My son, give me thine heart.'

Jim Elliott, one of the five missionaries to Ecuador martyred by the Aucas, said concerning his call to service, 'He is no fool who gives what he cannot keep to gain what he cannot lose.'

(Prov. 23. 26; Matt. 22. 37; Mark 10. 29, 30; 1 Pet. 3. 15)

214. Consecration.
Bondslave of Jesus Christ, Thine, Thine alone;
  Whom have I else in Heaven, or earth, or sea?
Naught that I have, my Lord, I call mine own:
  All that I am, O God, I pledge to Thee.

Against the doorposts of eternity,
  The high and holy place of Thine abode,
Pierce through mine ear the sign of slavery
  And point me any service, any road.

A slave! I would not question, would not choose.
  Man's praise or blame no more can trouble me;
Even my right to self to Thee I lose,
  And in that bondage find that I am free.
                                              —F.C.D.

(Exod. 21. 1-6; Rom. 12. 1)

215. Consecration. A girl was sent to a
finishing school by her wealthy parents. There
she learned science, art, dancing and other
things. One night she went to a revival
meeting and at the close of the service she
accepted Christ as her own personal Saviour.
She gave her heart to Christ, yielded to Him,
and decided she would dedicate her life to
missionary service.

She wrote home to her father and told him
of her decision. He went into a rage and wrote
to her immediately, saying, 'Get on the next
train and come home.'

She obeyed and returned to her home. As
her father met her, he said, 'I did not send you
to school to get religion. That is all right for
poor folk and half-wits, but not for a child in
your stratum of life. You will have to get this
religious notion out of your head. If by
tomorrow morning you have not decided to
give up this foolish notion of religion, you may
pack your suitcase and leave this home.'

She went to her room with a heavy heart. It
would mean loss of love, culture, money,
prestige. On her knees she fought it out. The
next morning she packed her suitcase. Before
leaving, she stepped over to the piano and
started to play and sing:

Jesus, I my cross have taken,
  All to leave and follow Thee;
Destitute, despised, forsaken,
  Thou, from hence, my all must be:
Perish every fond ambition,
  All I've sought and hoped and known;
Yet how rich is my condition,
  God and Heav'n are still my own!

She arose, and with tears streaming down her
face, turned toward the door. Before she could
open it, her father stepped out from behind the
curtain where he had been listening to her
playing, and with emotion said: 'Wait! I did not
know that Jesus Christ meant as much to you
as that. I did not know that you were willing to
give up father, mother, home and prestige just
for Jesus. Daughter, forgive me. I must be
beside myself. If such a great love can take
hold of your heart, there must be something
in it. Sit down here and tell me how I can
be a Christian.'
                                    —*Prairie Overcomer*

(Luke 14. 25, 27, 33; 18. 22, 29)

216. Consecration. Travelling from his own
province through Germany on his way to the
gay city of Paris, Count Zinzendorf, then a
young man, halted at the town of Dusseldorf,
where there was a fine collection of paintings.
He went into the Art Gallery to spend an hour
or two admiring the works of some of the great
Masters. Coming to a picture of Christ
suffering on the cross, he stood transfixed
before the scene and read the words that the
artist Steinberg had added to his painting: 'All
this I did for thee. What hast Thou done for
Me?' This was the turning point of his life.
Abandoning his journey to Paris, he returned
to his home and consecrated himself to the
Lord Jesus Christ. Devoting himself and his
wealth to the Master's service, he became the
leader of the Moravian brethren.

(1 Cor. 6. 20; Gal. 2. 20)

217. Consecration.
I bring my eyes to Thee,
  The eyes that looked beyond
The circle of Thy will,
  Of Eden's sacred bond:
With penitential tears now filled,
  To wash Thy feet—my fears are stilled.

My hair I yield to Thee,
  The glory, that was lost
In Eden's darksome hour,
  At disobedience' cost:
Now I will wipe Thy holy feet,
  And ne'er was worship e'er so sweet.

My lips I give to Thee,
  That once the fruit did taste—
Forbidden by Thy love.
  Then judgement came with haste:
And now these lips on Thee I'll spend
  To kiss Thy feet—My Saviour, Friend.

My hands I give Thee back,
  The hands that broke Thy will,
When plucking from the tree
  Desire's cup to fill;
But now with ointment filled for Thee,
  And 'Go in peace' Thou sayest to me.

And thus forgiven much,
  My love to Thee I give—
No more to seek my own,
  Henceforth for Thee to live:
For these Thy feet were bruised for me,
  As God in Eden said 'twould be.
                                    —Iscah Andrews

(Gen. 3. 6, 15; Luke 7. 37, 38; John 12. 3)

218. Consecration. In his poem *Morte
D'Arthur*, Lord Tennyson describes how King
Arthur, mortally wounded in battle, commanded his knight, Sir Bedivere, to take his
sword Excalibur, which he had received from
the lake nearby, and go and throw it into the
lake, then to return and report to the king
what he saw. In obedience the knight took the
sword and wended his way to the lakeside by
zigzag and rocky paths, and there, drawing out
Excalibur, with the bright winter sun shining
on it, he gazed long at the sword. Its hilt

sparkled with diamonds and jewels which scintillated in the moonlight. So he thought it better to conceal the sword somewhere in the waterflags: and, having done so, returned to the wounded king. In reply to Arthur's question, 'What is it thou hast seen? Or what hast heard?' he replied,

'I heard the ripple washing in the reeds,
And the wild water lapping on the crags.'

Knowing from his reply that his order had not been carried out, King Arthur rebuked his knight for telling this lie and again sent him to carry out his instructions and, having done so, to return and bring him word.

Again Sir Bedivere went to the side of the lake, but again the wonder of the jewellery on the hilt, and the exceeding preciousness of the sword, diverted him from obedience to his king; and he hid it a second time. When he returned to King Arthur and, in reply to Arthur's question, gave the same answer as before, the king was very angry and sent him again with the words:

'A man may fail in duty twice,
And the third time may prosper.'

This time Sir Bedivere hastened to the lake, drew the sword from its hiding-place in the bullrushes, and threw it into the lake. Then there rose 'an arm, clothed in white samite, mystic, wonderful,' caught the sword by the hilt, brandished it three times and drew it into the lake.

Sir Bedivere had returned the sword to the giver, and the giver had received it back. Thus should redeemed lives, given to those who believe, be yielded to the Giver.

(2 Sam. 23. 15-17; Rom. 6. 13; 12. 1)

219. Consecration. It was 'Missionary Day' in a Congregational church in Scotland many years ago, and a missionary from Africa had preached and told of how God was working and saving men and women in the dark continent. At the conclusion of his message, it was announced that the collection taken would be devoted entirely to the spread of the Gospel among African tribes. The large wooden collection plate was being passed round and came to the place where a young lad was seated. He was poor and had only a 'bawbee' to put in the plate. Seeing the large amount of silver coins in the collection, and ashamed of the poverty of his own offering, he asked the steward to put the plate on the floor. When this was done, he stepped into it and stood there for a moment or two. His action meant that he gave himself. That took place over a century ago. The lad grew to manhood and became a missionary to Africa where he was greatly used.

(1 Chron. 29. 5; Rom. 12. 1; 2 Cor. 8. 5)

220. Consecration. There is a fable well known in India of a poor beggar who lived in a State ruled by a Maharaja. The beggar had no home but put up every night in a free choultry—or lodging-house—sleeping on a mat on the floor, and covering himself in the cooler nights with old rags. His clothing was tattered and old, and, having no means of earning a livelihood other than begging, he used to go out in the morning after a meal of cold rice left over from the previous day and sit by the wayside with his beggar's bowl. For 'punyam' (merit), passers-by used to throw some grains of rice or copper coins his way, so he usually had enough rice for two meals a day, and enough money to buy sticks for a fire and a few vegetables, fish or dhall for curry, which he ate at the choultry.

One day he heard that on the morrow the Maharaja himself was coming that way in his chariot. That raised his hopes, as he said to himself, 'The Maharaja will not give me a handful of rice or a copper coin, or even a few annas, but nothing less than a golden "Varaha".' The next day he took up his usual position by the side of the road, and patiently awaited the Maharaja's coming. The sun stood overhead and still he waited in the noonday heat, but no sign of the ruler. Patiently he waited, still full of hope, until almost sunset and then he heard the welcome sound of the horses' hoofs and the chariot wheels. Stepping into the road, he brought the chariot to a standstill, approached the Maharaja and begged for alms. Instead of giving him anything, the Maharaja extended his hands and asked the beggar to give him something. Extremely disappointed and disgusted at a wealthy ruler begging from a poor beggar, he counted out five grains of rice from his bowl and placed them angrily in the hands of the Maharaja. 'Namasthe,' said the Maharaja, and continued his journey.

With a sore heart and very disappointed, the beggar went that evening to his choultry, took out his winnowing fan and began to clean his rice for his meal. As he did so, a small glittering object attracted his attention. Picking it up, he saw that it was a grain of gold. Laying it carefully on one side, he went on winnowing till he found another glittering golden grain, then another. Now the search began in real earnest, and a fourth was found among the rice. After another search he saw a fifth and put it with the others. But, no matter how long he searched after that, he found not another grain of gold.

Then the truth dawned on him. Five grains of rice given to the Maharaja had brought him in return five grains of gold. 'What a fool I was!' he exclaimed regretfully, 'If I'd known I'd have given him it all.'

We lose what on ourselves we spend:
We have as treasure without end
Whatever, Lord, to Thee we lend
Who givest all.

(Mal. 3. 10; Mark 12. 44; 2 Cor. 9. 6)

221. Consecration—of Jewels. The Princess Eugenia of Sweden, a devoted Christian lady and very liberal, had used up all the money she could control in doing good in various ways. Still, in visiting the poor, she found a number of sick persons who never could be cured, but who could be made comfortable, if they only had a hospital home. She wished to establish a hospital for incurables. But her money was all gone. She said to herself, 'May I not sell my diamonds?' She asked her brother, the king, about it. He consented. The diamonds were sold. The hospital was built. It was kept full of patients. With them this noble princess spent much of her time, talking and praying with them, and trying to lead them to Jesus. Among these was an old woman who was very ignorant and had been very wicked. The princess had laboured much over this woman and was very anxious to see her a Christian. But nothing seemed to make any change in her.

On one occasion the princess had to be absent for some weeks. She was going among the patients saying 'Goodbye'. The matron pointed to this old woman and said, 'You'll find her greatly changed.' As the princess came up to the bedside of the old woman, now near her end, she was greeted with these sweet words: 'I thank God that the blood of Jesus Christ His Son cleanseth from all sin, and that He has cleansed me from mine.' As she uttered these words, tears of grateful gladness flowed down her cheeks.

As the princess herself shed tears of joy when speaking of it to a friend, she said, 'In the tears of that saved soul I saw my diamonds again.'

—*The Indian Christian*

(Exod. 35. 27-29; 1 Chron. 29. 1-5; 1 Tim. 6. 19)

222. Consistency. It is the responsibility of the Christian to live consistent with the great Name he bears, with his profession of faith in the Lord Jesus Christ. One of the soldiers of Alexander the Great was called up to be court-martialled for desertion. 'What's your name?' asked the Commander of the Greek army. 'Alexander,' was the reply. 'Change your name or mend your manners,' said the Emperor.

(Eph. 4. 1; Col. 1. 10; Heb. 13. 20, 21)

223. Contentment.

> *There's discontent from sceptre to the swain,*
> *And from the peasant to the king again.*
> *Then whatsoever in thy will afflict thee,*
> *Give it a welcome as a wholesome friend,* ·
> *That would instruct thee to a better end.*
> *Since no condition from defect is free,*
> *Think not to find what here can never be.*
>
> —A. Nicholas

(Luke 3. 14; 1 Tim. 6. 6; Heb. 13. 5)

224. Contentment. A story is told of a king who went into his garden one morning and found everything withered and dying. He asked an oak that stood near the gate what the trouble was. He found it was sick of life and determined to die because it was not tall and beautiful like the pine. The pine was all out of heart because it could not bear grapes like

the vine. The vine was going to throw its life away because it could not stand erect and have such fine fruit as the peach tree. The geranium was fretting because it was not tall and fragrant like the lilac; and so on all through the garden. Coming to a Heartsease, he found its bright face lifted as cheery as ever.

'Well, Heartsease, I'm glad amidst all the discouragements to find one brave little flower. You do not seem to be the least disheartened.

'No, I am not of much account, but I thought that, if you wanted an oak or a pine or a peach tree, or a lilac, you would have planted one; but as I knew you wanted a Heartsease, I am determined to be the best little Heartsease that I can.'

(1 Tim. 6. 6; 1 Pet. 5. 5; Phil. 4. 11)

225. Contentment. Lord Congleton, coming downstairs one morning, in passing the kitchen door, heard the cook exclaim, 'Oh, if I had only £5, wouldn't I be content?' Thinking the matter over, and anxious to see one woman at least satisfied, he shortly after handed her a £5 note. She thanked him profusely. As he was leaving, he paused outside the door to hear if she would express her satisfaction and contentment, and thank God.

As soon as his shadow was invisible, she cried out, 'Why didn't I say ten?' The human heart is like the horse-leach's daughters: it ever cries, 'More! more!'

(Prov. 30. 15; 1 Tim. 6. 8; Heb. 13. 5)

226. Continuance. It has been well said that continuance is the test of reality.

> *If the Saviour's won your heart,*
> *And for Heaven you've made a start,*
> *Keep your eye upon the chart—*
> *And go on!*
>
> *Buy the truth and sell it not,*
> *Hold for God the bit you've got;*
> *Be content whate'er your lot—*
> *And go on!*
>
> *Feed on Christ the living Bread,*
> *Drink of Him, the Fountain Head;*
> *Think of why His blood was shed—*
> *And go on!*
>
> —W. Luff

(2 Kings 2. 6; John 6. 66-68; Acts 14. 22; 26. 22; Phil. 3. 13, 14)

227. Continuance. On his voyage to discover America, as day after day no land appeared, and again and again his sailors threatened mutiny and tried to persuade him to turn back, Columbus refused to listen to their entreaties and entered each day in the ship's log-book the two words—'Sailed on'.

(Exod. 14. 15; Num. 13. 30; Luke 9. 62; Heb. 6. 2)

228. Continuance. Some Christians are like hothouse plants, all right when the steam is on, with a special series of meetings or when a gifted minister of the Word or evangelist is among them. But when things are in their

usual way, those saints somehow always disappear. Hardy plants are what are wanted—full of sap all weathers, Christians living for God all the days no matter who comes or who goes.
(Josh. 24. 31; Ps. 73. 23; Luke 24. 53; 2 Tim. 3. 14)

229. Continuance.
Keep me from turning back.
My hand is on the plough, my faltering hand,
But all in front of me is untilled land;
What have I but this paltry grain,
These dwindling husks, a handful of dry corn,
These poor lean stocks? My courage is outworn:
Keep me from turning back.
(Luke 9. 62; 2 Tim. 4. 10)

230. Conversion—a Change of life. Conversion has been called a change of mind and a change of attitude, and this produces a change in the whole tenor of a life.

A young girl desiring baptism and admission to the Lord's supper in a town in Scotland was being interviewed by the elders of the local church who wanted to be sure she really had had a spiritual experience, for they considered her rather young.

First she was asked, 'Did you ever find out that you were a sinner?'

'Yes!' she replied without hesitation, 'I did indeed.'

The second question put to her was, 'Do you think, my girl, that you have undergone a change?' 'I know I have,' was the immediate reply.

'And do you think you are a sinner still?' she was asked.

'Yes,' she said, 'I know I am a sinner.'

'Well,' the question came, 'and what change has come over you?'

'Well,' she said, 'it's like this. Before I was converted I was running after sin. Now I am running away from it.'

There was in her both a change of attitude and a change of direction.
(Ps. 119. 59; Acts 11. 21; 1 Thess. 1. 9, 10)

231. Conversion—Change of Master. Horatio Bottomley, a very popular man and editor of a popular periodical, made a fortune. When his swindles were exposed, he was sentenced to seven years' imprisonment for embezzlement. Captain Tylor of the Church Army, hearing of him, determined to visit him and have a conversation with him in prison. As he approached the prisoner's cell, he wondered what he could say by way of introduction and decided to begin right away by telling the story of his conversion. So, when they met, Captain Tylor began, 'I was converted in Colston Hall, Bristol, when Canon Hay Aitken was preaching on the text, "Ye must be born again".'

'Was that in the year so and so?' asked Bottomley, specifying the year.

'Yes!' was Tylor's reply.

'And was it on a Friday night?' asked Bottomley.

'It was, but how did you know?'

'I too was there, but I curled my lip and walked out, saying, "It's not for me. I'm going to run my life in my own way, and shan't let anyone else manage it".'
(Josh. 24. 15; Rom. 6. 17-19; 10. 9, 10)

232. Conversion—Necessary for all. On one occasion H. P. Barker was having some Gospel meetings in a soap-manufacturing area, and the manager of one of the factories, who was a fine Christian man, asked him if he would like to see over his soap factory. Mr. Barker said he would be delighted, so, at the appointed hour, he went to the factory, was met by the manager and had the processes used in the manufacture of soap explained to him as they moved round the establishment. First, the manager took him to a number of vats filled with bad-smelling fats, and Mr. Barker was glad when they moved on because the stench was most unpleasant. After going round the various departments of the factory and explaining everything to his visitor, the manager had a lovely box of toilet soap brought and presented it to Mr. Barker, saying, 'The beautiful, useful, fragrant soap contained in this box was made from the evil-smelling fats you saw in those vats at the beginning of our tour round the factory.'

That night H. P. Barker preached on 'Conversion' and used the illustration of the conversion of the fats into fragrant soaps by means of a process known to the trade.

Next day he received a letter from one who had attended the meeting and heard his illustration. The writer said that he too was manager of a soap factory and invited Mr. Barker to come and visit it, 'for', said he, 'we do not use evil-smelling fats, but only the finest sweet-smelling oils for the manufacture of our soaps.' Mr. Barker wrote thanking him, but assuring him at the same time that a second visit to a soap factory was unnecessary. 'For', he said, 'whether the material used be bad-smelling fats or pleasant, sweet oils, it needs to be converted before it can become fragrant, useful soap.'
(Matt. 18. 3; Rom. 3. 23; Acts 15. 9)

233. Conversion—Providence of God in. A young man had been for some time under a sense of sin, longing to find mercy; but he could not reach it. He was a telegraph clerk, and being in the office one morning, he had to receive and transmit a telegram. To his great surprise, he spelled out these words, 'Behold the Lamb of God which taketh away the sin of the world!' A gentleman out for a holiday was telegraphing a message in answer to a letter from a friend who was in trouble of soul. It was meant for another, but he who transmitted it received eternal life, as the words came flashing into his soul.
—C. H. Spurgeon
(John 1. 29, 36, 37; Rev. 5. 9)

234. Conversion—of a Boxer. Bendigo was a prize-fighter who had been in Nottingham gaol. While there he had to attend the services on Sunday. One Sunday the subject was David's victory over Goliath, and Bendigo bawled out at the end, 'Bravo! I'm glad the little 'un won', and this was treated as a great joke by the other prisoners. The following Sunday he heard a sermon on Dan. 3, about the three Hebrew youths cast into the fiery furnace but saved by the Lord. Bendigo said to himself, 'If one Bendigo (Abednego) can be saved, why not another?' The last sermon he heard before finishing his time was about the seven hundred left-handed men in the book of Judges, and, remarking on this, Bendigo said, 'And I'm a left-handed man, of course I am, that was what beat the knowing ones I had to stand up against;' and added, 'Now, please God, I'll turn, and this Bendigo shall be saved too.'

When he finished his prison sentence his old chums were waiting for him and wanted him to go to the public-house, but he said to them, 'Look here, I will never again drink with any man in a public-house as long as I live.' They looked at each other and kept discreetly quiet, for they were afraid of his fists.

From that Bendigo continues his story: 'As I walked, I met a friend who wished me well, and he said, "Bendy, what do you say to coming up tonight to hear Undaunted Dick?" "Who's he?" said I, "I never heard of him." "Oh," says he, "he's a collier chap that was once in a bad way, and is now converted and turned preacher." "Ay," said I, "I'll go and hear him, he's one of my sort." So I went to hear him, and the next night I went again. It was bad weather and snowing hard, and I had to make my way home late at night across a park, and when I was half way across I couldn't hold out any longer. So, in the dark, with the snow coming down, I fell down on to my knees, and I asked the blessed Saviour to forgive me my many sins, and to blot them out in His blood and make me a new man; and when I got up I knew it was all done, I felt it in my heart.

'The next day I went again to hear Dick, and didn't I feel happy. I felt a peace and pardon in my soul, and I heard my Saviour saying, "My peace I give unto you".' There he made his first stand for God and gave his first public witness.
(Acts 11. 14; 16. 30, 31; 1 Tim. 1. 15, 16)

235. Conversion—of a Brahmin. Kasturi Sambamurthy was a Telugu Brahmin born in a very orthodox family but adopted by a rich uncle when a baby of only eleven months. He was invested with the sacred cord (Yagno-pavita) while still a boy and thus became a Dwija (twice-born one), though he knew nothing of the new birth. Very religious, he made a study of the world religions, learnt Sanskrit, and became well-versed in the Vedas, the sacred writings of the Hindus.

During the Dasara festival of 1912, in the month of October, the Holy Spirit began first to work in his heart. The question—'What is prayer?'—arose in the depths of his heart. He knew that his prayers as a Brahmin were all repetitions of Sanskrit prayers. Just at that time he was transferred to the Taylor High School, Narsapur, as a teacher there, and took on work as a munshi to a lady missionary in Narsapur, giving her tuition in the Telugu language. About that time he received direct from Scotland a book entitled *Answers to Prayer*, but could not understand how the sender knew about him or what his address and the yearning of his heart were.

During the festival days in January, 1918, while reading *Down Water Street*, he found himself weeping like a child, but could not understand why. From his heart came the cry, 'How can I find peace?' Then came the answer, 'The Son of Man has power on earth to forgive sins' (Mark 2. 10). But his proud heart objected—'How can I believe in the same God as some who are eaters of carrion and pork?' He found an excuse in the argument, 'If Jesus is omnipotent and Lord of the universe, He will bring me out in spite of my resistance.' Many believers were at that time praying for him. He prayed himself in Telugu but not in the name of the Lord Jesus.

One afternoon, while he was helping one of his missionary students to translate the first verses of John's Gospel into Telugu, a sudden flash of light illumined his mind, showing him that Jesus Christ was the Creator of the universe. After that he began to pray in the name of the Lord Jesus and read the Bible to his children, instructing them in its teaching. He could no longer remain happy as a Brahmin.

Three years went by, and the death of his mother and his wife (the latter a believer in the Lord Jesus Christ before she passed away) made it possible for him to come out boldly for the Lord. Then, after one of his daughters who was taken very ill with typhoid fever recovered, he left home, taking her with him, was baptised by the missionary, Mr. E. S. Bowden, and spent the remainder of his life till he was called Home in November, 1943, in humble, devoted service to his Lord and Master.
(1 Thess. 1. 9, 10; 1 John 5. 13)

236. Conversion—of a Crook. Jerry McAuley, the founder of the Water Street Mission in New York, at the age of 19 was sentenced to Sing Sing prison for a term of sixteen years and six months. In the prison chapel one morning, 'Awful Gardiner'—a notorious prize-fighter and an all-round ruffian whom Jerry had known prior to going to prison—was preaching. As Gardiner went on, with tears streaming down his face, telling of the love of Jesus, Jerry was convicted of sin. Gardiner quoted some passage of Scripture that impressed itself upon Jerry, and when they were dismissed and he had gone to his cell, he looked in the ventilator and found a Bible. Dusting it he tried to read but with some difficulty. He had never had one in his hands before, and he looked aimlessly to try to find the verse Gardiner had quoted. He never found that particular verse, but he did find that Jesus died for sinners, and the Holy Spirit showed him that he was a sinner.

'I've found Jesus,' he shouted. 'Oh, bless the Lord, I've found Jesus.' The unusual sound attracted the keeper, and he threw the rays of his dark lantern on Jerry as he was praising God in his lonely cell. In rough tones he shouted, 'What's the matter with you?' 'I've found Jesus,' replied Jerry. 'I'll put you in the cooler in the morning,' the keeper said, and took down his number. Jerry said, 'The Lord made him forget it, for I was never put in the cooler.' This was Jerry McAuley's conversion.

A wonderful revival broke out in the prison. Missionaries from the city went up and every opportunity was given them by the management. Jerry was the centre of all this activity. It resulted in his being pardoned by Governor John A. Dix, eight years of his sentence being remitted.

(John 1. 45; Acts 11. 21)

237. **Conversion—of a General.** I came to the Lord Jesus Christ and trusted Him as my Saviour when I was a boy at Charterhouse School, getting on for fifty years ago. It came to me in this way. I felt the burden of sin. Even boys can feel that, and I certainly did. And that burden was a very grievous burden to me.

One Sunday evening I suddenly realised that He had died in order to put away my sins and to blot them out. And God, for Christ's sake, that evening forgave my sins and blotted them out; and I have not been able to doubt from that day to this that that was a real and final transaction, and that all my sins—even those which I have committed since then, and they have been many—have all been put away once and for all. I could not doubt that, because it depends upon what He did, and not upon what I have done.

I would not dream of facing life in the army or out of it, without Christ. I do not know how people can go on trying to live without Him, especially in these troublous and anxious days in which we live.

—General Sir William Dobbie
(Matt. 11. 28; Acts 26. 22)

238. **Conversion—of a Jew.** I was born of Jewish parents in 1883 in Manchester, my father being a Sephardim or Spanish and Portuguese Jew. I learnt a little Hebrew and at eleven years of age went to a Jewish boarding school. In 1896 I went to Clifton College, which was the only school that had an orthodox Jewish house where the Jewish religion could be kept and where we had no work or games on the Sabbath. Shortly after I went to Clifton I had my Barmitzvah, which is something like the Church of England confirmation. I went to the synagogue and sang a portion of the law and recited a prayer in Hebrew. My parents gave a reception afterwards at our house and I received numerous presents. Altogether this is the most important day in the life of a young male Jew, as he is then considered to be himself responsible to God for his sins. I cannot say that I was 'touching the law blameless'. I did not keep the Sabbath or the whole law and was therefore condemned (Deut. 27. 26). Nevertheless I was considered quite religious by my friends.

With regard to my social life, I was a selfish and pleasure-loving person. I did a little dancing and horse and dog racing, and after my parents' death went every year to the South of France to see life and often spent a few days in Paris on my way back. The casinos were open on Sundays, and there were many gala dinners where we danced and were entertained by some of the best-known variety artists in the world. After that, play went on at the tables till all hours. I was also a great cinema fan. My great pastime, however, was card-playing, and I was an expert at bridge. I won a prize in one of the daily papers before I was 21 years of age and several other competitions and cups, as well as much money. Later on, Mr. Culbertson, an American, made bridge into a business, chiefly in the U.S.A., and he wrote books, spoke on the radio, and founded bridge schools. In 1933 he came over here and challenged us to a duplicate bridge match, and I was chosen to play for England.

We played at Selfridge's, and the match was so important that we had the hall muffled to stop all noise. There was a large room adjoining where lectures were given on the play of the most interesting hands. There were free drinks for all, and the scores were in the 'Stop-press'. We played for a whole week from 3 o'clock till midnight each day, with an interval for rest, dress and dinner. We were described as two of the greatest players in the world. I was often invited out, and made much of, but the war stopped all social and competitive bridge. However, I went to the cinema several times a week and played bridge from ten till one o'clock with an interval for dinner. I was averaging £700 a year free from tax. In fact, bridge was my god.

At this stage of my career the great and Almighty God took a hand in my life. Unlike some Jews of the present day, I had never read a word of the New Testament. I did not even know the names of the books, or who the Apostle Paul was. In the Old Testament I knew the five books of Moses, some of the better known stories and some of the Psalms which we sang at prayers in the synagogue. I then had my first introduction to the New Testament and was given a book called *Grace and Truth* by Dr. Mackay, and the first chapter, headed 'There is no difference', showed me that, no matter how religious I was, or what other people thought of me, I was a guilty sinner in God's sight and eternally lost.

I went to some meetings and met some believers, but it was not until some time later and in God's good time, that my eyes were opened and I saw that Jesus of Nazareth was the Jewish Messiah, the Son of God and the Saviour of the world, and that all the Old Testament prophecies were fulfilled in Him. So on September 3rd, 1942, I accepted Jesus Christ as my personal Saviour, Sinbearer and Lord, confessing to God that I deserved punishment for my sins, but asking for forgiveness, not on my own merits, but on the finished work of Christ on the cross, where He shed His precious blood for me. I was now a child of God and had passed from death to life.

The wonderful part is not that I heard God's voice and obeyed Him, but that I have no more desire for cards or for any other worldly amusement or ambition. All these attractions have fallen away like dead leaves, as I am now a new creature in Christ. I was baptized by immersion nine days after. Recently a friend of mine told me that I used to be a miserable-looking chap and that now I look quite different. Why? I had good health, and enough money to gratify my desires, but without Christ. I am now ready to meet my Maker.

—P. V. Tabbush (abridged)
(John 5. 24; Rom. 1. 16; 2 Cor. 5. 17)

239. Conversion—of a Sikh. A proud boy from a noble home in the Punjab entered a mission school but flared into open rebellion on being compelled to read the Christian Scriptures. Rather than receive religious instruction under compulsion, he left the school and became ringleader of a hostile gang which threw mud and stones at the preacher. His final protest was publicly to burn copies of the Gospel. Then a miracle began and his mind was so disturbed that he determined, a few days later, that unless he could find some answer to his problems, he would take his own life.

That night he found Christ, became His bondslave, and found in Him the answer to all his problems. He gave the rest of his life to proclaiming the Gospel of Jesus Christ in India, and then ventured into Tibet with the same glorious Gospel. From there he never returned.

That man was Sadhu Sundar Singh.

240. Conversion—of a Singer. The great singer, Jacques Hopkins, L.R.A.M., M.R.S.T., in writing the story of his conversion, described himself as a heathen while a student in the gay and wicked city of Paris. Before going there for musical studies, he had been a choir boy in the church. In the first World War, as one of 200 officers bound for the Persian Gulf, he embarked on a ship of which Captain E. Carré was captain, and his attention was drawn to him when he saw him rise to give thanks to God at the dinner table.

At the Saturday evening concert Hopkins sang 'There's a long, long trail a-winding,' and Captain Carré, interested in him because of his magnificent voice, went to his cabin to pray that he might be won for Christ. At the service on the following day Captain Carré

himself gave the message, and the singer's conscience was pierced. From that point Jacques Hopkins himself will tell of his conversion.

'Next day there followed a friendly talk which I can never forget. "Are you interested?" the captain enquired. "I certainly am," I replied, as he opened his well-worn Bible and showed me God's great provision in the death of His Son to meet my present and eternal needs.

'"You can start a new life from tonight," he remarked, while I drank in every word. "God is willing to forgive you on the ground of the perfect work of His Son through your acceptance of Christ as your own Lord and Master."

"It seems too good to be true," I replied.

"It all depends," the captain continued, "on what Christ did for you as your Sinbearer when He bore the fearful judgement due to the sinner. Now that sin has been punished in a perfect Substitute, God is able to forgive you on righteous grounds and give you everlasting life."

'There came a pause, then I said, "Captain, if I can have this, I'll have it! Tell me what I must do."

"Why not kneel down and tell the Lord you are willing to trust Him?" he replied.

'We knelt. The captain prayed very simply and pleaded for me. In a few broken words I prayed. "Lord, save me," and at that moment I surrendered myself to the Saviour.

'Some thousands of miles away, all unknown to me, an old lady, an intimate friend of the captain, was burdened in prayer for him, and was compelled to plead earnestly for him all through that Sunday. She felt there was some special reason. Months later she heard how wonderfully God had answered.'
(Acts 16. 30, 31; Rom. 10. 9)

241. Conversion—of a Youth. Conversion is the turning of man to God. A. T. Schofield, the Harley Street physician, was in his fifteenth year when he experienced its power. At that age, one summer's evening, he arrived at Mr. Charles Hanmer's Private Academy in Rhyl, N. Wales, went upstairs and found his bedroom. The boy who shared the bedroom with him asked him first if he were the new boy, and then enquired, 'Are you a Christian?' The new boy replied that he was not a Christian, knowing that, though he had been religiously brought up, his parents' teaching had fallen on deaf ears. Then his companion asked, 'Would you like to be one?' A. T. Schofield replied, 'It's no use liking. I know well I never shall be a Christian.'

His young mentor went off to a prayer meeting that was being held, to pray for the new boy, and, returning, tumbled into bed and fell asleep. But A. T. Schofield could not sleep, knowing that the lad who shared the bedroom with him was all right and he was all wrong. He tossed about with uneasy snatches of sleep till nearly 2 a.m., asking himself why he could not rest like the boy in the next bed. Suddenly there came to his mind the words, 'Because you won't take it.'

He realised then that he was very sick with the sin disease and was asking himself why he was not cured when all the time the medicine to heal his disease was within his reach. The remedy for his disease, he knew, was belief, true personal belief in Christ his Saviour. Then to his horror he saw that to believe in the medicine would do him no good: he must take it.

The Spirit of God was hovering over that lad, for he thought, 'I cannot do better than settle it now.' So kneeling on his bed, he solemnly and from his heart said aloud, 'O God! I take Thy Son, Jesus Christ, to be my Saviour this night,' and dropped off to sleep.

Next morning the master came and sat beside him, and said, 'We were praying for you last night; I'm so sorry you are not a Christian.' Immediately the Holy Spirit flashed into the youth's mind the words, 'If thou shalt confess with thy mouth the Lord Jesus and believe in thine heart that God hath raised Him from the dead, thou shalt be saved.' He knew he had believed in his heart, so it only remained for him to confess with his mouth.

So he said to the master, 'But I am one.'

'But you told us you were not,' said the master incredulously.

'No more was I last night,' replied A. T. Schofield.

'But when did you become one?' he said, completely puzzled.

'About two o'clock this morning,' the lad replied.

'What happened?' asked the master. Then the young convert told him all, and in telling his story, Dr. A. T. Schofield, himself adds, 'I rushed out of the house, threw my cap into the air, and ran round and round the playground to let off, as it were, some of the steam.' (John 1. 12; Rom. 10. 9; Col. 2. 6)

242. Convert. Four years after the *Titanic* went down a young Scotsman rose in a meeting in Hamilton, Canada, and said, 'I am a survivor of the *Titanic*. When I was drifting alone on a spar on that awful night, the tide brought Mr. John Harper of Glasgow, also on a piece of wreck, near me. "Man," he said, "are you saved?" "No!" I said, "I am not." He replied, "Believe on the Lord Jesus Christ and thou shalt be saved."

'The waves bore him away; but, strange to say, brought him back a little later and he said, "Are you saved now?" "No," I said, "I cannot honestly say that I am." He said again, "Believe on the Lord Jesus Christ and thou shalt be saved," and shortly after he went down. There, alone in the night and with two miles of water under me, I believed. I am John Harper's last convert.'
(Acts 16. 31)

243. Convictions—Courage of. Harry Shepler, a young man of whom the *Sunday School Times*

tells, was in the signal service. Being ordered one morning by a sergeant to report for duty at the canteen, he refused to do so, and the sergeant threatened to report him to the officer that day.

'All right,' said Shepler, 'go ahead. I did not enlist to be a bartender but a soldier, and I will not report at the canteen.'

He was duly reported to the major who sent for him. Shepler went with trembling knees and with a steady heart, for he knew he was right. The officer said to him, 'Are you the young man who disobeyed orders this morning?'

'Yes, sir, I am.'

'Why did you do it?'

'Simply because I do not believe it is right to do what I was asked to do. I enlisted to be a soldier and not a bartender.'

The major arose quickly from his stool and, extending his hand, said:

'Shepler, you are the kind of man we want. I am glad to see a fellow who has the courage of his convictions. You are not obliged to report at the canteen.'
(Acts 22. 1; 26. 2; 1 Cor. 16. 13; 1 Pet. 3. 15, 16)

244. Costliness—of Salvation. When D. L. Moody approached a man who was president of a colliery about his soul's salvation, the man listened patiently and courteously, then said, 'It's too cheap, I can't believe it is true. You ask me to do nothing except to accept Christ in order to obtain salvation. It is too cheap. It should cost more than that.'

D. L. Moody replied, 'Did you go down into the shaft of the colliery today?' 'Yes,' said the man, 'I did.' 'How far did you go down?' 'Oh, several hundred feet.' 'How did you go down?' D. L. Moody asked.

'Well, I pushed a button, the lift came up. I pushed another button, the lift went down.'

'That was all you did, just pushed a button?' Mr. Moody asked.

'Certainly,' the man replied, 'the coal company had spent thousands of pounds to sink the shaft and construct the elevators, but all I did was to push a button.'

'That's it, exactly,' said D. L. Moody. 'Salvation has been wrought out at a tremendous price. It is the costliest thing in the world. Yet God offers it to you free because of what God has done by His Son.'
(Rom. 4. 5; 6. 23; Gal. 3. 13; Eph. 2. 8, 9)

245. Courage.
True courage is not moved by breath of words:
While the rash bravery of boiling blood,
Impetuous, knows no settled principle.
(Acts 4. 18-20; 5. 28, 29)

246. Courtesy. 'Love does not behave itself unseemly but is always courteous, polite, and becoming in demeanour,' says J. Oswald Sanders in *Light on Life's Problems*. Then he recounts an incident told of Louis XIV of France.

On one occasion he was narrating a story before his courtiers at Versailles, when suddenly he ended it very lamely. A few minutes after, a prince left the room. The king then said, 'You must have noticed how lamely my story ended. I forgot that it reflected on an ancestor of the prince who has just left the room; and I thought it better to spoil a good story than to distress a good man.' That was courtesy.
(1 Pet. 3. 8)

247. Criticism. Some one has made the observation that, when we point the finger of criticism at anyone, the three fingers that are bent are pointing to ourselves, and the thumb is pointing upward to God in Heaven. So, by criticising another, and pointing the finger to find fault with another, we lay ourselves open to three times as much criticism of ourselves, and also point the finger of accusation at God.
(Matt. 7. 1-3)

248. Cross—of Christ.

The Rationalist says: 'Give me Christ without the cross.'

The Ritualist says: 'Give me the cross without the Christ.'

The redeemed soul says:

A Crossless Christ my Saviour could not be;
A Christless cross no refuge is for me;
But Oh, Christ crucified, I rest on Thee.'

In the Cross of Christ is seen—
the glorious climax of the Eternal plan,
the greatest crime of sin-benighted man,
the gravest crisis of a sinless life,
the grandest crown of Christ's triumphant strife.
(John 12. 24-27; Acts 2. 23; Gal. 6. 14)

249. Cross—Creator on the.
The Maker of the universe,
As Man, for man was made a curse;
The claims of laws that He had made
Unto the uttermost He paid.

His holy fingers made the bough
That grew the thorns that crowned His brow.
The nails that pierced His hands were mined
In secret places He designed.

He made the forest whence had sprung
The tree on which His body hung:
He died upon a cross of wood,
Yet made the hill on which it stood.

The sky that darkened o'er His head
By Him above the earth was spread:
The sun that hid from Him its face
By His decree was poised in space.

The spear that spilled His precious blood
Was tempered in the fires of God.
The grave in which His form was laid
Was hewn in rocks His hands had made.

The throne on which He now appears
Was His from everlasting years;
But a new glory crowns His brow
And every knee to Him shall bow.
(Gal. 3. 13; 5. 11; Phil. 2. 8; Col. 2. 13, 14)

250. Cross—Enemies of the. Cicero, the Roman author and orator, said, 'Let the very name of the cross be far away from Roman citizens, not from their bodies only, but from their thoughts, their eyes and their ears.'
(Gal. 5. 11; Phil. 3. 18)

251. Cross—Foolishness of the. 'A man crucified between two thieves on a Roman gibbet! You ask us to trust our all for this world and the world to come, to Him? That is the height of folly,' says the man of the world, speaking the 'wisdom of the world'. For 'the preaching of the cross is to them that perish foolishness'.

Dr. A. T. Schofield writes of a conversation he had with an unconverted relative who, referring to the cross used as a sign, said, 'I can't understand the practice of some Christians. They seem so heartless.'

'How?' asked Dr. Schofield.

'Look at that cross! Do you think that if I really loved a man and he was my dearest friend and had the misfortune to die on the gallows, I should erect them everywhere to his memory and tell everybody about him?'
(1 Cor. 1. 18; Gal. 6. 14)

252. Cross—God's Love in the. It has been said that the heart of Christianity is the Bible, the heart of the Bible is the cross, and the heart of the cross is the very heart of God Himself, for
Inscribed upon the cross we see,
In shining letters, 'God is Love'.
The Lamb Who died upon the tree
Has brought us mercy from above.
(John 3. 16; Gal. 2. 20; 1 John 3. 16)

253. Cross—Pardon through the.
In evil long I took delight,
Unaw'd by shame or fear,
Till a new object struck my sight
And stopped my wild career.

I saw One hanging on a tree
In agonies and blood,
Who fixed His languid eyes on me,
As near His cross I stood.

Sure never till my latest breath
Can I forget that look;
It seemed to charge me with His death,
Though not a word He spoke.

A second look He gave which said,
'I freely all forgive;
This blood is for thy ransom paid,
I died that thou may'st live.'

Thus while His death my sin displays
In all its blackest hue;
Such is the mystery of grace
It seals my pardon too.

With pleasing grief and mournful joy
My spirit now is fill'd,
That I should such a life destroy,
Yet live by Him I killed.
                                                    —John Newton
(Acts 10. 39, 40, 43; 13. 38, 39)

254. Cross—For the Penitent.

If the wanderer his mistake discern,
Judge his own ways and sigh for a return,
Bewildered once, must he bewail his loss
For ever and forever? No!—the Cross—
There, and there only (though the Deist rave,
And atheist, if earth bear so base a slave)
There, and there only, is the power to save.
There no delusive hope invites despair,
No mocking meets you, no deception there.
The spells and charms that blinded you before
All vanish there and fascinate no more.

—W. Cowper

(Acts 2. 23, 37; 1 Cor. 1. 23, 24; Gal. 3. 13)

255. Cross—For the Penitent.

He showed me the cross where He died for me,
And I end where I begin
With an eye that looks to my Saviour
And a heart that mourns for my sin.

(Lam. 1. 12; Matt. 27. 35, 36, 42; Acts 20. 21)

256. Cross—For the Sin-burdened. John
Bunyan, in *The Pilgrim's Progress*, tells how,
when the pilgrim with his burden arrived at
the cross, and looked by faith to the Saviour,
his burden of sin fell off and was buried in the
grave. He then exclaimed:

'*Blest cross! Blest sepulchre! Blest rather be*
The Man that there was put to shame for me.'

(Matt. 11. 28; Gal. 2. 20)

257. Cross—Symbol of Sacrifice. The cross
forces sacrifice into the heart of life. It con-
demns selfishness, the oldest idol in the world.
It reveals God's method of dying in sacrifice,
and being raised again in power—as the
process through which the individual lives.

—Dr. J. Kelman

(Gal. 2. 20; 6. 14)

258. Cross—Unreliability of everything except.
In the Alpine Museum at Zermatt is a broken
rope. It is stout: it looks strong: yet it failed
at a critical moment. Here is the story.

Edward Whymper, a famous wood engraver
and Alpine climber, had for many years been
ambitious to scale the dizzy heights of the
Matterhorn, but although many times reaching
the great shoulder on the Italian side, he had
never got to the top. On the day named he
started again, the more eagerly because a party
of Italians were to attempt it also on the same
morning.

His party consisted of four climbers and
three guides. The guides were two brothers,
named Tangwalder, and a famous guide,
Michel Croz. All went well until the top was
reached and for the first time they stood on the
dizzy peak enjoying a wonderful view, and, as
Whymper described it, 'one crowded hour of
glorious life'.

Then they re-roped themselves to descend
in the following order: Michel Croz, the guide,
first; then three climbers; then the senior
Tangwalder in front of Whymper and the
younger Tangwalder in the rear. Carefully

they were letting themselves down the fearful
precipice, Michel Croz out of sight of the rear
members helping the next man to find a footing
over the yawning abyss.

A startling cry rang out as a man fell on to
Croz, hurling him off his slender foothold.
The next two men were dragged after them, but
the experienced climbers above tightened the
rope between them and stood firm to bear the
shock as one man. The rope ran its length and
the blow came, but the cord snapped like a
thread. The horrified climbers above saw their
friends spreading their arms and legs in a
hopeless attempt to stop their slide over the
precipice. They fell on the great glacier 4,000
feet below.

For nearly an hour the remaining three stood
in terrified silence—petrified. At length the
guides began to weep, saying they could never
attempt the fearful descent. Mr. Whymper,
however, nerved them to the effort, and hours
later they arrived in Zermatt to tell their story.

The broken rope was examined. Why had it
not held? Alas! it was not a genuine Alpine
Club rope. Alpine ropes are distinguished by a
red strand running through them, and this
rope did not have one. How it was that a
substitute rope was carried on such an occasion
has ever since remained an inexplicable
mystery.

It has often been said that the saving power
of the Cross of Christ runs like a red cord
through the heart of the Bible. Are you joined
to the Saviour by this unbreakable cord? Or
have you some substitute to which you are
trusting? No other power will stand the strain;
every substitute will break when it is needed
most.

—*Prairie Overcomer*

(1 Cor. 1. 17, 18; Col. 2. 14, 15)

259. Crown.

As a soldier who shrinks from the danger
The joy of the soldier must lose,
So the crown of the Lord is withholden
If the cross upon earth we refuse.

—D. W. Whittle

(2 Tim. 2. 3, 12; 4. 7, 8)

260. Crown. Dr. W. Graham Scroggie
narrated the following incident. A minister
with a pastoral heart was once visiting a poor,
elderly sister who was a member of his congregation. Before praying with her prior to
leaving, he sympathized with her in her
troubles and struggles to keep body and soul
together, concluding with the words, 'Never
mind, my dear sister, you will receive your
crown by and by,' having in mind, no doubt,
the promise: 'Blessed is the man that endureth
temptation; for when he is tried, he shall
receive the crown of life, which the Lord hath
promised to them that love Him.' 'Yes,' she
replied, 'I know that, but I could be doing
with the half-crown now.'

(Rom. 12. 8; Gal. 2. 10; James 1. 12)

261. Crucifixion—of Christ. In a small village stood a chapel upon whose arch were inscribed the words, 'We preach Christ crucified', that all who entered the chapel or stood outside might understand the purpose for which the meeting-room had been built. For years godly men preached there and presented a crucified Saviour as the only means of salvation. But as those generations of godly preachers passed, there arose a generation that considered the cross and its message 'the gospel of the shambles', and began to preach salvation by Christ's example and teaching, without the necessity of His sacrificial death on the cross. And a little creeper made its way up the side of the archway and covered the final word of the inscription so that it was completely hidden from view. Now the inscription read, 'We preach Christ', and so they did, but not Christ crucified. After some time some asked why the sermons should be confined to Christ and the teachings of the Bible, so the preachers began to give discourses on the social gospel, politics and moral disarmament without Christ. And the little creeper crept along a little further and wiped out the third word of the inscription, so that it read simply, 'We preach'. Man's philosophies and social conditions had taken the place of Christ's Gospel. The Apostle Paul, one of the men who 'turned the world upside down' in the first century, determined when in cultured Corinth to know nothing among them but 'Jesus Christ and Him crucified'.

(1 Cor. 1. 18, 23, 24; 2. 2)

262. Crucifixion—with Christ. Many a believer will be fain to say, 'My old things have not passed away. My memory is loaded with the accumulated rubbish of unhallowed reading, conversation, deeds. Unholy scenes rise before my imagination and with the longing to be holy there co-exists the craving for things unholy. My heart is not pure but mixed.'

How can the old man be dealt with so effectively that he shall lose his power, with the evil which is all he can produce? Obviously this result would be obtained most simply and certainly if he could be killed, since a dead man has no power for mischief, being unable longer to suggest thoughts, inspire feelings or influence the will of another. But how can our old man be killed? Not by efforts of our own. Nor can he be persuaded to commit suicide. This death must be wrought by the power of God. What has God done in this matter?—Rom. 6. 8—'Was crucified,' i.e., was killed at the cross of Christ. The assurance that God offers to us is that our old man is not alive because he was crucified at Calvary. He turns our attention from ourselves and bids us consider what He wrought in Christ. Thus the matter stands as God reckons, and thus we are to reckon it to be true.

We must accept as being true in our case that which God says is true in Christ. We have no other evidence of the death of the old man

than the statement of God. We must face each day by telling the Lord that we take it for granted that by the power of the Spirit the death of the old man will be made good in our experience.

—G. H. Lang
(Rom. 6. 11; 7. 21; Gal. 2. 20; Col. 3. 3)

263. Crucifixion—with Christ. To one who asked George Muller the secret of his service, he replied, 'There was a day when I died, utterly died,' and, as he spoke, he bent lower until he almost touched the floor—'died to George Muller, his opinions, preferences, tastes and will, died to the world, its approval or censure, died to the approval or blame even of my brethren and friends, and since then I have studied to show myself approved unto God.'

(Rom. 6. 11; Gal. 2. 20; 5. 24)

264. Cup—Exchange of.
Refusing the cup that would deaden pain
To drink the cup that meant our gain,
He, Servant of all, trod a thorn-girt path
To bleed and to die and give all that He hath,
His soul crushed down in grief's dark hour
That others might gain by His sacrifice power.

His priestly garments He laid aside
To wash the feet of the weary and tried,
His majesty linked with service so low,
He dared to stoop, that He might show
His power to bend, His joy to serve,
And touched His lip to the cup's cold curve.
(Matt. 26. 39; 27. 34; Ps. 116. 13; 1 Cor. 10. 16)

265. Cup—Overflowing.
There is always something over when we trust
*   our gracious Lord;*
Every cup He fills o'erfloweth: His great rivers
*   all are broad.*
Nothing narrow, nothing stinted ever issues from
*   His store;*
To His own He gives full measure, running over
*   evermore.*
(Ps. 23. 5; James 1. 5)

266. Danger—in Delay. In the days when the American Northwest was being opened up, a young engineer went to build a bridge across a mountain chasm. After months of work they had almost finished the bridge, and one night he said to his men, 'Come after supper, and we will finish it in about an hour, and I will pay you a day's wages for that extra hour.'

'No!' they said, 'we have made other arrangements.'

'Come back,' he pleaded, 'and I will give you two days' wages.'

They said, 'No! but why do you want us back?'

He replied, 'If a great storm should come tonight in the mountain it would sweep the bridge away. We have not quite finished it.'

But they went their way, saying, 'It won't rain in months.' And that very night the rain-filled clouds emptied their floods upon the mountains, and they rushed down relentless in their power and swept the unfinished bridge away.

It is a parable of the soul that knows, and wishes, and yet presumes and delays and waits. How different was the response of the men of Nehemiah's day when they said, 'Let us rise and build.'

—*Sunday School Times*

(Neh. 2. 18; 2 Cor. 6. 2)

267. Danger—in Delay. Years ago in Pennsylvania, United States, a small town stood near a river. Just above the town a large dam was built across the river which held back a great volume of water. Then came extra heavy rains and the water rose to a height unknown before. Engineers were anxiously watching and asking: 'Will the dam hold?' Suddenly a crack was noticed in the dam. Immediately the engineers gave a warning. Word was passed round to all, 'Flee at once to the hills; the dam is breaking and a terrible flood will come.' But that dam had been there many years and no flood had been seen. Some doubted and said, 'What do these young fellows know about it?' And they refused to leave with those who left everything to fly for safety.

Then suddenly with a tremendous roar the dam burst and millions of gallons of water swept down the valley sending over three hundred to their death. When the catastrophe came there was no time to get away. Those who heeded the warning and left at once had time to reach safety, but those who did not obey the warning had no time to escape. Have you heard the voice of God warning you to flee from the danger that is coming? 'There's danger and death in delay.'

—A. L. Goold

(Gen. 19. 17; Matt. 3. 7; Acts 13. 40, 41; Rev. 6. 15, 16)

268. Danger—from Satan's wiles. The antlion is a little dark-looking creature that makes a hole in the sand, puts itself in the very centre and buries itself completely out of sight, except its horn which appears like a rusty needle sticking up in the sand. An observer of its tactics wrote:

'A little red ant came along seeking her food in her usual busy way. So she climbed upon the rim of the sandy cup and peeped over to investigate. Presently, suspecting danger, she turned to scramble off. Alas! it was too late; the sand rolled from under her feet, and down she went to the bottom, when in an instant that little black horn opened like a pair of shears, and "Clip" the poor ant had lost a leg. And now the poor thing struggles to climb up, but, one leg gone, she finds it hard work.

'The little monster does not move or show himself. He knows what he is about. The ant has got almost to the top and liberty when the sand slips, and down she goes. "Clip" go the shears, and another leg is gone. She struggles hard to rise, but she gets up but a little way

before she slips again, and a third leg is off. She now gives up the struggle, and the lion devours her in a few minutes; and then with a flip of his tail throws the skin of the ant entirely out of the cup, and the trap is now set for another victim.'

The same process is gone through with flies and other insects. No ant-lion was in sight, but the destroyer was there. The dead were pushed out of sight. 'Your adversary the devil, as a roaring lion, walketh about seeking whom he may devour.'

(2 Cor. 2. 11; 1 Pet. 5. 8)

269. Danger—of Sin's Pleasures. Spending a short holiday near the Needles, Isle of Wight, I was much interested in an account of how a certain nocturnal moth was caught by a London entomologist.

The gentleman made a special journey to Freshwater to collect some specimens of a species which is said to be found in no other part of the British Isles except the South Downs near the Needles.

Shortly after sunset he proceeded along the top of the cliff, armed with a pot of syrup and a brush, and whenever he came to a thistle, he just daubed it slightly with the syrup and passed on. About midnight he returned along the same path, but this time provided with a lantern, and as he stepped from thistle to thistle, his innocent victims were found clustering round the syrup, and fell, an easy prey, into the collector's hand.

What a solemn picture, I thought, of how Satan dupes his victims! He, too, stalks through the land, daubing the pleasures of sin with a delusive sweetness, and soon after his victims, intoxicated with the poisoned draught and hardened by the deceitfulness of sin, lose all consciousness of their terrible danger.

—*The Journey and its End*

(2 Tim. 2. 26; Heb. 3. 13; 11. 25)

270. Dangers—in the Christian Life.

Sometimes the lions' mouths are shut;
Sometimes God bids us flight or fly;
Sometimes He feeds us by the brook;
Sometimes the flowing stream runs dry.

Sometimes the burning flames are quenched;
Sometimes with sevenfold heat they glow;
Sometimes His hand divides the waves:
Sometimes His billows overflow.

Sometimes He turns the sword aside;
Sometimes He lets the sharp blade smite;
Sometimes our foes are at our heels;
Sometimes He hides us from their sight.

We may not choose, nor would we dare,
The path in which our feet shall tread;
Enough that He that path hath made,
And He Himself shall walk ahead.

The dangers that His love allows
Are safer than our fears may know;
The peril that His care permits
Is our defence where'er we go.

(Acts 27. 9; 2 Cor. 1. 10; 11. 26; Heb. 11. 35

271. Dangers—of the Present Day. General William Booth once said, 'I consider the greatest dangers of the twentieth century to be: i. Religion without the Holy Ghost; ii. Christianity without Christ; iii. Forgiveness without regeneration; iv. Morality without God; v. Heaven without Hell.
(Col. 2. 8; 1 Tim. 6. 3-5; 2 Pet. 2. 1; 2 John 8. 9)

272. David. In calling David, God—sought a man (1 Sam. 13. 14), chose a shepherd (Ps. 78. 70), found a servant (Ps. 89. 20), commanded a captain (1 Sam. 13. 14), and provided a king (1 Sam. 16. 1-13).

> *Latest born of Jesse's race,*
> *Wonder lights thy bashful face.*
> *Twofold praise thou shalt obtain*
> *In royal court and battle plain,*
> *Then come heartache, care, distress,*
> *Blighted hope and loneliness;*
> *Wounds from friend and gifts from foe,*
> *Dizzied faith and guilt and woe.*

(1 Sam. 13. 14; Acts 13. 22) —J. H. Newman

273. Death—Conqueror of. Well might old Trapp, the commentator, say: 'This is the boldest and bravest challenge that man ever rang in the ears of death. Death is here outbraved, called craven to the face, and bidden to do his worst.' 'O Death, where is thy sting, O Grave where is thy victory?' The apostle, however, is not yet done. 'The sting of death is sin and the strength of sin is the law. But thanks be unto God that giveth us the victory through our Lord Jesus Christ.' The battle has been fought and the victory gained by the Crucified One, of whom Renan wrote, 'Complete Conqueror of death, take possession of Thy Kingdom, whither shall follow Thee, by the royal road which Thou hast traced, ages of worshippers.'
—Dr. Brookes

> *He hell in hell laid low;*
> *Made sin, He sin o'erthrew;*
> *Bow'd to the grave, destroyed it so,*
> *And death by dying slew.*

(1 Cor. 15. 55-57; Heb. 2. 14)

274. Death—Conqueror of. Alfred Mace, a minister of the Word of God, and his father, Jim Mace, the world's champion pugilist at one time, were walking together one day along a street when a funeral cortege approached. 'Here he comes again, dad, and only been beaten once,' said the son to the father. 'Where is he?' said the pugilist, assuming a boxing attitude. 'There he is: his name is Death,' said the preacher.
(1 Cor. 15. 55-57; Heb. 2. 14)

275. Death—Conqueror of. In a village of West Godavari District, India, there lives a goldsmith named Mruthyamjayachari, formerly a Viswabrahman, but now a preacher of the Gospel. Convinced of the error and sin of idolatry, he turned to God from idols while still young, and began to serve the living and true God and to wait for His Son from Heaven. He has since been greatly used in winning many souls for Christ. His long name means 'Priest of Death's conqueror'. This is what he has in truth become, for Jesus Christ is death's Conqueror.
(Heb. 2. 13; Rev. 1. 5, 6, 18; 5. 9, 10)

276. Death—Facing. The following is the true account of an episode recorded in the *Readers Digest* some time ago. On a warm Thursday afternoon of October, 1958, over a hundred men went down to work in a mine in Springhill, Nova Scotia. That day a catastrophic earth tremor occurred 12,000 feet down. Seventy-five men were killed immediately and about twenty more were trapped in the pit. Twelve of these managed to get together to face what seemed certain death. One had a leg broken in three places: another had his leg badly crushed and turned black from internal bleeding: and still another, suffering excruciating pain, had had his shoulder dislocated and his ribs battered.

By Saturday evening their water supply was exhausted, and their only remaining lamp flickered its last glow, plunging the twelve men into darkness. One of the men, a Christian named Caleb Rushton, started humming a tune. 'Let's have a song,' said one of his mates, and Caleb sang to them the hymn— *The Stranger of Galilee*—with its stirring chorus:

> '*And I felt I could love Him for ever,*
> *So gracious and tender was He:*
> *I claimed Him that day as my Saviour,*
> *That Stranger of Galilee.*'

On Sunday morning Rushton brought the dial of his watch close to his face. 'It's going on 7. They'll be getting ready for church soon,' he said. Without another word those men began praying, some almost incessantly. Occasional drifts of methane brought an added danger: it could kill any one of them and the others would not know. But God heard and answered their cry for deliverance, although they were nearly a week facing death in some form or other. Truly the gates of death seemed to have opened to them. Rescuers arrived at 2.25 on Thursday morning, and they were taken to fresh air and to safety.
(Job. 38. 17; Ps. 9. 13; 107. 18, 19)

277. Death—and the Hereafter. In the city of Valladolid, the ancient capital of Spain, there stands a monument erected in commemoration of the great discoveries made by Christopher Columbus. The most notable feature of it is a lion represented as deliberately destroying one of the words which had formed Spain's national motto for centuries. The Romans, thinking they had come to the confines of the earth, pronounced the three words which became Spain's motto—'Ne Plus Ultra'. The lion of Castile is represented as tearing the 'Ne' away, making it read 'Plus ultra', 'more beyond' or 'something beyond'. Death is not the end: it is not annihilation. There is something beyond, a hereafter.
(Heb. 9. 27)

278. Death—and the Hereafter.

Who would fardels bear
To grunt and sweat under a weary life
But that the dread of something after death,
The undiscovered country from whose bourne
No traveller returns, puzzles the will
And makes us rather bear the ills we have
Than fly to others we know nothing of.

—Shakespeare in *Hamlet*

279. Death—and the Hereafter. A keen
Christian witness wherever he went, a minister
of the gospel was on a journey from London
to the North of England, and got into a
carriage in which three men and two women
were already seated. One of the men said to
him, 'May I ask you a question?' 'Certainly!'
answered the preacher. 'There was a man who
had a family, who was a good citizen, an
indulgent father, and brought up his family
well. At 60 he developed cancer. He was a
friend of Charles Bradlaugh and used to defy
God. To save trouble and expense he committed suicide. Where did he go?' The
minister of the gospel replied, 'That is a
simple question. He went to his own place,
where you will go and I shall go. Everybody
goes to his own place. But I have a Friend
Who has told me He has prepared a place for
me. His place shall be mine. The Lord Jesus
is arranging my future home.'
(John 14. 1-3; Acts 1. 25)

280. Death—and the Hereafter. Second
Lieutenant H. F. Sargood, a young officer
aged nineteen of the Middlesex Regiment,
wrote the following, his last letter from the
Front. It was found in his kit, having been
left there just before he went into action.

'My own dearest parents, I don't suppose
you will ever get this, and I certainly hope
you won't as it is only to be sent to you if I
am killed while on the "Trench Stunt". I
expect you have wondered (or will do so) how
I regarded the prospect of death, for of course,
the possibility of it is always before one. As
you know, I have always been expecting it, so
it has not taken me by surprise. As for the
rest, well, I have never been able to express it
to myself, so I don't suppose I can do any
better for you. Although I have not regarded
the prospect with pleasure (I should imagine
that in a young man that would be unnatural)
yet I can say that it caused me no fear. I have,
of course, such feelings to buck me up as the
thought of being an Englishman, a gentleman,
the descendant of soldiers, and so on; but
when it comes to the point such things are of
little or no value.

'No, I have an assurance which is of far
more use to me than any of these things, the
knowledge that Jesus Christ is my Saviour,
and that He will be with me after death, the
same as He has been with me for the last
three or four years. This has been of the
greatest comfort to me, and—under God—I
owe it all to you, my dearest parents, and I
could never, if I lived a thousand years, tell
you what I would want to, or thank you for
all that you have done for me, and especially
the best thing of all, in bringing me up in the
knowledge of my Saviour. And if I am killed,
remember that it is our Lord's will, and He
Who is our Friend, knows far better than we
what is good for us; and after all, none of us
would wish it otherwise, would we? I know
you wouldn't, and though it means more for
you than for me, yet I'm sure you wouldn't.

'And now, as I hope you will never get this,
I'll leave off. Good-bye, my dearest parents.
Don't sorrow.'

—A. Mercer

(Rom. 14. 8; 1 Cor. 15. 55)

281. Death—and the Hereafter. In the
Cathedral at Worcester, there is an ancient
slab, bearing as its inscription the solitary
word 'Miserrimus' (most miserable).

Down in the catacombs, those vast under-
ground chambers of the dead where the early
Christians endeavoured to hide from their
fierce persecutors—engraven on a stone
embedded in the well, stands this beautiful
word 'Felicissimus' (most happy).

Which of these two Latin inscriptions would
describe your condition were you to die?
(John 8. 24; Phil 1. 23; Heb. 10. 28)

282. Death—the Huntsman.

There's a keen and grim old huntsman
On a horse as white as snow.
Sometimes he is very swift
And sometimes very slow.
But he never is at fault,
For he always hunts on view,
And he rides without a halt
After you.

The huntsman's name is Death,
His horse's name is Time.
He is coming, he is coming
As I sit and write this rhyme;
He is coming, he is coming
As you read the rhyme I write;
You can hear his hoofs' low-drumming
Day and night.

You can hear the distant drumming
As the clock goes tick-a-tack,
And the chiming of the hours
Is the music of his pack.
You can hardly note their growling
Underneath the noonday sun,
But at night you hear them howling
As they run.

And they never check or falter,
For they never miss their kill.
Seasons change and systems alter,
But the hunt is running still.
Hark! the evening chime is playing:
O'er the long grey dawn it peals.
Don't you hear the death-hound baying
At your heels.

—Sir A. Conan Doyle

(Heb. 9. 27)

283. **Death—Impartiality of.**

The glories of our blood and state
  Are shadows, not substantial things.
There is no armour against fate:
  Death lays his icy hand on kings.
Sceptre and crown
  Must tumble down,
And in the dust be equal laid
  With the poor crooked scythe and spade.

　　　　　　　　　—James Shirley

(2 Sam. 14. 14)

284. **Death—Impartiality of.**

The boast of heraldry, the pomp of power,
  And all that beauty, all that wealth, e'er gave,
Await alike the'inevitable hour:
  The paths of glory lead but to the grave.

　　　　　　　　　—Thomas Gray

(2 Sam. 14. 14; Heb. 9. 27)

285. **Death—of Kings.**

　　　Within the hollow crown
That rounds the mortal temples of a king
Keeps Death his court; and there the antick sits,
Scoffing his state, and grinning at his pomp,
Allowing him a breath, a little scene,
To monarchise, be fear'd, and kill with looks;
Infusing him with self and vain conceit—
As if this flesh, which walls about our life,
Were brass impregnable; and humour'd thus,
Comes at the last, and with a little pin
Bores through his castle wall, and—farewell,
　　　King!

　　　　　　—Shakespeare in *Richard II*

286. **Death—Life through.**

Have you heard the tale of the aloe plant
  Away in a sunny clime?
By humble growth of a hundred years
  It reaches its blooming time;
And then a wondrous bud at its crown
  Bursts into a thousand flowers;
That floral queen in its blooming seen
  Is the pride of the tropical bowers.
But the plant to the flower is a sacrifice,
  For it blooms but once and in blooming dies.
Have you further heard of the aloe plant
  That grows in the sunny clime,
How every one of its thousand flowers,
  As they drop in the blooming time,
Is an infant plant that fastens its roots
  In the place where it falls to the ground;
And as fast as they drop from the dying stem,
  Grow lively and lovely around?
By dying, it liveth a thousandfold
  In the young that spring from the death of the
　　old.
Have you heard the tale of the pelican,
  The Arab's 'Gimel el Bahr,'
That lives in the African solitudes
  Where the birds that live lonely are?
Have you heard how it loves its tender young
  And cares and toils for their good?
It brings them water from fountains afar
  And fishes the seas for their food.
In famine it feeds them—What love can devise!
  The blood of its bosom, and feeding them dies.

You have heard these tales: shall I tell you one,
  A greater and better than all?
Have you heard of Him Whom the Heavens
　　adore,
  Before Whom the hosts of them fall?
—How He left the choirs and anthems above
  For earth with its wailings and woes,
To suffer the shame and pain of the cross,
  To die for the life of His foes.
O Prince of the noble! O Sufferer divine!
  What sorrow and sacrifice equal to Thine?
Have you heard this tale, the best of them all,
  The tale of the Holy and True?
He died, but His life in untold souls
  Lives on in the world anew.
His seed prevails and is filling the earth
  As the stars fill the sky above.
He taught us to yield up the love of life
  For the sake of the life of love.
His death is our life, His loss is our gain,
  The joy for the tear, the peace for the pain.
Now hear these tales, ye weary and worn,
  Who for Him do give up all.
Our Saviour hath said the seed that would grow
  Into earth's dark bosom must fall,
Must pass from the view and die away,
  And then will the fruit appear.
The grain that seems lost in the earth below
  Will return many-fold in the ear.
By death comes life, by loss comes gain,
  The joy for the tear, the peace for the pain.

(John 12. 24; Gal. 2. 20)

287. **Death — of Napoleon Buonaparte.**
Napoleon Buonaparte said, 'I die before my time; and my body will be given back to earth, to become the food of worms. Such is the fate which so soon awaits the great Napoleon.'

What a contrast to the words of Job: 'I know that my Redeemer liveth—and though after my skin worms destroy my body, yet in my flesh shall I see God!' (Job. 19. 25, 26)

288. **Death—the Preacher.** There is a preacher of the old school, and he speaks as boldly as ever. He is not popular, though the world is his parish, and he travels over every part of the globe, and speaks in every language under the sun. He visits the poor; calls upon the rich, and preaches to people of every religion and many of no religion, but the subject of his sermon is always the same.

He is an eloquent preacher—often stirs feelings which no other preacher could, and brings tears into eyes that seldom weep. He addresses himself to the conscience and the heart. His arguments none are able to refute; nor is there any heart that has remained wholly unmoved by the force of his weighty appeals. Most people hate him, for many quail in his presence, but in one way or another he makes everybody hear him.

He is neither refined nor polite. Indeed, he often interrupts the public arrangements and breaks rudely in upon the private enjoyments of life. He frequents the shop, the office and the mill; he appears in the midst of legislators, and intrudes upon fashionable and religious gatherings at most inopportune times. His name is Death.

You cannot take up a newspaper without finding that he has a corner in it. Every tombstone serves him for a pulpit. You often see his congregations passing to and from the graveyard. The sudden departure of that neighbour—the solemn parting with that dear parent—the loss of that valued friend—the awful gap that was left in your heart when that fondly loved wife, that idolized child, was taken—have all been loud and solemn appeals from this old preacher. One day he may take you for his text and in your bereaved family circle, and by your graveside, he may be preaching to others. Let your heart thank God this moment that you are still in the land of the living—that you have not, ere now, died in your sins!

—Whither Bound?

(Heb. 9. 27)

289. Death—Spiritual. Dr. Walter Lewis Wilson, in his book—*The Romance of a Doctor's Visit*—narrates that, on one occasion, going to a funeral, he had permission to ride to the cemetery with the undertaker in the hearse. As they went along, he said to the driver, a young man of thirty, 'What do you suppose the Bible means by saying, "Let the dead bury their dead"?' He replied, 'There isn't a verse like that in the Bible.' The Doctor assured him that there was, and he said then, 'It must be a wrong translation. How could a dead person bury a dead person?' The Doctor then explained the verse by pointing out to him, 'You are a dead undertaker in front of the hearse driving out to bury the dead friend at the back of the hearse. That person is dead to her family, and you are dead to God.' He quoted to him John 10. 10 and 1 John 5. 12. The conversation resulted in the conversion of the undertaker as he accepted eternal life through faith in the Lord Jesus Christ.

(Luke 9. 60; Eph. 2. 1; 1 Tim. 5. 6; 1 John 5. 12)

290. Death—Triumph in. A Chinese girl who saw Mr. Vinson before he was shot, heard the bandits threatening him. 'Aren't you afraid?' they asked him. 'No!' he replied, 'I am not afraid. If you shoot me, I shall go straight to Heaven.'

Afraid? Of What?
To feel the spirit's glad release,
To pass from pain to perfect peace,
The strife and strain of life to cease—
Afraid—of that?

Afraid to see the Saviour's face,
To hear His welcome and to trace
The glory gleam from wounds of grace?
Afraid—of that?
Afraid—of what?

A flash, a crash, a piercéd heart;
Darkness, light—O Heaven's art
A wound, of His the counterpart.
Afraid—of that?

To enter into Heaven's rest,
And still to serve the Master blest,
From service good to service best—
Afraid—of that?

291. Debt—Paid. There was a singular Oriental custom regarding settled debts. When the debt was settled, either by payment or cancellation, it was the usage for the creditor to take the cancelled bond and nail it over the door of him who owed it, that all might see it was paid.

—Dr. A. J. Gordon

(Col. 2. 14)

292. Debt—Paid.
He gave me back the bond:
It was a heavy debt;
And, as He gave, He smiled and said,
'Thou wilt not me forget.'

He gave me back the bond:
The seal was torn away,
And, as He gave it me, He said,
'Think thou on me alway.'

It is a bond no more,
Yet it shall ever tell
That all I owed was fully paid
By my Immanuel.

This bond I still will keep,
Although it cancelled be.
It tells me of the love of One
Who suffered there for me.

(Is. 53. 5; Luke 22. 19, 20; Col. 2. 14)

293. Debt—Paid.
From whence this fear and unbelief
Since God, my God, has put to grief
His spotless Son for me?
Can He, the righteous Judge of men,
Condemn me for that debt of sin
Which, Lord, was charged to Thee?

Since Thou hast my discharge procured
And freely in my place endured
The whole of wrath divine,
Payment God will not twice demand,
First at my bleeding Surety's hand
And then again at mine.
'It was exacted and He became answerable.'

(Isa. 53. 6; Rom. 3. 25; 1 Tim. 2. 6)

294. Debt—Paid. Nicholas II was one of the most beneficent Tsars of Russia, 'the father of the people'. On one occasion he was acting orderly officer to troops stationed in a lonely Cossack fortress. The Tsar was not actually living in the fortress, but billeted some miles away, but the sentries had to be ready and alert whenever the orderly officer came.

It was a cold blustering night and the wind howled mournfully round the tower and rattled the windows of an office in which a young man sat. Count Ivanovitch gazed with dull eyes at the fire; there was nothing he could do—he was smashed.

Ivan was the darling of society, both in Moscow and St. Petersburg; brave, dashing, handsome, he was everybody's favourite. His father had held high military rank and served the Tsar faithfully until his death. Now exposure and disgrace loomed before Ivan.

For months he had been living far beyond his means, and he was head over ears in debt. Then, poor foolish boy, he made what was bad so much worse, for he began to help himself from the regimental funds. He was always going to pay it back, but somehow he never did. It would be quite impossible now; his debts rose like a mountain before him. Tomorrow the military auditors were coming to the fortress to check up the accounts.

The table behind was all spread over with open account books and ledgers; he had been going through them again and again till his head ached. He would be courtmartialled and dismissed the Service—perhaps imprisoned. Yes, his career was smashed.

Gazing moodily into the fire, the wretched boy cried out, 'That is the only way out.' He got up and found his pistol and was bringing it back to the fire when the open ledgers and books on the table seemed to draw him. He sat down, went over them again and again then made some rough calculations on a sheet of paper; it was no good, so, pistol in hand, he went back to his seat by the fire.

There was no hurry, he had about five or six hours left. He stared into the fire and thought he saw in the burnt-out coals a picture of his wasted life. Then, because he was very young and unhappy, his eyes drooped and closed and he fell asleep still clutching the pistol.

At midnight the orderly officer arrived at the fortress and went his rounds. Coming along the corridor he was surprised to see a light under the door of the office at that hour. He opened it softly and looked in. A litter of books and ledgers open on the table and his friend, Count Ivanovitch, asleep in a chair with a pistol in his hand—that was what he saw.

Amazed, he went nearer to examine the books, and on the table he found a sheet of paper inscribed, 'What I owe;' a long, long list of figures followed and at the end a boyish scrawl: 'So great a debt, who can pay it?'

The orderly officer looked more closely at the sleeper and marked the misery and despair on his face, then he took up a pen, added a few words at the bottom of the page, quietly removed the pistol and went away. As dawn broke Count Ivanovitch awoke stiff and wretched. The day had dawned which was to bring the dreaded scrutiny. There was just one way out, but where was the pistol? He got up to search for it, then he went over to the table. It was not there; but he saw something at which he stared incredulously. It was just a sheet of paper covered with a long list of debts in his own writing, but something had been added since he fell asleep. Under his last

despairing question, 'Who can pay so great a debt?' was now written: 'I will, Nicholas, Tsar.'

Strange things happened at the fortress that day; dispatch riders and couriers came and went. Headquarters postponed the military audit for three months, and Count Ivanovitch was recalled to the capital for a period of duty at the Palace. He never forgot his interview with the Tsar, for it was the turning point to a life that henceforth became straight-forward, honourable and prosperous.

—Wing-Commander Knowles, A.F.C.,
R.A.F. (Abridged)

(Rom. 3. 24-26; Col. 2. 13-14; Philem. 18)

295. **Debt—Paid.** In his book *Studies in Bible Doctrine*, the late William Hoste uses an apt illustration. He writes, 'If a large sum was devoted by the Government to pay the debts of a community, wholly insolvent, on condition that each debtor made full disclosure of his affairs and accepted the offer, the sum might be more than required to pay the debts of all, but only those who fulfilled the conditions could actually say, "Our debts have been paid by the Government". Potentially all debts might be paid; actually only a proportion would be.'

W. R. Lewis of Bath, England, has a very enlightening article on *The Sovereignty of God*. In it he says, 'But while the death of Christ is universal in its efficiency, it is particular in its application, and if the sinner avails not himself of this provision, his guilt has not been expiated—he is guilty before God; his sins have not been borne away, his transgressions have not been removed, his debt has not been discharged, and if he dies in his sins, he will be answerable not only for his rejection of Christ, but also for every sin he has committed.'

(Acts 20. 21; Rom. 3. 25; Eph. 5. 6; Rev. 20. 12)

296. **Deceit.**

Oh, what a tangled web we weave,
When first we practise to deceive.

—Sir Walter Scott in *Marmion*

(1 Sam. 21. 12; 27. 10, 11; 30. 1; Rom. 16. 18)

297. **Deceit.** D. L. Moody said, 'Lying covers a multitude of sins—temporarily.' Martin Luther said, 'A lie is a snowball: the further you roll it, the bigger it becomes.'

298. **Decision—the Valley of.**

I stood at the crossroads amazed to see
The few on the Heaven-bound way:
While the broad road thronged with the motley crowd
Who lived only for today:
For the future, it seemed, they had never a thought,
Or what lay at the journey's end:
And I heard, as it were, Wisdom's warning voice,
'Be wise, lest to Hell you descend.'

(Deut. 30. 19; 1 Kings 18. 21; Prov. 9. 12)

299. Deity of Christ. What do we need in God that we do not find in Christ? God is not beyond Him, but in Him. He brings God: in Him God comes—Immanuel. In Jesus Christ we meet God. He is One with the inmost heart of God. His life is a personal disclosure of the Life of God.

Like man He walked, like God He talked;
His words were oracles, His deeds were miracles;
Of God the true expression, of man the finest
  specimen;
Full-orbed humanity, crowned with Deity;
No trace of infirmity, no taint of iniquity;
Behold the Man! Behold thy God!
Veiled in flesh the Godhead see,
Hail, Incarnate Deity!

(Isa. 9. 6; 40. 9; Matt. 1. 23; 8. 27; 27. 54; John 1. 1, 2, 14, 16; Rom. 9. 5; Col. 1. 15, 16)

300. Disappointment.

'Disappointment—His appointment,'
  Change one letter, then I see
That the thwarting of my purpose
  Is God's better choice for me.

His appointment must be blessing,
  Though it may come in disguise,
For the end from the beginning
  Open to His vision lies.

'Disappointment—His appointment,'
  Whose?—The Lord's Who loves me best,
Understands and knows me fully.
  He my faith and love would test.

For, like loving, earthly parents,
  He rejoices when He knows
That His child accepts, unquestioned,
  All that from His wisdom flows.

'Disappointment—His appointment,'
  'No good thing will He withhold;'
From denials oft we gather
  Treasures of His love untold.

Well He knows each broken purpose
  Leads to fuller deeper trust;
And the end of all His dealings
  Proves our God is wise and just.

(Acts 16. 6; Rom. 12. 2; 2 Cor. 1. 15, 16)

301. Discipleship—its Costliness. Henry Drummond, preacher and author, was once asked to address a meeting of a select West-End Club in London. On his arrival he found his audience assembled and everything arranged for him to give his message. He commenced his address with these words: 'Ladies and Gentlemen, the entrance fee into the Kingdom of Heaven is nothing: the annual subscription is everything.'

302. Discipleship—its Demands. 'It doesn't take much of a man to be a Christian, but it takes all there is of him,' said Thomas Huxley. (Luke 14. 33; Rom. 12. 1)

303. Discipleship—its Essentials. Peter Waldo, the probable leader of the pious Waldensians, was a rich merchant of Lyons, France. He was converted through the death of a friend at a feast. He then had the Scriptures translated by two erudite scholars into his own tongue and thereafter gave up all his wealth and followed his Lord. Everywhere he went he preached the claims of Christ, using the words, 'Look to Jesus! Listen to Jesus! Learn of Jesus!'

These are the prerequisites of discipleship. (Matt. 11. 29; 16. 24; Heb. 12. 1, 2)

304. Discoveries. Archimedes of Syracuse, who lived in the Third century B.C. was the greatest mathematician and mechanical engineer of his time. He was a pioneer in his day in the domain of mechanics, and a venerable philosopher. Hiero, King of Syracuse, charged him with the task of ascertaining whether a crown made for him by a local goldsmith was of pure gold or of an alloy of gold and some baser metal. It took him many days to find a solution to the problem set him. According to his custom he went to the public baths and entered the water with the problem of the gold crown on his mind. As he did so, he observed the changing level of the water, and after some thought splashed out of his bath, shouting at the top of his voice, 'Eureka!' This means 'I have found the solution'. Later he put his discovery to a practical test, and found that he could with certainty formulate his findings in the proposition that a body plunged in a fluid loses an amount of its weight which is equal to the weight of fluid displaced by it. This was to lead to many subsequent discoveries, but it enabled him to tell the king how much pure gold was in the composition of his crown. 'Eureka!'—he had the thrill of making a great scientific discovery.

The early Christians—Andrew, John, Peter, Philip and others, when they met Jesus of Nazareth, made the great discovery that He was the Saviour of the world, the Christ their Saviour. 'We have found the Messias,' said Andrew, using the same Greek word for 'found' that Archimedes had used for his discovery.

305. Discoveries. Sir James Simpson, the discoverer of chloroform, was asked as he neared the end of a life in which he had made many scientific discoveries, 'What is the greatest discovery you ever made?' He replied, 'The greatest discovery I ever made was that I was a lost, guilty sinner, and that Jesus Christ, the Saviour of sinners, is my Saviour.' (Job. 11. 7; 23. 3; Isa. 55. 6; John 1. 41, 45; 4. 29; 1 Tim. 1. 15)

306. Discoveries. Lord Kelvin, when asked by a student which of all his wonderful discoveries he considered the most valuable, startled the questioner by replying, 'To me the most valuable of all the discoveries I ever made was when I discovered my Saviour in Jesus Christ.' (Acts 22. 7, 8; Gal. 1. 15, 16)

307. Distrust. The folly of snap judgements of others is well illustrated by the story of the late Bishop Potter of New York. He was sailing for Europe in one of the great transatlantic liners. When he went on board, he found another passenger was to share the cabin with him. After going to see his accommodation, he came up to the purser's desk and inquired if he could leave his gold watch and other valuables in the ship's safe. He explained that ordinarily he never availed himself of that privilege, but he had been to his cabin and had met the man who was to occupy the other berth and, judging from his appearance, he was afraid that he might not be a very trustworthy person. The purser accepted the responsibility of caring for the valuables and remarked: 'It's all right, Bishop, I'll be very glad to take care of them for you. The other man has been up here and left his for the same reason.'

—*Sunday School Times*

(Gen. 31. 36-41)

308. Divide—The Great. Of Jesus Christ it is written, 'There was a division because of Him.' He divides man's destiny. All deserved hell, but He has 'brought life and immortality to light' and is 'leading many sons to glory', Heaven instead of Hell. He has divided Time in the reckoning of many countries into B.C. and A.D. He divides the human race into two classes—those 'in Christ' and those 'in Adam'. When He was on earth there was a division among the Jews as to His Person, His works and His words.

On a mountain in the Rockies in Canada, where there is a watershed, an arch of twigs has been erected, with the words plainly wrought on the rustic structure—'The Great Divide'. Drops of rain falling in the same shower separate there, some joining a stream that becomes a mighty river and flows to the Atlantic Ocean, others falling in the other direction into another stream that flows to join the Pacific Ocean. Though they fall in the same shower of rain, their destinies are hundreds of miles apart. So it is in families, classes in school, neighbourhoods, and places of business. Christ is the Great Divide, and the destiny of men for glory or despair is determined by the attitude of the individual to Him.

(Matt. 27. 22; John 7. 43; 9. 16; 10. 19)

309. Divide—The Great.

So from the heights of will
Life's parting stream descends,
And, as a moment turns its slender rill,
Each winding torrent bends.

From the same cradle's side,
From the same mother's knee—
One to long darkness and the frozen tide,
One to the peaceful Sea.

(Luke 12. 49-53)

310. Divide—The Great. At the funeral of Dr. David Livingstone a man who appeared to be a derelict of humanity was seen to be weeping bitterly. When someone asked if he were a near relative of the great missionary, he replied, 'No! but we were in the same class at school and worked at the same loom in the mill in Blantyre. Only I took the wrong road and have become a useless drunkard. David Livingstone when young began to follow and serve Jesus Christ, and that loyalty took him to Africa.'

(Gen. 24. 58; John 1. 12)

311. Divide—The Great. In 1839, when R. G. Wilder, missionary to India and founder of the *Missionary Review of the World*, graduated from Middlebury College, he divided first honours with his classmate, Foote. Strange to say, both had been born in the same year and on the same day.

Foote became a lawyer and rose rapidly in his profession. He amassed wealth and married a young woman of singular beauty. But in the midst of his prosperity, death took wife and daughter from him and, overcome with sorrow, he blew his brains out.

When Wilder turned from flattering prospects at home to devote his life to India, his twin-honour man said to him, 'Why bury yourself among the heathen, Wilder?' Wilder worked in India more than thirty years, preached in more than 3,000 cities and villages, scattered more than three million pages of tracts, and gathered into schools over 3,300 children of whom 300 were girls. He had Christ: his twin-honour friend Foote had not. Was not Wilder's the better choice?

In the case of those two brilliant men, also, Christ was the great Divide.

(Phil. 1. 21; 3. 7)

312. Divide—The Great. H. Delaney, the Scottish evangelist, was preaching in a hall in a town in Scotland. Describing the suffering love of the Lord Jesus Christ as He was mocked by Herod, questioned by Pilate, thorn-crowned, spat upon and scourged by Roman soldiers, and despised and rejected by the Jews, he said, 'And all were against Him, giving vent to their hatred and crying, "Away with Him! Crucify Him"! He stood alone: there was no one on His side. I wonder,' he added, 'if we had been there, how many of us would have taken His side.' It was a rhetorical question and the preacher did not expect an answer, but he got one; for a lad near the front of the Hall who had listened with rapt attention and been greatly moved by the story of such suffering and love, called out, 'I would, sir.' Stopping in his address for a moment, the preacher looked at the lad and said, 'And are you on His side now, my laddie?'

(Exod. 32. 26; Matt. 27. 22, 23)

313. Divide—The Great. 'In my College life,' said Arthur T. Pierson, 'there were two young men who were mightily moved by the Spirit of God on the same night. They walked down to the Chaplain's house, intending to go in and converse with him, and then in prayer surrender to the Lord Jesus Christ. When they got to the gate, one said to the other, "Jim, I think I won't go in", and he resisted all persuasions and parted at the gate. The man who went in and received Christ that night is one of the mightiest ministers of Christ in America today. The one who parted with him at the gate went into drink, into gambling and sensuality, went down to Cuba and was identified there with some rebellion where he was shot, and died in his sins. They parted for eternity at the gateway of the chaplain's house, and each man's future depended on the decision made at that moment.'

Your destiny may depend upon the decision made in these fateful moments.

—John G. Ridley
(Matt. 27. 22; John 1. 11, 12)

314. Divisions.

Aesop has a fable of three bulls that fed in a field together in the greatest peace and safety. A lion had long watched them in the hope of making prey of them, but found little chance so long as they kept together. He therefore began secretly to spread evil and slanderous reports of one against another till he fomented jealousy and distrust among them. Soon they began to avoid each other and each took to feeding alone. This gave the lion the opportunity it had been wanting. He fell on them singly and made an easy prey of them all.

It is true of God's people that—'united, they stand; divided, they fall.' (Ps. 133. 1; 1 Cor. 1. 10, 11; 3. 3).

315. Doubts.

'There is more faith in honest doubt,
 Believe me, than in half the creeds;'
So penned a poet (witless lout)
 To praise the doubter's doubtful deeds.

But let me whisper in your ear,
 'There's no such thing as honest doubt':
For doubt will doubtless disappear
 If it is honest out and out.

For doubt is very much like gout—
 The more 'tis nursed, the more it grows;
When fed on atheistic stout,
 It juggles, wriggles, cavils, crows.

Much of the doubt before our eyes
 Is most dishonest in its heart:
It poses under honest guise
 And shoots with skill its subtle art.

Its shafts have entered hall and hut,
 And into churches not a few;
The preacher cracks the doubtful nut
 And spreads the poison to the pew.

'Tis now thought doubtful not to doubt.
 Yes! we are taught to doubt our doubts.
All certainty is put to rout
 And no one knows its whereabouts.

Is there no knowledge to be had?
 Has God not spoken once for all?
Indeed He has: all doubt is mad,
 And destined to disastrous fall.

For God is God, and truth is true;
 All doubt is sinful in His sight;
And doubters will have cause to rue
 Their doubts through Hell's undoubted night.

—Thomas Baird
(Matt. 14. 31; John 8. 24)

316. Dreams.

During some revival meetings a woman under deep conviction of sin could not find peace. She asked the preacher and heard from him the way of peace, but was still in deep distress of soul. A friend, converted at the meetings, told her: 'I did nothing, Christ has done all. He "made peace by the blood of His cross".'

But she could not understand, and still thought she must do something for her own salvation. She went home, kneeled in prayer, fell asleep on her knees, and dreamed. In her dream she was falling over a precipice and clutched at a twig to save herself. A voice said, 'Let go the twig,' but still she clung to it with all her might. 'I cannot save you unless you let go the twig,' came the voice again. With strength almost spent, she let go and found herself in the arms of the Saviour. Then she awoke and saw how God in her dream had showed her clearly the way of salvation.
(Job 33. 14-16)

317. Duty—On.

The guard of the train had a rose in his buttonhole. A drunken man came along the platform and snatched it out. The guard went red but said nothing. An onlooker said, 'However did you keep your temper? You said nothing.' The guard replied simply, 'I'm on duty.'

As Christians, we should remember that, wherever we are and whatever happens to us, we are always 'on duty'.
(1 Pet. 2. 9)

318. Dwelling Deep.

It is said by those who have to do with submarines that, no matter how furious the storm upon the surface of the ocean, the vessel has but to submerge to certain depths to find a place whose calm no storm ever disturbs. The fact offers us a spiritual analogy. The deep things of life are always calm and steadfast. Exclaims the Apostle Paul: 'O the depths of the riches both of the wisdom and knowledge of God!' Elsewhere his prayer is that 'Christ may dwell in your hearts by faith; that ye, being rooted and grounded in love, may be able to comprehend with all the saints what is the breadth and length, and depth and height; and to know the love of Christ which passeth knowledge.' We live in a world that is being torn to pieces by the storms of human passion. Because of the terrors of this world conflict, our minds are disturbed and our hearts are distressed. In such a time we need more than ever to 'dwell deep' in the knowledge and love of God. There we shall find that inner peace and assurance that will enable us to look through the present chaos to the fulfilment of the eternal purposes.

—Selected

(Jer. 49. 8)

319. Dwelling Deep.

'O that we might dwell deep in the ocean of God's rest, not disturbed by the surface storm!'

Dwell deep, my soul; dwell deep within the ocean
Of God's rest, undisturbed by surface storm.
O let Him calm thy restless thought to silence,
The spirit—to His image He'll conform.

Dwell deep—so deep in His great love so tender;
It casteth—or should cast—out every fear.
God's rest, God's love, God's peace is all that's
needed.
O soul of mine, forget not He is near.

Dwell deep—stay there—'tis peace that passeth
knowledge.
Let nothing move thee, nothing cause alarm.
But if?—His words: 'And do ye not remember?'
'Return unto thy rest, my soul'—God's calm.

(Jer. 49. 8; Rom. 11. 33; Eph. 3. 17-19; Phil. 4. 7).

320. Dying Words—of Christians.

Martin Luther—'Our God is the God from Whom cometh salvation, God is the Lord by Whom we escape death.'
John Knox—'Live in Christ, live in Christ, and the flesh need not fear death.'
John Calvin—'Thou, Lord, bruisest me, but I am abundantly satisfied, since it is from Thy hand.'
John Wesley—'The best of all is, God is with us. Farewell! Farewell!'
Charles Wesley—'I shall be satisfied with Thy likeness—satisfied, satisfied.'
Richard Baxter—'I have pain (there is no arguing against sense); but I have peace, I have peace.'
Dr. Preston—'Blessed be God! though I change my place, I shall not change my company; for I have walked with God while living, and now I go to rest with God.'
Samuel Rutherford—'If He should slay me ten thousand times, ten thousand times I'll trust. I feel, I feel, I believe in joy and rejoice; I feed on manna. O for arms to embrace Him! O for a well-tuned harp!'
Mrs. Hemans—'I feel as if I were sitting with Mary at the feet of my Redeemer, hearing the music of His voice and learning of Him to be meek and lowly.'

(1 Cor. 15. 55; Phil. 1. 23).

321. Dying Words—of Unbelievers.

Voltaire—'I am abandoned by God and man. I will give you half of what I am worth if you will give me six months' life.'

When his doctor said, 'Sir, you cannot live six weeks,' he replied, 'Then I will go to hell and you will go with me.'

Lord Byron—'Shall I sue for mercy?—(A long pause)—Come, come, no weakness, let's be a man to the last.'

(John 8. 21).

322. Ears.

If you your ears would keep from jeers,
These things keep meekly hid—
Myself and I, and mine and my,
And how I do and did.

—H. Dennett

(Matt. 6. 2).

323. East—and West.

'East is East and West is West, and never the twain shall meet,
Till Earth and Sky stand presently at God's great Judgement-seat,'

wrote Rudyard Kipling. But they are meeting at the feet of a crucified and risen Saviour, at the Lord's table, at the Lord's Supper, won by the same glorious gospel that knows no distinction of caste, country, clime, culture or creed.

(Rom. 1. 14-16; Gal. 3. 28).

324. Easter.
The word is derived from the Anglo-Saxon 'Eastre'—the name of a Norse goddess whose festival was celebrated at the time of the vernal equinox. It marked the dawn of a new year, the end of the reign of winter and the advent of increasing light and heat. The festival was celebrated by Easter games, and special cakes were baked, of which representatives still exist in 'hot cross buns'.

The original derivation of the name is from the Greek 'Eos', the East, and it is also etymologically connected with the Latin 'Aurora', dawn. At first, Easter synchronised with the Jewish passover. The word occurs only once in the Bible, and there it is an erroneous translation, for the Greek word is 'Pascha', and the Revised Version and most other modern translations render it 'Passover'.

(Acts 12. 4).

325. Education — Modern.
A disgruntled school-teacher handed in her resignation with the following comment: 'In our public schools today, the teachers are afraid of the Principals, the Principals are afraid of the superintendents, the superintendents are afraid of the board, the board members are afraid of the parents, the parents are afraid of the children, and the children are afraid of nobody.'

—*Journal of Education*

(Eph. 6. 1-4; Col. 3. 20).

326. Emmaus.
In Emmaus, near Nabi Samwil, there is an old monastery once used in World War I as an advanced station. Major Vivian Gilbert in his *Romance of the last Crusade* tells that he went there to visit one of his company who had been mortally wounded, and found him in a cot in a special corner of the monastery set aside for the more serious cases, lying in his grey flannel army

shirt. Little more than a youngster, he was a general favourite with the men because of his cheery face and witty jokes on the march that had often set the company in a roar. Yet he was going to die very soon in a strange, foreign land thousands of miles from home.

The Major drew an empty ammunition box towards the bed and sat down. He told him the story of Emmaus, of how Christ appeared to His disciples just as night was coming on, and how, as He was about to go, one of them had entreated Him, saying, 'Abide with us, for it is toward evening, and the day is far spent;' and how He had stayed for a while, broken bread and blessed it, and given it to them. Just as the Major finished speaking, a ray from the setting sun stole in at the window and fell across the bed, lighting up the dying soldier's face. The strained, worried look had vanished, and a peaceful, almost happy and contented, expression had taken its place. His hand crept slowly from the side of the bed, and the Major took it in both of his. Then he whispered, 'Thank you for telling me that story, sir.'

'"Abide with me, fast falls the eventide" is mother's favourite hymn. I shall be able to sleep now. Good night, sir.' And then, lower still, he murmured, 'God bless you.'
(Luke 24. 13-32).

327. Encouragement. When Sir Walter Scott was a boy he was considered a great dullard. His accustomed place in the schoolroom was the ignominious dunce corner, with the high-pointed paper cap of shame on his head. When about twelve or fourteen years old he happened to be in a house where some famous literary guests were being entertained. Robert Burns, the Scottish poet, was standing admiring a picture under which was written the couplet of a stanza. He inquired concerning the author. None seemed to know. Timidly a boy crept up to his side, named the author, and quoted the rest of the poem. Burns was surprised and delighted. Laying his hand on the boy's head, he exclaimed, 'Ah, bairnie, ye will be a great man in Scotland some day.' From that day Walter Scott was a changed lad. One word of encouragement set him on the road to greatness.
—*Indian Christian*
(Deut. 1. 38; 3. 28; Is. 41. 7).

328. Encouragement. A young Member of Parliament, when making his maiden speech in the House of Commons, was overcome by intense nervousness. Gradually, however, his shyness in addressing the House vanished, and he said what he had to say and sat down. Then his nervousness returned and he felt that he had blundered. Just as he was undergoing this misery, a note was passed to him with only two words, 'You'll do.' They were initialled by the greatest Statesman of the day. The Member kept those kind words as a treasured souvenir and a perpetual encouragement.

Are there not many of us who are needing encouragement today—in the spiritual life? Encouragement to read, to pray, to act.
(Deut. 1. 38; 3. 28; Heb. 10. 24, 25).

329. Encouragement.
Lord, when I'm weary with toiling
And burdensome seem Thy commands,
If my load should lead to complaining,
Lord! show me Thy hands,
Thy nail-pierced hands,
Thy cross-torn hands.
O Saviour! show me Thy hands.

Christ! if my footsteps should falter
And I be prepared for retreat;
If desert and thorn cause lamenting,
Lord! show me Thy feet,
Thy bleeding feet,
Thy nail-scarred feet.
O Saviour! show me Thy feet.
O God; dare I show Thee my hands and my feet?
                    —Brenton Thoburn Bradley
(Luke 24. 40; Gal. 6. 17).

330. Encouragement. David, like Joshua, was emerging from desert obscurity into a place of prominence. Adversity was upon him. But instead of being discouraged, he encouraged himself in the Lord. Then he turned defeat into victory. If others do not encourage us, let us encourage ourselves in the Lord. How much He encouraged others! On the stormy lake, and in the upper room. He spoke words of cheer to the paralytic, and to the stricken women He administered words of comfort. When Paul lay in prison He said, 'Be of good cheer, Paul.'
                    —A. Soutter
David was greatly distressed and wept. No wonder, for he was enduring—Exile from his loved homeland—'eating the bitter bread of banishment'. Ingratitude from the people whom he had saved from Goliath and the Philistines: Postponement of his acceptance by his own people as their Divinely-appointed king: Losses of material possessions snatched from him at a single blow, and of all he held dear; and mutiny by his own followers, for 'the people spake of stoning him'.
Yet 'David encouraged himself in the Lord'.
(1 Sam. 30. 6; 2 Tim. 4. 17).

331. Enemy.
'In cases of defence, 'tis best to weigh
The enemy more weighty than he seems.'
                    —Shakespeare in *Henry V.*
(2 Cor. 2. 11; 11. 14; 1 Pet. 5. 8).

332. Enlargement. In Baptist Chapel, Friars Lane, Nottingham, Carey preached his memorable 'Missions' sermon, an address which still comes to the reader today with tremendous power. He read the fifty-fourth chapter of Isaiah, and his text was 'Enlarge the place of thy tent, and let them stretch forth the curtains of thy habitations; spare not, Lengthen thy cords and strengthen thy stakes; for thou shalt break forth on the right hand and on the left; and thy seed shall inherit the Gentiles, and make the desolate cities to be inhabited. Fear not.'

He packed his message into two biddings: 'Expect great things from God'. Christian enterprise is the fruit of Christian faith. And, 'Attempt great things for God'. The divine way out of failure and disgrace was a wider vision, a bolder programme. Then he pleaded for committal, for action. He bade them pledge themselves there and then, and dally and disobey no longer.

—R. W. Orr

(Is. 54. 2-3).

333. Enlargement. In his essay on 'On the other side of the hill', Dr. F. W. Boreham says, 'The desire to view the vast beyond is strong in everyone. On the pinnacle of one of the hills of the many in S. America, stands a large statue of Christ. It has more significance than was intended by those who placed it there. On the summit of the mountain-tops of our experience stands the Lord, pointing to the vast unexplored regions beyond.'

(2 Cor. 6. 13; 10. 15, 16; Phil. 3. 12-14).

334. Enthusiasm. 'Every great movement in the annals of history,' said Emerson, 'is the triumph of enthusiasm.'

It is derived, that magic name, from two Greek words: *en* meaning *in* and *theos* meaning *God*. Enthusiasm is literally 'God in us'. The enthusiastic man is one who speaks as if he were possessed by God.

This quality is the most effective, the most important, factor in advertising and selling goods and getting things done. The largest advertiser of any single product in the world came to Chicago thirty years ago with less than fifty dollars in his pocket. Wrigley now sells thirty million dollars worth of his chewing gum every year, and on the wall of his private office hang the framed words of Emerson: 'Nothing great was ever achieved without enthusiasm.'

—Dale Carnegie

(Neh. 2. 10; Rom. 12. 11).

335. Epistles. Dr. W. Graham Scroggie said, in one of his addresses, as he asked his audience to turn to Paul's Letter to the Romans, that he preferred the simple word 'letter' to the word 'epistle' to describe the didactic writings of Paul, Peter, James, John and Jude in the New Testament. Every child, he said, knew what a letter was, but there were many like the child in Sunday School who, when asked what an epistle was, replied that it meant the wife of an apostle.

336. Epistles of Christ. In olden times they had a kind of manuscript called 'Palimpsest', and on it bad things, mischievous things and plays, as well as dirty, obscene stories, were written. At that time skins were scarce and people often used those skins for recording portions of Scripture. They rubbed off the bad writing and wrote on them portions of the Gospel. What a different message the skins then conveyed!

(2 Cor. 3. 2, 3).

337. Eternal Life. A member of the congregation of John Brown, Haddington, Scotland, a godly old woman, was on her deathbed. On visiting her the minister desired, after the austere fashion of those days, to try her faith. 'Janet,' he enquired, 'what would you say if, after all He has done for you, God should let you perish?' 'Even as He will,' was the answer, 'If He does He'll lose mair than I will.' Our Lord's promise stands unchanged: 'I give unto my sheep eternal life and they shall never perish.'

(John 3. 14-16; 10. 28; 17. 2, 3).

338. Eternal Realities. Over the triple doorways of Milan Cathedral there are three inscriptions spanning the splendid arches. Above one is carved a wreath of roses, and underneath is the legend: 'All that pleases is but for a moment'. Over another is sculptured a cross, and underneath are the words: 'All that troubles is but for a moment'. While underneath the great central entrance to the main aisle is the inscription: 'That only is important which is eternal'.

—Selected

(2 Cor. 4. 18).

339. Eternal Security. An old coloured woman in one of the Southern States of U.S.A., who was very poor and ignorant, was very confident she was going to Heaven. 'What?' said one, 'nobody knows anything about you, and if you go to hell, the universe will be ignorant of it.'

'Yes, massa,' said she, 'it won't make no difference to the universe; but it will make a great difference to the Lawd. His honour would be gone.'

—Dr. A. T. Pierson

(John 10. 28; 6. 36, 37; 17. 2, 12).

340. Eternity. Graven on the pavement of a street in Dundee, Scotland, is the word 'Eternity'. It was first chalked there by Robert Annan, swimmer and life-saver, as he set forth to endeavour to save someone from drowning. The attempt cost him his life.

(Is. 57. 15; Heb. 9. 15; 1 John 5. 11; Rev. 20. 10).

341. Eternity.

Eternity! Eternity!
How long art thou. Eternity?
A little bird with fretting beak
Might wear to naught the loftiest peak,
Though but each thousand years it came;
Yet thou wert then, as now, the same.
Ponder, O man, eternity!

342. Eternity. 'We may travel the sea of life without Christ, but what about the landing? Outside the city of London there is a tombstone visible to those who pass that way, whose inscription proclaims:

'Passer by! Stop and think!
I'm in eternity; you're on the brink.'

(Heb. 5. 9; 2 Thess. 1. 8, 9).

343. Eternity.

Count the gold and silver blossoms spring has
scattered o'er the lea:
Count the softly-sounding ripples sparkling on
the summer sea;
Count the lightly-flickering shadows in the
autumn forest glade:
Count pale nature's scattered teardrops, icy gems
by winter made.
Count the tiny blades that glisten early in the
morning dew:
Count the desert sand that stretches under
noontide's dome of blue:
Count the notes that wood-birds warble in the
evening's fading light:
Count the stars that gleam and twinkle in the
firmament by night.
When thy counting all is done,
Scarce eternity's begun.

344. Eternity. A young man came to an aged Professor of a distinguished University and with pleasure informed him that the fondly cherished desire of his heart was fulfilled: he was to study law. 'Well, and when you have finished your study, what do you mean to do then!' asked the Professor. 'Then I shall take my degree,' said the young man. 'And then?' 'Then I shall get difficult cases and win fame by my eloquence and acuteness.' 'And then?' 'Then I shall be promoted and become rich.' 'And then?'——

After time has gone, eternity begins. What then?

—Dr. Octavius Winslow

(Heb. 9. 27).

345. Eternity. A thoughtful young woman, seriously minded, wrote on a card the following lines:

'To think of summers yet to come
That I am not to see!
To think a weed is yet to bloom
From dust that I shall be!'

A Christian friend, finding the card, picked it up, read it, and wrote on the other side:

'To think, when Heaven and earth are fled,
And skies and seas are o'er,
When all that can die shall be dead,
That I shall die no more!
Oh, where shall then my portion be?
Where shall I spend eternity?'

(Heb. 9. 27; Rev. 14. 11).

346. Eternity. In the city of Sydney, Australia, late one evening, a British naval officer walked down a well-known street.

Suddenly he heard a voice behind him which said: 'If you should be called into eternity within the next twenty-four hours your soul would be in either heaven or hell.' These arresting words of this unknown man burned their way into his soul until he felt his need as a sinner before God, unfit for His holy presence and unprepared for eternity. Later he sought to find the way of salvation and placed all his confidence in Christ and His work of redemption. He thus entered into possession of eternal life.

The remarkable thing is that several other people had the same experience in the same place by hearing the same words spoken by the same elderly Christian man. They too were awakened by those words to see their need as sinners and to prepare for eternity, and accepted Christ as their Saviour.

Francis Dixon, godly minister of Lansdowne Baptist Church, Bournemouth, narrated, from the personal testimonies of those who had had the experience, the details of several who had been led to consider what their eternal state would be on hearing the words of the Christian man on the street in Sydney, and had received the Lord Jesus Christ as a result. He told us in Coonoor how he had sought out that faithful brother in Sydney when he had been there on a visit and how the aged servant of Christ, on hearing of how God had blessed his simple words of witness, had broken down and wept with joy.

(Num. 23. 10).

347. Etiquette. Etiquette means 'a ticket'.— The old gardener at Versailles was in great distress. What pains he took with his flower beds! How patiently he mapped them all out in the evening! and how deftly he executed his own designs in the daytime! How he longed for summer that he might feast his eyes upon the perfect patterns and the beautifully pleasing flowers! But that joy was never his. For, as soon as he got his rare seed nicely sown, his fragile plants fondly set, and his delicate young cuttings tastefully arranged, the courtiers from the palace trampled them all down and reduced the poor gardener to tears. Season after season the noblemen and great ladies in their strolls among the beautiful terraces and graceful parterres, ruthlessly destroyed the labours of the old man's skilful hands;—till at last he could endure it no longer. He would appeal to the king. So right into the august presence of the great Louis XIV the poor gardener made his way and confided all his sorrows and disappointments to his royal master. The king, sorry for the old man, ordered little tablets— 'Etiquette'—to be neatly arranged along the sides of the flower beds, and a State order was issued commanding all the courtiers to walk carefully within the 'Etiquette'. So the old gardener not only protected his flowers but enriched our vocabulary with a new and startlingly significant word.

—Dr. F. W. Boreham

(1 Kings 2. 36-44; 1 Thess. 4. 6; 1 John 3. 4).

348. Evangelism. Evangelism is the sob of God. It is the anguished cry of Jesus as He weeps over a doomed city.

It is the cry of Paul, 'I could wish that myself were accursed from Christ for my brethren, my kinsmen according to the flesh.'

Evangelism is the heart-winning plea of Moses. 'Oh this people have sinned.—Yet now, if thou wilt, forgive their sin—; if not, blot me, I pray thee, out of the book which thou hast written.'

It is the cry of John Knox, 'Give me Scotland or I die.' It is the declaration of John Wesley, 'The world is my parish.' It is the sob of parents in the night, weeping over a prodigal child.

—Selected

(Luke 19. 41, 42; Rom. 9. 3; 1 Cor. 9. 16; Philem. 10).

349. Evangelist.

His ear hath heard the question: 'who to the lost will go?'
'Send me,' he cries, his sin-purged lips with altar fires aglow:
'I'll bear the living message of free forgiving love;
O let me win the wand'rers to the path that leads above.'

'Spite all the ties of nature, he leaves his friends and home,
A lonely witness o'er the world, despised and poor, to roam.
Nought takes he for his service, but freely in His name
Who sent him and supplies his need, the Gospel would proclaim.

Within his yearning bosom, love to the Saviour reigns:
In all the labours of his life no other power constrains.
Deep are his tender feelings, sweet is his pleading tone,
As he described the glories of yon Man on Heaven's throne.

His heart the heavy burden of sinful souls must bear;
He wrestles for them at God's throne through hours of midnight prayer.
Eternity before him more real than Time appears:
Oh, wonder not he pleadeth with the eloquence of tears!

Anointed by God's Spirit, trained at the Master's feet,
Commissioned and sent forth by Him, all furnished and complete.
No human art or wisdom his talent could assist:
A heavenly-moulded, God-sent man is the evangelist.

He is the weeping sower who shall with singing come,
Bringing his gathered sheaves from earth to Heaven's harvest home.
And when with joy he lays them down at the Master's feet,

His own 'Well done! thou faithful one,' will make his bliss complete.

—William Blane

(Ps. 126. 5, 6; Isa. 6. 8; Luke 14. 23; Rom. 1. 14, 15; 3 John 7).

350. Evolution. I know nothing of the origin of man except what I am told in the Scriptures, that God created him. I do not know anything more than that, and I do not know anyone who does.

—Sir J. W. Dawson

The entire monkey-ape theory is an entire fiction, set up as a scarecrow, which has been entirely set aside by modern archaeological research.

—Dr. Osborn

(Gen. 1. 26, 27; 2. 7).

351. Evolution. Darwin guessed that two hundred millions of years ago one or a few germs appeared on the planet and then, according to Darwin, they immediately went to work reproducing. Not quite according to kind, but with just enough variation to give us finally between two and three millions of species. Darwin thought we had two or three million. I am so conservative that I prefer the lowest estimate—a million species in the animal and vegetable world — but according to Darwin's guess, everything we now see came from one or a few germs of life. All the evolutionists believe this whether they call themselves Christian, theist or atheist. Our answer is that if it were true that all species came by slow development from one or a few germs, every square foot of the earth's surface would teem with evidences of change. If everything changed, we ought to find evidence of it somewhere, but because it is not true, they have not found a single thing, living or dead, in process of change. They have examined millions of specimens, from insects so small that you have to look at them with a microscope, up to mammals, but everything is perfect. They have not found one in process of change, and they have not been able to show that a single species ever came from another. Darwin said so while he lived and expressed surprise that, with two or three million species, they had not found a single one that they could trace to another; but he thought we should accept the hypothesis, even though the 'missing links had not been found'—not the missing link, but the missing links (plural) had not been found. If we have a million different species, we must have at least a million connecting links, one to link each species to another, but a scientist, speaking in London not long ago, said that if evolution were true, it would not be one link between two species, but there would be a million links between two species, and yet, with a million times a million links that must have existed if evolution be true, they have not found a single link.

—W. Jennings Bryan

(Gen. 1. 20-28).

352. Evolution. Whatever may be the effect on the religious opinions of adults or of scientific men of an adherence to this evolutionary theory of human origin, it is unquestionable that it is disastrous to the ethical development or spiritual life of the young or uneducated to lead them to believe that men were 'descended from monkeys', or that 'the chimpanzee or gorilla are man's nearest relations', which is the form in which this theory takes expression in the minds of the general public.

The reckless popularization of the theory of organic evolution without regard to the strong arguments which can be urged against it, constitutes a serious danger.

Biblical teaching is not inconsistent with any definitely ascertained facts with regard to early mankind, when carefully interpreted.

—Sir Ambrose Fleming,
M.A., D.Sc., D.Eng., F.R.S.
(President of the Victoria Institute and Philosophical Society of Great Britain: President of the Television Society; Fellow of University College, London, etc.).
(Gen. 1. 26, 27).

353. Evolution—Beliefs of.

Once I was a tadpole grubbing in the mire,
Till I became ambitious and started to aspire.
I rubbed my tail so vig'rously against the sunken
*   log*
It disappeared completely and I found myself a
*   frog.*
I struggled from my puddle and jumped upon dry
*   land,*
And the feeling that was in me was glorious and
*   grand;*
It made me kind o' frisky, so I hopped around a
*   tree*
Till I landed in the branches as happy as could be.
And there I spent some aeons evoluting without
*   fail*
Till I became a monkey and grew another tail;
But still I had ambitions, as aeons quickly sped,
So I climbed down from the branches and walked
*   the earth instead.*
Till my tail got tired with trailing on the hard
*   earth every day,*
And twice within my 'process' that appendage
*   passed away.*
Once again I evoluted, and, believe me if you
*   can—*
I woke one summer morning and found myself a
*   man.*

354. Evolutionist—Deathbed of an. Neither the biographers of Charles Darwin, nor writers on Evolution, relate the following story of the last days of Charles Darwin, as told by Lady Hope, at meetings in Northfield, Mass.

'It was on a glorious autumn afternoon, when I was asked to go and sit with Charles Darwin. He was almost bedridden for months before he died. Propped up with pillows, his features seemed to be lit up with pleasure as I entered the room.

'He waved his hand towards the window, as he pointed out the beautiful sunset scene beyond, while in the other hand he held an open Bible, which he was always studying.

"What are you reading now?" I asked.

"Hebrews," he answered, "Still Hebrews. The Royal Book, I call it." Then, placing his finger on certain passages, he commented on them.

'I made some allusion to the strong opinions expressed by many on the history of Creation, and then their treatment of the earlier chapters of the Book of Genesis. He seemed distressed, his fingers twitched nervously, and a look of agony came over his face as he said, "I was a young man with unformed ideas. I threw out queries, suggestions, wondering all the time over everything; and to my astonishment the ideas took like wildfire. People made a religion of them." Then he paused, and after a few more sentences on the holiness of God, and "the grandeur of this Book", looking at the Bible which he was holding tenderly all the time, he said:

'"I have a summer house in the garden which holds about thirty people; it is over there" (pointing through the open window). "I want you very much to speak here. I know you read the Bible in the villages. Tomorrow afternoon I should like the servants on the place, some tenants, and a few neighbours, to gather there. Will you speak to them?"

'"What shall I speak about?" ! asked.

'"Christ Jesus" he replied in a clear, emphatic voice, adding in a lower tone, "and His salvation. Is not that the best theme? And then I want you to sing some hymns with them. You lead on your small instrument, do you not?"

'The look of brightness on his face as he said this I shall never forget; for he added: "If you take the meeting at three o'clock, this window will be open, and you will know that I am joining with the singing".'

—*Christian Witness*

(Gen. 2. 7; John 1. 1-3).

355. Example.

I'd rather have example than precept any day,
I'm glad my Saviour walks with me, not merely
*   points the way.*
The eye's a better pupil and more willing than
*   the ear:*
Fine counsel is confusing, but example's always
*   clear.*
The greatest of all teachers was my Lord Who
*   lived His creed,*
For to see good put in action is what all His
*   people need.*
I may not fully understand the doctrines I've
*   received,*
But there's no misunderstanding how He loved
*   and how He lived.*

(John 13. 15; 1 Pet. 2. 21).

356. Example—Of Christ. Peter the Great of Russia had a big idea to improve Russia, which was then in a backward state compared with the rest of Europe. So he left his exalted position, became first an apprentice, then a skilled workman, and finally a teacher and demonstrator. He worked as a shipbuilder in Holland and at Deptford in England, and studied military science in Austria. The result was—St. Petersburg, whose name has since been changed, was founded by him. It rises out of the marshes, the capital and harbour for merchant ships many of which Peter himself piloted in.

He was an outstanding example of humility and diligence to his subjects. Our Lord Jesus Christ has given us a very much greater example of humility and service.
(John 13. 3-5, 14-16; 1 Thess. 1. 7).

357. Example—of Christ. At the close of an address a few years ago, a stranger accosted Dr. Stearns of U.S.A. and said, 'I don't like your preaching. I do not care for the cross. I think that instead of preaching the death of Christ, it would be far better to preach Jesus the Teacher and Example.'

Dr. Stearns replied: 'Would you be willing to follow Him if I preach Christ as the Example?' 'I would,' said the stranger, 'I will follow in His steps.'

'Then,' said the preacher, 'let us take the first step!—Who did no sin? Can you take this step?'

The stranger looked confused. 'No,' he said, 'I do sin. I acknowledge it.'

'Well, then,' said the Doctor, 'your first need of Christ is not as an Example, but as a Saviour.'

Expiation for sins comes first, then Christ's Example for our lives.
(1 Pet. 2. 21, 24).

358. Example—of Good and Great men. Men are by nature imitators. All persons are more or less impressed by the speech, the manners, the gait, the gestures, and even the habits of thinking of those around them. 'Example is the school of mankind,' said Burke, 'and they will learn from no other.'

In man, as in the lower animals, imitation is for the most part unconscious. Impressions are made without our knowing it. But though they are unheeded, the effects are more or less permanent. Though the force of example is for the most part spontaneous and unconscious, the young need not necessarily be the passive followers or imitators of those about them. Not only can they select their companions and decide which are most worthy of imitation, but their own conduct tends to fire the purpose and form the principles of their lives.

Let a young man seek, if possible, the society of men better than himself, and especially of those who do not possess the kind of fault to which he finds himself peculiarly liable, or who possessed it once but have conquered it. Their example is always inspiring. He corrects his own conduct by theirs, and becomes a partner in their wisdom. If they are stronger in will or character than he is, he becomes a participator in their strength.

Dr. Arnold's own example was an inspiration, as is that of every great teacher. In his presence young men learnt to respect themselves; and out of the root of self-respect grew up the manly virtues. The example of a good and great man is contagious and compels imitation.

        —S. Smiles
(Phil. 2. 5; 3. 17; 1 Thess. 4. 1).

359. Example—Of Parents. In the nursery the children were talking rather loudly, and mother went in and asked what they were quarrelling about. 'We're not quarrelling, mother,' said the eldest, 'we're just playing "Daddy and mummy".'

360. Exile. Madame de la Mothe Guyon, that notable prisoner for Christ's sake in the Chateau de Chillon, sang:

Nor exile I nor prison fear;
Love makes my courage great;
I find a Saviour everywhere,
His grace in every state.

Nor castle walls, nor dungeon deep,
Exclude His quickening beams;
There I can sit and sing and weep,
And dwell on heavenly themes.

There, sorrow for His sake is found
A joy beyond compare;
There no presumptuous thoughts abound,
Nor pride can enter there.

A Saviour doubles all my joys
And sweetens all my pains;
His strength in my defence employs,
Consoles me and sustains.

(Eph. 6. 20; Rev. 1. 9).

361. Exposition. Originality within the sphere of a creature, and in reference to a finite intelligence, consists in the power of interpretation. In its last analysis it is exegesis— the pure, genial and accurate exposition of an idea or truth already existing, already communicated, already possessed.

There has been no creation, but only a development; no absolute authorship, but only an explication. And yet how fresh and original has been the mental process! The same substantially in Plato and in the thousands of his scholars; and yet in every single instance there has been all the enthusiasm, all the stimulation all the ebullient flow of life and feeling that attends the discovery of a new continent or a new star.

'Then feels he like some watcher of the skies
When a new planet swims into his ken;
Or like stout Cortes, when with eagle eyes
He stared at the Pacific, and all his men
Looked at each other with a wild surmise,
Silent, upon a peak of Darien.'

        —Dr. G. Campbell Morgan
(Neh. 8. 8; Job. 13. 1; 32. 8; Acts 20. 27).

362. **Face—Of Christ.** A great painter had finished painting a scene in a room, in which the Lord Jesus Christ was the central figure, and he invited some friends to see it. They were all enamoured by the wonderful lace tablecloth, the product of the artist's genius. They talked only of that, the magnificent lacework. The painter took his brush, dipped it into his paints, with one bold stroke wiped out the lacework, and, addressing his friends, said, 'Fools, look at the Master's face.' They had almost missed the glory of the picture by looking at the lacework. We need to look beyond the lacework of Christendom to see the glory of the Face of Christ.

—*The Indian Christian*

(2 Cor. 3. 18; 4. 6).

363. **Face—of Christ.**

Is this the Face that thrills with awe
  Seraphs who veil their face above?
Is this the Face without a flaw,
  The Face that is the Face of love?
Yea, this defacéd, lifeless clod
  Hath all creation's love sufficed,
Hath satisfied the love of God,
  This Face—the Face of Jesus Christ.

—Christina Rosetti

'His visage was so marred more than any man and His form more than the sons of men.' (Isa. 6. 2; 52. 14; Rev. 20. 11).

364. **Face to Face.**

I had walked life's way with an easy tread,
Had followed where pleasures and comforts led,
Until one day, in a quiet place,
I met the Master face to face.

With station and rank and wealth for my goal,
Much thought for my body but none for my soul,
I had entered to win in life's mad race
When I met the Master face to face.

I had built my castles and reared them high
Till their towers had pierced the blue of the sky:
I had sworn to rule with an iron mace
When I met the Master face to face.

I met him, and knew Him, and blushed to see
That his eyes, full of pity, were fixed on me;
And I faltered and fell at His feet that day
While my castles melted and vanished away.

Faded, and vanished, and in their place
Naught else did I see but the Master's face:
And I cried aloud, 'O make me meet
To follow the steps of Thy wounded feet!'

My thought is now for the souls of men,
I have lost my life to find it again,
Ever since that day, in a quiet place,
That I met the Master face to face.

—Captain Edith Overall

(Hos. 2. 14; John 12. 21; Heb. 2. 9; 2 Cor. 3. 18).

365. **Face to Face.**

For though from out our bourne of time and place
  The floods may bear me far,
I hope to see my Pilot face to face
  When I have crossed the bar.

—Alfred, Lord Tennyson

(1 Cor. 13. 12; 2 Cor. 5. 8).

366. **Failure—the way to success.**

I held it truth with him that sings,
  To one clear harp in divers tones,
  That men may rise on stepping stones
Of their dead selves to higher things.

—Alfred, Lord Tennyson

(Acts 13. 13; 15. 37, 38; 2 Tim. 4. 11).

367. **Faith—Act of.** Someone wrote the following lines on the back of a £1 note:

This piece of paper in your hand
Declares to you that on demand
You twenty shillings will receive;
That simple promise you believe.
It puts your mind as much at rest
As if the silver you possessed.
So Christ Who died but now doth live
Doth unto you the promise give
That, if in Him you will believe,
You shall eternal life receive.
Upon the first you calmly rest.
Which is the safer? Which the best?
The Bank may fail: Heaven never can;
'Tis safer to trust God than man.

(John 3. 16; Rom. 4. 5).

368. **Faith—Activities of.** Faith is deaf to doubts, dumb to discouragements, blind to impossibilities, knows nothing but success. Faith lifts its hand up through the threatening clouds, lays hold on Him Who has power in Heaven and on earth. Faith makes the uplook good, the outlook bright, the inlook favourable and the future glorious.

Faith, mighty faith, the promise sees
  And looks to God alone,
Laughs at impossibilities
  And cries, 'It shall be done.'

369. **Faith—Certainty of.** Faith is simple. If it were not so, we would be kept in life-long perplexity, trying to perform it or to practise it, as if it were some great thing. Faith is sure. It does not conjecture, or speculate, or think; it is sure as soon as it knows that what is heard is really true. Nothing can shake the certainty of faith, save what invalidates the foundation on which it rests. Faith rests on divine testimony. We do not reason out the matter, nor think it out; we believe because God hath spoken. We hear the words of His mouth, and we say, 'Amen! I believe, whatever reason may say.'

—Cheyne Brady

(Rom. 4. 20, 21).

370. **Faith—Courage of.** Alexander the Great had a famous but poor philosopher in his court.

Being pressed for money, the philosopher made application to his patron for relief. Alexander had commissioned him to draw whatever cash he needed from the Treasury, so the philosopher presented a request for a very large sum. The Treasurer refused to honour the draft until he consulted his royal master, adding that he thought the amount exorbitant. Alexander replied, 'Pay the money at once. The philosopher has done me a singular honour. By the largeness of his request he shows the idea he has conceived both of my wealth and my munificence.'
(Phil. 4. 19).

371. Faith—Courage of. The Lord Jesus is here, and we have unlimited, unbounded faith in Him. That is the first thing touching the King: His unique power of drawing out faith in Himself. Where the agnostic and sceptic would fold their hands in despair, and curse Heaven for their miseries and troubles from which they saw no way of deliverance or escape, the man who knows Jesus Christ takes fresh courage of faith, and sets himself with steadfast perseverance, with indomitable courage, and with magnificent hopefulness, to raise the fallen and comfort the weak-hearted.
—Preb. F. S. Webster
(Ps. 45. 1; Heb. 10. 22, 38).

372. Faith—Definition of. 'Trust' is the word used in the Old Testament: 'faith' is the equivalent in the New Testament. 'Belief' is the precursor of both. Belief has to do with the head, trust and faith with the heart.
John G. Paton was making a translation of the Scriptures into the language spoken in the country where he was a missionary, and searched long for a word for 'Faith'. The natives had no word for 'believe'. One day, while working on his translation, a native entered his room and, tired out, flung himself down on one chair, resting his feet on another chair and remarking how good it was to 'lean his whole weight' on the chairs. Dr. Paton noted the word he had used for 'lean his whole weight'. He had his word for 'believe'.
(Acts 16. 31; Rom. 10. 9, 10).

373. Faith—Definition of. Do we need to define 'faith' to ourselves over again? Has not every use of the word by the Lord Himself in the Gospels long ago assured us that it means just personal reliance, personal entrustment? It is the open arms which in their emptiness embrace Christ, the open lips which receive Him as the Bread of the soul, the life, the all. As in justification, so in this its glorious sequel, our part is to take the promise as it stands, to take the thing in the envelope of promise, and to act upon its holy presence and reality.
—H. C. G. Moule, D.D.
(Rom. 4. 21; Heb. 11. 1, 11).

374. Faith—Essence of. In order to clarify what faith involved, C. H. Spurgeon used to employ this illustration. Suppose there is a fire on the third floor of a house, and a child is trapped in a room there. A huge, strong man stands on the ground beneath the window where the child's face appears, and he calls 'Jump! Drop into my arms.' 'It is a part of faith,' Spurgeon would say, 'to know that there is a man there; still another part of faith to believe him to be a strong man; but the essence of faith lies in trusting him fully and dropping into his arms.' Thus it is with the sinner and Christ.
(Is. 59. 16; Matt. 1. 21; Acts 16. 30, 31).

375. Faith—Essence of. The missionary's son, nearly five years of age, had been born and brought up in India, and had seen no near relatives except his parents. One day he said to his mother, 'I love my grandpa.' 'How can that be, my son?' replied his mother, 'You have never seen him and how can you love him?' 'But,' said the child, 'doesn't he send us letters, and doesn't he send presents for my birthday and at Christmas, and aren't we going on the big steamship soon to see him?'
'Whom, having not seen, we love; in Whom, though now we see Him not, yet believing, we rejoice with joy unspeakable and full of glory.'
(Heb. 11. 1; 1 Pet. 1. 8).

376. Faith—Meaning of. Dr. Chalmers went to see a Scottish woman in her time of trouble about her sin. She was trying to 'get faith'. On his way to her house he had to cross a stream over which there was a thin plank. Looking out of her window, she saw he was afraid to venture across on it, and, coming out, she called to him, 'Jist lippen to it.' That was her way of advising him just to trust himself to the plank.
Then he spoke to her about the way of salvation and used the illustration and her own words to explain to her how to trust the Saviour.
(Eph. 1. 12, 13; 3. 17; 1 John 5. 1).

377. Faith—Need of.
Faith is needed all the way,
Faith to toil and faith to pray,
Faith to learn and faith to teach,
Faith to practise, faith to preach;
Faith to start each day anew,
Faith to do our duty, too;
Faith to help the weak along,
Faith to bear, in patience, wrong;
Faith to smile, though sad within,
Faith to conquer every sin,
Faith to ask Him for His care
While we earthly trials bear;
Faith to smother every sigh,
Faith to live and faith to die.
(Matt. 6. 30; 8. 26; 14. 31; 17. 20).

378. Faith — Obedience of. Faith looks straight to the command in order to obey it, and takes the promise for her support. She pushes on her way, regardless of dangers.

Moses must go forward, though the next step lead the people into the sea. Whatever appearances may say to us, it is by advancing in the narrow way of obedience that we prove the truth of the promises, and the faithfulness, wisdom and power of our promise-keeping God.

—R. C. Chapman

Abraham's Call—Faith in the Promise 'I will bless thee'.
Obedience to the command 'Get thee out'.
Christ's Call to the sinner—Faith in the promise—'I will give you rest'.
Obedience to the command 'Come unto me'.
Christ Call to follow—Faith in the promise—'I will make you fishers of men'.
Obedience to the command 'Follow me'.
(Rom. 1. 5; 16. 26; Heb. 11. 6, 8).

379. Faith—Object of. A woman was famed for her sanctity and her beautiful life. When people visited her town, if they were interested in divine things, they almost always went to see her. One day someone went to see her, and when he was ushered into her room, he said, 'I am so glad to see you; you are the woman of the strong faith.' 'No, sir,' she replied. 'But,' he said, 'everybody tells me what great things you have done.' 'No, I am the woman of the weak faith in the strong Saviour,' she said.

—W. Y. Fullerton

(Luke 17. 6; Heb. 11. 33, 34).

380. Faith—Object of. There is no blessing outside of Christ: the person of Christ, the heavenly Man. The Gospel places before the sinner a risen, living Christ, as the object of faith and the end of the law for righteousness to every one that believeth. While the eye of faith is kept on the heavenly Christ, all is light, joy and peace; but, if turned in on self, and occupied with what it finds there, and what it feels, or with anything that may come between the heart and Christ, all will be darkness.

—W. P. Mackay

(Rom. 10. 4, 8-10).

381. Faith—Object of. A devout Christian was acting on a Royal Commission of which Professor Huxley was a member, and one Sunday he and the great scientist were staying in a little country town. 'I suppose you are going to Church,' said Huxley. 'Yes,' replied the Christian. 'What if, instead, you stayed at home and talked to me about religion?' 'No,' was the reply, 'for I am not clever enough to refute your arguments.' 'But what if you simply told me your experience—what religion has done for you?' So, instead of going to Church that morning, he stayed at home and told Huxley the story of his conversion and all that Christ had been to him. Presently there were tears in the eyes of the great agnostic as he said, 'I would give my right hand if I could believe that, but I can't.'
(Rom. 10. 17; Heb. 11. 1).

382. Faith—Object of. They who know what is meant by faith in a promise know what is meant by faith in the gospel; they who know what is meant by faith in a remedy, know what is meant by faith in the blood of the Redeemer; they who know what is meant by faith in a physician, faith in an advocate, faith in a friend, know, too, what is meant by faith in the Lord Jesus Christ.

—Bishop O'Brien

(Acts 3. 16; 4. 12; 10. 43; 13. 38, 39).

383. Faith—Object of. Some years ago I was one of the speakers at a large Convention in Travancore, now Kerala State. The pandal for the Convention was in the sandy dried-up bed of a river, and to reach it we had to cross a branch of the river that had not dried up. The brethren in charge of the arrangements had seen to it that every facility was provided for all who wished to attend the meetings, and had provided a strong plank from one side of the stream to the other. With several of the national brethren I arrived at the bank of the stream which seemed to be fairly deep. There was the plank over which I might cross to the other side, but I hesitated. 'Why do you hesitate?' they asked. 'You simply have to walk across the plank and in a few seconds you will be on the other side. This is the only stream that has to be crossed to get to the Convention pandal.' Still I hesitated and replied, 'Yes, but I do not think the plank is strong enough to bear my weight.' 'No need for any fears on that score,' said they, 'Hundreds have already crossed in safety before you came.' 'Yes,' I replied, 'that may be so, but I'm taller and heavier than those I have seen going across, and what is sufficient for them might not bear my weight.' To prove the strength of the plank two well-built, hefty fellows walked across together. 'Look,' they said, 'two of us are heavier than you, and the plank took us both together.'

'All right,' said I, 'I'll venture.' So, very slowly and hesitantly, I made my way across as they stood watching me with amused smiles. When I reached the other side, they said, 'Didn't we tell you you would be quite safe? Why didn't you take our word for it and trust the plank in the first place?' 'Yes,' I explained to them, 'you see it was not the strength of my faith that took me safely across, for my faith, as you know, was very weak. But it was the strength of the plank, the object in which you advised me to put my trust.'

—A. N.

(John 4. 42; Acts 16. 31; 2 Tim. 1. 12).

384. Faith—Power of. Faith sees the invisible, hears the inaudible, touches the intangible. All seen comes out of the unseen and returns thither. Into this realm comes faith, and it is at home. It knows God. It endures martyrdom since it sees Him Who is invisible.
(Heb. 11. 1, 27, 35-37).

385. **Faith—Proof of.** The story is told of a blind boy who was flying a kite and enjoying this pastime along with others of his own age. A passer-by, knowing him and wanting to give him a gentle teasing, said, 'Where is your kite? You don't know whether it is on the ground or up in the sky.' 'Oh yes,' said the blind lad, 'I do know. It is now quite a fair height up in the air.' 'How do you know that?' asked his friend, 'you can't see it.' 'No!' replied the boy, 'I can't see it, it is true, but I can feel the tug of the string.'

(Heb. 11. 3, 6; 1 Pet. 1. 8).

386. **Faith—Quality of.** It is not the quantity of faith, but the quality of faith, that is important. A grain of mustard seed and a pellet of dust are similar in appearance, but the difference is immense. The one has no life burning at the heart of it, while the other contains life as God kindled it. Faith that has in it the principle of life is a faith with God in it.
—F. B. Meyer

(Matt. 17. 20; Luke 17. 6).

387. **Faith—Realm of.**
Senses for the things of sense;
Reason for the things of thought and the mind;
Faith for the things of God.
—H. W. Warren

388. **Faith—Shield of.** This is the defence for the living saint and the dying saint. In olden days, when a warrior carried a shield almost as big as himself, those who recovered the slain after a battle would often use their shields that had been their protection in the battle as their biers to carry them to the burial. (Eph. 6. 16).

389. **Faith—Steps of.**
'The steps of faith
Fall on the seeming void, and find
The Rock beneath.
—J. G. Whittier
Abraham's steps of faith—He left all for God, left all with God, found all in God and yielded all to God.
(Heb. 11. 8, 9-10; 16-17; Rom. 4. 12).

390. **Faith—Strength of.** The other evening I was riding home after a heavy day's work. I felt very wearied and sore depressed, when swiftly, suddenly as a lightning flash, that text came to me, 'My grace is sufficient for thee'. I reached home and looked it up in the original, and suddenly it came to me in this way: 'My grace is sufficient for thee', and I said, 'I should think it is, Lord,' and I burst out laughing. I never fully understood the holy laughter of Abraham until then. It seemed to make unbelief so absurd. O brethren, be great believers! Little faith will bring your souls to heaven but great faith will bring heaven to your souls.
—C. H. Spurgeon

(Rom. 4. 20).

391. **Faith—Vision of.**
Faith sees in Christ on high enthroned
The cruel cross on which He groaned;
The crown which now His brow adorns
Was once a cruel crown of thorns.

And while the ages roll away,
Faith sees the increase of His sway
Till crowns and thrones and kingdoms fall,
And Christ is King and Lord of all.
(Heb. 2. 9; 11. 10).

392. **Faithfulness.** It costs to be faithful. It cost Abraham the yielding up of his only son. It cost Esther the risk of her life. It cost Daniel being cast into the den of lions. It cost Shadrach, Meshach and Abednego being put in a fiery furnace. It cost Stephen death by stoning. It cost Peter a martyr's death. It cost Paul his life. Does it cost you anything to be faithful to your Lord and King?
—Selected
(Matt. 25. 31; Luke 19. 17; 1 Cor. 4. 2; Rev. 2. 10).

393. **Faithfulness.** The hymn with the chorus 'Hold the fort, for I am coming!' written by P. P. Bliss, was suggested to him by an incident in the American Civil War. At Altoma Pass the fort being held by General Corse was besieged by the enemy under General Hood, who summoned it to surrender. Corse refused to surrender. Many were the casualties, but in spite of the hopeless situation the defenders remained faithful. Then a white signal flag across the valley, some twenty miles away, waved the message, 'Hold the fort, for I am coming'. General Sharman was marching to the relief of the beleaguered and faithful defenders.
(Rev. 2. 25; 3. 11).

394. **Father—in Heaven.** A missionary was crossing the River Godavari from Narsapur to Nagaram Island in a boat, setting out on a preaching tour. Equipped with gospel tracts, he handed one to each of those on the boat who could read. Opposite him sat a Brahmin gentleman who politely accepted a tract and, after scanning it through, began to question the missionary, asking what his native country was, how long he had been in India, where he resided in this land, what was his business and what business was taking him across the river. Then followed questions about the missionary's family. Was he married? Had he any children? When he heard that the family consisted of a wife and five sons, he said, 'God has certainly blessed you: you are a very rich man.' Then came the inevitable question, 'What salary do you receive?'
It is very often good to answer a question by asking one, so the missionary said, 'May I ask you one or two questions?' 'Certainly,' said the Brahmin. 'Are you a married man?' On receiving an affirmative reply, the missionary next asked what family he had; and he replied, telling him he had sons and daughters. 'Then

what salary do you pay them?' asked the missionary. 'Me,' said he, astonished, 'I don't pay them any salary. I provide them with food and clothing, educate them and meet their marriage expenses when the time comes. Isn't that sufficient?' he asked. 'Of course it is,' said the missionary. 'And you know?' he added, 'I am in the very same position as your children are. My Father provides me with food and clothing, equips me for my work here, and meets all my expenses as they arise, so that I don't have to look for a salary either.' 'You must have a very rich father' was the Brahmin's reply, as he looked the missionary up and down. 'Yes, indeed I have,' said the missionary. 'This great river belongs to my Father, and all the fruitful fields and fruit-bearing trees, and that sun shining down upon us and giving us light and warmth; yes, and the sky over our heads, and the moon and stars with which it is studded at night—all these belong to my Father.' 'I see,' said he, 'God is your Father.' (Matt. 6. 32; Luke 11. 2, 3; 1 Tim. 6. 17).

395. Favours—Asking. The great importunity of Sir Walter Raleigh, court favourite during part of the reign of good Queen Bess, wearied Queen Elizabeth. One day, when he came to ask a fresh favour from her, she turned and said, 'Raleigh, when will you cease to be a beggar?' Immediately came Raleigh's reply, 'When your Majesty ceases to be a benefactress and to grant me favours.'
(Matt. 7. 7; John 16. 23, 24; Phil. 4. 6).

396. Feelings.

For feelings come and feelings go,
And feelings are deceiving.
My warrant is the Word of God:
Naught else is worth believing.

Though all my heart should feel condemned
For want of some sweet token,
There is One greater than my heart
Whose Word cannot be broken.

I'll trust in God's unchanging Word
Till soul and body sever:
For, though all things shall pass away,
His Word shall stand for ever.

—Martin Luther

(1 Pet. 1. 23-25).

397. Feelings. A man once came to a preacher and said to him: 'I was filled with joy in the meeting yesterday, and now it has all gone—all—and I do not know what to do. It is as dark as night.'

'I am so glad,' was the reply. He looked at the servant of Christ with astonishment and said: 'What do you mean?'

'Yesterday God gave you joy, and today He sees you are resting on your emotions instead of Christ, and He has taken them away in order to turn you to Christ. You have lost your joy, but you have Christ none the less. Did you ever pass through a railway tunnel?' 'Yes, often.'

'Did you, because it was dark, become melancholy and alarmed?'
'Of course not.'
'And did you, after a while, come out again into the light?'
'I am out now,' he exclaimed, interrupting the servant of Christ; 'it is all right—feelings or no feelings.'

—Henry Durbanville
(Rom. 7. 24, 25; 8. 38, 39).

398. Feet of Jesus. In the Bible, Mary of Bethany is always found at the feet of Jesus—waiting at His feet in Luke 10. 39, weeping at His feet in John 11. 32, 33, and worshipping at His feet in John 12. 3.

I sit an infant at His feet
Where moments teach me more
Than all the toils and all the books
Of all the ages hoar.

(Deut. 33. 3).

399. Fellowship. Samuel Hebich has a very good illustration of the fellowship of saints, which he entitles being 'Fitly shoined togeder'. It is the 'Tale of a Tub', Hebich's tub.

'You and I cannot make a tob. It requires a cood carpenter to make a tob or it will hold no water, because it is not made of von piece of wood, but of many, and dey must be fitly shoined togeder. Dere are four tings to make a cood tob:-

1. It must haf a cood bottom.
2. Each of de pieces must be fitly shoined to de bottom.
3. Each von must be fitly shoined to his fellow.
4. Each von shall be kept close by de bands outside.

'Von piece may be narrow and de next piece be wide, yet it shall be a cood tob; but if a leetle shtone or a bit of shtick vill come between de pieces, it vill not do at all. If de pieces are near, but do not touch, it vill not do at all; and if all de pieces but von touch, and are fitly shoined togeder, and dis von fall in or out of de circle, it is no tob at all.

'Vat is de shmall shtick or shtone between de pieces of vood? It is de leetle quarrel, de hard vord, de dirty bit of money dat keep broder from being fitly shoined to broder. Vat is de piece of vood dat falls out of de circle? It is de proud, unforgiving spirit dat efry von can feel is in de meeting and vich causes all heavenly peace to run out. Oh, beloved, be fitly shoined togeder!'
(1 Cor. 1. 10; Eph. 2. 21; 4. 1-3, 16).

400. Fellowship—Broken. In the factory, work was going on apace and every machine was working and producing to its utmost limit. Suddenly a main machine came to a standstill, and the power had to be switched off, making the other machines also idle. The work had come to a standstill. What had happened? Just this—the belt round the main pulley shaft and that particular machine had snapped, and the whole shop was thrown idle.

Fellowship with God by His Spirit is like the belt. When it is preserved intact, the service of the Lord goes on apace; but, when fellowship is broken, the work comes to a standstill until fellowship is re-established. (Acts 2. 42; 1 Cor. 1. 9; Phil. 2. 1; 1 John 1. 3, 6, 7).

401. Fellowship—on Earth.

Four lines used to be displayed on the wall of a beloved brother's home, and how true they are in experience! They read:

To dwell above with saints we love—
Ah yes! that will be glory.
To live below with saints we know,
Well, that's another story.

C. H. Spurgeon once said that he would rather spend eternity in Heaven with some Christians than half-an-hour on earth. (Phil. 1. 27; 2. 1; 4. 2).

402. Fellowship—of Kindred Minds.

The hymn—'Blest be the tie that binds'—was written by Dr. John Fawcett, pastor of a small but poor Baptist congregation at Wainsgate, Yorkshire. His salary of £25 a year was totally inadequate, so he accepted a call to a large, influential Baptist Church in London. He preached his Farewell sermon and was loading his belongings on to waggons for removal to the metropolis, when sorrowing members of his congregation, showing deep affection and grief, pleaded with him not to leave them. The pastor and his wife were so overcome that they sat down and wept. 'Oh John, John, I cannot bear this,' said the poor wife. 'We shall not go,' said the good man. His decision to remain with them was hailed by his people with great joy. To commemorate the event Dr. Fawcett wrote the hymn. They had proved that the loving fellowship of saints was more to be desired than more money and more physical comforts. (Acts 2. 42; Phil. 1. 5; 1 Thess. 2. 7, 8).

403. Fellowship—Restoration to.

A story is told of a certain preacher who mourned over a backslider in his assembly who had once been a regular attender at the prayer meeting, but for months had not been seen in the place where prayer was wont to be made. His voice, formerly so much heard in prayer, was sorely missed, so, after one prayer meeting, the preacher went straight to the brother's house and found him seated before an open fire. The absentee, surprised, quickly placed another chair for his visitor and then waited to receive the expected rebuke. But not a word did the preacher say. Taking his seat before the fire, he silently took the tongs and, lifting a glowing coal from the midst of its fellows, laid it by itself on the hearth. Remaining silent, he watched the blaze die out. Then the absentee spoke: 'You needn't say a single word, brother; I'll be there next Wednesday night.' (Acts 2. 42; Heb. 10. 25).

404. Fight of Faith.

If life is always a warfare
  Between the right and the wrong,
And good is fighting with evil,
  For ages and aeons long—

Fighting with eager cohorts,
  With banners pierced and torn;
Shining with sudden splendour,
  Wet with the dew of morn;

If all the forces of heaven
  And all the forces of sin
Are met in the infinite struggle,
  The souls of the world to win—

If God's in the awful battle
  Where the darkling legions ride,
Hasten to sword and to saddle;
  Lord! let me fight on Thy side.

(2 Chron. 20. 15; Eph. 6. 12, 13; 1 Tim. 6. 12; 2 Tim. 4. 7).

405. Fig-Tree—Putting forth leaves.

Some of the latest statistics regarding Israel's citrus industry reveal astounding facts. In 1950-51, some 32,000 acres were under cultivation but by the end of 1956 the figure shot up to 50,000 acres and an increase to 62,500 acres by 1960. What does this mean in fruit? At an average of 320 cases per acre, it means an annual output of sixteen to twenty million cases. The fruit consists of Jaffa oranges, grape-fruit, lemons, mandarines and other citrine fruits.

Israel's chief competitor in the field of citrus fruit is Spain, but this is offset by the superior quality and taste of Israel's fruit. The significance of citrus to the economy of Israel is most conspicuous in the field of its international trade. In 1955, out of total exports amounting to 86 million dollars, citrus exports accounted for 31 million dollars. In 1956 the value of citrus bi-products amounted to 43 million dollars. While the nett profit on other industrial exports is only 30% to 33%, that on citrus is 70%. Citrus exports therefore reach the level of all the country's other exports combined and rank high among Israel's foreign exchange earning industries.

It is also interesting to note that there is growing ability to save on shipping costs. During the 1955-56 season 26% of all citrus exports were carried by vessels under the Israeli flag, involving a gross foreign exchange earning of one and a half million dollars, and with the expansion of the country's merchant marine, it is expected that an ever-increasing percentage of Israel's citrus will be carried by Israel's ships.

What does all this mean? When the Lord was asked—'What shall be the sign of Thy coming and of the end of the world?' He listed certain important events that would occur, many of which are happening around us today. In His discourse, He added the parable of the fig tree—'When his branch is yet tender, and putteth forth leaves, ye know that summer is nigh: so likewise ye, when ye shall see these things, know that it is near, even at the doors.'

Israel is that fig tree and when we see her developing into a healthy nation and expanding in accordance with God's Word, we may be sure that the Lord's return is imminent.

(Matt. 24. 32, 33).
—S. J. W. Chase

406. Fig Tree—Putting forth leaves. In the early days of 1958, after being present at an interesting Jewish service in a synagogue in Cochin we learnt, in conversation with a Jew who had taken part in the reading of the Scriptures in Hebrew, that, though formerly there were thousands of Jews in Cochin, in which there are three synagogues, there are now only a few hundred, scarcely sufficient for one of the synagogues. These few, too, will soon be in Palestine, travelling free of cost by one of the weekly planes, the cost being met by the Zionist movement. From all the cities of the East, Jews are returning in their thousands to their own land. The fig tree is certainly putting forth its leaves.

(Matt. 24. 32, 33).

407. Fire—of the Refiner. The Bible Dictionary tells us that the refiner sits before his crucible, fixing his eyes on the metal, taking care that the heat is not too great, and letting the metal stay in the crucible only so long as is necessary for all the dross to be consumed. The indication of this is the reflection of the refiner's own image in the glowing mass.

He sat by the furnace of sevenfold heat,
As he watched the precious ore;
And closer he bent with a searching gaze
As he heated it more and more.

He knew he had ore that could stand the test,
And he wanted the finest gold
To mould a crown for the King to wear,
Set with gems of a price untold.

So He laid our gold in the burning fire,
Though we fain would say to Him 'Nay!'
And He watched the dross, which we had not seen,
As it melted and passed away.

And the gold grew brighter and yet more bright,
But our eyes were so dim with tears—
We saw but the fire, not the Master's hand,
And so questioned with anxious fears.

Yet our gold shone out with a richer glow,
As it mirrored a Form above
That bent o'er the fire, though unseen by us,
With a look of ineffable love.

Can we think it pleases His loving heart
E'er to cause us a moment's pain?
Ah no! but He sees through the present cross
All the bliss of eternal gain.

So He waited there with a watchful eye,
With a love that is strong and sure;
And His gold did not suffer a bit more heat
Than was needed to make it pure.

(Job. 23. 10; Mal. 3. 3; 1 Pet. 1. 7).

408. Fire—Tried by. The steel that has suffered most is the best steel. It has been in the furnace, on the anvil, in the jaws of the vice. It has felt the teeth of the rasp and has been ground by emery. It has been heated and hammered and filed until it does not know itself, and it comes out a splendid knife. Misfortunes are God's best blessings, moulding influences which give shapeliness and edge, and durability and power.

(Job. 23. 10; 42. 12; 2 Cor. 12. 10).
—Henry Ward Beecher

409. Fire—Tried by. The refiner is never far from the mouth of the furnace when his gold is in the fire, and the Son of God is always walking in the flames when his holy children are cast into them.

(Isa. 43. 2; Dan. 3. 22-25; 1 Pet. 1. 7, 8).
—C. H. Spurgeon

410. Fish. In the Gospel records, fish as a provision for human needs occupies a prominent place in our Lord's miracles. There were two miracles in which loaves and fishes were used to feed large companies, and two miraculous draughts of fishes. The risen Lord had fish to feed His toiling, hungry disciples on the shore of the Sea of Tiberias, and directed Peter to find the tribute money in the mouth of a fish, He knew where the fish was, and He knew where the money was.

So, and because the Greek letters of the word for 'fish' spell out the initials of our Lord's titles, the fish became the symbol of the Christians in days of persecution and trouble. It is frequently seen in the catacombs. The Greek word for 'fish' has five letters, which form the initials of the Greek words in the following order—Jesus Christ, Of God the Son—Saviour.

(Matt. 14. 17-19; 17. 27; Mark 8. 7; Luke 5. 6; John 21. 11).

411. Fishermen. Jesus made saints and servants of fishermen who would otherwise have died in the obscurity of Capernaum, without anyone except their neighbours being aware of them.

(Luke 5. 10, 11; Acts 3. 1-11).

412. Fishermen.

Jesus said, 'I will make you fishers of men
If you follow Me.'

I watched an old man trout-fishing the other day, pulling them out one after another briskly. 'You manage it cleverly, old friend,' I said. 'I have passed a good many below who don't seem to be doing anything.' The old man lifted himself up and stuck his rod in the ground. 'Well, you see, sir, there be three rules for trout-fishing, and 'tis no good trying if you don't mind them. The first is, Keep yourself out of sight; and the second is, Keep yourself further out of sight: and the third is,

Keep yourself still out of sight. Then you'll
do it.' Good for catching men, too!
—Mark Guy Pearse
(Mark 1. 17; Luke 5. 10).

413. Fishermen. Hebich had eight points for
a successful fisher of men:

   i. Be in love with your work.
   ii. Have patience.
   iii. Study the habits of the fish.
   iv. Have enticing tackle.
   v. Learn the run of the fish.
   vi. Follow the moves of the fish.
   vii. Be in time.
   viii. Have live bait.

(Mark 1. 17; John 1. 41).

414. Food—Spiritual. In a family it is
always a red-letter day in the life of the
youngest when the older children are able to
exclaim delightedly, 'Look, baby's feeding
himself.' A Christian sister in Chagallu,
Godavari District, India, was illiterate when
she was converted, but learnt to read at the
age of 50 so that she might be able to 'feed
herself' with spiritual food from God's Word.
With so many Christians content to remain
spoon-fed, that woman is an outstanding
example of hunger for the Bread of life and
determination to obtain it first-hand. Not only
is she able to feed herself, but she is in a
position to pass on much to others.
(John 6. 35; Heb. 5. 12-14).

415. Fool—Answering a. Seeing John Wesley
coming along the street one day, a man
straddled the pavement and said to him: 'I
never get out of my way for a fool.' 'But I
always do,' replied Wesley, as he stepped aside
into the gutter. A fine illustration of fulfilling the injunction, 'Answer a fool according
to his folly.'
(Prov. 26. 5).

416. Fool—for Christ's sake. A red-hot
evangelist, dressed in a morning coat and
striped trousers, and wearing a topper, walked
down a busy street in London one day. As he
approached, people walking in the opposite
direction from him read with amusement,
smiles and jeers, the words he had had printed
in large letters on a card fixed to the ribbon of
his hat. The words were—'A fool for Christ's
sake.' When he passed, they turned to have
another look at the man they thought to be a
religious maniac, and could not help seeing
the card on the back of his topper which read,
'Whose fool are you?'
(1 Cor. 4. 10).

417. Fool—for Christ's sake. The late W.
Kelly, preacher and Bible expositor who has
written many commentaries on the Scriptures,
was a distinguished Hebrew and Greek scholar.
His nephew took the Classics course at the
University, and the Greek Professor was so
impressed with the accuracy, beauty and per-

fection of his Greek proses that he called him
and asked who helped him in his translations.
The young man confessed that he had the help
of his uncle, W. Kelly. 'I should like to meet
your uncle,' said the Greek professor. 'That
can, I think, be arranged, and I am sure it will
give him pleasure to meet you,' replied the
student.

So he brought his uncle along at a time
convenient to his Professor, introduced him
and left them together. As they conversed on
the Greek language, the Professor's eyes
opened wider and wider at Mr. Kelly's profound erudition and extraordinary knowledge
of the Greek language and usage. Then he
said, 'And may I enquire what your vocation is,
Mr. Kelly?' 'Certainly,' replied the expositor,
'I am a preacher and travel here and there all
over the country ministering the Word of God
to groups of Christians.' Taking a deep breath
of surprise, the Professor said abruptly, 'Man,
you're a fool.' Immediately came W. Kelly's
reply, 'For which world, Professor?'
(Mark 8. 35, 36; 1 Cor. 4. 10).

418. Forgiveness. The Duke of Wellington
was about to pronounce the death sentence on
a confirmed deserter. Deeply moved, the great
General said, 'I am extremely sorry to pass this
severe sentence, but we have tried everything,
and all the discipline and penalties have failed
to improve this man who is otherwise a brave
and good soldier.'

Then he gave the man's comrades an
opportunity to speak for him. 'Please, your
Excellency,' said one of the men, 'there is one
thing you have never tried. You have not tried
forgiving him.' The General forgave him and
it worked: the soldier never again deserted and
ever after showed his gratitude to the Iron
Duke.
(Ps. 103. 2; Luke 7. 47, 48; Eph. 1. 7).

419. Forgiveness — Absolute. A Christian
doctor in Scotland was very lenient with his
poor patients, and when he found that it was
difficult for them to pay his fees he wrote in red
ink across the record of their indebtedness the
one word—'Forgiven'. This was of such
frequent occurrence that his case book had
few pages where the red letters did not appear.
After his death his executors thought the
doctor's estate would be greatly benefited if
some of the 'Forgiven' debts could be collected.
After unsuccessful applications to the poor
patients, the executors took legal proceedings
to recover the amounts. But when the judge
examined the case book and saw the word
'Forgiven' cancelling the entry, he said, 'There
is no tribunal in the land that could enforce
payment of these accounts marked 'Forgiven';
and he dismissed the case.
—*Indian Christian*
(Luke 7. 48-50; Acts 13. 38, 39).

420. Forgiveness—from the Crucified Saviour.
In an Oxfordshire village an old saint lay dying.
For over eighty years she had been on pil-

grimage to Zion, until her face had grown bright with Heaven's approaching glory. An Anglo-Catholic priest, under the misapprehension that none of his parishioners could find access to the City unless he unlocked the gate, called to visit her. 'Madam,' he said, 'I have come to grant you absolution.' And she, in her simplicity, not knowing what the word meant, inquired, 'What is that?' 'I have come to forgive your sins,' was the reply. 'May I look at your hand?' she answered. Gazing for a moment at the hand of the priest, she said, 'Sir, you are an impostor.' 'Impostor!' the scandalized cleric protested. 'Yes, sir, an impostor. The Man Who forgives my sins has a nail print in his hand.'

—R. Moffat Gautrey

(Mark 2. 5-7; Matt. 26. 28; 1 Cor. 11. 24).

421. Forgiveness—for the Penitent. A Russian prince, through the prerogative of Napoleon, was permitted to bring pardon to one convict in a French prison. Every person he interviewed professed innocence and said he was unjustly punished. At last he found one who with sorrow confessed his guilt and acknowledged himself deserving of the punishment. To him he said, 'I have brought you pardon. In the name of the Emperor I pronounce you a free man.'

(Acts 10. 43; Col. 1. 14).

422. Forsaken.

"My God, my God, why hast Thou forsaken me?"

Yet once Immanuel's orphaned cry the universe hath shaken;
It went up single, echoless, 'My God, I am forsaken!'
It went up from His holy lips amid His lost creation
That no one else need ever cry that cry of desolation.

(Ps. 22. 1; Matt. 27. 46; Mark 15. 34).

423. Fragrance—Of Christ in the life.

They say that once a piece of common clay
Such fragrance breathed as from a garden blows;
'My secret is but this,' they heard it say,
'I have been near the rose.'

And those there are who bear along with them
The power with thoughts of Christ men's hearts to stir;
For having knelt to kiss His garment's hem,
Their garments smell of myrrh.

So grant, I pray Thee, Lord, that by Thy grace
The fragrance of Thy life may dwell in me;
That as I move about from place to place,
Men's thoughts may turn to Thee.

(Ps. 45. 8; 2 Cor. 2. 14, 15).

424. Fragrance—Of Christ in the life. Dr. F. W. Boreham tells of a visit to a town in the South of France. A number of women passed him, evidently going to their homes from their factory or place of occupation; and, as they passed, he noticed that their garments were fragrant. The reason, he ascertained, was that they were engaged in preparing scent from flowers, and it had distilled on their clothes. Those enjoying Christ's presence and engaged in presenting Him to others cannot but transmit His fragrance.

(Hos. 14. 6; 2 Cor. 2. 14, 15).

425. Fragrance — From Communion with Christ.

A Persian fable says—One day
A wanderer found a piece of clay
So redolent of sweet perfume
Its odour scented all the room.

'What art thou?' was the quick demand:
'Art thou some gem of Samarcand
Or spikenard rare in rich disguise?
Or other costly merchandise?'

'Nay, I am but a piece of clay.'
'Then, whence this wondrous sweetness, pray?'
'Friend, if the secret I disclose,
I have been living with the rose.'

(Song of Songs 2. 1; 2 Cor. 3. 18).

426. Fragrance—of Mary's gift.

She brought her gift of worship to adorn
The One she loved, and poured it on His brow—
That brow so soon to feel the platted thorn,
The mockery of those who came to bow.

She brought her gift of service freely there
And poured it out upon the Saviour's feet—
Those feet that had the piercing nails to bear,
The journey to the cross—God's Mercy Seat.

And when the women came with burial token
That dawn, she was not there among the rest.
The alabaster box already broken,
She had anointed Him and given her best:
The fragrance of her gift that filled the room
Had reached beyond the cross, beyond the tomb.

—Ruth Gibbs Zwall

(Song of Songs 1. 12; John 12. 3, 7; Luke 24. 1-10).

427. Fragrance—In Mary's Life.

The scent of precious ointment—how it lingered
Long after all the guests had gone away;
And Mary's hands, how sweet where she had touched it,
The alabaster box she brought that day.

It filled the empty room with love's anointing,
Reached to the neighbours on the busy street
And ministered in many deeds of kindness
To friend and stranger whom she chanced to meet.

In every task she found the fragrance with her—
The pitcher that she carried bore the scent,
The coins exchanged for food within the market—
She took the blessing everywhere she went.

The box, unbroken, could have kept its treasure
  And pleased the fancy of a dinner guest;
But Mary broke the box, and in the breaking,
  Her Lord, and all the world beside, were blest.
                                        —Ruth Gibbs Zwall
(John 12. 3-5; 2 Cor. 4. 7).

428. Fragrance—From Pleasure or Pain.

My garden has roses red,
  My garden has roses white,
But if, when the day is sped,
  I stand by the gate at night,
One fragrance comes when the day is sped
From my roses white and my roses red.

The roses of joy are red,
  The roses of pain are white.
But I think, when the day is sped,
  And I stand by the gate at night,
I shall just know this, when the day is dead,
  That a rose is sweet, be it white or red.
                                        —Percy Ainsworth
(2 Cor. 6. 10).

429. Freedom—True.

I am now, every way, in good terms with Christ. He hath set a banished prisoner as a seal on His heart, and as a bracelet on His arm. I love Christ's glooms better than the world's worm-eaten joys. My loss is gain; my sadness is joyful; my bonds, liberty; my tears, comfortable. This world is not worth a drink of cold water. Oh the sweet communion that hath been between Christ and His prisoner! He is the fairest sight I see in Aberdeen. He hath made me king over my losses, imprisonment, banishment. I dare not say one word; He hath done it, and I will lay my hand upon my mouth. If any other hand had done it, I could not have borne it. I am here the Lord's prisoner and patient, handled as softly by my Physician as a sick man under a cure.

I wish that your soul might be satisfied with Him. This clay idol, the world, would seem to you not worth a fig; time will eat you out of possession of it. When the eye strings break, and the breath groweth cold, and the imprisoned soul looketh out of the windows of the clay house, ready to leap into eternity, what will you then give for a lamp of oil?
                        —Samuel Rutherford (written in prison)
(Eph. 3. 1-3; 4. 1; 6. 20).

430. Freedom—True.

  Stone walls do not a prison make,
    Nor iron bars a cage;
  Minds innocent and quiet take
    That for an hermitage.
  If I have pleasure in my love
    And in my soul am free,
  Angels alone that soar above
    Enjoy such liberty.
                                        —Colonel Lovelace
(John 8. 36; Eph. 6. 20).

431. Freedom—True.

  A little bird am I
    Shut in from fields of air;
  Yet in my cage I sit and sing
    To Him Who placed me there;
  Well pleased His prisoner to be
    Because, my God, it pleaseth Thee.

  Naught have I else to do,
    I sing the whole day long;
  And He Whom most I love to please
    Doth listen to my song.
  He caught and bound my wandering wing,
    But still He loves to hear me sing.

  Thou hast an ear to hear,
    A heart to love and bless;
  And, though my notes were e'er so rude,
    Thou wouldst not hear the less;
  Because Thou knowest, as they fall,
    That same sweet love inspired them all.

  My cage confines me round;
    Abroad I cannot fly;
  But though my wing is closely bound,
    My heart's at liberty.
  My prison walls cannot control
    The flight, the freedom of the soul.

  O, it is good to soar
    These bolts and bars above
  To Him Whose purpose I adore,
    Whose Providence I love,
  And in Thy mighty will to find
    The joy, the freedom, of the mind.
                                —Madam de la Mothe Guyon
(Ps. 69. 33; Acts 16. 25; 2 Tim. 2. 8, 9).

432. Friend.

In his book *Behind the Brass Plate*, Dr. A. T. Schofield narrates the interesting story of Maria Vincent and Queen Victoria. Here it is abridged.

In the lifetime of Queen Victoria, Dr. Schofield, a Harley Street physician, was one day visiting, not professionally, a poor street in Paddington—Woodchester Street—and in one of the houses he found Maria Vincent, an old, rather dignified lady seated in her rocking-chair by an empty grate. She was a mere anatomy of skin and bones. A thin shawl was drawn over her shoulders, and she had an indescribable something on her head. The bare room had a bed in the corner, with one blanket. It was mid-October. She was over 70 and had not seen her husband, a jobbing gardener somewhere, for years.

'Well, Mrs. Vincent,' said the doctor, 'a friend told me you were very much alone, and I thought I'd look in for a chat. You ought to have a fire these cold days.'

'I ain't got no money for a fire,' said Maria.

'Well,' said Dr. Schofield, 'winter is coming and you'll never get through it without more warmth and more clothes on your bed. What about your friends? Why don't they help you?' Maria replied that her friends were all dead.

'What?' asked the doctor, 'not one friend alive?'

'Ne'er a one,' she replied, 'there's no one comes next or nigh me.'

'Hasn't the parish doctor seen you?' Maria replied that she didn't hold with doctors. 'What about your neighbours?' asked Dr. Schofield.

'Lor', sir,' replied Maria, 'I never belonged to the likes of them. I don't know any of their names. I didn't always live in this room.'

Then her visitor left, saying he would call in a week, and telling her to think hard and try to remember some friend who knew her.

Returning the next week, he heard her cough badly and remarked on it. She replied, 'I've got the Browntitus.' Then Dr. Schofield asked her again if she could remember any friend of hers who might still be alive.

'Well,' replied Maria, 'there might be one'. 'And who is that?' he asked.

'God!' said she. 'Hasn't he kept me alive these 72 years?'

Her visitor agreed and then asked if she had no earthly friend she could recall. To this Maria replied, 'There might be one, but, sir, she's forgotten all about poor Maria.'

'Who is it?' asked the doctor; and Maria replied, 'Queen Victoria.'

Dr. Schofield gasped. Then the old lady told her story.

She had once had a house on Southsea Common. The Queen and her mother, the Duchess of Kent, used at that time to go rowing on the river with eight sailors and a young coxswain. One day the coxswain was taken ill and brought into the nearest house, which was Maria's, and she nursed him till he died. Then the Duchess of Kent came soon after to her house with a beautiful white Indian shawl as a present from the Queen, who thanked her for all the care she had taken of the poor fellow, and said Maria was to be sure and let her know anything she wanted. 'But, sir,' continued Maria, 'she's forgot all about it. She is now an old lady, and has never heard of me, nor have I seen her from that day to this; and her mother, the Duchess, why, she's been dead a very many years.'

Dr. Schofield went home and wrote a letter to the Queen at Balmoral, telling her the story he had heard from Maria Vincent. In a few days he received in reply a beautiful letter from the Queen saying it was all true, and enclosing a postal order for a good many pounds. The doctor went to Maria's house and showed her the Queen's letter which she read slowly. As he read he could see in her face Matheson's 'Sunshine through the rain,' as expressed in his wonderful hymn. With the tears streaming down her cheeks and her eyes bright with joy, she exclaimed,

'Oh, sir, she's not forgotten me!'

She saw no postal order: she thought nothing of money, but the thought that her Queen had not forgotten her was too much for her.

'But that isn't all, Maria,' said the doctor, 'there's a piece of blue paper the Queen has sent. Can you write your name?'

'Lor', sir,' she said, 'I'm a scholar; I don't make my mark. I writes my name.' Maria took the order to the Post Office, received a stream of golden sovereigns which made her a richer woman than she had been since her far-off youth, and then went off to a large drapery store to buy things of which she stood badly in need.—A toque of gay satin in the millinery department, hand-sewn boots in the shoe department, a shawl of rainbow colours in the drapery department, and blankets for her bed. Next she ordered coal at the coal merchant's and provisions at the store.

She arrived home followed by a stream of boys with parcels, who had to fight their way through crowds of wondering women who blocked the way to her room.

An Irishwoman volunteered to go to Maria and ask all about what had happened. She said to Maria, 'Yer must have some good friends.' 'Oh, yes, I'm well off for friends,' replied Maria. 'Ah!' said the Irishwoman, 'that kind gentleman that comes to see you?' 'No!' said Maria, with unconcealed delight. 'And might I be so bold as to inquire who the friend might be?' 'The Queen,' said Maria casually, though absolutely bursting with pride. 'Oho! Queen Victorier?' 'Yes,' said Maria, 'she and me's old friends.'

Some months later, after a further supply from the Queen, Maria was transformed and looked ten years younger. Then Dr. Schofield learnt from her that she had another friend also, the Empress of the French, whom she had once helped in trouble. The Empress Eugenie had lost her husband while in Christchurch, and Maria Vincent had written her a letter and sent a piece of poetry with it. Dr. Schofield wrote to the Empress and received from her also a confirmatory letter, with a Postal Order for several pounds for Maria. Thus Maria had two earthly friends, one a Queen, the other an Empress, and she wanted for nothing till she left this world to enter the presence of the greatest Friend of all.

Each day He spreads a glorious feast,
    And at His table dine
The whole creation, man and beast,
    And He's a Friend of mine.

(Prov. 17. 17; 18. 24; John 15. 14, 15).

433. **Fruitfulness.** A 'fruitful bough whose branches run over the wall' grows from a strong, well-rooted, vigorous and healthy stock on the other side. The foremost disciples in spiritual life are the foremost in unselfish, persistent, untiring work for souls.
                    —Dr. A. T. Pierson
(Gen. 49. 22; John 15. 5; Phil. 1. 11).

434. **Fruitfulness.** The Godavari Delta in South India is a 'surplus' rice area, and is known all over India as a district of great fruitfulness. In the first half of the nineteenth century it was an unfruitful area, like many other parts of the vast sub-continent of India, until Sir Arthur Cotton, the great Christian engineer, carried out his irrigation scheme, had the dam constructed at Dowlaishwaram on the bank of the Godavari River, and canals dug

to carry the fresh water to all parts of the Delta. The river brings down the water which Heaven has sent from the skies; the canals bear the water to all parts of the district; and the whole district has become exceedingly fruitful.

And this is a parable of the fruitfulness of that part of India spiritually. The Heaven-sent Gospel was brought to the people living there in 1836, and from then on it has flowed through God-sent channels, till at the present time there are thousands whom God could use as channels of blessing to others.

(John 7. 38; 15. 4, 5).

435. Fulness. The Greek word 'Pleroma', in Eph. 1. 22, 23, translated 'fulness' suggests the picture of a Greek warship which contained three ranks of rowers. When the man-of-war was fully equipped, the boatswain, naval commander and rowers ready and on the alert, it had its full complement. The rowers were needed to make up its 'Pleroma'.

(Eph. 1. 22, 23; 5. 18).

436. Fulness. In the north of Ireland there is a little town called Ballymena. It is pretty rough on Roman Catholics in Ballymena—there are not very many of them. One lady I heard of there held a series of cottage meetings, and her next-door neighbour was one of the few Roman Catholics in the town. One night she said, 'We are having a cottage meeting tomorrow: will you come?' 'No,' she said, 'I'm not allowed to.' But the day after the cottage meeting the Roman Catholic was interested enough to find out how she had been getting on. And the lady said, 'Oh, we had a wonderful time. We had thirty-five in my little cottage and it was full.' 'Oh!' said the Catholic, 'that's interesting.' They had another meeting the following week and the next morning the same conversation. 'We had fifty-one in the cottage, and the place was full.' 'Oh, really!' 'We are having another meeting the third week; that'll be the last one. Would you come?' 'Oh no,' said the Roman Catholic, 'can't come!' But the next morning she was curious enough to say, 'Did you have a good meeting last night?' 'Wonderful!' 'How many did you have?' 'Sixty-two! and the place was full.' 'Now listen,' said this lady, 'that's a sheer impossibility.' 'Not impossible: nothing of the kind,' said her neighbour. 'But how did you get them in?' 'Oh!' she said, 'it was perfectly simple. We simply got rid of every stick of furniture and put it out in the garden! We emptied the house of everything that cluttered it up, and it was filled with people.'

Now listen, Christian, if you mean business, there's to be some furniture kicked out of your life in the name of the Lord. Stuff that clutters up your life.

—Alan Redpath

Emptied that Thou shouldest fill me,
A clean vessel in Thy hand
With no power but as Thou givest
Graciously with each command.

(Neh. 13. 8, 9; 2 Cor. 7. 1; Eph. 5. 18).

437. Fulness. Bishop Taylor Smith, when Chaplain-General, was passing a number of convalescent men seated in a corridor of a hospital. Seeing that they recognized him, he looked to God for a message, as was his wont.

There was an inverted bowl on the table. 'See that bowl!' he said. 'Turned down as it is, it is full of darkness, empty, useless. But convert it, turn it right way up, and immediately it is full of light, the sun shines in, and it can be useful, filled with whatever the bowl is used for. Just so are we. Until the Sun of righteousness shines into our hearts, all is darkness, and our lives are empty and useless!

(Eph. 5. 17-19).

438. Fulness—of the Holy Spirit. I remember one summer morning sitting with Moody in his home (I went there ten or eleven times from England) and he told me this. He said, 'I opened a hall on Sunday nights for everybody and the place used to be crowded every Sunday. Four old ladies sat right in front. They used to sit there and say, "Very good, very good, Mr. Moody, but there is something you haven't got." I never quite understood what they meant until one day I was going along Fifth Avenue, New York, and God seemed to come very near and I felt I must get alone. I knew a man living on the avenue and I went to him and said, "I want to have a room to be alone." To humour me the key was given.'

Moody told me that he first sat on the sofa, and God came very near to him. Finally he found himself on the very floor, entreating God to fill him with the Holy Spirit. This is almost too sacred a story to tell and yet I tell it to you because there are men and women who need to know that there is a face to face contact with the Eternal. I remember Moody saying, 'I would rather give up my right hand any day than to have missed that experience.' He told me that the next Sunday when he came back to Chicago, the old ladies in front were laughing and crying together, and they said, 'Oh, Mr. Moody, you have got it now.'

—Dr. F. B. Meyer

(John 7. 38, 39; Acts 4. 31; Eph. 5. 18; Col. 3. 16).

439. Fulness—of the Holy Spirit. 'The fulness of the Holy Spirit is a continuous appropriation of a continuous supply from Jesus Christ Himself; a moment-by-moment faith in a moment-by-moment filling and moment-by-moment cleansing. The moment I begin to believe, that moment I begin to receive, and as long as I go on believing, praise the Lord! I go on receiving.'

—Dr. Charles Inwood

(Eph. 5. 18).

440. Futility. When the game is not worth the candle, drop it at once. It is wasting time to look for milk in a gatepost or blood in a turnip, or sense in a fool. Never offer a looking-glass to a blind man; if a man is so proud that he will not see his faults, he will only quarrel with you for pointing them out to him. It is of no use to hold a lantern to a mole, or to talk of heaven to a man who cares for nothing but his dirty money.

It is not wise to aim at impossibilities—it is a waste of powder to fire at the man in the moon. It is never worth while to do unnecessary things. Never grease a fat sow, or praise a proud man. Don't make clothes for fishes. Don't paint lilies or garnish the gospel. Never bind up a man's head before it is broken, or comfort a conscience that makes no confession. Never hold a candle to show the sun, or try to prove a thing which nobody doubts.

I would advise no one to attempt a thing which costs more than it is worth. You may sweeten a dunghill with lavender but it will turn out a losing business in the long run.

Long ago my experiences taught me not to dispute with anybody about tastes and whims; one might as well argue about what you can see in the fire. It is of no use ploughing the air, or trying to convince a man against his will in matters of no consequence.

—C. H. Spurgeon

(Prov. 23. 9; 26. 4).

441. Gain.
'What things were gain to me,'
Lord Jesus! these I count for Thee but loss:
Mine be the fervent mind to follow Thee
And glory in Thy cross.

Too oft my foolish heart
Has listened to the false world's siren voice,
Yet, Lord, Thou knowest the eternal part
Is still, through grace, my choice.

One thing alone I'd do;
I've but Thyself, O blessed Lord, to please;
Let me press forward, with the prize in view,
Nor dream of rest or ease.

'What things were gain to me,'
'Tis these I've cast aside and prize no more;
'Tis the deep joy, O Christ, of knowing Thee,
That makes my cup run o'er.

If all should pass away,
Mine's an inheritance that will not fade;
What men call loss, seen in the coming day,
To richest gain is made.

That day is drawing near:
O welcome day! when Christ the Lord shall come,
When He no more shall be a 'Stranger' here,
But honoured as God's Son.

—K. B.

(Phil. 3. 7-14).

442. Garden. Is there no other King's garden? Yes, my heart, thou art, or shouldst be, such. How do the flowers flourish? Do any choice fruits appear? Does the King walk within and rest in the bowers of my spirit? Come, Lord, and let the heavenly wind blow at Thy coming, that the spices of my garden may flow abroad. Nor must I forget the King's garden of the Church. Rebuild and nourish her plants, ripen her fruits.

(Song of Songs 4. 12, 16). —C. H. Spurgeon

443. Gardens. In the Bible we read of many gardens. The early chapters of Genesis introduce us to the Garden of Eden and the last Chapter of Revelation presents a panoramic picture of the Paradise of God. Some of the gardens of Scripture are—i. the Garden of communion—Eden (Gen. 3); ii. the garden of agony—Gethsemane (John 18. 1); the garden of triumph in which was the empty tomb (John 19. 41); the garden of glory—Paradise (Rev. 2. 7)— and the garden of delight (Song of Songs 4. 10-16; 5. 1).

In a garden—on that night
When the Saviour was betrayed,
With what world-redeeming might
In His agony He prayed:
Till He drank the vengeance up
And with mercy filled the cup.

In a garden—on the Cross
When the spear His heart had riven,
And for earth's primeval loss
Heaven's best ransom had been given,
Jesus rested from His woes,
Jesus from the dead arose.

Emblem of the Church above!
Where, as in their native clime,
Midst the garden of His love,
Rescued from the rage of time,
Saints, as trees of life, shall stand,
Planted by His own right hand.

444. Gentleness.
Give me Thy gift of gentleness, most gracious Lord;
For when the way was rough, and darkly black,
The clouds of sorrow hung about life's track,
Till tears and anguish seemed my double part—
It was Thy gentleness that healed my heart!
And there are others—walking weary years,
With bleeding feet, the stony track of tears.
Oh, make me gentle, Lord; through me express
The healing grace of Thine own gentleness.
(2 Sam. 22. 36; Ps. 18. 35; 2 Cor. 10. 1; Gal. 5. 22).

445. Gethsemane.
One word—and skies aflame shall rock
Beneath the judgement's rending shock,
As angel legions earthward flee
To garrison Gethsemane;
And marshalled hosts surround their Lord,
Obedient to His will and word.

One word—and from the embattled skies
Ten thousand times ten thousand rise;
And shining cohorts line the road
With heaven, to light the feet of God;
One word—and sinless heralds bring
God's answer to the earth-born King.

One word—and Rome's imperial power
Had perished in that judgement hour.
One word—and Caiaphas had met
The doom he dared on Olivet;
And Jew and Gentile in their pride
Had sinned, and in their sinning died.

But He Whom heaven and earth obey,
Whom men forsake and friends betray,
With sorrow's crown upon His brow,
Stands silent 'mid the shadows now;
Through gates of sorrow He has come,
"As sheep, before her shearers, dumb."

And men and devils round Him wait,
With scornful insolence of hate;
With eyes that blaze, and tongues that flame,
They pour dishonour on His name;
And hell's contempt around Him fling,
"Behold the Man! Behold your King!"

Oh, earth that shuddered when He died!
Oh, heaven that darkened when He cried!
Oh, temple veil, now rent in twain!
Oh, dead, restored to life again!
God's mighty witnesses are ye—
He loved! He gave Himself for me.

Gethsemane's unspoken word
Will never now on earth be heard—
For human souls His life He gave,
It was Himself He would not save.
This is the wondrous mystery
Of death and life on Calvary.

—Dr. Heyman Wreford

(Isa. 53. 7; Matt. 26. 53).

446. Gift—Of God. During the Spanish War the late President Roosevelt, then a colonel, commanded a regiment of rough-riders in Cuba. He became much attached to his men and was greatly concerned when a number of them fell sick.

Hearing that Miss Clara Barton (the lady who devoted herself to the work of nursing the wounded soldiers) had received a supply of delicacies for the invalids under her care, Colonel Roosevelt requested her to sell a portion of them for the sick men of his regiment. His request was refused. The Colonel was very troubled; he cared for his men and was willing to pay for supplies out of his own pocket.

'How can I get these things?' he asked. 'I must have proper food for my sick men.'

'Just ask for them, Colonel.'

'Oh!' said Roosevelt, his face breaking into a smile, 'that's the way, is it? Then I do ask for them.' And he got them at once.

How often the Colonel's mistake is repeated in connection with the matter of salvation. People seem to expect to receive it in exchange for something that they can offer. One brings an earnest prayer; a second brings a vow or pledge to turn over a new leaf; a third brings an inwardly-made resolution to live a better and purer life; a fourth imagines that he can obtain this great blessing by religious rites.

Now the truth is that God's salvation can only be had as a free gift.

—*Indian Christian*

(Isa. 55. 1; John 4. 10; Rom. 5. 15; 6. 23; Eph. 2. 8).

447. Gift—of God. David Morse had been watching Rambhau, the old Indian pearl diver, going down and emerging from the water with a big oyster between his teeth. 'Look at this one, Sahib,' said the diver, 'I think it'll be good.' As the missionary took it and was prying it open with his pocket knife, Rambhau was pulling other small oysters from his loin-cloth.

'Rambhau, look!' exclaimed Morse, 'Why it's a treasure.'

'Yes, a good one,' shrugged the diver.

'Good! Have you ever seen a better pearl? It's perfect, isn't it?'

'Oh yes, there are better pearls, much better. Why, I have one'——His voice trailed off. 'See this one—the imperfections—the black specks here, this tiny dent; even in shape it is a bit oblong, but good as pearls go.'

The missionary, addressing the pearl-diver, said, 'There's only one way to Heaven. And see, Rambhau,' he said as they started up the dusty road, 'you are older now. Perhaps this is your last season of diving for pearls. If you ever want to see Heaven's gates of pearl you must accept the new life God offers you in His Son.'

'My last season? Yes, you are right. Today was my last day of diving. This is the last month of the year, and I have preparations to make.'

'You should prepare for the life to come,' said the missionary.

'That's just what I'm going to do. Do you see that man over there? He is a pilgrim. He walks barefooted and picks the sharpest stones, and every few rods he kneels down and kisses the road. The first day of the New Year I begin my pilgrimage. All my life I have planned it. I shall make sure of Heaven this time. I am going on my knees.'

'Rambhau, my friend! You can't. How can I let you do this when Jesus Christ has died to purchase Heaven for you?' But the old man would not be moved. He could not understand, could not accept the free salvation of Christ.

One afternoon the old pearl-diver called at the missionary's house and asked him to come to his house for a short time as he had something to show him. On the way to Rambhau's house, Morse learnt that the diver was setting out on his long pilgrimage in just a week's time, and his heart sank. Seated within Rambhau's house, while the owner left the room, the missionary wondered what he could say to the old man. Rambhau returned with a small but heavy strong box and said, 'I have had this box for years. I keep only one thing in it. Now I will tell you about it, Sahib Morse. I once had a son.' The old man's eyes moistened as he continued:

'My son was a diver too. He was the best pearl diver on the coasts of India. He had the swiftest dive, the keenest eye, the strongest arm, the longest breath, of any man who sought for pearls. What joy he brought me! He always dreamed of finding a pearl beyond all that had ever been found. One day he found it. But when he found it he had already been under water too long. He lost his life soon after.'

The old pearl diver bowed his head and for a moment his whole body shook. 'All these years I have kept the pearl,' he continued, 'but now I am going, not to return, and to you, my dear friend, I am giving my pearl.' He then drew from the box a carefully wrapped package. Gently opening the cotton, he picked up a mammoth pearl and placed it in the hand of the missionary. It was one of the largest pearls ever found off the coast of India, and it glowed with a lustre and brilliance never seen in cultured pearls. It would have brought a fabulous sum in any market. For a moment the missionary was speechless and gazed with awe. 'Rambhau,' he said, 'this is a wonderful pearl, an amazing pearl. Let me buy it. I would give you ten thousand rupees for it.'

'Sahib,' said Rambhau, stiffening his whole body, 'this pearl is beyond price. No man in all the world has money enough to pay what that pearl is worth to me. On the market a million rupees could not buy it. I will not sell it. You may have it only as a gift.'

'No, Rambhau, I cannot accept that. As much as I want the pearl, I cannot accept it that way. Perhaps I am proud, but this is too easy. I must pay for it, or work for it.'

The old pearl diver was stunned. 'You don't understand at all, Sahib. Don't you see? My only son gave his life to get this pearl, and I wouldn't sell it for any money. Its worth is in the life blood of my son. I cannot sell this, but do permit me to give it to you. Just accept it in token of the love I bear you.'

For a moment the missionary could not speak. Then, gripping the hand of the old man, he said in a low voice, 'Rambhau, that is just what you have been saying to God! He is offering you eternal life as a free gift. It is so great and priceless that no man on earth could buy it. No man on earth could earn it. No man is good enough to deserve it. It cost the life blood of His only Son to make the entrance for you into Heaven. In a hundred pilgrimages you could not earn that entrance. All you can do is to accept it as a token of God's love to you, a sinner. I will accept this pearl in deep humility, but won't you too accept God's great gift of eternal life, in deep humility, knowing that it cost Him the death of His Son to offer it to you?'

Great tears were running down the cheeks of the old man. The veil was lifting. He understood at last. 'Sahib, I see it now. I believe Jesus gave Himself for me. I accept Him.'

(John 3. 16; Rom. 6. 23; 2 Cor. 9. 15).

448. Gifts—of Grace.

He giveth more grace when the burdens grow greater,
He sendeth more strength when labours increase.
To added affliction He addeth His mercy,
To multiplied trials—His multiplied peace.
When we have exhausted our store of endurance,
When our strength has failed ere the day is half-done,
When we reach the end of our hoarded resources,
Our Father's full giving is only begun.
His love has no limit, His grace has no measure,
His power no boundary known unto men,
For out of His infinite riches in Jesus,
He giveth and giveth and giveth again.

(2 Cor. 9. 8; 12. 9).

449. Girdle—Of our High Priest.

He, of old the Man of Sorrows, pleads before the Father's face,
Knowing all the needed solace, claiming all the needed grace;
We, so faithless and so weary, serving with impatient will—
He, unwearied in our service, gladly ministering still.

Girded with the golden girdle, shining as the mighty sun,
Still His piercéd hands will finish all His work of love begun
On the night of His betrayal, in the glory of the throne,
Still with faithful patience washing all defilement from His own.

When the Father's house resoundeth with the music and the song;
When the bride in glorious raiment sees the One Who loved so long;
Then for new and blesséd service—girt afresh will He appear,
Stand and serve before the angels those who waited for Him here.

—T. P. in *Hymns of Ter Stegen and others*
(Exod. 28. 8, 39; John 13. 4, 5; Rev. 1. 13).

450. Giving.

The sixpenny piece tells its story:
I'm only a sixpence, a very small coin. I am not on speaking terms with the butcher. I am much too small to buy a pint of beer or even a lemon squash. I am not large enough to purchase a quarter pound of chocolates. A permanent wave won't look at me. They won't even let me in at the cinema show. I am hardly fit for a tip. But, believe me, when I go to church on Sunday, I am considered some money.

(Mal. 3. 8; 1 Cor. 16. 1, 2).

451. Giving.

From the sale of books alone John Wesley gave away between £30,000 and £40,000. He told Samuel Bradburn, one of his preachers, in 1787, that he never gave away anything less than £1,000 a year, and yet, when he died, his personal estate amounted to only a few pounds.

When earning £30 a year, he lived on £28 and gave the remaining £2 to the Lord. Next year his salary was doubled. He found that he lived comfortably on £28 a year, so, instead of raising his standard of living, he continued to live on £28 a year and gave the whole of his increase to God. So later God entrusted him with large and larger amounts.

(1 Chron. 29. 2-5; 2 Cor. 9. 8, 9).

452. Giving. There stood thirteen chests, each with a brazen, trumpet-shaped receiver into which the worshippers dropped their offerings; nine of them were marked 'for Jehovah', and four 'for the poor'. (In the temple court in Jerusalem).

The widow would fain manifest her love to the Lord and to her neighbour as well. If she casts the mite into His chest it will be known in heaven that one of the Lord's lovers has been in the treasury that day; if she casts it into the box marked 'for the poor' it will show her care for her fellows, but will it not seem to place human need above divine worship? The solution she adopts is both simple and costly; she will balance the claims of heaven and earth, and drop two mites into separate chests.

With eager joy the Lord called the attention of the twelve to her actions, and offers them a problem in the arithmetic of heaven.

She loved God and her neighbour.

—H. St. John

(Mal. 3. 10; Mark 12. 41-44; Gal. 2. 10).

453. Giving.

Give all thou canst,
High heaven rejects the lore
Of nicely calculated less or more.

(Mark 14. 3-9; 1 Cor. 16. 2; 2 Cor. 8. 12).

454. Giving. If you want to be rich, give; if you want to be poor, grasp! if you want abundance, scatter; if you want to be needy, hoard!

A man there was, and some did count him mad:
The more he gave away, the more he had.

(Prov. 11. 24, 25; 2 Cor. 9. 6).

455. Giving.

The wealth of earth, of sky, of sea,
The gold, the silver, sparkling gem,
The waving corn, the bending tree,
Are Thine: to us Thou lendest them.

And when Thine Israel, travel-sore,
With offerings to Thy court would come,
With free and willing hearts they bore
Gifts, even from their desert home.

We, Lord, would lay at Thy behest
The costliest offerings on Thy shrine;
But, when we give and give our best,
We only give Thee what is Thine.

(Exod. 35. 21-24; 2 Chron. 31. 10; 2 Cor. 8. 1-5).

456. Giving. A poor, blind woman in Paris put twenty-seven francs into a plate at a missionary meeting. 'You cannot afford so much,' said one.

'Yes, sir, I can,' she answered.

On being pressed to explain, she said, 'I am blind, and I said to my fellow straw-workers, "How much money do you spend in a year for oil in your lamps when it is too dark to work at nights?" They replied, "Twenty-seven francs." So,' said the poor woman, 'I find I save so much in the year because I am blind and do not need a lamp. I give this money to shed light to the dark, heathen lands.'

—Prairie Overcomer

(Exod. 35. 21-24; 2 Chron. 31. 10; Matt. 4. 16).

457. Giving. When the British Government sought to reward General Gordon for his brilliant service in China, he declined all money and titles, but accepted a gold medal inscribed with the record of his thirty-three engagements. It was his most prized possession. But after his death the medal could not be found. Eventually it was learned that he had sent it to Manchester during a severe famine, directing that it should be melted down and used to buy bread for the poor. Under the date of its sending, these words were found written in his diary: 'The last earthly thing I had in this world that I valued I have given to the Lord Jesus Christ.'

—Indian Christian

(Ps. 112. 9; 2 Cor. 9. 11).

458. Giving. The story is told of a farmer who was known for his generous giving, and whose friends could not understand how he could give so much and yet remain so prosperous. One day a spokesman for his friends said: 'We cannot understand you. You give far more than any of the rest of us, and yet you always seem to have more to give.'

'Oh, that is easy to explain,' the farmer said. 'I keep shovelling into God's bin, and God keeps shovelling back into mine, and God has the bigger shovel.'

—Dr. Herbert Lockyer

(Prov. 3. 9, 10; 2 Cor. 9. 8).

459. Giving. A little Chinese boy who lived in Manila in the Philippine Islands was saving up to buy a bicycle, but when he had saved about three pounds he decided there was something he wanted even more than a bicycle —and that was to help the Chinese people who were suffering in their own country so terribly because of the way Japan was smashing their homes and ruining their farms. He knew that many of those poor folks were starving, and he decided that he had better do something about it. So he went to a bakery and spent all the money that he had saved on sacks and sacks of bread. Then he dragged his sacks to the offices of the Chinese Relief Committee. The people there were very surprised to see all this bread and wondered what in the world they were going to do with it. They didn't want to hurt the little chap's feelings by telling him that if they tried to send it to China it would be stale and mouldy before it got there. So at last they decided to call it 'Patriotic bread', and sell it again to the Chinese people in Manila. It was amazing how quickly it was bought. At the end of the day the boy's three pounds had grown to ten.

'This is a great idea,' said the committee, and with the ten pounds they bought more bread and tied labels to it, telling that it was 'Patriotic bread' again. The Chinese women of Manila sold it outside shops and theatres, and everyone rushed to buy it. After three days the three pounds had grown to three hundred, and this large sum was sent to China in the boy's name.

But the story isn't finished yet. An American returned from Manila to the United States and she told this story to a great many people. Among those who heard it was Mr. Henry Ford, the motor car manufacturer, and his wife felt sorry that because of his unselfishness the boy didn't get his bicycle for which he had worked so hard. She sent twenty dollars to Manila and asked the China Relief Committee to buy a bicycle for the boy. They did so, and the wife of the American Commissioner presented it to him at a public ceremony attended by all the important people of the town.

But, although he now had his bicycle, the boy still wanted as much as ever to help the poor people of China, and so he decided to hire out the bicycle for two shillings an hour and send all the money to the relief fund.

The bicycle is now supporting a Christian home in China for fifteen orphan boys. And every word of this story is true.
—A. C. G. in *The Pilgrim* (written before China became Communist)
(2 Cor. 9. 11, 12).

460. Giving. 'Some people give according to their means, others according to their meanness.' There are three kinds of givers:

The flint never gives till it is well hammered, and then it yields only sparks.
The sponge gives only when you squeeze it and keep on squeezing it till it is dry.
The honeycomb gives freely and keeps on giving.
(Exod. 35. 21, 22; Acts 4. 34, 35; 2 Cor. 8. 12; 9. 7; Heb. 13. 16).

461. Giving. 'Give until you feel it: then keep on giving until you don't feel it,' said D. L. Moody. An old German said in his broken English, 'I likes to give villingly; when I gives villingly, it enjoys me so much I give again.'
What makes the Dead Sea dead? It is all the time receiving and never giving out.
(Matt. 10. 8; Acts 20. 35).

462. Giving. Dr. Paul White, the 'Jungle Doctor' recently told a group of business men about two Africans, lepers, with hands so eaten away that they were just bandaged stumps, who wanted to help the missionaries; so for weeks on end they worked in the deep saw-pit sawing logs into boards for a new part of the bush hospital. When the job was done, each received the sum of thirty shillings. The Doctor noticed them dividing the little pile of silver into two parts, and asked why. When told that one half was for the Lord, he said to them, 'But that's too much. God only asks for a tenth—three shillings, not fifteen shillings.' 'But, Bwana,' one of them quickly replied, 'we love Him far more than that.'
(Gen. 14. 20; Mark 12. 44; 2 Cor. 8. 1, 2).

463. Giving—our Best. On a black cloudy day the late Queen Mary was out walking in the vicinity of Balmoral. She walked rather far, and as the rain came down she stopped at a cottage and asked for the loan of an umbrella. The woman did not know the Queen so decided to give the stranger an old umbrella with a broken rib. Next morning a man in gold braid appeared at the cottage door and said, 'The Queen asked me to thank you for lending her the umbrella.' The woman in the cottage was dumbfounded and with tears flowing down her cheeks she said, 'What an opportunity I missed! Why did I not give the Queen the best umbrella I had?' Let us make sure we give to God the best we can.
(Mal. 1. 7, 8; John 12. 3).

464. Giving—our Best. The sister of Nietzsche tells that, when the thinker was a little boy, he and she decided on one occasion to take each of them a toy to give to the Moravian sisters in support of their missionary enterprise. They carefully chose their toys and duly carried them to the sisters. But, when they returned home, Nietzsche was restless and unhappy. His sister asked what ailed him. 'I have done a very wicked thing,' the boy answered. 'My fine box of cavalry is my favourite toy, and my best. I should have taken that.' 'But do you think,' his sister asked, 'that God always wants our best?' 'Yes!' replied the young philosopher, 'always, always!' The lad was then, at least, following the right course.
(Exod. 23. 19; Mal. 1. 7, 8; 3. 10).

465. Giving—Praying about. Pray about giving. The more we give, the more we have to give. I am as careful about investing God's money in a place where it will bring spiritual profits as I am in my own business investments. I feel worse about a bad investment made with God's money than with my own. God will hold us responsible if we do not give or if we give prayerlessly.
—John Wellons
(1 Tim. 6. 17-19).

466. Giving—our Tithe. We have given our tenth to the Lord for about 40 years and God has abundantly blessed us. During the last few years my wife and I have given much more than a tenth to God, and God has given us prosperity in much greater proportion. We took the responsibility to finance Gospel Broadcasts for thirteen weeks—a quarter of a year—and it looked as if we should find it very hard. But, before the weeks were finished, God raised our income for the period to more than five times the cost of the Broadcast, and many souls were won for Christ by the Gospel broadcast.

—Dr. F. J. Barton

(2 Cor. 9. 8; 1 Tim. 6. 17-19).

467. Giving—our Tithe. Charlie Page was a young man, broke, penniless and jobless. One day he stopped on the street to listen to a Salvation Army service. When the tambourine was passed round for the collection, he told the girl who held it out before him that he would like to give something but had nothing himself, even for his food. She gave him a dollar, saying, 'Take this: put ten cents in the offering, and hereafter give a tenth of all you get to God. Keep this up all your life, and you'll never be penniless again.' He did so, got a job, and began giving his tenth regularly. By and by he became a millionaire, and gave much more than a tenth, building Hospitals and helping in many ways to carry on the work of the Lord.

(Gen. 14. 20; Prov. 3. 9, 10).

468. Glory—of Christ. Truly God and truly Man, the Lord Jesus Christ was visible, audible and tangible (1 John 1. 1, 2). The Greek words used of our Lord's form as Man are:

1. *Character*—Heb. 1. 1, 2. Of this Alexander Clark says, 'Our word "character" is a direct transcription from the Greek, where it meant originally the sculptor's chisel, then the image chiselled out of marble or brass—the finished figure.' In Heb. 1. 1, 2, it means 'the reality of the Father's invisible glory that stamps itself visibly on the Son'. 'On the plastic flesh of a human life Jesus of Nazareth chiselled out for all to see and adore the character of His Father.'

2. *Eikon*—2 Cor. 4. 4; Col. 1. 15—meaning an image. Our Lord Jesus is the image of the invisible God.

3. *Morphē*—Phil. 2. 6, 7—meaning 'form'. 'Though in the very form of God with heavenly glory crowned,

Thou didst a servant's form assume, beset with sorrow round.'

4. *Homoiōma*—Phil. 2. 7—meaning 'likeness' indicates the outward likeness our Lord assumed in perfect Manhood.

5. *Schēma*—Phil. 2. 7—fashion: 'being found in fashion as a man'.

6. *Eidos*—Luke 9. 29—from which is derived the word 'idol'.

This is the word used at His transfiguration when 'they saw His glory' and 'were eye-witnesses of His majesty' (2 Pet. 1. 16-18).

469. Glory—of Christ.

He Who wept above the grave,
   He Who stilled the raging wave,
Meek to suffer, strong to save,
   He shall bear the glory.

He Who sorrow's pathway trod,
   He that every good bestowed—
Son of Man and Son of God—
   He shall bear the glory.

He Who bled with scourging sore,
   Thorns and scarlet meekly wore,
He Who every sorrow bore—
   He shall bear the glory.

Monarch of the smitten cheek,
   Scorn of Jew and scorn of Greek,
Priest and King, Divinely meek—
   He shall bear the glory.

On the rainbow-circled throne
   Mid the myriads of His own,
Nevermore to weep alone—
   He shall bear the glory.

Man of slighted Nazareth,
   King Who wore the thorny wreath,
Son obedient unto death—
   He shall bear the glory.

His the grand eternal weight,
   His the priestly-regal state;
Him the Father maketh great—
   He shall bear the glory.

He Who died to set us free,
   He Who lives and loves e'en me,
He Who comes, Whom I shall see,
   Jesus only—only He—
He shall bear the glory.

—William Blane

(Zech. 6. 13; Heb. 2. 9).

470. Glory—of Christ.

Ere seraphim had winged a flight,
   Where brightness knew no shades of night,
Amid the grand immortal light—
   He was there.

Where dwelt the Godhead three in One,
   Whose glories paled the brightest sun,
Ere mortal time had yet begun—
   He was there.

Majestic sweep! Lo, now I see
   The Christ upon a mother's knee
Upheld in feeble infancy—
   He was there.

And then in dark Gethsemane
   Beneath the shady olive tree,
Prostrated in soul agony—
   He was there.

And oh, my soul! I see Him now
   A crown of thorns upon His brow;
Creation groans and wonders how
   He was there.

'Mid rending rocks I hear Him cry—
'Eli, lama sabacthani':
The ransomed host can answer why
    He was there.

The scene is changed: behold the sight!
Clothed in all majesty and might,
The centre of all Heaven's delight—
    He is there.

—Mrs. McKendrick

(John 1. 1-4; 17. 4, 5; Heb. 1. 3; 2. 9).

471. Glory—of God.

When man at first was made by God in glory,
    glory, glory,
No sin nor sorrow found abode in glory, glory
    glory.
But soon, alas! our father fell from glory, glory,
    glory,
And rather chose the ways of hell than glory,
    glory, glory.
But God beheld our ruined race from glory,
    glory, glory,
And Jesus left His highest place in glory, glory,
    glory.
The wondering angels never saw such glory,
    glory, glory,
When mercy healed the broken law and gave it
    back its glory.

(2 Cor. 4. 6; 2 Thess. 2. 14).

472. Go!—Christ's Command. A classic in
the annals of the U.S. Coast Guard is the story
of Captain Pat Etheridge of the Cape Batterne
station. One night in the howling hurricane,
the look-out saw a distress signal from a ship
that had gone aground on the dangerous
Diamond Shoals, ten miles at sea. The lifeboats
were ordered out. One of the life-guards
protested, 'Captain Pat, we can get out there,
but we can never get back.'
'Boys,' came the reply that has gone down
in history, 'we don't have to come back.'
The Lord Jesus has given us our marching
order. He has commanded that the Gospel be
preached in all the world. He has not promised
His messengers an easy time. He has not given
the assurance of a safe return to the home
base—but He did say—'GO!'

Who answers Christ's insistent call
Must give himself, his life, his all,
His purpose aye unshaken.
Who sets his hand unto the plough
And glances back with anxious brow,
His calling hath mistaken.

—The Fields

(Matt. 28. 19; Mark 16. 15; Luke 9. 62).

473. God.

Thou art the Unapproached Whose height
    Enables Thee to stoop,
Whose holiness is undefiled
    To handle hearts that droop.

How Thou canst think so well of me
    And be the God Thou art
Is darkness to my intellect
    But sunshine to my heart.

—F. W. Faber

(Job 33. 12, 13; Acts 17. 24; Rom. 11. 33).

474. God. God writes with a pen that never
blots, speaks with a tongue that never slips,
and acts with a hand that never fails.

(Luke 18. 27; Heb. 6. 17, 18).

475. God—Greatness of. Dr. Bartoli in his
'Knox Club Lectures' described a picture he
saw in the 'Salon de Mai', Paris, an annual
exhibition of paintings and sculptures. In the
foreground, hands were seen raised toward a
beautiful radiant light. There were hands of all
kinds, shapes and colours: white, yellow, brown,
red hands; finely-chiselled, refined hands of
ladies; horned, rough hands of workmen and
artisans; powerful hands of strong men;
supple, long-fingered hands of musicians; fat,
podgy hands. In the light of the rising sun,
still visible, the sacred name of God shone
across the sky, and all hands all over the earth
were raised to God.
Everywhere in the world—among civilised,
cultured races, and among primitive and
aboriginal peoples, in the heat of tropical
climes and amid Arctic snows—man recognizes
a Creator, a God to Whom they may raise
their hands in worship and prayer.

(Exod. 20. 3, 20, 21; Rev. 5. 13, 14).

476. God—Greatness of. 'God is great in
great things and very great in little things,'
said Henry Dyer.
A party stood on the Matterhorn admiring
the scenery, the great things that came from
the hands of God. Among them was a
scientist who produced a microscope, caught a
fly and placed it under the glass. He reminded
the party that the legs of the house-fly in
England were naked. Then he showed them
the fly of the Swiss Mountains under the
microscope, with legs thickly covered with
hair, proving God's greatness in His provision
for little things.

(Gen. 1; Job. 38. 4-41; 39. 1-5).

477. God—Greatness of.

How great, how mighty, how sublime!
O'er every nation, every clime
He is the Lord. Oh tell His worth,
To Him alone they owe their birth!
Say, canst Thou make one tiny star
To guide the mariner from afar?
Or make a blade of grass to grow?
His marvellous wisdom—who can know?
The birds, the beasts, the flowers as well
God's power and greatness surely tell;
For ripened fruit and golden grain
He sends the sunshine and the rain.
In every vale and leafy glade
God's handiwork is there displayed.

Those rocks! Those mountains towering high
That rear their summits to the sky,
Where only eagles' pinions rise
Beyond the scan of mortal eyes.
To speak one message all combine—
'The hand that made them is Divine.'

But all creation's works alone
Could ne'er the heart of God make known.
Redemption's plan—so great, so vast—
Is e'en by angels' grasp surpassed.
Behold Him in a manger lie,
The Lord of earth, and sea, and sky.
See Him in Gethsemane
In such dreadful agony—
While those He loves in slumber sleep;
Their vigil they can never keep.
Hush! while on Calvary's Cross we gaze,
What words are these the Saviour says?
'Father, forgive them!' Oh what grace
To rebel sons of Adam's race,
Pardon from an offended God,
Pardon through the Saviour's blood?
'Tis finished!' now the Victor cries,
Then bows His sacred head and dies.

Surpassing wisdom, power and might
Revealing God in purest light,
Frail stammering tongues can never tell
Such love immense, unsearchable!
But when we see Thy face above
And know the fulness of Thy love,
With ransomed and unsinning heart
We'll shout, 'My God, how great Thou art!'
                                    —E. S. Haddow
(Job. 26. 7; Isa. 40. 9; Rom. 11. 33).

478. God—Greatness of.
Thrice blest is He to whom is given
The instinct that can tell
That God is on the field when He
Is most invisible.

For right is right, and God is God,
And right the day must win;
To doubt would be disloyalty,
To falter would be sin.
(Rom. 8. 28; 11. 33).   —F. W. Faber

479. God—Greatness of.
The hymn—'How great Thou art'—was written one summer evening in the year 1886 at a country place called Kroneback, Sweden. The author, Carl Boberg, relates that he had been invited, with other men, to a meeting of women who came together to sew for the benefit of missions. It was a beautiful day. All nature was arrayed in its summer finery. Both young and old enjoyed the hospitality of the home and roaming about the large estate.

Presently a storm cloud was seen above the horizon and before long the sky was overcast, lightning flashed across the dark heaven and a downpour drove the visitors under cover. Soon the rain stopped, however, and on the sky was seen a bow of promise. From a church across the bay, where a funeral was in progress, the bells pealed forth their doleful cadency.

Enraptured with the wonders of it all,

Boberg that evening gave expression to his feelings in the writing of the poem *O Store Gud*! nine stanzas long. It was first published in a couple of periodicals and then apparently forgotten. Several years later the author attended a meeting in the Province of Varmland and was surprised to hear the congregation sing his poem to the tune of an old Swedish melody. In 1890 the song was published by a Chicago publisher.

Carl Boberg was born in 1859 and died in 1940. He studied for the ministry and served a Mission Covenant Church. A number of his songs have a permanent place in Swedish hymnology and at least two have been translated into English.
                                    —*The Standard*

Besides the translation by S. K. Hine from the Russian which is so commonly sung, another by Prof. E. Gustav Johnson directly from the original Swedish appeared as early as 1925. The following is S. K. Hine's translation:

O Lord my God! When I in awesome wonder
  Consider all the works Thy hand hath made,
I see the stars, I hear the mighty thunder,
  Thy Pow'r throughout the universe displayed:

Chorus
Then sings my soul, my Saviour God, to Thee,
  How great Thou art, how great Thou art!

When through the woods and forest glades I
    wander
  And hear the birds sing sweetly in the trees;
When I look down from lofty mountain grandeur,
  And hear the brook, and feel the gentle breeze.

And when I think that God, His Son not sparing,
  Sent Him to die—I scarce can take it in;
That on the Cross, my burden gladly bearing,
  He bled and died to take away my sin:

When Christ shall come with shout of acclamation
  And take me home—what joy shall fill my
    heart!
Then shall I bow in humble adoration,
  And there proclaim, my God, how great Thou
    art.
(Ps. 145. 3-5).

480. God—Power of.
The day after the great earthquake of San Francisco, a newsboy was showing a dazed man the way through, and, as they walked, the boy philosophized thus: 'It took a long time to put all this stuff up, but God tumbled it over in a minute. Say, Mister, 'Tain't no use for a feller to think he can lick God.'
(Ezek. 21. 26, 27).

481. God—Power of.
They cannot shell His temple
  Nor dynamite His throne;
They cannot bomb His city,
  Nor rob Him of His own.
They cannot take Him captive,
  Nor strike Him dumb or blind,
Nor starve Him to surrender,
  Nor make Him change His mind.

They cannot cause Him panic,
Nor cut off His supplies;
They cannot take His kingdom
Nor hurt Him with their lies.
Though all the world be shattered,
His truth remains the same,
His righteous laws still potent,
And Father's still His name.

Though we face war and struggle,
And feel their goad and rod,
We know above confusion
There always will be God.

—Dr. Murray
(Isa. 40. 28; 43. 10-12; 45. 21, 22).

482. Gold. For centuries the effigy of the 'Black Prince' has stood in Canterbury Cathedral, but until a few years ago no one knew it was made of pure gold. Its blackness from centuries of grime and a coating of protective enamel was appropriate to the memory of the fourteenth century Edward, Prince of Wales, who fought so heroically in the wars with France and died before he assumed the throne. Recently the coating was removed, and Edward the 'Black Prince', so named because he wore black armour, stood forth a beautiful statue of gold! A critic has said, 'It is the most magnificent tomb and statue in England.'

There are times in our Christian experience when the fine gold becomes dim and tarnished, but God's desire for us is that all the grime should be removed in order that our life and witness might be bright and lustrous before men. The fine gold of Christian experience needs no dull covering. Let it shine!

—*Indian Christian*
(Job. 23. 10; 1 Pet. 1. 7).

483. Golgotha. Golgotha means 'the place of a skull'.

A skull is a human head shorn of its dignity and beauty, with no light in its eyesockets, an empty vacuum in the brain space, and with none of that grace of hair which is the sign of man's strength and woman's glory. It is Mark's way of reminding us that when a man rejects Jesus Christ, all the lights of the world die down; there is nothing left but a grinning, bony death's head.

—H. St. John
Mark 15. 22)

484. Gospel—For Man's need. A Christian worker once visited a poor woman in order to bring her a sum of money which she badly needed. He knocked at her door, not once or twice only, but got no response, and he had to go away disappointed with the money still in his pocket. Meeting her a few days later, he told her of his fruitless visit. She replied, with tears in her eyes, that she had heard him knocking, but thought he was the rent collector, and she dare not open the door, for she had not the money to pay the rent.

C. H. Spurgeon used this as an illustration

of the Gospel. He Who stands at the door and knocks has come with a gift; the knock is the Saviour's knock, not that of a taskmaster. The Gospel is good news; news of a debt paid, not of rent required. It is not a demand but a free gift, which no one has deserved or could win by merit, but which is offered to all. (Rom. 6. 23; 1 Cor. 15. 1, 3, 4)

485. Gospel—Message of the.
From the glory and the gladness, from His secret place;
From the rapture of His presence, from the radiance of His face—
Christ, the Son of God, hath sent me through the midnight lands;
Mine the mighty ordination of the piercéd Hands.
Mine the message grand and glorious, strange unsealed surprise,
That the goal is God's Beloved, Christ in Paradise.
Hear me, weary men and women, sinners dead in sin;
I am come from heaven to tell you of the love within;
Not alone of God's great pathway leading up to heaven;
Not alone how you may enter stainless and forgiven—
Not alone of rest and gladness, tears and sighing fled—
Not alone of life eternal breathed into the dead—
But I tell you I have seen Him, God's beloved Son,
From His lips have learnt the mystery He and His are one.

(Acts 26. 16-18; 1 Cor. 9. 16, 17; 15. 1-3)

486. Gospel—Power of the. When Paul says the Gospel is the power of God unto salvation he uses the word 'dunamis' which is related to the English word 'dynamite'. Dynamite blasts the rock in pieces. And that is just what the Gospel does in the spiritual realm. It blasts the rock-like resistance of the sin-hardened heart. The rough jailor in Philippi, the run-away slave Onesimus in Rome, and Saul the persecutor on the Damascus road, all had the hard core of their resistance broken by the Gospel. They knew its power and their trans-formed lives bore witness to it before all men. (Rom. 1. 16)

487. Gospel—Preaching of the. At this time, before we hear the shout of our descending Lord and rise to meet Him, shall we not come back with holiness of heart to the simplicity of our mission? Let us leave the civilizing of the world to the effect of the presence there of the Gospel of Christ, and let us give our time, our strength, our talents, our money, all that we are and have, to make Christ known to every creature in every land.

—C. I. Scofield
(Rom. 1. 15; 15. 19, 20; 2 Cor. 10. 16)

488. Gospel—Preaching of the. Some years ago I was asked by a group of young Christians

in the City of Glasgow to lead a discussion on the subject, 'Why preach the Gospel?' It immediately occurred to me that the letter of Paul the apostle to the Romans gave the authoritative answer to the question. We preach the Gospel: because of what man is, because of what God is, because of what the Gospel is, because of what Christ is, and because of what the Christian is.
(Rom. 1. 1-5; 18-32; 3. 23, 26; 1 Cor. 9. 16, 17)

489. Gospel—Preaching of the. An old Gospeller once advised his younger brethren to preach:

'A full Gospel—Christ and nothing less:
'A plain gospel—Christ and nothing more:
'A pure gospel—Christ and nothing else.'

A preacher once said: 'I preached philosophy and men applauded. I preached Christ and men repented.'

—A. P. Gibbs

(Gal. 1. 6-10)

490. Gospel—for the Saint.

Justified freely by grace from on high:
Portion of those who to God are made nigh:
We have the Spirit—that heavenly seal,
Foretaste of riches Christ will reveal.
Justified freely through faith, blood and grace,
Waiting in hope of seeing His face.

Sanctified wholly by God's sovereign will,
Through Him Who suffered that will to fulfil:
Of this the Spirit as witness is given,
Turning our hearts to Christ now in heaven.
Sanctified wholly, so let us each bear
Likeness to Him Whose glory we'll share.

Consecrate each to Thy service, we pray!
Help us to live for Thy glory each day,
Telling to others the tidings of love
Coming to us from heaven above.
Consecrate each, and the hands daily fill
Ever in service doing Thy will.

We're heirs of God, and joint-heirs with His Son–
Foretaste of heaven already begun.
Soon we'll be glorified, matchless display,
With Christ our Lord throughout endless day.
Justified, sanctified, serving the Lord,
Glorified soon—Oh, blessèd reward!

—W. Fraser Naismith

(Rom. 5. 1; 8. 1; 12. 1)

491. Gospel—Simplicity of the.

O how unlike the complex works of man
Heaven's easy, artless unencumbered plan!
No meretricious graces to beguile,
No clustering ornaments to clog the pile;
From ostentation, as from weakness, free,
It stands, like the cerulean arch we see,
Majestic in its own simplicity.
Inscribed above the portal from afar,
Conspicuous as the brightness of a star,
Legible only by the light they give,
Stand the soul-quickening words, 'Believe and live.'

Too many, shocked at what should charm them most,
Despise the plain direction and are lost.

—William Cowper

(John 3. 16; Rom. 1. 16; Eph. 2. 8-9)

492. Gospels—The Four.

Chronologically, Mark's Gospel was written first, then Matthew's, then Luke's, and last John's. In the Synoptic Gospels (Matthew, Mark and Luke) the emphasis is on our Lord's humanity: in John's Gospel it is on His Deity.

Matthew wrote especially for the Jews, Mark for the Romans, Luke for the Greeks, and John for the Christian Church: all four for the whole world.

In Mark, Jesus is depicted as the Servant of God, in John as the Son of God.

In Matthew, He is portrayed as the Ruler of men, in Luke as unique amongst men. Matthew and Mark provide the record of His official glories—as King and Servant: Luke and John delineate His personal glories—as Son of Man and Son of God. Rénan described Matthew's Gospel as 'the most important book ever written', and Luke's as 'the most beautiful book ever written'. Mark's Gospel might with truth be called 'the most concise book ever written', and John's 'the most heavenly book ever written'.

Matthew—Messiah, Israel's King, sets forth, by Israel slain;
But God decreed that Israel's loss should be the Gentiles' gain.
Mark tells us how in patient love this earth has once been trod
By One Who, in a Servant's form, was yet the Son of God.
Luke, the physician, writes of a more skilled Physician still
Who gave Himself, as Son of Man, to save us from all ill.
John, the beloved of Jesus, sees in Him the Father's Son,
The everlasting Word made flesh, yet with the Father One.

(Matt. 1. 1; Mark 1. 1; 10. 45; Luke 19. 10; John 1. 1; 20. 31)

493. Government. Our English word 'Government' is derived from the Greek word 'Kubernēsis', the act of steering. A 'kubernētēs' was a steersman who guided the ship. Hence the figure was transferred to the 'Ship of State', whose government consists of its steersmen. Steersmen are required also for the local churches of Christ.
(1 Cor. 12. 28; 1 Tim. 5. 17)

494. Grace. C. H. Spurgeon tells of an occasion when he was riding home one evening after a heavy day's work and feeling very wearied and depressed, until the verse—'My grace is sufficient for thee' came to him. He immediately compared himself to a little fish in the Thames, apprehensive lest, drinking so many pints of water in the river each day, it might drink the Thames dry, and hearing Father Thames say to it, 'Drink away, little fish, my stream is sufficient for thee.' Then he thought of a little mouse in the granaries of Joseph in Egypt, afraid lest it might—by daily consumption of the corn it needed—exhaust the supplies and starve to death; when Joseph came along and, sensing its fear, said, 'Cheer up, little mouse, my granaries are sufficient for thee.' Or again, he thought of himself as a man climbing some high mountain to reach its lofty summit, and dreading lest he might exhaust all the oxygen in the atmosphere, when the Creator Himself said, 'Breathe away, O man, and fill thy lungs ever; my atmosphere is sufficient for thee.'

(2 Cor. 12. 9)

495. Grace.

> There is a day that comes apace,
> Long looked-for by the blood-washed race
> That ends their earthly story:
> Their last day here of toil and strait,
> Whose sunset finds us at the gate,
> The very gate of glory.
> What would we wish that day to be,
> Whose nightfall brings with certainty
> The end of Time's brief measure?
> Oh! nothing better can we ask
> Than grace to fill our last day's task
> Entirely for His pleasure.
> —George Cutting

(John 1. 16; 2 Cor. 4. 15; 2 Cor. 9. 8)

496. Grace. Dwight L. Moody became so stirred in the preparation of his sermon on 'Grace', so wrought up in his search for truth, that he seized his hat, left his study, strode out into the street and accosted the first man he met with the abrupt enquiry: 'Do you know what Grace is?' The man happened to be a policeman on point duty, and the question and earnestness of D. L. Moody broke him down and was used to his conversion. Is it any wonder that a man, fired with such earnestness and intensity, exerted such power over audiences?

(Tit. 2. 11)

497. Grace. In the days of the American revolutionary war there lived at Ephrata, Pennsylvania, a plain Baptist pastor, Peter Miller, who enjoyed the friendship of General Washington. There also dwelt in that town one Michael Wittman, an evil-minded man who did all in his power to abuse and oppose that pastor. But Michael Wittman was involved in treason and was arrested, and sentenced to death. The old preacher started out on foot and walked the whole seventy miles to Philadelphia that he might plead for that man's life. He was admitted into Washington's presence and begged for the life of the traitor. 'No, Peter,' said Washington, 'I cannot grant you the life of your friend.' 'My friend,' exclaimed the preacher, 'he is the bitterest enemy I have!' 'What?' cried Washington, 'you have walked

seventy miles to save the life of an enemy? That puts the matter in a different light. I will grant the pardon.' And he did. And Peter Miller took Michael Wittman from the very shadow of death, back to his own home in Ephrata—but he went no longer as an enemy but as a friend.

—*Light and Liberty*

(Rom. 5. 10; 12. 20; 2 Cor. 8. 9)

498. Grace.

> *Grace when the sun is shining Lord,*
> *Grace when the sky is black,*
> *Grace when I get the unkind word,*
> *Grace on the too-smooth track,*
> *Grace when I'm elbowed into a nook,*
> *Grace when I get my turn,*
> *Grace when the dinner will not cook,*
> *Grace when the fire won't burn.*
>
> *Grace when my duties all go wrong,*
> *Grace when they all go right,*
> *Grace when it's gladness, praise and song,*
> *Grace when I have to fight,*
> *Grace when my clothes are fresh and new,*
> *Grace when they're worn and old,*
> *Grace when my purse is empty too,*
> *Grace when its full of gold.*
>
> *Grace when the saved ones don't act saved,*
> *Grace when they all blame me,*
> *Grace when denied the good I've craved,*
> *Grace when I get my plea,*
> *Grace when the midnight hours I tell,*
> *Grace when the morn is nigh,*
> *Grace when I'm healthy, strong and well,*
> *Grace when I come to die.*
>
> *Lord Jesus, hear and grant the grace:*
> *My need to Thy store I bring,*
> *That, the proper one in the proper place,*
> *I may glorify Thee, my King.*

(John 1. 16; 2 Cor. 12. 9)

499. Grace. It was the eve of Waterloo, 18th June, 1815. The rain was coming down steadily and relentlessly, and round the farmhouses of Hougemont and La Haye Saint the sheaves of corn grouped in stooks looked soddened and spoilt.

Napoleon had ordered Marshall Ney to place picked sentries to patrol these strategic farms, and so prevent Marshal Blücher and the German army from joining their British allies.

Now in the large cornfield outside the wall of La Haye Saint, a tall Corporal of the Old Guard had been detailed for sentry duty. He did his beat, up and down, in the pitiless rain. On one side, in the far distance he could see the sullen glow of British camp fires. On the other, no sign of the Prussian. Up and down— up and down! he was getting weary and he was feeling stiff and chilled. The corn stooks looked inviting; underneath them it was dry; one big sheaf turned over would make a good mattress. The foe would not be abroad on such a night as this; not a sound anywhere but the swish and splash of the rain. Oh for twenty minutes' rest and warmth, no officers likely to be about—no one would know! He looked each way—nothing stirred but that monotonous swish of the steady rain. Bien! He rolled up his greatcoat for a pillow, laid down the dry sheaf, and taking off his tall 'shako', and placing his long musket with its fixed bayonet by his side, was soon comfortably esconced and clear of the rain, and a few minutes more and he was fast asleep.

Now that night Napoleon was taking no chances in spite of his orders to Ney. So, telling his orderly to bring out his favourite horse, 'Marengo', and muffled up in his well-known long cloak, the two started to make a tour of the sentries round the farmhouses. All, alert, challenged these riders till the great cornfield was reached. The rain had at last ceased, the clouds were breaking and scurrying away. Napoleon strained his shaded eyes to find a sentry there and failed. So leaving Marengo with his orderly, he quietly went round the field. No sentry anywhere! A fitful ray of light from a still fitful moon, shines on something bright in the middle of the field. Stealthily he makes for it, to find a musket and bayonet on the damp ground, and a sentry asleep under a stook! Quietly the Emperor picks up the musket and stands like a statue, keeping guard, yet watching his man. Presently the moon shines on the sleeping sentry who wakes, rubs his eyes, looks, misses his musket, rolls out on hands and knees and, looking up, meets the bent head and the stern eyes of the Emperor.

'Mon Dieu! c'est l'Empereur!' Springing to attention, he stands shaking before Napoleon. Falling on his knees, he falters out, 'Sire, take my bayonet and kill me yourself.' It is said that Napoleon replied, 'Corporal! you know your fate tomorrow morning, but listen—I have kept your watch and guard—your life is spared. Resume guard!' What would not that soldier do for his Emperor?
—E. Matheson

(2 Cor. 8. 9; Tit. 2. 11)

500. Gratitude. John A. Clarke of Katanga used to tell of an exhausted band of native carriers at the close of a long march, falling so fast asleep around their camp fire that they allowed it to die out. A watching lion saw his opportunity and seized one of the men. His cries awoke the others, and they drove the lion off, leaving the man fearfully mangled. Wrapping him up in a blanket they carried him to the missionary who patched him up as best he could. To the astonishment of all the man made a good recovery, for no bones had been broken. As he left the missionary, he said, 'I will return.'

Long after, a group of Africans appeared at the Mission house. The leader said, 'You don't recollect me.' 'No,' said John A. Clarke. 'I am the man you healed at such and such a place,' said the African. 'These are my wives and children: they carry my goods. I am yours, you saved my life; these are yours; all I have is yours.'

Such was the response of gratitude for a life saved.
(Ps. 116. 12; 2 Cor. 9. 15)

501. Greatest Blessings.
Man's greatest wisdom is to know
The Christ of God Who loved him so,
And came into this world of woe
To break the clinchéd chains of sin
And give him wondrous peace within.

Man's greatest joy is to possess
The peace of God and righteousness,
And Jesus' name 'fore men confess.
It makes the heart with rapture swell
Beyond the power of tongue to tell.

Man's greatest blessing is to have
A living hope beyond the grave
Though foes assail and Satan rave,
To be assured when life is done
That he shall reign above the sun.
(Phil. 3. 10; 4. 4, 7)

502. Greatness. Dr. F. W. Boreham in an essay on 'A Tonic of big things' writes— 'Immensity is magnificent medicine. That is one reason, if we may let the cat out of the bag, why the doctors send us to the seaside. We forget the tiddly-winking in the contemplation of the tremendous. We lose life's shallow worries in the vision of unplumbed depths.'

Then he goes on to tell of Gladstone's visit to Dr. Chalmers, who never seemed to indulge in small talk. Of him Gladstone said, 'Everything about him was massive, monumental, magnificent.—He had nothing to say. He was exactly like the Duke of Wellington who said of himself that he had no small talk.'
(Exod. 11. 3; Num. 12. 3; Ps. 18. 35; Luke 1. 32; 9. 48)

503. Grumbling. It is usually not so much the greatness of our troubles as the littleness of our spirit that makes us complain.
—Jeremy Taylor

(1 Cor. 10. 10)

504. Guest—The Perfect.
She answered by return of post
The invitation of her host.
She caught the train she said she would,
And changed at junctions as she should.
She brought a light and smallish box
And keys belonging to the locks.
Food strange and rare she did not beg
But ate the homely scrambled egg.

When offered morning tea, she drank it;
She did not crave an extra blanket,
Nor extra pillows for her head;
Made no complaints about her bed.
She never came downstairs till ten;
She brought her own self-filling pen;
Nor once by look or word or blame
Exposed her host to open shame.
She left no little thing behind
Excepting loving looks and kind.
—R. Hennicker Heaton
(Luke 10. 5-7; 38-42; 1 Cor. 10. 27)

505. Guidance—By Christ's Commands.

Just to ask Him what to do all the day,
And to make you quick and true to obey;
Just to know the needed grace He bestoweth,
Every bar of time and place overfloweth;
Just to take the orders straight
From the Master's own command!
Blessed day! when thus we wait
Always at our Sovereign's hand.

(Ps. 32. 8; Prov. 8. 34)

506. Guidance—for the Depressed. The poet, William Cowper, who wrote the comforting hymn, 'God moves in a mysterious way His wonders to perform,' that ends with the verse:

Ye fearful saints, fresh courage take:
The clouds ye so much dread
Are big with mercies, and will break
In blessings on your head,

was subject to fits of depression and temporary insanity. On one occasion he was on the way to throw himself into the River Ouse and thus commit suicide. He hired a postchaise, but the coachman, purposely losing his way, brought him back home. The cloud over his spirit had by this time lifted and Cowper wrote the hymn.

(Ps. 43. 3-5; Isa. 42. 16)

507. Guidance—of Israel.

For o'er the ark there hovered high
The mystic guide and shield,
A cloud when day o'erspread the sky,
A flame when night concealed.
That pointed out their devious way
Or told their armies when to stay.

But oh! how changed from these glad times,
That wonder how reversed!
They wander still o'er different climes,
But joyless and accursed;
Their remnant scattered far and wide,
Without a God, without a Guide.

—Henry Rogers

(Exod. 13. 21; Neh. 9. 12, 19; Ps. 32. 8; Hos. 3. 4, 5)

508. Guidance—by the Pillar.

God's leadings often crossed their inclination:
The pillar went too fast or went too slow;
It stayed too long to suit their restless temper
Or, when they wished to stay, it bade them go.
It kept them so uncertain of the future:
It wrote 'If God permit' on every plan;
It seemed to mock the wisdom of the wisest
And make a child of every full-grown man.

(Num. 10. 29-36; Neh. 9. 19)

509. Guidance—by the Providence of God. In my district there was a boarding-house for travellers, which I visited. Among others I met there was a youth named Peter McGhee, to whom I often spoke about his soul, but who did not then decide for Christ. Many years after, when travelling with my husband, we had occasion one day to wait at a little station near my home. While there, Mr. Scroggie entered into conversation with a woman in the waiting-room. As he was speaking to her, I observed a man listening at the door, and asked him if he would come inside, which he was quite ready to do. Upon my husband asking him if he were a Christian, he said very decidedly that he was. My husband took a few little books out of his pocket to give to this man, and, in so doing, he was strangely led to slip a half-crown into one of them.

As the man looked through the books, the piece of money dropped on the floor. He exclaimed, 'Thank God! I never meant to tell anyone but I must tell you. As I passed through this village just now, I went in to see a poor widow, and found her in great distress. On asking the reason, she said that she had not the money to pay the rent, and she had never missed before. Asked as to how much it was, she replied 'Half a crown!' I am but a labourer myself, and have nothing to spare, but I felt I must give the poor widow the money; at the same time I wrote on a slip of paper, "The Lord will provide," and here I have only walked up to the station, and He has given it back to me.'

Going the same way, we travelled together. My husband asked our friend if he had ever been to Newburgh, my native village. He said, 'No, but there is a young man works alongside of me, a very bright Christian, who was converted through one of Mr. Mitchell's daughters named Jeannie; do you know her?'

Mr. Scroggie said, 'I do, as she happens to be my wife, and sits by my side.' You will guess I was eager to know the young man's name, and was told it was Peter McGhee. We never had met before, never have seen him since; we never even knew his name, but in the providence of God we had to cross each other's path in this remarkable way that I might enter into the joy of past sowing.

—Mrs. James J. Scroggie

(Gen. 24. 27; Eccl. 11. 1; John 10. 3)

510. Guidance—by the Spirit and the Word. I never remember in all my Christian course that I ever sincerely and patiently sought to know the will of God by the teaching of the Holy Ghost through the instrumentality of the Word of God but I have always been rightly directed. But, if honesty of heart and uprightness before God were lacking, or if I did not patiently wait on God for instruction, or if I preferred the counsel of my fellow-men to the declarations of the Word of God, I made great mistakes.

—George Muller

(Ps. 25. 9; 32. 8; Rom. 12. 2; Col. 1. 9)

511. Guidance—by the Spirit and the Word. Dr. F. B. Meyer was crossing from Dublin to Holyhead one very dark night, and asked the Captain of the ship, 'How do you find Holyhead harbour on such a dark, starless night as this?' The Captain replied, 'Do you see those three lights just ahead? These must be lined up one behind the other in one straight line of vision, and I follow them, keeping the ship in line with the three, until I safely enter the harbour. Dr. Meyer, using the illustration, compared the three lights to the light of God's Word, the inward conviction begotten within the heart by the Holy Spirit, and the Divine arrangement of circumstances in the believer's life.

(Ps. 73. 24; Acts 16. 6-9; Col. 1. 9)

512. Guidance—by Yielding to the Lord.

I said, 'Let me walk in the fields,'
    God said, 'No, walk in the town.'
I said, 'There are no flowers there;'
    He said, 'No flowers, but a crown.'
I said, 'But the sky is black,
    There is nothing but noise and din!'
He wept as He sent me back:
    'There is more,' He said, 'there is sin.'

I said, 'But the air is thick,
    And fogs are veiling the sun;'
He answered, 'Yet souls are sick,
    And souls in the dark undone.'
I said, 'I shall miss the light,
    And friends will miss me, they say;'
He answered, 'Choose ye tonight
    If I am to miss you or they.'

I pleaded for time to be given;
    He said, 'Is it hard to decide?
It will not seem hard in Heaven
    To have followed the steps of your Guide.'
I cast one look at the fields,
    Then set my face to the town;
He said, 'My child, do you yield?
    Will you leave the flowers for the crown?'

Then into His hands went mine,
    And into my heart came He,
And I walk in the light divine
    The path I had feared to see.

(Ps. 32. 8; 36. 9; Isa. 42. 16; Jer. 10. 23; Acts 16. 6-9)

513. Guide—The Unfailing.

Harold St. John, using one of his very apt illustrations, told of a group of ten American ladies who called themselves 'the Society of the Queen's Daughters'. They decided to make a trip to the Holy Land, and crossed by ship to Palestine. Immediately they realised their need of a guide, so they obtained the services of a dragoman who knew the country well. Before undertaking to guide them around the country and explain to them the points of interest in the various localities visited, he laid down three conditions to which the ladies readily agreed, viz. to entrust all their luggage to him, always to let him go before them and never to go before him or act on their own initiative, and to have absolute and implicit confidence in him to make all necessary arrangements in advance for their travel and comfort. The ladies accepted the terms but failed to keep the conditions. With regard to the first condition, they were willing to leave the larger, bulkier and heavier trunks and suitcases in his charge but wanted to hold on to the smaller cases and 'vanity bags', but on his insisting, they handed

these over also. All went well until they had to change trains at an important junction, and the ladies, instead of waiting for their guide, seeing a train on the opposite platform, rushed across and installed themselves comfortably in corner seats. The dragoman looked in and said, 'I'm sorry, ladies, but this train isn't going anywhere. Did you not agree to let me go before and guide you?' So they all had to dismount and follow the guide to another platform where their train was awaiting them. Later they had to ride on camels along the edge of a desert to the South of Damascus, and their guide informed them that they would have to spend a night in the desert. Then they began to worry as to what would happen. Would there be sleeping facilities? What about food? What protection would there be from marauders and wild beasts? But at nightfall they reached an oasis and found there that their guide had made every arrangement for their comfort. Tents were pitched, with cots and bedding ready for their use. There were basins and fresh water: there was a sumptuous meal ready for them, and the camp fire had been lit to keep wild beasts away.

So it is with the Christian and his Guide to Heaven, and 'they who trust Him wholly find Him wholly true.'

(John 10. 27; 21. 22; 1 Pet. 5. 7)

514. Halo.

Dr. Curtis Lee Laws, Editor of the *Watchman Examiner* once went out shopping and visited several shoe shops looking for shoes. At last, weary and tired out, he came to the last shop in the place where shoes were obtainable. The assistant brought him all the shoes in stock that were anything like his size, but not one seemed to fit him. He was just about to make an impatient remark, when the assistant said, 'I like your sermons, Dr. Laws.' 'How do you know me?' he asked. 'Oh,' said the assistant, 'I often come to hear you preach.'

'I'll take that pair of shoes,' said Dr. Laws, 'they don't fit too badly.'

In narrating this in an address to Bible students, he added, 'You see, I couldn't lose my halo.'—'Be courteous.'

(1 Pet. 2. 9; 3. 8)

515. Hand—The Master's.

Mendelssohn one day went into a little village church and sat listening for a time to the organist as he sat playing. After a time he went up to him and asked to be allowed to play the organ. 'I never allow anyone to play my organ,' said the organist. The stranger persisted and he reluctantly yielded. Quietly the stranger took his place at the instrument and, as his hands moved gently over the keys, there burst from that little organ such strains of music as never before had filled that place of worship. The organist was spellbound, and when, on asking the stranger who he was, he learnt that it was

Mendelssohn, the organist said, 'How could I have kept my organ from the great Master-player?'

(Rom. 6. 13; 12. 1, 2; 1 Pet. 3. 15)

516. Hand—The Master's. It was advertised in one of our large cities that a great violinist would play on a violin worth a thousand dollars. The theatre was packed. Many came as much to see the fine violin as to hear the music. The violinist came out and played, and the people were enraptured. But suddenly he threw the violin down and stamped on it, crushed it into matchwood and walked off the stage. The people were shocked, and thought the man must have lost his mind to destroy such a lovely and costly instrument. Then the manager came on and addressed the audience, saying, 'Friends, the violinist has not been playing on the thousand-dollar violin yet. The instrument you have heard he bought at a second-hand store for 65 cents. He will play on the thousand-dollar violin now.'

And so he did, and there were few people in the audience who could tell any difference. He simply wanted to show them that it is the violinist rather than the violin that makes the music. You may be a 65-cent fiddle, but the Master will make music upon you if yielded to Him.

—*Sunday School Times*

(Acts 4. 13-14; Rom. 12. 1, 2)

517. Hand—The Master's.

'Twas battered and scarred, and the auctioneer
  Thought it scarcely worth his while
To spend much time on the old violin,
  But he held it up with a smile.

'What am I bidden for this?' he cried.
  'Who'll start the bidding for me?
A dollar— one dollar: then two—only two:
  Two dollars are bidden; say three.

'Three dollars once: three dollars twice:
  Going for three!' But lo!
From the back of the crowd a grey-haired man
  Came forward and picked up the bow.

Then, wiping the dust from the old violin
  And tight'ning the loosened strings,
He played a melody passing sweet,
  The kind that haunts and clings.

The music ceased, and the auctioneer,
  With a voice that was soft and low,
Said, 'Now what is bid for the old violin?'
  And he held it up with the bow.

'A thousand dollars: who'll make it two?
  Two—two thousand: say three.
Three thousand once, three thousand twice,
  Three thousand—gone!' said he.

The people cheered, but some exclaimed,
  'We do not quite understand
What changed its worth:' and the answer came,
  ''Twas the touch of a Master's hand.'

And many a man with soul out of tune,
  And battered and scarred by sin,
Is auctioned cheap by the thoughtless crowd,
  Just like the old violin.

But the Master comes, and the foolish crowd
  Never can quite understand
The worth of a soul, and the change that is
    wrought
  By the touch of the Master's hand.

O Master! I am the tuneless one:
  Lay, lay Thy hand on me,
Transform me now, put a song in my heart
  Of melody, Lord, to Thee.

(Rom. 6. 16; 12. 1, 2; 2 Cor. 3. 18)

518. Hands—Filled for service.
'What is in thy hand, Abel?'
'Nothing but a wee lamb, O God, taken from the flock. I purpose offering it to Thee, a willing sacrifice.'
And so he did. And the sweet smell of that burning has been filling the air ever since, and constantly going up to God as a perpetual sacrifice of praise.
'What is in thy hand, Moses?'
'Nothing but a staff, O God, with which I tend my flock.'
'Take it, and use it for me.'
And he did; and with it wrought more wondrous things than Egypt and her proud king had seen before.
'Mary, what is that thou hast in thy hand?'
'Nothing but a pot of sweet-smelling ointment, O God, wherewith I would anoint Thy Holy One, called Jesus.'
And so she did; and not only did the perfume fill all the house in which they were, but the Bible-reading world has been fragrant with the memory of this act of love, which has ever since been spoken of 'for a memorial of her.'
'Poor woman, what is that thou hast in thy hand?'
'Only two mites, Lord. It is very little; but then it is all I have and I would put it into Thy treasury.'
And so she did; and the story of her generous giving has ever since wrought like a charm in prompting others to give to the Lord.
'What is that thou hast in thy hand, Dorcas?'
'Only a needle, Lord.'
'Take it and use it for Me.'
And so she did; and not only were the suffering poor of Joppa warmly clad, but, inspired by her loving life, 'Dorcas Societies' still continue their benign mission to the necessitous poor throughout the world.

—*The Monthly Broadcast*

(Exod. 4. 2; Mark 12. 42; John 12. 3; Acts 9. 39)

519. Happiness. It has been said that Happiness consists of three things—i. something to love: ii. something to do: iii. something to hope for. For the believer, Christ is the One he loves; His service is the something he has to do: and His approval and eternal companionship the what he hopes for.

—Scripture Truth

(Phil. 4. 4, 5; Col. 3. 24)

520. Happiness. Augustine Birrell was Secretary of State for Ireland in the early days of the Asquith administration, and among the most brilliant essayists of the closing days of the nineteenth century. He and his wife were driving through London one day and came to a mansion of magnificent proportions that took their breath away. Mrs. Birrell looked at it enviously, asked whose it was, and remarked how happy the owner must be to possess such a place. Mr. Birrell said it belonged to 'Barney Barnato', one of the world's richest men and partner with Cecil Rhodes. 'Perhaps,' he added, 'for all his wealth he is not happy.' In recording the incident later, Mr. Birrell stated that it was almost at that hour that Barnato jumped overboard from a boat coming from South Africa to end his unhappy life. Wealth does not bring happiness.

(Eccl. 5. 12, 13; 1 Tim. 6. 9, 10)

521. Happiness. Where is happiness found? NOT IN WEALTH.—*John B. Rockfeller*, a Christian millionaire, said, 'I have made many millions, but they have brought me no happiness. I would barter them all for the days I sat on an office stool in Cleveland and counted myself rich on three dollars a week.' Broken in health, he employed an armed guard.

W. H. Vanderbilt said 'The care of 200 million dollars is too great a load for any brain or back to bear. It is enough to kill anyone. There is no pleasure in it.'

John Jacob Astor left five million, but had been a martyr to dyspepsia and melancholy. He said, 'I am the most miserable man on earth.'

Henry Ford, the automobile king, said, 'Work is the only pleasure. It is only work that keeps me alive and makes life worth living. I was happier when doing a mechanic's job.'

Andrew Carnegie, the multi-millionaire, said, 'Millionaires seldom smile.'

(Deut. 33. 29; Eccl. 5. 12; 1 Pet. 4. 14)

522. Happiness—not found in Fame. Lord Byron, the poet, wrote:

My days are in the yellow leaf:
The flowers, the fruit of love are gone:
The worm, the canker and the grief
Are mine alone.

(Eccl. 2. 10, 11)

523. Happiness. There is an Eastern tale of a wealthy king who ruled a vast domain, lived in a magnificent palace and had a luxurious court. In spite of all his authority and power, and in spite of his extensive possessions, he was very unhappy. Among the servants in his court there was a renowned sage whose counsel the king frequently asked in times of difficulty and crisis. This sage was summoned to the king's presence. The monarch asked him how to get rid of his anxiety and depression of spirits, how he might be really happy, for he was sick in body and mind. The sage replied, 'There is but one cure for the king. Your Majesty must sleep one night in the shirt of a happy man.'

Messengers were dispatched throughout the realm to search for a man who was truly happy. But everyone who was approached had some cause for misery, something that robbed them of true and complete happiness. At last they found a man—a poor beggar—who sat smiling by the roadside and, when they asked him if he were really happy and had no sorrows, he confessed that he was a truly happy man. Then they told him what they wanted. The king must sleep one night in the shirt of a happy man, and had given them a large sum of money to procure such a shirt. Would he sell them his shirt that the king might wear it? The beggar burst into uncontrollable laughter, and replied, 'I am sorry I cannot oblige the king. I haven't a shirt on my back.'

(Eccl. 2. 3-11)

524. Harmony. On London Bridge there stood alone, and sad, a century ago, a poor old beggar man. He scraped away wretchedly on his old miserable violin in the attempt to draw a few pennies from the passers-by, but no one seemed to listen or stop, and his poor old heart was down in his toeless boots, and cold. A stranger passed along the bridge and suddenly halted beside the poor old fiddler, and listened while the weary, wistful eyes searched his face for, 'Charity, for the love of God!' Instead of the hoped-for penny the stranger asked for the fiddle; he would help with a tune.

The stiff, numbed fingers were glad to pass the old thing over, and the new hands began to play a low, plaintive melody that made the first passer-by find a tear start from his heart on the way to his eye, and he stopped and threw a penny in the old beggar's tattered hat, but still lingered, for the tune was going on. Then another stopped; another penny, and he lingered too. Then another, another, and yet they came and stopped. In the red heap of coppers in the old man's hat were even now appearing the white gleam of sixpences and shillings, and here and there the yellow glint of half-sovereigns and sovereigns. In a few minutes there was a dense crowd of thousands of people massing more and more on the bridge, while yonder big policeman, instead of saying 'Move on!' placed himself, with tears in his eyes, within hearing of the wondrous strains. Still from this decrepit old violin, melody, like an echo of the song that the angels sang, floated over their heads, and the decrepit old hat became brimful of coins.

'It is Paganini! It is Paganini!' passed the whisper along.

Aye, it is the Master—the Master Player!

Poor beggars are we on the ancient Bridge of Sighs, scraping to bring melody out of time-worn, sin-wormed hearts; poverty-stricken, joyless, with no resources to meet life's sorrows, fierce temptations, misfortunes, and out of them draw sweetness and strength.

Then a Stranger passes by, and stands, listening to our pitiful attempt to make music out of life. With loving, tender eyes, He gazes into ours, and pride and self-sufficiency melt away: humbly we hand Him our poverty-stricken hearts.

In a moment, fulness of joy, laughter and gladness fill our souls. The Hand that was pierced has taken the instrument, and made it anew. The Heart that was broken for us pours life and love into ours. The Master has come, the Lord of the Human Heart, the Controller of time and eternity. We have found Life's harmony in His fellowship. It is Jesus! It is Jesus!

All my life was wrecked by sin and shame,
Discord filled my heart with pain;
Jesus swept across the broken strings,
Stirr'd the slumb'ring chords again.

—The Pilgrim
(Luke 18. 35-43; Philem. 11)

525. Heart. In Kansas city, during the great Gipsy Smith revival years ago, an old preacher came into the room where the Gipsy was sitting after the service. Thousands were being blessed and hundreds saved. The older minister placed his hands upon the evangelist's head and felt about it. 'I am trying to find the secret of your success,' he said.

'Too high! Too high! My friend, you are too high,' Gipsy said. 'The secret of whatever success God has given me is not up there but down here,' and he placed his hand upon his heart.

The other day I heard this man preach, this Gipsy born in a tent, won by his Gipsy father who never had a day's schooling from men, and yet who preached to multitudes for sixty years. And as he preached, again and again the tears coursed down his cheeks, and my own heart was stirred and warmed and blessed.

—Dr. John R. Rice
(Exod. 36. 2; Ps. 39. 3; 2 Cor. 6. 11)

526. Heart. Two young officers in Bangalore, India, once invited Samuel Hebich, of the Basle Mission, to dinner. He accepted the invitation and while with them he behaved as a perfect gentleman, chatting pleasantly, and was very sociable and genial. The officers were agreeably surprised. After dinner, the officers lighted up their cigars, and one said to the guest, 'Mr. Hebich, will you have a game of cards?' He agreed. Before the cards were dealt, Hebich said to them, 'Shentlemen, I play cards, but I always bring my own cards:' and then pulled out ten cards. The first he showed them had a man's heart on it. 'Shentlemen,' he said, 'dis is trump! so are your hearts. You infite me to dinner and tink

you vill have much fun mit de old man. Now, I show you your hearts. See in it de defil, and not de Lord Jesus, sits on de trone. You haf all de defil's beasts in your hearts. You haf de peacock of pride, de shakal of deceit, de snake of enfy, de rat of greed, de dog of efil desires, and de gluttony and intemperance of de dirty fulture. Yes, all lust is in your heart as big as de elephant. God's Holy Spirit cannot enter your hearts because of dose efil beasts. Drife out de defil's menagerie.'

The result of Hebich's words was seen in the conversion of the two young officers.
(Prov. 4. 23; Mark 7. 20-23)

527. Heaven. Early in the sixteenth century Peter Martyr wrote to the Pope about a scheme to find a land of immense wealth, eternal summer and perpetual youth. The Pope gave his blessing, and ships were fitted out to sail westward in search of that land. They sailed round Florida and visited many islands, but could not find the object of their search. They failed because they searched in the wrong place.

Dreams cannot picture that world so fair:
Sorrow and death cannot enter there:
Time does not breathe on its fadeless bloom.
Beyond the seas and beyond the tomb—
It is there.

(Col. 1. 5; Rev. 22. 1-5)

528. Heaven.
There is a land where shadows never deepen,
And sunset glories fade not into night,
Where weary hearts shall win the boon of endless
blessing,
And faith is lost in sight.

A land where sad farewells are never spoken,
Where every loss of life is richest gain,
Where stumbling feet at last shall find a haven,
And hearts have no more pain.

A land where those who sigh for long-lost faces,
The loved of life whose going brought us pain,
Shall find them in the brightness of the Father's
glory,
Where we shall meet again.

On that bright strand the blood-washed ones of
Jesus
Are safe; no more the weary feet shall roam;
They find at last all that the heart has longed for,
Within God's house at home.

(John 14. 2, 3; Rev. 22. 1, 5)

529. Heaven. Some time ago Charles E. Fuller announced that he would be speaking the following Sunday on 'Heaven'. During that week a beautiful letter was received from an old man who was very ill, and the following is part of his letter.

'Next Sunday you are to talk about Heaven. I am interested in that land, because I have held a clear title to a bit of property there for over fifty-five years. I did not buy it. It was given to me without money and without price. But the Donor purchased it for me at tremendous sacrifice. I am not holding it for speculation since the title is not transferable. It is not a vacant lot. For more than half a century I have been sending materials out of which the greatest Architect and Builder of the Universe has been building a home for me which will never need to be remodelled nor repaired because it will suit me perfectly, individually, and will never grow old. Termites can never undermine its foundations for they rest on the Rock of Ages. Fire cannot destroy it. Floods cannot wash it away. No locks nor bolts will ever be placed upon its doors, for no vicious person can ever enter that land where my dwelling stands, now almost completed and almost ready for me to enter in and abide in peace eternally, without fear of being ejected.

'There is a valley of deep shadow between the place where I live in California and that to which I shall journey in a very short time. I cannot reach my home in that City of Gold without passing through this dark valley of shadows. But I am not afraid because the best Friend I ever had went through the same valley long, long ago and drove away all its gloom. He has stuck by me through thick and thin, since we first became acquainted fifty-five years ago, and I hold His promise in printed form, never to forsake me or leave me alone. He will be with me as I walk through the valley of shadows, and I shall not lose my way when He is with me.

'I hope to hear your sermon on Heaven next Sunday from my home in Los Angeles, California, but I have no assurance that I shall be able to do so. My ticket to Heaven has no date marked for the journey—no return coupon—and no permit for baggage. Yes, I am all ready to go and I may not be here while you are talking next Sunday evening, but I shall meet you there some day.'

—*Messenger of Peace*

(1 Pet. 1. 3-4; Ps. 23. 4)

530. Heaven.

Oh think! To step ashore and that shore Heaven:
To breathe new air, and that celestial air;
To feel refreshed and know 'tis immortality.
Oh think! To pass from storm and stress
To one unbroken calm; to wake and find it Glory.

(Ps. 17. 15; John 14. 2)

531. Heaven.

A preacher, passing through an institution, was asked by a woman: 'Sir, what work of man will be in Heaven?' 'None, my dear lady,' he replied, thinking to escape quickly. 'Oh, yes, there will; can you not tell me?' she persisted. 'No, I cannot, but will you not tell me?' said the preacher. 'Yes, sir,' she replied, 'it will be the print of the nails in the hands and feet of the Lord Jesus Christ. That is the only work of man that will be seen in heaven.'

532. Heaven.

It has been said that the light of heaven is the Face of Jesus Christ: the joy of heaven is the presence of Jesus Christ: the melody of heaven is the name of Jesus Christ: the harmony of heaven is the praise of Jesus Christ: the theme of heaven is the work of Jesus Christ: the employment of heaven is the service of Jesus Christ: and the fulness of heaven is the Lord Jesus Christ Himself.

(Rev. 5. 6-10)

533. Heaven—Home in.

A good friend of the 'long ago', when passing out of sight under almost tragic circumstances, had a glorious departure. I came to know him in Malaya, where he was a young missionary. It was on the eve of his sailing for home on his first furlough, after five years in the East, when he was taken suddenly ill. The doctors gave him two days to live.

But all his thoughts were fixed on home, his old parents, and the girl he loved and hoped to marry; moreover, he imagined he was getting better, instead of being at death's door. A mutual friend broke the news of his real condition to him. For a moment he seemed overwhelmed with the shock, then joy appeared to fill his soul as with beaming face he calmly said, 'Ah, I was going home, to my earthly home. Now I am going home to the Heaven I've so often preached above.' How indisputable is the God-given inward knowledge that the saved soul revels in, for 'he that believeth on the Son of God hath the witness in himself'.

—Capt. E. G. Carre

(Phil. 1. 23; 1 John 5. 10)

534. Heaven—Home in.

Heaven is the centre of the Christian's universe and he is bound to it by eight golden links:
Our Father is there—Matt. 6. 9: our Saviour is there—Heb. 9. 24: our home is there—John 14. 2: our name is there—Luke 10. 20: our life is there—Col. 3. 1-3: our heart is there—Matt. 6. 19-21: our inheritance is there—1 Pet. 1. 3-5: and our citizenship is there—Phil. 3. 20 (R.V.)

—Henry Durbanville

535. Heaven—Home in.

A child was sitting in a field of flowers,
With naught of care to veil the sunlit hours:
'Whose child art thou?' She lifted up her head;
'I am my mother's child,' the maiden said.
'Where dost thou dwell?' The simple lips replied,
'I live at home, upon the mountain-side.'
No sweeter words, though round the earth we roam,
Can be than those two words—mother and home.
An aged pilgrim, when the day grew late,
Sat reading David at her garden gate:
'Art thou a daughter of the heavenly King?'
'I am my Father's child Whose praise I sing.'
'Is this your dwelling-place, the home you love?'
'I have a better Home in Heaven above.'
No sweeter words have been to mortals given
Than those two golden words—Father and Heaven.

—William Wileman

(John 14. 2, 3)

536. Heaven—No disappointment in.

There's no disappointment in Heaven,
  No weariness, sorrow or pain;
No hearts that are bleeding and broken,
  No song with a minor refrain.
The clouds of our earthly horizon
  Will never appear in the sky,
For all will be sunshine and gladness,
  With never a sob nor a sigh.

I'm bound for that beautiful city
  My Lord has prepared for His own;
Where all the redeemed of all ages
  Sing 'Glory' around the white throne.
Sometimes I grow homesick for Heaven
  And the glories I there shall behold;
What a joy that will be when my Saviour I see
  In that beautiful city of gold.

We'll never pay rent for our mansion:
  The taxes will never come due;
Our garments will never grow threadbare,
  But always be fadeless and new.
We'll never be hungry nor thirsty
  Nor languish in poverty there;
For all the rich bounties of Heaven
  God's sanctified children shall share.

There'll never be crepe on the door-knob,
  Nor funeral train in the sky;
No graves on the hillsides of glory,
  For there we shall nevermore die.
The old will be young there for ever,
  Transformed in a moment of time;
Immortal, we'll stand in His likeness,
  The stars and the sun to outshine.

(John 14. 2, 3; Rev. 22. 1-5)

537. Hell.

Hell is not what we make of our lives down here (Luke 16. 22, 23), nor is it annihilation (Luke 16. 23), nor soul sleep in an unconscious state (Luke 16. 23-25), nor purgatory to fit the soul for heaven (Luke 16. 26). It is not a place or state that makes communication with those living on earth possible (Luke 16. 26-29), nor is it the final state of those who perish (Rev. 20. 11-15). The Lord Jesus made all this abundantly clear in the incident He narrated in Luke 16, which is not a parable. What then is Hell?

It is the place of the departed spirits of those who have lived and died without Christ. Jesus said to the Pharisees:- 'Ye shall die in your sins; whither I go, ye cannot come.' (John 8. 21)

538. Hell.

On an American troopship during the Second World War, the soldiers crowded around their chaplain, asking, 'Do you believe in hell?' He answered, 'I do not.'

'Well, then,' they said, 'will you please resign, for if there is no hell we do not need you; and if there is a hell we do not want to be led astray.'

(Ps. 9. 17; Prov. 9. 18; Luke 16. 23; 2 Pet. 2. 4)

539. Hell.

In January, 1833, Samuel Hebich was in Mangalore. The residential surgeon there was seriously ill, and Hebich went to visit him, but was again and again refused admission. Finally his persistence won, and at last he was shown in. The surgeon said to him, 'I'm too weak to talk to you.' As Hebich was about to go, he asked, 'Is there a hell?' 'Certainly,' replied Hebich, 'unless the Word of God lies.' On a subsequent visit the surgeon said to him, 'I am not a very great sinner, hence I hope for salvation.' Hebich's reply was, 'I am so great a sinner that, without a Saviour, I must go to hell.' Later on the surgeon said to him, 'What a great sinner I am!' Then he added, 'Almost it would have been too late.' The surgeon died trusting in the Lord Jesus Christ to save him from the penalty due to his sins, to save him from hell.

540. Help—in time of need.

Queen Elizabeth's favourite, Essex, was angry because the Queen, on account of his insolence, took from him his monopolies. He then behaved in a treacherous way, was tried by the Council and condemned as a traitor. He remembered a ring the Queen had formerly given him, with the words, 'When in difficulty, send this to me and I will help you.' He took the ring and gave it to a boy, with a present, telling him to take it to a lady, his friend, to give to Queen Elizabeth. By mistake the boy delivered the ring to another lady, a Countess who was the enemy of Essex, and it was never given to the Queen. How often Satan robs us of our help from above. The further history of the ring was this. It was passed on to Sir Thomas Warner, and placed on his coat-of-arms, with the motto, 'I hold from the King.'

—Selected

(Heb. 4. 16)

541. Hiding-place.

In 1732, the 'Volture', a British sloop of war, crept up the Hudson River to anchorage above Stony Point. In the dark, a young man wearing a heavy coat stepped from the 'Volture' into a small boat that had come out from the shore. This coat purposely covered the bright regimentals of a British Army Officer. The boat with muffled oars was rowed back to the shore, and in fulfilment of pre-arranged plans the strange man from the 'Volture' who was to be known as Mr. Anderson, was met by a man on shore. Soon the pair were seated in a nearby house—locked in—with deep plans and heavy bargaining.

Of course, we have guessed the names of this pair—General Arnold of the American Forces and Governor Clifton's adjutant general, Major André. Finally, Arnold handed over his plans and received his guarantee of reward.

While attempting to return to New York by land, Major André was captured and the plans were discovered in his stockings. He was court-martialled and publicly hanged from a lofty tree and buried in a nearby shallow grave. The British army went into mourning for him and in 1821 his remains were brought to England and deposited in Westminster Abbey.

This remarkable poem was found in his pocket after his execution:

Hail, Sovereign Love, which first began
The scheme to rescue fallen man!
Hail, matchless, free, eternal grace,
Which gave my soul a hiding-place!

Against the God Who built the sky
I fought with hands uplifted high—
Despised the mention of His grace,
Too proud to seek a hiding-place.

Enwrapt in thick Egyptian night,
And fond of darkness more than light,
Madly I ran the sinful race,
Secure—without a hiding-place.

But thus the eternal counsel ran:
Almighty Love, arrest that man!
I felt the arrows of distress,
And found I had no hiding-place.

Indignant, Justice stood in view;
To Sinai's fiery mount I flew;
But Justice cried with frowning face—
'This mountain is no Hiding-place.'

Ere long a heavenly voice I heard,
And mercy's angel soon appeared:
He led me with a beaming face
To Jesus as a Hiding Place.

On Him almighty vengeance fell,
Which must have sunk a world to hell.
He bore it for a sinful race
And thus became their Hiding Place.

Should sevenfold storms of thunder roll
And shake the globe from pole to pole,
No thunderbolt shall daunt my face,
For Jesus is my Hiding Place.

Apparently this man was saved and trusting the Lord, and the Lord was hiding him.
(Ps. 32. 7; Isa. 32. 2)

542. Hitherto—Henceforth.

Hitherto the Lord hath helped us,
Guiding all the way;
Henceforth let us trust Him fully,
Trust Him all the day.

Hitherto the Lord hath loved us,
Caring for His own;
Henceforth let us love Him better,
Live for Him alone.

Hitherto the Lord hath blessed us,
Crowning all our days;
Henceforth let us live to bless Him,
Live to show His praise.

—Frances Ridley Havergal
(1 Sam. 7. 12; 2 Cor. 5. 15)

543. High Priest—Aaron and Christ.

Holiness on the head,
Light and perfections on the breast,
Harmonious bells below, raising the dead
To lead them into rest.
Thus are true Aarons drest.

Profaneness in my head,
Defects and darkness in my breast,
A noise of passions ringing me for dead
Unto a place where is no rest;
Poor priest, thus am I drest.

Only another Head,
I have another heart and breast,
Another music, making live, not dead,
Without Whom I could have no rest
In Him I am well drest.

Christ is my only Head,
My alone only heart and breast,
My only music, striking me e'en dead,
That to the old man I may rest
And be in Him new drest.

So holy is my head,
Perfect and light in my dear breast,
My doctrine tuned to Christ (Who is not dead
But lives in me while I do rest).
Come, people, Aaron's drest.

—George Herbert
(Exod. 28. 29-36; Col. 2. 19; 1 Pet. 1. 16)

544. High Priest—Aaron and Christ.

As of old, on Aaron's breastplate Israel's names
in beauty shone,
So upon His priestly bosom Jesus ever bears His
own.

Names unworthy, yet in mercy all are graven on
His heart,
Bound by heavenly ties unto Him, never,
nevermore to part:

Precious and elect each jewel, special treasure in
His sight.
Every name a gem that sparkles 'neath the soft
and golden light.

Borne, besides, upon His shoulders: strong to save
and keep is He;
Set within the golden ouches of His glorious
Deity;

Wreathen, golden chains so perfect, bonds of
strong eternal love,
Clasp us now to Him for ever—joined by God to
Him above.

Blest memorials of the ransomed, ever borne
before our God,
Tokens of complete atonement by the Saviour's
precious blood.

Jesus, the Son of God, our great High Priest, is able to succour, sympathize and save to the uttermost all that come to God by Him.
(Exod. 28; Heb. 2. 18; 4. 15; 7. 25)

545. Holiness—of God. The following is the translation of a Telugu Hymn:

Holy, holy, Lord most holy; Thine intrinsic
holiness
E'en the angels in the glory cannot fathom or
express.

Holy Father! all excelling wisdom, power and
strength are Thine,
As from Thy celestial dwelling radiant right-
eousness doth shine.

Holy Son! in incarnation Man of truth and
    boundless grace,
Bringing by Thy death salvation to our sinful
    fallen race.
Holy Spirit! Great Bestower from Heaven's
    precious treasure-store!
Love and joy and grace and power on Thy saints
    Thou still dost pour.
Holy Father, Son and Spirit—God the blessed
    Trinity!
Glory, honour, power and merit be eternally to
    Thee.

                                    —A.N.

(Isa. 6. 3; John 17. 11; Heb. 7. 26; Eph. 4. 30)

546. Home. Six things necessary to make a house really a Home should be found in every Christian home:
i. The architect—integrity: ii. the upholsterer—tidiness: iii. the heating—affection: iv. the lighting—cheerfulness: v. the ventilator—industry: vi. the protecting roof—God's blessing.
(Mark 2. 1)

547. Home—Heavenly.
He laid him down upon the breast of God
    In measureless delight—
Enfolded in the tenderness untold,
    The sweetness infinite.

                    —Machthild of Hellfde
(Ps. 116. 15; 2 Cor. 5. 8; Phil. 1. 23)

548. Home—Heavenly. The following lines were written after the death of Dr. Morrison, of Glasgow, Scotland, in the Doric, the dialect of lowland Scotland:

Ye're hame;
A weel-bund sheaf o' gowden grain;
Ripe, ripe for God and God alane,
Who waled ye for His very ain,
An' took ye hame.

Ye're hame.
The whisperin' hills o' this dear airt
Brocht ye awa' frae a' apairt,
An' God an' you spak hairt to hairt
O' His dear hame.

Ye're hame.
But oh, hoo blithe the hameward road,
Hoo licht the unco heavy load
To you who walked sae near tae God
The hale road hame.

Ye're hame.
Ye're safely doon life's staney brae,
But hame is so sae far away;
Ayont death's burn whaur nicht is day,
And God is hame.

                        —Gilbert Rae

(John 14. 2, 3; 2 Cor. 5. 8)

549. Honesty. About the middle of the year 1911, Mr. McAlpine, founder of the Bakery business in Melbourne which still bears his name, was lying on what proved to be his deathbed.

Dr. Wolston, of Edinburgh, a well-known physician, was due to arrive in a day or two. Mr. McAlpine asked that, if necessary, the funeral might be postponed until his arrival, as he had a particular reason for wishing the doctor to take the service at the graveside, in accordance with an old understanding between them.

Speaking in front of the open grave, Dr. Wolston told this story:

A partnership of seven miners was being 'grubstaked' in New Zealand by a local storekeeper. They were very unfortunate, and when the amount owing reached £400, they decided to clear out. Packing their belongings, they all left one night, but when some miles away, one stopped and said he couldn't go on; he meant to go back and face the storekeeper, and tell him everything. His mates jeered at him, but back he went.

Naturally, their ingratitude angered the storekeeper, who thought they might have got jobs and made some effort to repay him. He told the returned miner that, as a partner, he was responsible for the whole debt. 'All right,' was the reply, 'if ever I can, I'll pay you.'

Going back to the abandoned claim and getting some help, he struck gold almost at once, and in a week or two was back at the store with a bag containing over 100 ounces of small nuggets and gold dust. The storekeeper heartily congratulated him and refused to take more than one seventh of the debt. But the miner insisted. 'Well,' said the storekeeper, 'I'm your friend for life.'

'That miner's body now lies in the grave before you,' said Dr. Wolston. 'He was afterwards converted and became a most successful business-man.' Then the preacher urged all present to accept the Lord Jesus Christ as their Saviour, insisting on the truth of the words, 'Godliness is profitable unto all things, having the promise of the life that now is, and of that which is to come.' After the service was over, an old man came up to him and said, 'I am the seventh and last of the band of miners. The story is true: all the other five died poor. I am in the Old Men's Home and we made nothing by defrauding the storekeeper.'

(Rom. 12. 17; 1 Tim. 4. 8)

550. Hope—Purchase of. It is recorded in Roman history that, when the Gauls were encamped around Rome, the very lands on which the Gauls had erected their tents were bought and sold—a great proof of their confidence in the future destiny of Rome.

                    —William Kelly
(Jer. 32. 1-25; Luke 12. 33; Col. 1. 5)

551. Humility. William Gladstone said, 'Humility as a sovereign grace is the creation of Christianity.'
Lowliness of heart is good soil for the seed of
    faith.
(Phil. 2. 5, 6; 1 Pet. 5. 5, 6)

552. Humility.

The saint that wears Heaven's brightest crown
In deepest adoration bends:
The weight of glory bears him down
The most, when most his soul ascends.
Nearest the Throne itself must be
The footsteps of humility.

(Eph. 3. 8; 1 Cor. 15. 9; James 4. 10)

553. Humility. When Dr. Morrison, well-known missionary to China, wrote home, asking that an assistant be sent him, a young man eager to go appeared before the committee. He looked to them so unpromising, so rough and 'countrified', that they said, 'He will never do for a missionary.' But he was so anxious to be employed in missionary labours, the committee made a proposal to send him out as a servant. Asked if he was willing, he replied with a bright smile: 'Yes, most certainly. I am willing to do anything, so that I am in the work. To be "a hewer of wood and drawer of water" is too great an honour for me when the Lord's house is a-building.' That young rustic afterwards became Dr. Milne, a most efficient missionary, founder and principal of the Anglo-Chinese College of Malacca.

—*The Prairie Overcomer*

(Prov. 15. 33; Luke 7. 6; Phil. 2. 5, 6; 1 Pet. 5. 6)

554. Humility.

Do what you can, being what you are:
Shine as a glow-worm if you cannot be a star.
Work like a pulley if you cannot be a crane;
Be a wheel-greaser if you cannot drive a train.

Be the pliant oar if you cannot be the sailor.
Be the little needle if you cannot be the tailor.
Be the cleaning besom if you cannot be the
*   sweeper:*
Be the sharpened sickle if you cannot be the
*   reaper.*

(Jer. 45. 5; 1 Cor. 7. 20)

555. Humility.

You have a famous cook, 'tis true;
*   Your menage is the best.*
You are a splendid hostess too,
*   And such an ideal guest.*
But can you eat of humble pie
*   A truly generous slice,*
Without one soft, regretful sigh
*   As if it tasted nice?*

You're lithe and young as anything:
*   You're quite a sport at hockey,*
And you alone on deck can sing
*   When winds and waves are rocky.*
You mount the highest horse in town
*   With ease that's good to see;*
But, say, can you do climbing down
*   With real agility?*

You can from any instrument
*   Draw music sweet and clear;*
Like Orpheus, 'tis your gay intent
*   To soothe and charm the ear.*
Harp, viol, 'cello—all of these
*   Your servants. Let me see!*
Can you play second fiddle well
*   And make a melody?*

(Luke 14. 10; Phil. 2. 22)

556. Humility. A certain French Marquis was raised to his grand and exalted state from very humble surroundings. He had been a shepherd in his earlier days, and so, in his palace, he had one room known as 'the shepherd's room'. In that room were reproductions of hills and valleys and running streams and rocks and sheepfolds. Here were the staff he had carried and the clothes he had worn as a lad when herding his sheep. When asked one day the meaning of this, he replied, 'If ever my heart is tempted to haughtiness and pride, I go into that room and remind myself of what I once was.' Such humility would have saved Nebuchadnezzar and Belshazzar.

—*Sunday School Times*

(Deut. 26. 5; Ps. 78. 70, 71; Prov. 15. 33; Isa. 51. 1; 1 Cor. 15. 9, 10)

557. Humility.

The bird that soars on highest wing
*   Builds on the ground her lowly nest,*
And she that doth most sweetly sing
*   Sings in the shade when all things rest;*
In lark and nightingale we see
*   What honour hath humility.*

(Prov. 15. 33; 22. 4; Acts 20. 19; Luke 18. 14)

558. Hymns. During a circus performance in Dublin, at the time of the great revival under Moody's preaching when Sankey's hymns were being sung everywhere, one clown, pretending to be dejected, said to the other, 'I feel quite moody tonight. How do you feel?' 'Oh!' said the other, 'I'm sankeymonious.' Contrary to what was expected, this was met with hisses, and the whole audience rose and sang, 'Hold the fort, for I am coming.'—D. J. Beattie

(Jude 18)

559. Illumination.

*   The sacred page*
With calm attention scan. If on thy soul,
As thou dost read, a ray of purer light
Break in, oh, check it not; give it full scope,
Admitted, it will break the clouds which long
Have dimmed thy sight, and lead thee till at last,
Convictions, like the sun's meridian beams,
Illuminate thy mind.

(Ps. 19. 8; 119. 130; Luke 24. 45; John 16. 13)

560. Illustrations. These exist for the purpose of making clear the truths to be presented. Illustrations are like windows that let in the light; but these should not be too numerous, for one's sermon should not resemble a glasshouse. A gospel address should not consist of an endless string of anecdotes, with a few odd texts interspersed to keep it from falling apart; but should be a setting forth of the truth of Scripture, for this alone can give authority to the message. The sermon does not exist for the sake of the illustrations but vice versa. These illustrations, though necessary, are purely incidental.

Henry Ward Beecher has pointed out that illustrations serve a sevenfold purpose.

(a) They assist argument.
(b) They help the hearer to remember.
(c) They stimulate the imagination.
(d) They rest the audience.
(e) They provide for various classes of hearers.
(f) They bridge difficult places.
(g) They enforce the truth.

—Alfred P. Gibbs
(Matt. 13. 3; Gal. 4. 24)

561. Illustrations. Let your illustrations be such as shine into your sermon, and not illustrations you drag in. You have heard men preach, and tell a story. The story has really no vital relationship with their message. They put it in, and it relieves the congregation, making them smile at the moment, perhaps, but it has no relation to the sermon. One of the most skilful in this matter that I have known was John Henry Jowett.—Dr. Jowett's illustrations always shone into his main theme. You never went away with the illustration as the supreme thing; it was there illuminating. I remember hearing him in Birmingham, when he said: 'Human and Divine divisions of humanity are radically different. Divine divisions are perpendicular, human divisions are horizontal.' Well, there we were. He picked up his hymn book, held it upright, and said, 'I will show you what I mean. That is perpendicular division to the right, to the left: that is Divine.' Then, holding it flat—'This is horizontal—upper, middle, lower classes: that is human.'

—Dr. G. Campbell Morgan

562. Image—Broken.

Old events have modern meanings;
    Only that survives
Of past history which finds kindred
    In all hearts and lives.

Mahmood once, the idol-breaker,
    Spreader of the faith,
Was at Sumnat tempted sorely,
    As the legend saith.

In the great pagoda's centre,
    Monstrous and abhorred,
Granite on a throne of granite,
    Sat the temple's Lord.

Mahmood paused a moment, silenced
    By the silent face
That, with eyes of stone unwavering,
    Awed the ancient place.

Then the Brahmins knelt before him,
    By his doubt made bold,
Pledging for their idol's ransom
    Countless gems and gold.

Gold was yellow dirt to Mahmood,
    But of precious use,
Since from it the roots of power
    Suck a potent juice.

'Were yon stone alone in question,
    This would please me well,'
Mahmood said; 'but with the block there
    I my truth must sell.

'Wealth and rule slip down with fortune,
    As her wheel turns round;
He who keeps his faith, he only
    Cannot be discrowned.

'Little were a change of station,
    Loss of life or crown,
But the wreck were past retrieving
    If the Man fell down.'

So his iron mace he lifted,
    Smote with might and main,
And the idol on the pavement,
    Tumbling, burst in twain.

Fifty times the Brahmin's offer
    Deluged on the floor.

—J. Russell Lowell

The dearest idol I have known,
    Whate'er that idol be,
Help me to tear it from its throne
    And worship only Thee.

(Hos. 14. 8; 1 John 5. 21)

563. Image—The Lost. Michael Angelo lingered before a rough block of marble so long that his companion remonstrated. In reply, Michael Angelo said, 'There's an angel in that block and I'm going to liberate him.' Oh, what unbounding love would manifest itself in us towards the most unlovable—the most vile—if only we saw what they might become, and in our enthusiasm for souls we cried out, 'There's the image of Christ—marred, scarred, well-nigh obliterated—in that dear fellow, and I'm going to make that man conscious of it.'

—A. E. Richardson
(2 Cor. 3. 18)

564. Image—Nebuchadnezzar's.

'Our God is able, mighty King, to save us from
    the flame;
He can prevent thee hurting us—Almighty is His
    name.
From thy strong hand He will us keep; and His
    shall be the praise
When thou, and all this throng, to Him shall
    humble worship raise.

'If not, what then? Why, then the flame our
    bodies shall consume.
Far better that brief agony than one, long,
    living doom,
To feel the conscience burn with shame that we
    should faithless prove,
And in the hour of trial deny the Holy One we
    love.

'He will deliver: "but if not", Thy royal will be
    done:
And we now cheerfully will look our last upon
    yon sun.
For be it known to thee, O King, thy gods we will
    not serve;
Thy golden image we contemn! From this we will
    not swerve.
'We make our choice with one accord: we serve
    Jehovah high,
And Him alone; and for His name we ready are
    to die.
And we shall choose His servants' lot and order
    our estate;
So do thy worst: we will not bow before thy
    image great.'

—G. H. Lang

(Dan. 3. 16-18)

565. Imagination. Fancy plays like a squirrel
in its circular prison, and is happy. Imagination is a pilgrim on the earth, and her home is
in Heaven. Shut her from the fields of the
celestial mountains, bar her from breathing
their lofty, sun-warmed air; and we may as
well turn upon her the last bolt of the tower of
famine, and give the keys to the keeping of the
wildest surge that washes Capraja and
Gorgona.

—John Ruskin

(1 Chron. 29. 18)

566. Immanuel's Land. Anne Ross Cousins
has rendered in exquisite poetic form some of
the last words of Samuel Rutherford. Several
of the verses are found in many of our hymn
books. These are omitted here, and a selection
made from the remaining stanzas.

Oh! well it is for ever,
    Oh, well for evermore,
My nest hung in no forest
    Of all this death-doomed shore;
Yea, let the vain world vanish,
    As from the ship the strand,
While glory—glory dwelleth
    In Immanuel's land.

There the red Rose of Sharon
    Unfolds its heartmost bloom,
And fills the air of Heaven
    With ravishing perfume;
Oh! to behold it blossom,
    While by its fragrance fanned,
Where glory—glory dwelleth
    In Immanuel's land.

The King there in His beauty
    Without a veil is seen;
It were a well-spent journey,
    Though seven deaths lay between:
The Lamb, with His fair army,
    Doth on Mount Zion stand,
And glory—glory dwelleth
    In Immanuel's land.

E'en Anwoth was not heaven—
    E'en preaching was not Christ:
And in my sea-beat prison
    My Lord and I held tryst:

And aye the murkiest storm-cloud
    Was by a rainbow spann'd,
Caught from the glory dwelling
    In Immanuel's land.

Fair Anwoth by the Solway,
    To me thou still art dear!
E'en on the verge of Heaven
    I drop for thee a tear.
Oh! if one soul from Anwoth
    Meet me at God's right hand,
My Heaven will be two Heavens
    In Immanuel's land.

Deep waters cross'd life's pathway,
    The hedge of thorns was sharp;
Now these all lie behind me—
    Oh! for a well-tuned harp!
Oh! to join Hallelujah
    With yon triumphant band,
Who sing, where glory dwelleth
    In Immanuel's land.

I have borne scorn and hatred,
    I have borne wrong and shame;
Earth's proud ones have reproached me,
    For Christ's thrice-blessed name.
Where God His seal set fairest
    They've stamped their foulest brand;
But judgement shines like noonday
    In Immanuel's land.

They've summoned me before them,
    But there I may not come—
My Lord says, 'Come up hither!'
    My Lord says, 'Welcome Home!'
My kingly King at His white throne
    My presence doth command,
Where glory—glory dwelleth
    In Immanuel's land.

(Isa. 7. 14; 8. 8)

567. Impressions. Youth is the impression-
able age. There is a stone in the British
Museum in London which is as hard as any
steel, and yet there is on it the imprint of a
little bird's foot. There was a time when that
stone was soft and plastic, and took on that
impression, and it has retained it down
through the years. Youth is the plastic time
in life. A Telugu proverb says, 'The sapling
will bend, but—will the tree?'
(Deut. 4. 9, 10; Prov. 22. 6)

568. Inside. 'Is it getting night?' said an old
Scottish woman ninety-seven years of age.
And her aged Scottish husband by her side,
realizing that she was dying, bent down close
to her and said, 'Yes, Janet, it is getting night.'
She was wandering a bit and was back in the
olden days with her loved ones, but she knew
that the end was near. She was still a moment,
and then said, 'Are the boys all in?' 'Yes,' he
said, 'the boys are all in, Janet.' (The last one
had come home three years before).
    She was again still a moment more, then she
said, 'I will soon be in.' 'Yes, Janet, you will
soon be in.' 'And you will soon come too,'
she asked. 'Yes!' he said, 'by the grace of
God I will soon come too.' She reached out her

thin hands in order that she might clasp them round his neck and draw him down to her side, as she said, 'And He will then shut us all in.' 'All in!'

I wonder if you can say it, with the boys all in, the girls all in. It is a sad thing to have a boy that is a wanderer and a girl that is lost.
—J. Wilbur Chapman

Soon Thy saints shall all be gather'd—Inside the veil,
All at home—no more be scatter'd—Inside the veil.

(Gen. 7. 1; Rev. 21. 27)

569. Incarnation. Sadhu Sundar Singh used to illustrate the incarnation mystery in this way. A simple countryman was being shown a red glass bottle full of milk. They asked him what was in the bottle. 'Wine? Brandy? Whisky?' he replied, questioningly. He could not believe it was filled with milk till he saw the milk poured out from it. The redness of the bottle hid the colour of the milk. So, he said, it was and is with our Lord's humanity. Man saw Him tired, hungry, suffering, weeping and thought He was only man. 'He was made in the likeness of men,' yet He ever is 'God over all, blessed for ever.'

(John 1. 14; Rom. 9. 5; Phil. 2. 7, 8; 1 Tim. 3. 15)

570. Incarnation. Handley Bird, for many years a missionary in India, used to illustrate the incarnation of our Lord by the following story. A father, walking-stick in hand, took his young son for a walk. The lad asked his father to let him have the stick for a little while and, when his father acceded to his request, he began to use the stick to play golf with the stones and to swipe the shrubs growing by the roadside. By and by he poked it into a nest of ants which, hurt, disturbed and terrified, began to scurry off in all directions. The lad, tender-hearted, was sorry for what he had done, and, looking up into his father's face, he said, 'Oh, father, I'm sorry these poor ants have been hurt and are scurrying off in terror. I love them and am sorry for them. Oh father, won't you tell them how sorry I am for them and how I love them.' The father, looking at his son with an amused smile, said, 'I am glad you have such a tender, compassionate heart toward these little creatures. I would gladly give them your message and tell them how you feel toward them, but I can't. In order to be able to do so, I should have to be born an ant and speak to them in their language, for they cannot understand our language.'

(John 1. 14; Rom. 5. 8)

571. Incarnation.

Angelic hosts to men the mystery tell—
Th' Almighty deigns on earth with men to dwell
As Man, the virgin's son, Immanuel,
God here with us.

'His own received Him not;' Rejected, He
Sin's bonds to break and Satan's slaves to free,
Endures the curse and hangs upon a tree;
Christ died for us.

Rising, He conquers Death, the monster hoary,
Bids His redeemed proclaim on earth His story,
Enters and fills our hearts with hopes of glory;
Christ lives in us.

Formed in a virgin's womb, Eternal Son!
Thou becam'st dead, Thou true life-giving One!
Live now Thy life through lives Thy death has won—
Christ formed in us.

Soon shall the Saviour to our longing eyes
Appear. The dead in Christ shall rise:
With them caught up, we'll meet Him in the skies—
Christ come for us.

—A.N.

(John 1. 14; 1 Tim. 3. 15; Gal. 2. 20)

572. Indifference. Napoleon's soldiers often used to sleep on the march. They were moving onward, yet asleep and indifferent to all around them. Thousands are like them in spiritual matters. They are 'passing onward, quickly passing' in the journey of life, yet indifferent to their need of eternal life in Christ and to the claims of God upon their lives.

(Jonah 1. 6; Eph. 5. 14)

573. Infidelity. D. L. Moody on one occasion met a man in the enquiry room after one of his powerful gospel messages and asked him, 'Are you a Christian?' The man replied, 'I'm, a practical Christian.' 'Ah!' said Mr. Moody, 'when were you converted?' 'I never was converted. I don't believe the Bible,' was the reply. 'Do you believe Webster's Dictionary?' asked D. L. Moody. 'Yes!' said the man. 'Well! Webster says that one who doesn't believe the Bible is an infidel. Call yourself by your right name,' said Mr. Moody.

(John 8. 24; 1 John 5. 10)

574. Infidelity. No more subtle praise of an institution could be imagined than the scandal which immediately attaches to any sin in it. To a young infidel scoffing at Christianity because of the misconduct of its professors, Dr. Mason said, 'Did you ever know of an uproar made because an infidel went astray from the paths of morality?' The infidel admitted that he had not.

'Then don't you see,' said Dr. Mason, 'that by expecting those who profess Christianity to be holy, you admit it to be a holy religion, and thus pay it the highest compliment in your power.'

(2 Tim. 2. 19; 1 Pet. 1. 16)

575. Infirmities. Wilberforce did not like himself. He was a diminutive edition of a man and never enjoyed good health. For twenty years he was under doctor's orders and had to take drugs to keep body and soul together.

Yet he stopped the British slave trade. Boswell once went to hear him speak and said afterwards: 'I saw what seemed a mere shrimp mounted upon the platform, but, as I listened, he grew and grew till the shrimp became a whale.'

The most stimulating successes in history have come from persons who, facing some kind of limitations and handicaps, succeeded splendidly in spite of all. Once, when Ole Bull, the great violinist, was giving a concert in Paris, his A string snapped and he transformed the composition immediately and finished magnificently on three strings.

The Apostle Paul who was one of those that 'turned the world upside down' as a missionary, and who has given the Christian Church, under the inspiration of the Holy Spirit, such a wealth of doctrine in his Epistles, said of himself that his bodily presence was weak and his speech contemptible: and he suffered with 'a thorn in the flesh'.

(Rom. 8. 26; 2 Cor. 12. 7, 10)

576. **Influence.** I rejoice, now that our beloved brother, Harold St. John, has been called into the Lord's presence, to recount an incident that could happen only to a man who 'walked with God'.

He was staying in an hotel in Rome and when an English lady approached him, and said, 'May I presume to speak to you without an introduction on the basis that we are both British people in a foreign country?' 'Why, madam, certainly,' he replied, to which she responded, 'I wish to ask you a personal question. Will you please tell me the secret of your serenity? I have been watching you for two days and I perceive you live in a different world from mine.' This led to a conversation which ended in her kneeling in a secluded corner of the hotel lounge and accepting his Lord as hers.

—R. A. Laidlaw

(1 Pet. 2. 9)

577. **Influence—Spiritual.** When I was saved, during a mighty movement of the Spirit of God in Glasgow, Scotland, a young lady was also saved. Her name was Helen Ewing. She was just a slip of a girl, but at the very threshold of her new life in Christ, she crowned Him as absolute Lord and was filled with the Spirit. The rivers of living water just simply flowed from that young girl's life. Although she died at the age of twenty-two, all Scotland wept. I know hundreds of missionaries all over the world wept and mourned for her.

She had mastered the Russian language and was expecting to labour for God in Europe. She had no outstanding personality; she never wrote a book, nor composed a hymn; she was not a preacher, and never travelled more than two hundred miles, so far as I know, from her home. But when she died people wrote about her life story. Although she died so early in life, she had led a great multitude to Jesus Christ. She arose early each morning about five o'clock to study God's Word, to commune, and to pray. She prayed for hundreds of missionaries. Her mother showed me her diary—one of her diaries—and there were at least three hundred different missionaries for whom she was praying. It showed how God had burdened that young heart with a ministry of prayer. She had the date when she started to pray for a request and then the date when God answered her petition. She had a dynamic prayer life that moved God and moved man.

I was talking one day with two university professors in London City. We were talking about dynamic Christianity, when one of them suddenly said, 'Brother Stewart, I want to tell you a story.' And he told me that in Glasgow University there was a remarkable young lady who, wherever she went on that campus, left a fragrance of Christ behind her. For example, if the students were telling dirty stories, someone would say, 'Sh—Helen is coming—quiet,' and then she passed by and unconsciously left the power behind her.

—James Stewart

(Gal. 2. 20; Eph. 5. 18; Phil. 1. 21)

578. **Iniquity—of the holy things.** There is forgiveness, not only for our omissions of duty but for our duties themselves, not only for our prayerlessness but for our prayers; not only for our long rejection but for our sins in coming to Him; not only for our unbelief but for our faith; not only for our past enmity but for our present, cold-hearted love; not only for the sins we bring to Christ but for our way of bringing them; for the impure motives that defiled our service, and also for the sin mingling with our worship, when standing within the veil, in the sanctuary where the Majesty of the Holy One has its abode.

—Dr. Bonar

(Exod. 28. 38)

579. **Inspiration.** I once had a conversation with a group of young men on the subject of the inspiration of the Bible. Most of them opposed me. I reminded them of the numerous prophecies in the Old Testament concerning the Messiah, which were literally fulfilled in Christ. One of them was sharp enough to see the force of the argument, and he admitted that these prophecies were undoubtedly written hundreds of years before Christ was born, and that He fulfilled them in every detail, but he endeavoured to parry its force by advancing the theory that Christ had intentionally planned his actions in accordance with the Messianic programme, in order to establish His religion, so that there was, after all, nothing very wonderful in the fact that these prophecies were fulfilled.

This sounded very neat and ingenious, but I asked my friend to explain to us how Christ, in accordance with this theory, was able to arrange to be born in the very village—one of the smallest in Judaea—where the prophet Micah foretold that the Eternal One should be born on earth. I asked him what precautions He had taken, if a man as we are, to ensure being born at the very time and in the very family that the Scriptures had forecast. My friend was not inclined to surrender his position without a struggle, so he contended that Jesus, seeing that He happened to be born in this particular village, at this particular time, had been seized with the idea of carrying out the remaining details requisite to establish His Messianic claims.

My reply, in substance, was as follows: 'Well and good. In accordance with this, you will now perhaps tell us why Jesus was allowed to make arrangements for two thieves to be crucified with Him in order to fulfil Isaiah's predictions in his 53rd Chapter. You must tell us whether Judas arranged with the chief priests to betray Jesus in order to fulfil the word of the prophet; and, after Judas had hanged himself, who it was that arranged for a potter's field to be bought with the money which the betrayer flung down in the Temple, and whether it was done in order to fulfil the prophecy to that effect! You will also doubt-less show us how, while hanging on the Cross, Jesus persuaded the four Roman soldiers who crucified Him to divide His outer garments into four parts and to cast lots for His inner robe, as the 22nd Psalm had accurately described! You will also need to explain whether His enemies gave Him vinegar to drink in His agony in order to fulfil the 69th Psalm. If your theory is to hold good, you must explain to us how it was that, after Jesus was dead, the soldiers decided not to break His legs, as they did to the two thieves by His side. Did they desire to make Him fulfil the type of the Passover lamb in the twelfth chapter of Exodus, and the ninth of Numbers, or the reference in the 34th Psalm?—How did Jesus arrange all these details should be fulfilled in Himself?

My friend had nothing more to say.
—Arthur Gook
(Luke 24. 27, 44; John 5. 39; 2 Pet. 1. 21)

580. Invitation. I was in residence at the London Hospital as house-physician when Moody and Sankey were holding their services in a large building erected for the purpose at Stratford. Sitting in the crowded hall one afternoon, I found at the close of the service that immediately in front of me was a dis-guished-looking man who did not move when the rest went out. The choir was softly singing on the platform what I fear I must describe as doggerel, being an endless repetition of the words:

Come to Jesus! come to Jesus! come to Jesus just now!
Just now, come to Jesus! come to Jesus just now!

I leaned over and asked my neighbour how he liked the address. He turned round and said, 'Excuse me, sir, it was very powerful; but as my feelings are slightly agitated I would rather not say any more. I don't wish to speak at present'. And there he sat a little longer, while the choir still kept crooning the same endless invitation.

How little we really see with our eyes! All the greatest things elude us, or are only dimly perceived by the finer vision of the spirit. Anyhow, I was quite unconscious of the divine drama which was being enacted on that wooden form in front of me in that somewhat squalid building that afternoon. 'Well!' I replied, 'here is my address, and if at any time you would care for a chat, come and see me at the hospital.'

Three days after, the card of a city solicitor was brought up to my room, and as he entered I recognized my neighbour at Moody and Sankey's, though he was completely changed. His face had wholly lost its heavy and dull look, and was animated and sparkling with joy.

'Dr. Schofield,' he exclaimed, as he held out his hand, 'I cannot stop away. I must tell you my joy. Do you know, sir, my sins are all forgiven? Do you know that I, a respectable lawyer, have the greatest difficulty in not telling every one of the great change come over me?'

'I suppose it was at Moody and Sankey's service,' I asked.

'It was,' he replied, 'but it wasn't the address.' I looked surprised. 'Nor it wasn't what you said to me,' he added. 'The fact is, I am very fond of choral singing and am a member of the Temple Church where I hear some of the finest singing in the world.'

'I'm afraid Moody and Sankey's choir was hardly up to your standard.'

'Well, no, it wasn't,' he replied, 'but it has done more for me than any other choir in the world.'

'Tell me,' I said.

'While you were talking, I was listening to that choir. You know how it kept at it—"Come to Jesus! Come to Jesus!" Well, the first fifty times I didn't mind, but when it kept on unceasingly, and after I had heard it about a hundred times, I began to think. And as it still went on I realised the truth of the Saviour's words, "Come unto me, all ye that labour and are heavy laden and I will give you rest" (Matt. 11. 28). I thought I had better come. So I took the Lord Jesus as my Saviour there and then, and went home rejoicing, and ever since my joy has been growing and growing; I don't know how to contain it. You see, I'm a prosy city lawyer, and this is the last thing on earth I ever thought would happen to me. But, Oh I praise God it has.'
—Dr. A. T. Schofield
(Matt. 11. 28; John 6. 37)

581. Invitation. Miss Ada Habershon in her 'memoirs' tells how, at one of D. L. Moody's services, in a tent, right in the very front sat Deacon Abraham's daughter-in-law and her baby. The little one's eyes were fixed on Moody as he spoke. The Lord's loving invitation—'Come!' he repeated again and again with

outstretched arms. And the baby responded, with its little arms stretched out as if to go to him.
(Matt. 11. 28)

582. Invitation.

If you come to God as a braggart comes
In the pride of your own way,
Then the God of grace will hide His face
And send you empty away.

If you come to God as a beggar comes
With the plea of your bitter need,
Then the King of kings will give good things
And make you rich indeed.

(Luke 18. 10-14; John 7. 37; Rev. 22. 17)

583. Iron—Nails of.

Gold is for the mistress, silver for the maid,
Copper for the craftsman cunning at his trade.
'Good!' said the Baron, sitting in his hall,
'But iron, cold iron, is master of men all.'

So he made rebellion 'gainst the king, his liege,
Camped against his citadel and summoned it to
*   siege;*
'Nay,' said the cannoneer on the castle wall,
'But iron, cold iron, shall be master of you all.'

Woe for the Baron and his knights so strong,
When the cruel cannon balls laid 'em all along!
He was taken prisoner, he was cast in thrall,
And iron, cold iron, was master of it all.

Yet the king spake kindly (Ah! how kind a lord!)
'What if I release thee now and give thee back thy
*   sword?'*
'Nay,' said the Baron, 'mock not at my fall,
For iron, cold iron, is master of men all.'

'Tears are for the craven, prayers are for the
*   clown,*
Halters for the silly neck that cannot keep a
*   crown.*
As my loss is grievous, so my hope is small,
For iron, cold iron, must be master of men all.'

He took the wine and blessed it: He blessed and
*   brake the bread:*
With His own hands He served them, and
*   presently He said,*
'See! these hands they pierced with nails outside
*   my city wall*
Show iron, cold iron, to be master of men all.

'Wounds are for the desperate, blows are for the
*   strong,*
Balm and oil for weary hearts all cut and bruised
*   with wrong.*
I forgive thy treason, I redeem thy fall,
For iron, cold iron, must be master of men all.

'Crowns are for the valiant, sceptres for the bold!
Thrones and powers for mighty men who dare to
*   take and hold!'*
'Nay!' said the Baron, kneeling in his hall,
But iron, cold iron, is master of men all;
Iron out of Calvary is master of men all.'
                                              —Rudyard Kipling

(Col. 2. 14, 15; Gal. 6. 14)

584. Israel.

God Who in Israel's bondage and bewailing
*   Heard them and granted them their heart's*
*   desire,*
Clave them the deep with power and with pre-
*   vailing,*
*   Gloomed in the cloud and glowed into the fire,*
Fed them with manna, furnished with a fountain,
*   Followed with waves the rising of the rod,*
Drew them and drove, till Moses on the mountain
*   Died of the kisses of the lips of God.*
                              —F. W. H. Myer—*St. Paul*

(Ps. 77. 20; 78. 13-25; 106. 9-23)

585. Israel.

They and they only, amongst all mankind,
Received the transcript of the Eternal Mind,
Were trusted with His own engraven laws
And constituted guardian of His cause.
                                              —William Cowper

(Rom. 9. 4, 5)

586. Ittai.

'Wherefore goest thou with me?' said the king
*   disowned—*
Said the king despised, rejected, disenthroned.
'Go, return unto thy place, to thy king of yore—
Here a pilgrim and a stranger, nothing more.

'Not for thee the cities fair, hills of corn and
*   wine—*
All was portioned ere thou camest, Nought is
*   thine.*

'Wandering forth where'er I may, exiled from
*   mine own,*
Shame, rejection I can grant thee; that alone.'

Then unto the crownless king on the Kedron's
*   shore,*
All the wilderness before him, Ittai swore,

'As the Lord lives and the king, ever lord to me,
Where in death or life he dwelleth I will be.'

'Go—pass over;' spake the king; then passed
*   Ittai o'er;*
Passed into the place of exile from the shore.

He and all his little ones, granted by that word,
Shame, rejection, homeless wandering with their
*   lord.*

'Go—pass over;' words of grace spoken, Lord,
*   to me,*
That, in death or life, where Thou art I might be.

'He who serves Me,' spake his lips, 'let him
*   follow Me,*
And where I am shall My servant ever be.'

Follow, where His steps lead on, through the
*   golden street;*
Far into the depths of glory, track His feet.

Till unto the throne of God, of the Lamb I come;
There to share the blessed welcome—Welcome
*   home!*
                      —P.G. in *Hymns of Ter Stegen and others*

(2 Sam. 15. 19-22; John 12. 26)

587. Jacob. Jacob lifted up his *feet*—Gen. 29.
1—(Marginal Reading)—After Bethel, the
House of God.—Jacob the pilgrim.

Jacob lifted up his *eyes*—Gen. 33. 1—After
Peniel, the Face of God.—Jacob the priest.

Listen! Listen! Jacob, the schemer!
You, who with your fiery glance,
Made and moulded circumstance,
You, whose restless, roving brain,
Planned, contrived, and planned again.
Wrestling, grappling, striving then,
And manipulating men—
You were once a dreamer.

Poor homeless head, with stony pillows under,
Say, have you quite forgotten all the wonder?
Frail, earth-bound man, whose faculties divining
The heavenly ladder shining,
Looked upon God, and, looking, chose the good:
Have you forgotten His similitude?

'All these things are against me!' Yet those
*   things,*
Those very things, were God's machinery
For working out your heart's imaginings,
For turning hope to blessed certainty.
Oh, man who walked by sight,
You should have known the darkest hour of night
Is just before the earliest streak of grey.
Your wagons, all the time, were on their way!
Faith? Yes, but with a flaw,
Here was a man who trusted when he saw!
And yet,
The Holy One has set
His name beside two men of saintly will,
And calls Himself the 'God of Jacob' still,

That you and I,
Lacking in Faith, maybe, or Gentleness,
May yet stretch out weak hands of hopefulness,
And find the God of Jacob very nigh.
                                        —Fay Inchfawn
(Ps. 46. 7, 11)

588. Jehovah.

I'll follow Thee, and step by step along the track
*   I'll walk;*
Believing that Thy promises shall never come to
*   nought;*
Jehovah-Shammah, blessed Name, whate'er the
*   danger be,*
Thy promise is salvation sure, and Thine the
*   victory.*

The Lord of hosts my refuge is, Jehovah-nissi
*   too.*
Jehovah-jireh as my God provides the journey
*   through;*
I trust Thee, simply trust Thee, lay my troubled
*   fears to rest:*
I follow where Thou leadest, for my Father
*   knoweth best.*
                                        —E. Rowat

589. Jews. The Heritage of the Jews—a law
defied, a land defiled, a Lord denied:

The Hatred of the Jews—for his peculiarity
and prosperity, and as his punishment:

The Hope of the Jews—not legislation, or
segregation, or assimilation, or annihilation,
but

the Salvation of Jehovah (Jesus).
                              —Hyman J. Appleman
(Esther 3. 8; John 4. 22; Rom. 9. 4, 5)

590. Jews. Frederick the Great of Prussia
asked his chaplain to prove the authenticity
of the Bible in two words, and the chaplain
immediately replied, 'The Jews, your Majesty!'
(Num. 23. 9; Deut. 4. 25-27)

591. Jews.

Amazing race! deprived of land and laws,
A general language and a public cause;
With a religion none can now obey,
With a reproach that none can take away:
A people still whose common ties are gone,
Who, mixed in every race, are lost in none.
                                        —George Crabbe
(Num. 23. 9; Deut. 4. 25-27)

592. Jews. The poet, Lord Byron, wrote
concerning the Jews:

Oh! weep for those that wept by Babel's stream,
Whose shrines are desolate, whose land a dream;
Weep for the harp of Judah's broken shell;
Mourn—where their God had dwelt, the godless
*   dwell.*

Tribes of the wandering feet and weary breast,
How shall ye flee away and be at rest?
The wild dove hath her nest, the fox his cave;
Mankind their country, Israel but the grave!

Israel is a miracle. She became a self-governing
State in 1948. Right before our eyes now,
prophecy concerning them is being fulfilled on
every hand.
(Isa. 18. 2, 7; Hos. 3. 4, 5; Matt. 24. 32)

593. Jews.
Pride and humiliation hand in hand
*   Walked with them through the world where'er*
*   they went;*
Trampled and beaten were they as the sand,
*   And yet unshaken as the continent.*
                                        —H. W. Longfellow
(Deut. 28. 37; Isa. 18. 7)

594. Jews—their History. Under six conditions, as revealed in Scriptures.

Condition	Period	Years (approximate)	References
Promise	Abraham to Moses—Jewish family—Nation viewed as in Abraham's loins.	From 2000 to 1571 B.C.	Gen. 12. 1-4; 15. 4-7; 17; 22. 17, 18; 26. 3-5; 28. 13-15; Exod. 3. 1-8
Law	Moses to Christ. Israel as a nation, led out by Moses the lawgiver, who was succeeded by Joshua and the Judges.	From 1491 B.C.	John 1. 17; Acts 7. 14-36
Royalty	David to Zedekiah. Israel as a Kingdom.	From 1063 B.C.	1 Kings 12; Acts 13. 20-23
Captivity	Israel to Assyria, Judah to Babylon. Babylonian, Medo-Persian, Grecian & Roman Empires.	From 721 B.C. and 608 B.C.	2 Kings 13. 3; 24. 15; Jer. 21. 10; Dan. 1. 2; Luke 2. 1; 21. 24
Dispersal	Romans destroyed Jerusalem, and scattered the people.— Desolation of the land.	A.D. 70	Deut. 28. 64; Jer. 24. 9, 10; Hos. 9. 17
Restoration	Present Time. Great increase in the number of Jews returning to Palestine. In the early years of the 20th century there were 45,000 Jews in Palestine: in 1957—nearly two million.	20th Century	Jer. 31. 8-10; 32. 36-44; Amos 9. 14, 15; Zech. 14; Luke 21. 24-27

—C. A. Fletcher

595. Jews—their Months.

1. *Abib*—April (Called Nisan in Esth. 3. 7)—Sprouting, budding, resurrection (Exod. 13. 4; Deut. 16. 1)

2. *Zif*—May—Blossom, or flower month: fruit. In the 4th year of his reign Solomon began to build the house of the Lord, and the Foundations were laid in the month Zif (1 Kings 6. 1, 37)

3. *Sivan*—June—Their covering (from Siv—the Moon, to which the Assyrians dedicated it). On the 23rd day of Sivan, in the 12th year of his reign, Ahasuerus the Persian king decreed war (Esther 8. 9)

4. *Thammuz*—July—sacred to the idol, Tammuz (Ezek. 8. 14)

5. *Ab*—August, the twelfth month of the Syrian year, from which it was doubtless borrowed

6. *Elul*—September—the gleaning month. On the 25th day of Elul the wall of Jerusalem was completed (Neh. 6. 15)

7. *Ethanim*—October—the perennial, never-ending. The Talmud calls this month Tisri. In this month Solomon brought up the ark (1 Kings 8. 2).

8. *Bul*—November—Rain-god. In the eleventh year of his reign Solomon finished the house (1 Kings 6. 38).

9. *Chisleu*—December—Hunter, from Orion, Mars. In this month Nehemiah enquired about Jerusalem (Neh. 1. 1), and God spoke to Zechariah the prophet, censuring the people (Zech. 7. 1).

10. *Tebeth*—January—Winter. In the 7th year of the reign of the Persian monarch, Ahasuerus, Esther was taken to his house (Esther 2. 16).

11. *Sebat*—February—Smite thou. Zechariah the prophet saw judgement impending in his first vision in this month (Zech. 1. 7).

12. *Adar*—March—Fire-god. Many things happened in this month in Israel's history:

The House of God was completed (Ezra 6. 15)

The Jews cast Pur (Esther 3. 7, 13)

The Jews had to fight for their lives on the 13th day of Adar (Esther 8. 12)

The Jews observed the 14th and 15th days (Esther 9. 15, 21), in the 12th year of Ahasuerus' reign.

596. Job—Book of. I call this book, apart from all theories about it, one of the grandest things ever written with pen. One feels, indeed, as if it were not Hebrew; such a noble universality, different from noble patriotism or sectarianism, reigns in it. A noble book, all men's book.—There is nothing written in the Bible, I think, of equal literary merit.

—Thomas Carlyle

The greatest poem of ancient and modern times.

—Alfred, Lord Tennyson

It is magnificent and sublime as no other book in the Bible.

—Martin Luther

597. John—the Apostle.

I'm growing very old. The weary head
That hath so often leaned on Jesus' breast
In days long past that seem almost a dream,
Is bent and weary with its weight of years.
I'm old—so old I cannot recollect
The faces that I meet in daily life:
But that dear Face and every word He spoke
Grow more distinct as others fade away,
So that I live with Him and the holy dead
More than the living.

(John 21. 20; Rev. 1. 9)

598. Joined—to the Lord. The apostle Paul speaks of our being joined to the Lord. Our union with Him can never be broken and therefore we are eternally secure. The story is told of a shipwreck in the Georgian Bay of Canada. The mate of the ship leaped into a boat with six or seven strong men and a timid girl. One by one the strong men lost their hold as the boat was turned over and over by the raging billows. Every one perished except the girl, the reason being that the mate had taken the precaution to bind her with ropes to the prow of the boat. She drifted to the shore where she was rescued and she lived for many years to relate her way of deliverance. How thankful we should be that we are joined to the Lord!

—Indian Christian

(1 Cor. 6. 17; Eph. 2. 21)

599. Jordan.

Christ is a sure help to the children of Zion,
But if thou hast any false props to rely on,
Thy soul is deluded; think what thou art doing!
Oh, cast them away ere they sink thee in ruin!
For none but Jehovah has power to deliver
And bear up thy soul in the midst of the river.

The clouds gather blackness, the night is fast coming:
The river swells high and the billows are foaming.
On what wilt thou lean when thy strength is all wasted?
The reeds will all fail and thy hopes will be blasted.
O cry unto Jesus thy soul to deliver
And bear up thy spirit when crossing the river.

But in thy true character am I mistaken?
Hast thou in thy folly thy Saviour forsaken?
O come again to Him for peace and for pardon,
Or soon thou must sink in the swellings of Jordan!
Thy soul from all danger He then will deliver,
And nothing will harm thee when crossing the river.

But if on His mercy thy soul is relying,
Thou hast nothing to fear, either living or dying.
The footmen and horses shall fall down before thee,
And Jordan shall open thy passage to glory:
And when thou art landed safe over the river,
We'll sing of salvation for ever and ever.

(Jer. 12. 5)

600. Jordan—the Swellings of. 'If thou hast run with the footmen, and they have wearied thee, how canst thou contend with horses?' Surely the meaning is clear. God is telling Jeremiah that if he has had difficulties in his service, that is not the end, there are more to follow. Worse things are to befall him; greater dangers he must meet. Already he has run with footmen, but now he must contend with horsemen. 'And if in a land of peace thou thinkest thyself in security, how wilt thou do in the swelling of Jordan?' (J.N.D.) What does this mean? Certainly it has no reference to the death that awaits the sinner. Many a time has this verse been hurled at the unsaved at the street corner, but it has no reference to them. Jeremiah's condition under Josiah was comparatively one of peace. Under the godless kings to come how would he get on? His future difficulties would be like 'the swellings of Jordan' or 'the jungles of Jordan'. It would be hard to run there. His first sufferings were like a stream; his coming trials would be like a river in flood. Surely this was a discouraging prospect to God's servant. True, but God's servant must learn and learn again that his resource is in God alone.

—A. L. Goold

(Jer. 12. 5)

601. Joseph—God's purpose for.

Heaven's favourite down a darksome pit they cast,
His rich-hued robe and lofty dreams deriding;
Then, from his tears their ruthless faces hiding,
Sell him to merchants, who with spicery passed.
The changeful years o'er that fair slave fled fast:
Behold him now in glorious chariot riding,
Arrayed in shining vesture, and presiding
O'er Egypt's councils—owned by Heaven at last.
In pit or palace, God's own hand was weaving
The 'many-coloured' texture of his days,
The brightest tints till last in wisdom leaving.
So when in dismal paths our feet are sinking,
Let us be looking soon for lightsome rays,
For our wise Father 'thoughts of peace' is thinking.

—Richard Wilton

(Gen. 37. 3, 31, 32; 45. 13)

602. Joy—the Christian's. Principal Rainy, of whom a child once remarked that she believed he went to heaven every night, because he was so happy every day, once used a fine metaphor about a Christian's joy. 'Joy,' he said, 'is the flag which is flown from the castle of the heart when the King is in residence there.'

(Hab. 3. 18; John 15. 11; 1 Pet. 4. 13)

603. Joy—the Christian's. There is joy in retrospect, as we look at the past; there is joy of aspect, as we look at the present; there is the joy of prospect, as we look forward to the future.

There is the joy of memory, the joy of love, the joy of hope. There is the joy of the peaceful conscience, the joy of the grateful heart, the joy of the teachable mind, the joy of the trustful soul, the joy of the adoring spirit, the joy of the obedient life, and the joy of the glowing hope. 'In Thy Name do they rejoice.' That is where we get our joy: in Thy name, in the revelation of God.

—Dr. W. H. Griffith Thomas
(Neh. 8. 10; Ps. 16. 11; Luke 24. 52; Rom. 15. 13)

604. Joy—In Presence of the angels. One of the famous tombs in India has a marvellous architecture. 20,000 men took twenty-two years to erect it and the buildings around it. Standing there, if you speak or sing, the echo comes from the height of 150 feet, as if from heaven itself. It is not an ordinary echo. The sound is drawn out in sweet prolongation. So from sin's tomb the voice of believing, penitent prayer brings back an echo of joy from Heaven itself.
(Luke 15. 7, 10, 24, 32)

605. Judge. In the city of Hyderabad, Deccan, India, there was a judge who, on his way to court one day, saw a child on the railway line right in the way of a fast-approaching train. Taking his own life in his hands, he dashed on to the line and drew the child into safety just in time.

He went on to the court, and an hour later sat as judge in the criminal court, listened to the jury's verdict on a murderer and pronounced the death sentence. He had that day been both a saviour and a judge.
(John 5. 24-27)

606. Judgement. A young minister of the Gospel was confronted—as the congregation expected—with an able young sceptic, Burt Olney. At the close of the first service Olney said, 'You did well, but, you know, I don't believe in the infallibility of the Bible.' 'It is appointed unto men once to die, but after this the judgement,' was the young man's calm assertion.

'I can prove to you there is no such thing as a judgement after death,' declared the sceptic.

'But men do die,' the young preacher declared, 'for it is appointed unto men once to die, but after this the judgement.'

'But that's no argument,' the sceptic protested. 'Let's get down to business and discuss this matter in regular argument form.'

The minister shook his head. 'I am here to preach the Word of God and not to argue over it.'

Olney, annoyed, turned away with the remark, 'I don't believe you know enough about the Bible to argue about it.'

'Perhaps you are right,' was the calm rejoinder, 'but please remember this—"It is appointed unto men once to die, but after this the judgement".'

The very tree-toads Olney heard on the way home sang the verse, and the stream he crossed, and the frogs seemed to croak, 'Judgement, judgement, judgement.'

The next morning he called at the parsonage. 'I've come to see you about that verse of Scripture you gave me last night,' he said. 'I've spent a terrible night with those words burning their way into me. I can't get rid of them. Tell me what I must do to be saved. I've got to get rid of this torture.'

When he left, he was a child of God through faith in the finished work of Christ.
(Heb. 9. 27, 28; John 5. 24)

607. Judgement.

The world is grown old, and her pleasures are past;
The world is grown old, and her form may not last;
The world is grown old and trembles for fear,
For sorrows abound and judgement is near.

The sun in the Heaven is languid and pale;
And feeble and few are the fruits of the vale;
And the hearts of the nations fail them for fear,
For the world is grown old and judgement is near.

The king on the throne, the bride in her bower,
The children of pleasure all feel the sad hour;
The roses are faded, and tasteless the cheer,
For the world is grown old and judgement is near.

The world is grown old! But should we complain
Who have tried her and know that her promise is vain?
Our heart is in Heaven; our Home is not here,
And we look for our crown when judgement is near.

—Reginald Heber
(Acts 24. 25; Rom. 2. 2, 3; 1 Tim. 5. 24; 2 Tim. 4. 1; Jude 6, 15)

608. Judgement. The most horrifying thing on the Western plains is the dreaded prairie fire. Until the fall rains set in, the dry scorching summer months are spent in fear and suspense. Every suggestion of haze or smoke is intensely watched. But, when once fired and swept by a breeze, its speed strikes terror to man and beast as it unmercifully consumes all in its way. Many, powerless to escape, have perished, and their farms been reduced to ashes.

Others, with presence of mind, seeing their danger, have resorted to one way of escape and have been saved by it. They have stooped and fired the long dry grass at their feet, and then, as soon as the blaze had burned off a space, taken refuge by standing where the fire had been. Thus, in time, they were saved from the oncoming devouring flames. Of course, it is no time to trifle, but a case of life or certain death.

Yet more solemn and terrifying will be the coming wrath and judgement of God upon this world that has crucified, and ignored the grace of, His beloved Son. It is 'reserved unto fire against the day of judgement' (2 Pet. 3. 7).

But thanks be unto our gracious God who has provided a place of safety where the fire has already been. On Calvary's cross Christ was, as it were, enveloped in the 'fire' of God's righteous judgement to save the trembling sinner that has fled to Him for refuge (Heb. 6. 18).

(1 Pet. 3. 18; 2 Pet. 3. 9, 10)

609. Judgement. Donald Campbell worked down at the docks. One day, when they had a few spare minutes after unloading the coal from a boat, one of his fellow-workers informed him that he wasn't a Christian but a killjoy. To prove his point, the fellow, to the pleasure of the bystanders, proceeded to quote part of Ecclesiastes 11. 9—'Rejoice, O young man, in thy youth and let thy heart cheer thee all the days of thy youth, and walk in the ways of thine heart, and in the sight of thine eyes.'

Soon their mirth vanished. Picking up a piece of chalk, Donald walked over to the blackboard (on which quantities were marked up) and wrote the last part of the verse: 'but know thou that for all these things God will bring thee into judgement.' His accusers were forced to withdraw, confused and crestfallen.

—James Cordiner
(Eccles. 3. 15; 11. 9; Heb. 9. 27)

610. Judgement.

Mine eyes have seen the glory of the coming of the Lord:
He is trampling out the vintage where the grapes of wrath are stored.
He hath loosed the fatal lightning of His terrible swift sword.
His truth is marching on.

I have seen Him in the watchfires of a hundred circling camps;
They have builded Him an altar in the evening dews and damps;
I can read His righteous sentence by the dim and flaring lamps;
His day is marching on.

—Julia Ward Howe
(Isa. 63. 1-4; Rev. 6. 15, 16; 20. 11)

611. Justice. Pandit Kharak Singh, an old man, and a Sanskrit scholar, was asked while preaching in the bazaar in a town in India, how he could reconcile the death of Christ Jesus for men—the death of the guiltless for the guilty—with the justice of God.

He replied, 'Our ideas of the justice of God, or of justice at all, are very crude and imperfect. For example: a man steals 20 rupees and spends it. He is caught and punished as a thief. But the stolen money is not restored to the man from whom it was stolen—justice is not done to him; and the thief suffers for his crime. This is man's justice—loss and pain.

Or suppose a man was to kill three children. He should be hanged three times that strict justice may be done. The children are not restored to life—justice is not done to them. Neither are they restored to their parents or to the community. The man who killed them is put to death, and thus man's justice again is resolved into loss and pain!

'But God's justice is different. It results in gain and joy! Lost souls are found, losses are made good, happiness takes the place of misery, and all because the Son of God gave Himself a willing sacrifice to save men and restore them to God' (Isa. 45. 21; Rom. 3. 24-26)

612. Justice. Peter the Great of Russia condemned his own son Alexei to death for intrigues and high treason against the Tsar, and the sentence was duly carried out. Peter suffered intensely in the interests of justice. This family tragedy was the greatest grief in his life. The sentence of death has been passed on sinful man, but a sinless substitute has taken the penalty and exhausted the sentence for all who will accept and believe in Him.

Justice God will not twice demand,
First at my bleeding Surety's hand,
And then again at mine.

(Rom. 3. 26; 1 Pet. 3. 18).

613. Justification. A friend took William Callahan, a 'down and out', into a Gospel service and he was gloriously saved. Then he tried to live down his old reputation but found it very hard. The police kept him shadowed, not believing the work of grace in his life. After five years he went to Chicago and, through the aid of a Christian lawyer, got his photos from the police. He did not want to be known as a crook. Then he employed a lawyer to get his photo from the penitentiary at Joliet and to have his Bertillon measurements there destroyed. The reply came from the warden: 'You may have got the records from the Chicago police, but you can't get them away from the State of Illinois.'

Some time after, nervous and in poor health, while staying at a Sanatorium in Battle Creek, with three Governors present including Atgeld of Illinois, he made a speech at a function, telling of his conversion and attempt to get his records from Joliet. When he got through, Governor Atgeld was wiping his eyes and said, 'I'll see what I can do for you.' A month later Mr. Callahan received a letter from Executive Mansions, Springfield, State of Illinois:

'My dear Mr. Callahan, It gives me pleasure to enclose your photograph from the Penitentiary of Joliet, and to tell you that your records and measurements there have all been destroyed. There is no record, except in your memory, that you were ever there. You have the gratitude and best wishes of your friend, John P. Atgeld.'

—Silas Fox
(Isa. 44. 22; Rom. 3. 23, 24; Heb. 10. 17)

614. Justification. Just over a hundred years
ago, a woman was buried in an old churchyard
in Enfield. Six lines on her tombstone show
that she knew that not character but Christ,
saves:

If friendship, kindness, truth, goodwill and love
Could prove a passport to the realms above,
The soul that tenanted this mouldering frame
To God's right hand might justly lay a claim.
But her own works she scorned as worthless
dust:
Her Saviour's merits were her only trust.
— H. P. Barker

(Rom. 3. 28; Gal. 2. 16)

615. Justified.

Plead Thou my cause, Thou Advocate divine!
I have no words—no argument, save Thine.
Speechless, I stand before the bar of God;
Guilty!—Lost! unless redeemed by blood.

Base my behaviour—
I need a Saviour—
'Mercy!' my only plea;
Take Thou my case, Lord,
I trust Thy grace, Lord,
I will leave my whole defence with Thee!

Plead Thou my cause, Thou Advocate divine;
I need no words—no argument, save Thine;
Show but the wound prints in Thy hands and side,
And I stand before Thee—Justified!
— F. Gilbert

(Rom. 3. 24, 25; 1 John 2. 1)

616. Justified. It was the Saturday before
August Bank Holiday when the Polish S.S.
Dabrowski berthed by London Bridge, and
English stevedores moving the cargo found the
Polish stowaway, Antoni Klimowicz. Fainting
with hunger and thirst, he just managed to cry,
'Tell the English police!' when the Captain
and the political Commissar seized him, and
locked him in a cabin.

Saturday, Sunday, Bank Holiday Monday,
the London newspapers bore sensational head-
lines, 'Can Klimowicz be saved?' It appeared
there were diplomatic difficulties. The Polish
Captain refused to surrender him. Thousands
of Polish refugees swelled a fund to engage the
best lawyers.

But on the Monday, the captive stowaway
felt the ship casting off, and soon, to his
dismay, he saw the Thames growing wider and
wider as the ship went down towards the sea.
Soon the friendly shores of Britain would
disappear, and then it would be the open sea—
and what beyond? Imprisonment, perhaps
worse!

And yet, salvation was near. The greatest
legal mind in the land—that of Lord Goddard,
the Lord Chief Justice, had been searching for
a way to be 'just and the justifier' of the man
who had appealed for mercy. It was discovered that on a previous visit Antoni
Klimowicz, as a sailor, had attempted to
smuggle something, and the police had re-
frained from prosecuting. So he could be

lawfully brought to a British court of law to
answer for his misdeed.

Four hundred policemen raced down the
Thames, and opposite Tilbury a few of them
boarded the Polish ship. The cabin door was
broken down. Did the poor stowaway protest
that he was innocent of the charge of smuggling?
Did he 'go about to establish his own righteousness'? No, he gladly submitted to justice.

'Guilty! Fined one farthing'! Ten thousand
refugees in Britain would willingly have paid
his fine ten thousand times. Antoni Klimowicz
walked out of the court—back to bondage?
No! For what his own fulfilling of the law
could never do, mercy had done—giving him
liberty and a new life in Britain. He was free.

Shortly afterwards he invited to tea the two
London stevedores who carried his desperate
plea to the authorities. How much *we* owe to
the One Who heard our cry as sinners and
Who never turns away anyone who seeks
refuge with Him! Perhaps Antoni Klimowicz
learnt of that Saviour's love from the Polish
New Testament, which he gratefully received
from the writer.
— Stuart K. Hine

(Rom. 3. 26; 8. 3; 10. 3)

617. Keeper—Jehovah His People's. 'Jehovah
is my Keeper.'

The Assyrian came down like a wolf on the fold,
And his cohorts were gleaming with purple and
gold;
Like the leaves of the forest when summer is
green,
That host, with its banners, at sunset was seen.
Like the leaves of the forest when autumn has
blown
The host on the morrow lay withered and strown.
For the Angel of Death spread his wings on the
blast,
And breathed in the face of the foe as he passed;
And the eyes of the sleeper waxed deadly and
chill,
And their hearts but once heaved and for ever
grew still:
And there lay the steed with his nostrils all wide,
Though through it there rolled not the breath of
his pride.
And the tents were all silent, the banners alone,
The lancets unlifted, the trumpets unblown.
And the might of the Gentile, unsmote by the
sword,
Had melted like snow in the glance of the Lord.
— Lord Byron

(2 Chron. 32. 21, 22; Ps. 121. 5; Jude 24)

618. Kindness.

Let me be a little kinder, let me be a little blinder
To the faults of those about me; let me praise a
little more.
Let me be, when I am weary, just a little bit more
cheery;
Let me serve a little better those that I am
striving for.
Let me be a little braver, when temptation bids
me waver;

*Let me strive a little harder to be all that I
should be.*
*Let me be a little meeker with the brother that
is weaker;*
*Let me think more of my neighbour and a little
less of me.*

(Eph. 4. 32; Col. 3. 12; 1 Cor. 13. 4)

619. King—Christ the. Writing on Psalm 45
—'the things . . . touching the king'—Dr.
Alexander McLaren says:

'There is no doubt that this Psalm was
originally a marriage hymn for some Jewish
king. All attempts to settle who he was have
failed, for the very significant reason that
neither the history nor the character of any of
them correspond to the Psalm. Its language is
a world too wide for the diminutive stature and
stained virtues of the greatest and best of them.
And it is almost ludicrous to fit its glorious
sentences even to a Solomon. They all look
like little David in Saul's armour. So then,
we must admit one of two things. Either we
have here a piece of poetic licence, or "a
Greater than Solomon is here".'

The three great themes of the Psalm are—
the grace, the glory and the gladness of Christ
the King.

(Ps. 45; Heb. 1. 8)

620. King—Crowned with thorns.
Full many a king a golden crown has worn,
But only one a diadem of thorn:
Full many a king has sat on jewelled throne;
But only One hung on a Cross alone:
*Through garlanded gay streets, cheered by the
crowd*
*Great kings have ridden—One, with His head
bowed*
Beneath the burden of His Cross, passed on
To die on Calvary, one King, but one:
All other kingdoms pass, are passing now—
Save His Who wore the bramble on His brow.

(John 19. 5, 14, 19)

621. King—Earthly and Heavenly. The
following lines were found on the body of a
dead airman during World War II and
published in Sandes Soldiers' Home Magazine.

Those who are called by an earthly king
And are bidden to meet with the great,
Who are asked to dine at the Royal Court
In earthly splendour and state,
They come from his presence with face alight,
With a proud and a lifted head,
They are eager to tell what they saw and heard
And repeat what the great one said.

But we who have supped with the King of kings
And have eaten the heavenly bread,
Are we eager to say what we saw and heard
And tell what the King hath said?
Are we proud that the King has called us 'Friends'
And bidden us seek His face?
Do we tell the world of His matchless love?
Do we speak of His wondrous grace?

(2 Pet. 1. 16-18)

622. King—Eternal. Admirers of Charlemagne (Charles the Great) set up his corpse in
its grave, crowned the pulseless temples, and
put a sceptre in the bloodless fingers. What
grim mockery? Charlemagne is dead, though
his fame remains. The King of kings, our
Lord Jesus, crucified as King of the Jews, is
alive for evermore.

(1 Cor. 15. 25; Ps. 2. 6; Rev. 1. 18; 19. 16)

623. King—Lord of hosts.
Tell me no more of the splendour
Of the courts of mighty kings;
Speak to me not of the grandeur
Of the brightest earthly things;
For how shall I care for the glitter
Of gold or pearl or gem?
Or how shall mine eyes be dazzled
By yon monarch's diadem?
Or how shall this heart be ravished
By the choicest earth can boast,
Now that mine eyes have seen Him,
The King, the Lord of Hosts?

For who will gaze on a candle
While the noonday sun shines clear?
Or who will turn to the servant
While the Master standeth near?
Or why should one leave the palace grand
To stand in courtyard bare?
Or who depart from the Throne-room
While the monarch sitteth there?
And how can I leave His service
For the highest earthly posts
Now that mine eyes have seen Him,
The King, the Lord of hosts?

As he that enjoys the sunlight
Needeth not that the stars should shine:
So I ask not for earthly light,
Having guidance all divine:
As a bride careth not who chideth
If her lover but agrees,
So I care not who condemneth
If but the Lord I please.
To afford His heart some gladness
Is the prize this heart seeks most,
Now that mine eyes have seen Him,
The King, the Lord of hosts.

So offer me not the baubles
Which the blinded worldlings seek,
For mine eyes have seen the King of kings;
Mine ears have heard Him speak;
And I cannot but be satisfied
With His favour full and free;
I cannot but His bidding do
As He enables me.
The world has no attractions left:
How mean is all it boasts,
Now that mine eyes have seen Him,
The King, the Lord of hosts.

—G. H. Lang

(Isa. 6. 5; Rev. 19. 16)

624. King—Love for the. When Robert Bruce
was fleeing from the English, when they
invaded Scotland, he came to a poor old
Highland woman's house, and asked for a

night's lodging. 'Who are you?' said she. 'I am a stranger, and a traveller,' said the King. 'All strangers and travellers are welcome here,' said she, 'for the sake of one.' 'And who is that one?' asked the king. 'Our good King Robert the Bruce,' said she, 'whom, though he is hunted by hounds and horns, I acknowledge to be the rightful king of all Scotland.' She could not enthrone Him except in her heart, but she would if she could; and in his rejection she acknowledged him as her rightful king.

—Indian Christian

(1 Chron. 12. 31; John 18. 36, 37; Heb. 2. 9; 1 Pet. 3. 15)

625. King—Voice of the. One of the great and good Tsars of Russia frequently visited the cities and towns of his kingdom incognito to see how his subjects fared. On one occasion, dressed in a peasant's garb, he knocked at the door of an inn. The innkeeper, who answered the door, listened to the 'peasant's' request for a night's accommodation, and was about to dismiss him with the words, 'There are many of the king's nobles in this inn tonight, and there is no room for a peasant here. You must seek a lodging elsewhere,' when one of the knights, having heard the voice and recognised the accent of his liege lord, rushed to the door and, bidding the king enter, said, 'The dress may be that of a peasant, but the voice is the voice of my lord, the King.'

(Jer. 14. 8; Luke 2. 7; Matt. 2. 2; 1 Pet. 3. 15)

626. King—and the King of kings. One Saturday King George V and Queen Mary were out in the country with Lord Stamfordham, and came to a humble little cottage. Desiring to sit down and rest for a few minutes, the Queen asked if she might enter. The good woman who answered the door ran inside and cried, 'O William, here's the king and queen. Whatever shall we do?' 'Let 'em come in, of course,' said William.

When the royal visitors were seated in the spotless little parlour, they noticed a family Bible in a prominent position. 'I am glad to see you have got the good Book,' said the king. 'Ay, your Majesties,' said William, 'would you like to hear about my conversion?' 'Of course I should,' said the king. The story was told with enthusiasm.

The queen, with tears in her eyes, turned to the good wife. 'And have you had an experience like that?' Yes! she had, and she too told how she was saved. When they rose to go, the king and queen, much affected by the incident, thanked them and said simply, 'We love Him too, you know.'

(Ps. 72. 11; Phil. 2. 10)

627. Kingdom—Christ's.

The kingdoms of the earth go by
In purple and in gold;
They rise, they flourish and they die,
And all their tale is told.

One kingdom only is Divine,
One banner triumphs still:
Its king a servant, and its throne
A Cross upon a hill.

(Isa. 32. 1; Dan. 2. 37-39; John 19. 2, 3; Rev. 19. 16)

628. Kingdom—Christ's. Peter McKenzie, the famous Methodist preacher, was being shown over Madame Tussaud's Waxworks in London. Coming to one object, his guide said, 'This is the chair in which Voltaire sat and wrote his atheistic blasphemies.'

'Is that the chair?' asked Peter; and then, without seeking permission, he stepped over the cord, sat down on the chair, and sang as only a real believer could:

Jesus shall reign where'er the sun
Doth His successive journeys run;
His kingdom stretch from shore to shore
Till moons shall wax and wane no more.

Which would you rather have—McKenzie's faith or Voltaire's atheism?

—Selected

(Ps. 72. 8; 1 Cor. 15. 25)

629. Kingdom—Christ's. In Damascus a temple was built centuries ago. When Christianity spread, this was used as a place for Christian worship and an inscription put on the arch: 'Thy kingdom O Christ, is an everlasting kingdom, and Thy dominion endureth throughout all generations.'

Mohammedans took possession and made it a mosque. The inscription remained. The mosque has been burnt several times, but the inscription still remains. 'He must reign.'

(Luke 1. 33; Rev. 22. 5)

630. Kinsman—Christ our. Jesus Christ is the Condescension of Divinity and the Exaltation of Humanity. He, the Son of God, became the Son of Man that sons of men might become sons of God. We see Him in His manhood bearing grief for us, bearing grief with us, and bearing grief like us.

(Heb. 2. 14; 2. 17, 18; 4. 15)

631. Kinsman—Christ our.

And didst thou love the race that loved not Thee?
And didst Thou take to Heaven a human brow?
Dost plead with Man's voice by the marvellous sea?
Art Thou a Kinsman now?

O God, O kinsman loved, but not enough,
O Man, with eyes majestic after death,
Whose feet have toiled along our pathways rough,
Whose lips draw human breath!

By that one likeness which is ours and Thine,
By that one nature which doth hold us kin,
By that high Heav'n where, sinless, Thou dost shine
To draw us sinners in.

By Thy last silence in the Judgement-Hall,
By long foreknowledge of the deadly tree,
By darkness, by the wormwood and the gall,
I pray Thee, visit me.—

Come, lest this heart should, cold and cast away,
Die ere the Guest adored she entertain,—
Lest eyes which never saw Thine earthly day
Should miss Thy heavenly reign

—F. W. Faber

(Heb. 2. 11-15; 1 John 4. 2)

632. Kiss—Told in a Cross. The lines which follow were suggested by the story of an aged African woman who, on hearing of God's love in the gift of His only Son, rather disturbed the meeting by continually protesting, 'That's not love! that's not love!' And, when pressed for her meaning, she explained that the word 'love' was not strong enough to express what was involved in the gift of an only Son.

A father one day to his own little son
A letter of love had penned;
He could scarcely read, so young he was,
So, just at the very end,
'To show him my love,' the father said,
'I will close it with a kiss;
That simple sign he will surely know:'
And he made a sign like this—X.
Yes, right at the end, where he signed his name,
He added a simple cross,
And the letter was sent,
And he knew what it meant,
The kiss that was told in a Cross.

And God wrote a letter, a wonderful Book;
He wrote it o'er earth and sky;
A book that the humble in heart could read,
When lifting their hands on high,
And, looking at stars so far away,
And looking at flowers so near,
They noted the care-free birds' sweet song:
In them God's care they did hear.
Yes, over it all He signed His name
On sea, on earth, on sky,
And the letter was sent,
And they knew what it meant
Who lifted their heads on high.

And then, when the course of time had run,
A letter of love was sent.
It was writ so plain that all might read
And know what the sender meant.
For there, at the end, where all might see—
A sign that they could not miss—
He placed in the language of childhood's day
The sign of a child's pure kiss.
But why, if it told us of God's great love,
Oh! why was there only one?
My eyes fill with tears—I sob as I see
'Twas the Cross of His only Son.
And the letter was sent;
Do you know what it meant—
God's love in the Cross of His Son?

—F. Howard Oakley

(John 3. 16; Rom. 5. 8)

633. Kneeling. In the centre of the great Cathedral of Copenhagen is Thorwaldsen's figure of 'Christ'. Dr. Stanley Jones of India once entered the Cathedral, and describes his experience in the following words: 'As I walked along, a Danish friend drew nearer to me and whispered, "You will not be able to see His face unless you kneel at His feet".' In Mark's Gospel there are three mentions of Kneeling at the feet of the Lord Jesus Christ:

1. Mark 1. 40—A Leper, asking for Cleansing from his disease.
2. Mark 10. 17—A rich young ruler, asking how to inherit eternal life.
3. Mark 15. 19—The Roman soldiers, kneeling in mockery before the Lord Jesus.

(1 Kings 8. 54; Dan. 6. 10; Acts 21. 5)

634. Knowledge. There is an Arabic proverb which says:

He that knows not and knows not that he knows not is a fool: shun him.
He that knows not and knows that he knows not is a child: teach him.
He that knows and knows not that he knows is asleep: wake him.
He that knows and knows that he knows is a wise man: follow him.

(Job 19. 25; 2 Tim. 1. 12; 1 John 5. 15, 19, 20)

635. Knowledge—of God. One cold winter afternoon the philosopher Thomas Carlyle was sitting before the open fireplace in his library. The door opened and the new pastor of a local church entered the room. After Carlyle and the young minister had spoken for a few moments, the young minister asked the great philosopher, 'What do you think this parish needs most?' Carlyle, without hesitation, replied, 'What this parish needs is a man who knows God otherwise than by hearsay.'

David Hume said of John Brown of Scotland, 'That old man preaches as if Christ were at his elbow.' How much we need men of this kind today.

—Indian Christian

(Hos. 6. 6; 8. 2; Col. 1. 9, 10; 2 Pet. 1. 1-4; 2. 20; 3. 18)

636. Knowledge—of God.

Strong Son of God, immortal love,
Whom we, that have not seen Thy face,
By faith, and faith alone, embrace,
Believing where we cannot prove.

Thine are these orbs of light and shade;
Thou madest life in man and brute;
Thou madest death; and lo! Thy foot
Is on the skull which Thou hast made.

Thou seemest human and divine;
The highest, holiest manhood Thou;
Our wills are ours, we know not how;
Our wills are ours to make them Thine.

Our little systems have their day;
They have their day and cease to be:
They are but broken lights of Thee,
And Thou, O Lord, art more than they.

Let knowledge grow from more to more,
But more of reverence in us dwell;
That mind and soul, according well,
May make one music as before,
But vaster.

—Alfred, Lord Tennyson

(Dan. 11. 32; Col. 1. 10; 2 Pet. 3. 18)

637. Knowledge—of the Good Shepherd.
Some years ago a great actor was asked at a drawing-room function to recite for the pleasure of his fellow-guests. He consented and asked if there was anything they specially wanted to hear. After a minute's pause an old minister of the Gospel asked for Psalm 23. A strange look came over the actor's face; he paused for a moment, then said, 'I will, on one condition—that after I have recited it, you, my friend, will do the same.'

'I!' said the preacher, in surprise, 'I am not an elocutionist, but, if you wish it, I shall do so.'

Impressively the actor began the Psalm. His voice and intonation were perfect. He held his audience spellbound, and, as he finished, a great burst of applause broke from his guests. As it died away, the old man rose and began to declaim the same Psalm. His voice was not remarkable: his tone was not faultless; but, when he finished, there was not a dry eye in the room.

The actor rose and his voice quivered as he said, 'Ladies and gentlemen, I reached your eyes and ears: he has reached your hearts. The difference is just this: I know the Psalm but he knows the Shepherd.'

(Ps. 23. 1; 2 Tim. 1. 12)

638. Knowledge—of the Way of Salvation.
The knowledge of how to be saved is far better and more essential than the knowledge of sciences and philosophies. The Telugu people have a proverb that says, 'A washerman is better than a scholar': and everybody will admit that, in certain circumstances, this is true. Telugu school Primers used to contain a story that illustrates this.

On a wide river an old ferryman had been plying his boat for years, taking passengers across for a very modest sum. One day, the story goes, three learned Pandits came to cross, and entered his boat. The clouds were threatening overhead, and gusts of wind were rising, betokening a storm. However, the ferryman undertook to take the three scholars across. As they proceeded, one of them said to the old man, 'Do you know anything about astrology?' The ferryman replied, 'No, master, I have never been to school. I cannot read or write, and from childhood I have been doing this job, rowing great and learned men like you from one side of this great river to the other.' 'Alas!' said the Pandit, 'a good part of your life has been wasted.' The second pandit next addressed the old man and asked him if he had ever learnt the philosophy of their great religion. Again, the ferryman replied, 'I have just said that I have never been to school and have only been trained to do the work I am now doing.' 'Alas!' exclaimed the second pandit, 'half of your life has been lost.' The third scholar then asked him if he knew any of the Shastras—Psychology, Biology, etc.—and he was again replying, 'No! sir, I have never had the opportunity of studying them,' when a fierce gust of wind caught the little boat and a huge wave dashed over it. The boat capsized in the middle of the river, and all four were thrown into the water. As the ferryman was striking out for the shore after vainly struggling to retrieve his boat and oars, he saw the three pandits struggling in the water, and shouted to them 'Gentlemen, do you know anything about "Swimmology"?' Alas! they did not. 'Then,' he said, 'all your lives will be lost.'

(John 17. 3; Acts 4. 13)

639. Lamb of God. C. H. Spurgeon was to preach in the Crystal Palace, London, so he went, with a friend, to try the acoustics of the building the evening before the day for which the meeting was scheduled. He arranged that he should speak from the rostrum, and his friend should stand in one or two places near the rear of the building and listen—those were the days before loud-speakers had been invented. Mounting the rostrum, the great preacher shouted the words, 'Behold the Lamb of God that taketh away the sin of the world.' This was repeated several times so that its audibility could be tested in various parts of the Palace. Then they left, satisfied that Spurgeon's voice could be heard all over the vast building.

But they had not noticed that a workman was engaged in completing some repairs to the roof. He heard the text and went home later under deep conviction of sin. As a result of the plain quotation of the Word of God, the workman was saved.

(John 1. 29; 1 Pet. 1. 18, 19)

640. Laughter.

Laugh and the world laughs with you;
Weep and you weep alone;
This grand old earth must borrow its mirth,
It has troubles enough of its own.
Sing, and the hills will answer;
Sigh, it is lost on the air;
The echoes bound to a joyful sound
But shrink from voicing care.

Be glad, and your friends are many;
Be sad, and you lose them all;
There are none to decline your nectared wine,
But alone you must drink life's gall.
There is room in the halls of pleasure
For a long and lovely train,
But one by one we must all file in
Through the narrow aisles of pain.

Rejoice and men will seek you;
Grieve and they turn and go—
They want full measure of your pleasure,
But they do not want your woe.

—Ella Wheeler Wilcox

(Eccles. 3. 4; 7. 3; 10. 19; Luke 6. 21)

641. Laziness. A stranger, passing along a road and uncertain of his way, saw a shepherd lad lying by the roadside while the sheep were grazing contentedly in nearby pastures. Approaching the boy, the stranger asked the way. The boy, scarcely looking up, stretched out his arm nonchalantly and said, 'That way.' The stranger thanked him, but said, 'My laddie, if you can show me anything lazier than that, I'll give you a shilling.' Without looking up, the lad said, 'Put it in my pocket.' (Prov. 12. 27; 13. 4; 19. 24; 21. 25; 26. 14; Matt. 25. 26)

642. Leading—the Lord's. 'He leadeth me.'
'In pastures green?' Not always. Sometimes He
Who knoweth best in kindness leadeth me
In weary ways, where heavy shadows be;

Out of the sunshine, warm, and soft, and bright;
Out of the sunshine into darkest night.
I oft would faint with sorrow and affright.

Only for this: I know He holds my hand;
So, whether led in green or desert land,
I trust, although I may not understand.

And by 'still waters'? No, not always so.
Oftimes the heavy tempests round me blow,
And o'er my soul the waves and billows go.

But when the storm beats loudest, and I cry
Aloud for help, the Master standeth by,
And whispers to my soul, 'Lo, it is I.'

Above the tempest wild I hear Him say,
'Beyond this darkness lies the perfect day;
In every path of thine I lead the way.'

So whether on the hilltops high and fair
I dwell, or in the sunless valleys where
The shadows lie—what matters? He is there.

So where He leads me I can safely go;
And in the blest hereafter I shall know
Why, in His wisdom, He hath led me so.

(Ps. 23. 2; 78. 53; Isa. 42. 16; John 10. 3)

643. Leaning—on the Lord. A well-known missionary, Fidelia Fisk, was once instructing a class of heathen women. She was obliged, on account of the custom of the country, to occupy a sitting posture on the floor, without any support to her back, and, as she had just recovered from an illness, she became very tired. One of the women who was a believer noticed this, left the circle and sat down right behind her, placing her back to Miss Fisk's back, who acknowledged the kindness and timeliness of the act and leaned gently against the prop offered to her. 'No! No!' said the Christian woman, 'if you love me, lean hard.' (John 13. 23)

644. Leaning—on the Lord.
Child of my love, lean hard,
And let me feel the pressure of thy care.
I know thy burden, child, I shaped it,
Poised in my own hand, made no proportion
In its weight to thy unladed strength;
For soon as I laid it on, I said,
'I shall be near and when he leans on me,
This burden shall be mine, not his.'

So shall I keep my child within the circling arms
Of mine own love. Here lay it down, nor fear
To impose it on a shoulder which upholds
The government of worlds. Yet closer come:
Thou art not near enough: I would embrace thy
*   care,*
So I might feel my child reposing on my breast.
Thou lovest me! I know it! Doubt not then,
But, loving me lean hard.

(Ps. 55. 22; 1 Pet. 5. 7)

645. Leaves—Nothing but.
The Master came to the fig tree
And saw the foliage there
Of thick and shady branches,
To hungry eyes so fair;
But He found that it was barren
And bore no luscious fruit,
For life was gone, and very soon
'Twas withered to the root.

The Master came to the Temple
And saw the worship there,
The riches and the customs,
To Jewish eyes so fair;
But to Him 'twas all corruption,
His house a den of thieves,
And all its boasted glory
Was fruitless, only leaves,

The Master comes to our fireside
And sees the family there:
And one goes off to the pictures,
Another to Vanity Fair.
For, instead of family worship
And intercessory prayer
The saints are torn to pieces,
Their failings all laid bare.

The Master to the assembly
Has come! what sees He here?—
The busy round of service
And meetings held so dear.
But He sees the strife and divisions,
And His Holy Spirit grieves
To find that many efforts
Are fruitless, mostly leaves.

—Adapted

(Mark 11. 12-21)

646. Leaving—All with Jesus.
Leaving all with Jesus, heart and mind at rest;
For whate'er betideth, Jesus knoweth best;
Though no ray of sunshine o'er my path is shed,
Soon the mists will vanish and the night have fled.

Leaving all with Jesus, though I may not see
For the length'ning shadows that encompass me;
Darkness radiant seemeth, shadows disappear;
Joy effaces sorrow when my Lord is near.

Leaving all with Jesus, striving to be pure;
Strong in Him enduring, though the world allure;
Trusting, yet hard striving wrong thoughts to
subdue,
Through Him overcoming all that is not true.

Leaving all with Jesus, leaning on His might;
Prayerful, watchful, anxious to be led aright;
There's no time for sighing, resting on His Word;
All in all is Jesus, trusted and adored.

—E. Middleton

(Heb. 13. 5)

647. Lending—to the Lord.

Peter lent a boat to save Him from the press;
Martha lent a home, with busy kindliness.
One man lent a colt, another lent a room;
Some threw down their clothes, and Joseph lent
a tomb.
Simon lent his strength the cruel cross to bear;
Mary spices brought His body to prepare.
But nought have I to lend—no boat, no house, no
lands.
Dwell, Lord, in my heart and use these feeble
hands.

(1 Sam. 1. 28; Luke 5. 3; 10. 38; 19. 33, 34;
22. 11, 12; 23. 26; 24. 1)

648. Letter—writing.

If you with pen would talk to men,
Of five laws be aware:
With courtesy and courage write,
Let calm control, correctness cite,
And round it off with care.

(Philem. 1; 2 John 1, 2, 12; 3 John 1)

649. Liberty.

During the dark days of the struggle for liberty in Italy, most of the people looked upon Garibaldi as their great liberator. Prisoners, hurried away to loathesome dungeons, would be encouraged as they passed along the streets, by friends whispering in their ears, 'Courage! Garibaldi is coming.' Men would steal out at night and chalk on the walls and pavements, 'Garibaldi is coming!' And when the news of his approach to the city was announced, they would shout, 'Garibaldi is coming.' He came, and they regained their freedom, never to be enslaved again. But someone far greater than Garibaldi has come, the great Deliverer, bringing redemption and liberty to the slaves of sin and Satan.

(Rom. 7. 24, 25; 8. 2; Gal. 3. 13; Heb. 2. 14, 15)

650. Liberty—or Licence.

There are in London three sorts of dogs; there is the dog on a chain with a master who regularly pays his tax; this dog has law but no liberty; there is the stray dog for whom no tax is paid, who steals his meals where he can, and he has liberty but no law; and, lastly, there is the dog that has, and understands, the law of liberty.

In like manner these three classes are exemplified in the young life of this great metropolis. We have thousands of young men and women who, in their parents' country homes, are under strict law with little liberty. These come up to London, and find themselves at liberty with no law, and unless they join the third class who understand the law of liberty, their liberty soon degrades into licence, and they, like the dogs of which we have spoken, soon alas! reach their inglorious end.

Some years ago I had a collie called 'Jock', a thoroughbred; a beautiful dog, with large lustrous eyes, sent to me by a dear friend, and when he arrived in London, he was perfectly wild, for he had never seen a city. The first thing, therefore, that I had to do was to buy a strong collar and chain, and put him at once 'under law'. Within the four walls of the house he could not go far wrong, and whenever he went out he held up his neck to have the chain put on, which gave him no more than six feet of liberty. He would give a bound on the doorstep as if to go right away, but was at once pulled up by the chain, which alone prevented his liberty degenerating into licence.

There can be no doubt that law is a most valuable power for keeping both dogs and men clean and respectable; and indeed, as we shall see, it is essential up to a certain point. But one day my dog reached that point; he came to me in the hall as usual to have his chain put on, but I knew a great change had taken place in that dog's spirit. I said, 'No chain today, Jock, you can go where you like.' I opened the door and for the first time he was apparently free. I say apparently, because he was not really free, although he had no chain. He bounded away and vanished round the corner, but in a moment or two back he came, and without my saying a word trotted quietly by me.

What was the invisible chain that brought him back without fail? It was the simple fact that the dog had given me his heart from which he could not run away. There is nothing on earth like the heart of a dog for faithfulness and unflinching loyalty, quite irrespective of the worthiness of the master. Once it has given its heart it cannot take it back; and the only language it knows and expresses in its beautiful eyes are the words of Ruth: 'Where thou goest I will go, where thou lodgest I will lodge.' This, then is the law of liberty, for the law of liberty is the law of love.

—Dr. A. T. Schofield

(Prov. 23. 26; Rom. 6. 14; Gal. 5. 13; James 2. 12; 1 Pet. 2. 16)

651. Life—Attitudes to.

'I hate life, yet I hate to die,' said Voltaire.
'For me to live is Christ: to die is gain,' said the Apostle Paul.

Only one life, 'twill soon be past;
Only what's done for Christ will last.

(Phil. 1. 21; Col. 3. 24; 1 Tim. 4. 8; 6. 12)

652. Life—Brevity of.

Tomorrow and tomorrow and tomorrow
Creeps on this petty pace from day to day
To the last syllable of recorded time,
Till all our yesterday's have lighted fools
The way to dusty death. Out! Out! brief candle!
Life's but a walking shadow, a poor player
That struts and frets his hour upon the stage
And then is heard no more. It is a tale,
Told by an idiot, full of sound and fury,
Signifying nothing.

—Shakespeare in *Macbeth*

(Job. 14. 1; Ps. 103. 15, 16; James 4. 14)

653. Life—The Christian.

Out of the running of things down here,
Out of success and the glow of its sphere,
Out of the plans to push people on,
In a scene of today that tomorrow is gone.

Out of it all as time passes o'er,
Feel we our path to be more and still more.
Earth has its fav'rites, the world has its own;
On plods the pilgrim unwanted and lone.

Out of it all, yet rejoicing in hope,
Helpless so often, yet ever held up,
Strengthened in spirit by succour divine—
Blest compensation! How can we repine?

Life that is better than earth can afford,
Life where we happily rest in the Lord,
Christ as its centre, and Christ as its sun,
Life of all lives, with what joy we speed on!

(Col. 3. 1-4)

654. Life—the Christian.

Life is too brief
Between the budding and the falling leaf,
Between the seedtime and the golden sheaf,
For hate and spite.
We have no time for malice and for greed;
Therefore, with love make beautiful the deed;
Fast speeds the night.

Life is too swift
Between the blossom and the white snow's drift,
Between the silence and the lark's uplift,
For bitter words.
In kindness and in gentleness our speech
Must carry messages of hope, and reach
The sweeter chords.

Life is too great
Between the infant's and the man's estate.
Between the clashing of earth's strife and fate,
For petty things.
Lo! we shall yet who creep with cumbered feet,
Walk glorious over heaven's golden street,
Or soar on wings. —Margaret E. Sangster

(Rom. 6. 4; 2 Cor. 5. 14-17; Gal. 2. 20)

655. Life—Elixir of.
During the reign of Queen Elizabeth I, known as 'Good Queen Bess', a certain Dr. Dee, a magician, undertook to provide the queen with an elixir of life that would guarantee perpetual youth and ever-lasting life. He had also a scheme for trans-muting base metals into gold and bringing enormous wealth to the realm. There was also a Dutchman named Cornelius Lanoy who had his laboratory at Somerset House, and did research work there to try to find the 'Elixir of Life'.

(John 3. 16; 11. 25, 26)

656. Life—Eternal.

This world's a city with many a crowded street:
Death is the market place where all men meet.
If life were merchandise that gold could buy,
The rich would live, the poor alone would die.

(John 5. 39, 40)

657. Life—Eternal.
The following incident was told concerning the ministry of Lord Adalbert Cecil, so greatly used of God in Canada and elsewhere.

It was evening and 'the Chief' had paid an unusually late visit to the ward. He had just quitted it, accompanied by the House Surgeon and the 'Sister', when, pausing a moment at the open door of the sitting-room, he said to her, 'It is a pity, Sister, about that splendid young fellow at the top of the ward. We have done our very best for him, but he will be dead before morning.'

Startled out of her usual calm, the Sister answered, 'Oh! Is that possible, Doctor? But you told him he was doing fine, and he is expecting to live.'

'Well, he has put up a grand fight for life, and there was no use in depressing him. He will probably be unconscious in a few hours and never know he is dying.' With these words the great Surgeon moved on.

The Sister stood for a moment, hesitating. Then she said to the House Surgeon, 'Will you not tell him, Doctor? His friends are all far away in the north, and there has been no time for anyone to come down, and he may have something to settle, or some last message to send. It is hard for them that he should not know. Do tell him.'

'No, no, I will not tell him. It is easier for him not to know,' said the House Surgeon. Then, as he also passed on, he looked back and said, 'You can tell him if you like.'

The night Nurse was already at her post, and the lights had been turned down in the ward when the Sister took her seat by the side of the one who was dying.

'This is kind of you to come and pay me another visit, Sister,' he said. 'You heard what the doctor said—"I am doing fine". Does he think it will be long before I can be moved?'

'You will write to my mother, won't you, and make the best of it to her?'

The Sister was silent a moment or two. Then she said gently, 'I am afraid the doctor made you think what is not true. Andrew, You are very gravely hurt. There is more danger than was thought of at first.'

It was Andrew's turn to be silent for a full minute; then, as a look of fear and dismay came into his eyes, he said, 'You do not mean I am dying, Sister.' Again there was a pause. It was night, all was quiet, there was nothing to distract and to take off the solemnity of knowing he had God and Eternity to face. Presently, with quivering lips, he asked, 'How long, Sister?'

She dare not hide from him the stern truth. And then came a long, despairing cry, 'But I can't die, Sister. I can't die. I am not ready to die.' And then the momentous question was eagerly asked, 'What must I do to be saved?' She had said to the doctor, 'He might have something to settle,' but she had thought of earthly things, the things of time. He had indeed something to settle, and it meant for all eternity, but all she could say was, 'I don't know, Andrew; I am not saved.' Then a pleading voice, now very low, said, 'Won't you pray for me? Do pray.' And the sad answer came, 'I can't. I don't know how to pray.'

At last surely a Spirit-given thought came to her, as she said, 'I will tell you what I can do, Andrew, if it will be of any comfort to you; I will sit up with you tonight and read the Bible to you.' Andrew caught at the suggestion as a drowning man might catch at a rope thrown to him, and said, 'Oh! do, do.'

She took up a Bible that was lying quite near. She hardly knew where to begin, but the Bible fell open at the Gospel of St. John, and she read in a low, clear voice of one who came to the Lord Jesus by night and got his questions answered. She read of the need of man, and of God's love and His promise to meet that need. She read slowly, distinctly, and he listened eagerly, trying to grasp something to answer the now all-absorbing anxiety of his soul.

Pausing a moment, she read on of the woman who got her thirst quenched, and her heart satisfied. Still there was no word from the suffering man, and a grey look was stealing over his face, and yet his eyes besought her to go on. Finally she came to John 5. 24, 'Verily, verily, I say unto you, he that heareth My Word and believeth on Him that sent Me, hath everlasting life, and shall not come into condemnation but is passed from death unto life.' She looked up as she finished reading it, and saw a change in his face: the haggard look of agony—the struggling to grasp something that was unattainable—was fast disappearing as he said, 'Stop there, Sister, Light is coming in. I see—I see!' Very weak was the voice as he said, 'Leave me alone, Sister, but come back soon. Thank you, oh, thank you.'

She left him for half-an-hour—alone with God. When she returned his face was radiant. 'I have heard His Word—I believe the Lord Jesus Christ bore my sins when He was lifted up, and He has received me—just as I was—all guilty, all unprepared. It is not death for me, Sister, it is Everlasting Life—He has given it to me. I have passed from death unto life.'

After a minute or two's rest he spoke again: 'Sister, promise me you will meet me in Heaven. You can never say again that you do not know the way. Promise me.'

'I promise, Andrew,' she said, 'not to rest until I know, but I cannot grasp it as you have. It is not clear to me.'

'Thank God it is settled and you have been

the means. Thank you—thank you. Tell my mother Christ saved me at the eleventh hour. Peace! Peace!' These were his last conscious words. Very soon, as the Surgeon had said, he sank into profound unconsciousness, only to awaken 'with Christ', with the Good Shepherd Who had sought and found His lost sheep.

And what of the Sister? The arrow of conviction had entered her breast. Four dreary years, a ray of hope coming sometimes, to be quickly followed by darkness and despair. She accepted an invitation to hear Lord A. P. Cecil preach. She waited behind afterwards while prayer was going on. Lord Adalbert asked her into a side room, trusting to be given the right message for this troubled soul. At first nothing seemed to touch her. Finally, he turned to John 5. 24. Suddenly the light broke in, and like Andrew, she, too, said, 'I see! I see!' She went away a new creature to praise and thank God that for her also, all was settled.

—Arthur Mercer (slightly abridged)
(John 5. 24, 25)

658. **Life—for a Look.** An obscure man preached one Sunday to a few persons in a Methodist Chapel in the South of England one snowy day. Among them was a lad of fifteen years, driven in by the snowstorm. 'Look unto Me and be ye saved' was the text.

'Young man!' he said, 'you look miserable. Only look!' The young man looked and was saved, and received eternal life. He was Charles Haddon Spurgeon.

(Isa. 45. 22; Num. 21. 8, 9; John 3. 14, 15)

659. **Life—Peaceful and Pure.**
There's a Man in the Glory
Whose life is for me.
He's pure and He's holy,
Triumphant and free;

He's wise and He's loving—
Tender is He,
And His Life in the Glory
My Life may be.

There's a Man in the Glory
Whose Life is for me.
His peace is abiding;
Patient is He.

He's joyful and radiant,
Expecting to see
His Life in the Glory
Lived out in me.

(Gal. 2. 20; Col. 3. 3, 4)

660. **Life—Present and Eternal.**
So this is life, the world with all its pleasures,
Struggles and tears, a smile, a frown, a sigh,
Friendship so true, and love of kin and neighbour?
Sometimes 'tis hard to live—always, to die!
The world moves on, so rapidly the living
The forms of those who disappear replace,
And each one dreams that he will be enduring—
How soon that one becomes the missing face

In life or death—and life is surely flying,
The crib and coffin carved from the self-same tree
In life or death—and death so soon is coming—
Escape I cannot, there's no place to flee—
But Thou, O God, hast life that is eternal;
That life is mine, a gift through Thy dear Son.
Help me to feel its flush and pulse eternal,
Assurance of the morn when life is done.

Help me to know the value of these hours,
Help me the folly of all waste to see;
Help me to trust the Christ who bore my sorrows,
And this to yield for life or death to Thee.
In all my days be glorified, Lord Jesus,
In all my ways guide me with Thine own eye;
Just when and, as Thou wilt, use me, Lord Jesus,
And then for me 'tis Christ, to live or die.
                                    —Will H. Houghton
(Phil. 1. 21; 1 Tim. 4. 8)

661.   Life—Present and Future.
The tissues of the life to be
    We weave with colours all our own,
And on the fields of destiny
    We reap what we have sown.
Still shall the soul around it call
    The shadows gathered here,
And painted on the eternal wall,
    The past shall reappear.

(1 Tim. 4. 8)

662.   Life—in this World.
So he died for his faith. That is fine—
    More than most of us do.
But stay! Can you add to that line
    That he lived for it, too?

It is easy to die. Men have died
    For a wish or a whim—
—From bravado or passion or pride.
    Was it harder for him?

But to live, every day to live out
    All the truth that he dreamt,
While his friends met his conduct with doubt,
    And the world, with contempt.

Was it thus that he plodded ahead,
    Never turning aside?
Then we'll talk of the life that he led—
    Never mind how he died.

(Phil. 1. 21; Gal. 2. 20)   —Ernest Crosby

663.   Light. Samuel Hebich was a missionary
whose labours were greatly blessed in India.
Realizing the great need of the 'white heathen',
as he termed them, he spent much time
visiting the garrisons, and many British officers
and soldiers were led to the Lord through his
ministry.

After a few sultry days in Madras, one day
an officer, during the hottest hours, was lying
in his room lazily smoking a cigarette,
dreamingly listening to the slow creaking of
the punkah above his head. A step sounded
on the verandah and grew more and more
distinct as the owner drew near with an even
firm tread. Then in walked Mr. Hebich, a tall,
strange-looking man, with a long, loose black
coat and a huge umbrella.

The officer felt embarrassed, even in his own
rooms, but Mr. Hebich, who seemed quite at
home, advanced into the room, saying, 'Goot
day!' and politely motioned the officer to a
seat. After a short silence he said, 'Get down
de Book.' His hearer knew at once which
Book was meant, and fetched the Bible which
he never read himself, though he possessed a
copy. 'Open de fierst chapter of Shenesis and
read,' said Hebich. The officer obeyed and
read: 'In the beginning God created the heaven
and the earth. And the earth was without
form and void; and darkness was upon the
face of the deep.' 'Dat will do! Shut de Book.
Let us pray!' said Hebich. So they knelt down
and Hebich prayed. After this, his strange
visitor bowed and said farewell, shaking hands
very solemnly before leaving.

The following day the officer was lounging
in his large arm-chair, unoccupied as on the
previous day, but feeling a turmoil within.
Once again there was a sound of footsteps and
Hebich appeared. Again—'Get down the
Book'; and again 'Open de fierst chapter de
book of Shenesis and read.' Again the officer
read, and continued on with 'And the Spirit of
God moved upon the face of the waters.'
'Dat vill do,' said Hebich. 'Let us pray.'
This time the officer listened to the prayer—
such a prayer as he had never heard before—
Hebich talked as to an intimate friend, telling
God his Father about the young officer, and
imploring Him to reveal to him his need that
he might find salvation and flee to the open
arms of the Redeemer. Again he took leave as
on the previous day.

If ever a man was humbled, convinced that
he was a sinner, and realised his need of a
Saviour, that officer did. How he spent the
time till the next day he did not know. The
next day at the same hour he heard the footsteps again. His Bible lay open before him.
He rose to meet Hebich and took his hand.
'Oh, Mr. Hebich,' he said, 'it is all plain to me
now. What must I do?'

Looking at him with true love, Hebich said,
'And God said, let there be light, and there was
light.' 'Believe on the Lord Jesus Christ and
thou shalt be saved.' They knelt together, the
light shone into the officer's heart, and he
prayed from the heart, without a book, for the
first time in his life.

The British officer who was thus saved in
Madras was the grandfather of Lieut.-General
Sir William Dobbie, whom we honour today
as a great general and the valiant defender of
Malta during the second World War. Captain
G. S. Dobbie, of the Africa Evangelistic Band,
another grandson, was also engaged wholly in
the work of the Lord.
(Gen. 1. 1-3; Ps. 119. 130)

664.   Light.
The restless millions wait the Light
Whose dawning maketh all things new.
Christ also waits, but men are slow and few.
Have we done all we could? Have I? Have you?
(2 Cor. 4. 3-6)

665. Light. At the 1938 Empire Exhibition held in Bellahouston Park, Glasgow, Scotland, many groups of Christian assemblies combined to make the Gospel known to the large numbers of visitors to the Exhibition. One of the spheres of witness was a Kiosk in Royal Mile Avenue where Bibles, New Testaments and portions of Scripture were displayed for sale, and many were sold. Millions of tracts were also distributed free, and not a few visited the evangelist in charge for conversations on spiritual matters. Numbers thus came into the light of the knowledge of the glory of God in the face of Jesus Christ.

In the large window of the kiosk was an open Bible, open at John, Chapter 8, with the words of the Lord Jesus, 'I am the Light of the World', underlined in red ink, and a hand pointing to the verse. Underneath were printed the words: 'The only Way out of the Dark.'

The whole world was lost in the darkness of sin: The light of the world is Jesus.

(John 8. 12; 9. 5; 2 Cor. 4. 6)

666. Light.—'The Light of the World' is the title of a famous picture by Holman Hunt, the artist. It portrays the Lord Jesus Christ, thorn-crowned, and carrying a lantern in his left hand, knocking at a closed-door.

It is said that the artist, after completing the picture, showed it to some friends who praised the merit of the painting. One of them pointed out what he considered an omission on the part of the artist. 'You have put no handle on the door,' he said to Holman Hunt, who replied immediately, 'You forget—the handle is on the inside.'

(John 1. 9; Rev. 3. 20)

667. Light.

A tender child of summers three,
Seeking her little bed at night,
Paused on the dark stair timidly,
'Oh Mother! take my hand,' said she,
'And then the dark will all be light.'

We older children grope our way,
From dark behind to dark before:
And only when our hands we lay,
Dear Lord, in Thine, the night is day,
And there is darkness nevermore.

Reach downward to the sunless days,
Wherein our guides are blind as we,
And faith is small and hope delays:
Take Thou the hands of prayer we raise,
And let us feel the light of Thee.

—John Greenleaf Whittier

(Eph. 5. 8)

668. Light. Dr. F. B. Meyer told how at one time in his life, ministering in Regent's Park Chapel in London, having a very dead and difficult time, with dwindling congregations and nobody listening, he became so discouraged. 'But,' he said, 'every time I stood up to speak something came between me and God, and I knew it was wrong, and I knew it was sin. The Lord had everything else in my life, but I thought that I could keep this to myself and enjoy it, and indulge it. But one Sunday,' said Dr. Meyer, 'after coming back from church, I thought about how it had been a miserable day; I had been so dead and useless and fruitless, so lacking in Holy Spirit anointing, and I went into my study and knelt at my desk, and said, "Lord, You've had every key into every part of my life except one. I can't fight this battle any more". And when Dr. Meyer told that story he said, 'The Lord never took that key: He took the door off, and in place of the door He put a window, and ever since that day the light of the knowledge of the glory of God has shone into my heart in the face of Jesus Christ.'

—Alan Redpath

(2 Cor. 4. 6)

669. Light. I was coming up to London from Cambridge one morning and a country minister was sitting opposite me. I said to him, 'Were you preaching yesterday?' He said, 'Yes, I was.' I said, 'Did you preach a good sermon?' He replied, 'That is not for me to say.' I said, 'You tell me your sermon and I will say.'

'Well!' he replied, 'I was preaching on "The Lord is my light", and I pointed out to my people that light is invisible and that God is invisible, that we only know of the existence of light by the manifestation of it through the mists and in the dust of the atmosphere. It is only thus that we realise that light exists. And then I told them how we should not know God except that He shone in the person of our Lord Jesus Christ. "He that hath seen me hath seen the Father".' I said to him, 'Top marks!'

'The Lord is my Light and my Salvation.'

—Bishop Taylor Smith

(Ps. 27. 1; John 1. 4, 5; 2 Cor. 4. 6)

670. Light. Once I saw a huge stone being removed from the place where it had been fixed. All sorts of tiny creatures had lived under that stone. They had always lived in the darkness, and when the light of the sun struck them on the stone being removed, they began to run with great fear in all directions. They could not live in the light. When the stone was replaced in its former position you should have seen the hurry and bustle of those creatures to get back to where they had been. It was with great relief that they hurried back to be under the stone.

—Sadhu Sundar Singh

(John 3. 19, 20; 2 Cor. 4. 3-6)

671. Likeness. C. H. Spurgeon received one day a copy of Andrew Bonar's Commentary on Leviticus. It so blessed him that he returned it, saying, 'Dr. Bonar, please place herein your autograph and your photograph.' The book was returned to him with the following note from Dr. Bonar:

'Dear Spurgeon, here is the book with my

autograph and with my photograph. If you had been willing to wait a short season, you could have had a better likeness, for I shall be like Him; I shall see Him as He is.'

(Ps. 17. 15; 1 John 3. 2)

672. Likeness. Gipsy Rodney Smith, preaching at Dallas, Texas, had a petition from coloured ministers asking for a meeting exclusively for negroes. They came in thousands. There was a good deal of punctuating of his address with 'Hallelujahs' and 'Amens'.

Suddenly an aged coloured woman called out, 'Gipsy Smith, may I ask a question? Looking at her, he said, 'Certainly, my sister, what is it?' 'What colour are we going to be when we get to Heaven? Shall be white or black?' Everybody was waiting breathlessly for the answer. 'My dear sister, we are going to be just like Christ,' replied Gipsy Smith. And 'Amen' rang out all over the hall.

(Rom. 8. 29; Phil. 3. 20, 21; 1 John 3. 2)

673. Lilies.

The God of heaven has decked this earth
With lilies wondrous fair,
Placed here, as gems of beauteous worth,
The objects of His care.
Their great Creator knows their needs:
No toil or care they know.
In Providence He clothes and feeds
The lilies, and they grow.
Great Solomon, earth's richest king,
Most gorgeously displayed
In all the glories wealth could bring,
Was never so arrayed.
The lily's clothed: the raven's fed;
He marks the sparrow's fall.
Be sun or cloud above your head,
'Your Father knoweth' all.

—A.N.

(Song of Songs 2. 2; Matt. 6. 28-30)

674. Lips. When about, like Moses, to speak inadvisedly with our lips, we do well to remember the following rhyme:

If you your lips would keep from slips,
Five things observe with care—
Of whom you speak, to whom you speak,
And how, and when, and where.

(Job 2. 10; Ps. 106. 33; Prov. 14. 3; 1 Pet. 3. 10)

675. Listening well. A story is told about the great Paderewski, who, after a concert in a mid-western town, was found behind the stage, silent, preoccupied. Someone asked him what was the matter. Was he ill? 'No! No!' he answered, 'but some friends of mine were missing—the greyhaired couple fourth row back. They were not in their usual seats.' Then he explained, 'I didn't know them well. I never spoke to them, but I liked the way they listened and I always played for them.' Many a preacher has been encouraged in giving his message by seeing regular attenders whom he may not know well, listening attentively.'

(Luke 8. 18)

676. Little Things. To illustrate to his students the power of little things, Professor Tait had a heavy iron joist suspended from the roof of the laboratory by a strong cord, and then began to throw small paper pellets at it, striking it square each time. At first there was no perceptible movement of the joist, but after a continuous barrage of paper pellets, the iron joist commenced to sway from side to side and swing like a pendulum.

(1 Kings 13. 20-22)

677. Little Things. A holy life is made up of a multitude of little things. It is the little things of the hour, and not the great things of the age, that fill up a life like that of Paul and John, of Rutherford, or Brainerd, or Martyn. Little words, not eloquent speeches, little deeds, not miracles or battles, not one heroic effort or martyrdom—these make the true Christian life. The little constant sunbeam, not the lightning; the waters of Siloah 'that go softly' in their meek mission of refreshment, not the waters 'of the rivers great and many' rushing down in torrent noise and force; are the true symbols of a holy life. The avoidance of the little evils, the little sins, little inconsistencies, little weaknesses, little follies . . . the avoidance of such little things as these goes far to make up at least the negative beauty of a holy life.

—Dr. Horatius Bonar

(Song of Songs 2. 15)

678. Living Water. 'The Samaritan woman in John 4 left her waterpot and went away with the Well.'

'The woman, forgetful of her errand, and only conscious of that new wellspring of life that had risen within her, left the unfilled waterpot by the well and hurried into the city.'

—Edersheim

Jesus gave her water that was not in the well:
She went away singing,
And came back bringing
Others for the water that was not in the well.

(John 4. 13-15; 28, 29)

679. Locusts. In April, 1932, the first colony of locusts to be established in the British Isles was living in the Natural History Museum, South Kensington, London, in a glass case, with desert and tropical grasses, and lit by a powerful electric lamp to represent the African sun. London thus became the international centre for war against locusts whose invasion of Asia and Africa could cause millions of pounds' damage annually.

(Joel 1. 4; 2. 3-5)

680. Look up!

To all who are sick and weary
  Who feel you must 'lie up',
My word to you is lie on your back,
  For then you must 'look up'.

You could of course lie on your face
  Looking at dull, grey ground,
Or lie on your side, whichever you like,
  Looking at things around.

But it's better far to lie on your back,
  Relax and be quite still;
For as you lie down you must 'look up'
  And so fulfil His will.

—F. H. Oakley

(Ps. 4. 4; 5. 3; Luke 21. 28)

681. Lord—Himself.

Not an angel from the glory, flying swift on
    joyous wing;
Not an envoy sent expressly, with a message
    from the king;
But Himself Whom angels worship; but Himself,
    the very Word;
All Divine, intensely human; sympathizing, risen
    Lord.
Not with trumpets, not with heralds, driving
    back in tones severe;
But with gracious held-out sceptre, and the smile
    that draws thee near—
Coming slowly, gentle, lowly, He to Whom all
    power is given,
Strong to save thee, wise to guide thee, pledged
    to bring thee safe to Heaven;
Coming nearer than thy nearest, those who
    would, but cannot, aid,
Proving truer than thy dearest, those who
    watched with thee and prayed.
Love itself, unfathomed, deathless; love which
    ne'er misunderstands,
Love untiring, love desiring, stretching forth
    beseeching hands.
Not thy merits, not thy virtues, not the record of
    thy deeds,
But His joy in utter giving, and His knowledge
    of thy needs,
By His blood-signed deed of purchase, by His
    right to claim and bless,
Right to beautify and clothe thee in His own pure
    righteousness.
His the stripping, His the bruising, His the
    piercéd hands and feet;
Thine the healing, thine the life-stream, Heaven's
    river full and sweet.
No more doubtings, no more distance, no more
    room for sinful fear—
He Himself is thine for ever, always able, always
    near.

—K. Staines

(Luke 24. 15)

682. Lord—Himself.

Canaan's vineyard rich was planted
  By the God of Heaven's own hand:
Blessings great, divinely granted,
  Centred in the promised land.

Luscious fruits beyond appraising
  God's beneficence declared;
But, in place of fruitful praising,
  Barren murmurings were heard.

Murm'ring sons of Israel's children
  Treasured hatred greater still:
Placed, as stewards in God's garden
  By th' Almighty's sovereign will,
Prophets, messengers from Heaven
They entreated as they willed:
All were from the vineyard driven—
  Some they stoned and some they killed.

Matchless grace! amazing story—
  'I will send Mine only Son,'
And the Lord Himself His glory
  Veiled, and came, the lowly One,
And Creation donned her mourning,
  Filled with wonderment to see
Man his mighty Maker spurning,
  Slaying Him upon a tree.

Gaze thereon, my soul, and ponder
  O'er thy ruin there exprest,
And confess, in grateful wonder,
  By His dying thou art blest.
Wondrous love!—all thought transcending—
  He Himself for me has given,
On this truth all else depending—
  'Twas the Lord Himself from Heaven.

All the hosts of hell defeated,
  Victor over death's domain,
Midst us at His table seated
  Stands the Lord Himself again.
Let us round His table gather,
  Hear His words—'Remember Me!'
View His Cross, adore the Father,
  As the Lord Himself we see.

That same Jesus Who, ascending,
  Passed through Heaven's portals wide,
Soon will come, from Heaven descending,
  To receive His blood-bought bride.
Yes! Himself, and not another,
  We shall see His form most fair,
And, His own caught up together,
  We shall meet Him in the air.

But while here, by foes surrounded,
  Think that He Himself was tried:
He has all our foes confounded;
  He Himself is by our side.
As our Shepherd, forth He leads us,
  Our High Priest, for us He pleads,
For the conflict fits and feeds us,
  And Himself, our Captain, leads.

—A.N.

(Matt. 21. 37; Luke 24. 15; John 21. 7; 1 Cor.
11. 26; 1 Thess. 4. 16)

683. Lordship—of Christ.

'God first! My interests must always come
    second to His, never first.'
'Seek ye first the kingdom of God.'

Dr. Graham Scroggie was one time speaking
along these lines, and at the close of the service
he was approached by a young woman a
professing Christian, who had been greatly
stirred.

'And why don't you yield?' inquired Dr. Scroggie.

'I'm afraid I should have to do two things if I did,' responded the girl.

'What are they?' asked Dr. Scroggie.

'I play the piano in a concert hall, and I fear I would have to give it up,' she replied.

'And the other?'

'I am afraid God would send me to China as a missionary.'

Opening his Bible at Acts 10. 14, Dr. Scroggie explained to the young woman the absurdity of Peter's answer. A slave never dictates. And to say, 'Not so,' and then use the word 'Lord' was impossible.

'Now,' said Dr. Scroggie, 'I want you to cross out the two words, "Not so" and leave the word "Lord"; or else cross out "Lord" and leave "Not so".'

Handing her his pencil he quietly walked away. For two hours she struggled. Then he returned. Looking over her shoulder, he saw a tear-stained page, but the words 'Not so' were crossed out. With a glad light in her eyes she left and went home, repeating over the one word, 'Lord'. No longer would she dictate. She was now His disciple and He her Lord and Master.

—Oswald J. Smith

(Acts 10. 14, 36; Rom. 10. 9; Col. 3. 24; 1 Pet. 3. 15)

684. Love—God's.

Could we with ink the ocean fill,
Were the whole sky of parchment made;
Were every stalk on earth a quill
And every man a scribe by trade;
To write the love of God above
Would drain the ocean dry;
Nor could the scroll contain the whole,
Though stretch'd from sky to sky.
—Meir Ben Isaac Nehorai—
(Adapted Modern Version)

(John 3. 16; Tit. 3. 4)

685. Love—God's.

A preacher went one day, 'tis said,
To see a neighbour's vane;
Beneath the weathercock he read
A motto clear and plain—
Writ just above was 'God is Love.'
Said he unto his friend,
'How reads this sign?
Can Love divine
Like changing weather, wet or fine,
On varying winds depend?'

'Not so', quoth he. This outward form
The Gospel shall proclaim;
In days of calm or days of storm,
God's Love is still the same;
Nor has it ceased though winds blow East;
Wherever we may rove,
Should winds blow North, South, East, or West,
Love always gives the very best,
And God is always Love.'
—Phyllis Skene

(1 John 3. 1; 4. 8)

686. Love—God's.

Love has a hem to its garment
That touches the very dust;
It can reach the stains of the streets and lanes,
And because it can, it must.

(Tit. 3. 3-5)

687. Love—God's.

John 3. 16—'For God so loved the world'—
        Heaven's brightest beam.
'That He gave His only-begotten Son'—Earth's greatest theme.
'That whosoever believeth in Him should not perish'—God's simplest scheme.
'But have everlasting Life'—Life's purest stream.

Dr. Jewett writes on this verse, John 3. 16—

'The biggest thing with which the mind can cope is the infinite love of God. All the explorations of eternity will never reach a limit in its unsearchable wealth. The biggest thing you and I will ever know is the love of God in Jesus Christ our Lord.

'A diamond is "of the first water" when it is without flaw or taint of any kind. Love can be degraded by the taint of jealousy: it can be debased by the taint of envy: it can be vulgarized by a strain of carnal passion.

'The test of purity is the Revelation of the Love of God. Its brilliance is its holiness. "God is Light and in Him is no darkness at all". There is nothing shady, nothing questionable, nothing compromising in God's love. Its brilliance is "of the first water". The dazzling whiteness of eternal Light and eternal Love is God's holiness.

'Sunbeams can move among sewage and catch no defilement. The holy love of God ministers in the deepest depths of the human mind, is deeper than sorrow, deeper than death, deeper than sin.

'God's love imparts its own loveliness until one day we shall be altogether lovely.'

(John 3. 16; 1 John 3. 1, 16)

688. Love—God's.
During the time that Handley Moule was Bishop of Durham, a very serious colliery disaster took place, and the man of God, Bible in hand, went to the pit-head to endeavour to comfort the sorrowing wives, mothers and sisters, and other relatives who, gathered there, were weeping and mourning the loss of their loved ones. Almost at a loss for words to express his deep sorrow and sympathy in such tragic circumstances, he opened his Bible, and the bookmark fell out. As he picked it up, the Holy Spirit gave him the message for those passing through deep sorrow. On it was worked in silken threads the text 'GOD IS LOVE'. On one side the words stood out lovely and clear, but the other side showed a mass of tangled threads. Holding up the wrong side, with the tangled threads first, he showed it to the weeping relatives and said, 'This disaster, with the sorrow and loss it brings you, is like these tangled threads. It is

unintelligible to you: you cannot understand it. But look,' he said, turning the other side so that all could see, 'like everything in our lives that we cannot understand, it tells that "God is Love".'

(Rom. 8. 28, 38, 39; 1 John 4. 8)

689. Love—God's.

Love ever gives, forgives, outlives;
And ever stands with open hands;
And while it lives, it gives,
For this is love's prerogative
To give, and give, and give.

(John 3. 16; 2 Cor. 9. 15)

690. Love—of Jesus.

From off the throne eternal He came to earth
below—
From off the throne eternal He came to bear our
woe,
He came to scorn and hatred, He came to shame
and loss,
He came to be a victim, to die on Calvary's
cross—
To die alone in darkness, with none His grief to
share
(And though He looked for sympathy, no
sympathy was there)
Alone, amid the darkness He died for you and
me;
Oh! the mighty love of Jesus, it could not greater
be.

Tell me of earth no longer, tell me of earth no
more—
The mighty love of Jesus has made my heart run
o'er;
Oh, it is all so wondrous, it doth my thoughts
confound—
I can but bow and worship with reverence
profound.
That He should leave the glories of that bright
home on high,
For me to come and suffer, for me, for me to
die—
Is love beyond all measure, unbounded, full and
free;
Oh! the wondrous love of Jesus, it could not
greater be.

My heart and my affections how can I now
retain?
Oh! how can I but love Him Who once for me
was slain.
Ah no! I could not, would not, my love for Him
deny—
For Him Who came to suffer—for me, for me to
die.
This love I cannot measure—'tis love that has no
end—
'Tis love that all things earthly completely doth
transcend;
Eternal, uncreated, unmeasured, full and free;
Oh! the mighty love of Jesus, it could not greater
be.

A never-failing fountain is the precious love of
Christ—
Its overflowing fulness hath my yearning heart
sufficed;
A depth without a bottom, a sea without a shore,
Where my thirst has all been quenched, to wake
again no more;
Or if it wakes, 'tis only to drink again more deep
From that never-failing fountain, whose waters
upward leap.
—So great, so vast, so mighty, unmeasured, full
and free
Oh, the deep, sweet love of Jesus that satisfieth
me.   —John Macdonald

(Gal. 2. 20; Rom. 8. 35; Eph. 5. 2, 25; 1 John 4. 19)

691. Love—of Jesus.

Can you count me the leaves of the forest trees
Or the sand on the sea-washed shore,
Or the flowers bedecking the fragrant leas,
Or the grain in the harvest store?
If you can, then I'll tell you His love to me
Who died for my sins on Calvary's tree.

Can you count me the locks of glossy hair
On the blooming, youthful head?
Can you count me each particular star
That shines when the day is sped?
If you can, then I'll tell you His love to me
Who died for my sins on Calvary's tree?

Can you count me the blades of grass that grow
In the meadows all around,
Or the sparkling, glittering drops of dew
At the sun's uprising found?
But you cannot, and oh! I cannot tell
The depths of His love to me
Who died for my sins on Calvary's tree.

(John 15. 13; Gal. 2. 20; Eph. 5. 2)

692. Love—Impelling. In 'Assembly Annals'

Dr. H. A. Cameron relates the following incident:

'Over in Scotland it used to be the custom in the time of harvest for the women in farming districts to help in making and binding the sheaves after the mower had cut down the grain. On one occasion, a mother named Hannah Lamond, offered her services in that time of labour and to make the work easier took with her her little child, thinking that she could place it safely within easy reach where she could look at it now and then. But, busily occupied as everyone was, the reapers did not notice that an eagle which had its nest on a nearby mountain, had swooped down and snatched the sleeping child from its little bed among the sheaves, and carried it off, flying with its talons firmly fixed in the child's clothing. However, it had not risen far when the anguished cry went up: 'The eagle has taken awa' Hannah Lamond's bairn.'

'Consternation took hold of the men and women, and in their commotion they ran as rescuers to the foot of the rock where high up the eagle had its eyrie, and to which it had transported the child to become food for its eaglets. Some of the men made a valiant effort to scale the face of the rock but unable to get a footing they fell back defeated, and it seemed a hopeless task to recover the bairn before it would be destroyed by the eagle and torn to pieces. Among the men there was a sailor accustomed to climbing places where there was but little foothold, and he did his best to ascend that precipitous cliff, but after a vigorous endeavour he also gave up the attempt and acknowledged himself beaten. The people were frantic, yet helpless, and the child's case seemed absolutely hopeless.

'But who is this that now essays to do what all others had failed to accomplish? It is Hannah Lamond. Impelled by mother love she begins to ascend that vertical rock, and bit by bit, here and there finding a little projection upon which to place her foot, she gradually rises away from the plain, and at last accomplishes the seemingly impossible by reaching the eagle's nest. There the bird of prey with flapping wings and powerful beak, tries to beat her back and keep its victim, now lying in the nest among the eaglets, but, desperate though the bird's efforts are, they are not equal to the courage and determination of the mother of the child as she rescues it from death and destruction.

She now begins the more perilous descent, more difficult far than the first journey, and, marvellous to tell, she comes back as surely if not as swiftly as before. And great is the rejoicing among her friends, as they welcome her returning safe and sound from her heroic and dangerous task, another proof that "love will find a way" where everything else fails.'

(John 15. 13; Rom. 5. 6-8; Gal. 2. 20)

693. Love—Sacrificial.

He gave His back to the smiters, the gentle Son
   of Man;
Then the smiters smote till their work was done,
And the thornless field was ploughed so deep
That a golden sheaf of life I reap;
   'He gave Himself for Me.'

He gave His brow to the thorn-crown, the mighty
   Prince of Peace;
Then they soiled His face, and they bowed their
   knees
To the kingliest King Whose love so strong
Fills my heart with joy, my lips with song;
   'He gave Himself for me.'

He gave His side to the spear-thrust, the Holy
   Son of God;
Then they stabbed Him deep, till water and blood
Flowed out in the stream, whose cleansing grace
Makes sinners meet for the heavenly place;
   'He gave Himself for me.'

He gave His heart to the judgment, the sinless
   Judge of all;
Then the wrath of man and the wrath of God
Broke out in the storm that raged until
My debt was paid—my shameful bill;
   'He gave Himself for me.'

          —A. C. Rose
(Isa. 50. 6; Lam. 1. 12; Gal. 2. 20; 1 John 4. 10)

694. Love—Sacrificial.

Love is the true Economist:
   She breaks the box and gives her all,
Yet not one precious drop is missed
   Since on His head and feet they fall.
Love is the truest Providence,
   Since beyond time her gold is good;
Stamp'd o'er man's mean three hundred pence
   With Christ's 'She hath done what she could.'

(Mark 14. 3-9; John 14. 15)

695. Love—Sacrificial.
The following verses were written by Sir Cecil Arthur Spring-Rice on Jan. 12, 1918, his last night as British Ambassador in Washington, U.S.A.

I owe to thee, my country,
All earthly things above,
Entire and whole and perfect,
The service of my love,
The love that asks no questions,
The love that stands the test,
That lays upon the altar
The dearest and the best;
The love that never falters,
The love that pays the price,
The love that makes, undaunted,
The final sacrifice.

And there's another country
I've heard of long ago,
Most dear to them that love her,
Most great to them that know.
We may not count her armies,
We may not see her King;
Her fortress is a faithful heart,
Her pride is suffering.
And soul by soul, and silently,
Her shining bounds increase,
And all her ways are gentleness,
And all her paths are peace.

(2 Cor. 5. 14, 15; Phil. 3. 20, 21; Heb. 11. 15, 16)

696. Love—Wonderful.
Arriving at Chester at 2 a.m. on a cold winter's night, after a rough passage across the Irish Channel, I found I should have five or six hours to wait before the train would arrive to take me the rest of my journey.

The station is a dreary place to wait in at this hour, and season. It is cold, desolate, and terribly draughty, being open from end to end, and not a terminus. I went to the waiting-room and found an old porter, apparently the only man left on the premises at that hour, sweeping out the room. I could not help noticing his face, as it had such a happy, patient look.

'Are you here all night?' I said.

'For many, many years, sir, I've been on night duty here; but I'm almost worn out now.'

'It must be very cold for you, you don't look very strong.'

'No, sir, I'm not, and I'm almost racked to death with the rheumatics, but oh, sir, I've had such a blessed time this night, although the cold has gone right through my old bones.'

Curious to know, and but half suspecting the old porter's source of comfort, I said that there was not much comfort in being frozen to death with cold.

'Oh! sir,' said the old man, his face all lighting up, 'it is not that, but what I've been a-thinking of before you came in was that blessed Jesus; and what love it was of Him to go and take a body that could feel, and go through all His sorrow and suffering down here that He might be able to understand all my cold and pain this night, while He's up there in Heaven. I know His feeling for me, and He knows and understands all I suffer; and when I think of Him a-feeling for me and loving me up there, I seem as if I didn't half mind the pain. Oh! 'tis a wonderful thing—His love—isn't it, sir?'

Through God's mercy I was enabled to share my fellow-pilgrim's enjoyment of the Good Shepherd's love, and a happy time we spent together talking of the One dear to both our hearts.

—Dr. A. T. Schofield

(Gal. 2. 20; Heb. 2. 18; 4. 15)

697. Love's Language. In his *Child's History of England*, Charles Dickens tells the following interesting story:

This is the romance of the father and mother of Thomas à Becket who, for asserting and maintaining that the power of the clergy was superior to the king's power, was murdered by the knights of Henry II in Canterbury Cathedral of which he was Archbishop.

Gilbert Becket, Thomas à Becket's father, a London merchant, made a pilgrimage to the Holy Land and was taken prisoner by a Saracen lord who had one fair daughter. She fell in love with him and told him she wanted to marry him, and was willing to become a Christian if they could escape to a Christian country. He returned her love till he found an opportunity to escape with his servant Richard, and returned to England. Then he forgot the fair Saracen maiden.

But the Saracen lady had not forgotten Gilbert. She left her father's house in disguise to follow him and made her way to the coast. The merchant had taught her two English words, 'London' and 'Gilbert'. She went among the ships, saying again and again the same word 'London'. Sailors showed her a ship bound for London, and she paid her passage with some of her jewels and arrived in London.

As the merchant was sitting one day in his office, Richard, his servant, came running in, saying, 'Master! there is the Saracen lady. As I live, she is going up and down calling "Gilbert! Gilbert"!' The merchant saw her in the crowd and went to her. She saw him and fainted in his arms. Soon after they were married.

698. Lover.
Mender of bruised reeds—
O patient lover!
'Tis love my brother needs—
Make me a lover,

That this poor reed may be
Mended and tuned for Thee—
O Lord, of even me
Make a true lover.
Kindler of smoking flax,
O ardent lover!
Give what Thy servant lacks—
Make me a lover,
That this poor flax may be
Kindled, aflame for Thee—
O Lord, of even me
Make a true lover.

—Amy Carmichael

(Isa. 42. 3; John 13. 34, 35)

699. Magnitudes. 'The author of this pamphlet can assert from the authority of experience that, after the satisfactory discharge of his parish duties, a minister may enjoy five days in the week of uninterrupted leisure for the prosecution of any science.' So wrote Thomas Chalmers in 1805, having been ordained two years before to minister the Gospel in Kilmany, Fife, and having continued to give lectures in chemistry and mathematics in St. Andrews.

Twenty years after, when these words were slung in his teeth, Dr. Chalmers acknowledged his error and said, 'And what, sir, are the objects of mathematical science? Magnitude and the proportions of magnitude. But *then*, sir, I had forgotten two magnitudes. I thought not of the littleness of time. I recklessly thought not of the greatness of eternity.' (Ps. 103. 15-17; Isa. 40. 6-8; 1 John 2. 17)

700. Man. Man is a tripartite being, consisting of body, soul, and spirit. Body has been defined as world consciousness, soul as self-consciousness and spirit as God-consciousness. These three faculties are brought out in the words for 'Man' in different languages.

Man's body: Latin — Homo — cognate with 'humus', the ground.
Hebrew—Adam—red earth.
Man's mind: Sanskrit — Manushya — from 'manu'—to think.
Anglo-Saxon — Man — cognate with the Sanskrit.
Man's spirit: Greek—Anthropos (from which is derived 'anthropology', science of man)—he who looks upward.

(Job. 7. 17, 18; 15. 14, 16; Ps. 8. 4-9; 144. 3, 4; Heb. 2. 5-9)

701. Man.
So fair is man that death (a parting blast)
Blasts his fair form and makes him earth at last.
So strong is man that, with a gasping breath,
He totters and bequeaths his strength to death.
So wise is man that, if with death he strive,
His wisdom cannot teach him how to live.
So rich is man that—all his debts being paid—
His wealth's the winding sheet wherein he's laid.

—Francis Quarles

(Job 14. 1, 2; Ps. 90. 9, 10; Eccles. 12. 5-7)

702. Man. What a piece of work is man; how noble in reason! how infinite in faculty! in form and moving how express and admirable! in action how like an angel! in apprehension how like a god! the beauty of the world! the paragon of animals!

—Shakespeare in *Hamlet*

(Ps. 8. 4-6; Heb. 2. 6-8)

703. Man. Bishop Taylor-Smith told this incident in the Assembly Hall, Sydney. He was travelling on a vessel which carried as a passenger a major of the Army who was a notorious evil-liver. One day, in the smoking room, this man attacked the Bishop, saying:

'If God has given man desires, cravings—physical desires, I mean—I suppose He means he should gratify them?'

'Before I answer,' replied Bishop Taylor-Smith, 'let me ask you a question. Is man composed simply of physical desires? Is man body only, or is he mind as well as body?'

The major said, 'Of course, he is mind as well.'

'You grant me that point. Now I want to ask you this—If God has given a man mental desires as well as physical desires—desires for knowledge—then He has given him those intellectual desires that he may gratify them. Do you agree?'

'Yes,' said the major.

'Then go a step further,' urged the Bishop. 'Is man only mind and body? Has he not a spirit as well? And if a man has spiritual desires, then, according to your own reasoning, God has given him spiritual desires that he may gratify them.' Then, looking the major in the face, he added, 'If you gratify your spiritual desires, and your mental desires, then you may gratify your physical desires.'

At that moment an officer came in carrying a lantern in which was a candle. Taking it from him, the Chaplain-General, as he was then, said, 'Look here, major! Here is a candle, lighted; notice the fat, which is like the body, the wick we will call the mind, and the flame—the spirit. Stand it upright as it is meant to burn, and it gives a pure, useful light. Turn it over, the light flickers, the candle begins to stink.' Then he said, 'If all I hear of you is true, that is what you are doing. Keep the fat in the proper place.'

Two years afterwards they met again, and the major thanked Bishop Taylor-Smith and said, though he didn't like being exposed before all in the smoking room of the ship, the reproof had been blessed and used to the salvation of his soul, and the cleansing of his life. (Gen. 1. 27; Rom. 1. 24, 28, 30; 1 Thess. 5. 23)

704. Man. The Sphinx—in ancient mythology—was supposed to have propounded a riddle, 'What animal goes on four legs in the morning, on two at noonday, and on three in the evening?' The riddle remained unsolved till Oedipus appeared and gave the right answer—'Man!' In infancy the human babe goes on all fours; during life's course he walks upright on two legs; and in the eventide of life he leans on a staff.
(Ps. 8. 4-6; 39. 4; 90. 10)

705. Man.

How readily upon the Gospel plan
That question has its answer, 'What is man?'
Sinful and weak, in every sense a wretch,
An instrument whose strings upon the stretch,
And strained to the last cord that he can bear,
Yields only discord in the Maker's ear.

But what is man in his own proud esteem?
Hear him—himself the poet and the theme:
A monarch clothed with majesty and awe,
His mind his kingdom and his will his law,
Grace in his mien and glory in his eyes,
Supreme on earth and worthy of the skies.

—William Cowper

(Job 15. 14-16; Dan. 4. 30; 1 Tim. 2. 5)

706. Man—in the Glory.

There's a Man in the glory I know very well,
I have known Him for years and His goodness can tell;
One day in His mercy He knocked at my door,
And, seeking admission, knock'd many times o'er
But when I went to Him and stood face to face,
And listen'd awhile to His story of grace,
How He suffer'd for sinners and put away sin,
I heartily, thankfully welcomed Him in.
We have lived on together a number of years,
And that's why I neither have doubtings nor fears,
For my sins are all hid in the depths of the sea;
They were carried down there by the Man on the tree.

I am often surprised why the lip should be curled
When I speak of my Lord to the man of the world;
And notice with sorrow his look of disdain
When I tell him that Jesus is coming again.
And yet at His coming I'm sure he would flee
Like the man in the garden who ate of the tree.
Is the Man in the glory a stranger to you?
A stranger to Jesus! What, do you not know
He is washing poor sinners much whiter than snow?
Have you lived in a land where the Bible's unknown
That you don't know the Man Who is now on the throne?
The question of sin I adoringly see
The Man in the glory has settled for me!
And as to my footsteps, whatever the scene,
The Man in the glory is keeping me clean;
And therefore I'm singing from morning till night,
The Man in the glory is all my delight.

—George Cutting (abridged)

(1 Tim. 2. 5; Heb. 2. 9)

707. Man—of God.

There is no glory halo round his devoted head;
No lustre marks the sacred path in which his footsteps tread;
Yet holiness is graven upon his thoughtful brow,
And unto God and God alone his high-born soul shall bow.

He often is peculiar and seldom understood,
And yet his power is felt by both the evil and the
    good;
For he lives in touch with Heaven a life of faith
    and prayer;
His sympathies, his hopes, his joys—his all is
    centred there.
He is a chosen servant among God's many sons;
He bears His sayings on his lips, and on His
    errands runs.
No human frown he feareth, no earthly praise
    he seeks;
But in the dignity of Heaven his burning message
    speaks.
                                    —William Blane
(2 Kings 4. 9; Ps. 90-title; 1 Tim. 6. 11, 12)

708. Man—Moods of.

Within my earthly temple there's a crowd,
There's one of us that's humble, one that's proud,
One that's broken-hearted for his sins,
One that's unrepentant, sits and grins,
One that loves his neighbour as himself,
One that cares for nought but fame and pomp and
    pelf.
From much corroding care I should be free
If I could once determine which of these is me.
(Rom. 7. 21-24; Gal. 5. 17)

709. Manifestation.

There was a famous trial in Paris about the end of the nineteenth century, investigating the fraud of a certain Madame Humbert. A country girl of humble origin but clever and ambitious, she was anxious to figure in the best Parisian society. She had married above her station and gave out that she was immensely wealthy. She told how, while travelling, an old gentleman in the next compartment was taken seriously ill, and she had been able to save his life. As a result he had bequeathed all his property to her. The deeds of this property were supposed to be in a certain safe which Madame Humbert kept in her salon, and which was sometimes on view, bearing on its front a plentiful supply of sealing wax. On the strength of this she borrowed money to the extent of millions of francs. This went on for several years till her creditors became uneasy.

Then the matter was brought to court. The judge decided that the safe should be opened in the presence of witnesses. When it was opened, it was found to contain only a copper coin not worth a halfpenny. The manifestation revealed her poverty and bankruptcy as well as her deceit.

'We must all be made manifest at the judgement seat of Christ.'
(Mark 4. 22; 1 Cor. 4. 5; 2 Cor. 5. 10)

710. Maranatha.

'Maranatha'—word of greeting
    Passed between the saints of old;
Let our lips repeat when meeting,
    Heirs of glory must be told—
'Maranatha! Maranatha!'
    Jesus comes, ye saints, behold!

Maranatha, word of promise
    By the Faithful and the True—
Precious parting words of Jesus,
    'I will come again for you.'
Maranatha, Maranatha,
    Soon His glory we shall view.

Maranatha, word of gladness,
    Cheering star of hope is this,
Smiling through the rifts of sadness
    Till the cloudless dawn of bliss.
Maranatha, Maranatha!
    Shine, Thou blessed star of peace!

'Maranatha', this our anchor
    Safely cast within the veil;
Winds and waves may rage with anger,
    As across Life's sea we sail.
Maranatha, Maranatha!
    Lo! the haven fair we hail.

Oh! 'tis true our Lord is coming;
    Surely, quickly He will come;
As we muse, this word we're humming—
    Here we would no longer roam.
Maranatha, Maranatha!
    Come, Lord Jesus, take us home.
(1 Cor. 16. 22)

711. Mark—and his Gospel.

Mark, having become the interpreter of Peter, wrote down accurately everything that he remembered of the words and deeds of our Lord without, however, recording in order what was said and done; for neither did he hear the Lord nor follow him; but as I said, he attended Peter who adapted his instructions to the needs of his hearers. Mark committed no error in writing certain matters just as he remembered them. He took thought for one thing, not to omit or falsify any of the things that he had heard.
                                    —Eusebius

Mark, the disciple and interpreter of Peter, handed down in writing the things which his Master proclaimed.
                              —Irenæus (180 A.D.)

Note the prominence of Peter in Mark's Gospel.
(1 Pet. 5. 13)

712. Marks—of a Christian.

When Christian and Faithful in Pilgrim's Progress were passing through Vanity Fair, the citizens observed in them certain marks that distinguished them from themselves. Bunyan has set those down very clearly in the narrative of his 'Immortal Dream'. The following Indian fable illustrates some of the marks that distinguish a true believer in Jesus Christ from an unbeliever.

It is said that one of the many millions of crows that can be seen and heard anywhere in India one day saw a very happy covey of doves feeding together and living in perfect unity and goodwill. Anxious to join them, he realised that his raven-black feathers contrasted strongly with the white or light grey coats of the doves. So, finding a heap of white ashes, he rolled in them until his coat appeared, if not white, to be a light grey hue. Then he assayed to join himself to the doves. Their immediate reaction was to edge away from the intruder and finally to fly off altogether. The wise crow noticed that his walk was different from the doves! He hopped: the doves walked, putting one foot down after another. After some practice at this new kind of locomotion, the crow came another day to where the doves were, a fresh layer of ashes covering his black feathers, and walked along carefully in imitation of the walk of the doves. He made some success, and was about to become friendly when he smelt a carcase some little distance away. Leaving the grains the doves had permitted him to share with them, he flew over to the carcase and was soon enjoying himself feeding on the dead body. The crow found great difficulty next day in approaching the doves, though he came with a light grey coat and imitated their walk almost to perfection. Realising that his eating habits had offended them, he made up his mind that no carcase should divert him from enjoying their company that day. So in time, he struck up a friendship with them and was sharing their meal when another crow—jet-black—came and perched on an overhead branch. Looking down, it recognized a brother crow and immediately began to make its satisfaction known in a series of 'Caws'. Its brother crow among the doves, forgetting himself, fittingly replied—'Caw! Caw!' That was the grand finale. Its hypocrisy was detected and it was ever after boycotted by the doves. Its walk was different: its food was different: its talk was different. The true Christian is marked off in these three respects from the man of the world.

(Eph. 4. 1, 17; 5. 1, 8; 4. 29; 1 Pet. 2. 2, 3)

713. Marriage. Abraham Lincoln, afterwards President of the United States and victor in the war against the negro slave trade in America, wrote the following verses at the age of 17, and sang them on the occasion of his sister's marriage.

The woman was not taken
From Adam's feet, we see:
So we must not abuse her—
The meaning seems to be.
The woman was not taken
From Adam's head, we know:
To show she must not rule him—
'Tis evidently so.
The woman—she was taken
From under Adam's arm:
So she must be protected
From injuries and harm.

(Gen. 2. 21, 22)

714. Marriage. The following lines are true when the presence of the Lord Jesus Christ is realised. Three essentials to a happy marriage are: the presence of the Lord Jesus Christ at the wedding (John 2. 2), in the home (Mark 2. 1) and all along life's journey (Luke 24. 15).

We two make home of any place we go;
We two find joy in any kind of weather;
Or if the earth is clothed in bloom or snow,
If summer days invite or bleak winds blow,
What matters it if we two are together?
We two, we two, we make our world, our weather.

715. Martyrs. A week before the slaughter of the Ecuador missionaries, of whom Nate Saint was one, he was reading to his children before bedtime. As he read the account of Stephen's stoning, he broke down and wept over the martyr's wonderful spirit as he faced death. From various remarks he had made in recent weeks, we gather that he seemed to know that the effort was going to cost him his life.

Fortified by his mother's faith, little Stephen Saint (five years) inquired concerning his father: 'How long will it take him to get to Heaven?'

—*Life*

Five years before, Jim Elliott, another of the Auca martyrs, wrote in his diary: 'When it comes time to die, make sure all you have to do is to die.'

(Phil. 1. 21; 2 Pet. 1. 14)

716. Martyrs.
Hallowed martyrs, who with fervent zeal
And more than mortal courage greatly dared
To preach the name of Jesus; they, who stood
The undaunted champions of eternal truth,
Though maddened priests conspired, though
*   princes frowned,*
And persecution with ingenious rage
Prepared ten thousand torments.

(Matt. 23. 34-37; Acts 12. 2; 2 Tim. 4. 5; Heb. 11. 35-38)

717. Martyrs.
The blood of martyrs, living still,
*   Makes the ground pregnant where it flows,*
And for their temporary ill
*   Thereon eternal triumph grows.*

(Gen. 4. 10; Matt. 23. 35)

718. Martyrs. The martyrs presented their bodies as living sacrifices in full assurance of submissive faith that their sorrows would not be in vain. 'Be of good cheer, Master Ridley,' said Latimer, as they stood bound at their stakes, 'by the grace of God we shall this day light such a candle in England as shall never be put out.' And so it was.

—A. C. Rose

(Acts 8. 2-5; 9. 4, 5, 15; 17. 6; 2 Tim. 4. 6)

719. Martyr—Stephen the first Christian.
He heeded not reviling tones,
Nor sold his heart to idle moans,
Though cursed and scorned and bruised with
*   stones;*
But, looking upward, full of grace,
He prayed, and from that Holy Place
God's glory smote him on the face.

(Acts 7. 54-60)

10

720. Master. God is the only Master Who always gives His servants the wages they work for. Serve Him in your business, and every hour you spend in your counting-house or in your works—whether you make money or lose it—will increase your treasure in Heaven. Serve God in your profession and whether you are successful or not in your professional life, every hour of labour will discipline you for the higher activities on the other side of death.

—H. W. Dale

Queen Elizabeth in the sixteenth century called on a prominent merchant and proposed to entrust to him some important business on the continent. When he pleaded that if he went abroad on the Queen's business his own business at home would suffer, Elizabeth replied, 'You attend to my business and I shall see that yours suffers no loss.'

(John 12. 26; Acts 27. 23; Col. 3. 24)

721. Measurements. When God measures a man He puts the tape round his heart, not his head.

It isn't the size of your banking account
And the people of wealth you have met,
The number of dresses and hats that you buy,
The amount of regard you can get.

It isn't the size of the house that counts,
And the crowds you entertain,
The number of cars that stand outside
And the servants you retain.

The value of jewels upon your hand
And the silver that you possess,
The number of miles you have travelled abroad,
The important folks you impress.

It's the size of your heart and the sympathy,
The breadth of your mind and love,
The value and height of your loyalty
That matters to Him Who's above.

(Rom. 12. 14-16; 2 Cor. 6. 11-13)

722. Measuring. 'Measuring themselves by themselves.'

A little boy came to his mother, saying, 'Mummy, I am as tall as Goliath! I am nine feet high!'

'Why do you say that?' asked his surprised mother. 'Well, I made a little ruler of my own and measured myself with it and I am just nine feet tall.'

Some of the boy's elders are doing the same thing. If they don't 'measure up' according to the accepted standards, some folks make their own rulers, set their own standards. We must remember that 'not he that commendeth himself is approved, but whom the Lord commendeth.'

—*Christian Victory*

(2 Cor. 10. 12-18)

723. Memory System. The following is the best:

Forget each kindness that you do
As soon as you have done it;
Forget the praise that falls to you
As soon as you have won it;

Forget the slander that you hear
Before you can repeat it;
Forget each slight, each spite, each sneer,
Wherever you may meet it.

Remember every kindness done
To you, whate'er its measure;
Remember praise by others won
And pass it on with pleasure;
Remember every promise made
And keep it to the letter;
Remember those who lend you aid
And be a grateful debtor.

Remember good, remember truth,
Remember Heaven's above you,
And you will find, through age and youth,
That many hearts will love you.

(Heb. 13. 2, 3, 7, 16)

724. Merciful—The. When William Ewart Gladstone was Chancellor of the Exchequer, he sent down to the Treasury for certain statistics upon which to base his budget proposals. The statistician made a mistake. But Gladstone was so sure of this man's accuracy that he did not take time to verify his figures. He went before the House of Commons and made his speech, basing his appeal on the incorrect figures that had been given him. His speech was no sooner published than the newspapers exposed its glaring inaccuracies.

Mr. Gladstone was naturally overwhelmed with embarrassment. He went to his office and sent at once for the statistician who was responsible for his humiliating situation. The man came full of fear and shame, certain that he was going to lose his position. But instead, Gladstone said: 'I know how much you must be disturbed over what has happened, and I have sent for you to put you at your ease. For a long time you have been engaged in handling the intricacies of the national accounts, and this is the first mistake that you have made. I want to congratulate you, and express to you my keen appreciation.' It took a big man to do that, big with the bigness of the truly merciful.

The worst of men do not so much need our forgiveness as the best of men need the forgiveness of God; and one would have thought that the wonderful mercy shown to us by our gracious Father would make the forgiving of our brother man for any injury he may have done to us, a very simple matter.

—Henry Durbanville

(Matt. 5. 7; Eph. 4. 32)

725. Mercy. Dr. Alexander Whyte used to tell how on one occasion he went into a solicitor's office and was asked if he had any message for an old sinner. Staggered by the utterance, he repeated the text he had chosen for his next sermon: 'He delighteth in mercy,' and was thanked for the only word that could have afforded comfort. The verse overflows with kindness.

(Mic. 7. 18)

726. Mercy.

The quality of mercy is not strained;
It droppeth as the gentle rain from Heaven
Upon the place beneath, It is twice blest:
It blesseth him that gives and him that takes.
'Tis mightiest in the mightiest: it becomes
The throned monarch better than his crown.
His sceptre shows the force of temporal power,
The attributes to awe and majesty
Wherein doth sit the dread and fear of kings:
But mercy is above this sceptred sway:
It is enthroned in the heart of kings:
It is an attribute of God Himself,
And earthly power doth then show likest God's
When mercy seasons justice.

—Shakespeare in *Merchant of Venice*
(Ps. 106. 1; 107. 1; Luke 18. 13, 14; 1 Tim. 1. 13)

727. Mercy. A mother sought from Napoleon the pardon of her son. The Emperor said it was the man's second offence, and justice demanded his death.

'I don't ask for justice,' said the mother, 'I plead for mercy.'

'But,' said the Emperor, 'he does not deserve mercy.'

'Sir,' cried the mother, 'it would not be mercy if he deserved it, and mercy is all I ask.'

'Well, then,' said the Emperor, 'I will have mercy.' And her son was saved.

This little incident gives us a good idea of the meaning of mercy. We think of clemency as another word for mercy, but mercy is the 'gracious attitude of one who sits in the seat of authority toward one who has given offence by breaking of the law, or by some violation of those canons of conduct which constitute offence'. This is at least part of its meaning.

Grace is the unmerited favour of God toward the undeserving: mercy is His pitying kindness toward the hell-deserving. Grace bestows what we do not deserve: mercy does not mete out to us what we deserve.

(Exod. 34. 6, 7; Mic. 6. 8; Heb. 4. 16)

728. Mercy.

Blind Bartimaeus at the gates
Of Jericho in darkness waits.
He hears the crowd—he hears a breath
Say, 'It is Christ of Nazareth!'
And calls in tones of agony—
'Iesou eleeson me.'

The thronging multitudes increase,
'Blind Bartimaeus, hold your peace.'
But still, above the noisy crowd,
The beggar's cry is shrill and loud,
Until they say, 'He calleth thee.'
'Tharsei, egerai, phonei se.'

That said the Christ, as silent stands
The crowd, 'What wilt thou at my hands?'
And he replied, 'O give me light!
Rabbi, restore the blind man's sight!'
And Jesus answers, 'Hupage
He pistis sou sesike se.'

Ye that have eyes, yet cannot see
In darkness and in misery,
Recall these mighty voices three,
'Iesou, eleeson me!'
'Tharsei, egeirai hupage!'
'He pistis sou sesike se.'

—H. W. Longfellow
(Mark 10. 46-52)

729. Messenger—of Christ. Every Christian is a messenger sent by his Master to take the Message of the Gospel to the whole world.

The character of the messenger is illustrated in the following extract from an article in the March, 1899, Philistine Magazine. During the war between Russia and Japan, every Russian soldier who went to the front was given a copy of the 'Message to Garcia'. The Japanese, finding the booklets in possession of the Russian prisoners, concluded that it must be a good thing, and accordingly translated it into Japanese. And on an order of the Mikado, a copy was given to every man in the employ of the Japanese Government, soldier or civilian. Over forty million copies of 'A Message to Garcia' have been printed.

—Dale Carnegie

A Message to Garcia

When war broke out between Spain and the United States, it was very necessary to communicate quickly with the leader of the Insurgents. Garcia was somewhere in the mountain fastnesses of Cuba—no one knew where. No mail or telegraph message could reach him. The President must secure his co-operation, and quickly.

What to do!

Some one said to the President, 'There is a fellow by the name of Rowan will find Garcia for you, if anybody can.'

Rowan was sent for and given a letter to be delivered to Garcia. How the 'fellow by the name of Rowan' took the letter, sealed it up in an oilskin pouch, strapped it over his heart, in four days landed by night off the coast of Cuba from an open boat, disappeared into the jungle and in three weeks came out on the other side of the Island, having traversed a hostile country on foot, and delivered his letter to Garcia—are things I have no special desire now to tell in detail. The point that I wish to make is this: McKinley gave Rowan a letter to be delivered to Garcia; Rowan took the letter and did not ask, 'Where is he at?'

There is a man whose form should be cast in deathless bronze and the statue placed in every college of the land. It is not book learning young men need, or instruction about this and that, but a stiffening of the vertebrae which will cause them to be loyal to a trust, to act promptly, concentrate their energies: do the thing—'Carry a message to Garcia'.

General Garcia is dead now, but there are other Garcias. No man who has endeavoured to carry out an enterprise where many hands were needed, but has been well-nigh appalled at times by the imbecility of the average man—

the inability or unwillingness to concentrate on a thing and do it.

—Elbert Hubbard

(Matt. 28. 19, 20; Mark 16. 15, 20; Acts 8. 4; Rom. 1. 15; 2 Cor. 10. 16; Rev. 1. 9)

730. Midst—Christ in the.

He sat in the midst of the sages
As Teacher from Heaven above:
To them He interprets the pages
That speak of His Father's love.

He stands in the midst of the stricken
To comfort their hearts so sad:
His hands and His side that are riven
Are tokens that make them glad.

He walks in the midst of the churches,
Inspector and Potentate:
With eyes that are flaming He searches
And sees their declining state.

He waits in the midst of the fewest
Who gather to plead His name:
He sends to the least and the lowest
And grants them whatever they claim.

He hangs in the midst of two felons.
As Saviour He sheds His blood:
And thus He has opened for millions
The way to the heart of God.

—D. Hine-Butler

(Ps. 22. 22; Matt. 18. 20; Luke 2. 46; 24. 36; John 19. 18; Rev. 2. 1)

731. Millennium.

Every tiger madness muzzled, every serpent
passion killed,
Every grim ravine a garden, every blazing desert
tilled,
Robed in universal harvest, up to either pole she
smiles,
Universal ocean softly washing all her warless
isles.

(Ps. 72. 16; Isa. 65. 23; Mic. 4. 3; Rev. 22. 3-5)

732. Miracles.
The Parables of the Lord Jesus Christ are spoken miracles: His miracles are acted Parables.

In the Healing of the nobleman's son in John 4. 46-54 notice—

it was 'the nobleman' who *besought* Jesus:
it was 'the man' who *believed* His word:
it was 'the father' who *knew* it was at the same hour that Jesus spoke that the miracle of healing took place.

—C. Hewlett

(John 4. 47, 50, 53)

733. Miracle—of Preservation.
The streets of the Dutch city of Leyden were deserted, except for small groups of men, walking fearfully to the tower in the centre of the city. The leaves had been stripped from the trees and eaten by the residents. From the quaint little houses came the anguished cries of babies pleading for food.

Outside the city walls a Spanish army lay in formidable entrenchments while the Spaniards waited for the public officials of Leyden to announce surrender. But no surrender came. Leyden refused to bow to the Spanish king, who sought to stamp out the Protestant faith.

For days which ran into months, the starving Dutch held out. Conditions grew worse, until even dogs, cats and rodents had to be eaten. Surrounded on all sides of their rectangular city, the people of Leyden had only one masterful weapon—prayer.

One day in August, in the year 1574, carrier pigeons flew into besieged Leyden with a message from William of Orange, the Dutch leader. 'The dikes which hold back the ocean have been cut and soon the sea water will drown out your besiegers,' William wrote.

The destitute people of Leyden rejoiced, firing a cannon to acknowledge receipt of the message. In the Spanish camp there was some fear, but the inexperienced officers finally convinced themselves that this was only a futile gesture of the Dutch ruler. 'He thinks he can rule the ocean as he does his subjects,' they scoffed. After all, they said, the ocean was twenty-two miles from Leyden!

A vigilance from the city's highest tower began, and each day the news was discouraging. 'I cannot see the water coming,' one watcher after another reported. Only prayer kept hope alive in the hearts of the people of Leyden.

Finally, at the end of the fateful month, pigeons were sent back to William. 'Soon we shall perish,' a note read, 'surely we have been forgotten.' An answer came immediately. William of Orange wrote, 'Rather will we as a whole land perish and all our possessions perish in the waves than forsake thee, O Leyden.'

Again, there was rejoicing, but the more sceptical wanted action, not words. Then a few days later, they saw the Dutch ships sailing toward the city. The ocean cascading through the dikes, had furnished water on which the fleet could float. But, within five miles of Leyden, the water became too shallow. The fleet was stalled.

The Spaniards laughed derisively. 'How can William bring the sea to the walls of Leyden?' they jeered. 'Look, he is helpless, a fleet inland!'

Suddenly, from out of the north-west blew a wind which quickly developed into a gale blowing southwest. In its path the waters of the North Sea were lashed furiously into the land. The Dutch fleet was able to move again. Panicky and overwhelmed by this miracle of the dikes, the Spanish army fled.

At the wharves, the people caught bread and other food thrown by valiant sailors aboard the ships. The celebrations in the town lasted for many days.

—The Young Soldier

(Ps. 106. 9-11; Heb. 11. 29)

734. Miracle—of Provision.

'Whatsoe'er He bids you, do it!'
  Though you may not understand;
Yield to Him complete obedience,
  Then you'll see His mighty hand.
'Fill the waterpots with water'—
  Fill them to the very brim;
He will honour all your trusting—
  Leave the miracle to Him.

Bring to Christ your loaves and fishes,
  Though they be but few and small;
He will use the weaker vessels—
  Give to Him your little all.
Do you ask how many thousands
  Can be fed with food so slim?
Listen to the Master's blessing—
  Leave the miracle to Him.

O ye Christians, learn the lesson!
  Are you struggling all the way?
Cease your trying, change to trusting,
  Then you'll triumph every day.
'Whatsoe'er He bids you, do it!'
  Fill the pots up to the brim,
But remember 'tis His battle—
  Leave the miracle to Him.

                                        —T. H. Allen

(John 2. 5-7; Mark 6. 37-44)

735. Mirror—Reflecting Christ. Harold St. John wrote: 'In a noble palace in the city of Venice, I once saw a magnificent ceiling beautifully painted, but the chamber was so lofty that the visitor could only see a confused vision of gorgeous colours. In the centre of the room stood a table inlaid with a horizontal mirror so skilfully placed that as one gazed into it, the picture above was reflected in its full beauty of form and hue.' It is as we gaze into the mirror of Scripture that the greatness and glory of our Lord comes into full view.

                                —Indian Christian

(John 5. 39; 2 Cor. 3. 18)

736. Mirror—Revealing Self. There is an allegory that reads something like this: A man was complaining of his neighbours. 'I never saw such a wretched set of people,' he said, 'as there are in this village. They are mean, greedy of gain and careless. They are for ever speaking evil of one another.'

'Is it really so?' asked the angel who was walking with him. 'It is indeed,' said the man. 'Why, only look at this fellow coming toward us. I know his face though I cannot tell his name. See his little, sharp, cruel eyes darting here and there. The very droop of his shoulders is mean and cringing, and he slinks along instead of walking.'

'It is clever of you to see all this,' said the angel, 'but there is one thing which you do not perceive.'

'What is that?' asked the man.

'Why, that is a looking-glass we are approaching.'

The Scottish poet, Robert Burns, put the moral to that fable in this way:

'O wad some power the Giftie gi'e us
To see oorsel's as ithers see us.'

(James 1. 23-25)

737. Missionary—Aim of the. The missionary, Robert Moffat, wrote in an autograph album:

My album is the savage breast,
Where tempests brood and shadows rest,
Without one ray of light;
To write the name of Jesus there,
And see that savage bow in prayer,
And point to worlds more bright and fair—
This is my soul's delight.

(Rom. 1. 14; Col. 3. 9-11)

738. Missionary—Bible's Emphasis on.

The first message at the birth of Christ was a missionary message—Luke 2. 10;

The first prayer Christ taught was a missionary prayer—Matt. 6. 10:

The first disciple, Andrew, became the first missionary—John 1. 41:

The first message of the Risen Lord was a missionary message—John 20. 17:

The first command of the Risen Lord to his disciples was a missionary command—John 20. 21:

The first apostolic sermon was a missionary sermon—Acts 2. 17-39:

The first reason the Lord gave for Christian love was a missionary reason—John 13. 35:

The first coming of Christ was for missionary work—Luke 6. 13-21:

The second coming of Christ is to be hastened by missionary work—Matt. 24. 14:

Our Saviour's last wish was a missionary wish—Matt. 28. 19:

The last wish of the departing Lord should be the first wish of His waiting people.

(Mark 16. 15)

739. Missionary—Call of. 'My son, if God has called you to be a missionary, your Father would be grieved to see you shrivel down into a king.' said C. H. Spurgeon.

(Acts 26. 17-19)

740. Missionary—Dr. Livingstone at Victoria Falls.

O Livingstone! Thou hero of my youth,
In toil and travel great and strong for truth!
Man of the humble heart and mighty mind,
Lover of Africa, friend of mankind!
What raptures thrilled thy mighty soul when first
'Mosi-out-tunga' on thy vision burst.

                                        —William Blane

(Rom. 15. 20; 2 Cor. 10. 15; 11. 26)

741. Missionary—Guide for. The Acts of the Apostles that has been more fittingly called 'the Acts of the Holy Spirit through the apostles', is the perfect text-book for missionary

service. It certainly does not offer a stereo-
typed pattern for missionary work, but it does
provide—
   Principles to regulate the missionary's service,
   Precepts to be obeyed in service, and
   Practices to guide the missionary in service.
(Acts 8. 4; 13. 1-4)

742. Missionary—Responsibility of.
               The Scorn of Job!
'If I have eaten my morsel alone,'
   The patriarch spoke with scorn.
What would he think of the church, were he
      shown
   Heathendom, huge, forlorn,
Godless, Christless, with soul unfed,
   While the Church's ailment is fulness of bread,
Eating her morsel alone?

'We do not well, with good tidings for all,'
   Said the lepers four at the gate,
'To tell them not, lest mischief befall
   If till morning light we wait.'
Dare we lose time ere we gladly spread
   The tidings good of the living Bread?
Dare we eat our morsel alone?

'I am debtor alike to the Jew and the Greek,'
   The mighty apostle cried,
Traversing continents souls to seek
   For the love of the Crucified.
Centuries, centuries, since have sped:
   Millions are famishing: we have bread,
Yet we eat our morsel alone.

Ever of them that have largest dower
   Shall Heaven require the more.
Ours are affluence, knowledge, power,
   Ocean from shore to shore:
And East and West in our ears have said:—
   'Give us, give us your living Bread:'
Yet we eat our morsel alone.

'Freely as ye have received, so give,'
   He bade Who hath given us all.
How shall the soul in us longer live
   Deaf to their starving call,
For whom the blood of the Lord was shed,
   And His body broken to give them bread
If we eat our morsel alone?
(Job 31. 17; Mark 6. 37; Rom. 1. 14)

743. Missionary—Triumph of the. A story is
told of an old Fijian chief and an infidel who
visited the Fiji islands. The man said to the
chief: 'You are a great chief, and it is really
a pity that you have been so foolish as to
listen to the missionaries who only want to
get rich among you. No one nowadays would
believe any more in that old book which is
called the Bible; neither do men listen to that
story about Jesus Christ; people know better
now, and I am sorry for you that you have
been foolish.'
   When he said that, the old chief's eye flashed,
and he said: 'Do you see that great stone
over there? On that stone we smashed the
heads of our victims to death. Do you see
that native oven over yonder? In that oven
we roasted the human bodies for our great

feasts. If it had not been for those good
missionaries, for that old Book and the great
love of Jesus Christ which has changed us
from savages into God's children, you would
never leave this spot! You have to thank God
for the Gospel, otherwise you would be killed
and roasted in yonder oven, and we would
feast on your body in no time!'
                                —Dr. Donald Barnhouse
(Rom. 1. 15, 16)

744. Missionary—Urge of the. Is the kingdom
a harvest field? Then I thought it reasonable
that I should seek to work where the work was
most abundant and the workers fewest.
Labourers say they are overtaxed at home;
what, then, must be the case abroad, where
there are wide-stretching plains already white
to harvest, with scarcely here and there a
solitary reaper?
   To me the soul of an Indian seemed as
precious as the soul of an Englishman, and the
gospel as much for the Chinese as for the
European, and as the band of missionaries was
few compared with the company of ministers
at home, it seemed to me clearly to be my duty
to go abroad.
   But I go out as a missionary not that I may
follow the dictates of commonsense, but that I
may obey that command of Christ, 'Go into
all the world and preach'. This command
seems to me to be strictly a missionary
injunction; so that, apart altogether from
choice and other lower reasons, my going
forth is a matter of obedience to a plain
command; and in place of seeking a reason
for going abroad, I would prefer to say that I
have failed to discover any reason why I
should stay at home.
                          James Gilmour of Mongolia
(Mark 16, 15; John 4. 34-36; Rom. 15. 20, 21

745. Missionary—Vocation of. The wife of
Dr. Donald Fraser, Mrs. Agnes Fraser, has
recounted this episode concerning her
illustrious missionary husband:
   'What is your husband?' asked a Johannesburg business man one day in the steamer, as
he watched Dr. Donald Fraser pacing the deck.
   'He's a missionary.'
   'A missionary! Dear me! Do you mean to
tell me that a man like him could not get a
better job than that?'
   'If he could, you may be sure he would have
jumped at it,' replied Mrs. Fraser.
   'But surely,' he began—then stopped and
looked at Mrs. Fraser, realised what she meant,
got up and strolled off to consider that strange
phenomenon.
(Rom. 1. 1; 1 Cor. 9. 16; 1 Tim. 1. 12)

746. Missionary—Zeal of. The Premier of
Australia said that, when the Great War broke
out, the Australian Commonwealth at once
offered to do what they could to back Great
Britain. They asked what was the most useful

thing that they could do, and the reply came—
'Build us ships: we want ships'.

The Australians do not build ships, so smiled and began to till the fields, sow seed, and reap harvests to send food to the motherland. Grain was gathered, put into sacks, and brought down to the water's edge to wait for the ships. But the ships never came. The mice got in, and then found their way into towns and villages and cities, carrying disease with them—a disease that attacked the eyes of many and blinded some.

And all the time Great Britain said, 'Ships! ships! ships!'

God is saying to His people today, 'Ships, ships!' The mice of Modernism have crept in and blinded many in the churches of the saints. And so missionary zeal has flagged. Still the Lord says—'Go ye . . . and preach.'
(Mark 16. 15; Acts 13. 4)

747. Missionary Hymn. The hymn 'From Greenland's icy mountains' is a unique example of spontaneous writing. Reginald Heber wrote it in twenty minutes. He was then Rector of Hodnet, and was on a visit to his father-in-law, Dr. Shipley. On the Saturday before Whitsunday, 1919, he learnt that on the Sunday a special collection was to be taken for the propagation of the Gospel in foreign lands. His father-in-law asked Heber to write something suitable to sing on that occasion, and in a very short time he had composed three verses. In a few minutes he sat down and wrote the last verse.
(Luke 13. 29; Acts 1. 8; 2 Cor. 10. 16)

748. Model Church.
How beautiful the church must be
*   Where Watchful is the porter;*
Whilst Prudence has the oversight
*   With Patience as exhorter.*

Where Harmony conducts the praise
*   And Reverence the worship;*
Whilst Loyalty accords to Christ
*   The undisputed Lordship.*

Humility pervades the place
*   And Piety sweet smileth;*
Whilst Purity her fragrance breathes
*   And Gentleness beguileth.*

Simplicity adorns the walls
*   And Grace is captivating;*
Benevolence is prominent
*   Whilst Zeal is operating.*

Here Mercy wears her diadem
*   And Meekness conquers friction;*
Whilst Trust exerts its influence,
*   Joy adds the benediction.*
                              —T. Baird
(1 Thess. 1. 2, 3, 7)

749. Money—Definition of. A prize was once offered for the best essay on 'Money', and the winner's summing up of the subject was as follows:
'Money is a very useful commodity, and can purchase everything but happiness. It is a passport everywhere but to heaven.'
(Luke 16. 9, 10; 18. 23, 24; 1 Tim. 6. 7, 8)

750. Money—Eternal Life without. Isaiah speaks the language of the trader when he says, 'Ho, every one that thirsteth, come ye to the waters, and he that hath no money—Yea, come buy wine and milk without money and without price.' Spurgeon says about this invitation: 'The difficulty with other traders is to get you up to their price; but my difficulty is to get you down to mine, for the Bread of Heaven is without price.'
(Is. 52. 3; 55. 1)

751. Money—Heaven without.
At the Devil's booth are all things sold:
Each ounce of dross costs its ounce of gold.
For a cap and bells our lives we pay,
Bubbles we earn with a whole soul's tasking;
'Tis Heaven alone that is given away,
'Tis only God can be had for the asking.
                              —J. Russell Lowell
(Isa. 55. 1; Rom. 5. 15; 1 Pet. 1. 18)

752. Money—Limitations of. Money will buy a bed but not sleep, books but not brains, food but not appetite, finery but not beauty, medicine but not health, luxury but not culture, amusement but not happiness, a crucifix but not a Saviour, a temple of religion but not Heaven.
(Ps. 49. 6-8; Eccles. 5. 12)

753. Money—Love of. Way's translation of 1 Tim. 6. 7-10, with his footnote, is very illuminating.
        A Hymn of Contentment
v. 7. Nothing did we bring into the world, to teach us to remember that we can carry nothing out.
v. 8. But while we have food and clothing, with these will we content us.
v. 9. But they that crave to be rich fall into temptation's snare, and into many witless and baneful desires, which whelm men in pits of ruin and destruction.
v. 10. For the love of money is a root whence springs all evils. Some have clutched thereat, have gone astray from the faith, and have impaled themselves on anguish manifold.
Footnote—The metaphor of this and the lines which follow may be taken from the wild beast which, leaping at the bait hung over a pit, falls in, and is impaled on the stake below.

754. Money—Possession of.
Whereunto is money good?
Who has it not wants hardihood:
Who has it has much trouble and care:
Who once has had it has despair.
                              —H. W. Longfellow
(Ps. 62. 10; Prov. 13. 8; 30. 8; 1 Tim. 6. 8, 9)

755. Money—Spending.

I'm feeling very rich today,
For Jesus holds my purse.
I need not count its scanty store
As all the assets at my door;
Behind it stands a wealthy name,
And vast resources I may claim
Since Jesus holds my purse.

My Cashier never lets me want
Since He controls my purse:
Debit and credit always meet.
I marvel at His counsel sweet
Concerning purchases I make,
Or money given for His dear sake
While He controls my purse.

I'd face the world in great alarm
If Judas held my purse.
He'd call the gifts of humble love
Naught but a waste, treasure above
Uncertain quantity and poor.
My life would barren be, I'm sure,
If Judas held my purse.

And thus I live a carefree life
For Jesus holds my purse.
Since money is a sacred thing,
Both joy and sorrow it may bring
According as we do His will,
Or find our hearts rebellious still.
Let Jesus hold your purse.

756. Money—True Happiness not in.

This is illustrated in the history of two kings, Croesus, King of Lydia, born in 590 B.C., had immense wealth and lived luxuriously. He filled his house with all manner of costly treasures. He thought he was the happiest of mortals. Solon, one of the seven wise men of Greece, paid him a visit and was received into a magnificent chamber. Solon showed no surprise or admiration. The king, angry at his indifference, asked Solon, 'Why do you not think me the most truly happy?' Solon replied, 'No man can be esteemed truly happy but he whose happiness God continues to the end of his life.'

Cyrus, noted for his liberality, was a king loved by his people. He was rich but gave much away. 'My treasures,' he said, 'are the hearts and affections of my people.'
(1 Tim. 6. 17-19)

757. Money—True Wealth not in.

Riches are not gold, nor land, estates, nor marts:
The only gold worth having is found in human
*   hearts.*
(Zech. 4. 2; Luke 12. 33, 34)

758. Money—Uses of.

Dug from the mountain-side, washed in the glen,
Servant am I or the master of men;
Steal me, I curse you; earn me, I bless you;
Grasp me and hoard me—a fiend shall possess
*   you;*
Live for me, die for me, covet me, take me—
Angel or devil, I am what you make me.
(1 Tim. 6. 9, 10, 17)

759. Morale.

The world's moral decay is a forecast of death: the deepening iniquity, above all else, must reach a limit compelling the miraculous intervention of God. The murders in the United States between 1912 and 1918 exceeded by 9,050, the total American death-roll in the first World War—59,377 murders; and 135,000 undiscovered murderers were then at large in the United States. 'To realise,' says Judge Kavanagh of the Superior Court of Chicago, 'the prevalency of this invisible class, it is only necessary to consider that we have unconfined in the United States more killers than we have clergymen of all denominations, or male teachers in our schools, or all lawyers, judges and magistrates put together, and three times the combined number of our editors, reporters and writers; and 52,000 more slayers at large than we have policemen. Within a decade burglary increased 1,200%; and in one year the thefts from common carriers reached £20,000,000; the postal authorities estimated that £60,000,000 was lost through fraudulent schemes; and the Bankers' Association reported £10,000,000 stolen through false cheques. The world's moral fall culminates in a scene in Moscow impossible in any capital in the world before the first World War—a huge bonfire in which a figure labelled 'God Almighty' was burned, while hundreds locked arms and sang and danced as the effigy crashed into cinders.

World War II has been followed by an even greater increase in murders, robberies, sex crimes and embezzlement in Great Britain as well as other countries.
(2 Tim. 3. 1-8; 2 Pet. 2. 12)

760. Morality.

Your morality may keep you out of jail, but it takes God's grace and Christ's atoning sacrifice to keep you out of hell. Salvation is in the cross, not in the commandments.
(Eph. 2. 8; Tit. 3. 5)

761. Mortification—Of Self.

It is said of Mahmoud, the mighty conqueror of a large part of India, that he caused the destruction of all the idols in every town which he entered. In his great career of conquest, he laid siege to the important city of Guzarat. Entering the city at last, he forced his way to the costly shrine of the Brahmins. There he saw a gigantic image, fifteen feet high. Mahmoud gave immediate orders for its destruction. The Brahmins of the temple flung themselves at his feet and begged him with many entreaties to spare their god as the fortunes of the city depended upon him. A poet has described what happened thus:

Ransom vast of gold they offer,
Pearls of price and jewels rare,
Purchase of their idol's safety,
This their dearest will he spare.

And there wanted not who counselled
That he should his hand withhold;
Should that single image suffer,
And accept the proffered gold.

But after further reflection Mahmoud replied
that he would rather be known as the breaker
than as the seller of idols, and he struck the
image a blow with his battle-axe. His soldiers
seeing this followed their leader, and made
short work of the huge image, which was
smashed to pieces. It proved to be hollow
inside and was the hiding-place of a vast
treasure. No wonder the Brahmins begged
that their idol might be spared. Thousands of
most precious gems fell at the conqueror's feet
as the image was shattered by the blows of
the soldiers.

From its shattered side revealing
Pearls and diamonds, showers of gold;
More than all that proffered ransom,
More than all a hundredfold.

Such an idol is self. It offers much if only it be
spared, but this cannot be. True wealth and
heavenly treasure is secured to those who have
learned the secret of losing their life for Christ's
sake. Did not Christ declare: 'He that loveth
his life shall lose it; and he that hateth his life
in this world shall keep it unto life eternal'
(John 12. 25). The way of the cross is the way
of death to the self life.

—Jesse Webb

(Rom. 8. 13; Col. 3. 5)

762. Mortification—Of Self. Look at the
candle. What is it used for? Is it not for
giving light? If it is to give light it must burn
and make itself less and less. But if the candle
were to protest and say, 'I will not burn and
become less and less; I cannot suffer hurt,
neither can my form be changed,' then what
would be its value? In the same way, those who
determine not to put self to death will never see
the will of God fulfilled in their lives. Those
who ought to become the light of the world
must necessarily burn and become less and
less. By denying self we are able to win others.

—Sadhu Sundar Singh

(John 12. 25; Phil. 2. 15; Col. 3. 5)

763. Moses.

Moses, the patriot fierce, became
The meekest man on earth,
To show us how love's quick'ning flame
Can give our souls new birth.

Moses, the man of meekest heart,
Lost Canaan by self-will,
To show, where grace has done its part,
How sin defies us still.

Thou, who hast taught me in Thy fear,
Yet sees me frail at best,
O grant me loss with Moses here,
To gain his future rest!

—John Henry Newman

(Num. 12. 3; Ps. 105. 26; 106. 32, 33)

764. Moses—Antithesis of life of.

Moses was the child of a slave, yet the son of a
Princess:
He was born in a hut, but reared in a Palace:
He inherited extreme poverty yet enjoyed
immense wealth:
Educated for a court, he did his greatest work
in a desert:
He was the mightiest of warriors, yet the
meekest of men:
Moses possessed the wisdom of this world, yet
had the faith of a little child:
His funeral was not attended by a single human
creature: but the Creator Himself was
present:
His death created no great stir on earth,
but occasioned a great commotion in
Heaven.

(Exod. 2. 10; Num. 12. 3, 7; Deut. 34. 5-7;
Jude 9)

765. Moses—Character of. Meekness is not
weakness. On the contrary, it is the sign and
cause of strength. The ox lies still while the
geese are hissing. The mastiff is still while the
curs are yelping. Moses was king in Israel
because of his great meekness among a
provoking people.

(Num. 12. 3; Heb. 3. 5)

766. Moses—Education of. Dr. Flinders
Petrie was the greatest archaeologist of modern
times, and his work opened the way for our
knowledge of ancient Egypt. Other Egypt-
ologists also rendered great service in this field
of study. Dr. Smith in the *Moody Monthly*
referred to this and, quoting from Dr. Petrie's
book, *The Wisdom of the Egyptians,* he gives
some idea of how large may have been the
range of knowledge acquired by Moses in
Egypt. The Egyptians studied:- observational
Astronomy, instrumental Astronomy, Arithmetic and Geometry, Writing, Drawing and
Design, Musical Instruments, Building, Miner-
ology, Chemistry, Metal Working, Agriculture,
Transport, etc. The subject-headings dealt
with in the chapter on Instrumental Astronomy
are—the sun's altitude, star observation,
constellations, planets, the Zodiac, transits,
and so on. A formidable list!

—Indian Christian

(Acts 7. 22)

767. Moses—Funeral of.

By Nebo's lonely mountain,
On this side Jordan's wave,
In a vale in the land of Moab
There lies a lonely grave.
And no man knows the sepulchre,
And no man saw it e'er,
For the angels of God upturned the sod
And laid the dead man there.

That was the grandest funeral
That ever passed on earth;
But no man heard the trampling
Or saw the train go forth—
Noiselessly as the daylight
Comes back when night is done,
And the crimson streak on ocean's cheek
Grows into the great sun.

Noiselessly as the springtime
Her crown of verdure weaves,
And all the trees on all the hills
Open their thousand leaves;
So without sound of music,
Or voice of them that wept,
Silently down from the mountain's crown
The great procession swept.

Perchance the bald old eagle,
On grey Beth-peor's height,
Out of his lonely eyrie
Looked on the wondrous sight;
Perchance the lion stalking,
Still shuns that hallowed spot,
For beast and bird have seen and heard
That which man knoweth not.

This was the truest warrior
That ever buckled sword;
This the most gifted poet
That ever breathed a word.
And never earth's philosopher
Traced with his golden pen
On the deathless page truths half so sage
As he wrote down for men.

And had he not high honour?—
The hill-side for a pall,
To lie in state while angels wait,
With stars for tapers tall;
And the dark rock-pines, like tossing plumes,
Over his bier to wave,
And God's own hand in that lonely land
To lay him in the grave.

In that strange grave without a name,
Whence his uncoffined clay
Shall break again, O wondrous thought!
Before the judgement day,
And stand with glory wrapt around
On the hills he never trod,
And speak of the strife that won our life,
With the incarnate Son of God.

O lonely grave in Moab's land!
O dark Beth-peor's hill!
Speak to these curious hearts of ours,
And teach them to be still.
God hath His mysteries of grace,
Ways that we cannot tell;
He hides them deep, like the hidden sleep
Of him He loved so well.
—Cecil F. Alexander (two stanzas omitted)
(Deut. 34. 6)

768. **Mounting up.** Some flightless birds are equipped with wings. Of these there are two classes:-
(i) those that cannot fly because of their tremendous weight or enormous stature:- e.g. the ostrich, the emu, the cassowary:

(ii) those which, through lack of persecution from land creatures, become lazy and never trouble to fly, finding by experience they can get good food with ease. The result is that ultimately their wings become useless for flying:- e.g. the penguin, kiwi, domestic fowls. (Isa. 40. 31)

769. **Mounting up.** In Philadelphia the capital of Pennsylvania, U.S.A., above the city hall, is the statue of William Penn, 25 feet high itself, yet resting on the topmost point of the dome. In autumn, when birds from the North fly South to a warmer clime—often in the twilight or at night—bodies of dead birds are frequently found in the morning among the masonry and on the pavement around the Town Hall. One morning over a hundred dead birds were found, mostly young ones. Flying in the dark and flying low, they struck and stunned themselves on the statues and fell.
That is just the tragedy in the lives of some young Christians. They fly too low, too near the world. We must mount up higher.
(Isa. 40. 31)

770. **Name—Good.**
Good name in man or woman, dear my lord,
Is the immediate jewel of their souls;
Who steals my purse steals trash; 'tis something,
*   nothing;*
T'was mine, 'tis his, and has been slave to
*   thousands;*
But he that filches from me my good name
Robs me of that which not enriches him,
And makes me poor indeed.
                    —Shakespeare in *Othello*
(Prov. 22. 1; Acts 22. 12)

771. **Name—of Jesus.** Dr. Stewart tells of a little company of Russian peasants who had met for worship, knowing full well their gathering was illegal. While their worship was proceeding, suddenly the door was flung open and there entered an agent of the secret police, with a body of men. 'Take these peoples' names,' he commanded. The names were written down. One old man stopped him and said, 'There is one name you have not got.' The Officer said in surprise, 'I assure you you are mistaken. I have them all.' The peasant insisted that one name was missing from his list.
'Well, we'll prove it. We'll count again. —Thirty!—you see,' said the officer, 'I have them all, every one.'
But still the peasant persisted, 'There is one name you haven't got.'
'Who is it then?' asked the officer.
'The Lord Jesus Christ,' was the answer, 'He is here.'
'Ah!' answered the officer, 'that is a different matter.'
(Matt. 18. 20; Phil. 2. 10)

772. Name—of Jesus.

Jesus, dishonoured and dying,
A felon on either side—
Jesus, the song of the drunkards,
Jesus the Crucified!
Name of God's tender comfort,
Name of His glorious power,
Name that is song and sweetness,
The strong everlasting tower.
Jesus the Lamb accepted,
Jesus the Priest on His throne—
Jesus the King Who is coming—
Jesus Thy Name alone!

—C.P.C. in *Hymns of Ter Stegen & others*
(Matt. 1. 21; Matt. 27. 37; Acts 4. 12)

773. Name—of Jesus. A group of Bedouin women were listening for the first time to the preaching of the Gospel. It was all new to them, and one woman was afraid that she might even forget the name which had fallen so sweetly on her ears. 'Tell me the name again,' she pleaded; and returned to her wandering life with the name of 'Jesus' as her one link with eternal truth.

Tell me the name again, lest I forget it,
The name of Him Who died to set me free.
'Tis Jesus, Saviour; ne'er wilt thou forget it
If thou wilt let His love lay hold on thee.

His name above all other names is glorious,
A place of refuge in the day of strife;
To trust Him fully is to be victorious
In every hour and circumstance of life.

'Tell me the name,' then when the day is dawning,
Ere through the busy world my way I take,
'Tis 'Wonderful'—He'll gild the dullest morning
If thou wilt live thy life for Jesus' sake.

Tell me the name, when noontide finds me
viewing,
With anxious eyes, the problems that oppress;
'Tis 'Counsellor'—thy failing strength renewing:
He'll teach thee wisdom, banish thy distress.

Tell me the name, when life's short journey
ending,
My senses fail, my mortal eyes grow dim;
'Tis 'Prince of Peace,' all human peace trans-
cending,
He'll give thee rest, thou shalt abide with Him.

Tell them the name—its beauty, its perfection—
Who never heard our blessed Master's fame:
Tell of His life, His death, His resurrection;
Tell of His power to save—tell them the name!

—J.D.McK

(Isa. 9. 6; Acts 3. 6; 10. 43; Phil. 2. 10, 11; Heb. 1. 4)

774 Names. Dr Clifton N. Howard, Chairman of the World Peace Commission, attended the opening session of the Conference for Limitation of Armaments at Washington, U.S.A. Among the High Commissioners attending, an interesting and extraordinary personality representing 350 million people attracted much attention. While every head was uncovered he kept his hat on—a white turban closely wound round his dark-skinned, dignified head. Around his neck was a string of beads which he fingered with reverence, pushing them from right to left one by one until he made a complete circuit of his neck. He was a Mohammedan nobleman, this Commissioner from India, and sat in silence moving his lips in inaudible speech as he pushed his beads.

Dr Howard, introduced to him by an official, asked, What is the significance of that string of beads around your neck?'

'That is not a string,' he replied, 'but a golden cord that binds my soul to Allah.'

And the beads?' enquired Dr. Howard.

'Beads! these are not beads, but gems of glory, jewels of joy, pearls of Paradise! This is my rosary. Each of these gems—jewels—pearls—ninety-nine in all, one short of 100—is a name of Allah, the God of the Moham-medans, the God of the Koran, and I have a better speaking acquaintance with Allah than you have with your Christ. I know my God by His full name and I challenge you to match my rosary.'

Dr. Clifton N. Howard could not take up the challenge, he was ashamed to say, for he did not know his Bible well enough, and was not on such a close speaking acquaintance with the Lord Jesus Christ. But after study and search he found 208 names for our Lord Jesus Christ in the Bible: all gems of glory, jewels of joy, pearls of Paradise.

He listed seven names from Heaven given to our Lord in Incarnation at His birth—Jesus, Son of God, Son of the Highest, Immanuel, Saviour, Christ and Lord.

He listed seven more in John Chapter 1—The Word, the Lamb of God, the Son of God, Messias, Jesus of Nazareth, Rabbi, and King of Israel.

He discovered that the name of Jesus occurred over 700 times in the New Testament. Jesus—the name high over all—means Jehovah Saviour.

Jesus, the name high over all,
In hell, or earth, or sky;
Angels and men before it fall,
And devils fear and fly.

Jesus, the name to sinners dear,
The name to sinners given:
It scatters all their guilty fear,
It turns their hell to Heaven.

(Prov. 18. 10; Matt. 1. 21; Isa. 9. 6; Acts 4. 12)

775. Natural Man. There is a story told of Catherine the Great of Russia who was by birth a German and had not a drop of Slav blood in her veins. She did her utmost to become a Russian to the Russians, and to master their language. Once, when her doctor was, as was the custom in those days, bleeding her for some ailment or other, she remarked to him, 'There goes the last drop of German blood, I hope.'

(1 Cor. 2. 14; 15. 22; 2 Cor. 5. 17)

776. Needle—Eye of a. Shakespeare makes allusion to this in *Richard II*:

'*It is as hard to some, as for a camel*
To thread the postern of a needle's eye.'

Evidently he understood it not to mean a literal needle but the Needle Gate, so called because it was so narrow and difficult to pass through.

The word Luke, the beloved physician, uses in his Gospel record for a 'needle' is different from that the other Synoptics use. Luke uses the word for a surgeon's needle. We infer, therefore, that our Lord meant an ordinary needle used for sewing.
(Mark 10. 25; Luke 18. 25)

777. Needs—All our. We can never use the language of the Laodicean church and say, 'We have need of nothing.' Our needs are great but the Lord's resources are inexhaustible. Here are some kinds of needs mentioned in the New Testament:
1. *Material*—Matt. 6. 32; Phil. 4. 12, 16— 'Your Father knoweth'.
2. *Physical*—Luke 9. 11—'All who had need of healing'.
3. *Personal*—Luke 10. 42—Quiet time alone with the Lord, at His feet.
4. *Moral*—John 13. 10—Daily cleansing: need to wash our feet.
5. *Social*—1 Cor. 12. 21—Need of fellowship: fellow-members of Christ.
6. *Spiritual*—Heb. 10. 36—'Ye have need of patience'.
7. *Mental*—James 1. 5—'If any man lack wisdom let him ask of God'.

(Phil. 4. 19)

778. New Birth. Mr. Spurgeon tells of a simple countryman who took his gun to the gunsmith for repairs. After examining it, the latter said: 'Your gun is in a very worn-out, ruinous, good-for-nothing condition. What sort of repairing do you want for it?'

'Well,' said the countryman, 'I don't see as I can do with anything short of a new stock, lock, and barrel. That ought to set it up again.'

'Why,' said the smith, 'you had better have a new gun altogether.'

'Ah,' was the reply, 'I never thought of that. It strikes me that's just what I do want, a new stock, lock and barrel. Why, that's about equal to a new gun altogether, and that's what I'll have.'

That is just what God says concerning poor human nature 'A new man altogether'.
—*Prairie Overcomer*
(2 Cor. 5. 17)

779. New Creation. The first creation was on probation in its head, Adam, and failed. The new creation was also on probation in its Head, Christ Jesus; but it did no fail. Christ is no longer on probation, neither are those who have believed on Him unto salvation.
—Selected
(Rom. 5. 14, 15; 1 Cor. 15. 22; 2 Cor. 5. 17; Col. 1. 28)

780. New Heaven.
We look still beyond for a wondrous new heaven
Its glories the finite can ne'er comprehend;
Without sin or sorrow, without night or morrow,
And oh, what a wonder, without e'er an end!
—J. Danson Smith
(2 Pet. 3. 13; Rev. 21. 1-5)

781. New Heaven and New Earth.
Where all is new and never shall be old,
For time is not, nor age, nor slow decay,
No dying eyes, no hearts grown strange and cold,
All pain, all death, all sighing fled away.
(2 Pet. 3. 13; Rev. 21. 1-5)

782. New Life. I have seen in the autumn when the trees had shed their leaves that two or three have stuck fast on the branches, and have clung to them through all the storms of winter. But, when the spring has come and the sap has begun to ascend, the leaves have disappeared, pushed off by the rising tide of life.
—Dr. A. J. Gordon

In the experience of the believer in the Lord Jesus Christ, this is what Dr. Chalmers called 'the expulsive power of a new affection'.
(2 Cor. 5. 17)

783. New Life. I will never forget the day Grace Armstrong was converted. It was at a Sunday afternoon meeting in Chicago. She just slid down on her knees and sobbed as though her heart would break. No one could console her. Then as she went out, her girl friends told her that it would soon pass away.

'No, girls,' responded Grace, 'this will never pass away.'

And when young men telephoned her and invited her to the theatre, without a moment's hesitation she answered 'No!' Old things had passed away in a single moment. All things had become new. Christ was now in her heart and she had a new affection. She loved the prayer meeting, loved to stand and sing for her Saviour on the street corner, loved to do personal work, loved above everything else the house of God. Grace is now with the Lord, but oh, what a wonderful testimony she left before she went home.

When I was a missionary among the Indians near Alaska, I lived for some time on what is called 'hardtack'. 'Dog biscuit' I suppose would be the name in civilization. Now, it was hard, so hard that only by warming it could I manage to penetrate it with my teeth. Nevertheless I thoroughly enjoyed and relished it.

But there came a day when I returned to civilization and began to eat bread and butter once more. And, what do you think? Why, I have never wanted hardtack since. Not once have I pined for the old days and cried, 'Oh, for a bit of hardtack once more.' And why? Simply because I have found something better.

—Oswald J. Smith

(2 Cor. 5. 17)

784. New Life. John Masefield has described how 'Saul Kane' came upon a new world because Christ made him a new man. He existed through a wild career of coarseness, wickedness, of poachings, drinkings, imprisonments. One dissolute night he tore his clothes to shreds, ran wild through the street, clutched and rang the fire bell, till, his rage subsiding, he crept back to the public-house. But there came an end, a complete break with the past, the discovery of a new world, because new eyes saw it, and a new heart felt it.

I did not think, I did not strive,
The deep peace burnt my me alive;
The bolted door had broken in,
I knew that I had done with sin.
I knew that Christ had given me birth
To brother all the souls on earth,
And every bird and every beast
Should share the crumbs broke at the feast.

O glory of the lighted mind.
How dead I'd been, how dumb, how blind!
The station brook, to my new eyes,
Was bubbling out of Paradise;
The waters rushing from the rain
Were singing Christ has risen again.
I thought all earthly creatures knelt
From rapture of the joy I felt.

—John Macbeath

(Acts 3. 8, 9; 2 Cor. 5. 17)

785. New Year.

Ring out, wild bells to the wild sky,
The flying cloud, the frosty light;
The year is dying in the night;
Ring out, wild bells, and let him die.

Ring out the old, ring in the new,
Ring, happy bells, across the snow;
The year is going, let him go;
Ring out the false, ring in the true.

Ring out the grief that saps the mind,
For those that here we see no more;
Ring out the feud of rich and poor,
Ring in redress to all mankind.

Ring out the want, the care, the sin,
The faithless coldness of the times;
Ring out, ring out my mournful rhymes,
But ring the fuller minstrel in.

Ring out false pride in place and blood,
The civic slander and the spite;
Ring in the love of truth and right,
Ring in the common love of good.
Ring out old shapes of foul disease,
Ring out the narrowing lust of gold;
Ring out the thousand wars of old,
Ring in the thousand years of peace.

Ring in the valiant man and free,
The larger heart, the kindlier hand;
Ring out the darkness of the land,
Ring in the Christ that is to be.

—Alfred, Lord Tennyson

(Ezek. 36. 26; John 3. 7)

786. New Year. January, the first month of the year, gets its name from the Roman god, Janus or Januarius, who was represented as having two heads, and two pairs of eyes, each pair looking in the opposite direction from the other, and each head facing a different direction from the other.

New Year is often stock-taking time with business men, and it is good for the Christian, too, to take stock, to look back into the past and trace the good hand and kindness of the Lord amid much failure on his part, and to look forward to a new year of opportunity, of privilege and responsibility. Instead of good resolutions, he will make a full and fresh consecration of himself and all his powers to the Lord.

(Exod. 12. 2)

787. New Year. Charles Lamb, in one of the *Essays of Elia*, tells us that he was shy of novelties—new books, new faces, new friends, new years. In this respect he differed from the poet, Tennyson, who welcomed in the new year.

788. News. Tennyson on one occasion spent a holiday with a Methodist family in a Lincolnshire village. On his arrival, he asked his hostess if she had any news for him. 'Why, Mr. Tennyson,' she replied, 'there's only one piece of news that I know—Christ died for all men.' 'Well,' responded the poet, 'that's old news, and good news, and new news.'

This word *NEWS* is a very interesting one, and is composed of the initial letters of the four main points of the compass—North, East, West, South. News is gathered from all quarters, but the best of all news comes, not from around us, but from above us.

—Indian Christian

(Acts 13. 26; 1 Cor. 15. 3, 4)

789. News—Bad; but God—

Bad news has come, and heart and mind are
*   sobered,—*
*   We did not think that things would come to*
*   this:*
We deemed that God would surely send deliver-
*   ance;*
*   We asked that what was threatened we might*
*   miss.*

But it has come—the thing we deemed unwanted!
*   Bad news, indeed, it seems to us today;*
We cannot think that God has failed to hear us,
*   But cannot fathom why He answers 'Nay'.*
What shall we do?—Succumb or get down-
*   hearted?*

That were indeed the easy road to tread;
With hope and trust cast over—faith abandoned—
And God, the God Who loves—why, deemed
as dead.

Bad news indeed! But God abideth faithful!
Some fresh unfolding of His power He'll show;
Thus, unto Him, Whose love is quite unending,
Whose care and power are limitless—we'll go.
　　　　　　　　　　　—J. Danson Smith
(Rom. 8. 28; Phil. 2. 26, 27; 4. 19)

790. Nothing—Argument about. It was in a
commercial hotel. A few travellers were
present, comparing notes and gossiping on all
sorts of topics. Some of them were Christians,
and ready to take advantage of any opportunity
that arose of testifying for their Master. One
of them, addressing another, said: 'Rees is here
and boasting loudly that he is ready to tackle
any Christian about their religion and knock
the bottom out of all their arguments in
support of it. What do you say to meeting
him?' The other replied, 'Very well, I'll meet
him: arrange it as soon as you can.' Rees was
a bold and blatant infidel, who boasted he
could upset the Christian faith and confute its
ablest defenders. The Christian who calmly
undertook its defence believed his faith,
founded upon the Holy Scriptures, to be
impregnable, and feared no defeat.

The arrangements were soon made, the
opponents facing each other, and an eager
audience looked on. The Christian opened
the discussion with the Bible on his knee, and,
pointing to it, said: 'You say that the things in
this Book are nothing to you?' 'I do,' said the
infidel, boldly. 'You say that the salvation it
speaks of for saving a lost humanity is nothing
to you?' 'I do,' again replied the other.
'And,' went on the Christian, 'you say that the
Saviour that this Book speaks of, whose name
is Jesus, the Son of God Who shed His blood
on the Cross of Calvary for sinners, is nothing
to you?' 'I do,' replied the infidel emphatically.
'Well!' answered the believer, 'don't you
think that all the people around us here would
put us down as a pair of arrant fools to have
an argument about *Nothing*? Man, if there is
nothing in it, and you're quite sure of it, why
do you bother your head about it? As there's
nothing in it, why trouble about it? No man
interests himself much about nothing! Why,
you can't even defend nothing, for there's
nothing to defend! And why attack that
which, by your own admission, has nothing
in it.'
(Lam. 1. 12)

791. Nothing—to pay.
Nothing to pay?—No, not a whit;
Nothing to do?—no, not a bit;
All that was needed to do or to pay
Jesus has done in His own blessed way.

Nothing to do?—No, not a stroke;
Gone is the captor, gone is the yoke;
Jesus at Calvary severed the chain,
And none can imprison His freeman again.

Nothing to fear?—No, not a jot;
Nothing unclean?—no, not a spot;
Christ is my peace, and I've nothing at stake;
Satan can neither harass nor shake.

Nothing to settle?—All has been paid;
Nothing of anger?—Peace has been made;
Jesus alone is the sinner's resource;
Peace He has made by the blood of His cross.

What about judgement?—I'm thankful to say
Jesus has met it and borne it away;
Drank it all up when He hung on the tree,
Leaving a cup full of blessing to me.

What about terror?—It hasn't a place
In a heart that is filled with a sense of His grace;
My peace is divine and it never can cloy,
And that makes my heart bubble over with joy.

What about death?—It hasn't a sting;
The grave to a Christian no terror can bring,
For death has been conquered, the grave has
*　　been spoiled,*
And every foe of his armour despoiled.
(Luke 7. 42; John 19. 30; Rom. 4. 4, 5; 1 Cor.
15. 54-57)

792. Numbers—Scripture.

One—unity, light: hence light in the soul
and spiritual rebirth. There are two words in
Hebrew, 'echad' signifying a collective unit
(Deut. 6. 4) and 'yacheid' (Gen. 22. 2).

Two—separation, division: hence redemption
and witness (Exod. 8. 23). God's witnesses
were in pairs and Christ's apostles were sent
out two by two.

Three—Trinity, Divine perfection (Isa. 6. 3;
Num. 6. 23-27). God is Spirit, Light and Love.
The tabernacle had three parts. The inscription
on the Cross was in three languages. Christ's
temptation was threefold and His resurrection
on the third day. There were three patriarchs,
Abraham, Isaac and Jacob.

Four—creation and the material world
which was constructed on the fourth day.
There are four seasons and four directions;
there were four world empires. In the presentation of the life of our Lord four 'Gospels' are
used. The good seed of the Word of God falls
on four kinds of soil in the field which is the
world.

Five—Divine grace and power amid human
weakness. Israel went out from Egypt five in a
rank. There were five ingredients in the
anointing oil and the sweet incense.

Six—the number of man. Man was created
on the sixth day. The giant, Goliath, was six
cubits high and had six pieces of armour. The
golden image in Dan. 3. was sixty cubits by six.
Six words are used in the Bible for 'man', and
the number of man—in Rev. 13—is 666.

Seven—spiritual perfection. In Isa. 11. 2
there is a sevenfold description of the Spirit
resting on Christ. There are seven spirits in
Revelation, and the 'new song' is mentioned
seven times in the New Testament.

Eight—resurrection and regeneration. Eight persons were saved in the ark. The eighth day was the day of circumcision. There are 8 authors in the New Testament, and 88 occurrences of the Lord's title—'Son of man'.

Nine—finality. Nine is the last of the digits. Amen occurs 99 times in the Bible. On the cross our Lord cried at the ninth hour, 'Father, into Thy hands I commend my spirit'. The fruit of the Spirit is ninefold, and the gifts of the Spirit are nine.

Ten—perfection of order. In Gen. 1. 'And God said' occurs ten times. God gave ten commandments on Sinai. The holiest of all in the Tabernacle was $10 \times 10 \times 10$. The Millennium will be $10 \times 10 \times 10$ years.

Eleven — disorganization, disintegration. Eleven sons of Jacob in Gen. 32. 22: Joseph, the long-lost son, saw eleven stars in his dreams (Gen. 37. 9).

Twelve—governmental perfection. There were twelve tribes and twelve apostles. On the tree of life there will be twelve fruits. The new Jerusalem is described as having 12 foundations and 12 gates.

793. Obligations. When some men discharge an obligation, you can hear the report for miles around.

—Mark Twain

794. Obscurity.

An unknown man supplied the beast
Whereon the lowly Saviour passed
Along the way triumphantly,
Proclaimed the promised king at last.
An unknown man supplied the room
Where once the Saviour broke the bread
And gave the wine—His flesh and blood:
His life, by which our lives are fed.

(Luke 19. 33; 22. 10, 11)

795. Obstacles. The story is told of a king who placed a heavy stone in the road and then hid and watched to see who would remove it. Men of various classes came and worked their way round it, some loudly blaming the king for not keeping the highways clear, but all dodging the duty of getting it out of the way. At last a poor peasant on his way to town with his burden of vegetables for sale came, and, contemplating the stone, laid down his load, and rolled the stone into the gutter. Then, turning round, he spied a purse that had lain right under the stone. He opened it and found it full of gold pieces, with a note from the king saying it was for the one who should remove the stone. Under every obstacle our King has hidden a blessing. We can turn back from a cross or go round it, but we are eternal losers if we do. We cannot dodge the cross without dodging God's blessing, and we cannot refuse it without endangering our crown. He is watching.

—*Indian Christian*

(Luke 14. 27; John 11. 39)

796. Occupied—for the Lord. 'Occupy till I come'—'Be occupied, be in business, till I come'.

An Eastern Allegory.

A merchant, going abroad for a time, gave two of his friends each two sacks of grain to take care of against his return. Years passed by. When he came back, he applied to them for the return of the grain.

The first took him into his storehouse and showed him the two sacks as he had received them, now mildewed and worthless. The other led him into the country and showed him fields of grain growing and ripening, the produce of the two sacks which he had used as seed.

'Give me the two sacks,' said the merchant, 'and keep the rest.'

(Luke 19. 13)

797. Old Age.

They say that I am growing old,
I've heard them tell it times untold,
In language plain and bold;
But I'm not growing old.
This frail old shell in which I dwell
Is growing old, I know full well—
But I am not the shell.

What should I care if Time's old plough
Has left its furrows on my brow?
What though I falter in my walk?
I still can watch and pray and talk.
My hearing may not be so keen
As in the past it may have been;
Still I can hear my Saviour say,
In whispers soft, 'This is the Way!'

(2 Cor. 4. 16)

798. Old Age. An aged gardener was asked how old he was. 'I am an octogeranium,' he replied, making a charming blunder which was really an improvement on the meaning of the word he meant to use. The octogenarian who is also an octogeranium—that is to say, the old man with a young soul, the veteran with an open mind, the ancient pilgrim who maintains the forward look—that person is one of the most attractive of human types.

With that story came another equally beautiful one from America, about a fine old warrior well on in his eighties. He was told that a friend of his, aged 75, had said that a man is at his best in his seventies; but the octogenarian would have none of it. 'He will know better when he grows up' was his comment.

—Henry Durbanville

(Josh. 14. 6-12; Isa. 46. 4)

799. Old Age. They say I am growing old because my hair is silvered, and there are crow's feet on my forehead, and my step is not as firm and elastic as before. But they are mistaken; that is not me. The knees are weak but the knees are not me. The brow is wrinkled but the brow is not me. This is the house I live in: but I am young—younger than I was ever before.

—Dr. Guthrie

800.   Old Age. When John Quincey Adams was a very old man someone asked him how he was keeping, and he said: 'Thank you, John Quincey Adams is very well himself, sir; but the house in which he lives is falling to pieces. Time and seasons have nearly destroyed it. The roof is well worn, the walls shattered. It trembles with every gale. I think John Quincey Adams will soon have to move out. But he himself is very well, sir.'

—Henry Durbanville
(Prov. 16. 31; 2 Cor. 4. 16)

801.   Old Age. Some four hundred names of the most noted men in all times, from all lines of activity, were chosen. There were statesmen, painters, warriors, poets, and writers of fiction history, and other prose works. Opposite to the name of each man was indicated, his greatest work or achievement. This list was then submitted to critics, to learn their opinion of the greatest work of each man submitted. The names of their greatest works were accepted, or altered, until the list was one that could be finally accepted. After this was done the date at which the work was produced was placed after the name, and so the age was ascertained at which the individual was at his best. The list was then arranged according to decades.

It was found that the decade of years between sixty and seventy contained thirty-five per cent of the world's greatest achievements. Between the ages of seventy and eighty, twenty-three per cent of the achievements fell; and in the years after the eightieth, six per cent.

In other words, sixty-four per cent of the great things of the world have been accomplished by men who had passed their sixtieth year, the greatest percentage, thirty-five, being in the seventh decade.

The figures for the other periods of life are interesting. Between the fiftieth and sixtieth years are found twenty-five per cent, between forty and fifty ten per cent. These, all totalled together, leave the almost negligible quantity of one per cent to be attributed to the period below the age of forty.

Two great classes of work fall below the forty year limit. These are the deeds which require the extreme of physical power and vim, as the conquests of Alexander the Great; and the beautiful expression of the lyric poetry, which is typified by the nervous, supersensitive temperament of such men as Shelley and Keats.

—Martin Sherwood
(Ps. 92. 14)

802.   Old Age.
They call it going down the hill when we are
  growing old,
And speak with mournful accents, when our tale
  is nearly told:
They sigh when talking of the past, the days
  that used to be,
As if the future were not bright with immortality.
But oh! it is not 'going down'; 'tis coming
  higher, higher,
Until we almost see the Home our longing hearts
  desire;
For when the natural eye grows dim, it is but dim
  to earth,
While the eye of faith grows keener to see the
  Saviour's worth.
Those bygone days, the days of joy, we wish not
  back again;
For—were there not so many days of sorrow and
  of pain?
But in the days awaiting us, the days beyond the
  tomb,
Sorrow shall never find a place, but joy eternal
  bloom.
For though in truth the outward man must perish
  and decay,
The inward man is still renewed by grace from
  day to day.
They who are planted by the Lord, unshaken in
  the root,
E'en to old age shall flourish still, and even bring
  forth fruit.
It is not years that make men old; the spirit may
  be young,
Though for the threescore years and ten the
  wheels of life have run.
God has Himself recorded in His blessed Word
  of truth
That 'they who wait upon the Lord' shall still
  renew their youth.
Yes, when the eyes now dimmed with years
  behold with joy the King,
And ears now dull with age shall hear the harps
  of Heaven ring,
And on the head now hoary shall be placed the
  crown of gold,
Then shall we know the lasting bliss of never
  growing old.

—J.G.D.
(Ps. 92. 14; 2 Cor. 4. 16)

803.   Opinions—Man's and God's.
Man calls sin an accident, but God calls it an
  abomination:
man calls sin a blunder, but God calls it blind-
  ness:
man calls sin a chance, but God calls it a choice:
man calls sin a defect, but God calls it a disease:
man calls sin an error, but God calls it an
  enormity:
man calls sin fascinating, but God calls it fatal:
man calls sin infirmity, but God calls it iniquity:
man calls sin a luxury, but God calls it lawless-
  ness:

man calls sin a mistake, but God calls it madness:
man calls sin a trifle, but God calls it a tragedy:
man calls sin weakness, but God calls it wicked-
ness.
(John 9. 41; James 2. 9, 10; 1 John 3. 4)

804. Opportunity. In one of the cities of
ancient Greece stood a statue chiselled by
Lysippus. It had wings, a lock of hair on the
forehead, and was bald at the back. Under-
neath were chiselled out in Greek letters the
questions and answers:
'Who made thee?'—'Lysippus made me.'
'What is thy name?'—'My name is Oppor-
  tunity.'
'Why hast thou wings on thy feet?'—'That I
  may fly swiftly over the earth.'
'Why hast thou a forelock?'—'That men may
  seize me as I come.'
'Why art thou bald on the back of thy head?'—
  'Because, when I am gone, none can lay
  hold of me.'
Hence we have the proverbial expression—
'Take time by the forelock.'
(Acts 24. 25; 2 Cor. 6. 2)

805. Opportunity.
Of all sad words of tongue or pen,
The saddest are these, 'It might have been.'
              —*J. G. Whittier in Maud Muller*
(2 Sam. 18. 32, 33)

806. Opportunity.
Remember three things come not back:—
The arrow sent upon its track:—
It will not swerve, it will not stay
Its speed: it flies to wound or slay.

The spoken word, so soon forgot
By thee; but it has perished not;
In other hearts 'tis living still
And doing work for good or ill:

And the lost opportunity
That cometh back no more to thee.
In vain thou weep'st, in vain dost yearn;
These three shall never more return.

(2 Cor. 6. 2)

807. Optimism. You cannot be optimistic
with misty optics about spiritual things: you
must have your vision clear and spiritual.
(Matt. 6. 22; 2 Pet. 1. 8, 9)

808. Orderliness. A planter in Kentucky
engaged a negro as a mule-driver. To test him
he handed him a new whip, climbed into a seat
behind a pair of mules, and asked the new
driver if he could use the whip. To prove his
skill, Sam flicked a butterfly on clover blossom,
then killed a honey-bee with another swing of
the whip. Further along they came to a hornet's
nest beside the highway, with two or three
hornets at the entrance.
'Can you hit them?' asked the planter.
'Yes, sah, I kin, but I ain't goin' to. Dey's
organized,' replied Sam.
(Ezek. 37. 10; Phil. 1. 27)

809. Out-and-out—for God. There used to be
an American firm of tentmakers, Wilson by
name. They manufactured tents, awnings,
covers, campcots, and such-like canvas articles.
On the catalogues they sent out they printed
such advertisements as—'A good Bargain:'
then followed a short description of one of
their products:
Underneath—'A Better Bargain'—'The gift
of God is eternal life through Jesus Christ
our Lord.'
'Excellent Covers'—strong and durable:
Then below this—'A Better Covering still—
'Blessed is the man whose transgression is
forgiven, whose sin is covered.'
One of their customers wrote in complaining
about the advertisements, and said, 'Unless
you stop this "Jesus" stuff, we'll stop our
orders.'
The advertisements continued as before. A
year later, the customer wrote, '"Jesus" stuff or
no "Jesus" stuff, we can't duplicate them.'
(Rom. 12. 11; Col. 3. 17, 23)

810. Palestine. Out of Hebrew Palestine and
its ancient rigours and wars came the Psalms
of David, the prophecies of Isaiah, the cosmo-
graphy of Job. And out of it, nearly two
thousand years ago, came the most wonderful
thing that has ever happened on this planet:
the birth of a male child to the betrothed wife
of an obscure Jewish carpenter which changed
and transfigured the potentialities of the human
mind and spirit. For Jesus Christ of Nazareth,
born in the strange, wild, war-racked country of
this turbulent, restless race, discovered and
revealed to man something far more wonderful,
and in the long run far more powerful, than
gunpowder, steam power, or the use of atomic
energy.
It is well for a Christian to bear all this in
mind when he contemplates the alarms and
excursions, the murders, threats and horrors
now once again rending the land of Palestine,
and in which the Jews today, in the full and
irresistible process of one of their historic and
periodic returns to their chosen land, are the
leading actors.
                                        —Selected
(Deut. 34. 4; Rom. 9. 4, 5)

811. Paradoxes—of the Christian.
How strange is the course that a Christian must
  steer,
How perplexed is the path he must tread;
The hope of his happiness rises from fear,
And his life he receives from the dead.
His fairest pretensions must wholly be waived,
And his best resolutions be crossed;
Nor can he expect to be perfectly saved
Till he finds himself utterly lost.
When all this is done, and his heart is assured
Of the total remission of sins;
When his pardon is signed and his peace is
  procured,
From that moment his conflict begins.
(2 Cor. 6. 9, 10)

812. Pardon. A shamefaced employee was summoned to the office of the senior partner to hear his doom. The least that he could expect was a blustering dismissal; he might be prosecuted, and even go to prison for years. The old man looked straight at him and asked if he were guilty. The clerk stammered out that he had no defence. 'I shall not prosecute you for the sake of those who love you,' said the old man. 'If I let you stay, can I trust you?' When the surprised and broken clerk had given assurance and was about to leave, the senior partner continued: 'You are the second man who has fallen and been pardoned in this business. I was the first. What you have received I received. It is only the grace of God that can keep us both.'

Ps. 32. 1, 2; 2 Cor. 5. 19; Luke 7. 42, 43)

813. Passover—and the Lord's Supper.

'We see in Paul a man beside whose achievements even a colossus like Napoleon seems a pigmy, and Alexander the Great the creature of an instant.'

(1 Tim. 1. 12; 2 Tim. 4. 17)

816. Payment—by another. My husband was invited to preach for a time in Inverness-shire, and proposed taking me and the children to my father's home for the time-being. That this might be possible the Lord sent, from some source unknown to us, a five pound note, and we were enabled with this to set out. When we started from Glasgow two women with large baskets filled with fruit entered the carriage. The passengers rather demurred to the baskets being there, and thought they should have been in the baggage van. However, the women seemed quite willing to stand or do anything to accommodate the passengers if only the baskets could remain, so we all

THE JEWISH PASSOVER	THE LORD'S SUPPER
Annual.	Frequent.
A lamb roast with fire on the table.	Bread and wine on the table.
Looked forward to the Cross.	Looks backward to the Cross.
Redeemed commemorate their Deliverance.	Redeemed remember their Deliverer.
Family communion.	Church communion.
Testimony to their children.	Testimony to the whole world.
'Put away all leaven.'	'Purge out the old leaven' of malice.
A Supper before the journey.	A Supper during the pilgrimage.

The Passover was the great central feast of Israel. It was to them what the Lord's Supper is to the Christian. In fact, the two are linked most intimately by our Lord, in that it was during the celebration of the one that He instituted the other. Both spoke of the same blessed event, the death of Christ. The one set forth that death in prospect; the other declared that death as having already taken place. (Exod. 12. 24-27; Luke 22. 7-20; 1 Cor. 5. 7, 8; 11. 23-26)

814. Patience. When Stanley went out in 1871 and found Livingstone, he spent some months in his company, but Livingstone never spoke to Stanley about spiritual things. Throughout those months Stanley watched the old man. Livingstone's habits were beyond his comprehension, and so was his patience. He could not understand Livingstone's sympathy for the Africans. For the sake of Christ and His gospel, the missionary doctor was patient, untiring, eager, spending himself and being spent for his Master. Stanley wrote, 'When I saw that unwearied patience, that unflagging zeal, those enlightened sons of Africa, I became a Christian at his side, though he never spoke to me about it.'

(2 Cor. 6. 4; 12. 12; Gal. 6. 9; Heb. 10. 36)

815. Paul. In his book, *Turning Points in History*, the first Earl of Birkenhead wrote,

settled down agreeably. Half-way between Glasgow and Perth there was a halt for the tickets to be examined. As the inspector came near to our carriage, to our amazement one of the women got down and hid under the seat of the carriage, and the other woman spread an old shawl over her. She remained in this position until the train started again, the ticket examiner thinking, no doubt, that it was a bundle of luggage.

When she rose my husband looked at her and said, 'You have been able to hide this time, but the Lord Jesus is coming one of these days, and you will not be able to hide under the seat then.' The poor woman did not answer, but burst into tears, and when she could speak she said, 'I have a husband in Glasgow out of work, and four little children starving with hunger. This woman and myself started with this fruit in time, as we thought, to catch the cheap train for the Cattle Show in Perth, but we missed it, and we had only enough money between us to pay for one ordinary ticket, and this woman has got it.' Again she cried, and then she continued, 'With the thought of not getting to the show to sell this fruit the faces of my dear children came before me, and they seemed to say, "O mother, do something!" so I felt I must go without a ticket.' We were all very touched with the poor woman's grief, and my husband said, 'Well, supposing I pay the fare between those two places, how would that do?' The woman gave him such a look as much as to say, 'You, a complete stranger, pay my fare?' She said, 'But I have not a copper.' He said. 'You do not need a copper if I pay it, and I will.'

The poor woman could scarcely take it in. As we neared Perth, and made a halt at the siding, where Perth tickets were collected, the woman who had the ticket whispered to her companion, 'I think you had better hide again.' She faintly answered, 'I think I had better.' She was just about to get down again when my husband said, 'Don't you believe me? I told you I would pay your fare.' She said, 'But the inspector is coming.' 'That does not matter,' said my husband. So then she sat up in her seat and simply trusted my husband. The inspector came right in this time, but before he could ask any questions it was all settled. One would have thought the woman would have dried her tears then, but she burst afresh into weeping—ah, but they were tears of joy and of gratitude, and, turning to her basket, she filled both hands with fruit, and put it into my lap, saying, 'It is all I can do.'

We parted from them both at Perth, probably never to meet again on earth, but I trust that this simple incident may have been used of God to their salvation.

Jesus paid it all; all to Him I owe.
Sin had left a crimson stain—He washed it
  white as snow.

—Mrs. James Scroggie
(1 Cor. 6. 19, 20; Col. 2. 14; 1 Pet. 1. 18)

817. Peace.

Three Christian brothers met one day
  To speak of things divine;
They had so much of Christ to say,
  With joy their faces shine.
The first one said, 'My brothers dear,
  By virtue of Christ's blood,
My heart retains no guilty fear,
  I now have "Peace with God".' (Rom. 5. 1)

The second brother answered bold,
  'You lag on heaven's road;
I grasp the truth with higher hold,
  I have the "peace of God".' (Phil. 4. 7)
The third dear brother drew up tall;
  He laughed and scarce could cease:
'My brothers dear, I beat you all—
  I have the "God of Peace".'

They all had peace, they all were right,
  But peace in diverse measure;
The third had scaled the highest height
  Of Heaven's exalted pleasure.

—T. Baird

(1 Thess. 5. 13)

818. Peace.
The people of Sahebjina Muvada, a hamlet with a population of 65, in Dahegam taluq, Ahmedabad district, has established a unique record of peaceful community life.

The humble, unsophisticated but greatly tolerant inhabitants of this village have not witnessed a single feud in the village during the past sixty years. Nor has any dispute reached the courts, as the villagers themselves ironed out their differences without any outside mediation.

The village has no panchayat, but their unity and organization enabled them to complete local development works costing over Rs. 32,000 in the last two years. Their own contribution amounted to more than Rs. 10,000.

Sahebjina Muvada has a small primary school, and now there is a proposal to construct a playground.

The above was reported in the Madras daily newspaper, 'The Mail'.

The above picture of peaceable living may well be taken as an object-lesson for us all. Would that every group of Christians in the land enjoyed the same tranquillity. We profess to have peace with God through faith in our Lord Jesus Christ. Peace is the Christian's birthright. 'Peace I leave with you: My peace I give unto you,' said the Saviour ere He left earth for Heaven. Time and again the Scriptures call us to a life of peaceful living. We profess to follow the Prince of Peace. When we keep close to Him our peace remains unbroken and unmarred. It is when Christians follow their Lord afar off that strife takes the place of peace, and calm tranquillity is interrupted by the storm.

—*Indian Christian*
(John 14. 27; 1 Thess. 5. 13; 2 Thess. 3. 16)

819. Peace.
Not peace that grows by Lethe, scentless flower,
  There in white langours to decline and cease;
But peace whose names are also rapture, power,
  Clear sight and love, for these are parts of
    peace.

(Rom. 16. 20; 2 Cor. 13. 11; Heb. 13. 20, 21)

820. Peace.
They laid the Pilgrim in a large upper chamber, facing the sun-rising. The name of the chamber was Peace.

—John Bunyan in *Pilgrim's Progress*
(John 14. 27)

821. Peace.
One morning in 1875 Canon Gibbon of Harrogate preached from the text: 'Thou wilt keep him in perfect peace whose mind is stayed on Thee.' The Hebrew is 'peace, peace' instead of 'perfect peace'. Bishop Bickersteth wrote the hymn, putting each first line in the form of a question and giving the answer in each second line:
'Peace, perfect peace—in this dark world of sin?
The blood of Jesus whispers peace within.'
(Isa. 26. 3, 12; 2 Thess. 3. 16)

822. Pearl.
A pearl is found beneath the flowing tide,
And there is held a worse than useless thing,
Spoiling the shell-built home where it doth cling,
Marring the life near which it must abide.

In Matt. 13. 45, 46, three stages in the story of the pearl are indicated:
i. The formation of the pearl—work of the Pearl-oyster:
ii. The finding of the pearl—work of the Diver:
iii. The financing of the project—work of the Gem-dealer.

823. Pearl.

Tale of tenderness unfathomed
    Told by God to me—
Tale of love, mysterious, awful—
    Thus God's love must be.

God the Seeker—one fair image
    Ever in His thought,
Pure and radiant, and faultless,
    Yet He found it not.

Not amongst His holy Angels,
    Was there one so bright;
Not amongst His stars of glory
    Dwelt His heart's delight.

Yet there was a depth unfathomed
    In a lonely place;
One great deep of endless sorrow
    Darkness on its face.

Restless sea of black pollution
    Moaning evermore,
Weary waves for ever breaking
    On a barren shore.

There below in midnight darkness,
    Under those wild waves,
Lies the treasure God is seeking,
    Jewel that He craves.

Down beneath those sunless waters
    He from Heaven has passed,
He has found His heart's desire,
    Found His pearl at last.

All He had His heart has given
    For that gem unpriced—
Such art thou, O ransomed sinner,
    Yea, for such is Christ.
      —C.P.C. in *Hymns of Ter Stegen & others*
(Matt. 13. 46)

824. Pebbles.

Five little pebbles lay in a brook,
Five little pebbles hid in a nook.
'What are we good for?' one said to another.
'Little or nothing, I'm thinking, my brother.'
Wearing away day after day—
It seemed that for ever those pebbles must stay.

If they were flowers ever so gay,
Doubtless someone would take them away;
Or if they were big stones that builders could use,
Perhaps then some builder those big stones
    would choose.
Wait, little pebbles, rounded and clean,
Long in your loneliness lying unseen,
God has a future waiting for you
Five little pebbles, sturdy and true.

Five little pebbles hid in a brook.
David came down and gave them a look,
Picked them up carefully out of the sand:
Five little pebbles lay in his hand.
Hark! there is shouting and fighting today,
And boldly these pebbles are borne to the fray:
One of them chosen and put in a sling.
Would we have thought that a stone could thus
    wing?

Onward it sped with a might not its own:
Onward it sped, by a shepherd boy thrown;
Swift as an arrow, straight as a dart!
For the whole nation that stone did its part,
Striking the giant's great, terrible head,
Laying him low—a mighty man dead.

Five little pebbles found in a brook
Are mentioned with honour in God's holy Book.
Be thou a pebble, contented and low,
Ever kept clean by His Spirit's pure flow,
Hidden and ready till Jesus shall look
And choose you, and use you, a stone from the
    brook.
(1 Sam. 17. 40)

825. Penalty—paid.
Two men who had been friends in their youth met years later in the police court of a great city, one on the judge's bench, the other in the prisoner's dock. Evidence was heard, and the prisoner found guilty. In consideration of their former friendship the judge was asked to withhold sentence.

'No,' he said, 'that cannot be; justice must be done and the law upheld.' So he gave sentence: 'Fifty dollars fine, or fourteen days at hard labour.'

The condemned man had nothing wherewith to pay, so prison was before him. Then the judge, having fulfilled his duty, stepped down beside the prisoner, paid his fine, put his arm about him, and said, 'Now, John, you are going home with me to dinner.' Not even God can overlook sin. He must be faithful and just. But for us the Judge was crucified! 'Lo! guilt is gone, and I am free.'
      —*Sunday School Times*
(Hab. 1. 13; Rom. 3. 24, 26)

826. Perseverance.
King Robert the Bruce of Scotland, pursued after a battle in which he had suffered defeat by the enemy, took refuge in a lonely cave, and began to think out his plans. Tempted to despair, he had almost lost heart and decided to give up, when his eyes were directed to a spider in the cave, carefully and painfully attempting to make its way up a slender thread to its web in the corner above. The king watched as it made several unsuccessful attempts to get to the top, and thought, as it fell back to the bottom again and again, how its efforts typified his own unsuccessful efforts to gain the victory and rid Scotland of its enemies. He never seemed to get to the place at which he was aiming—just like the spider. But he continued to watch the spider's movements.

'Steadily, steadily, inch by inch,
Higher and higher he got,
Till a neat little run, at the very last pinch.
Put him into his native cot.'
The king took courage and persevered, and
the example of the spider brought its reward.
Eph. 6. 18; 1 Cor. 15. 58)

827. Perseverance. After Sir Walter Raleigh's
introduction to the favour of Queen Elizabeth,
he wrote with a diamond on the window pane:
'Fain would I climb, but that I fear to fall.'
The Queen saw the words that he had written,
and wrote with a diamond underneath it:
'If thy heart fail thee, do not climb at all.'
(Phil. 3. 12; Col. 1. 23)

828. Perseverance. Sir Ernest Shackleton
died while steaming southward on the good
ship 'Quest' to explore the Antarctic. The first
thing that attracted one's eyes on going
aboard the 'Quest' were these lines from
Kipling engraved on a brass plate:

If you can dream and not make dreams your
    master;
If you can think and not make thoughts your
    aim;
If you can meet with triumph and disaster,
    And treat those two impostors just the same;

If you can force your heart, and nerve, and sinew
    To serve your turn long after they are gone;
And so hold on when there is nothing in you
    Except the will which says to them, 'Hold on;'

If you can fill the unforgiving minute
    With sixty seconds' worth of distance run,
Yours is the earth and everything that's in it,
    And what is more, you'll be a man, my son.

'The spirit of the Quest', Shackleton called
these verses.

                  —Dale Carnegie

(2 Kings 2. 1-12)

829. Perseverance. Mrs. Josephine Butler,
whose features displayed her marked determination and purposeful character, brought about
the reform of workhouses and the establishment of homes of refuge for the poor and
underprivileged in Britain during the nineteenth century. She stoutly opposed the
Contagious Diseases' Acts which, largely as a
result of her untiring perseverance, were
repealed in 1886.

John Macbeath in his book 'The Face of
Christ' tells us that, when she saw for the first
time her portrait painted by G. F. Watts, who
had a deep veneration for her heroism, she
said but a few words. But when she came
down to dinner that evening, she had written
what her delicate and sensitive nature had
prevented her from saying to the artist. This
is what she wrote:

'When I looked at that portrait which you
have just done, I felt inclined to burst into
tears. I will tell you why. I felt sorry for her.
Your power has brought out of the depths of
the past the record of a conflict which no one
but God knows of. It is written in the eyes
and the whole face. Your picture has brought
back to me all that I suffered, and the sorrow
through which the Angel of God's presence
brought me alive.'

John Macbeath adds: 'her passion was
kindled by the passion of Jesus Christ. She had
seen her Lord, and from that hour life was
never the same again.'
(Esther 8. 3-6; Eph. 6. 18; Phil. 3. 13)

830. Peter. A Keswick speaker some years
ago told the following story:

I remember hearing a Welsh preacher tell
of a dream that he had. He visited a certain
town and, walking through the streets, saw
placarded on hoardings advertisements of two
meetings. He read the bills. One stated that
a meeting would be held in a certain hall at a
certain hour, and the preacher was to be the
Angel Gabriel. He thought, 'I'd like to go and
hear him.' The other notice was of another
meeting at the same time, but in a different
place, to be addressed by the Apostle Peter.
He thought, 'And I'd like to hear Peter.' He
was reading the two bills again when suddenly
someone said, 'I see you are trying to make up
your mind which of these two you will go to
hear. If I may be allowed to advise, go and
hear Peter. I've heard them both; Gabriel sent
me to enquire of Peter who spoke words
through which I was saved. My name is
Cornelius.'
(Acts 10. 3-6; 11. 13, 14)

831. Peter.
I think that look of Christ might seem to say:
'Thou, Peter, art thou then a common stone
Which I at last must break my head upon,
For all God's charge to His high angels, may
Guard my foot better? Did I yesterday
Wash thy feet, my beloved, that they should run
Quick to deny me 'neath the morning sun;
And do thy kisses, like the rest, betray?'
The cock crows loudly—'Go and manifest
A late contrition but no bootless fear.'
(Luke 22. 60, 61)

832. Philosophy.
'Tis said Philosophy hath charms
    Which prove celestial birth,
That Science, with distending arms,
    Grasps Heaven in grasping earth.

I know not, neither have I tried
    Their claims to disallow:
A trusting soul is satisfied
    With neither why nor how.

They come from God if they be right:
    If true, they lead to Him;
But who would shun the noonday light
    To grope 'mid shadows dim?

And who would leave the Fountain Head
    To drink the muddy stream,
Where men have mixed what God hath said
    With every dreamer's dream?

How dim is every earthly light
When suns celestial glow!
No earthly visions lure the sight
Where God His face doth show.

           —William Blane

(Col. 2. 8)

833. Photograph. It was necessary for me some years ago to get some passport photographs. Awful agony! When I received the photograph from the photographer I opened it and, well, I was a little disappointed. So I wrote to the photographer, and he said, 'Well, that is only a passport photograph. Would you like some touched-up prints?' That sounded better, so I ordered some. But to my disappointment the American consulate only wanted the passport photograph. I offered them the other, but no, they wanted the passport photograph that was not touched-up. The two were completely different. You would not have recognised the same person. The touched-up photograph was what I wanted other people to think that I was; but the passport photograph was the ugly reality. And all I could do was to submit to the diagnosis, and give the man the thing he wanted.

           —Alan Redpath

(Luke 13. 11-13; Rom. 7. 18, 24)

834. Photograph. In the days when there were fewer cameras and fewer photographs, and when it was an event in one's life to have one's photo taken, an evangelist with a party of friends was enjoying a pleasant Saturday afternoon in Rouken Glen, Glasgow, Scotland, on a lovely summer day. He carried with him a little leather case containing his Bible and, as he walked along, a company of young people out for an afternoon's enjoyment approached him and said, 'Please will you take our photograph,' thinking that the little leather case contained a Vest-pocket Kodak.

Without a moment's hesitation the evangelist said, 'O, I have it already.' The spokesman of the party asked in surprise, 'When did you take it? You must have got us on the hop.' 'Well, anyway I have it here, and here it is,' said the preacher as he pulled out his well-worn Bible, opened it at Romans 3, and began to read to them from verse 9 to verse 23. 'This is God's photograph of every one of us,' he said, as he concluded his reading with the words, 'For all have sinned and come short of the glory of God.'

(Rom. 3. 23)

835. Pilgrimage.

We're bound for yonder land
Where Jesus reigns supreme;
We leave the shore at His command,
Forsaking all for Him.

'Twere easy, did we choose,
Again to reach the shore—
But that is what our souls refuse,
We'll never touch it more.

(Heb. 11. 14-16)

836. Pilgrimage.

Strangers and pilgrims here below,
This earth, we know, is not our place—
And hasten through this vale of woe;
And, restless to behold Thy face,
Swift to our heavenly country move,
Our everlasting home above.

(Phil. 3. 20, 21; Heb. 11. 13; 13. 14; 1 Pet. 2. 11

837. Pilgrimage. The following are some of the last words of John G. Bellett:

My pilgrim days are waning;
The voice of Him I love
Has called me to His presence
In my Father's house above.
Long, long, by faith I've known Him,
But now I'm going to see
The One that sits in Heaven—
The Man that died for me.

But ere I left the desert,
I longed that I might know
What joy His blessed presence
Could give me here below,
A few more fleeting moments—
Oh, I would nearer be
My precious, loving Saviour,
The Man that died for me.

He gave me all I asked for,
And more than I can tell;
He filled my heart with rapture,
With joy unspeakable;
The loving hand of Jesus
Seemed gently laid on me—
I had for my Companion
The Man that died for me.

The glories of the Kingdom
Are coming bye-and-bye;
And I shall see my brethren,
Be crowned with them on high.
I know that I shall reign, but,
Before it all for me
There's a time alone with Jesus,
The Man that died for me.

To fall asleep in Jesus,
'Tis what I think of now;
To be for ever with the Lord,
Before Himself to bow!
O yes, with Him Who stayed to call
Zacchaeus from the tree;
With Him Who hung upon the cross—
The Man Who died for me.

It is the Man Christ Jesus—
With Him I'm going to dwell;
The very man of Sychar
Who sat upon the well;
Whose matchless love filled that poor heart,
And gave her eyes to see
That He was God's anointed,
The Man that died for me.

To leave the world that cast Him out,
And be with Him up there,
Before the kingdom glories
Or the many crowns appear!

Oh, the Man of Sychar—
It is Himself to see!
Perfection of perfections,
I long to be with Thee.
(John 14. 2, 3; Phil. 1. 23; 3. 20, 21; 1 John 3. 2)

838. Pilgrimage.
O Thou, by long experience tried,
Near Whom no grief can long abide,
My Lord! how full of sweet content
I pass my years of banishment.

All scenes alike engaging prove
To souls impress'd with sacred love;
Where'er they dwell, they dwell in Thee
In heaven, on earth, or on the sea.
To me remains nor place nor time;
My country is in every clime;
I may be calm and free from care
On any shore since God is there.

While place we seek or place we shun,
The soul finds happiness in none;
But with a God to guide the way,
'Tis equal joy to go or stay.

Could I be cast where Thou art not,
That were indeed a dreadful lot;
But regions none remote I call,
Secure of finding God in all.

My country, Lord, art Thou alone:
No other can I claim or own;
The point where all my wishes meet,
My law, my love, life's only sweet.

I hold by nothing here below;
Appoint my journey and I go.
Though pierced by scorn, opprest by pride,
I feel the good—feel naught beside.

No frowns of men can hurtful prove
To souls on fire with heavenly love:
Though men and devils both condemn,
No gloomy days arise for them.
                        —Madame de la Mothe Guyon
(Col. 1. 27; Heb. 13. 13, 14)

839. Place—His own. Dr. Alexander Dickson quaintly suggests the following analysis of the verse—'That he might go to his own place'
1. Every man has his own place, here and hereafter.
2. Every man makes his own place, here and hereafter.
3. Every man finds his own place, here and hereafter.
4. Every man feels that it is his own place when he gets there.
(Acts 1. 25)

840. Pleasure. Dr. Samuel Johnson liked very much a poem of Philip Doddridge, the writer of the hymns, 'O God of Bethel', and 'O happy day'. The poem was—
Live while you live, the epicure would say,
And seize the pleasures of the perfect day.
Live while you may, the sacred preacher cries,
And give to God each moment as it flies.
Lord, in my life let faith united be:
I live to pleasure as I live to Thee.

A modern version of the above is—
The worldling says—'I live to Pleasure as I die to God.'
The ascetic says—'I live to God as I die to Pleasure.'
The Christian says—'Lord, in my life, let both united be;
I live to Pleasure as I live to Thee.'
(1 Tim. 4. 4, 5; Heb. 11. 25)

841. Pleasures of sin. In the West Indies there grows a beautiful and attractive flower, but on being plucked it ceases to be beautiful, and emits a most unpleasant odour. It is called by the natives 'the dead horse'—about the best name that could be given it.
                        —J. T. Mawson

842. Pleasures of sin. Another illustration of sin's pleasure is the sugar-coated pill our mothers used to give us when we became sick in childhood days. We loved those pills at first —they were so sweet—but when we had sucked the sugar off, they were so bitter that we wanted to spit them out. Sin's pleasures first, then the remorse and pain.
(Heb. 11. 25)

843. Pleasures of sin. At the foot of the Kaylass Mountains there is a district which is full of sweet-scented flowers. Once I had to walk through an area which contained a garden of these flowers several miles long. The beauty and fragrance of the flowers gave me great pleasure. Just then a man came out of the jungle and said in great haste, 'You must not stand here; this is a place of danger; many have died here.' I was taken by surprise and asked him, 'Is this place poisonous, or are poisonous creatures to be found here?' The answer he gave me was full of meaning. 'I don't know anything about that,' he said, 'but if you take in the scent of these flowers for a little while, sleep will overpower you. And once asleep there is no waking you out of this sleep. Some have been known to sleep in this way for ten or twelve days, and this ends in death. Since I live in the forest near by I endeavour to let people who are ignorant of this danger know all about it.' When I heard this I thought as follows. This flower cannot hurt of itself. But when its aroma is inhaled, there is no longer any desire for food or aught else. God wishes us to use the world and the blessings around us for our good but if we allow these things to draw us aside and to allure and stupefy us we will suffer great spiritual loss. Not only so, we will be robbed of the desire for spiritual sustenance and the lust for money and other things will in the end result in death.
                        —Sadhu Sundar Singh
(Mark 4. 19; Heb. 3. 13)

844.   **Pleasures of sin.**

Pleasures are like poppies spread:
You seize the flower, the bloom is shed;
Or like the snowfall in the river,
A moment white—then melts for ever;
Or like the borealis race,
That flit ere you can point their place;
Or like the rainbow's lovely form,
Evanishing amid the storm.

—Robert Burns

(Heb. 11. 25)

845.   **Possessions.**

Let me hold lightly things of the earth;
Transient treasures, what are they worth?
Moths can corrupt them, rust can decay;
All that bright beauty fades in a day.
Let me hold lightly temporal things—
I who am deathless, I who wear wings.

Let me hold fast, Lord, things of the skies;
Quicken my vision, open my eyes!
Show me Thy riches, glory and grace,
Boundless as time is, endless as space.
Let me hold lightly things that are mine—
Lord, Thou dost give me all that is Thine!

—M. S. Nicholson

(2 Cor. 4. 18)

846.   **Potters.** The names of potters appear frequently on jar handles. The pots usually bear royal marks. Israel's pots show heathen traces in times when the Bible deplores national apostasy, and none in times of national fidelity.

The ruler of a country in the East usually had his own potters employed to supply him with what was needed for the use of the royal household.

(1 Chron. 4. 14, 23)

847.   **Power.** Five young College students spent a Sunday in London, and were anxious to hear some well-known preachers. They found their way on a hot Sunday to Spurgeon's Tabernacle. While they were waiting for the doors to open, a stranger came up to them and said, 'Gentlemen, would you like to see the heating apparatus of this church?' They were not particularly anxious to do so on a broiling day in July, but at once consented. They were taken down some steps and a door was thrown open. Then their guide whispered, 'There, Sirs, is our heating apparatus.' They saw before them 700 souls bowed in prayer seeking for blessing on the service about to be held in the tabernacle above. Their unknown guide was C. H. Spurgeon himself.

The Prayer meeting is the Power-house of the church.

(Acts 4. 31, 32)

848.   **Power.** Sir Astley Cooper, on visiting Paris, tells that a certain surgeon asked him how many times he had performed a certain feat of surgery. He replied, 'Thirteen times.' 'Ah, but, Monsieur,' replied the French surgeon, 'I have done it 130 times.'

'And how many times did you save the life?' continued the curious Frenchman, after he had looked in blank amazement into Sir Astley Cooper's face.

'I saved eleven out of thirteen,' said the English surgeon. 'How many did you save out of 130?'

'Ah, Monsieur, I lose dem all, but the operation was very brilliant.'

(Acts 4. 16; 1 Thess. 1. 5-10)

849.   **Power.** C. H. Spurgeon, in his young days, got a 'penny-farthing' cycle, new and silver-plated, and was very proud of it. One day, riding along the road, he met another cyclist on a boneshaker.

'Difficult to ride a machine like that, isn't it?' said Spurgeon.

'Not a bit!' said the man, and off he started. Spurgeon did his best to follow, but was soon left far behind. Spurgeon had the machine, the man had the power.

(Acts 1. 8; 4. 13)

850.   **Power.** After the death of a great painter a young Italian boy went to the studio and asked for the great artist's brush. He tried it but found he could not paint any better with it than with his own. He lacked the master's power.

(Matt. 28. 18; Luke 24. 49; Mark 16. 20)

851.   **Power.** Dr. J. Wilbur Chapman was once asked what was the secret of his power. He replied, 'I find that I have power just in proportion as my soul is saturated through and through with the Word of God.'

(Col. 3. 16)

852.   **Poverty.** George Bowen came from the U.S.A. to India as far back as 1848 and remained in that country, without ever visiting his homeland, till his death in 1888. His outlook was aggressive—he wanted to see moral earthquakes, even churchquakes. He had no time for formality and lived a life of holy poverty. Once it was his turn to entertain the missionaries in the city at the monthly breakfast which followed a time of prayer and Bible reading, and since he had only four pice in his possession, he hoped that none would stay for food. Three did, so a napkin was placed on the table, cold tea brought in from the night before, and some bread. His four pice was spent on sugar; an orphan boy who lived with him had two pice which the boy spent on plantains. Then Bowen said, 'I am sorry to be so shortcoming in the rites of hospitality, but in the providence of God I find myself compelled to treat you just as I am accustomed to treat myself.'

To the end he was a great believer in street preaching. After some years he moved into a better living room about 20 feet square, opening on the street. Later he occupied a corner behind some stocks of books in the shop of the Tract Society, sleeping, in the hot weather, on the counter with some papers for

a pillow. Seeing his threadbare shirts, a friend gave him Rs.25 for new ones. He handed the money to the Mission Treasury and kept wearing the old ones. His income was Rs.5 a month! His health was good: for five years he did not take a drop of medicine. But he suffered from frequent headaches—a sore enough affliction! Despite shabby clothes and frayed trouser ends, Bowen was the friend of governors, and some time in the 70's the Prince of Wales came to his tiny room to convey to him Queen Victoria's thanks for the blessing Bowen's books had been to her. Bowen was a wonder to many.
(James 2. 5)

853. **Practice.** 'Christianity refuses to be proved first and practised afterwards: its practice and its proof go hand in hand,' wrote I. R. Illingworth.

The sermons of a certain preacher were magnificent, but his life was so inconsistent with his profession that, when he was in the pulpit, his congregation wished he would never leave it; and, when he was out of the pulpit, they wished he would never enter it again.
(1 Cor. 9. 27; Col. 2. 6)

854. **Praise.** It is always a token of revival, it is said, when there is a revival of psalmody. When Luther's preaching began to tell upon men, you could hear ploughmen at the plough singing Luther's psalms. Whitefield and Wesley had never done the great work they did if it had not been for Charles Wesley's poetry, and for the singing of such men as Toplady, Scott, Newton, and many others of the same class. When your heart is full of Christ, you want to sing.

—C. H. Spurgeon
(Eph. 5. 18-20; Col. 3. 16)

855. **Prayer.**
Arrested suns and tranquilled seas declare
To Heaven and earth th'omnipotence of prayer,
That gives the hopeless hope, the feeble might,
Outruns the swift and puts the strong to flight,
The noontide arrow foils and plague that stalks
   by night.

—Colton
(Josh. 10. 13, 14; Ps. 91. 1-6; James 5. 17, 18)

856. **Prayer.** Prayer is the golden key that can open the wicket of mercy. Prayer is the slender nerve that moves the muscles of Omnipotence.
(Luke 22. 31, 32; Col. 4. 12)

857. **Prayer.** Archimedes was the great pioneer in the realm of mechanics. It was he who ran through the town of Syracuse shouting, 'Eureka, Eureka' (I have found it) after he had made an important discovery. During a state of war he turned to King Hiero and said, 'Give me a lever and a place to rest it, and I will move the world.'

Result: the enemy's ships were completely destroyed, and the siege lifted. Small wonder that Plutarch said, 'All other weapons lay idle and useless; his were the only offensive and defensive arms of the city.' God too has given His people a power by which they move the world: 'Prayer moves the hand that moves the universe.' Are we using that power?

—*Indian Christian*
(Matt. 17. 21; 1 Thess. 5. 17; 1 Tim. 2. 1-3)

858. **Prayer.** He was a Christian and he prayed. He asked for strength to do greater things, but he was given infirmity that he might do better things. He asked for power that he might have the praise of men: he was given weakness that he might feel the need of God.

—Selected
(2 Cor. 12. 8-10)

859. **Prayer.**
Lord, what a change within us one short hour
Spent in Thy presence will prevail to make!
What heavy burdens from our bosom take!
What parched lands refresh as with a shower!
We kneel, and all around us seems to lower:
We rise and all the distant and the near
Stands forth in sunny outline, brave and clear.

We kneel, how weak; we rise, how full of power!
Why therefore, should we do ourselves this wrong
Or others—that we are not always strong,
That we are ever overborne with care?
That we should ever weak or heartless be,
Anxious or troubled, when with us is prayer,
And joy and strength and courage are with Thee?

—R. C. Trench
(Dan. 6. 10, 11; 9. 3, 4; Acts 1. 14)

860. **Prayer.**
  When you pray at morn or sundown,
  By yourself or with your own;
  When you pray at rush of noontide,
  Just make sure you touch the Throne.

  When you pray in hours of leisure,
  Waiting long and all alone,
  Pour not out mere words as water,
  But make sure you touch the Throne.

  When you pray in busy moments,
  Oft to restless hurry prone,
  Brevity will matter little
  If you really touch the Throne.

  When amid the congregation
  Of God's saints in prayer you groan,
  He will hear your voice and answer
  If you really touch the Throne.

  When you pray as those sick people
  Who of old God's power have known,
  As they touched His garment's border,
  So make sure you touch the Throne.

  When you pray as Christ directed,
  In the manner clearly shown,
  In His name and by His Spirit,
  You will always touch the Throne.
(Esther 5. 2; Heb. 4. 16)

861. Prayer. Mr. Spurgeon once came to Bristol. He was to preach in the three largest Baptist chapels in the city, and he hoped to collect three hundred pounds, which were needed immediately for his orphanage. He got the money. Retiring to bed on the last night of his visit, Spurgeon heard a voice which, to him, was the voice of the Lord, saying, 'Give those three hundred pounds to George Muller.' 'But, Lord,' answered Spurgeon, 'I need it for my dear children in London.' Again came the word, 'Give those three hundred pounds to George Muller.' It was only when he had said, 'Yes, Lord, I will,' that sleep came to him.

The following morning he made his way to Muller's Orphanages, and found George Muller on his knees before an open Bible, praying. The famous preacher placed his hand on his shoulder and said, 'George, God told me to give you these three hundred pounds.' 'Oh,' said Muller, 'dear Spurgeon, I have been asking the Lord for that very sum.' And those two prayerful men rejoiced together.

Spurgeon returned to London. On his desk, he found a letter awaiting him. He opened it to find it contained three hundred guineas. 'There!' cried he with joy, 'the Lord has returned my three hundred pounds with three hundred shillings interest.'

—Henry Durbanville
(Phil. 4. 6; James 5. 16)

862. Prayer.
More things are wrought by prayer than this
*   world dreams of:*
For what are men better than sheep or goats
If, knowing God, they lift not hands of prayer
Both for themselves and those who call them
*   friend.*
—Alfred, Lord Tennyson
(1 Tim. 2. 1-3, 8)

863. Prayer.
How can I cease to pray for thee? Somewhere
In God's great universe thou art today;
Can I not reach thee with His tender care?
Can He not hear me when I pray?
(1 Sam. 12. 19, 23)

864. Prayer. Some 500 years ago in London, a number of poor men were praying for liberty to read the Bible. On the spot where that prayer meeting was held stand the buildings of the Bible Society today.
(Acts 4. 31; 6. 4)

865. Prayer.
Strong is the lion—like a coal
His eyeball—like a bastion mole
His chest, against his foes;
Strong the gier-eagle on his sail;
Strong against tide th'enormous whale
Emerges as he goes.

But stronger still in earth or air,
And in the sea, the man of prayer,
And far beneath the tide;
And in the seat to faith assigned,
Where ask is have and seek is find,
Where knock is open wide.
(1 Sam. 12. 23; Ps. 106. 23; Dan. 2. 18-20;
James 5. 17)

866. Prayer. Dr. Norman McLeod was in a small boat with a boatman, some ladies, and a well-known ministering brother who was as conspicuous for his weak and puny appearance as Dr. McLeod was for his gigantic size and strength. A fearful gale arose. The waves tossed the boat sky-high in their furious sport. The smaller of the two preachers was frightened out of his wits. He suggested that Dr. McLeod should pray for deliverance. The ladies eagerly seconded the devout proposal. But the breathless old boatman would have none of it. He instantly vetoed the scheme. 'Na! Na!' he cried, 'let the wee mannie pray, but the big ane maun tak' an oar if ye dinna a' want to be drooned.'
(Neh. 4. 9, 15, 16)

867. Prayer-meeting. Mrs. Prayer Meeting died recently at the First Neglected Church in Worldly Avenue. Born many years ago in the midst of great revivals, she was a strong, healthy child fed largely on testimony and spiritual holiness, soon growing into world-wide prominence, and was one of the most influential members of the famous Church family.

For the past several years Sister Prayer Meeting had been in failing health, gradually wasting away. Her death was caused through lukewarmness and coldness of heart. Lack of spiritual food, coupled with lack of faith, shameless desertion and non-support, were contributing causes of her death. Only a few were present at her last rites, sobbing over memories of her past beauty and power. Carefully selected pall-bearers were asked to bear the remains tenderly away, but failed to appear. The body rests in the beautiful cemetery of Bygone Glories, awaiting the summons from above.
—*The Grace Ambassador*
(Acts 12. 5; Matt. 18. 19, 20; Heb. 10. 25)

868. Prayer—to Men and to God.
Man's plea to man is that he nevermore
Will beg, and that he never begged before;
Man's plea to God is, that he did obtain
A former suit and therefore sues again.
How good a God we serve that, when we sue,
Makes His old gifts the examples of the new!
(Ps. 40. 1-4, 11, 17)

869. Prayer—a Minister and. Visitors to the famous Gallery in St. Paul's Cathedral, London, can hear the guide's whisper travel around the whole dome, the sound bouncing back many times from the smooth walls. If you put your ear close to the wall, you can hear what is said on the opposite side of the dome, even though it may be said in the lowest of tones.

A number of years ago, a poor shoemaker whispered to his young lady that he could not afford to marry her as he hadn't money enough to buy any leather, and his business was ruined. The poor girl wept quietly as she listened to this sad news.

A gentleman on the other side of the gallery, which is 198 feet across, heard this story and the shoemaker's whispered prayer, and he decided to do something about it. When the young shoemaker left St. Paul's the gentleman followed him, and after finding out where he lived, had some leather sent along to the shop. Imagine how delighted the poor man was! He made good use of this gift, and his business prospered so that he was able to marry the girl of his choice.

It was not till a few years later that he learned the name of his unknown friend. It was the Prime Minister of Great Britain, W. E. Gladstone.

There is always one above who hears our whispered sorrowings and prayers, and will take action. No matter how low we whisper He can hear. We cannot always tell our human friends about things, but God always knows, so we can tell Him all in prayer, and He will hear and answer.
(Phil. 4. 6)

870. Prayer—a Moment's.

I cannot tell why there should come to me
    A thought of someone miles and miles away,
In swift insistence on the memory,
    Unless there be a need that I should pray.

Too hurried oft are we to spare a thought
    For days together for some friend away:
Perhaps God does it for us, and we ought
    To read His signal as a call to pray.

Perhaps just then, my friend has fiercer fight;
    Some overwhelming sorrow or decay
Of courage, darkness, some lost sense of right,
    And so, in case my friend needs prayer, I pray.

Friend, do the same for me, if I, unsought,
    Intrude upon you on some crowded day;
Give me a moment's prayer in passing thought;
    Be very sure I need it, therefore pray.
                        —E. Middleton

(Eph. 6. 18, 19)

871. Prayer—Monica's. For many years Monica had prayed that her profligate son might be saved. When she learned that he was thinking of taking a ship from Carthage to Rome, she earnestly petitioned the Throne of grace that Augustine might be restrained from going to such a centre of corruption and sin.

But during the night he secretly took his departure and the mother was left, weeping and praying, behind.

The mother stood on the shore and filled the ear of the Almighty with groans and lamentations. But in Rome Augustine found the Saviour, and Monica, who had seen him depart for a season, had the joy of knowing that it had only been that she might receive him for ever.
(Philem. 15)

872. Prayer—Muller's in the fog. Charles Inglis, the well-known evangelist, tells the following story of George Muller, and it is worthy of a place under the heading of 'Answered Prayers'.

When I first came to America, thirty-one years ago, I crossed the Atlantic with the Captain of a steamer who was one of the most devoted men I ever knew, and when we were off the banks of Newfoundland he said to me: 'Mr. Inglis, the last time I crossed here, five weeks ago, one of the most extraordinary things happened that has completely revolutionised the whole of my Christian life. Up to that time I was one of your ordinary Christians. We had a man of God on board, George Muller of Bristol. I had been on that bridge for twenty-two hours, and never left it. I was startled by someone tapping me on the shoulder. It was George Muller. "Captain," he said, "I have come to tell you that I must be in Quebec on Saturday afternoon." (This was Wednesday). 'It is impossible,' I said. 'Very well, if your ship can't take me, but I have never broken an engagement in fifty years.' 'I would willingly help you. How can I? I am helpless,' said the Captain.

'Let us go down to the chart room and pray,' said George Muller.

I looked at the man of God, and I thought to myself, what lunatic asylum could the man have come from? I never heard of such a thing.

'Mr. Muller,' I said, 'do you know how dense the fog is?'

'No,' he replied, 'my eye is not on the density of the fog, but on the living God Who controls every circumstance of my life.' He got down on his knees and prayed one of the most simple prayers. I muttered to myself, 'That would suit a children's class where the children were not more than eight years old.'

The burden of his prayer was something like this: 'O Lord, if it is consistent with Thy will, please remove this fog in five minutes, Thou knowest the engagement Thou didst make for me in Quebec for Saturday. I believe it is Thy will.'

When he finished I was going to pray, but he put his hand on my shoulder and told me not to pray. 'First, you do not believe He will; and second, I believe He has, and there is no need to pray.'

And, as George Muller said, the fog had lifted.
(Ps. 34. 4, 6, 17)

873. Prayerlessness. Just before a large evangelistic campaign, I was asked by a number of Christian leaders to address a meeting for Christian workers. The object of the meeting was to awaken a sense of our responsibility toward those around us who are unsaved.

I felt impelled to use an allegory showing the sinfulness of prayerlessness. And I know that the Holy Spirit spoke to many because of the response following the special service. The story follows:

In one of our munition plants employing 500 men, there was an excellent canteen and lounging room. After the men had lunched each day, they developed an informal open forum where, for the balance of their lunch period, they discussed topics of general interest.

One day their discussion centred on Christianity and hypocrisy. Some very harsh and cruel things were said about Christians.

In the company was a Christian fellow named William James. When Bill could stand it no longer, he rose to his feet and said, 'Men, you have been saying some very hard things about Christians. Now I admit that there are hypocrites in the church, but I also want you to know that there are quite a lot of sincere Christians, and I, myself, very humbly claim to sincerely believe in Jesus Christ as my personal Lord and Saviour.'

He was about to sit down when a man said, 'Just a minute, Bill. I would like you to answer some questions. I take it from what you have said that you believe the Bible to be the Word of God?'

'I certainly do,' said Bill. 'I believe it from cover to cover.'

'Then, do you believe that all men out of Christ are lost and on their way to outer darkness?'

'Yes,' he said, 'I do.' And so the dialogue proceeded:

Question: Do you think that most of us men are out of Christ and therefore lost?

Bill: Yes, boys, I am very sorry indeed to say I do believe that.

Question: Do you believe in the efficacy of prayer?

Bill: Yes, I have had many answers to my prayers in the past.

Question: How long have you worked here with us?

Bill: Four years.

Question: How often in that period have you spent a night in prayer for our lost souls? Bill's head doesn't seem quite so high as he says, I am sorry boys, but I cannot say I ever spent a night in prayer for you.

Question: How often have you spent half a night in prayer for us?

Bill: I'm sorry, but I cannot say I ever spent half a night in prayer for you.

Question: Bill, we'll take your word for it —quickly add together all the time you've spent in prayer for us during the last week: how much would it be all told?

Bill: I'm sorry, fellows, but I cannot say that I have spent any time in prayer for you this last week.

Questioner: Well, Bill, that's just the kind of hypocrisy we've been talking about.

Could this have happened to you? Are you guilty of the sin of Prayerlessness? Do you lightly promise others that you will pray for them and about their circumstances and forget as soon as the words have left your lips?

—Robert A. Laidlaw (Slightly abridged) (1 Sam. 12. 23)

874. Prayerlessness.

From a convert in Uganda
Comes to us a story—grander
In the lesson that it teaches
Than a sermon someone preaches;
For it tells what sore temptations
Come to them, what need of patience,
And a need—all else outweighing—
Of a place for private praying.

So each convert chose a corner
Far away from eyes of scorner.
In the jungle, where he could
Pray to God in solitude.
And so often went he thither
That the grass would fade and wither
Where he trod, and you can trace
By the paths each praying place.

If they bear the evil tidings
Of a brother's late backslidings,
And if some are even saying,
'He no longer cares for praying;'
Then they say to one another,
Softly and so gently, 'Brother,
Do forgive us now for showing
On your path the grass is growing.'

And the erring one, relenting,
Soon is bitterly repenting.
'Ah, how sad I am at knowing
On my path the grass is growing;
But it shall be so no longer,
Prayer I need to make me stronger;
On my path I'll oft be going—
Soon no grass will there be showing.'

(Matt. 6. 6; Luke 18. 1; 1 Thess. 5. 17)

875. Preacher. I had the privilege of a great friendship with Dr. Parker in the last ripe years of his life, and I was in his vestry one day when a man came in. Dr. Parker had preached that morning a great sermon, and this man said, 'I want to thank you for that sermon. It did me good.'

Dr. Parker looked at him and said: 'Sir, I preached it because it had done me good. I had given a message that had come out of his own life, something that had gripped him.

—Dr. G. Campbell Morgan
(Matt. 13. 52; 2 Cor. 4. 5; Gal. 1. 15, 16)

876. **Preacher.** A Christian of discernment had the privilege of hearing Dr. Talmage. When asked his opinion of the preacher, he remarked, 'A wonderful preacher.'

The same man went to hear C. H. Spurgeon, and when asked concerning him, he gave his opinion expressing it in the words, 'What a wonderful Saviour!' The man had not been impressed so much by Spurgeon's oratory as by the Saviour Whom he preached.
(1 Cor. 1. 23, 24; 2 Cor. 4. 5; 1 Thess. 1. 5)

877. **Preacher.** 'God had only one Son, and He made Him a Preacher.'

Like his great Master, Teacher and Example, every preacher should have—

1. The innocence of a lamb
2. The wisdom of an owl
3. The cheerfulness of a cricket
4. The friendliness of a squirrel
5. The complacency of a camel
6. The adaptability of a chameleon
7. The diligence of a beaver
8. The fleetness of a deer
9. The vision of an eagle
10. The agility of a panther
11. The patience of an ox
12. The endurance of an elephant
13. The tenacity of a bulldog
14. The strength and courage of a lion.

(Mark 1. 38, 39; 1 Cor. 9. 16; 19-23)

878. **Preacher.** It was related of Dr. Norman Hall that one morning very early, he stood on the summit of Snowden in Wales with 120 others attracted by the prospect of a beautiful sunrise. As they stood watching the sun tinge the mountains and lakes, Dr. Hall was called upon to give a message. He was so over-powered with emotion that he could not speak, but he began to pray and noticed that tears rained down the faces of the people. A super-human stillness came over them all and they quietly dispersed.

Years later Dr. Hall was visiting the same place and was reminded of the previous occasion by one who told him that forty had been converted that morning. 'But I did not preach to them,' he said, 'I only prayed.'

'Stranger still,' said his friend, 'none of them could speak English and they couldn't under-stand your prayer.' God had spoken.
(Zech. 4. 6; 1 Cor. 2. 3-5)

879. **Preacher. Lines written of Dr. Elmslie.**

He held the lamp of truth that day
So low that none need miss the way,
And yet so high, to bring in sight
That picture fair, the world's great Light,
That, gazing up, the lamp between,
The hand that held it scarce was seen.

He held the pitcher, stooping low,
To lips of little ones below,
Then raised it to the weary saint
And bade him drink when sick and faint.
They drank:—the pitcher thus between,
The hand that held it scarce was seen.

He blew the trumpet soft and clear
That trembling sinners need not fear,
And then with louder note and bold
To raze the walls of Satan's hold.
The trumpet coming thus between,
The hand that held it scarce was seen.

And when the Captain says, 'Well done!
Thou good and faithful servant, come,
Lay down the pitcher and the lamp,
Lay down the trumpet—leave the camp,'
The weary hands will then be seen
Clasped in His pierced ones, naught between.
(2 Cor. 4. 5-8; 2 Tim. 4. 6-8)

880. **Preacher.** Late one Saturday night a man called to see a preacher. 'You cannot see him,' said his wife, 'he's buried in his sermon.

'The lady was right,' said the caller, who heard the sermon next day.

881. **Preacher.** An aged Christian sent the following lines to his son:

You want to be a preacher, lad, to tell the Old,
Old Story,
The story that is ever new, that leads men on to
glory.
Our Master left instructions clear, to go to
every creature,
So, if you would be faithful, you must also be a
'Reacher'.
Yes, we must all be reachers, lad, whatever be the
distance.
The Shepherd sought until He found; and should
you meet resistance,
Don't be put off—seek on—if crowds won't have
you as a teacher,
Seek out some lonely soul and make yourself into
an 'Each-er'.
                              —*Indian Christian*
(Mark 1. 39; John 4. 4-7; Acts 8. 5; 26-27)

882. **Preacher.** Dr. J. H. Jowett says the path over which a sermon must travel to produce action is:

First—enlighten the mind
Second—captivate the judgement
Third—arouse the conscience
Fourth—conquer the will

When you are complimented for a message, don't be too well satisfied. Somebody says, 'I learned some new things today.' That is only the first step. Another says, 'I see that truth more clearly: you have convinced me.' That is only step number two. You see a man moved to tears and he shakes with emotion under the message. He is aroused, he is stirred, but the one thing most needful for him is to yield—to obey—to act. Soul-winning preachers aim at action.
(1 Thess. 1. 5, 9, 10)

883. Preaching. Count Zinzendorf adopted the motto of Tholuck—'I have one passion, and it is He—only He.'

Martin Luther's preaching aroused the church from a thousand years' slumber during the Dark Ages—the devil's millennium. It is easy to understand why, when we discover how Luther preached. He said, 'I preach as though Christ was crucified yesterday; rose again from the dead today; and is coming back to earth tomorrow.'

—*Herald of His Coming*
(1 Cor. 1. 23; 2. 2; Acts 17. 18; 1 Thess. 4. 13-17)

884. Preaching. The meaning of preaching can be learnt from four Greek words used in the New Testament to translate the word 'preach'.

1. *Kerusso*—to proclaim, to herald. This is used of the public proclamation of the Gospel. (Matt. 11. 1; Mark 1. 4; 3. 14; 16. 20; Rom. 10. 15, etc.)

2. *Euaggelizo*—to tell good news. From this word are derived our terms—'evangel', 'evangelist', 'evangelize'. (Matt. 11. 5; Luke 4. 18; 7. 22; 1 Cor. 1. 17; Gal. 1. 8; Heb. 4. 2, etc.)

3. *Kataggello*—to tell thoroughly. (Acts 4. 2; 13. 38; 15. 36; Col. 1. 28)

4. *Laleo*—to talk. (Mark 2. 2; Acts 11. 19; 14. 25, etc.)

Of the 112 times, the word 'preach' is found in the New Testament, on only six instances does it mean a formal discourse. Thus to preach, in the New Testament sense of the term is to proclaim as a herald the message of the King of kings and Lord of lords; to tell the good news, to tell thoroughly all the truth of the gospel, holding back nothing, but declaring 'the whole counsel of God'; to talk to others, as we meet them on the highways, or in their homes, of the love of God as revealed in the gift of His Son, and of the salvation He has secured for whosoever will believe on Him.

—Alfred P. Gibbs

885. Preaching. A young preacher in a college town was embarrassed by the thought of criticism that he was likely to receive from such a cultured congregation. He sought out his father, an old and wise minister of the Gospel, and said, 'Father, I find it hard to outline a sermon I can preach to these people. If I cite anything from geology, there is Professor A—the geology professor, before me. If I use an illustration from history, there is Professor B—ready to trip me up. If I choose English literature for some allusion, I am afraid the whole English department will rise and challenge me. What shall I do?'

The sagacious and godly old man replied, 'Preach the Gospel, my son! They probably know very little about that.'
(Mark 16. 15; 1 Cor. 2. 1, 2)

886. Preaching. More and more, as I get older and go on preaching, I find that, if I take a text, I need the whole Bible to explain it.
—Dr. G. Campbell Morgan
(Luke 24. 27; Acts 13. 15, 16; 1 Cor. 15. 3, 4)

887. Preaching. A negro of standing was once introducing a negro preacher to his audience, and said:

'Bruddahs and sistahs, dis bruddah's gwine to preach a powahful sermon dis mo'nin'. He's gwine to define de undefinable: he's gwine to explain de unexplainable; he's gwine to dispense wid de indispensable; he's gwine to prove de unprobable; an' he's gwine to unscrew de unscrutable.'

888. Preaching. There is a message for all classes of people in the Scout motto: 'Be prepared'.

It is—A mandate from the Sovereign of the Universe—Matt. 24. 44
A message for the sinner from God—Amos 4. 12
A maxim for the servant of Christ—2 Tim. 2. 21
A motto for the soldier of Jesus Christ—Acts 21. 13.

889. Preparation—for Death. There is an old story of a king of bygone days and his 'clown' or 'jester', who sometimes said very foolish things and sometimes made very wise utterances. One day the jester had said something so foolish that the king, handing him a staff, said to him, 'Take this, and keep it till you find a bigger fool than yourself.'

Some years later, the king was very ill and lay on his deathbed. His courtiers were called; his family and his servants also stood round his bedside. The king, addressing them, said, 'I am about to leave you. I am going on a very long journey, and I shall not return again to this place: so I have called you all to say "Goodbye".' Then his jester stepped forward and, addressing the king, said, 'Your Majesty, may I ask a question? When you have journeyed abroad visiting your people, staying with your nobles, or paying diplomatic visits to other courts, your heralds and servants have always gone before you, making preparations for you. May I ask what preparations your Majesty has made for this long journey that he is about to take?'

'Alas!' replied the king, 'I have made no preparations.'

'Then,' said the jester, 'take this staff with you, for now I have found a bigger fool than myself.'
(Amos 4. 12; Matt. 24. 44; 25. 10)

890. Preparation—of Sermon. In the days when Mr. Handley Bird was carrying on aggressive gospel work in Madras city, he asked a young missionary who had come to visit him from the mofussil to preach the Gospel in the Sunday evening service. After vainly searching for a message, the missionary came to Mr. Bird and said humbly, 'I'm sorry I haven't been able to prepare an address.'

Mr. Bird's characteristic reply was, 'Brother, go and prepare yourself.'
(Eph. 6. 15)

891. **Presence of Christ.** When in the city of Aberdeen, my good host took me round the granite city, pointing out the places of importance and acting as my guide to the places for which the city was deservedly noted. I remarked on the absence of slums in the granite city, and he said, 'Well, there are just a few streets where the people are very poor, and the tenements are not so imposing as the other buildings in Aberdeen. Would you like to visit one of these streets?' he asked. I said I would very much like to see such a place if it did exist in their granite town. He took me to one of the back streets and, as we walked along, he pointed up to one of the tenement rooms about three storeys up, and said, 'Do you see that room there? Formerly, there was a fine old saint of God living there. She was well known everywhere for her cheerfulness amid much poverty and sickness, and was always radiant with the beauty of Christ. Once, when an evangelist was preaching at the Gordon Mission, he was told about this sister and went to visit her. When he went in and saw her bright radiant face, in the midst of such poverty, he said to her, 'My dear sister, they tell me the Lord Jesus Christ visits this place.' 'Na, na! ma laddie, ye're wrang!' was her reply. Thinking she was a bit hard of hearing and had not caught his words, he repeated what he had said, and again she replied, 'Ye're wrang! ye're wrang!' Convinced now that she must be very deaf, he fairly shouted into her ear, 'Sister, doesn't the Lord Jesus Christ visit your home?' Shaking her head again, she said, 'Ye're wrang! ye're wrang! He bides here.'
(Gal. 2. 20; Matt. 28. 20)

892. **Presence of Christ.** Samuel Rutherford, writing from prison in Aberdeen three centuries ago, persecuted for his faith, and writing his famous 'Letters' to his parishioners, ended one of them with this sentence: 'Jesus Christ came into my prison-cell last night, and every stone in it glowed like a ruby.'

—*Indian Christian*
(Luke 24. 15, 32; 2 Tim. 4. 17)

893. **Presentation—of Self to God.** 'Yield yourselves to God'; 'Present your bodies a living sacrifice.'

A certain preacher had two daughters, one of them older than the other. One Monday morning the minister was sitting in his study in London, feeling that the previous day had been a bad day, without blessing—and he was very unhappy. Mummy was making the breakfast downstairs, and suddenly turned to the children and said, 'Run upstairs and tell daddy breakfast's ready!' So they both ran upstairs; but the big one outran her little sister, dashed into the study, jumped on to daddy's knee, put her arms round daddy's neck and kissed him, and said, 'Daddy, breakfast's ready!' The little one came puffing and panting, and looked somewhat crestfallen as she took in the situation. And big sister said something rather catty to little sister: 'I've got all there is of daddy today!' And daddy looked at that little girl, and held out to her his arm that was free—and she ran into the study and jumped on to the other knee, and he hugged her and put his arm right round her. And that little girl looked at her big sister and said, 'You may have all there is of daddy; but daddy's got all there is of me.'

Listen. You have got all there is of Jesus. Has He got all there is of you?

—Alan Redpath
(Rom. 6. 13; 12. 1; 1 Thess. 5. 23)

894. **Pride.** The life and death of our Lord Jesus Christ are a standing rebuke to every form of pride to which men are liable.

Pride of birth and rank—'Is not this the carpenter's son?' Matt. 13. 55

Pride of wealth—'The Son of man hath not where to lay His head.' Luke 9. 58

Pride of respectability—'Can any good thing come out of Nazareth?' John 1. 46

Pride of personal appearance—'He hath no form nor comeliness.' Isa. 53. 2

Pride of reputation—'A friend of publicans and sinners.' Luke 7. 34

Pride of learning—'How knoweth this man letters, having never learned?' John 7. 15

Pride of superiority—'I am among you as he that serveth.' Luke 22. 27

Pride of success—'He is despised and rejected of men.' Isa. 53. 3

Pride of ability—'I can of mine own self do nothing.' John 5. 30

Pride of self-will—'I seek not mine own will but the will of Him that sent me.' John 5. 30

Pride of intellect—'As my Father hath taught me, I speak.' John 8. 28.

Pride has been classified into a few categories:- Pride of face, pride of race, pride of place, pride of pace, pride of grace.

895. **Priesthood—of Christ.**

Christ bears the names of all His saints,
For them death's night He braved,
He holds them on His shoulders strong,
And on His heart engraved.

In all His holiness complete,
They stand without a flaw;
Where wisdom, grace and glory meet,
In love divine, not law.

The blood, which as a Priest He bore
For sinners, was His own.
The incense of His prayers and tears
Now perfumes Heaven's throne.

'Tis here my weary soul finds rest,
  Though I am frail the while.
I read my name upon His breast,
  Enjoy my Father's smile.
(Ex. 28. 12, 29, 30, 31; Heb. 2. 17; 4. 14, 16)

896. Priesthood—Holy.

The race of God's anointed priests shall never
  pass away;
Before His glorious face they stand, and serve
  Him night and day.
Though reason raves, and unbelief flows on, a
  mighty flood,
There are, and shall be to the end, the hidden
  priests of God,
His chosen souls, their earthly dross consumed
  in sacred fire;
To God's own heart their hearts ascend in flames
  of deep desire;
The incense of their worship fills His Temple's
  holiest place;
Their song with wonder fills the Heavens, the
  glad new song of grace.

—G. Ter Stegen

897. Procrastination.

A gentleman standing by Niagara saw an eagle swoop down upon a frozen lamb encased in a piece of floating ice. The eagle stood upon it as it drifted towards the rapids. Every now and then the eagle would proudly lift its head into the air to look around him, as much as to say: 'I am drifting on towards danger. I know what I am doing. I shall fly away and make good my escape before it is too late.'

When he reached the edge, he stooped, spread his powerful wings, and leaped for flight; but alas! while he was feeding on the carcase, his feet had frozen to its fleece. He leaped and shrieked, and beat upon the ice with his wings until he went over into the chasm and darkness below.
(Job. 36. 18; Matt. 3. 7; Acts 24. 25; 2 Cor. 6. 2)

898. Procrastination.

There is a Russian folk-song that narrates how a man, wishing to build a house, kept putting off commencing the building, after all the materials had been collected, until he came to die, when it was too late.

And there in solemn silence stood
The piles of stone and piles of wood,
Till Death, who in his vast affairs
Ne'er puts off things as men do theirs,
Winked at our hero as he passed:
'Your house is finished, Sir, at last
A narrow cell, a house of clay,
Your mansion for an endless day.'
(Luke 12. 19, 20; 2 Cor. 6. 2)

899. Procrastination.

'To-morrow', he promised his conscience,
'Tomorrow I mean to believe.
Tomorrow I'll think as I ought to,
Tomorrow my Saviour receive.
Tomorrow I'll conquer the habits
That hold me from Heaven away.'

And ever his conscience repeated
One word, and one only—'Today!'
Tomorrow! tomorrow! tomorrow!
Thus day after day it went on.
Tomorrow! tomorrow! tomorrow!
Till youth with its vision was gone,
Till age and his passions had written
The message of fate on his brow,
And forth from the shadows came Death
With the pitiless syllable, 'Now!'
(Prov. 27. 1; Heb. 3. 7, 8, 15; 4. 7)

900. Procrastination.

In D. L. Moody's early days in Chicago, a man who attended regularly seemed on the verge of decision for Christ. Moody urged him to accept Christ. 'No, Mr. Moody, I cannot. My business partner is not a Christian, and if I accept Christ, he would ridicule me.'

Finally, annoyed at D. L. Moody continually urging him, he ceased attending. One day the man's wife came to Mr. Moody's house and said to him, 'Mr. Moody, my husband is very ill. Doctors say he cannot possibly live. Won't you come down and speak to him before he dies?'

D. L. Moody hurried to the home, found the man ready to listen, and brought him to the point of decision. The man seemed to accept Christ. To everyone's surprise he got better. Mr. Moody visited him in convalescence. 'Now God has been so good to you and raised you up, so of course, as soon as you are able to come to the Tabernacle, you will make a public confession of your acceptance of Christ.' 'No, Mr. Moody, I cannot do that,' he said, 'for my partner would ridicule me, and I cannot stand ridicule.'

Finally he said, 'I am going to move to Michigan. Then I will.' D. L. Moody told him the Lord could keep him in Chicago just as well as in Michigan, but he would not listen.

Just a week later he had a relapse. D. L. Moody was again called and went to his bedside. The dying man said, 'I don't want you to talk to me. It will do no good. I've had my chance and thrown it away.' Then Mr. Moody quoted the verse, 'Him that cometh unto Me I will in no wise cast out,' and asked, 'May I pray with you?' 'No, it won't do any good'. D. L. Moody knelt to pray, but could not. The sinking man kept repeating, 'The harvest is past, the summer is ended, and I am not saved,' till he died.
(Jer. 8. 20; 2 Cor. 6. 2)

901. Procrastination.

The *City of Cairo* sailed from Liverpool for the East on Nov. 3, 1922. There were a few missionaries on board, but many of the passengers were Dundee folks going to Calcutta for the first time, or returning to their posts in the Jute Mills there. Sunday evening afforded an opportunity for preaching the Gospel, with the consent of the Purser, and a missionary bound for Madras preached on the subject, 'What shall I do then with Jesus which is called Christ?' As he presented

Christ crucified, the passengers seemed to listen with rapt attention.

The next morning, in the lounge, one of the men going to the Jute Mills in Calcutta, having left his wife in Dundee, came to the missionary for a talk, and after expressing appreciation of the message he had heard the previous day, said it took him back in thought to early days, when in the Sunday School and Gospel meetings he had listened to the same old story. The missionary put before him his responsibility and pleaded with him to accept Christ without further delay and take his stand for Him. 'I will when I get to Calcutta, after this voyage is over,' said the man. 'But why not now?' pleaded the missionary. 'You may never reach Calcutta.' Pleading that he could not get away from his companions and that they expected him to accompany them when they got off at the various ports of call, he put off deciding.

After Port Said, when they seemed to have a rollicking time, he began to drink more, and had his liquor iced as the ship went into hotter climes. One day, one of his companions came to the missionary, and said, 'Padre, come to—'s cabin. He's very ill, and we have sent for the ship's doctor. He took an interest in your sermon the other Sunday, and likes you: so he would like to see you.' The missionary went in, and tried to speak to him, but the colic pains he was enduring were so bad that he could not pay much attention. Next morning, the missionary went again to see him, but he was unconscious by that time, and the doctor had given up hope of saving his life.

Later in the day he passed away without gaining consciousness, and his friends stood and looked sorrowfully on as he was buried at sea.

Too late! too late! will be the cry:
Jesus of Nazareth has passed by.
(Luke 18. 37; Heb. 3. 13-15)

902. Prodigal Son. Someone asked Charles Dickens once what was the best short story in the English language, and his reply was— 'The Prodigal Son'.
(Luke 15. 11-32)

903. Prodigal Son. Dr. Draper, a Salvation Army doctor in India, once visited a dying man of 25, when he was about the same age himself. The young man was lying in hospital dying of T.B. He had been visited by many Christian people who had spoken to him about his soul, but he could not grasp the truth or understand the simple way of salvation. Dr. Draper read to him the story of the Prodigal Son, and it was the means of the young man's conversion.

904. Prodigal Son. Two preachers had been invited to a Gospel tea-meeting somewhere in London, and they went together, having carefully prepared their messages. When they arrived and saw the audience, composed of the very poor and not very literate who lived in the slums in that area, they looked at one another. 'The sermon I have ready won't do here, I'm afraid,' said J. B. Watson. 'Nor mine,' said J. Stephen. 'I'll tell you what,' said J. B. Watson to his fellow-preacher, 'I'll take the prodigal son out to the far country, and you bring him home again.'
(Luke 15. 11-24)

905. Prodigal Son. Dr. A. T. Schofield narrates a wonderful story connected with a rough wooden bell-handle at Carlton Hall in the Dukeries.

The family had become very earnest Christians, and had started a mission hall in the village. They also held on Wednesday afternoons a family meeting for prayer for members of the family that were away from home, and especially for the eldest son—at that time the family prodigal, literally 'spending his substance on riotous living' in the 'far country' in Australia.

A great letter-writer, he delighted to recount his excesses in long weekly epistles. In spite of many prayer meetings, those letters, distressing in their tone, continued, and the mothers and daughters began to fear that their prayers were unheard, when suddenly a miracle took place. It appears the boy lived some twenty miles from the post town, and when he had written his weekly letter, he used always to ride through the bush to post it, returning the next day.

One afternoon, at Carlton Hall, they had just got their weekly letter, full of racing news, when the girls saw that a second letter from him was lying on the table. His mother opened it, little imagining what it contained. She read somewhat as follows:

'I was riding yesterday through the bush with my letter to you in my pocket. I think I must have got about half-way when, like Saul going to Damascus, I was suddenly arrested by a wonderful vision. Like a lightning flash I got an intense conviction that I was a lost man, riding to destruction. I reined in my horse, burst into a violent perspiration, and was so weak that I had to dismount and lean against the saddle. After some minutes I decided to go on and returned home slowly, my one desire being to relieve my agony.

'I found the Bible you gave me, at the bottom of my box, but could get no comfort from it; so next day I rode off to see the Bishop, but got no peace or rest from him. And now, dear mother, do tell me how I am to be saved from this awful condition. I am in intense suffering and long for your reply.'

Deciding that a letter was far too slow, they determined to send a telegram, and, after prayer, there came vividly into their minds the somewhat unsuitable words, 'And when they had nothing to pay, he frankly forgave them both.' They immediately sent that message to the prodigal son.

On receiving it he saw in a moment he was freely forgiven through the merits and work of

12   161

Christ. The prodigal, having come to himself, now 'arose and returned to his father'. The mother, hearing he was returning to England, had a bell put immediately over her bed, and it was the handle of that bell that had attracted Dr. Schofield's attention.

(Luke 7. 42; 15. 12-21)

906. Promise. When Christian and Hopeful lay helpless prisoners in Doubting Castle, the property of Giant Despair, Christian said, 'What a fool I am, thus to be in a stinking dungeon, when I may as well walk at liberty! I have a key in my bosom, called Promise, that will, I am persuaded, open any lock in Doubting Castle.' Then he pulled it out of his bosom and began to try at the dungeon door, whose bolt, as he turned the key, gave back, and the door flew open with ease, and Christian and Hopeful both came out. Then he went to the outward door that leads into the castle yard, and with his key opened that door also. After that he went to the iron gate, for that must be opened too, but that went desperately hard; yet the key did open it.

Escaping from By-path meadow, they went over the stile, where they erected a pillar with this notice: 'Over this stile is the way to Doubting Castle, which is kept by Giant Despair, who despiseth the King of the Celestial country and seeks to destroy his holy pilgrims.'

Then they sang:

'Out of the way we went, and then we found
What it was to tread upon forbidden ground.
And let them that come after have a care
Lest they, for trespassing, his prisoners are,
Whose castle's Doubting and whose name's Despair.'

—John Bunyan in *Pilgrim's Progress*
(Acts 12. 10; 2 Cor. 1. 20; 2 Pet. 1. 4)

907. Providence—Divine.

Back of all that foes have plotted, or that friends have wisely planned,
Human schemes or work of demons, moves a hidden higher Hand.
Man's horizon is but finite; present mysteries ensnare;
Wrongs in vain cry for avenging, Hope is tempted to despair.
But when God unveils the future, His exact and full reward
Will reveal an even balance in the judgements of the Lord.
Through the mystic fabric, woven on the great historic loom,
Runs the golden thread of purpose, not the iron threads of doom.
Warp and woof are heaven's making, pattern beautiful and wise,
Pattern hidden on the earth-side, perfect to celestial eyes.
Every action, every actor, great or little, foe or friend,
Like converging paths of empire to one golden milestone tend,

All minutest threads inwoven into God's complete design,
Perfecting its colour pattern, filling out its grand outline.
Yet God's agents act with freedom, choosing whether love or hate,
Close alliance—bold defiance—slaves to no relentless fate.
True the hand Divine is hidden—moving secret and unseen
Through the acts of life's long drama, managing each shifting scene.
Nothing happens accidental. All that man ascribes to chance
Choice of God has first determined—nothing can escape His glance,
Men may cast their lots and gamble with their deeds as with their dice,
Count capricious Fortune mother of their virtue or their vice;
Man proposes, God disposes; all things His design fulfil;
Every human wrath unconscious serves to execute His will.
This the goal of all the ages—highways, by-ways, higher bend,
And despite all foes and factions, God is Victor in the end.
So man's festival of Purim, read in Faith's illumined sense,
Shall be seen in realms eternal as the Feast of Providence.

—Dr. A. T. Pierson

(Esth. 3. 7-13; 9. 25, 26; Dan. 2. 37; 4. 25; 5. 23, 24; Rom. 11. 33)

908. Provision—Divine. One of the many interesting stories of the Bible is that of Elijah and the ravens. You remember that God sent ravens to bring His servant food, when he was at the brook, hiding from Ahab. Sometimes we seem to think that such wonderful things happened long ago, but that they do not happen any more. But in this we are mistaken. God still cares for His people. He is always near, when they need Him.

David Brainerd was a famous missionary who went to the Indians to preach the Gospel. As a result of his labours, many of the Indians found their Saviour. Brainerd was a man of prayer. In his diary he tells of his experiences on his many travels. And he often mentions how the Lord heard and answered his prayers.

One day, on one of his many journeys to visit an Indian tribe, he was overtaken by a severe storm. He looked for a place of shelter and eventually found one in a hollow log of a very large tree. While there, he prayed for the Indians and also that the Lord would take care of him and his needs.

When meal time came, he was hungry, but there was nothing to eat. He noticed a squirrel approaching the tree. The squirrel chattered a while. When the little animal disappeared, Brainerd noticed that he had left a few nuts behind. The missionary ate those nuts.

Three days the storm continued, and for three days Brainerd remained in the log. Each day the squirrel came to deposit some nuts at the entrance. David Brainerd knew that the Lord had sent that squirrel.

—*Indian Christian*

(1 Kings 17. 5-7; Phil. 4. 19)

909.   **Psalm—Twenty-third.**
The harp strings lie rusted and broken,
The kingdom has gone to decay:
The harpist king sleeps in Mount Zion
Not far from the ancient gateway.

But the sweet tender Psalm of the shepherd
Sings on through the wearisome years;
The shepherd may sleep, but his message
Still lives to dispel mortal fears.

(Ps. 23)

910.   **Psalms—David's.** David's Psalms are:
1. Psalms of tribulation—
   for David's Psalms had ne'er been sung
      If David's heart had ne'er been wrung:
2. Psalms of jubilation—
   for David's Psalms had ne'er been sung
      If David's harp had ne'er been strung:
3. Psalms of inspiration—
   for David's Psalms had ne'er been sung
      Had David's God ne'er touched his tongue.

911.   **Psalms—Jesus Christ in the.**

Psalm 22	Psalm 23	Psalm 24
Saviour	Shepherd	Sovereign
Sword	Staff	Sceptre
Suffering	Supplying	Splendour
The Cross	The Crook	The Crown
Gloom	Goodness	Greatness
Grace	Guidance	Glory
The Good Shepherd	The Great Shepherd	The Chief Shepherd
Propitiation	Provision	Prospect
Pardon	Peace	Power
Wrath	Walk	Welcome
Cry	Comfor	Conquest
Misery	Mercy	Majesty
Rejection	Refreshment	Reigning
He dies	He lives	He is coming
Yesterday	Today	For ever.

—Stewart Lavery

912.   **Psalms—Imprecatory Psalms.**
1. Not one psalm is purely imprecatory:
2. Only one psalm is half, or more than half, imprecatory:
3. Only fifteen psalms out of one hundred and fifty contain imprecations:
4. Out of 2,350 or more verses in the Psalms, about 65 contain imprecations:
5. Some of the imprecations are not prayers but predictions, with future tense verb:
6. The authorship of eleven of the imprecatory psalms is ascribed to David:
7. Imprecations are fewest in Books III and IV.

In considering the Imprecatory Psalms, four things must be taken into account: David's character, David's circumstances, David's convictions and David's creed.

(Ps. 83. 15, 16; 139. 19-24; 1 Cor. 16. 22)

913.   **Putting on Christ.** When the Roman youth reached manhood, he put on the Toga Virilis, the robe of manhood. The day was one of special ceremonial, a great day for him.

When the Hindu youths of certain castes reach manhood, they put on the Yagnopavitam, or sacred cord. The day is one of special ceremonial, a great day for the youth who is invested with the sacred cord.

So the believer at his baptism acknowledges that he has 'put on Christ'—a new robe of righteousness to display to the world, a new cord of holiness that links him with the holiness of his God, a 'Holy Father'.

(Gal. 3. 27)

914.   **Putting on Christ.** In Rome Augustine Monica's hitherto profligate son, found the Saviour. The verse that was used to his conversion was the exhortation of the Apostle Paul to the believers in Rome:

'Put ye on the Lord Jesus Christ, and make not provision for the flesh, to fulfil the lusts thereof.'

(Rom. 13. 14; Col. 3. 10, 12)

915.   **Pyramids of Scripture.** Many have gazed in wonder on the Pyramids in Egypt, Some have admired displays of gymnastic pyramids. Here are samples of Scripture Pyramids that the believer can contemplate with wonder and admiration:

Glory.   Weight of glory
   Eternal weight of glory
Exceeding and eternal weight of glory
More exceeding and eternal weight of glory
a far more exceeding and eternal weight of glory

Prayer.   Ask
   All that we ask
All that we ask or think
Above all that we ask or think
Abundantly above all that we ask or think
Exceedingly abundantly above all that we ask or think
Able to do exceedingly abundantly above all that we ask or think.

(2 Cor. 4. 17; Eph. 3. 20)

916.   **Quarrels.**
Two it takes to make a quarrel:
One can always end it.

(Phil. 4. 2)

917. Question—The Unanswerable. Some years ago, a Scottish friend of mine, while walking the streets of Johannesburg, South Africa, happened to glance in the gutter, and saw a piece of paper on which was written in large letters: 'Five thousand pounds reward!'

Moved with curiosity, to say nothing of the desire to possess the substantial reward, he stooped down and retrieved the paper. It turned out to be a four page gospel tract. On opening it he read: 'Five thousand pounds will be paid to the person or persons who can answer the following question: "How shall we escape, if we neglect so great salvation"?' Needless to say, the reward remains unclaimed unto this day!

—Alfred P. Gibbs

(Heb. 2. 3)

918. Question — The Unanswerable. An American student, rather nervous, had to take an examination which had two parts, oral and written. He did not mind the written examination, but looked forward to the oral exam. with some misgivings. Asking advice of one of his friends, he was told that it would be fatal to show any hesitancy, as the examiners would put that down to ignorance. He must give some sort of answer, or, if he did not know any answer, try to give the impression that he had a good knowledge of the subject.

Entering the examination room, he was asked by one of the oral examiners a difficult question in science related to a sphere or branch of that particular subject with which he was not at all familiar. Nevertheless, he put on a good face and, not being able to give any answer to the question, he said, 'I'm sorry, I've covered that ground and know the answer, but have just forgotten it for the moment.'

'What a tragedy!' said the examiner, 'Scientists have been searching for an answer to that question for the last two thousand years.'

(Heb. 2. 3)

919. Questions—Challenging. Oh, friends, better load up with a few interrogation points. You cannot afford to be silent when God and the Bible and the things of eternity are assailed. Your silence gives consent to the bombardment of your Father's house; you allow a slur to be cast on your mother's dying pillow. On behalf of the Christ Who for you went through the agonies of crucifixion on the rocky bluff back of Jerusalem, you dare not face a sickly joke. Better load up with a few questions, so that next time you will be ready. Say to the scoffer, 'My dear sir, will you tell me what makes the difference between the condition of women in China and the United States? What do you think of the Sermon on the Mount? How do you like the Golden rule laid down in the Scriptures? Are you in favour of the Ten Commandments? In your large and extensive reading have you come across a lovelier character than Jesus Christ? Will you please to name the triumphant death-beds of Infidels and Atheists? How do you account for the fact that among the out-and-out believers of Christianity were such persons as Benjamin Franklin, John Ruskin, Thomas Carlyle, Babington Macaulay, William Penn, Walter Scott, Charles Kingsley, Horace Bushnell, James A. Garfield, Robert E. Lee? How do you account for their fondness for the Christian religion? Among the innumerable colleges and universities of the earth, will you name me three started by infidels and now supported by infidels? Down in your heart are you really happy in the position you occupy antagonistic to the Christian religion? Go at him with a few such questions and he will look at his watch and say he has an engagement, and must go.

—Dr. Talmage

(Isa. 41. 21; 1 Pet. 3. 15)

920. Questions—Christ, the Master's.

Have ye looked for my sheep in the desert,
For those who have missed the way?
Have ye been in the wild, waste places,
Where the lost and wandering stray?
Have ye trodden the lonely highway,
The foul and darksome street?
It may be you'd see in the gloaming
The print of My wounded feet.

Have ye carried the living water
To the parched and weary soul?
Have ye said to the sick and wounded,
'Christ Jesus can make thee whole?'
Have ye told My fainting children
Of the strength of the Father's hand?
Have ye guided the tottering footsteps
To the shore of the Golden Land?

Have ye stood by the sad and weary,
To soothe the pillow of death,
To comfort the sorrow-stricken,
And strengthen the feeble faith?
And have ye felt, when the glory
Has streamed through the open door,
And flitted across the shadows,
That there I have been before?

Have ye wept with the broken-hearted
In their agony and woe?
Ye might hear Me whispering beside you,
"Tis the pathway I often go.'

(Luke 15. 4-6; Acts 1. 8; 20. 35)

921. Race—The Christian. In one of the attempts to scale Mount Everest before the final successful attempt in 1953, Mallory and his friend made a final dash for the summit but failed, and to-day lie buried somewhere in the eternal snows. They failed in spite of their tremendous determination, intrepid courage, the discipline of long training, and the personal sacrifice of money and life, to reach the highest point of the highest mountain in the world. When one of the party, having returned

to London, was giving a lecture, he had on the platform behind him a magnificent picture of Everest and, as he concluded his address, he turned round and apostrophised the mountain thus: 'We tried once to conquer you, and failed; we tried again, and you beat us; but we shall yet beat you, for you cannot grow bigger, but we can.'
(Phil. 3. 13, 14)

922. Race—The Christian. Atalanta, a beautiful Arcadian girl, daughter of King Schoenus, vowed never to marry. She had many suitors so, to free herself from them, she challenged them to a race, she carrying a dart while they carried nothing. Being exceedingly swift of foot, she felt sure she could outstrip all the competitors. The lovers started first, and she was to kill all she overtook, but, if one reached the goal before her, she promised to marry the successful suitor. Hippomenes ran with three golden apples in his hand, and as she gained on him, he threw down one of the apples after the other. Fascinated by the glittering gold, so easy to obtain, Atalanta stooped each time to pick them up, and thus Hippomenes won the race.
(1 Cor. 9. 24-27; Heb. 12. 1-3)

923. Race—Pressing on in the.
> Lord, make me deaf and dumb and blind
> To all 'those things which are behind':
> Deaf to the voice that memory brings
> Accusing me of many things,
> Dumb to the things my tongue could speak,
> Reminding me when I was weak;
> Blind to the things I still might see,
> When they come back to trouble me.
> Let me press on to Thy high calling
> In Christ, Who keepeth me from falling.
> Forgetting all that lies behind—
> Lord, make me deaf, and dumb, and blind:
> Like Paul, I then shall win the race
> I would have lost but for Thy grace!
> Forgetting all that I have done—
> 'Twas Thee, dear Lord, not I, who won.

(Phil. 3. 12-14)

924. Rahab.
> Rise up, rise up, Rahab,
>   And bind the scarlet thread
> On the casement of thy chamber,
>   When the battle waxeth red.
>
> From the double feast of Gilgal,
>   From Jordan's cloven wave,
> They come with sound of trumpet,
>   With banner and with glaive.
>
> Death to the foes of Israel!
>   But joy to thee and thine,
> To her who saved the spies of God,
>   Who shows the scarlet line.
>
> 'Twas in the time of harvest,
>   When the corn lay on the earth,
> That first she bound the signal
>   And bade the spies go forth.

> For a cry came to her spirit
>   From the fair Egyptian coasts,
> And a dread was in her bosom
>   Of the mighty Lord of Hosts.
>
> And the faith of saints and martyrs
>   Lay brave at her heart's core,
> As some inward pulse were throbbing
>   Of the kingly line she bore.
>   —C. F. Alexander

(Josh. 2. 18-21; 6. 23-25; Heb. 11. 31; James 2. 25)

925. Rainbow.
> Triumphal arch, that fill'st the sky
>   When storms prepare to part,
> I ask not proud Philosophy
>   To teach me what thou art.
>
> When o'er the green undeluged earth
>   Heaven's covenant thou didst shine,
> How came the world's grey fathers forth
>   To watch the sacred sign!
>
> And when its yellow lustre smiled
>   O'er mountains yet untrod,
> Each mother held aloft her child
>   To bless the bow of God.
>
> Nor ever shall the Muse's eye
>   Unraptured greet thy beam;
> Theme of primeval prophecy,
>   Be still the prophet's theme!
>
> The earth to thee her incense yields,
>   The lark thy welcome sings,
> When glittering in the freshen'd fields
>   The snowy mushroom springs.
>
> How glorious is thy girdle cast
>   O'er mountain, tower and town,
> Or mirror'd in the ocean vast
>   A thousand fathoms down.
>
> As fresh in yon horizon dark,
>   As young thy beauties seen,
> As when the eagle from the ark
>   First sported in thy beam.
>
> For, faithful to its sacred page,
>   Heaven still rebuilds thy span,
> Nor lets the type grow pale with age
>   That first spoke peace to man.
>   —Thomas Campbell

(Gen. 9. 13-16)

926. Rank—Keeping. The Greek word— Atakteo—in 2 Thess. 3. 7, translated 'unruly', and 'disorderly', is a military figure used for soldiers marching out of order or out of rank.
    The story is told of a proud mother watching the regiment, in which her son was being trained, march past, and remarking to her neighbour: 'They're a fine lot o' men, but they're a' oot o' step except oor Jock.'
(1 Thess. 5. 14; 2 Thess. 3. 7, 11)

927. Reading the Bible.

*Christian, wheresoe'er you are—read the Word
    and pray;
Make God's Word your guiding star—still read
    —still pray.
Keep your Bible near at hand,
Whether you're on sea or land,
Speak with God just where you stand—
Read the Word and pray.*

*When you've nothing much to do—read the
    Word and pray;
When you're very busy too—still read—still
    pray.
When the world with many toys
Its seductive arts employs,
Would you taste of heavenly joys?
Read the Word and pray.*

*When your patience has been tried—read the
    Word and pray;
When you feel self-satisfied—still read—still
    pray.
When you're happy, when you're sad,
When some trial you have had,
This will make your spirit glad—
Read the Word and pray.*

*Daily, if you'd win the fight—read the Word and
    pray;
Every morning, every night—still read—still
    pray.
Then you'll see the Saviour's face,
Full of Glory, full of Grace,
Shining out in every place;
Read the Word and pray.*

*Toiling up the Heavenly road—still read—still
    pray;
This will ease your heavy load—still read—still
    pray.
Feet are hastened, hearts are joyed,
Fears are quelled and doubts destroyed.
Christ Himself fills every void—
Read the Word and pray.*

—Frank Gilbert

(John 5. 39; 1 Thess. 5. 17)

928.

928. Ready—Always or never? Admiral
Fisher said the Navy never required time for
preparation for war: it was always ready to
strike, for the Navy was always at war, fighting
fog and storm at sea. A Christian should never
lose his alertness.

—John MacBeath

There was a king of England called Ethelred,
who was never ready to meet his enemies, and
had to try to buy them off. He earned the
nickname 'Ethelred the Unready'. In his reign
the Danes made many successful invasions of
his land.

(Matt. 24. 43, 44; 25. 10)

929. Rebekah.

*On, ever on, with swift unvarying pace,
My camel bears me through the deserts wide;
Last eve a laughing girl, to-day a bride,
And having not yet seen my bridegroom's face.*

*My father's house I shall not see again.
Brothers and girlhood friends—I left them all
To answer that strange, new, resistless call
That draws me on across this weary plain.*

*Sometimes I think that all is but a dream:
This unknown servant and his wondrous prayer,
The camels at the well, the gifts he bare—
But see! Upon my arms the bracelets gleam.*

*No dream, but truth! Palm-trees against the
    sky,
And one comes forth to greet us—this is he!
Give me my veil; help me down speedily!
My lord, behold thy handmaid: here am I.*

—F. Sullivan

(Gen. 24)

930. Redeemer—My. 'I know that my
Redeemer liveth' was Jenny Lind's, the
Swedish Nightingale's, favourite text. The
words are inscribed on her tomb at Great
Malvern Cemetery. In the 'Messiah' this was
the part she loved so passionately to sing.
Born in Sweden in 1820, she became the 'queen
of song', 'the slim girl with the marvellous
voice'. She wrote to Professor Blackie the
following words: 'My unceasing prayer is that
what I give to my fellows may continue to live
on through eternity, and that the Giver of the
gift, and not the creature to whom He lent it,
may be praised.' Asked why she abandoned
the stage at the very height of her success, she
replied, laying her finger on the Bible, 'When
every day it made me think less of this, what
could I do?'

(Ruth 4. 4-6; Job 19. 25; 1 Pet. 1. 18)

931. Redemption—in Christ.

*His, by reason of Creation:
His, He paid the price for me.
His, through the life-giving Spirit,
His because I want to be.*

(1 Cor. 3. 23; 6. 19, 20; 1 Pet. 1. 18; Song of
Songs 2. 16)

932. Redemption—by the Creator. Secretary
Lincoln said that the historic likeness of his
father that would go down to posterity was
that one in the noble 'Emancipation Group' in
Washington where the Martyr-President stands
with his outstretched hand above the freed
slaves. In the hearts of all Christ's redeemed
and in the heavenly anthem Christ Jesus will be
enthroned as our Liberator, our Redeemer
Who has 'loosed us from our sins in His
blood'.

(Eph. 1. 7; Rev. 1. 5; 5. 9)

933. Redemption—by the Creator. A little
boy worked very hard, and, with a fine piece of
wood and some tools, made himself a fine little
yacht. He was very proud of it, and used to go
to the lake with the other boys who had their
yachts also, and sail it on the tranquil waters
of the lake near his home. One day it drifted

away out of sight, carried by a strong breeze and all the lad's efforts to reach it or even follow it with his eye, were unsuccessful. Some days later, as he was going through the busy street where most of the shops were, he saw the yacht in a shop window. He went in and claimed it as his lost yacht. But in spite of all his claims, and his repeated assertion that he had made it with his own hands, the shopkeeper said, 'If you want it, you must pay for it.' He returned home, counted up his little savings in his money box and found he had just sufficient to meet the cost of the yacht. So he went in and bought it back. 'You're twice mine!' he exclaimed, as he looked thankfully and proudly at his little yacht: 'I made you and I've purchased you.'

(1 Cor. 6. 19, 20)

934. Redemption—Price of. Richard Coeur de Leon, captured by his treacherous enemy in Europe as he returned from a Crusade in the Holy Land, was thrown into prison. A colossal ransom was demanded for his redemption. The people of England submitted to heavy taxation and paid willingly, and many rich nobles contributed large sums, that their king might be set free. Hence the term—'a king's ransom'—is used to connote a tremendous amount of money.

Another Crusader, Sir Grimbald, was captured by the Saracens and held to ransom. To emancipate him and redeem him from death, his beautiful wife willingly gave the ransom price his captors demanded—her lily-white right hand.

(Job 33. 24; 1 Tim. 2. 5, 6; 1 Pet. 1. 18)

935. Reformation—Uselessness of. During a visit in 1904 to a remote part of the Transvaal, I was lodging at a small house on the veldt. On retiring to rest at night, I could not help noticing the extremely dirty state of the bedroom floor. It looked as if it had not been cleaned for months. I determined that the following day I would call the landlady's attention to it, and ask her to have it scrubbed.

The next morning, however, I saw what had escaped my notice the evening before. The floor was of such a nature that no scrubbing could make it any cleaner. It was made of big clods of dirt, dried and hardened in the sun, and trodden down till a solid surface was formed, as level and smooth as any ordinary floor.

Of course I gave up the idea of asking the landlady to scrub it. The more such a floor was scrubbed the worse it would become. No amount of soap and water would do it any good.

—Whither Bound?

The same kind of floor is found in many houses in India. The floor of many of the houses of the poor is made of mud and cowdung, mixed, and dried hard. Such a floor can be made very even, and many of the labouring class who do not possess beds and sleep on mats on the floor prefer it to cement or stone floors for comfort and heat in the cool season. The floor can be swept, but scrubbing with soap and water would only make it soft and muddy. The sinner's condition in the sight of God is like this. No amount of reformation can improve it: he must be made anew.

(Isa. 64. 6; John 3. 6, 7; 2 Cor. 5. 17)

936. Refuge. In the Hindu myths of their gods there is a story of Sibi Chakravarthi, an emperor of ancient India. One day there flew to him for refuge a dove chased by a hawk. He gave it shelter, and the hawk, approaching the Emperor, demanded that the claims of justice should be satisfied, for the Creator had ordained that the dove should be the food of the hawk and other birds of prey which He had created. Sibi asked how the claims of justice could be met, and was told that justice demanded either that the dove should be handed over to it, or its weight in flesh from the body of the Emperor. Scales were brought at the command of Sibi, and the flesh cut off and put in one pan of the scales, with the dove in the other pan, until the scales balanced.

(Ps. 46. 1, 7, 11; Deut. 33. 27; Mark 10. 45)

937. Refuge. 'Other refuge have I none.' Charles Wesley, shortly after his conversion in 1738, sat one summer day in his study. A little bird, pursued by a hawk, flew in through the open window and sought refuge in his bosom, where the baffled hawk dare not follow. This incident led to the writing of the familiar hymn, 'Jesus, Lover of my soul'.

(Num. 35. 15; Ps. 59. 16; Jer. 16. 19)

938. Refuge.

O lovely Man! none can with Thee compare,
  My Hiding-place from every wind that blows;
In Thee my heart is freed from anxious care,
  I know Thy love to me unceasing flows.

My covert from the wild and stormy blast,
  Whose fury would my trusting soul alarm;
In Thee I shelter till the storm is past,
  Safe in Thy keeping nought can do me harm.

From Thee the living streams of life abound,
  Whose healing waters make the spirit whole;
Who drinks of Thee eternal life hath found,
  And ne'er again shall thirst the longing soul.

Thou Rock of ages, in Thee is my rest,
  Beneath Thy shadow in a weary land;
A pilgrim, on my way supremely blest,
  To Thee above, Whose love the way has
  planned.

—W. E. Earl

(Isa. 32. 2)

939.   Refusal. There was an old woman who lived in a small cottage not far from Balmoral Castle in Scotland. When Queen Victoria was living in the castle she was very fond of visiting some of the old people who lived near by.

One afternoon this old lady was in her cottage alone. She was in a very bad temper because she had quarrelled with her nearest neighbour, and because some of her friends had been gossiping about her. She shut the door, locking herself in, saying to herself, 'Aye, I'll keep myself to myself in the future. I won't let them in when they try to get a dish o' tea out o' me.' Presently she heard a soft knock at the door. She set her lips and nodded her head.

'Knock away,' she whispered. The knock was repeated louder now.

'Knock away till doomsday,' she called out in an angry voice. 'I'll no let ye in.' The knock wasn't repeated and footsteps outside were heard going away from the house. The old woman nodded and smiled.

'They won't trouble me now for a bit,' she assured herself. But she did not smile the next day when she was told that her queen had stood outside her door and had knocked for admission, and she had refused to let her in. The queen never visited her again.

Someone greater than all the kings and queens of earth is knocking at the heart's door of men and women and they won't let Him in. Some day He will knock for the last time. That last time may be nearer than we expect, therefore we ought to 'swing the heart's door widely open' and let Him in now.

—*Messenger of Peace*

(Rev. 3. 20; Hos. 4. 17; 5. 15)

940.   Refusal—The Great. When G. F. Watts was painting his famous picture of 'The Great Refusal', he said of it, 'Now I am doing a man's back—little else but his back to explain, "He went away sorrowful, for he had great possessions". Fancy a man turning his back on Christ rather than give away his goods! They say his back looks sorry. I don't know. It is what I meant his back to express.' Demas, too, presents to us the study of a back. Demas deserted Paul.

—*Herbert S. Seekings*

(Matt. 19. 22; 2 Tim. 4. 10)

941.   Remembrance.

Let us forget the things that vexed and tried us,
The worrying things that caused our souls to fret,
The hopes that, cherished long, were still denied us,
Let us forget.

Let us forget the little slights that pained us,
The greater wrongs that rankle sometimes yet;
The pride with which some lofty one disdained us,
Let us forget.

But blessings manifold, past all deserving,
Kind words and helpful deeds, a countless throng;
The fault o'ercome, the rectitude unswerving
Let us remember long.

The sacrifice of love, the generous giving,
When friends were few, that handclasp warm and strong,
The fragrance of each life of holy living,
Let us remember long.

Whatever things were good and true and gracious
Whate'er of right has triumphed over wrong,
What love of God or man has rendered precious,
Let us remember long.

(Phil. 1. 3; 3. 13; 4. 8)

942.   Repentance. In the early years of the twentieth century, in the town of Wishaw, Lanarkshire, Scotland, on a Saturday night, a faithful preacher of the Gospel might be heard preaching 'repentance toward God and faith toward our Lord Jesus Christ', and repeating again and again the warning, 'Turn or burn! Turn or burn!'

(Prov. 9. 4; Acts 2. 38; 20. 21; 1 Thess. 1. 9)

943.   Repentance.

Nay, but much rather let me late returning,
Bruised of my brethren, wounded from within,
Stoop with sad countenance and blushes burning,
Bitter with weariness and sick with sin.

Straight to Thy presence get me and reveal it,
Nothing ashamed of tears upon Thy feet;
Show the sore wound and beg Thy hand to heal it;
Pour Thee the bitter, pray Thee for the sweet.

(Luke 7. 37-48; 1 John 1. 9)

944.   Responsibility. What is our attitude toward our responsibilities? Responsibility for the Christian has been defined as 'our response to God's ability'. There are five possible attitudes:

1. We may *shirk* our responsibilities: 2. we may *shelve* them, hoping that some time or other we shall be able to fulfil them: 3. we may *shoulder* them, and wear ourselves out bearing their full weight: 4. we may *shed* them after having made an attempt to fulfil them: or 5. we may *share* them. It is in following the fifth course that we shall best be able to fulfil the law of Christ and bring glory to God.

(Gal. 6. 2-6)

945.   Rest—in Christ. Unregenerate men labour to find rest but miserably fail. Byron had a long search for it and said sadly in the end:

Count o'er the joys thine hours have seen,
Count o'er the days from anguish free;
And know, whatever thou hast been,
'Twere something better not to be.

Augustine, on the other hand, by the grace of God and through faith in the Lord Jesus Christ, could write: 'Oh God! Thou hast made us for Thyself, and our souls are restless till they rest in Thee.'

(Matt. 11. 28, 29; Ps. 37. 7)

946. Rest—in Christ. William Nicholson once wrote a letter to a friend of mine, and finished up with a characteristic phrase, 'Yours restfully, Billy'. To more intimate friends he usually signed, 'Yours till hell freezes'—but this is the more effective, 'Yours restfully'. And that's what God means to you and me.

If you had been in Palestine when Christ was walking this earth, I am sure one of the first things that would have impressed you in His life would have been the restfulness. When He stood up and said to those gathered round Him, 'Come unto me, all ye that labour and are heavy laden, and I will give you rest,' they did not ask themselves, 'What on earth is He talking about?' They knew. They saw it in His life. It was one of the things that drew them round Him to listen to His words. The restfulness of that life which was far busier than any of ours. And His peace and His rest He comes to give to us.

—L. F. E. Wilkinson

(Ps. 37. 7; Heb. 4. 9-11)

947. Restoration.

Canst Thou restore, O mighty God,
  The years so long gone by?
So devastated, desolate!—
  In barren waste they lie.
I started out to serve Thee, Lord,
  When youth's responsive hour
Gave promise that the seed then sown
  Would burst forth into flower.

But oh! the barrenness of years.
  No effort of my own
Can reap a harvest from the fields
  The cankerworm hath mown.
The locust of my faithlessness
  Hath blasted and destroyed
The harvest that in course of years
  The Master had enjoyed.

Wilt Thou restore? Then, Lord, in faith
  Before Thy feet I bow,
Confess to Thee my shame and loss.
  Fulfil Thy promise now.
Thus cleansed and sanctified, made meet
  To do the humblest task;
To be well-pleasing in Thy sight,
  My Lord, is all I ask.

—Mrs. G. Henderson, India

(Joel 2. 25)

948. Restoration.

And when with grief you see your brother stray,
Or in a night of error lose his way,
Direct his wandering and restore the day.
To guide his steps afford your kindest aid,
And gently pity whom you can't persuade;
Leave to avenging heaven his stubborn will,
For, O remember, he's your brother still.

—Dean Swift

(Gen. 4. 9; Gal. 6. 1)

949. Results. A preacher once approached C. H. Spurgeon and said: 'How do you account for the fact that though I preach the same gospel as you, I do not get anywhere near the same results?' Spurgeon replied: 'But you surely don't expect results every time you preach, do you?' 'O no,' answered the man. Then Spurgeon exclaimed: 'Then that is one reason why you don't get any!' The farmer who sows his seed in the spring, does so with every expectation of reaping in the fall.

—Alfred P. Gibbs

(1 Thess. 1. 5, 6)

950. Resurrection of Christ. Dr. Torrey relates an incident that came under his notice in New York. A brilliant lawyer in that city approached a prominent clergyman and asked him if he believed in the bodily resurrection of Christ. The latter, strongly affirming his belief in it, asked if he might have the pleasure of furnishing material in support of his belief. To this the lawyer gladly acquiesced, and after thoroughly examining the evidence put before him, frankly confessed that the resurrection of Jesus was established beyond doubt. 'But,' he added, 'I am no nearer salvation than I was, for I find the trouble is not with my head, but with my heart.'

(Rom. 10. 9; 1 Cor. 15. 14-21)

951. Resurrection of Christ.

Yes, the Lord is risen,
And death's gloomy prison,
Stript of bolt and bars, lies robbed
Of all its power to harm;
And the blood is speaking
Peace to spirits breaking
With the dreadful sense of sin's
Unconquerable charm.

—J. Boyd

(Luke 24. 5, 6; 2 Tim. 2. 8)

952. Resurrection of Christ. At a large Missionary Convention in the Central Hall, Westminster, London, in October, 1929, a missionary who had been serving the Lord in Brazil—Harold Wildish—now in the West Indies, narrated an incident in his experience of preaching the gospel to a group of primitive South American Indians in Brazil. With some other preachers, he had been telling the wonderful story of the coming, the death and the resurrection of our Lord Jesus Christ. After the preaching had finished for the night, and before the company dispersed, he heard their conversation on the subject of the preachers' discourses. Most had been greatly moved by the story of the cross and sufferings of our Lord Jesus Christ, and thought it wonderful that He should endure such grief and pain and die to redeem them from sin and hell. Then one of them remarked, 'Yes! it's wonderful. But how can a dead man save us?' Another who had followed the teaching carefully to the end, replied, 'Yes! but didn't you hear? He rose again from the dead. He's alive, He's risen.'

(Matt. 28. 5, 6; Acts 2. 31-36)

953.   Resurrection of Christ. Among leaders of thought early in the eighteenth century were Gilbert West and Lord Lyttleton. A well-known story tells that these two men believed the Bible to be an imposture and that they determined to expose it. To do this, they decided that they must begin by exposing the two greatest miracles by writing a book. Lord Lyttleton chose 'The Conversion of Paul', and Gilbert West 'The Resurrection of Christ'. Their tasks led them on to a careful examination of the Bible accounts of these two events, and they took about a year to complete their task. When they had finished their books, they met together and something like this passed between them:

'I have written my book,' said Lord Lyttleton, 'and I have a confession to make. When I came to study all the evidence for the story of the conversion of St. Paul, and weighed it up by all the known laws of evidence, I found that St. Paul was miraculously converted in spite of himself. I am now a Christian and have written my book on that side, and not against it.' Gilbert West replied: 'I have a similar confession to make. I have found the resurrection of Jesus Christ to be a proved fact, and I, too, have become a believer, and have written my book on that side.'

One day, while I was busy writing my own book on the Resurrection, a man came to see me. He said, 'I was looking at a second-hand bookstall in the city, and I came across an old book on the Resurrection. They only wanted a penny for it, so, as I knew you were writing a book on the subject, I bought it for you. Is it any use to you?' I thanked him warmly and looked at it. You may imagine my surprise when on opening it, I read: 'Observations on the History and Evidences of the Resurrection of Jesus Christ' by Gilbert West. Printed in Dosley, 1747.

It was the very book which Gilbert West had written as related above. Very significant is the motto he had written on the title page—

'Blame not before thou hast examined the Truth; understanding first, and then rebuke.' —Eccles. 11. 7.

To me this shabby old book proves the truth of the story.

—C. C. Dobson (Abridged)

Acts 17. 18, 31, 32; 1 Cor. 15. 3, 4)

954.   Resurrection of Christ.

Never woke a fairer morn
Since creation's primal ray,
Than the hour of golden dawn
On the Earth's first Easter day;
Jewelled meadows! Skylarks winging,
Lilies blooming! Bluebells ringing,
All the earth with gladness singing,
Alleluia! Easter morn!

Never lived a greater joy
Than that breathless moment when
Angels standing near the tomb
Whispered, 'Lo! He lives again!'
Spread the truth to every nation!
Sing abroad in exaltation!
Hail the God-sealed confirmation!
Alleluia! Easter morn!

Never came a nobler hope
Than the promise of that hour,
When, triumphant over death,
Love proclaimed redeeming power.
Man immortal! Ever growing,
Greater power! Greater knowing!
Life in endless overflowing!
Alleluia! Easter morn!

—Alfred Grant Walton

(1 Cor. 15. 20; 42-45; Eph. 1. 19, 20; Phil. 3. 10)

955.   Resurrection of Christ. Years ago, on Princes Street, Edinburgh, with its beautiful setting, one of the many shop windows displaying art treasures in beautiful paintings attracted the eye of a passing gentleman. He was gazing intently at a painting of the 'Crucifixion', with the Saviour extended on the Cross, the multitude watching, Mary and some others standing by. It had been a long time since this man had allowed any thoughts like those suggested by the canvas to enter his mind, but the artist's portrayal brought back the memory of long forgotten truths, and he was impressed and troubled.

Suddenly he became aware of the presence at his side of a little ragged laddie who was also looking intently at the painting with its wondrous story of Calvary.

'That's Jesus, sir, on the cross. They nailed Him there with that crown of thorns on His head, and killed Him, sir. He was a good man. He died for us, and that's His mother standing there, sir, looking at what they did to Him. The gentleman felt a lump rise in his throat as the boy continued—'And He died, sir, for our sins and they buried Him yonder, sir.' It was too real, and the man turned away to continue his walk in Princes Street. He felt a tugging at his coat tails. Turning round he saw the boy who had been telling the story standing looking into his face. The boy blurted out breathlessly, 'I forgot to tell you, sir. I forgot to tell you He rose again.'

(Luke 24. 6; 1 Cor. 15. 3, 4, 20)

956. Resurrection of the Christian. Over the magnificent mausoleum that holds the mortal remains of Queen Victoria and those of her royal husband are inscribed the words: 'Here at last I will rest with thee and with thee in Christ I shall also rise again.'
(John 6. 40; 1 Cor. 15. 20-23)

957. Resurrection of the Christian.
No longer must the mourners weep,
  Nor call departed Christians dead;
For death is hallowed into sleep,
  And every grave becomes a bed.
(John 11. 11-13, 25; 1 Thess. 4. 13-18)

958. Resurrection of the Fallen Believer. Often the believer falls. But it is one thing to fall down: it is another thing to lie where one falls. Let us make sure that we rise after falling. Scripture abounds with examples of those who, having fallen, rose again to do great things for God.

An old cathedral stood on the site of the present St. Paul's in London. It perished in the great fire of 1666. After the fire the brilliant young architect, Christopher Wren, designed a new cathedral which took 35 years to erect. The first stone that Wren picked up from the ruins of the old building bore a Latin inscription, whose meaning is 'I shall rise again'.
(Luke 22. 60-61; Acts 3. 6, 7; 13. 13; 15. 37, 38; 2 Tim. 4. 11; Phil. 3. 10)

959. Retrospect.
He was better to me than all my hopes, He was
  better than all my fears.
He made me a bridge of my broken works and a
  rainbow of my tears.
The billows that bounded my seagirt path but
  carried my Lord on their crest:
When I dwell on the days of my wilderness
  march, I can lean on Him for the rest.

He emptied my hands of their treasured store
  and His covenant love revealed.
There was not a wound in my aching heart but
  the balm of His breath had healed.
O! tender and true was the chastening sore in
  wisdom that taught and tried,
Till the soul that He sought was trusting in Him
  and nothing on earth beside.

He guided by paths that I could not see, by ways
  that I have not known.
The crooked was straight and the rough made
  plain as I followed the Lord alone.
I praise Him still for the pleasant palms and the
  water springs by the way,
For the glowing pillar of flame by night and the
  sheltering cloud by day.
(Deut. 8. 2; Ps. 77. 11)

960. Riches and Poverty of Christ.
My Master was so very poor,
  A manger was His cradling place;
So very rich my Master was—
  Kings came from far to gain His grace.

My Master was so very poor,
  And with the poor He brake the bread;
So very rich my Master was
  That multitudes by Him were fed.

My Master was so very poor,
  They nailed Him naked to a Cross;
So very rich my Master was
  He gave His all and knew no loss.
(Luke 2. 12; 9. 58; 2 Cor. 8. 9)

961. Robes—High-Priest's.
In priestly robes, blue, gold, and purple, drest,
Up that steep mountain-side his way he wended;
Weeping, the people watched as he ascended
With fearless footsteps to his last, long rest.
At length he reached the cloud-enveloped crest,
By son and brother mournfully attended,
Whose hands removed (his priestly duties ended)
The glorious robes and splendour on his breast.
With that rich dress he saw his son invested,
Then—Israel's priest no more—lay down to die,
And in his grave sublime and lonely rested;
Not like that wondrous priest of ours possessing
'Dyed garments' changeless as His Deity,
For ever living, loving, pleading, blessing.

—Richard Wilton
(Num. 20. 27-29; Heb. 7. 23, 24)

962. Rock of Ages. A Welsh lady, when she lay dying, was visited by her minister. He said to her, 'Sister, are you sinking?' She answered him not a word, but looked at him with incredulous eye. He repeated the question, 'Sister, are you sinking?' She looked at him again as if she could not believe he would ask such a question. At last, rising a little in her bed, she said, 'Sinking! Sinking! Did you ever know a sinner to sink through a rock? If I had been standing on the sand, I might sink; but thank God, I'm on the Rock of Ages, and there is no sinking there.'

—C. H. Spurgeon
(Ps. 40. 2; Luke 6. 47, 48; 1 Cor. 10. 4)

963. Rock of Ages. Augustus Toplady was one day overtaken by a severe thunderstorm in Burrington Combe, a rocky glen running into the heart of the Mendip Hills. There was no habitation anywhere near, and no place to which he could turn for shelter from the storm. Looking about him, he saw two massive pillars of rock, a deep fissure in the centre of a precipitous crag of limestone, and took refuge there. Standing there in safety, he escaped the storm. Finding a piece of paper lying near, he picked it up and with his pencil wrote the famous, familiar hymn, first published in 1775, 'Rock of Ages, cleft for me, Let me hide myself in Thee.'
(Deut. 33. 27; Isa. 26. 4 margin; 32. 2)

964. Rod—Moses.

—That mystic rod
Of old stretched o'er the Egyptian wave
Which opened, in the strength of God,
A pathway for the slave.

—John Greenleaf Whittier

(Exod. 4. 2; 14. 16; 17. 5, 6)

965. Sacrifice.

Camest Thou far, Beloved,
To seek for Thine own?
From Heaven's high wonder and glory
I travelled alone,
From height that thine eye ne'er beholdeth,
Past planet and star,
Down distances measureless, shining;
Yea, I came far.

Didst Thou leave much, O Beloved,
In coming for me?
My home in the Love of my Father
I gave up for thee;
For aye through the song and the music
My heart heard thy call.
I gave up my freedom, my glory;
Yea, I left all.

Didst Thou bear much, O Beloved,
That I might be free?
The thorn-crown, the mocking, the scourging,
The death on the tree—
The wrath of my God—ah! This sorrow
The thought cannot touch—
I died from the stroke of His anger:
Yea, I bore much.

—Gospel Steward

(Phil. 2. 5-8)

966. Sacrifice. Dan Crawford was but a lad
of nineteen when he left for Africa, an only
son. In the little company at the Glasgow
station stood his mother. When a friend spoke
a word of comfort, she replied, 'He spared not
His Son.'

Twenty-two years passed before she saw him
again. Yes, twenty-two years while he toiled
in Africa, without a furlough. He had buried
his son, and there, amid loneliness indescribable, fever-stricken again and again, time after
time nigh unto death, he lived and toiled and
suffered. At fifty-six he died.

—Oswald J. Smith

(John 20. 21; Rom. 8. 32)

967. Sacrifice. The story is told by the
Persians of the great Shah Abbas, who reigned
magnificently in Persia, but loved to mingle
with the people in disguise. Once, dressed as a
poor man, he descended the long flight of
stairs, dark and damp, to the tiny cellar where
the fireman, seated on ashes, was tending the
furnace.

The king sat down beside him and began to
talk. At meal time the fireman produced some
coarse, black bread and a jug of water and
they ate and drank. The Shah went away, but
returned again and again, for his heart was
filled with sympathy for the lonely man. He
gave him sweet counsel, and the poor man
opened his whole heart and loved this friend,
so kind, so wise, and yet poor like himself.

At last the emperor thought, 'I will tell him
who I am, and see what gift he will ask.' So he
said, 'You think me poor, but I am Shah Abbas
your emperor.' He expected a petition for
some great thing, but the man sat silent, gazing
on him with love and wonder. Then the king
said, 'Haven't you understood? I can make you
rich and noble, can give you a city, can appoint
you as a great ruler. Have you nothing to ask?'

The man replied gently, 'Yes, my lord, I
understood. But what is this you have done, to
leave your palace and glory, to sit with me in
this dark place, to partake of my coarse fare,
to care whether my heart is glad or sorry?
Even you can give nothing more precious. On
others you may bestow rich presents, but to me
you have given yourself; it only remains to ask
that you never withdraw this gift of your
friendship.'

(Mark 10. 45; Gal. 2. 20; Eph. 5. 2, 25)

968. Sacrifice.

Oh, Thou wast crowned with thorns, that I might
    wear
A crown of glory fair:
'Exceeding sorrowful' that I might be
Exceeding glad in Thee:
'Rejected and despised,' that I might stand
Accepted and complete at Thy right hand.

Wounded for my transgressions, stricken sore,
That I might 'sin no more':
Weak, that I might be always strong in Thee,
Bound, that I might be free:
Acquaint with grief, that I might only know
Fulness of joy in everlasting flow.

Thine was the chastisement, with no release,
That mine might be the peace;
The bruising and the cruel stripes were Thine,
That healing might be mine:
Thine was the sentence and the condemnation,
Mine the acquittal and the full salvation.

For Thee revilings and a mocking throng,
For me the angel song:
For Thee the frown, the hiding of God's face,
For me the smile of grace:
Sorrows of hell and bitterest death for Thee,
And Heaven and everlasting life for me.

(Isa. 53. 3-6; 2 Cor. 8. 9; 1 Pet. 2. 24)

969. Sacrifice. 'He saved others: Himself He
could not save.'

There was an old Greek epigram which said:
'When you go home, tell them of us and say—
For your tomorrow we gave our today.'

(Matt. 27. 42)

970. Safety. The Scottish writer, McDonald,
tells us this affecting story:

A new minister was visiting an aged woman
who spoke to him of her trust in God for the
safety of her son who was at sea.

'But,' said the minister, 'you say two of your sons have been drowned for all you say of safety.'

'It would be a strange thing for an old woman like me to believe that safety lay in not being drowned. What is the bottom of the sea, sir?'

'The hollow of God's hand,' said the minister, and bowed his head before her greater wisdom.
(Isa. 40. 12)

971. **Salvation—An Allegory.** A man had fallen into a deep, dark pit and lay in its miry bottom, groaning and utterly unable to move. Someone passed by closely enough to see his plight, but walked on with stately tread, without giving any help. Another approached the edge of the pit and said, 'Poor fellow! I'm sorry for you: it's your "karma" (fate). If ever you get out, don't get in there again.' A priest next came by and said, 'Poor fellow! I am very much pained to see you in that plight. If you could but scramble up half way, I could reach you and help you up the rest of the way.' But the man was entirely helpless.

Next came one, bearing in His hands, feet and side the marks of deep wounds, and He, hearing the man's groans, had pity on him, and, reaching down to where he was, laid hold of him with His strong arm and lifted him up, saying, 'Go and sin no more.'
(Isa. 59. 16; Acts 16. 30, 31; Rom. 5. 6; Luke 10. 30-34)

972. **Salvation.** In a house on the bank of the River Godavari, in S. India, lived a Christian and his wife. He had some land under cultivation on the other side of the river, and kept a small rowing boat in the water, tied to a post on the bank just outside his house, so that, when occasion required, he might cross the river and see to the crops growing on his land. One day a gust of wind snapped the rope that fastened the boat to the shore, and the little boat with the oars in it drifted out to midstream. It was a squally day, and they were rather concerned about the boat, but could see no way of getting it back.

A young man, 'Pearl of Wisdom' by name, the brother of the owner of the house, insisted on trying to recover the boat, and, heedless of the warnings of all, plunged into the river and commenced to swim toward the boat. Though a strong swimmer, he found that the wind was carrying the boat further and further away from the shore, and when he reached the middle of the river, with no hope of reaching the boat, his strength gave out. Exhausted and unable to swim further, he threw up his hands and shouted for help. His cries reached the shore, and, as no one could venture out on the river in such a storm, the distressed relatives stood weeping and wringing their hands. He was unable to save himself and there was none to save him, so they had almost abandoned all hope when round a bend in the river they saw a small fishing smack making its

way toward the drowning young man. The fishermen had seen his plight and were sparing no pains to cover the distance at the utmost speed in an endeavour to save him from drowning.

Shouts of hopeful encouragement from the shore took the place of their wails of distress. The little band of relatives and friends watched intently as the fishermen drew nearer and nearer to the drowning man. At length—as the young man was going under—the smack drew alongside, and the fishermen dexterously raised the drowning man from the water and placed him safely in the boat, to the accompaniment of shouts of joy: 'He's saved! He's saved,' they cried. But there was still danger on the stormy waters, and they might well have said, as each moment he was brought nearer the shore in spite of the angry waves, 'He's being saved.' At last he reached the shore and was lifted safely on to terra firma—saved completely, with no more danger. He was home.

The believer is saved from sin's Penalty, sin's Power and will be saved from sin's Presence.
(Acts 16. 31; Rom. 5. 9, 10; 1 Pet. 1. 5, 9)

973. **Salvation.** Henry Moorhouse, during his first visit to America in evangelistic work, was the guest of a cultured and wealthy gentleman who had a daughter just coming into womanhood and looking forward with bright anticipation to a gay and worldly life. One day she entered the library and found the evangelist reading his Bible. Begging his pardon for the intrusion, she was about to retire, when he looked up, and, calling her by name, said in his quiet and kindly way, 'Are you saved?'

She could only reply, 'No, Mr. Moorhouse, I am not.'

Then came another question, 'Would you like to be saved?'

She thought for a moment of all that is meant by salvation, and of all that is meant by the lack of salvation and she frankly answered, 'Yes, I wish I were a sincere Christian.'

Then came the tender appeal, 'Would you like to be saved now?'

Under this searching question her head dropped, and she began to look into her heart. On the one hand her youth, her brilliant prospects, her father's wealth and position in society, made the world attractive. On the other hand stood Christ. She replied, 'Yes, I want to be saved now.'

The supreme moment in her life was reached. Mr. Moorhouse asked her to kneel beside him and to read aloud the fifty-third chapter of Isaiah. This she did in a tone that became tremulous and broken by sobs. 'Read it again,' said Mr. Moorhouse gently, 'and where you find "we", "our", and "us" put in "I", "my", and "Me".'

The weeping girl read it again. 'He is despised and rejected of men; a man of sorrows, and acquainted with grief; and I hid as it were my face from Him; He was despised and I esteemed Him not. Surely He hath borne my griefs, and carried my sorrows; yet I did esteem Him stricken, smitten of God, and afflicted.'

Here she broke down completely as she thought for the first time of her personal relation to the Lord Jesus in His sufferings. But, wiping away her blinding tears, she read on, 'He was wounded for my transgressions, He was bruised for my iniquities; the chastisement of my peace was upon Him; and with His stripes I am healed. I like a sheep have gone astray; I have turned to my own way; and the Lord hath laid on Him all my iniquities.'

She was silent for a moment, and then exclaimed with deep emotion, 'Oh, Mr. Moorhouse, is this true?'

'Dear child,' he answered, 'does not God say it?'

Again she was silent for a time, but at length looking up, no longer through the tears of sorrow, but in joy and adoring gratitude and inexpressible love, she said, 'Then I am saved, for all my iniquities have been laid upon Him, and no stroke remains for me.' She arose from her knees with the peace of God filling her heart and soul.

—*Indian Christian*

(Isa. 53. 3-6; Acts 16. 31)

974. Salvation. Is God indifferent to all that is happening? By no means. God is working for the eternal blessing and salvation of all who will turn to Him in repentance and faith. The world is doomed, but He is taking out of the world a people for Himself, i.e. all who respond to the call of the gospel. The world is like a ship whose crew has mutinied and murdered the Captain (the owner's son) and thrown his body overboard. Now the question arises as to who can guide the ship. Attempts are made by one and another, but all ends in failure and disaster, for the ship strikes a rock and is heading for destruction. The owner hears what has happened and orders a lifeboat to be sent out immediately to save the crew. 'But they have murdered your son,' the lifeboatmen exclaim. 'I will pardon their awful crime,' replied the owner, 'and save every man who will jump into the lifeboat. The ship is doomed and lost, but I will save out of it all who will accept saving.'

—John Weston

(Luke 19. 10; Acts 4. 12; 1 Tim. 1. 15)

975. Salvation—by Good Looks. Some time ago I was tramping over the fields of England with a grand old farmer; a fine man with cheerful face and twinkling eyes. He was proud of his land and kept pointing out his cows and crops. Suddenly he turned to me and said, 'You know, I was saved by my good looks.'

Somewhat surprised, I said, 'Saved by your good looks? I've heard of being saved by the wonderful grace of God. I've heard of being saved by the precious blood of Jesus our Lord.

But I confess I've never heard of a man being saved by his good looks, though you are a good-looking man. Explain yourself.'

He chuckled. 'I'll tell you how it happened. Some years ago a preacher came knocking at our farmhouse door. He asked could I please lend him my barn for some gospel meetings. I wasn't using it at the time, so I consented. He soon got busy, fixed it up with chairs and then went round the village inviting folk to come.

'After several nights had passed my wife said to me, "Why don't you go down and see how that man is getting on?" So that night I dropped in and found a seat. The barn was full and the people were singing heartily. As the singing finished the preacher gave out his first text, taken from Isa. 45. 22: "Look unto Me, and be ye saved, all the ends of the earth, for I am God, and there is none else." He pictured the cruel cross and Jesus, the Lamb of God, bearing away the sin of the world. He told of the suffering and shame that Jesus endured and of the precious blood He shed that sinners might be forgiven and cleansed. Sitting there, I gazed at the amazing sight, and with those inner eyes of my soul, I saw Him dying for me, and knew that He alone could pardon my sin. Yes, I looked to Jesus on the cross, and proved for myself His promise, "Look unto Me and be ye saved".

'But then,' continued the old farmer, 'the preacher turned to a second text, Heb. 12. 2: "Looking unto Jesus, the author and finisher of our faith, Who for the joy that was set before Him endured the cross, despising the shame, and is set down at the right hand of the throne of God." He pictured a *risen* Saviour, *able* to save to the uttermost all that come unto Him—*able* to keep us from stumbling—*able* to present us faultless before His throne—*able* to empower us to live victoriously. Why, I had never thought I could be a real Christian; but somehow that sight of the mighty risen Lord Jesus showed me that He could do the job not only for me, on the Cross, but also in me day by day. And so I looked to Jesus on the Throne and proved that He is the Author and Finisher of our faith.

'Then,' the old man went on, 'before the preacher closed his talk that night he gave us one more wonderful verse in Titus 2. 13: "Looking for that blessed hope, and the glorious appearing of the great God and our Saviour Jesus Christ." What a thrill it was to hear that this same Jesus is actually coming again for His own blood-bought people. It seemed too good to be true, but the promise is there in the Bible, "I will come again and receive you unto Myself, that where I am, there ye may be also".'

As the old farmer finished I just put my arms around him and said, 'Bravo! That's wonderful. Now I understand how you were saved by your good looks—looking into the face of Jesus and tasting of His great salvation.'

—H. Wildish

(Acts 4. 12, Heb. 2. 3)

976. Salvation—So Great. The Salvation God offers is 'so great' because-

1. Announced by an incomparable Preacher:
2. Attested by infallible proofs:
3. Accomplished at an infinite price:
4. Administered by an invincible prince:
5. Accompanied by inestimable privileges.

How shall we escape if we neglect so great salvation?

(Heb. 2. 3, 4, 7, 9, 10, 14, 18)

977. Salvation—Twofold. About 65 years ago an English young lad on a visit to a rural community in Scotland set out to enjoy a swim in a small lake. Seized with cramp while some distance from the shore, he shouted for help, and a young farmer boy in a nearby field plunged into the lake and brought him to the shore.

Years passed before the two met again. The city youth came again to ask the boy who had saved his life what plans he had for the future, and learnt that his ambition was to study medicine. So the youth's parents, who were wealthy, put at the young farm lad's disposal the money needed for his education.

The farm lad graduated and embarked on a career of scientific research. In 1928 he found that a new drug called penicillin killed all germs. The name of the farm lad who became famous as a doctor was Alexander Fleming.

The London youth also had risen to fame. He went to the Near East to meet Roosevelt and Stalin during the Second World War, and was there stricken with pneumonia. His condition was critical, so penicillin, the drug discovered by Sir Alexander Fleming, the farm boy who had saved his life in youth, was flown out to the sick man, and his life was again saved. For the second time Alexander Fleming had saved the life of Winston Churchill, then Prime Minister of Britain.

Heb. 7. 24, 25)

978. Satan. Peter McKenzie, the eloquent Wesleyan preacher, once said that, whenever he was going to preach on 'Satan', he invariably found some hindrance or other come in his way.

Satan is called—'the god of this world,' 'the prince of this world,' 'the prince of the power of the air' and 'Lucifer, son of the morning'. (Isa. 14. 12; John 12. 31; 14. 30; 16. 11)

979. Satan. Napoleon Bonaparte, with his staff officers around him, once spread a large map of the world on a table before him, put his finger on a kingdom coloured red, and said to them, 'Messieurs, if it were not for that red spot I could conquer the world.' That red spot was the British Isles.

In like manner Satan might place a huge map of the universe before his cohorts, put his finger on a place red with the blood of the Saviour, and say to them, 'If it were not for that red spot, I could conquer the universe.'

That red spot is the Cross on Golgotha's Hill where the Lord of glory died to save sinners from Satan's power.
(Col. 2. 15; Heb. 2. 14)

980. Satan.
The devil may wall you round
But he cannot roof you in;
He may fetter your feet and tie your hands
And try to hamper your soul with bands
As his way has ever been.
But he cannot hide the face of God
And the Lord shall be your light,
And your eyes and your thoughts can rise to the
*   sky*
Where His clouds and winds and birds go by,
And His stars shine out at night.

The devil may wall you round;
He may rob you of all things dear,
He may bring his hardest and roughest stone,
And think to cage you and keep you alone,
But he may not press too near;
For the Lord has planted a hedge inside,
And has made it strong and tall,
A hedge of living and growing green;
And ever it mounts and keeps between
The trusting soul and the devil's wall.

The devil may wall you round,
But the Lord's hand covers you,
And His hedge is a thick and thorny hedge,
And the devil can find no entering wedge
Nor get his finger through.
He may circle about you all day long;
But he cannot work as he would,
For the will of the Lord restrains his hand,
And he cannot pass the Lord's command
And his evil turns to good.

The devil may wall you round,
With his grey stones, row on row,
But the green of the hedge is fresh and fair,
And within its circle is space to spare,
And room for your soul to grow;
The wall that shuts you in
May be hard and high and stout,
But the Lord is sun and the Lord is dew,
And His hedge is coolness and shade for you,
And no wall can shut Him out.
                                    —Annie Johnson Flint
(Job. 1. 6-12; Ps. 104. 9)

981. Satan. Albert Durer's pictures representing Satan as a monster with horns and a tail are not true to the Scriptural representations of the Adversary. Satan is portrayed as 'a roaring lion seeking whom he may devour' but is often 'transformed as an angel of light'.

A Scotsman, seeing Schaefer's painting of the 'Temptation of the Lord', said, pointing to Satan, 'If that chiel cam' tae me in such an ugly shape, I think he'd hae a teugh job wi' me too.'

(Matt. 4. 1-11 2 Cor. 11. 14)

982. Saviour. F. B. Meyer, just before passing into glory, said, 'You will tell the others I am going home a little sooner than I thought. Then tell them not to talk about the servant but to talk about the Saviour.'
(Gal. 2. 20; Phil. 1. 19, 20)

983. Saviour—God our.

O Jesus Saviour, born in lowly station,
*   A virgin's Son, in David's royal line!*
Men to redeem from every tribe and nation,
*   Thou didst stoop down and die, and I am Thine.*

When I look back and see in History's pages
*   The story of Thy world-wide triumphs told—*
While o'er the globe to Thee, the Rock of Ages,
*   Men turn from sin Thy beauty to behold—*

Then sings my soul, my Saviour God, to Thee—
*   How great Thou art, how great Thou art!*
Before Thy lofty throne I bow the knee
*   And there confess how great Thou art.*

And since I know the Babe of Bethlehem's manger
*   Is Lord of Heav'n Whom myriad hosts acclaim*
Yet here amid the poor, on earth a stranger,
*   He died to save me—I extol His name.*

He Who on earth was scorned, despised, rejected,
*   Who now in Heav'n sits on His glorious throne,*
Is coming soon, the King so long expected,
*   To rule the universe and bless His own.*
                                                    —A.N.

(Luke 2. 11; Acts 5. 31; Titus 2. 11-14)

984. Scars. An infidel fireman once rescued a little boy from a burning cottage. To do so he had to climb a hot piping, and his hands were badly scarred. The woman who cared for the boy perished in the fire. The question arose as to who would take the boy. A couple came forward, saying, 'We should like to have him; we have plenty of money and no children of our own; we would give him a good education and a good start in life.'

Others offered the boy a home. Then the fireman spoke up: 'I should like to have him,' and he showed his scarred hands. All agreed that he had the greatest claim to the child. Some objected, knowing the man was an unbeliever.

However, the boy was adopted by the fireman who proved a good father to him and loved him as his own child. One day he took him to an Art Gallery. The boy caught sight of a painting of Christ on the Cross, and asked the man, 'Who was that, daddy?' The man tried to silence the boy, and quickly drew him away from the picture, which so impressed the child who gave him no peace till he had heard the gospel story. As the man was saying that Jesus let them put Him on the Cross for our sins, the truth shone into his heart, and he believed and yielded himself to the One Who has the greatest claim on each one of us.
                                          —Constance Barnett
(Isa. 52. 14; 53. 5, 6; 1 Cor. 6. 19, 20)

985. Science—and the Bible. Some say that science and the Bible are not in harmony, that they are antagonistic one to another. But the fact is not only that they are in harmony, but the Bible often has anticipated discoveries of science by thousands of years, and many scientific references in the Bible have now been proved to be true. Let us look at some examples.

It is generally regarded that Columbus (1451-1506) was among the first to establish the fact of our earth's roundness, yet centuries before, the Hebrew prophet announced—'It is He that sitteth upon the circle of the earth' (Isa. 40. 22) Moreover, when our Lord spoke of His second coming He referred to a night scene (in bed), a morning scene (grinding), and a midday happening (men in the field), and showed that all these things would be witnessed simultaneously when He appeared, which of course is an indirect reference to the rotundity of the earth.

It was recently discovered that the moon had an influence on plant life. But in the Bible it has been foretold—'For the precious things put forth by the moon' (Deut. 33. 13, 14), which gives evidence of the fact that the writer knew of the power of the moon to affect plant life thousands of years ago.

Dr. Harvey (1578-1657) was the first scientist who discovered that the life of the flesh is in the blood. But thousands of years ago Moses wrote—'the life of the flesh is in the blood' (Lev. 17. 11). Scientists have analysed the body of man and discovered it is made up of 14 elements. They have also analysed the dust of the earth, and found it also is composed of 14 elements. 'God formed man,' Moses tells us, 'of the dust of the ground' (Gen. 2. 7).

Sir Isaac Newton, father of physics, established the law of gravitation in the seventeenth century. But thirty centuries before the advent of Newton, Job wrote—'He stretcheth out the north over the empty place and hangeth the earth upon nothing' (Job. 26. 7). In the year 1643 Torricelli invented the barometer and hence discovered air has weight. But centuries before, in the sacred book it was written that 'God makes weight for the winds' (Job. 28. 25).

Galileo was the first to discover that the number of stars is uncountable. But 2,200 years before Galileo, Jeremiah said that 'the host of heaven cannot be numbered' (Jer. 33. 22).

The law of transmission of light is vividly described in these passages—'Let there be light and there was light' (Gen. 1. 3) and— 'By what way is the light parted' (Job. 38. 24).

It has been truly said by Sir John Herschel, the famous astronomer, 'All human discoveries seem to be made only for the purpose of confirming more and more strongly the truth contained in the sacred Scriptures.'
(1 Pet. 1. 25)

986. Sea—Parable of the.

The sea one day, in restless mood,
   And ceaseless ebb and flow,
Was heard to voice its discontent
   While rolling to and fro.
'Oh! how I wish that I could rise
   To yonder blessed light,
Instead of always tossing here
   And pitching day and night!

'O wind! kind wind! grant me your aid,
   I want to reach the sky,
And if you'll only blow enough,
   I can if I but try.'
'All right! All right!' the wind replied,
   'I'll do my best for you:'
And so it started blowing hard
   And furiously too.

The sea went mounting up and up,
   And higher in the air,
But soon came tumbling down again,
   And that in great despair.
'I feel I never shall mount up,
   Though all the winds would aid,
So I must just be water still,
   For water I was made.'

But hark! the sun is speaking now;
   'Oh, foolish, foolish sea!
Lie still and I will draw thee up,
   And I will set thee free.
Keep thou within my influence
   And I will change thee so
That, even if thou wished it much,
   Thou couldst not dwell below.

'I'll change thee into that which gives
   Refreshment from on high;
I'll let thee bear my gift of love
   O'er scenes both parched and dry.
Trust not to thy poor efforts vain—
   The changing power is mine.
Yours is the lot to rest content,
   To dwell just where I shine.'
                —F. Howard Oakley
(John 7. 37; Philem. 6, 7)

987. Sects.

'He follows not us'—the crowning sin,
   The old sectarian cry;
We must have nought to do with him,
   And that's the reason why.
'Tis true that he believes as we,
   Is born again, we trust;
But him we must forbid, you see,
   Because he's not of us.

'He is a Christian,' we admit,
   'As much as we ourselves,
Yet—at the Supper such must sit
   Below, and by themselves.
'Partakers all of that "one Bread",
   Of the "one Body" too;
Yet, though by the "one Spirit" led,
   We cannot eat with you.'

Within the Holiest with God,
   With us they worship thus;
Yet we refuse them at our board
   Because they're not of us.

O strange delusion, hateful pride!
   Denial of grace divine;
Whilst you Christ's brethren set aside,
   They on His breast recline.
                —S. Levermore
(Mark 9. 38; Luke 9. 49, 50)

988. Sects.

It's rather queer, I must confess,
   That folks in sects contend
That they're not sects, but simply saints,
   And hence their course defend.

All other folks are sects, they say,
   And 'we're the Church indeed';
But Bible proof that they are right
   We fail to find or read.

And organised? Yes, organised:
   But here they disagree.
Some say they are, but others not—
   Their members are all free.

Denominations? No, they shout,
   But fellowship we claim.
Why then do they reject the saints
   Who will not bear their name?

Another sect is on the way,
   Absorbing all the rest—
Interdenominational—
   They hope 'twill be the best.

But some folks live outside the camp
   Of men: Christ is their Head.
Though little, poor, despised and few,
   They rest on what He said.

Their perfect safety is in Christ—
   From men and methods free:
Like Mary, Timothy and Luke
   They're in Paul's company.
(1 Cor. 1. 10-13; 3. 3, 4)

989. Seed.

If you plant for a year, plant grain.
If you plant for ten years, plant trees.
If you plant for 100 years, plant men.
If you plant for Eternity, plant the Word.

An old Professor of Biology used to hold a little brown seed in his hand. 'I know just exactly the composition of this seed. It has in it nitrogen, hydrogen and carbon. I know the exact proportions. I can make a seed that will look exactly like it But if I plant my seed it will come to nought; its elements will be simply absorbed in the soil. If I plant the seed God made, it will become a plant, because it contains the mysterious principle which we call the 'life principle'.

The Bible looks like other books. We cannot understand altogether its marvellous power. Planted in good ground it shows that it has the life principle in itself: it brings forth spiritual fruit.

          —Quotation by Constance Barnett
(Ps. 126. 6; Luke 8. 11; 1 Pet. 1. 23)

990. Self. Alexander the Great had a wonderful horse, Bucephalus. This spirited creature had defied every attempt to tame him, and the soothsayers of those days foretold that the man who could mount and ride him would conquer the world

Alexander, at that time a young man, determined to succeed where others had failed After many fruitless efforts, he found that the cause of the horse's restlessness was its aversion to its own shadow. Then he deduced a simple remedy, and turned the horse's head toward the sun.

(Rom. 7. 16-18; Gal. 2. 20; Col. 3. 1, 2)

991. Separation. In the American Civil War, when the Northern States were pitted against the South in the fight for the freedom of the slaves, the soldiers of both sides had their own distinctive battle-dress. It is said that a man who lived near the border between North and South, uncertain on which side to throw his weight, thought he would escape the fire of both sides by a compromise. He donned the tunic of the Northerners and the trousers of the Southerners. But, in the battle, he found that, instead of being secure, his danger was doubled, for the tunic he wore drew the fire of the Southern army and his trousers the fire of the Northern army.

(Matt. 12. 30; Heb. 13. 13; Exod. 32. 26)

992. Separation—to the Lord. In the New Testament, separation and sanctification are two aspects of the same attitude of the believer in the Lord Jesus Christ. Separation indicates that he is set apart or separated from everything that is evil: Sanctification connotes being set apart to God and to all that is good Dr. Thomas Guthrie has presented the practical aspect of this in the Christian's life in the following sentences:

'If the world is growing less to your sight, it shows that you are retreating from it, rising above it, and, upborne in the arms of grace, are ascending to a higher region; and if, to your eyes, the fashion of this world seems passing away, it is because we ourselves are passing—passing and passing on the way to heaven. Sin never changes. If objects which once seemed lovely look loathesome now, if pleasures once desired are detested now, if what we once eagerly sought we now shun and shrink from, it is not because sin is changed, but—blessed be God, and praise be ascribed to His grace—we are changed.'

(Rom. 12. 1, 2; 1 Cor. 6. 11; 2 Cor. 6. 14-18)

993. Separation—to the Lord.
Set apart for Jesus! Is not this enough,
Though the desert prospect's often wild and rough?
Set apart for His delight,
Chosen for His holy pleasure,
Sealed to be His special treasure!
Could we choose a nobler joy,
And would we if we might?

Set apart to love Him, and His love to know!
Not to waste affection on appearing show.
Called to give Him life and heart,
Called to pour the hidden treasure
That none other claims to measure,
Into His beloved hand!
Thrice blessed set apart.

Set apart for ever, for Himself alone!
None to see our calling gloriously shown!
Owning, with no secret dread,
This our holy separation;
Now the crown of consecration
Of the Lord our God shall rest
Upon our willing head.

(John 17. 16, 17; Rom. 12. 1, 2)

994. Separation—from the World.

I cannot give it up, the little world I know,
The innocent delights of youth, the things I cherish so!
'Tis true I love my Lord and want to do His will,
And oh! I may enjoy the world and be a Christian still.

I love the hour of prayer, I love the hymns of praise;
I love the blessed Word that tells of God's redeeming grace.
But I am human still, and while I dwell on earth
God surely will not grudge the hours I spend in harmless mirth!

These things belong to youth, and are its natural right—
My dress, my pastimes, and my friends, the merry and the bright.
My Father's heart is kind: He will not count it ill
That my small corner of the world should please and hold me still.

And yet—'outside the camp'—'twas where my Saviour died:
It was the world that cast Him forth, and saw Him crucified.
Can I take part with those who nailed Him to the tree?
And where His name is never praised, is there the place for me?

Nay, world! I turn away, though thou seem fair and good;
That friendly, outstretched hand of thine is stained with Jesus' blood.
If in thy least device I stoop to take a part,
All unaware, thine influence steals God's presence from my heart.

Farewell! Henceforth my place is with the Lamb Who died.
My Sovereign! While I have Thy love, what can I want beside?
Thyself, dear Lord, art now my free and loving choice,
'In Whom, though now I see Thee not, believing I rejoice.'

Shame on me that I sought another joy than this,
Or dreamt a heart at rest with Thee could crave
   for earthly bliss!
Those vain and worthless things I put them all
   aside;
His goodness fills my longing soul, and I am
   satisfied.

Lord Jesus! let me dwell 'outside the camp' with
   Thee!
Since Thou art there, then there alone is peace
   and home for me.
Thy dear reproach to bear I'll count my highest
   gain,
Till Thou return, the banished King, to take Thy
   power and reign.

                —Margaret Mauro

(Gal. 6. 14; Heb. 13. 13)

995. Separation—from the world. Sir Walter Scott and others have in their writings demonstrated the deadly feuds that existed among the Scottish clans. At times, the hatred was so bitter that it meant death for a man of one clan to show himself or make free in the territory of a hostile clan. Each clan had its own tartan, and by this, as well as by personal appearance and habits, those belonging to the various clans could be recognized.

It is said that a youth of the Clan Macdonald, full of the energy and initiative of youth and tired of the confines of his own clan's territory, devised a scheme for exploring the magnificent mountains, lakes, streams and ravines of his neighbours. He decided to sew on his kilt and plaid the tartans and badges of some of the surrounding clans and, thus fortified, to sally forth footloose and enjoy the beauties of the territory of his neighbours. When challenged in the clachans of the Mackintoshes, he showed his tartans, and said, 'Look! I belong to you: Am I not wearing your tartan?' In the McGregor territory he met with the same challenge, and gave a similar reply, showing the McGregor tartan, badges and marks. Likewise in the territory of Clan McKenzie. The narrative does not record how he fared, or whether he escaped the Highlandman's dirk.

The same is an allegory. There are Christians who, not content with the spiritual wealth in Christ, and weary of 'this light bread', the Bread of life, turn to the world, its varied attractions, amusements, prosperity and fashions for satisfaction. On occasions, they can say to the worldling, 'We are like you. What's the harm in having a little innocent pleasure and enjoyment?—drink, the theatre, the cinema, the latest fashions, etc.?' Thus so many forget that they are a separated people, set apart for Christ by Whose precious blood they have been redeemed.

(Heb. 13. 12-14; 1 Pet. 2. 11; John 17. 16)

996. Service—for Christ.
I gave my service, but with heavy heart,
And with it went but little love or trust:
He was my Master, I must serve or die,
And so I gave my service, for I must:—is the
   voice of Destiny.

Then, o'er the dreary dulness of my road
There came the kindling ray of better thought:
I owed my service to a loving God,
And so I gave my service, for I ought:—is the
   voice of Duty.

And lo! the Master made the service sweet,
And, like a ray of glory from above,
There came the knowledge that to serve was joy,
And so I give my service, for I love:—is the voice
   of Devotion.

(2 Sam. 15. 34, 37; John 12. 26; Acts 27. 23; Rom. 12. 1)

997. Service—of the Lord. In Napoleon's expedition to Russia, a Russian peasant was captured, forced into Napoleon's service, and branded on the arm with the letter 'N'. When he understood what it meant, he chopped off the arm that had been branded rather than serve his country's enemy, Napoleon.

(Gal. 6. 17; Col. 3. 24)

998. Service—His Majesty's. In India, as in other countries that were under British rule, the letters O.H.M.S. (On His Majesty's Service, or On Her Majesty's Service) used to be printed on official documents. In those days, a little lad, the son of devoted missionaries in the district now called West Godavari, asked and received from his Canadian parents an explanation of the letters on such official envelopes, which came in fairly frequently.

In his prayers with his parents, he used to express his desire in the following way: 'Lord, I'm just like a Government letter. No matter what becomes blurred or defaced on me, please keep the letters—O.H.M.S.—on me clear.'

(Acts 16. 17; Rom. 1. 1; 1 Thess. 1. 9; Rev. 22. 3)

999. Service—the Master's.
Thou canst not choose but serve: man's lot is
   servitude.
But thou hast this much choice, a bad lord or a
   good.

(Col. 3. 23, 24; 2 Tim. 2. 24-26)

1000. Service—the Master's. At the close of an address by D. L. Moody, a highly-educated man said to him coldly, 'Excuse me, but you made eleven mistakes in your grammar tonight.' Mr. Moody replied, 'I probably did. My early education was very faulty. But I am using all the grammar I know in the Master's service. How about you?'

(Acts 4. 13, 14; Col. 3. 17, 23, 24)

1001. Service—the Master's.
   Not outward sphere, but inward heart,
   The love wherewith we do our part:
   Not how large gifts we hold in trust,
   But how far used or left to rust.
   Not how much done, but how well done,
   Faithful to many souls or one.

Seeking the Master's will to find
And lean on Him with peace of mind:
Content to fail in human eyes,
His smile the one reward and prize.
In any sphere serve Him alone
Till cross is left for crown and throne.
(Matt. 25. 21, 23; 1 Cor. 3. 9-15)

1002. Service—Unmeasured.

How far in service must I go,
    What sacrifices bring
To God, Whose loving hands bestow
    Each good and perfect thing?
How much of time and thought should I
    Devote to Him Who died?
What is my debt to Him, and why,
    And how, may I decide?

A measured service bound would be,
    A service mean and small:
He did not ask 'How much?' from me:
    He gave Himself, His all.
He did not ask how far to go.
    How far was not to say
What bound? How far? I only know
    That He went all the way.

1003. Shadows—and Substance.

I need no earthly altar,
    I need no earthly priest,
I need no earthly fasting,
    I need no earthly feast.

I need no earthly temple,
    I need no sabbath day;
As substance of the good things came,
    The shadows passed away.

The altar spake of sacrifice—
    On it the lamb was slain:
The altar cross of Calvary
    Makes other altars vain.

And fasts and feasts are blended
    With such stupendous skill
They now consist in simply this—
    The doing of God's will.

The earthly temple passed away—
    'Twas built of cold, dead stones:
In place God builds a new abode,
    But 'tis of living stones.

The earthly Sabbath passed away,
    A shadow at its best.
The substance came in One Who said,
    'Come unto Me and rest.'

                                                        —F. H. Oakley
(Col. 2. 17; Heb. 8. 5)

1004. Sheep.

John Nelson Darby, an esteemed servant of Christ, having once been asked to see a poor boy who was dying in some wild district in Ireland, narrated the following account of his visit. He says:

After upwards of an hour's toilsome walking (for the roads, which in some places led over steep hills, were in others scarcely passable on account of the heavy marshes), on entering the miserable hovel, I looked around me, and at first found no sign of any inhabitant, except an old woman who sat crouching over the embers of a peat fire. She rose as I entered, and, with the natural courtesy of the Irish poor, offered me the low chair, or rather stool, on which she had been seated. I thanked her, and passing on to the object of my visit, discovered in one corner of the hut a heap of straw, on which lay the poor sufferer. Some scanty covering, probably his own wearing apparel, had been thrown over him; but as to bed or bedclothes, there was none discernible in this miserable dwelling. I approached, and saw a young lad of 17 or 18 years of age, evidently in a state of extreme suffering and exhaustion, and it was to be feared in the last stage of tuberculosis. His eyes were closed, but he opened them on my approach, and stared at me with a kind of wild wonder, like a frightened animal. I told him as quietly as possible who I was, and for what purpose I had come, and put a few of the simplest questions to him respecting his hope of salvation. He answered nothing; he appeared totally unconscious of my meaning. On pressing him further, and speaking to him kindly and affectionately, he looked up, and I ascertained from the few words he uttered that he had heard something of a God and future judgement, but he had never been taught to read. The Holy Scriptures were a sealed book to him, and he was, consequently, altogether ignorant of the way of salvation as revealed to us in the Gospel. His mind on the subject was truly an utter blank.

I was struck with dismay, and almost with despair. Here was a fellow creature, whose immortal soul, apparently on the verge of eternity, must be saved or lost for ever; and he lay before me now, the hand of death close upon him; not a moment was to be lost, and what was I to do? What way was I to take to begin to teach him, as it were, at the eleventh hour, the first rudiments of Christianity?

I had scarcely ever before felt such a sinking within me. I could do nothing; that I knew full well, but on the other hand, God could do all; I therefore raised up my heart and besought my Heavenly Father for Christ's sake to direct me in this most difficult and trying position, and to open to me, by His spirit of wisdom, a way to set forth the glad tidings of salvation, so as to be understood by this poor benighted wanderer. I was silent for a few moments, whilst engaged in inward prayer and gazing with deep anxiety on the melancholy object before me. It struck me that I ought to try to discover how far his intelligence in other things extended, and whether there might not be reasonable hope of his understanding me, when I should commence to open to him (as I was bound to do), the Gospel message of salvation. I looked down upon him with an eye of pity which I most sincerely felt, and I thought he observed that compassionate look for he softened towards me as I said, 'My poor boy, you are very ill; I fear you suffer a great deal.' 'Yes, I have a bad cold; the cough takes away my breath and hurts me greatly.' 'Have you had this cough for long?' I asked. 'Oh yes, a long time—near a year now.' 'And how did you catch it? A Kerry boy, I should have thought, would have been reared hardily and accustomed to this sharp air.' 'Ah,' he answered, 'and so I was until that terrible night; it was about this time of year, when one of the sheep went astray. My father keeps a few sheep upon the mountains, and this is the way we live. When he reckoned them that night, there was one wanting, and he sent me to look for it.' 'No doubt,' I replied, 'you felt the change from the warmth of the peat fire in this little hut to the cold mountain blast.' 'Oh, that I did; there was snow upon the ground, and the wind pierced me through; but I did not mind it much, as I was so anxious to find father's sheep.'

'And did you find it?' I asked, with increased interest. 'Oh, yes; I had a long weary way to go, but I never stopped until I found it.' 'And how did you get it home? You had trouble enough with that too, I dare say. Was it willing to follow back?' 'Well, I did not like to trust it, and besides it was dead beat and tired, so I laid it on my shoulders, and carried it home that way.' 'And were they not all at home rejoiced to see you, when you returned with the sheep?' 'Sure enough, and that they were,' he replied. 'Father and mother, and the people round that heard of our loss, all came in next morning to ask about the sheep, for the neighbours in these matters are mighty kind to each other. Sorry they were, too, to hear that I was kept out the whole dark night; it was morning before I got home, and the end of it was, I caught this cold. Mother says I will never be better now; God knows best. Anyways, I did my best to save the sheep.'

'Wonderful!' I thought: 'here is the whole Gospel history. The sheep is lost, the father sends his son to seek for and recover it. The son goes willingly, suffers all without complaining, and in the end sacrifices his life to find the sheep, and when recovered, he carries it home on his shoulders to the flock, and rejoices with his friends and neighbours over the sheep that was lost, but is found again.' My prayer was answered, my way was made plain, and by the grace of God I availed myself of this happy opening. I explained to this poor dying boy the plan of salvation, making use of his own simple and affecting story. I read to him the few verses in the fifteenth chapter of Luke's Gospel, where the care of the shepherd for the strayed sheep is so beautifully expressed, and he at once perceived the likeness, and followed me with deep interest while I explained to him the full meaning of the parable.

The Lord mercifully opened not only his understanding, but his heart also, to receive the things spoken. He himself was the lost sheep, Jesus Christ the Good Shepherd Who was sent by the Father to seek for him, and who left all the joys of that Father's heavenly glory, to come down to earth and search for him and other lost ones like himself. He received it all. He understood it all. (Luke 15. 3-7)

1005. Sheep—gone astray. Somewhere about the year 1842, a young Scottish lad, George Clephane, stepped ashore in Canada to try and begin life anew. Although only in his early twenties, George had fallen a victim to drink. The change of country did not solve George's problem, and he got mixed up with the wrong kind of people in Canada. He spent his substance on riotous living. One cold morning he was picked up on the roadside in a state of complete collapse, the result of a drunken carousal and exposure to the elements. Shortly afterwards he died and was buried in the town of Fergus, Ontario. The news of his death stirred great sorrow in his old home in Fife, but most of all in the heart of his youngest sister, Elizabeth Cecilia. She had been born in Edinburgh, and the news of her brother's death arrived shortly before she was due to celebrate her twenty-first birthday. Through good report and evil report she had never ceased to love the black sheep of the family, and never wavered in her conviction that God loved him too. The thought burned itself into her mind that somehow in his dying hours, her brother had come to Jesus and been saved. The conviction shaped itself into an immortal hymn. She wrote it down to comfort her own soul:

There were ninety and nine that safely lay
In the shelter of the fold.

She locked the poem away in her desk. She died in 1869, her poem still unpublished. It was not the only one she had written.

The poem—'There were ninety and nine'—found its way into a Glasgow paper in 1874. It so happened that Moody and Sankey were in Scotland at the time. They had just finished a mission in Glasgow and were setting out for Edinburgh, and Sankey bought a newspaper at a Glasgow station. As he glanced through it hurriedly, his eye caught sight of Elizabeth Clephane's poem, half hidden in a corner of the page. He cut the poem out and placed it in his musical scrapbook. At the noon meeting on the second day in Edinburgh the subject was 'The Good Shepherd' on which Mr. Moody preached his sermon. When Mr. Moody finished, he asked Dr. Bonar to say a few words. At the conclusion of Dr. Bonar's message, Mr. Moody asked Ira D. Sankey if he had a solo appropriate to the subject with which to close the service. Sankey, lifting up his heart in prayer to God for help, placed the little newspaper slip on the organ, and began to sing note by note the hymn to the tune to which it is still sung. The hymn reached the heart of that Scottish audience, and Mr. Moody was greatly moved. And so the hymn, born under such strange circumstances, was launched upon the world. It has found its way into almost every hymnary, and has been a ministering angel to lead many a lost soul back home to God.

— *Workers Together*

(Luke 15. 1-7)

1006. Sheep—gone astray.
'Twas a sheep, not a lamb, that strayed away
In the parable Jesus told;
A grown-up sheep that had gone astray
From the ninety and nine in the fold;

Out on the hillside, out in the cold,
'Twas a sheep the Good Shepherd sought;
And back to the flock, safe in the fold,
'Twas a sheep the Good Shepherd brought.

And why for the sheep should we earnestly long,
And as earnestly hope and pray?
Because there is danger if they go wrong,
They will lead the lambs astray.

For the lambs will follow the sheep, you know,
Wherever the sheep may stray;
When the sheep go wrong, it will not be long
Till the lambs are as wrong as they.

And so with the sheep we earnestly plead,
For the sake of the lambs today;
If the lambs are lost, what terrible cost
Some sheep will have to pay!
(Isa. 53. 6; Luke 15. 4; 1 Pet. 2. 25; 5. 3)

1007. Silence. Silence may be 'golden', but more often it is guilty. The normal thing for a Christian is to speak of what he knows, to deal frankly against error, and to maintain freedom of discussion whenever challenged by an honest appeal to plain facts. But to shut up like a clam is sin by omission—failure to study God's Word or fear of the cost of voicing unpopular testimony.

Spirit-led use of truth will help those who are 'approved' (rightly dividing—2 Tim. 2. 15) and will manifest those who do the opposite (1 Cor. 11. 19). How can we be right when we are so fearful, evasive and unwilling to investigate? Why fear to be a witness if one knows whereof he speaks? If one has no faith for the problem—only hearsay, supposition and self-reasoning—he should confess it and ask God for help.

Silence will not be 'golden' at the judgement of works if to speak was our duty and we left it undone for any excuse.

— *Selected*

(Prov. 2. 6; 2 Cor. 12. 19; Eph. 6. 19, 20)

1008. Sin—Cleansing from. One Sunday evening a young man was walking along a street on his way to a place of pleasure when he was met by a man who thrust a small piece of paper into his hand. The young man took it and read by the light of the nearest lamp the words: 'Though your sins be as scarlet, they shall be as white as snow'. A sneer passed over his face as he read, and throwing the paper from him he hurried on.

'Though your sins be as scarlet, they shall be as white as snow' doesn't apply to me, at any rate. I'm an infidel and do not believe anything of the kind,' thought he.

'Though your sins be as scarlet, they shall be as white as snow.' Bother the thing, I can't get rid of it! Sins? Conscience? Yes; but I acknowledge neither a future nor a God, and therefore am not responsible. What do I care to have my sins made white, to use the figure, seeing that I own no duties beyond those necessary to natural existence?

'Though your sins be as scarlet, they shall be as white as snow.' I am an infidel. I don't believe the Bible. I don't believe in a future or anything beyond the still, dark grave, so here's for a short life and a merry one.

'Though your sins be as scarlet, they shall be as white as snow.' It is very forceful and poetical. Certainly that Bible is a wonderful book. Granted, for the sake of argument that it is true and that a God exists. I can easily understand how religious people who believe in a future either of joy or suffering cling to such sentences with a tenacity proportioned to their belief.

'Though your sins be as scarlet, they shall be as white as snow.' Admirable writing! Terse, forceful language! I wonder who wrote it. God, I suppose. God? Why, there is no God. I forgot myself. If I could only remember my principles, and how logical and well founded the arguments are which support them, I shall be all right.

'Though your sins be as scarlet, they shall be as white as snow.' That thing again! Will nothing put a stop to this? Here is a meeting house. I may as well turn in and see what they have to say. He entered and was shown to a seat near the door.

A solemn silence reigned. The preacher had just read the text from the pulpit, and paused a moment before repeating it. Then in a gentle voice he pronounced the words—'Come now and let us reason together, saith the Lord: though your sins be as scarlet, they shall be as white as snow; though they be red like crimson, they shall be as wool.'

The ante-room of that meeting Hall was always open for a short time after the service for the reception of those whom the message of the Lord had touched. That evening there was an anxious enquirer who prayed with tears, 'Jesus, though my sins be dyed deeper than the deepest scarlet, do Thou make them whiter than the purest snow.' And before he left that evening he knew his sins were forgiven and his iniquities pardoned, through the precious blood of Christ.

(Ps. 32. 1; Isa. 1. 18)

1009. Sin—Definition of. The English word 'sin' is connected with the verb 'to be'. The French is 'ils sont' (they are), the Latin 'sunt', and its present subjunctive 'sint' (they may be). The jurors in a law court try to find out about the prisoners if 'they are' guilty: God's message to David was 'thou art the man'.

The Greek word—'Hamartia' means 'missing the mark'.

Other words used for sin are 'Iniquity'—inequality, like ruts in the road: 'transgression' or 'trespass', meaning crossing over, or encroachment. 'Wrong' is cognate with the Anglo-Saxon word 'wrung'—used of a twisted cloth: so implies something awry, something twisted.

(Rom. 3. 23; Ps. 103. 10-12; 1 John 3. 4)

1010. Sin—Defilement of. There is an Indian fable of a swan that, pitying a poor pig in its muddy environment, began to describe the beautiful country further up the river, with the green banks and rising slopes, and invited the pig to join the happy company of white swans that lived there. The pig was willing enough to go, but asked the question, 'Is there any mire up in that fine country?' 'Oh no!' replied the swan, 'it is clean and free from mud and mire.' 'Then,' said the pig, 'I'm sorry I cannot accompany you. I must stay here in the mire.'

(2 Pet. 2. 22)

1011. Sin—Detection of. The thief was sure that the church was a safe hideout. Just inside he spied a rope up to the garret. Up he climbed, only to hear the church bell ringing his whereabouts.

A Mexico city man snatched a woman's purse and dashed into a doorway to hide. It turned out to be the door of a police station, where he was questioned and later identified by his victim.

Shoplifting in a department store in Rochester, New York, a man picked up an alarm clock and headed for the nearest exit. The clock, concealed under his coat, went off before he could get out of the store and brought detectives running.

A Canadian who had a custom-built radio stolen from his automobile advertised in the local paper for a custom-built radio. The first person to contact him about the advert. was the thief.

A Glasgow pickpocket got a sixty-day prison term after trying his luck on an excursion boat carrying twenty police officers and their wives.

Police in Palo Alto seized a suspect as he stood in a post office admiring his 'wanted' poster.

—*New York Times Magazine*

(Num. 32. 23)

1012. Sin—Given a foothold. There is a fable that illustrates the folly of giving sin a foothold in one's life.

An Arab sat comfortably in his tent, sheltered from the cold, biting air of the desert. His camel outside felt the cold, and, looking through the canvas flap, requested its master to let it put its head in. The master grudgingly gave his consent. Then, addressing its master, the camel said, 'My nose is warm and comfortable, but my shoulders are very cold. Won't you just let me get my shoulders and forelegs in?' it pleaded. After a while, permission was given to the camel to put its shoulders inside the tent. Again the camel approached its master and mildly pleaded in a pitiful, moving voice, for leave to get its hump and part of its body under the canvas, for, while its head was comfortably warm, its hinder parts were still shivering with the cold. Reluctantly the master agreed. By this time the camel was almost all inside the tent, and again requested that it might bring in its hind legs also. When, after some time, the master agreed to this also; the camel came right in and, looking round the small tent, said to its master, 'This tent is too small for you and me. You had better leave.' Beware of giving sin a foothold in your life.

(John 8. 34; Rom. 6. 14; 7. 11; Eph. 4. 27)

1013. Sin—Hidden up. There was an Indian prince who was a leper, but his leprosy was known to very few. When he appeared in public, he always wore a large jewel on his forehead, which sparkled and glittered in the light of the many lamps in his court. Only when he was alone did he remove the jewel, and then his mirror revealed to him the leprous spot where the jewel had been. Knowing of his leprous condition, he had devised this means of hiding it from the public and covering it up.

'He that covereth his sin shall not prosper.'

(Ps. 32. 1; Prov. 28. 13)

1014. Sin—Propitiation for.

Eternal light! Eternal Light!
How pure that soul must be,
When placed within Thy searching sight,
He shrinks not but with calm delight
Can live and look on Thee.

Oh, how can I whose native sphere
Is dark, whose eyes are dim,
Before th'Ineffable appear
And on my naked spirit bear
The uncreated beam?

There is a way for man to rise
To that sublime abode,
An offering and a sacrifice,
A Holy Spirit's energies,
An Advocate with God.

—T. Binney

(Ps. 51. 3-5; 1 John 2. 1, 2)

1015. Sin—Results of. When Leonardo da Vinci was painting his masterpiece, 'The Last Supper', he sought long for a model for his Christ. At last he located a chorister in one of the churches of Rome who was lovely in life and features, a young man named Pietro Bandinelli.

Years passed, and the painting was still unfinished. All the disciples had been portrayed save one—Judas Iscariot. Now he started to find a man whose face was hardened and distorted by sin—and at last he found a beggar on the streets of Rome with a face so villainous he shuddered when he looked at him. He hired the man to sit for him as he painted the face of Judas on his canvas. When he was about to dismiss the man, he said, 'I have not yet found out your name.' 'I am Pietro Bandinelli,' he replied, 'I also sat for you as your model of Christ.'

The sinful life of years so disfigured the once fair face of the young man that it now looked as though it were the most villainous face in all Rome! Sin degrades! Sin debases!

—*Indian Christian*

(Isa. 1. 4-6)

1016. Sin—Results of.
Sin, like a bee, into the hive may bring
A little honey, but expect the sting.
(Heb. 3. 13; 11. 25; James 1. 15)

1017. Sin—Results of. A Public Utilities Company, seeking a franchise in a large city, sent an unscrupulous representative to interview a city official whose vote was sorely needed. When the official intimated that his vote was not for sale, the representative exclaimed: 'Think of the money, man! It's the bargain of a lifetime. You'll never have another chance to make as much so easily!'

'So easily!' replied the official. 'Listen, friend! No one ever yet got a bargain in sin. It's the highest-priced thing in the market. You tell me that all I have to do is to vote "right". Well, it isn't. That's only the beginning of what I'll have to do. I'll have to carry the consciousness of my dishonesty to the grave. I'll have to live with a remorseful Conscience. I'll have to pose before my wife and children as someone I know I am not. Don't tell me it's a bargain.'

—T. Baird

(Num. 32. 23; Heb. 3. 13)

1018. Sin—Shame of. In the early part of the American War a young woman of 22 years died at the Commercial Hospital, Cincinnati, one morning in the dead of winter. She had once possessed an enviable share of beauty and had been greatly sought after for the charms of her face, but had become a prostitute. Highly educated and accomplished in manners, she had spent her young life in shame and died friendless as a broken-hearted outcast of society.

Among her personal effects was found, in manuscript, the poem 'Beautiful Snow', which was taken to the editor of *National Union* and appeared in print the morning after the girl's death. When the poem appeared in the paper, the girl's body had not been buried, and the American poet, Thomas Buchanan Reed, was so impressed by the stirring pathos of the poem that he followed the corpse to its final resting-place.

Some of the stanzas of the poem entitled 'Beautiful Snow' are as follows:

Oh! the snow, the beautiful snow!
Filling the sky and the earth below:
Over the housetops, over the street,
Over the heads of the people you meet,
Dancing, flirting, skimming along—
Beautiful snow!—it can do nothing wrong;
Flying to kiss a fair lady's cheek,
Clinging to lips in frolicsome freak;
Beautiful snow, from the heavens above,
Pure as an angel, gentle as love!

Once I was pure as the snow, but I fell,
Fell like the snowflakes, from heaven to hell,
Fell, to be trampled as filth in the street,
Fell, to be scoffed, to be spat on and beat,
Pleading, cursing, dreading to die;
Selling my soul to whoever would buy;
Dealing in shame for a morsel of bread,
Hating the living and fearing the dead.
Merciful God! have I fallen so low,
And yet—I was once like the beautiful snow!

Once I was fair as the beautiful snow,
With an eye like its crystal and heart like its glow;
Once I was loved for my innocent grace—
Flattered and sought for the charms of my face;
Father, mother, sister and all,
God and myself I have lost by my fall;
The veriest wretch that goes shivering by
Will make a wide swoop lest I wander too nigh:
For all that is on or above me, I know
There is nothing so pure as the beautiful snow.

How strange it should be that this beautiful snow
Should fall on a sinner, with nowhere to go!
How strange it should be, when night comes again
If the snow and the ice struck my desperate brain;
Fainting, freezing, dying alone,
Too wicked for prayer, too weak for a moan
To be heard in the streets of the crazy town,
Gone mad in the joy of the snow coming down—
To lie, and to die, in my terrible woe,
With a bed and a shroud of the beautiful snow.

The following verse has been added by another pen:

Helpless and foul as the trampled snow,
Sinner! despair not; Christ stoopeth low
To rescue the soul that is lost in its sin,
And raise it to life and enjoyment again:
Groaning, bleeding, dying for thee,
The Crucified hung, made a curse on the tree;
His accents of mercy fall soft on thine ear—
'Is there mercy for me? Will He heed my prayer?
O God! in the stream that for sinners doth flow,
Wash me, and I shall be whiter than snow!'
(Isa. 59. 2; James 1. 15; Ps. 51. 7)

1019. Sins—Forgiven. Sheila O'Gahagan was a factory girl in Ireland. Broken down in health, she was advised to try the effect of a holiday by the seaside. In her heart of hearts she was perplexed by a problem that struck much deeper than that of her health—the problem of her sins.

One day she sat, with her Bible on her knee, looking out on the waves breaking on the Giant's Causeway, and came upon the passage in Micah: 'Thou wilt cast all their sins into the depths of the sea.' As she surveyed the horizon, she said to herself: 'My sins are all cast into the depths of the sea.'

A few months later she died, and the following verse was found in her desk:

I will cast in the depths of the fathomless sea
All thy sins and transgressions, whatever they be;
Though they mount up to heaven, though they
　　sink down to hell,
They shall sink in the depths, and above them
　　shall swell
All the waves of my mercy, so mighty and free:
I will cast all thy sins in the depths of the sea.
(Ps. 103. 12; Isa. 38. 17; 44. 22; Mic. 7. 19; Heb. 10. 17)

1020. Sinners—Saints confessed. *Augustine* said—Lord, save me from that wicked man, myself. *John Knox* confessed—In youth, in mid-age, and now, after many battles, I find nothing in me but corruption. *John Wesley* acknowledged—I am fallen short of the glory of God; my whole heart is altogether corrupt and abominable, and consequently my whole life, seeing an evil tree cannot bring forth good fruit.

In his beautiful hymn *Charles Wesley* wrote —Vile and full of sin I am. *Augustus Toplady*, the writer of 'Rock of Ages' said—O that such a wretch as I should ever be tempted to think highly of himself! I that am myself nothing but sin and weakness, in whose flesh naturally dwells no good thing.
(Isa. 64. 6; Luke 5. 8; 1 Tim. 1. 15)

1021. Sinners—Saved. Dr. Charles Berry, the gifted preacher, was asked by a Lancashire girl with a shawl over her head and clogs on her feet, 'Are you a minister?' When she found that he was, she said, 'I want you to come and get my mother in.' On further questioning, he gathered that the girl's mother was dying and wanted to be saved. Dr. Berry tried to get out of it, but the girl persisted, and so he went. When he spoke to the dying woman about Christ the beautiful Example and Teacher, she said, 'That's no good to me. I don't want an Example: I'm a sinner!' Then Dr. Berry told her the old story of God's love in Christ's dying for sinners. 'That's what I want,' said the woman, 'that's the story for me.' So he got her in and got in himself, and from that night preached a full gospel.
(1 Tim. 1. 15)

1022. Sincerity. In the Greek original of the New Testament the word used means 'judged in the sunlight'; and the English word is derived from the Latin—'sine cera', which means 'without wax'. In the days when art flourished in ancient Greece, it was the common practice to repair with 'invisible' wax any vase or statue that had, as a result of carelessness or misadventure, been damaged.

A rich man or a person of high rank might employ a sculptor to chisel his bust in marble. Sometimes, if the chisel slipped, the end of the nose would be chipped off. Rather than go to all the trouble of making a new bust, the sculptor would so mend the features with wax that the flaw could not be detected unless by very close scrutiny, and palm off on the customer his defective workmanship. If the client happened to be a knowing person, he would carry the finished statuette out of the studio into the open before paying for it, and examine it carefully in the sunlight: otherwise, in course of time, he would have the chagrin of seeing the nose drop off his statuette in the heated room of his house. The statue was not 'sincere', not 'without wax', and could not bear careful scrutiny in the sunlight.
(Josh. 24. 14; 2 Cor. 2. 17; Phil. 1. 10)

1023. Slander. Hannah More had a good way of dealing with talebearers. Whenever she was told anything that was derogatory of another, her invariable reply was: 'Come, we will go and ask if this is true.' The effect was sometimes ludicrously painful. The talebearer was taken aback, stammered a qualification, or begged that no notice be taken of the statement. But the good lady was inexorable; off she took the scandalmonger to the scandalized to make inquiry and compare accounts. It is not likely that anybody ever a second time ventured to repeat a gossipy story to Hannah More.

But what if the report is true? Even if it be true, by repeating it unnecessarily you violate the law of Christian love. Listen to this:

If you are tempted to reveal
A tale by someone told
About another, make it pass,
Before you speak, three gates of gold.

Three narrow gates: first, Is it true?
Then, Is it needful? In your mind
Give truthful answer. And the next
Is last and narrowest—Is it kind?

And if to reach your lips at last,
It passes through these gateways three,
Then you may tell the tale, nor fear
What the results of speech may be.
　　　　　　　　　　　　—Henry Durbanville
(Ps. 15. 1-3; 101. 5; 1 Tim. 3. 11; Titus 3. 2)

Note—The word translated 'slanderer' is in the feminine, and literally means 'she-devil'.

1024. Slander. An evangelist, when someone approached him with a story about a sister, said to the gossip, 'Before you say anything about that person, I should like to ask you three questions:
First, will it do me any good if you tell me your story?
Second, will it do you any good to tell it?
Third, will it do the sister about whom you have come to tell me any good?'
Needless to say, the slander was never uttered.
(2 Thess. 3. 11; 1 Tim. 5. 13; 1 Pet. 4. 15)

1025. Slander. Two friends were inseparable. One day one of them heard a story about his friend, believed it without making enquiries as to its truth, and passed it on. As it went, it grew. His friend heard of it, and their friendship was broken. The man thus maligned was taken seriously ill and lay on his deathbed. His friend who had spread the slander, heard of his illness and came to see him, confess his wrong, and ask his forgiveness, which was readily given by the dying man.

'Now,' said the dying man, 'I want you to do something for me. Take my feather pillow and scatter the feathers in the garden.' Though he thought it a strange request, the visitor carried it out and returned to his friend's bedside. 'Now', said the dying man, 'go and gather the feathers up again.' 'That is impossible,' said the other. 'Just so,' said the wronged man, 'I frankly and willingly forgive you for scattering those stories about me, but even my forgiveness cannot revoke the evil that has been done. Slanderous stories scattered abroad cannot be recalled.'

(Titus 3. 2; James 4. 11; 1 Pet. 2. 1)

1026. Sodom.

'Get ye up from the wrath of God's terrible day!
Ungirded, unsandalled, arise and away!
'Tis the vintage of blood, 'tis the fulness of time,
And vengeance shall gather the harvest of crime!

The warning was spoken; the righteous had gone,
And the proud ones of Sodom were feasting alone;
All gay was the banquet; the revel was long,
With the pouring of wine and the breathing of
*   song.*

'Twas an evening of beauty; the air was perfume,
The earth was all greenness, the trees were all
*   bloom;*
And softly the delicate viol was heard,
Like the murmur of love, or the notes of a bird.

And beautiful maidens moved down in the dance,
With the magic of motion and sunshine of glance;
And white arms wreathed lightly, and tresses fell
*   free*
As the plumage of birds in some tropical tree.

Where the shrines of foul idols were lighted on
*   high,*
And wantonness tempted the lust of the eye;
Midst rites of obsceneness, strange, loathsome,
*   abhorred,*
The blasphemer scoffed at the name of the Lord.

Hark! the growl of the thunder—the quaking of
*   earth!*
Woe, woe to the worship, and woe to the mirth!
The black sky has opened—there's flame in the
*   air—*
The red arm of vengeance is lifted and bare!

Then the shriek of the dying rose wild where the
*   song*
And the low tone of love had been whispered
*   along;*
For the fierce flames went lightly o'er palace and
*   bower,*
Like the red tongues of demons, to blast and
*   devour!*

Down—down on the fallen the red ruin rained,
And the reveller sank with his wine-cup undrained.
The foot of the dancer, the music's loved thrill,
And the shout and the laughter grew suddenly
*   still.*

—John Greenleaf Whittier

(Gen. 19. 24, 25; Jer. 50. 40; 2 Pet. 2. 6; Jude 7)

1027. Sodom. Deut. 29. 23—'And that the whole land thereof is brimstone, and salt, and burning, that it is not sown, nor beareth, nor any grass groweth therein, like the overthrow of Sodom, and Gomorrah, Adamah and Zeboim, which the Lord overthrew in his anger, and in his wrath.'

From these words we can understand that Moses, writing about 500 years after the destruction of the cities of the plain, was narrating the fact that the salt, the brimstone and the burning that took place in this area centuries before his time, had left very apparent results upon the face of the earth, and he was able to draw the attention of the people of his day to the evidences of the judgement, that could be observed by them whilst passing through that area.

—Walter J. Beasley

Now the ruins of the catastrophe, and indeed, all the remaining undisturbed materials are right here at Jebel Usdum. Here is the stratum of rock-salt, here the overlying marl mixed with free sulphur, and the whole region round about attests the disruptive character of some event that scattered the salt and the sulphur far and wide, encrusted the mountain peaks and so blasted the earth that it took twenty-five hundred years of climatic influences to wash out, and make the plain again 'as the garden of the Lord'.

—Professor Kyle

(Gen. 19. 24-26; 13. 10)

1028. Soldiers of Jesus Christ. During the revival of 1859, Dudley A. Tyng was the leader of a remarkable Gospel Mission in Philadelphia. The Sunday before his death was outstanding in that at least 1000 people were converted. A few days later, while watching a mule at work threshing corn on a H.P. machine, as he patted the animal on the neck, the sleeve of his coat became entangled in the machinery and his arm was torn off. From his deathbed he sent a message to the meeting being held in the Y.M.C.A., Philadelphia: 'Tell them to stand up for Jesus.' George Duffield, who preached the funeral sermon, wrote the words of the well-known hymn:

Stand up, stand up for Jesus
Ye soldiers of the Cross.

(Eph. 6. 13, 14; 2 Tim. 2. 3)

1029. Son of God. Sir Harry Lauder, who lost his only son in the first Great World War, was visited in New York by a man who told him a beautiful and touching story. In

American towns any household that had given a son to the War was entitled to place a star on the window pane. 'Well,' said Sir Harry, 'a few nights before he came to see me, this man was walking down a certain avenue in New York, accompanied by his wee boy. The lad became very interested in the lighted windows of the houses, and clapped his hands when he saw the star. As they passed house after house, he would say, "Oh, look, daddy, there's another house that has given a son to the war! And there's another! There's one with two stars! And look, there's a house with no star at all!"

'At last they came to a break in the houses. Through the gap could be seen the evening star shining brightly in the sky. The little fellow caught his breath. "Oh, look, Daddy," he cried, "God must have given His Son, for He has got a Star in His window." He has indeed!' said Sir Harry, when he repeated the story.

For God so loved the world that He gave His only begotten Son, that whosoever believeth in Him should not perish, but have everlasting life.
(John 3. 16; 2 Cor. 9. 15; 1 John 4. 14)

1030. **Song.** Brother Ira D. Sankey has recalled with a song:

My life flows on in endless song;
Above earth's lamentation
I hear the sweet, not far-off hymn
That hails the new creation.
Through all the tumult and the strife
I hear the music ringing;
It finds an echo in my soul—
How can I keep from singing?
—C. H. Spurgeon
(Rom. 8. 19-22; Rev. 5. 9)

1031. **Sorrow.** The Arabs have a saying that all sunshine makes the desert. It is even so. Just as sun and shower are alike needful for the development of the flower, so are joy and grief for the culture of the soul.
From vintages of sorrow are deepest joys distilled;
And the cup outstretched for healing is oft at Marah filled.
God leads to joy, through weeping; to quietness, through strife;
Through yielding, unto conquest; through death, to endless life.
—Henry Durbanville
(Exod. 15. 23-27; 2 Cor. 6. 10)

1032. **Sorrow.**
I walked a mile with Pleasure;
She chatted all the way
But left me none the wiser
For all she had to say.

I walked a mile with Sorrow,
And ne'er a word said she:
But oh, the things I learnt from her
When Sorrow walked with me.
(Eccles. 7. 3; 2 Cor. 7. 10)

1033. **Spectacle.** In 1 Cor. 4. 9 Paul speaks of himself and his fellow-labourers, the other apostles, as a spectacle to the world, and to the angels and to men. The word he uses for 'spectacle' means a semi-circular building in which plays were acted, an amphitheatre where gladiators were forced to fight in the arena.

1034. **Spirit—Holy.** When the Spirit came to Moses, the plagues came upon Egypt, and he had power to destroy men's lives; when the Spirit came upon Elijah, fire came down from Heaven; when the Spirit came upon Joshua, he moved around the city of Jericho, and the whole city fell into his hands. But when the Spirit came upon the Son of Man, He gave His life, He healed the broken-hearted.
—D. L. Moody

When the Spirit comes into the believer, He makes Christ dearer, Heaven nearer and the Word of God clearer.
(Judg. 6. 34; Luke 4. 1, 18; John 16. 13-15)

1035. **Saliva.** It is said that saliva in the East represents a man's essential nature or being. To use one's spittle in healing suggested profound sympathy. Lightfoot has much to say on the use of the spittle in medicine.
—H. St. John

Ellicott remarks that 'we know from the pages of Pliny and Tacitus, and Suetonius, that the "saliva jejuna" was held to be a remedy in cases of blindness, and that the same remedy was used by the Jews is established by the writings of the Rabbis.'
(Mark 7. 33; 8. 23; John 9. 6)

1036. **Stand.** At the Battle of Waterloo when the fight was grim and hard, an officer galloped up to the commander, the Duke of Wellington, reporting on behalf of his superior that they were being destroyed where they were, that they could not hold the position, and that they must have reinforcements. Said the Iron Duke, 'Tell him to stand.' The soldier galloped back and delivered the message. Presently another officer came with the same request. The Duke's answer was the same, 'Tell him to stand.' He went back, and a third came, begging in the name of his superior for the needed help. 'I have no help to send you,' said the Duke, 'Tell him to stand.' He saluted and said, 'You will find us there, Sir.' And when the battle was fought and won, there they were, all of them, dead in their place. They were prepared to stand—and to die in their stand.
(Eph. 6. 11-14)

1037. **Stewardship.** In the writings of the early Christian fathers is found 69 times a saying of our Lord Jesus not recorded in the Gospels 'Show yourselves approved bankers'. How can we do this? i. In detecting counterfeits—1 Thess. 5. 21. ii. In guarding the deposit entrusted to us: 1 Tim. 6. 20; 2 Tim. 1. 14.

1038. Stones.

A stone I surely am! but of what kind?
Ah! let this thought most deeply grip the mind,
For there are stones and stones which, as you see,
Do neither in their size nor shape agree.

Am I a living stone? Or am I dead?
Have I been blasted from dark nature's bed?
Or do I still within my rock-home lie?
—Unreached by God's great power—dead and
*   to die.*

If saved— a stepping-stone I may become
To raise a brother from some sinful slum;
And watch him rise to heights of moral worth,
And claim an honoured place, through grace, on
*   earth.*

Or I may be a heartless stumbling-stone!
O'er which my fellow falls and breaks a bone;
And have him crippled for the rest of life,
Unfit to stand erect amid the strife.

Or—awful thought!—I may a millstone be
And drown my brother deep in sin's dark sea,
Then watch the bubbles rise, which indicate;
How absolutely helpless was his fate.

Or I may be a grindstone hard and round,
Upon whose wheel some fellow may be ground:
A lord of sweated labour—what reck I
Should fellow-beings near me sink and die?

Yea, I may even be a rolling-stone
And to a life of wandering be prone;
But all such stones are useless as a whole,
They simply oscillate from pole to pole.

Not only are we stones; but stones we cast—
The Stone of judgement at a brother's past;
Ye who are sinless—only ye alone—
Possess the right to cast the Judgement-stone.

                                          —Tom Baird
(1 Pet. 2. 5, 8; Matt. 18. 6; John 8. 7)

1039. Strength. The following lines were
found in the bedroom of General Gordon:

        God imparteth by the way
        Strength sufficient for the day.
(Deut. 33. 25; Dan. 11. 32; Eph. 6. 10)

1040. Strength.

Be strong!
We are not here to play, to dream, to drift:
We have hard work to do and loads to lift:
Shun not the struggle; face it, 'tis God's gift.

Be strong!
Say not the days are evil: who's to blame,
And fold the hands and acquiesce! Oh shame!
Stand up, speak out, and bravely, in God's name!

Be strong!
It matters not how deep entrenched the wrong,
How hard the battle goes, the day how long:
Faint not! fight on!—Tomorrow comes the song.

                                  —Maltbie D. Babcock

(Josh. 1. 6, 7, 9; Eph. 6. 10; 2 Tim. 2. 1)

1041. Study. 'Search the Scriptures', said the
Lord Jesus Christ, using the Greek word
which implies a strict, diligent, curious search
such as men make when seeking gold, or
hunters when hunting game.
(John 5. 39)

1042. Study—Daily.

        If the Saviour's won your heart
        And for Heaven you've made a start,
        Study well your Bible chart,
        And go on.

        Bear in mind that what you know
        Proves itself by what you show;
        Let your life be all aglow,
        And go on.

        Never from your purpose turn!
        Daily from your Master learn.
        Walk with Jesus, then you'll burn
        And go on.

        Buy the truth and sell it not:
        Praise the Lord for what you've got;
        Be content whate'er your lot,
        And go on.
(Acts 17. 11; 2 Tim. 3. 14-17)

1043. Study—How to. In the study of the
Scriptures, 'on the threshhold of your task you
will find a host of lurking demons to lure you
away from it,' warns Dr. Samuel Zwemer.
In this, as in all branches of study, 'con-
centration is the secret of success,' as Emerson
has said.
    D. L. Moody said: 'I never saw a useful
Christian who was not a student of the Bible.
If a person neglects the Bible there is not
much for the Holy Spirit to work with. We
must have the Word.' And Bengel's advice is
very sound: 'Apply yourself wholly to the
Scriptures, and apply the Scriptures wholly to
yourself.'

1044. Study—Prayerfully.

My pail I'm often dropping deep down into the
*   well.*
It never touched the bottom, however deep it fell.
And though I keep on dipping by study, faith and
*   prayer,*
I have no power to measure the living water there.
(John 4. 11; Acts 17. 11)

1045. Study—What to. The subjects for the
Christian's study programme can be remem-
bered easily from an acrostic on the word
'study'.
Study the Scriptures: by reading, searching,
    comparing and meditating.
Theology: the knowledge of God Who has
    revealed Himself in His Word.
the Universe: the wisdom and power of God
    in all His works.
Doctrine: acquainting ourselves with sound,
    systematic teaching.
Yourself: remembering Paul's exhortation to
    Timothy—'Take heed to thyself and to the
    doctrine.'
(1 Tim. 4. 13, 15, 16; 2 Tim. 2. 15)

1046. Substitution. In Napoleon's time, in one of the conscriptions, a man who was balloted to a place and did not want to go, had a friend who offered to go in his place. His friend joined up in his name, was sent off to the front, and was killed in action.

Some time after, Napoleon wanted more men, and by mistake the first man was balloted a second time. 'You cannot take me: I am dead,' he said; 'in such and such a battle you left me buried on the field. Look up your books and see.'

They looked and found he had been killed in action. 'It must have been a substitute,' they said. 'Yes, true!' he replied, 'he died in my stead and the law has now no claim on me.'
(1 Pet. 3. 18)

1047. Substitution.

Under an Eastern sky,
Amid a rabble's cry,
A man went forth to die
For me.

Thorn-crowned His blessed head,
Blood-stained His every tread;
Cross-laden, on He sped
For me.

Pierced through His hands and feet,
Three hours there o'er Him beat
Fierce rays of noontide heat
For me.

Thus wast Thou made all mine:
Lord, make me wholly Thine:
Grant grace and strength divine
To me.

In thought and word and deed
Thy will to do: O, lead
My soul, e'en though it bleed
To Thee.

(Mark 10. 45; 15. 22-34)

1048. Substitution. J. T. Badclay, in his book, *The Russian Conquest of the Caucasus*, tells of a brave leader in the Caucasus who, in the middle of the last century, was struggling to maintain the independence of his people. He was Shamil of the tribes of Dagestan. On one occasion, when defeatism was prevalent among his countrymen, Shamil proclaimed that whoever would contend for capitulation with the Russians would be beaten with a hundred heavy lashes. An offender was caught. To Shamil's embarrassment and grief he found it to be his own mother. Following a period of fasting, prayer and meditation, he instructed that the penalty should be executed. After the fifth stroke, however, he stopped the executioner, had his mother withdrawn, and then, baring his own back, insisted on taking the full weight of all the remaining 95 strokes. His tribesmen were so impressed by their leader's justice, sincerity and willingness to suffer that no one again mentioned negotiations with the enemy.

—*Sunday School Times*

(Isa. 53. 5, 6)

1049. Substitution.
Scarlet robe!—Sins of my heart were placed upon
my King.
His heart, not mine, was pierced for every evil
thing:
In Him no sin—He is my perfect rest—
I see Him now with gold about His breast.

Thorny crown!—Sins of my head were placed
upon His brow.
His head, not mine, was scarred: by faith I see
Him now:
He knew no sin, He is eternal Light—
Ancient of days, with hair of purest white.

Withered reed!—Sins of my hands were placed
in His right hand.
His hands, not mine, were nailed in death's dark,
lonely land:
He did no sin, so now in highest heaven,
In His right hand the stars He holds are seven.

—I. Gauba

(Matt. 27. 28, 29; Rev. 1. 13-16)

1050. Success. Many years ago a lad of sixteen left home to seek his fortune. All his worldly possessions were tied up in a bundle. As he trudged along he met an old neighbour, the captain of a canal-boat, and the following conversation took place:

'Well, William, where are you going?'

'I don't know,' he answered. 'Father is too poor to keep me at home any longer, and says I must now make a living for myself.'

'There's no trouble about that,' said the captain. 'Be sure you start right and you'll get along fine.'

William told his friend that the only trade he knew anything about was soap-making, at which he had helped his father while at home.

'Well,' said the old man, 'let me pray with you once more, and give you a little advice, and then I will let you go.' They both knelt down on the tow-path: the dear old man prayed earnestly for William and then gave him this advice:

'Someone will soon be leading soap-maker in New York. It can be you as well as anyone. I hope it may. Be a good man; give the Lord all that belongs to Him of every dollar that you earn; make an honest soap; give a full pound, and I am certain you will yet be a prosperous and rich man.'

When the boy arrived in the city, he found it hard to get work. Lonesome, and far from home, he remembered his mother's words and the last words of the canal-boat captain. He was then led to 'seek first the kingdom of God and His righteousness'. He remembered his promise to the old sea-captain, and the first dollar he earned brought up the question of the Lord's part. In the Bible he found that the Jews were commanded to give one tenth; so he said, 'If the Lord will take one tenth, I will give that.' And so he did, and ten cents of every dollar was sacred to the Lord.

Having regular employment he soon became a partner; after a few years his partner died, and William became the sole owner of the

business. He now resolved to keep his promise
to the old captain; he made an honest soap,
gave a full pound, and instructed his book-
keeper to open an account with the Lord,
carrying one tenth of his income in that
account. He prospered. His business grew:
his family was blessed: his soap sold, and he
grew rich faster than he had ever hoped. He
then gave the Lord two-tenths, and prospered
more than ever; then he gave three tenths,
then four tenths, then five tenths. He educated
his family, settled all his plans for life, and
thereafter gave the whole of his income to the
Lord.

What was the name of this lad? William
Colgate! And who has not heard of Colgate's
soap?

—J. Oswald Sanders

(Ps. 1. 3; Prov. 3. 9, 10)

1051. Success. Someone asked General
Booth of the Salvation Army on one occasion
the secret of his success. He hesitated a second,
and then, with tears in his eyes, said, 'I will tell
you the secret. God has had all there was of
me to have.'

(Rom. 12. 1, 2)

1052. Suffering—and Glory. Rom. 8. 18
reads—I consider that the sufferings of this
present while are not worth comparing with
the glory that is to be revealed in us.

Some time, when all life's lessons have been
  learned
  And suns and stars for evermore have set,
The things which our weak judgements here have
  spurned,
  The things o'er which we grieved with lashes
  wet,
Will flash before us out of life's dark night,
  And we shall see how all God's plans are right,
And what then seemed reproof was love most true.
But not today. Then be content, poor heart,

  God's plans like lilies pure and white unfold;
We must not tear the close-shut leaves apart.
  Time will reveal the calyxes of gold.
And if, through patient toil, we reach the land
  Where our tired feet, with sandals loosed, may
  rest,
Where we shall clearly see and understand,
  I think that we shall say, 'God knew the best'.

1053. Suicide. All America was shocked by
the recent cases of suicide among university
students. One said that he had sucked all the
juice out of the orange. Another, that he had
had all the thrills there are in life, and he was
now going to get the thrill of death. Still
another wanted to find out what was on the
other side. At the door of the rationalistic,
evolutionary teaching of today must be laid
the blame. No young man commits suicide
whose life is anchored in God; but robbed of a
future hope, life is barren and worthless.

—Oswald J. Smith

1054. Supplies.

Through the meadows, past the cities, still the
  brimming streams are rolled,
Now in torrents, now expanding into silver lakes
  of gold,
Wafting life and increase with them, wealth and
  beauty manifold.

Whence descends the ceaseless fulness, ever
  giving, never dry?
Yonder, o'er the climbing forest, see the shining
  cause on high—
Mountain snows their watery treasure pouring
  everlastingly.

(Ps. 104. 10-15; 145. 16)

1055. Sympathy. In the *Tempest*, one of
Shakespeare's plays, he makes the heroine,
Miranda, say, 'Oh, I have suffered with those
that I saw suffer': that was sympathy. What a
contrast to the picture in Milan of a little
cherub trying to feel one of the points of the
Saviour's crown of thorns! He has a look of
incredulous wonder on his face, for he has
been told it meant agony, but he cannot feel
it. Our High Priest is 'able to be touched with
a feeling of our infirmities', because He Himself 'suffered, being tempted'.

1056. Sympathy.

There is starlight through the shadows for the
  feet that have to tread
In the path of secret sorrow, with the hidden tears
  unshed.
There's the glory of the sunset flaming red down
  in the west,
When the storm is hushed to stillness and the
  waters sink to rest.

There's a lamp that God has lighted where the
  shadowed pathways are,
And it sheds a softened radiance like the shining
  of a star;
There's a haven of sweet refuge from the deeply
  hidden pain,
Where the heart that long has suffered sees
  God's rainbow through the rain.

There's an angel in the shadows—oftentimes in
  human guise,
Who, in silent understanding, sees the tears that
  blind our eyes;
For the words may be unspoken, quiet waters
  running deep—
When the sympathy of friendship is outpoured on
  those who weep.

There's a twilight in the evening when the throb
  of pain is stilled,
And the heart, through human friendship, with
  the peace of God is filled;
And the twilight touches softly all the valley we
  have trod,
When a true friend's love sustains us, like an
  angel sent from God.

(1 Cor. 12. 26; Heb. 12. 11)

1057. Tabernacle — Acrostic on. The tabernacle in the wilderness was:

1. Tripartite and Typical,
2. Appointed by the Almighty,
3. Bound together by Bars,
4. Entered from the East,
5. Rested on Redemption,
6. Needful for a Nomadic Nation,
7. Adorned within and Anointed,
8. Carried by Chosen men,
9. Lighted by the Lord's priests,
10. Erected again at Each Encampment.

1. It was of three parts, the court, the holy place and the Holiest of all, and it is a type of Christ. 2. Its purpose was that Jehovah might dwell among His people (Exod. 25. 8). 3. Bars of wood overlaid with gold typify Christ's true humanity and His essential deity (Exod. 26. 24-29). 4. The gate of the court and the door of the tabernacle were on the East (Exod. 38. 13-16; Num. 3. 38). 5. Each board rested on two sockets of silver, which is the emblem of redemption (Exod. 26. 15-25). 6. It could be easily taken down and put together again. 7. Its inner curtains of fine twined linen, and blue, purple and scarlet, had cherubim worked on them (Exod. 26. 1-6): and, when erected, the tabernacle was anointed (Exod. 40. 9). 8. The three Levite families were responsible for its transport (Num. 4). 9. The Shechinah glory over the Holiest of all gave divine light, and the lampstand in the holy place artificial light (Exod. 40. 34-38; Num. 8. 1-4). 10. See Num. 9. 15-23.

1058. Tabernacle—Furniture of.

The Kohathites upon their shoulders bear
The holy vessels covered all with care.
The Gershonites receive an easier charge,
Two waggons full of cords and curtains large.
Merari's sons four ponderous waggons load
With boards and pillars of the House of God.
　　　　　　　　　—R. Murray McCheyne
(Num. 4)

1059. Talk. Diogenes the sage once said: 'We have two ears and only one tongue that we may hear more and speak less.'

Talk may be cheap, but we often pay dearly for it.
(Ps. 39. 1; 141. 3; Col. 4. 6; James 1. 26; 3. 2)

1060. Talkativeness. Talkativeness is utterly ruinous to deep spirituality. The very life of our spirit passes out in our speech, and hence all superfluous talk is a waste of the vital forces of the heart. In fruit growing it often happens that excessive blossoming prevents a good crop, and often prevents fruit altogether; and by much loquacity the soul runs wild in word bloom and bears no fruit. I am not speaking of sinners, nor of legitimate testimony for Jesus, but of that incessant loquacity of nominally spiritual persons—of the professors of purifying grace. It is one of the greatest

hindrances to deep, solid union with God. Notice how insignificant trifles are magnified by a world of words; how things that should be buried are dragged out into gossip; how a worthless non-essential is argued and disputed over; how the solemn, deep things of the Holy Spirit are rattled over in light manner.

See the evil effects of so much talk. First, it dissipates spiritual power. The thought and feeling of the soul are like powder and steam—the more they are condensed, the greater their power. The true action of the heart, if expressed in a few Holy Ghost selected words, will sink into minds to remain for ever, but if dissipated in any rambling conversation, is likely to be of no profit.

Second, it is a waste of time. If the hours spent in useless conversation were spent in secret prayer, or deep reading, we should soon reach a region of spiritual life and divine peace beyond our present dreams.

Third, loquacity inevitably leads to saying unwise, or unpleasant, or unprofitable things. The Holy Spirit warns us that 'in the multitude of words there wanteth not sin'. We must settle this personally. I must guard my speech as a sentinel does a fortress. The cure for loquacity must be from within. To walk in the Spirit we must avoid talking for talking's sake, or merely to entertain.

　　　　　　　　　　　　　　　—Selected
(Prov. 10. 19; 17. 27; Eccles. 5. 2, 3; Eph. 4. 29)

1061. Teaching of Christ.

He talked of grass, and wind, and rain,
Of fig-trees, and fair weather,
And made it His delight to bring
Heaven and earth together.

He spake of lilies, vines, and corn,
The sparrow and the raven;
And words so natural, yet so wise,
Were on men's hearts engraven.

Of yeast with bread, and flax, and cloth,
Of eggs, and fish, and candles.
See how the whole familiar world
He most divinely handles.

　　　　　　　　　　　　　—T. T. Lynch
(Matt. 13. 3, 34)

1062. Temptation of Man. Of Genesis 3 George Whitefield said, 'Moses unfolds more in that Chapter than all mankind would have been capable of finding out of themselves though they had studied it to all eternity.'
(Gen. 3. 1; 2 Cor. 11. 3)

1063. Temptations. Temptations divide the world into two classes; those who fail and go down under them and those who meet them successfully and gain strength of character through overcoming them. To the one class they are stumbling-blocks; to the other they are stepping-stones. To the one they are hindrances; to the other they are helps. It is not our temptations but the way we respond to them that counts.

—H. O. Fanning

(Matt. 4. 1; Luke 22. 31, 32; 1 Cor. 10. 13; James 1. 12)

1064. Testimony. A soldier lay, bleeding to death from wounds, on the battlefield. Seeing a surgeon, he said faintly, 'Oh, doctor, please!' The doctor got down, dressed his wounds, gave him all possible relief, and ordered him to be conveyed to hospital.

'What's your name, doctor?' asked the wounded man.

'Oh, no matter!' replied the surgeon.

'But, doctor,' he said, 'I want to tell my wife and children who saved my life.'

(Ps. 66. 16; Acts 1. 8; 1 Tim. 1. 12-16)

1065. Testimony. A nurse in a Glasgow hospital is responsible for the following story of a Christian's last testimony in song.

A man came into the hospital for an operation on his tongue. In reply to his enquiries concerning the future, the surgeon told him that he would probably be able to speak with sufficient plainness to make himself understood, but he would never be able to sing again. Whereupon the sufferer said that, if that were the case, he must have one more song before his tongue was touched. In the presence of the doctors and nurses, he burst forth into song in Cowper's hymn, 'There is a fountain filled with blood', and concluded thus:

Soon in a nobler, sweeter song,
I'll sing Thy power to save
When this poor lisping, cancerous tongue
Lies silent in the grave.

The patient never recovered from the operation.

(Rev. 5. 9, 10)

1066. Thanksgiving. A Christian in great perplexity prayed but found no relief in prayer. Looking up from where he knelt, his eye alighted on a card, 'Try Thanksgiving!' He did, and the Lord gave him peace and removed his cares.

(Phil. 4. 6; 1 Tim. 2. 1)

1067. Thanksgiving. A well-known Christian in a small town in Scotland was afflicted with nasal catarrh. Dr. Adams of Hamilton, Lanarkshire, a nose, throat and ear specialist, operated on him, and the operation gave him the relief he wanted. He was so helped that he sat down, after he had paid the doctor's fee, and wrote a letter of thanks. In a day or two he received a reply from the surgeon saying he was going to keep the letter among his prized papers, as it was the first letter of thanks he had ever received.

(Ps. 100. 4; Col. 2. 7; 1 Tim. 4. 4)

1068. Thirst. After the Second World War, under the caption 'The Drink that made history' a popular monthly magazine published an article which described how the turning of the tide at El Alamein in the Eastern section of North Africa was due to a fortuitous circumstance that blasted the last hopes of the Nazis of gaining Alexandria. It concerned a supply of water.

The strength of the British forces in and around El Alamein, and of the German forces pressing down upon them, was almost equal. Both sides were hard pressed for drinking water: and thirst is a terrible thing to endure in the heat of the desert sands. The British forces had laid pipes from a known source of good water to their encampment, but, as was the custom, for the purpose of putting the pipelines to the test, the pipes were first filled with sea water as an economy measure. This was a procedure of which all the British troops in the North African campaign were aware. Nazi patrols, reconnoitring, came upon this pipeline just a day after it had been laid. The information was immediately transmitted to their camping quarters, and before long the Nazi soldiers, in desperation with thirst, made their way to where the pipes had been located, struck a hole in one with a pickaxe, and one after another gulped down the liquid that gushed from the hole in the pipe. Having consumed quantities of water without restraint, they did not realise that the water was salt till they experienced the agony that followed. Driven to desperation by suffering that far eclipsed their original thirst, they decided to surrender in a body; and the British forces in El Alamein were surprised to see a large company of enemy troops approach, with swollen tongues lolling out of their mouths, their hands stretched upright above their heads as a sign of surrender. The first act of the prisoners was to seize the water bottles of their captors and pour down their burning throats the sweet, living water for which their whole beings were gasping.

That was the incident that proved to be the turning-point in the campaign. Had it happened a day earlier, the pipes would have been empty: had it occurred a day later, they would have been full of good, drinking water.

Physical thirst is a terrible thing, a pang that racks the human frame, and is accompanied by an indescribably intense longing for satisfaction. It has its counterpart in the spiritual being of men. Detecting its intensity in mankind, the Lord Jesus—when here on earth as Man—said, 'If any man thirst let him come unto me and drink.' There are many who, like those German soldiers, in order to obtain a temporary satisfaction, turn to whatever bears the slightest resemblance to a thirst-quencher. Millions are vainly endeavouring to slake their thirst with the useless and transient pleasures of sin. These are positively harmful and produce, sooner or later, an agony of remorse and disappointment. Only One can satisfy the thirsty soul, and the

only way to find satisfaction is to come to Him, surrender to His claims and receive His gift.
(Jer. 2. 13; John 4. 10-14; 7. 37; Isa. 44. 3; Rev. 21. 6)

1069. Thirst. The explorer, Coulthard, who perished of thirst in the Australian desert, left behind, in the place of his last encampment, the feebly-scrawled lines: 'Lost, lost, for want of water.'
(John 7. 37; Luke 16. 24)

1070. Thoughts. It has been said, 'We are not what we think we are, but—what we think, we are.'

A naughty little weed one day
Poked up its tiny head.
'Tomorrow I will pull you up,
Old Mr. Weed,' I said.
But I put off the doing till,
When next I passed that way,
The hateful thing had spread abroad
And laughed at my dismay.

A naughty little thought one day
Popped right into my mind.
'Oh no!' I cried, 'I'll put you out
Tomorrow, you will find!'
But once again I put it off,
Till like the little weed,
The ugly thing sprang up apace
And grew into a deed.
(Rom. 12. 2; Phil. 4. 8)

1071. Thoughts. Sow a thought, you reap an action; sow an action, you reap a habit: sow a habit, you reap a character: sow a character, you reap a destiny.
(Prov. 12. 5; Ps. 19. 14; 2 Cor. 10. 5)

1072. Thoughts. A young man went up from his home in the country to the city to take his degree in the University there. As a resident student, he had his own room in the hostel. After he had settled in, his mother, a godly, devoted Christian, decided to pay him a visit. She found that he was comfortably ensconced, and was taking an interest in the various courses of study to prepare him for his degree: but she was very shocked to see the kind of pictures he had fixed to the walls of his room in the hostel. They were portraits of semi-dressed artistes, film stars, and suggested much that was sensual, and unbecoming a young man who had been reared and trained at home as he had. The mother said not a word.

Instead of expressing her displeasure, she went home, had her photo taken, and sent him the very best that the photographer could provide, with the request that he would hang it in his room. The next time she visited him, all the other pictures were gone: only his mother's photograph adorned the wall. When she asked him about it, he replied, 'You see, mother, I could not have those pictures alongside of yours. They would be out of place.'
(Rom. 8. 6; Phil. 4. 8; Col. 3. 1, 2)

1073. Threats. Chrysostom, summoned before the Roman Emperor Arcadius, and threatened with banishment, is said to have replied: 'Thou canst not banish me, for the world is my Father's house.'

'Then I will slay thee,' exclaimed the Emperor wrathfully.

'Nay, but thou canst, for my life is hid with Christ in God.'

'Your treasures shall be confiscated,' was the grim reply.

'Sire, that cannot be. My treasures are in heaven, as my heart is there.'

'But I will drive thee from men and thou shalt have no friends left.'

'That you cannot do either, sire, for I have a Friend in heaven Who has said, "I will never leave thee, nor forsake thee".'
(Acts 4. 17, 21, 29; 9. 1; Col. 2. 3)

1074. Throne.

On the Father's throne of glory
Is a Man divine;
There my heart, O God, is tasting
Fellowship with Thine.
Called to share Thy joy unmeasured,
Now is heaven begun;
I rejoice with Thee, O Father,
In Thy glorious Son.

Here, who follows Him the nearest
Needs must walk alone;
There, like many seas the chorus,
Praise surrounds the throne.
Here a dark and silent pathway;
In those courts so fair
Countless hosts, yet each beholding
Jesus only, there.

—T.P. in *Hymns of Ter Stegen and others*
(Rev. 3. 21; 4. 9; 5. 6-10)

1075. Time.

When as a child I laughed and wept, Time crept;
When as a youth I dreamt and talked, Time walked;
When I became a full-grown man, Time ran;
When older still I daily grew, Time flew;
Soon shall I find in travelling on, Time gone;
And face eternity begun, Time done.

1076. Time.

Time was—is past: thou canst not it recall:
Time is—thou hast: employ the portion small.
Time future is not and may never be:
Time present is the only time for thee.
(2 Cor. 6. 2)

1077. Titles of Christ.

Forth from Zion's citadel
Who is this led out to die,
As those voices rise and swell
'Crucify! crucify!'?
Mocking rulers make reply,
'Christ the King of Israel.'

Simon whom they did compel
  After Him to bear His cross,
Saw His anguish and could tell
  How the soldiers dice did toss,
How He died to bear our loss—
  Christ the King of Israel.

Hushed by every heart and tongue!
  There, to save our souls from hell
He in agony is hung,
  Numbered thus with thieves among.
'Twas for us—O mark it well—
  Christ, the King of Israel.

Like a wounded wild gazelle,
  Stricken sore and mortally,
From His parchéd lips there fell
  Groans of dire extremity:
'Why hast Thou forsaken me—
  Christ the King of Israel?'

Finished what the Scripture saith
  And the prophet's words foretell:
Silenced now each infidel.
  See! He bows His head in death,
And He yields His parting breath—
  Christ the King of Israel.

Here, beside His cross is found
  Mercy without parallel.
This indeed is holy ground;
  Let your sandals be unbound
While we linger near its spell—
  Christ the King of Israel.

Praises be for what befell
  On that dark and dreadful day.
Everywhere let people say,
  'This our guilty fears can quell:
Christ has borne our sins away—
  Christ the King of Israel.'

Hail we Him, Emmanuel,
  Throned upon the royal tree,
Who in distant islands dwell;
  And from henceforth none but He
Shall our God and Saviour be—
  Christ the King of Israel.

              —R. Randall

(Mark 15. 32)

1078. Tongue. A loose tongue will often get you into a tight corner.

When Demaratus was asked whether he held his tongue because he was a fool or for want of words, he replied, 'A fool cannot hold his tongue.'

Simonides said that he never repented having held his tongue but was often sorry that he had spoken.
(Prov. 12. 19; 15. 2, 4; James 3. 2-8)

1079. Tongue.

'The boneless tongue, so small and weak,
Can crush and kill,' declares the Greek.

'The tongue destroys a greater horde,'
The Turk asserts, 'than does the sword.'

A Persian proverb wisely saith,
'A lengthy tongue—an early death.'

Or sometimes takes this form instead,
'Don't let your tongue cut off your head.'

'The tongue can speak a word whose speed,'
The Chinese say, 'outstrips the steed.'

While Arab sages this impart,
'The tongue's great storehouse is the heart.'

From Hebrew writ this maxim sprung,
'Though feet should slip, ne'er let the tongue.'

The sacred writer crowns the whole:
'Who keeps his tongue doth keep his soul!'
(Prov. 21. 23; 1 Pet. 3. 10)

1080. Training. The mountain goat which lives in the higher reaches of the mountains must in due season teach her offspring how to jump from crag to crag.

When they come to the edge of a ledge which mother has selected, the little fellow naturally hesitates, so mother promptly pushes him over the cliff. Terrified, the young goat manages to strike his feet against a jutting rock, and then he bounces safely to a trail below. Mother knows that there is a ledge below, and a trail that her son can jump to, for she has made these jumps many times before, and she will not lead her offspring into a task he is incapable of. The feet of a mountain goat are made 'nonskid.' In like manner God trains His people. It is through God-appointed trials that our faith is strengthened.

              —Christian Victory

(Deut. 32. 11; James 1. 12)

1081. Traitor. The story has often been told of Mr. H. St. John standing in the private chapel of Keble College, Oxford, contemplating Holman Hunt's masterpiece, 'The Light of the World'. Suddenly, the silence was broken by a crowd of tourists led by a guide, a man with a particularly strident voice. After a hasty explanation of the painting, he announced, 'The original of this picture was sold for £5,000.' Without a moment's hesitation Mr. St. John stepped forward and said very quietly, 'Ladies and gentlemen, may I say that the true Original of this picture was sold for thirty pieces of silver?' After a moment's silence, the crowd of people passed out of the chapel without another word.
(Matt. 26. 14-16)

1082. Traitor.

Thirty pieces of silver for the Lord of life they
    gave:
Thirty pieces of silver—only the price of a slave,
But it was the priestly value of the holy One of
    God:
They weighed it out in the temple, the price of the
    Saviour's blood.

Thirty pieces of silver laid in Iscariot's hand:—
Thirty pieces of silver, and the aid of an armed
    band,
Like a lamb that is brought to the slaughter, led
    the Holy Son of God
At midnight from the garden where His sweat
    had been as blood.

Thirty pieces of silver burned in the traitor's
    brain:
Thirty pieces of silver! but oh! it is hellish gain:
'I have sinned and betrayed the guiltless,' he
    cried with a fevered breath
And he cast them down in the temple and rushed
    to a madman's death.

Thirty pieces of silver lay in the House of God:
Thirty pieces of silver, but oh! 'twas the price of
    blood.
And so, for a place to bury the stranger in, they
    gave
The price of their own Messiah Who lay in a
    borrowed grave.

It may not be for silver: it may not be for gold;
But still by tens of thousands is this precious
    Saviour sold.—
Sold for a godless friendship, sold for a selfish
    aim,
Sold for a fleeting trifle, sold for an empty name!
Sold in the mart of science! sold in the seat of
    power!
Sold at the Shrine of Fortune! sold in Pleasure's
    bower!
Sold, where the awful bargain none but God's
    eye can see:
Ponder, my soul, the question, 'Shall He be sold
    by thee?'

Sold! O God, what a moment! stifled is con-
    science' voice:
Sold! and a weeping angel records the awful
    choice:
Sold! but the price of the Saviour to a living coal
    shall turn,
With the pangs of remorse for ever deep in the
    soul to burn.
                                            —William Blane
(Exod. 21. 32; Zech. 11. 12, 13; Matt. 26. 15;
27. 3, 4)

1083. Traitor.
Still, as of old, man by himself is priced:
For thirty silver pieces Judas sold himself, not
Christ.
(Matt. 27. 3, 4; Acts 1. 18)

1084. Transfiguration of Jesus. In Raphael's
famous painting of the Transfiguration the
artist has portrayed two scenes on a single
canvas. In the upper part the Saviour shines
in a blaze of supernatural light. Moses and
Elias are doing homage to Him, and the
favoured three lie prostrate at His feet. In the
lower zone, earthbound souls are seeking
salvation and yearning with deep emotion for
the healing of the stricken child.
                                            —H. St. John
(Mark 9. 2-8; 14-27)

1085. Transformation.
    No more the power of human mind
        Nor strength of human will,
    But vision of the open face
        The newborn heart to fill.

Rejoicing in that fadeless light
    Reflectors we shall be;
While walking with Him, we become
    Like Him whose face we see.
                                            —F. H. Oakley
(2 Cor. 3. 18)

1086. Transformation.   Biographers   of
Fenelon tell us that he lived in such intimate
fellowship with God that his very face shone.
Lord Peterborough, a sceptic, was obliged to
spend a night with him at an inn. In the
morning he rushed away, saying, 'If I stay
another night with that man, I shall be a
Christian in spite of myself.' Someone else
said of him, 'His manners were full of grace,
his voice full of love, and his face full of glory.'
(Exod. 34. 29; 2 Cor. 3. 18)

1087. Transformation.   Archibald Orr Ewing,
a successful business man in Glasgow, went to
China as a missionary. Through communion
with his Lord Jesus Christ, his features
became so radiant that the people there gave
him a new name—'Mr. Glory-face'.
(Exod. 34. 29; 2 Cor. 3. 18; 4. 6)

1088. Transformation.   A Christian leader, a
servant of Christ known for his devoutness and
gracious manner, was calling at a home on a
pastoral visit to the family, and knocked at
the door. The knock was answered by a little
girl, the daughter of the house, who, on
opening the door and seeing the stranger,
immediately ran inside, saying, 'O mother,
come: Jesus is at the door.'—'Reflecting as a
mirror the glory of the Lord and changed into
the same image from glory to glory.'
(2 Cor. 3. 18)

1089. Transformation.   The   word   'Meta-
morphoo', the Greek for 'transform', occurs
three times in the New Testament: Matt. 17. 2;
Rom. 12. 2 and 2 Cor. 3. 18.
    From that Greek word we get our English
term—'metamorphosis'.   The   entomologist,
when he uses the term, envisages the transformation of the caterpillar through the
chrysalis stage into the beautiful winged
butterfly. It is a change of form and appearance
from ugliness to beauty, but it also suggests a
change of habits and manner of life.
(1 Cor. 6. 9-11)

1090. Transformation.
Look on His face: so shall His light Divine
On Thee in radiancy and beauty shine:
Walk in His steps; the path that Jesus trod
Shall lead thee safely on to Heaven and God.
List to His voice, and thou shalt ever hear
His words of comfort, peace, thy heart to cheer.
Put thou thy hand in His, and thou shalt see
How strong, how firm His hold on thee shall be.
(2 Cor. 3. 18)

1091. Transformation.

Gazing on the cloudless glory of the Lord they love,
While on high He fills with radiance those bright courts above,
Day by day a change is passing o'er each upturned brow,
Soon to shine with Christ in glory, though so dimly now.

(2 Cor. 3. 18; 1 John 3. 2; Dan. 12. 3)

1092. Transformation.

He who sets out to change individual lives may be an optimist; but he who sets out to change society without first changing the individual is a lunatic.

—Dr. S. M. Zwemer

(Acts 26. 18)

1093. Transformation.

A British vessel landed Mr. and Mrs. Paton on an island under armed guard and stood by while the crew built the missionaries a house in which to dwell. Then they sailed away, convinced that they would never see the courageous couple again.

What followed constitutes one of the greatest and most thrilling romances of all time. The people with whom the Patons worked were brutal and cruel almost beyond hope. After a short time Mrs. Paton died of a tropical disease that was swift and deadly. Her husband buried her, and so low were the standards of the natives that they demanded her body for their feast. John Paton had to lie upon her grave, musket in hand, ten days and nights, aided only by his dog. This was the only way he could preserve his wife's body. When he was sure that the dear form was corrupted so as to be inedible, he retired to his lonely house and began the translation of the Bible into the native tongue. For thirty years he laboured with those people. Then a commission of the British Government visited the Islands and published an official document of congratulation, saying that the 'cannibals' of the New Hebrides had now become the most advanced and cultured of all the native tribes who lived under the British flag. In those thirty years a race had been transformed and redeemed by the cultural power of the wonderful Word.

—Harry Rimmer

(Ps. 119. 105; 2 Cor. 3. 18)

1094. Transformation.

There is a story told of an American who went over to Paris and, wishing to buy his wife a little gift, purchased a phosphorescent, mother-of-pearl match-box container; and the beauty of it was that in the dark it was said to radiate a wonderful light. He packed it in his trunk, took it home to the U.S.A., and after the family welcome dinner asked for the lights to be put out. In the dark he took the match-box container from his pocket to present it to his wife, but, when he looked at it, it was as black as the darkness around. Then he said, 'That is just what they palm off on foreigners. I've been swindled.' Next day his wife, a bit curious, discovered on the box a few words in French. She took it down to some friends who had a French maid and had it translated. That night, in the darkness, it was all aglow, for she had followed the instructions written on the box, which said: *'If you keep me all day long in the sunlight, I will shine for you all night long in the darkness.'*

(2 Cor. 4. 6; Phil. 2. 15)

1095. Transience of Earthly things.

Once in Persia reigned a king, who upon his signet ring
'Graved a maxim true and wise which, if held before the eyes,
Gave him counsel at a glance fit for every change and chance:
'Even this shall pass away.'

Trains of camels through the sand brought him gems from Samarcand;
Fleets of galleys through the seas brought him pearls to match with these,
But he counted not his gain treasures of the mine or main;
'What is wealth?' the king would say: 'Even this shall pass away.'

In the revels of his court, at the zenith of the sport,
When the palms of all his guests burned with clapping at his jests,
He, amid his figs and wine, cried, 'Oh, loving friends of mine!
Pleasures come, but not to stay: Even this shall pass away.'

Fighting on a furious field, once a javelin pierced his shield,
Soldiers with a loud lament bore him bleeding to his tent.
Groaning from his tortured side, 'Pain is hard to bear,' he cried,
'But with patience, day by day, even this shall pass away.'

Towering in the public square, twenty cubits in the air,
Rose his statue carved in stone. Then the king, disguised, unknown,
Stood before his sculptured name musing meekly, 'What is fame?
Fame is but a slow decay—Even this shall pass away.'

Struck with palsy, sere and old, waiting at the Gates of gold,
Said he with his dying breath, 'Life is done, but what is death?
Then, in answer to the king, fell a sunbeam on his ring,
Showing by a heavenly ray: 'Even this shall pass away.'

(Heb. 11. 25; James 4. 14)

1096. Trials. John Wesley was one day walking along the road with a friend who, sore vexed and troubled, expressed his doubts of God's goodness. 'I don't know what I shall do with all my worries and troubles,' said he. Wesley noticed a cow looking over a stone wall, and put the question, 'Why does a cow look over the wall?'

'Because it can't see through it, I suppose,' replied his friend.

'Precisely!' said Wesley. 'So, if you can't see through your troubles, try looking over them: and look up to God.'

1097. Trials.

Pressed out of measure and pressed to all length;
Pressed so intensely, it seems beyond strength:
Pressed in the body and pressed in the soul,
Pressed in the mind till the dark surges roll:
Pressure by foes, and pressure by friends:
Pressure on pressure, till life nearly ends.
Pressed into knowing no helper but God;
Pressed into loving the staff and the rod:
Pressed into liberty where nothing clings,
Pressed into faith for impossible things.
Pressed into living a life in the Lord,
Pressed into living a Christ-life outpoured.
(Ps. 73. 26; Job. 23. 10; 2 Cor. 1. 8)

1098. Trials. A jeweller gives as one of the surest tests for diamonds the 'water test'. He says: 'An imitation diamond is never so brilliant as a genuine stone. If your eye is not experienced enough to detect the difference, a simple test is to place the stone under water. The imitation diamond is practically extinguished. A genuine diamond sparkles under water and is distinctly visible. If you place a genuine stone beside an imitation under water, the contrast will be apparent to the least experienced eye.'

Many seem confident of their faith so long as they have no trials; but when the waters of sorrow and affliction overflow them, their faith loses its brilliancy. It is under these circumstances that the true children of God shine as genuine jewels.
(Job. 23. 10; Isa. 43. 1, 2; 1 Pet. 1. 7)

1099. Triumph. Paul uses several times the figure of a Roman triumphal procession. On the triumphant Roman conqueror great honours were conferred. When he returned from the field of battle victorious he received a great ovation in his capital. He had a magnificent entry into the capital attended by the spoils of war, and by princes, nobles and generals whom he had taken captive. White horses, or elephants, or lions, or tigers, drew his splendid chariot. Fragrant odours were diffused, and flowers were scattered along the way while incense was burned on the altars. The whole city was filled with the smoke of the sacrifices, and with aromatic perfumes.

It is from the same Greek word that Paul uses that we derive our English word 'triumph'.
(2 Cor. 2. 14; Eph. 4. 8; Col. 2. 15)

1100. Trust.

Until I learned to trust
I never learned to pray,
And I did not fully learn to trust
Till sorrow came my way.

Until I felt my weakness,
His strength I never knew;
Nor dreamed till I was stricken
That He could see me through.
(Ps. 34. 6; 56. 3, 11; Isa. 12. 2; 26. 4)

1101. Trust.

Have you lifted anchor and hoisted sail?
Does your ship sail out to sea?
Do you tremble at peril and dread the gale
Where the waves and winds are free.
THEN TRUST IN GOD!

Is your old sail salt with the frozen foam?
And grey as the seagull's wing?
Do you long for land and native home,
When the great waves clutch and cling?
THEN TRUST IN GOD!

O the sea of Faith hath storms, God knows;
And the haven seems very far,
But he is God's true child who goes
With his eyes on the polar star.
THEN TRUST IN GOD!

With his hands on the canvas, his foot on the ropes,
Filling each sail with wind and glee,
With dauntless courage and quenchless hopes
Sail the ships o'er the infinite sea.
THEN TRUST IN GOD!

And the Infinite Christ Who stilled the waves
On the Sea of Galilee.
Speaks a message of peace to each troubled heart
That sails o'er the infinite sea.
THEN TRUST IN GOD!
(Prov. 3. 5; Isa. 26. 4; Acts 27. 24, 25)

1102. Truth. The late Dr. A. T. Pierson told the following story of General Robert E. Lee. Hearing General Lee speak in the highest terms to President Davis about a certain officer, another officer, greatly astonished, said to him. 'General, do you not know that the man of whom you spoke so highly to the President is one of your bitterest enemies, and misses no opportunity to malign you?' 'Yes,' replied General Lee, 'but the President asked my opinion of him, and I gave him a true answer, he did not ask his opinion of me.'
(Prov. 12. 17; Zech. 8. 16; Eph. 4. 25)

1103. Truth—Eternal. Truth is a queen who has her eternal throne in heaven, and her seat of empire in the heart of God.   —Bossuet
(Deut. 32. 4; Isa. 65. 16; John 8. 32; Rom. 3. 7)

1104. Truth—Ever true.

Since truth is always true
And only true can be,
Keep me, O Lord, as true to truth
As truth is true to Thee.

—T. Baird

(Eph. 4. 25; Heb. 6. 18)

1105. Truth—Future reign of.

Careless seems the Great Avenger; history's
*   pages but record*
One death-grapple in the darkness 'twixt false
*   systems and the Word,*
Truth for ever on the scaffold, Wrong for ever on
*   the throne:*
Yet that scaffold sways the future, and behind the
*   dim unknown*
Standeth God within the shadows keeping watch
*   above His own.*

                    —J. Russell Lowell

(2 Tim. 4. 4; Titus 1. 1, 14)

1106. Truth—Girt with. At the battle of
Bothwell Brig, the ammunition of the
Covenanters ran out. They were waiting for
a barrel of bullets, but instead, a barrel of
raisins was sent to them. So they sat down in
defeat. Today, as then, the soldiers of Jesus
Christ must have less confectionery and more
of the Truth of God. We must have our loins
girt about with truth.
(Eph. 6. 14)

1107. Truth—Hand of.

       The nimble lie
Is like the second hand upon the clock;
We see it fly: while the hour hand of truth
Seems to stand still, and yet it moves unseen,
And wins at last, for the clock will not strike
Till it has reached its goal.

                —H. W. Longfellow

Ps. 43. 3; Prov. 23. 23)

1108. Tyrants. Tyrants were unconstitutional
monarchs who ruled Greek cities or states in
the seventh to the third centuries B.C. Under
the rule of these upstarts many cities and
states attained their great power and splendour.
    They were not necessarily bad or cruel rulers.
They were often patrons of the Arts and
Literature. But they were usurpers, men who
rose to power out of party strife and general
unrest.
    Dionysius, the Tyrant of Syracuse, started
life as a clerk in a public office. He ruled
Syracuse, the capital or principal city of
Sicily, for thirty years, and concentrated in it
the 'greatness and glory of the Greek world in
the West'. Timoleon was a Greek general who
made himself master of Corinth, and later was
chosen by popular vote to attack Syracuse, of
which he became the Tyrant, ruling well for
many years. Hiero II, another General, rose
to be Tyrant and was acclaimed as king, ruling
wisely and maintaining peace for fifty years.
    The name 'tyrannus' (tyrant) is of obscure
origin. Today it has acquired a meaning far
removed from its original one of 'king' or
'monarch', but we have seen in Europe and
are seeing in the Middle East and Egypt a
remarkable recrudescence of the movement
which played such a notable part in Greek

history. Hitler, Mussolini, Stalin, and Nasser,
all men of the people, with no hereditary rights
or claims to kingship, forced their way to
supreme authority by a 'will to power' similar
to that of the Greek tyrants. History will
record the use they made of the authority
they obtained.
    We are reminded of the tyrant we read of in
the Book of Daniel, that king 'who shall do
according to his will', who shall exalt himself,
and 'magnify himself above every god, and
shall speak marvellous things against the God
of gods, and shall prosper till the indignation
be accomplished'. These tyrants already
mentioned prospered till the indignation was
accomplished, or will prosper till the indignation be accomplished, and we know what
befell some of them.
(Dan. 11. 36; Acts 19. 9)

1109. Unchanging God. Galileo was one of
the world's greatest leaders in scientific
discovery. His revolutionary teachings raised
the ire of the cardinals. He was finally
summoned to appear before the Inquisition.
There he confessed his error in having taught
his new theories, especially that which related
to the earth revolving round the sun, but as
he walked away he is said to have muttered
defiantly—'But it moves, just the same.'
True—the Divine laws abide. God's will
directs God's laws, and God's Word enshrines
them. Human prejudice may war against
God's laws but it cannot change them. Then
let us cleave to the Lord Who changes not and
to the Word of His grace.

                —*Indian Christian*

(Acts 17. 24-27; Mal. 3. 6; Heb. 1. 10-12)

1110. Unchanging God.

'We are shaking the world,' he said—
'With our conflict of black shirt and red.
We are clearing the stage
For a saner age,
And the old taboos are dead.'
Said the old, old woman, 'Shake on!
I have watched men shaking this eighty years, my
*   son.'*

'We have conquered the air,' he said,
'And distance and time are fled.
Our liners race
Through realms of space
With their silver wings outspread.'
Said the old, old woman, 'Such fuss!
The birds could do it before they heard of us.'

'We have finished with God,' said he.
'From the shackles of myth break free!
There is little need
Of an outworn creed,
And a futile Deity.
Said the old, old woman, 'Let be!
God sits at my fireside, waiting to talk with me.'
(Isa. 40. 21-23; 43. 11; Mal. 3. 6)

1111. Unchanging Christ.

When from my life the old-time joys have vanished—
Treasures, once mine, I may no longer claim—
This truth may feed my hungry heart, and famished:—
Lord, Thou remainest! Thou art still the same!

When streams have dried, those streams of glad refreshing—
Friendships so blest, so pure, so rich, so free;
When sun-kissed skies give place to clouds depressing—
Lord, Thou remainest, still my heart hath Thee.

When strength hath failed, and feet, now worn and weary,
On gladsome errands may no longer go—
Why should I sigh, or let the days be dreary?
Lord, Thou remainest! Could'st Thou more bestow?

Thus through life's days—whoe'er or what may fail me—
Friends, friendships, joys—in small or great degree—
Songs may be mine—no sadness need assail me,
Since Thou remainest, and my heart hath Thee.
—J. Danson Smith

(Heb. 1. 11; 13. 8)

1112. Unchanging Christ.

'Thou remainest!' What a comfort in this transient scene of life,
When our hopes so full of promise crash to earth in life's mad strife.

'Thou remainest!' friends have failed us—friends that were, while skies were blue;
But as sorrow's darkening shadows overspread, they proved untrue.

'Thou remainest!' wealth has vanished; comforts too have taken wing;
Poor our lot of earthly treasure, yet our hearts can gaily sing.

'Thou remainest!' health has left us: bloom of youth has ebbed away,
Beauty gone and charm departed, things of time born for a day.

'Thou remainest!'—hope is kindled. Come what may, yes, weal or woe,
'Tis enough our hearts to comfort—'He remains!' all else may go.
(Heb. 1. 11; 13. 8)

1113. Unfailing God.

He faileth not, for He is God:
He faileth not: He's pledged His Word:
He faileth not: He'll see you through,
This God with whom we have to do.
(Zeph. 3. 5; Josh. 1. 5; 21. 45; 23. 14)

1114. Unity. Mr. J. A. Abbott, Vice-President of the L.A.D. Motors Corporation of Brooklyn, spoke to the employees of his organization on the subject of Loyalty and Co-operation. He closed his address with this ringing verse from Kipling's *Second Jungle Book*:

'Now this is the Law of the Jungle—as old and as true as the sky;
And the Wolf that shall keep it may prosper, but the Wolf that shall break it must die.
As the creeper that girdles the tree-trunk, the Law runneth forward and back—
For the strength of the Pack is the Wolf, and the strength of the Wolf is the Pack.'
—Dale Carnegie
(Ps. 133. 1-3; Acts 1. 14; 4. 31, 32; Phil. 1. 27)

1115. Unity—Dwelling together in.

E'en as the ointment whose sweet odours blended
From Aaron's head upon his beard descended,
And, falling thence, with rich perfume ran o'er
The holy garb the High Priest wore:
So doth the unity that lives with brothers
Share its best blessings and its joys with others.
—Rumphuyzen
(Ps. 133; Gal. 3. 28; Eph. 4. 3)

1116. Unity—in Face of Enemy. If there is one thing more than another required in the Church of God to-day, it is that we present a united front to the enemy. There is a great need of aggressive unity. Just before the battle of Trafalgar, Nelson inquired of Admiral Collingwood where his captain was, and learned that he and Captain Rotherham were not on good terms with each other. Sending a boat for the captain, he placed the hands of Collingwood and Rotherham together, pointed to the enemy's ships, and earnestly looking them both in the face, he uttered the simple words: 'Look, yonder is the enemy.' It was enough; disagreements were forgotten, and victory was gained.
—Hy. Pickering

(Phil. 1. 27; 4. 2)

1117. Unity—in Face of Enemy. Achilles and Agamemnon were fighting in the Trojan War against the Trojans. At the siege of Troy, Achilles, in a fit of jealousy, sat sullen in his tent and refused to co-operate. This nearly lost the Greeks their victory over the Trojans.
(1 Cor. 1. 10; Phil. 4. 2)

1118. Unity. On a hot sultry night a small company of Christians was vainly trying to be comfortable on the front steps of a dwelling in a certain city in one of the Western States of America. Suddenly one of the party proposed that they all go to the prayer meeting at the 'First Church'. 'What put that notion into your head?' queried one of the party. 'Oh, it's so hot here, I can't stand it any longer. I thought if we went down there we would get cooled off. It is the coolest place I know.'

A member of an East London church was asked how they were getting on at the church of which he was a member. 'We are quite united,' he replied, 'for we are all frozen together.' Alas! there are perhaps many prayer meetings characterized by this type of unity.
(Acts 1. 14; 4. 31, 32; Jude 20)

1119. Unity—Family. There is in South India a story of a wealthy landowner who had some very quarrelsome sons, always jealous of one another and always at strife among themselves. On his deathbed he called them and divided his property among them. Then he called for some sticks to be brought, nicely tied into a bundle, and asked them one by one, beginning at the eldest, to break the bundle. So long as they were thus closely bound together, they could not break any of the sticks. 'Now,' he said to the eldest, 'untie the bundle, and try to break the sticks singly.' This was not difficult, and soon each of the sticks, broken one by one, lay before them in two pieces.

The father thus taught them that—united they stood: divided they fell.

(Acts 2. 1, 2; 4. 31, 32; Phil. 1. 27; 2. 2)

1120. Unity—Family. Coming together is a beginning: keeping together is progress: working together is success in the Christian assembly: for,

As One Flock, we are gathered together—John 10. 16

As One Family, we dwell together—Ps. 133. 1

As One Body, we are joined together—Eph. 4. 16

As One Temple, we are framed together—Eph. 2. 21

As One Household, we are built together—Eph. 2. 19, 20

As One Kingdom, we are to strive together—Phil. 1. 27

As One Hierarchy, we are raised up together—Eph. 2. 6.

1121. Unity—Maintaining. In 1747 there arose differences and disunity among the Moravian brethren, a group of local churches whose influence and missionary effort were widespread. Count Zinzendorf, with representative elders, arranged to hold a Conference at which the differing views on the subject of their controversy might be aired and discussed amicably among themselves. The leaders came—some from long distances to the place at which the Conference was to be held, arriving on the appointed day, each prepared to contest the view he supported and confident that it would receive the acceptance of the majority. They arrived about the middle of a week.

In his wisdom Count Zinzendorf proposed that they should spend some time over the Word and in prayer, and suggested a Bible Reading. The book chosen was the first Epistle of John, and they spent the remaining days till the end of the week becoming familiar with the teachings of that letter, and learning that one of its main lessons was 'love for all the brethren'. They agreed that on the first day of the week, like the disciples in the early Church, they should come together to break bread, and in so doing were reminded that they, being many, were 'one Body!' The reading and study of God's Word and the fellowship at the Lord's Supper had a very salutary effect on all, and the result was that when, on Monday morning, they commenced to examine the matters on which they differed, their differences and disputes were quickly settled, each bowing to the Word of God and thus helping to 'keep the unity of the Spirit in the bond of peace'.

(1 Cor. 10. 16-17; Eph. 4. 3; Phil. 1. 10)

1122. Universe. Imagine a mighty globe described in space, a globe of such stupendous dimensions that it shall include the sun and his system, all the stars and nebulae, and even all the objects which our finite capacities can imagine. Yet, what ratio must the volume of this great globe bear to the whole extent of infinite space? The ratio is infinitely less than that which the water in a single drop of dew bears to the water in the whole Atlantic Ocean.

—Sir Robert S. Ball

(Ps. 19. 1; Isa. 40. 12)

1123. Unprincipled people. Captain Anything in the 'Holy War' was an accommodating creature, not much concerned about which side he served so long as it was safe. Dean Swift called a man of his type an 'Anythingarian', and Dante showed his regard for this unsatisfactory creature by giving the 'Anythings' a very unpleasant place in his 'Inferno'.

The man who takes sides may have his embarrassments, but the man who refuses to take sides does not escape embarrassments. He often finds that his neutral position only increases and aggravates them. 'Mr. Anything,' says Bunyan, 'became a brisk man in a broil, but both sides were against him because he was true to none.'

—John Macbeath

Mr. Anything probably believes that—

'A merciful Providence fashioned him hollow
That he might the better his principles swallow.'
(Gal. 4. 9)

1124. Urim and Thummim. A preacher in England had frequent conversations with an uneducated cobbler who, nevertheless, was well acquainted with the Word of God.

One day he mentioned the cobbler's remarkable knowledge of the Bible to a young friend. His friend boasted that he could ask some questions the cobbler would not be able to answer. On being introduced to the man, the visitor asked, 'Can you tell me what the Urim and Thummim were?' The cobbler replied, 'I don't know exactly; I understand that the words apply to something that was on the breastplate of the high priest. I know the words mean "Lights and Perfection" and that through the Urim and Thummim the high priest was able to discern the mind of the Lord. But I find that I can get the mind of the

Lord by just changing a few letters. I take this blessed Book, and by usin' and thummin' it, I get the mind of the Lord.'

—Dr. H. A. Ironside

(Exod. 28. 30; Ezra 2. 61-63; Deut. 33. 8; Ps. 119. 105; Col. 1. 9)

1125. Usefulness — Asses and Horses. Balaam's ass saw what her master could not see, and sat down in the way in defiance of Balaam, but in obedience to God. Then the ass spoke God's message to the perverse prophet after he had mercilessly beaten his beast three times. The ass saved Balaam. Not long ago an English duke and three companions were doing some Alpine climbing. A blizzard burst on them: the donkey refused to go a step forward. A couple of guides came to the rescue and found that they (donkey and all) were within a step or two of a deep crevasse. The donkey had saved them. Men can be more stupid than donkeys. In England about thirty years ago a poor widow lived with her three girls. She took in washing for a living. Once she had no bread, and, kneeling down, she prayed, 'Lord, if you will only send food for the children, I don't mind for myself.' A knock came to the door, and the baker asked if she wanted any bread that day. 'No, thank you,' she said, for she would not go into debt for anything. The baker drove his van to the next street. Suddenly the horse bolted back and stood at the widow's house. Knocking again, the baker asked the same question and got the same answer. This time the baker whipped his horse and drove off to a street further on. For the third time the horse ran back. Addressing the widow, the baker said: 'My horse has come back here three times, and I don't understand it at all. It's something far above my thinking. I've had the horse fifteen years and she's never done such a thing before, so I'm going to give you all that's left in the van.' Several loaves of bread as well as other foodstuffs were handed to the widow. Now, if God can use asses, can He not use the weakest of us? If God can use horses, can He not use all of us? One more question? If the widow had gone into debt to buy bread that day, would God have wrought for her in such a wonderful way?

—Alpha in the *Indian Christian*

(Num. 22. 28; Matt. 21. 7)

1126. Valley—Passing through.

We are passing through the Valley,
    And the road is sometimes steep,
And the mountains all around us
    Often make the shadows deep.
'Tis the narrow Vale of Baca,
    'Tis the valley full of shade;
But we're only passing through it,
    So we need not be afraid.

Far away the land of Beulah
    Wrapped in sunlight may be seen,
And this little bit of valley
    Is now all that lies between.
Just beyond it is the sunshine,
    Just beyond it is our home.
When we reach it, 'twill not matter
    By what valley we have come.

One there is Who trod the Valley,
    And He suffered much from thirst.
He was weary, worn and footsore
    As He trod the way the first.
But His footsteps made the pathway
    Which we now may safely tread,
And it makes the road more easy
    When we know He's just ahead.

Just before He left the Valley
    And emerged into the light,
All His friends He gathered round Him
    E'er He vanished out of sight.
Words of comfort then were spoken
    To the travellers in the vale.
Not one promise that He made them
    Has been ever known to fail.

—W. D. Morrow

(Ps. 23. 4; 84. 6; Isa. 43. 1, 2; John 16. 33)

1127. Valley—Vision across.

I stood upon the hillside
    In driving mist and rain.
The wind was round me whistling
    A sobbing, sad refrain.
But away across the valley
    The hill was bathed in light,
And in its golden glory
    Was radiantly bright.

But would I reach that hillside
    This valley I must tread:
The glory of the sunlight
    Is to the valley wed.
And so, methought, how often
    The story of our years
Is but a glimpse of glory
    Through vision cleared by tears.

—F. H. Oakley

(Deut. 11. 11; 1 Sam. 17. 3; 1 Kings 20. 28; Luke 3. 5)

1128. Values.

'Rabbi! begone! Thy Powers
Bring loss to us and ours:
Our ways are not as Thine—
Thou lovest men—we, swine.
Oh get Thee gone, Omnipotence, and take this
    fool of Thine!
His soul? What care we for his soul? Since we
    have lost our swine.'
The Christ went sadly: He had wrought for them
    a sign
Of love and tenderness divine—
They wanted swine!
Christ stands without your door and gently
    knocks,
But if your gold or swine the entrance blocks,
He forces no man's hold, He will depart
And leave you to the treasures of your heart.

—John Oxenham

(Mark 5. 15-18)

1129. Vanity Fair. Then I saw in my dream, that when they were gone out of the wilderness, they presently saw a town before them, and the name of that town was 'Vanity'; and at that town there is a fair kept called Vanity Fair because the town where it is kept is lighter than vanity; and also because all that is there sold, or that cometh thither, is vanity.

The fair is no new-erected business, but a thing of ancient standing. I will show you the original of it.

Almost five thousand years ago, there were pilgrims walking to the Celestial City, as these two honest persons were; and Beelzebub, Appolyon and Legion, with their companions, perceiving the path that the pilgrims made, that the way to the city lay through this town of Vanity, they contrived here to set up a fair; a fair wherein should be sold all sorts of vanity; therefore at this fair are all such merchandises sold, as houses, lands, trades, places, honours, preferments, titles, countries, kingdoms, lusts, pleasures, and delights of all sorts as whores, bawds, wives, husbands, children, masters, servants, lives, blood, bodies, souls, silver, gold, pearls, precious stones and what not.

Now, as I said, the way to the Celestial City lies just through this town, and he that will go to the City, and yet not go through this town, must needs go out of the world. The Prince of princes Himself, when here, went through this town to His own country.

Now these pilgrims, as I said, must needs go through this fair. Well, so they did: but behold, even as they entered into the fair, all the people of the fair were moved and the town itself as it were in a hubbub about them, and that for several reasons:

First, the pilgrims were clothed with such kind of raiment as was diverse from the raiment of any that traded in the fair. The people, therefore, made a great gazing upon them: some said they were fools, some they were bedlams, and some they were outlandish men.

Secondly, and as they wondered at their apparel, so they did likewise at their speech, for few could understand what they said; they naturally spoke the language of Canaan, but they that kept the fair the men of the world; so that, from one end of the fair to the other, they seemed barbarians each to the other.

Thirdly, but that which did not a little amuse the merchandisers was, that these pilgrims set very light by all their wares; they cared not so much as to look upon them, and if they called upon them to buy, they would put their fingers in their ears, and cry, 'Turn away mine eyes from beholding vanity,' and look upwards, signifying that their trade and traffic was in heaven.
(Eccles. 1. 2; 2. 11; Eph. 4. 17)
                                        —Pilgrim's Progress

1130. Vessel—Meet for the Master. When King George V was opening the Conference on Disarmament, a special room was prepared in New York so that the king's message might be relayed through the United States of America. Just at the critical moment, a man tripped over the cable and broke it, and twenty minutes would be required to repair it. Something had to be done.

Mr. Vivian, who was in charge, threw himself into the breach, seized one end of the cable in one hand and the other end in the other, and stood there as the king's message passed through his body. Then he fell down and was taken to hospital. His body was the vessel used to convey, uninterrupted, the king's message.
(Phil. 1. 20; 2 Tim. 2. 21; 4. 11)

1131. Vicarious Death.
> *In peace let me resign my breath*
> *And Thy salvation see.*
> *My sins deserve eternal death,*
> *But Jesus died for me.*

These lines were written by Dr. Valpy, who gave them to a friend Dr. Marsh, the author of the *Life of Captain Hedley Vicars*, and the verse became a great blessing to him. Dr. Marsh gave the lines to his friend, Lord Roden, who was so impressed that he got Dr. Marsh to write them out, and then fastened the paper over the mantelpiece in his study. There, yellow with age, they hung for many years.

Some time after this an old friend, General Taylor, one of the heroes of Waterloo, came to visit Lord Roden at Tollymore Park. Lord Roden noticed that the eyes of the old veteran were fixed for a few moments on the motto over the mantelpiece.

'Why, General,' said Lord Roden, 'you will soon know those lines by heart.'

'I know them now by heart,' replied the General with feeling—and the simple words were the means of bringing him to know the way of salvation. Some two years after, the physician who had been with the old General while he lay dying, wrote to Lord Roden to say that his friend had gone, and that his last words were Dr. Valpy's lines which he had learnt to love in his lifetime.

Years afterwards, at the house of a neighbour, Lord Roden happened to tell the story of the old General and these lines; and among those who heard it was a young officer in the British army. He listened carelessly enough. A few months later, Lord Roden received a message from the officer that he wanted to see him, as he was in a rapid decline. As the Earl entered, the dying officer extended both his hands and repeated the lines, adding, 'That is God's message of comfort and peace to me in this illness.'

And so the simple lines presenting the vicarious death of the Lord Jesus Christ for sinners became a blessing to many.
(1 Cor. 15. 3; Gal. 2. 20; 1 Pet. 3. 18)

1132. **Vicarious Death.** In the North of Scotland, where the main railway line crosses a gulley—bridged by a viaduct—one night a fearful storm raged, and the little burn under the viaduct became a raging torrent.

A young shepherd, a Highland laddie, sheltered his sheep as best he could for the night, and in the morning, long before dawn, he set out to see how they fared. As he made his way up the hillside he noticed, to his dismay, that the central column of the viaduct had gone, and the bridge was broken. He knew the mail train was due and, if not warned, would be dashed to pieces and many lives lost. He made his way up as best he could, wondering if he would be in time. As soon as he reached the rails he heard the pound of the mighty engine. He stood and beckoned wildly, but the engine-driver, making up time, drove on. The train drew nearer, and still he stood, beckoning it to stop. At last it came to where he stood, and he flung himself in front of the engine. The driver applied the brakes and managed to stop the train in its own length. The stop was sudden and the passengers, awakened, came to see what was the matter. The driver said,

'It has been a close shave this time. We might all have been lost. Come and I'll show you the one who saved us tonight.'

A little way along they saw the mangled remains of the shepherd laddie who gave his life for them, dying that they might live.
(1 Thess. 5. 10; Tit. 2. 13, 14)

1133. **Vicarious Sufferings.**

Wounded for me, wounded for me:
There on the cross He was wounded for me.

Lady Kinnaird used to relate the following story. The Duke of Windsor, then Prince of Wales, arranged to visit a hospital in London where some of the sorest wounded and mutilated soldiers in the first Great World War were being treated. The Medical Superintendent met him and was showing him round. 'I hear you have in this hospital some of the worst-wounded men in the War,' said the Prince. 'How many altogether?' On learning that there were 36, the Prince asked to be permitted to go round their ward and see them all. He was taken into a ward, and saw badly wounded soldiers all lying comfortable in the hospital beds, and receiving the best attention. He went round the ward, had a cheery word for all, made enquiries as to their near relatives, wives, families, etc., and encouraged them with words of hopefulness. Then, turning to the Medical Officer, he said, 'Doctor! you told me there were 36 badly wounded men: I have only seen 30 in this ward. Where are the other six?' 'Your Highness!' said the doctor, 'the others are in such a pitiable condition that we thought it well to spare you the pain of visiting them.' 'But, doctor, I must see them all, every one.' So they went on into another ward where lay five men, terribly disfigured and wounded,

some of them blind, some having lost limbs, and all just physical wrecks. The Prince was deeply moved, and showed his affection for the men in every possible way, speaking words of cheer and comfort. 'But where is the thirty-sixth man?' he asked. 'I must see him also.' The Medical Superintendent, realising that the Prince was not to be put off, led him into a ward apart, where lay a young man in a very pitiable condition—blind, disfigured, maimed —a wreck of a fine physique he had once possessed. The Prince, stooping down, kissed the man on the forehead, and, as he rose, with tears streaming down his cheeks, he turned to the doctor and said, 'Doctor, wounded for me, wounded for me.'
(Isa. 53. 5; Rom. 4. 25)

1134. **Victory.** The news of the result of the Battle of Waterloo was eagerly awaited by the people of Great Britain, for so much depended on it. Somehow or other the message came with one word short, and only two words got across—'Wellington defeated'. The country was plunged into mourning, and great was the lamentation until the mistake was discovered, and the omitted third word arrived—'Napoleon —so that it read 'Wellington defeated Napoleon'. Their sorrow was turned into joy, and great rejoicings followed the mourning. Christ was the glorious Victor at the Cross, where so much for the whole world depended on the issues of the conflict with Satan.

In what might seem defeat
He won the meed and crown,
Trod all our foes beneath His feet
By being trodden down.

(Col. 2. 15)

1135. **Victory.** It is told of Hannibal that when he came, in utter amazement and grief, into the presence of his father who had been crucified by the Romans, he lifted up his hand before that Roman cross and swore by all his gods that he would fight to the death the power that had crucified his father.

The Christian's conflict is with sin and Satan in light of the Cross, and in all these things 'we are more than conquerors through Him that loved us'.
(Rom. 8. 37; 1 Cor. 15. 57; Heb. 12. 2-4)

1136. **Victory—at the last.** Some of us have been like the tribe of Gad, of whom we read in Gen. 49. 19, 'A troop shall overcome him; but he shall overcome at the last.' Our adversaries for a while were too many for us, they came upon us like a troop. Yes, and for the moment they overcame us, and they exulted greatly because of their temporary victory. Thus they only proved the first part of the heritage to be really ours, for Christ's people, like Gad, shall have a troop overcoming them.

This being overcome is very painful, and we should have despaired if we had not by faith believed the second line of our Father's benediction, 'He shall overcome at the last.' 'All's well that ends well,' said the poet, and he spoke the truth. A war is to be judged, not by first successes or defeats, but by that which happens 'at the last'. The Lord will give to truth and righteousness victory 'at the last', and, as Mr. Bunyan says, that means for ever, for nothing can come after 'the last'.

—C. H. Spurgeon

(Rom. 8. 36, 37; Rev. 5. 5, 10)

1137. Victory through Trust in Christ. A painter once painted the devil playing a game of chess with a young man whose eternal soul was at stake. The scene showed the devil with a look of glee on his face as he checkmates the young man whose look of despair acknowledges defeat. There appears no other move for him to make.

A great chess player came across the work of art and, after carefully studying the game, he set up a chess board with the pieces in a similar position. After much thought and time, he saw that defeat could be turned into victory. By making just one certain move on the young man's behalf, the devil was placed in a position of utter defeat.

In the game of life, youth has no chance against the wiles of the devil who is determined to ruin the soul. But at Calvary the Lord Jesus intervened and made a 'move' that enables youth today, who trust in Christ, to have complete victory.

'Thanks be unto God Who giveth us the victory through our Lord Jesus Christ.'

—*Youth for Christ Magazine*

(Rom. 8. 37; 1 Cor. 15. 57)

1138. Vine. The world's biggest vine is reputed to be found in Scotland—a country with a cold, uninviting climate. Known as the Kippen vine, it was planted 65 years ago, covers 8 acres, and 8 men and women work on it all the year round. It produces an average annual crop of 2,000 bunches of grapes. Cuttings from this vine have been sold to growers in Commonwealth countries, to Switzerland, and even to sunny Spain. Every year thousands of people from all over the world come to see it. Despite adverse climatic conditions this vine grows on. These climatic hindrances have been brought under control.

—*Indian Christian*

(John 15. 1-8; Rom. 5. 5; Gal. 5. 22)

1139. Virgin Mary. A little lad in Central Africa had learned to read the New Testament in the mission school. Some time later, the Roman Catholic fathers persuaded him to be baptized into the Roman Catholic Church. They gave him a medal to wear on which was a representation of the virgin. 'It will be easier for you to pray when you look at that,' they said, 'and the mother of Jesus will pray to her Son for you.'

Several months passed, and the boy returned to the evangelical mission. Asked the reason why he did not go to the Catholics, he said, 'I read in the Gospels that Mary lost Jesus when she was on a journey; so I thought, if she forgot her own little boy, she will surely forget me: so I am going to pray straight to Jesus.'

—The Good Samaritan

(Luke 2. 44-49; John 2. 5)

1140. Vision—Clear.

The glories of the sunrise sky
That greet the dawn of day
We all may see but must rise up:
Yes, it is MUST, not MAY.

Yet even then a little thing,
If held too near the eye,
Can hide the vast expanse o'erhead:
Yes, even hide the sky.

So help me, Lord, to vision clear
Throughout the coming day,
To see, and know that Thou art near
To guide me in Thy way.

—F. H. Oakley

(Acts 26. 19; Eph. 1. 18, 19)

1141. Vision—Spiritual. Among his stories of the great Revival in Scotland, Woodrow tells of a devout minister, who, once a year, visited a distant parish. On the road he was accustomed to alight from his grey pony at a little wayside inn nestling in a lonely hollow out among the heather-covered hills. When he drew rein for the first time at this cosy little hostelry, the daughter of the house tripped out and took charge of his beast. He at once became interested in her. She was a typical Scots lassie, with rosy cheeks and laughing eyes, who did everything in her power to make his visit restful and pleasant. Eager to make the most of the opportunity, he engaged the girl in conversation and soon came to grips on the matter of her soul's salvation.

Unable to lead her to a definite decision, he extracted a promise that, until they met again, she would daily offer a prayer, 'Lord, shew me myself!' On his return a year later, the sparkle and gaiety had vanished, the brightness had left her eyes, and she could talk of nothing but her wickedness and waywardness, her faithlessness and her need. He again tried to persuade her to trust the Saviour, but she could not believe such love could be intended for her.

She promised again to offer another daily prayer he taught her, 'O Lord, shew me Thyself.' On his return the next year he saw in her face settled peace and overflowing gratitude. The first prayer brought her to herself: the second gave her a vision of her Saviour and led her to Him.

(Isa. 6. 1-7)

1142. Voice—Echo of our Master's. Crossing the Channel the other day, as we were nearing the pier, we heard a loud clear voice ringing over the boat. It came from a small dirty-looking boy standing near the engine-room. We could not hear what he said, but we could feel that the great wheels were beginning to revolve more slowly.

Again the clear tones were heard, and suddenly the motion of the engines was reversed and the paddles began to turn in an opposite direction. At first it appeared as if the boy had the entire control of the vessel, and certainly he seemed quite capable of guiding her.

The orders he gave were with authority, and with the utmost confidence; there was no hesitation in his manner or in his voice. On approaching nearer to him the mystery was explained.

His eyes were intently fixed on the little bridge above his head, where stood the captain. It was some time, however, before we discovered how he gave his orders to the boy. He seldom spoke, and then but a word, and yet the boy kept shouting down below as if moved by some unseen power.

At last we found that it was by short, sharp movements of the hand that the captain gave his orders. Quite unintelligible as they were to us, to the boy all was clear, every movement had its meaning, and no sooner did a little wave of the hand say 'forward' than the voice was heard, 'Full speed ahead', and instantly the mighty engines moved in obedience.

We pondered over this, and wished we were more like the captain's boy. The boy was (like John the Baptist of old) simply 'a voice', but as the Baptist's voice derived all its importance because it was the Lord's, so did the boy's because it was but an echo of the captain's.

—Dr. A. T. Schofield

(Matt. 3. 3; John 1. 23)

1143. Voyage—Guidance on Life's. The Captain of the ship is the man who might be supposed to know. He is a specialist. And Paul sets over against his nautical erudition the unsatisfying words, 'I perceive'. It is a case of Reason on the one hand and Revelation on the other.

That is the exact point at which the world has always missed its way. Adam believed the captain of the ship. Later Noah predicted a flood. Again the insistent voice of Revelation was scouted.

There can be no doubt about it. The unseen world is the triumphant world. The spiritual is, after all, the sane and safe. The only way of avoiding shipwreck in Church and State is clearly to pay heed to 'the things spoken by Paul'.

—Dr. F. W. Boreham

(Acts 27. 10, 11)

1144. Voyage—Shipwreck and its cause. An old pilot, trusted and wise, one night many years ago, was taking his vessel up between the coasts of Wales and Ireland. He had been over the course innumerable times without disaster. This night, nearing port and home, he was running full steam ahead. With his keen eye he watched compass and chart. Suddenly with a sickening, crashing sound, on the hidden rocks went the vessel. Loss of life, loss of ship, marked the wreck. Later, in investigating the wreckage, close and interested examination revealed that someone, in seeking to clean or tamper with the compass, had slipped a thin knife blade into the compass box, near the needle, and the blade had broken off. That little piece of foreign steel was sufficient to deflect, though only slightly, the needle by which the clear-eyed pilot was steering the boat. When he thought he was on the true course, he was really rushing toward the rocks. Such a little thing—such a mighty wreck!

(1 Kings 13. 11-26; James 3. 4)

1145. Vows. There is a story in India of one who went on a voyage to another country and was returning by ship to his own country when they encountered stormy seas. In great fear of drowning he prayed to his god, and vowed to sacrifice ten fat oxen if his life were saved. The storm passed over and the sea became calm again.

Before he landed at the port, he reconsidered his promise of ten oxen, and thought the god might be satisfied with five. On his way home, he again thought over his vow, and feared he was still too generous, so he vowed to sacrifice two oxen if he reached home safely without mishap.

Arrived home, he retired to rest, but could not sleep, and vowed that he would the next day take one fat bullock from his herd and make a public sacrifice to his god in thanksgiving for his preservation and safe return. But, awaking in the night, he again changed his mind, and thought his goat might be a good substitute for an ox. When he told his wife the next morning that he intended offering the one goat they had to their god in gratitude for the preservation of his life, she strongly objected, saying that it had just begun to give a seer of milk daily and she could not afford to lose that milk. 'All right,' said he, 'I shall take to the temple a large basket of peanuts: and these will surely be better and more pleasing to the god than an animal sacrifice.' So he prepared the basket of peanuts and was on his way to the temple, when it occurred to him that he had not tasted peanuts for some considerable time. So he began to take a few and liked them so well that he had eaten them all by the time he reached the temple. All that was left to pay the vow that he had made was a basket of husks.

(Deut. 12. 10, 11; 23. 23; Eccles. 5. 5; Mal. 1. 14)

1146. Vows. A Christian in a South Indian town where there was a large assembly, lay at death's door with typhoid fever. At that time the assembly was very poor and met in a schoolroom 150 years old, and too small for the congregation of God's people. They very much needed a hall sufficiently spacious for the increasing numbers being added to the local church, and there was only Rs.2,000 in hand.

The sick brother then made a vow that, if the Lord restored him to health, he would provide a commodious hall for the local assembly. When he recovered from his sickness, Satan tempted him to break his vow and withhold the money, but the Lord had the victory and the hall was built and called 'Bethany', which means 'the house of the poor'. It not only provided what was so much needed for the assembly but became, as the years passed, the birthplace of many souls. The brother who fulfilled his vow and gave so generously for the construction of the hall was granted renewed health and prospered in his business.

(Gen. 28. 20; Judg. 11. 39; Eccles. 5. 4, 5)

1147. Waiting on the Lord. Frequently a merchant receives—a day or two ahead—a card from a firm of manufacturers or suppliers to this effect: 'Our Mr. — — will have the pleasure of waiting on you on such and such a day.' The commercial traveller arrives and waits, not outside the shop door, but inside. He sits or stands in the presence of the merchant, converses with him in a friendly way, and expects to receive an order for supplies. If he receives none, he takes leave and promises to wait on him again when the merchant's stock is less.

In exactly the same way God wants us to wait upon Him, not at a distance, but in His presence, within the veil.

(Isa. 40. 31; Prov. 8. 34; Heb. 10. 19)

1148. Walking with God.

He 'walked with God!' Could grander words be written?
Not much of what he thought or said is told:
Not where or what he wrought is even mentioned;
He 'walked with God'—brief words of fadeless gold!

How many souls were succoured on his journey—
Helped by his words, or prayers, we may not know;
Still, this we read—words of excelling grandeur,
He walked with God while yet he walked below.

And, after years, long years, of such blest walking,
One day he walked, then was not, God said 'Come!
Come from the scene of weary sin-stained sadness!
Come to the fuller fellowship of Home!'

Such be the tribute of thy pilgrim journey
When life's last mile thy feet have bravely trod—
When thou hast gone to all that there awaits thee,
This simple epitaph—'He walked with God'.
                                   —J. Danson Smith

(Gen. 5. 22-24; Heb. 11. 5)

1149. Warning—The Divine.

There is a time we know not when, a place we know not where,
That marks the destiny of men for glory or despair.
There is a line by us unseen that crosses every path,
That marks the boundary between God's patience and His wrath.
To pass that limit is to die, to die as if by stealth:
It does not dim the beaming eye or pale the glow of health.
The conscience may be still at ease, the spirits light and gay:
That which is pleasing still may please, and care be thrust away.
But on that forehead God has set indelibly a mark
Unseen by man, for man as yet is blind and in the dark.
And yet the doomed man's path below as Eden may have bloomed:
He did not, does not, will not know, or feel that he is doomed.
He thinks, he feels that all is well: his every fear is calmed;
He lives, he dies, he wakes in hell not only doomed but damned.
O! where is this mysterious bourne by which our path is crossed
Beyond which God Himself hath sworn that he who goes is lost?
How long may we go on in sin? How long will God forbear?
Where does hope end, and where begin the confines of despair?
An answer from the skies is sent:—Ye who from God depart,
While it is called today, repent, and harden not your heart.

(Job. 36. 18; Heb. 3. 7, 8, 15; 4. 7)

1150. Warnings of Danger. The road signs for motorists on all main highways are instructive for travellers to eternity. Dangerous crossings or bends are indicated before the motorist comes to them, and we are warned to 'Keep Death off the road', and to pursue a 'Safety first' policy in preference to speeding. Frequently too the warning is reinforced by a large hoarding containing the words—'You have been warned'.

God's Word is replete with warnings to travellers to eternity, so that none can say they have not been warned.

(Ps. 19. 11; Ezek. 33. 4-6; Matt. 3. 7; Acts 20. 31)

1151. Water of Life. A ship in distress off the Canadian coast, with its fresh water supply completely exhausted, sent out an S.O.S. for fresh water. The reply came back immediately: 'Let your buckets down!' They had sailed into the fresh water of the River St. Lawrence. (Rev. 21. 6; 22. 17)

1152. Water Supply. Water, water everywhere! The atmosphere often contains as much as 50,000 tons of water over one square mile of the earth's surface at summer temperature. All our food contains water—in watery fruits as much as 95 per cent. About 70 per cent of the human body is water.

In industry the great raw material is water. It takes 10 gallons of water to produce one gallon of petrol; 24 gallons to produce a pound of paper; 70 gallons to make a pound of woollen cloth; and 65,000 gallons to produce a ton of highly finished steel. In highly industrialized countries the need of still greater supplies of water is of paramount importance. Water supply is a big industry in the U.S.A. By weight of material handled it is 7 times as big as all other industries put together.

In Iceland there is an abundance of drinking water, so pure and clear and free from bacteria that no purification is needed. Springs of hot water are used for heating houses, schools and public buildings, and this hot water is so clean that it corrodes neither concrete nor iron and can be used even in cooking. In India how much we would appreciate such a boon!

The Bible has a lot to say about water. In John's Gospel, for example, chapter after chapter is occupied with it. Pots of water, a well of water, pools of water, a lake of water, rivers of water, and a basin of water (chapters 2, 4, 5, 6, 7, 9, and 13). John tells us how Christ transformed the water, drank of the water, and walked on the water (2. 9; 4. 7; 6. 19). The disciples baptized in it and the Lord applied spiritual lessons from the water. But in chapter 5 He dispensed with the need of it. Why?

The sick folks at the pool of Bethesda were looking to the water instead of looking to the Lord Who provided it. How sad that men should be occupied with the creature or the created thing rather than with the Creator.

When the Lord took the poor impotent man's case in hand it is not surprising that He healed him without any reference to the water. This man had been an invalid for years before Christ was born in Bethlehem, but in an instant the Saviour loosed him from his long-standing sickness and made him fully whole. This wasn't a water-cure but a wonder-cure genuinely and miraculously wrought by the divine Healer, and all without money and without price.

The moral is clear and plain. Make sure that you go straight to the Lord Himself for deliverance when the need arises.

Now the frail vessel Thou hast made, No hand
but Thine can fill—

The waters of the earth have failed, And I am
thirsty still.
Oh! Peace of God that passeth thought, I daily
hourly sing,
My heart is at the secret source of every living
thing.
—A. Soutter

(John 4. 10; 5. 3)

1153. Way to Heaven. A gentleman was driving in his car through a town in Renfrewshire, Scotland, the town of Kilmacolm, and stopped to hail a roadmender and ask him please to tell him the way to Glasgow. After giving him explicit directions, the roadmender asked, 'Excuse me, sir, but do you know the way to Heaven?' 'No, I don't,' replied the gentleman in the car. 'Jesus said, "I am the Way",' said the roadmender. Thanking him, the man drove on to Glasgow, turning over in his mind the roadmender's words. On his return to London, the same man was involved in a fatal road accident, and taken to hospital where, after arranging his affairs, he died. Ten days later two young men wearing black ties, and in deep mourning, arrived in the town of Kilmacolm, enquiring for a roadmender who, as a witness for the Lord Jesus Christ, had told their father the way to Heaven. He had commissioned them to take the journey after the funeral service was over, and to thank the Christian roadmender for pointing out the way to Heaven when he showed their father the way to Glasgow: 'and,' they added, 'he understood and is now in Heaven.' (John 14. 6)

1154. Ways of God. God's ways are behind the scenes, and He moves all the scenes He is behind.
—J. N. Darby

(Ps. 77. 13-19)

1155. Ways of God.
His ways are ways of pleasantness,
And all His paths are peace.
His words are words of graciousness
And love which ne'er shall cease.
His works are works of holiness
And victory over sin.
His wounds are wounds of tenderness:
He only wounds to win.
—F. H. Oakley

(Ps. 18. 30; Prov. 3. 17)

1156. Will of God.
His Plan for today is all that I ask;
With Him I can leave the 'Tomorrow'.
So by faith I can walk, and with Him I can talk:
Just today, with its joy or its sorrow,
He my pathway hath planned, and, led by His
hand,
Through the fire while the gold He's refining,
Be it trial or test, He knows what is best,
So I travel where love's light is shining.

With no plan of my own, but with Him on the
   Throne,
   And to Him all my problems confiding,
He gives me a song as I journey along,
   And His 'fulness of joy' is abiding.
Though the path may be steep, and the storm
   round me sweep,
   Yet my soul He is constantly feeding;
And my strength He renews and with fresh
   power endues,
   As I walk where my Master is leading.

Just His will for today, just to watch and to pray,
   To be still when to me He is speaking,
Just to kneel at His feet, in that secret retreat,
   Where His face I am constantly seeking.
His plan for today, let it bring what it may,
   Be it 'fulness of joy' or 'deep sorrow',
In His love let me rest, for He knows what is
   best,
   So with Him I can leave the 'tomorrow'.
                —Alfred Easterbrook
(Matt. 6. 34; Eph. 5. 17; Col. 1 .9)

1157. Will of God—How to ascertain.

1. I seek at the beginning to get my heart
into such a state that it has no will of its own
in regard to a given matter.

Nine-tenths of the trouble with people is
just here. Nine-tenths of the difficulties are
overcome when our hearts are ready to do the
Lord's will, whatever it may be. When one is
truly in this state, it is usually but a little way
to the knowledge of what His will is.

2. Having done this, I do not leave the result
to feeling or simple impression. If I do so, I
make myself liable to great delusions.

3. I seek the will of the Spirit of God through,
or in connection with, the Word of God.
The Spirit and the Word must be combined.
If I look to the Spirit alone without the Word
I lay myself open to great delusions also. If
the Holy Ghost guides us at all, He will do it
according to the Scriptures and never contrary
to them.

4. Next I take into account providential
circumstances. These often plainly indicate
God's will in connection with His Word and
Spirit.

5. I ask God in prayer to reveal His will to
me aright.

6. Thus, through prayer to God, the study of
the Word and reflection, I come to a deliberate
judgement according to the best of my ability
and knowledge, and if my mind is thus at
peace, and continues so after two or three
more petitions, I proceed accordingly.

In trivial matters, and in transactions
involving most important issues, I have found
this method always effective.
                —George Müller
(Rom. 12. 1, 2; Col. 1. 9)

1158. Witness.

Make me a witness, Lord,
   So faulty I and weak,
My trembling word can scarce be heard,
   So loud my failings speak.

Make me a witness, Lord;
   Subdue my will to Thine
That, led by Thee, in meek accord,
   My lamp may brightly shine.

Make me a witness, Lord,
   That all at home may see
A constant daily growth in grace,
   And glory give to Thee.

Make me a witness, Lord,
   To those I daily meet,
That I may be Thy messenger
   In neighbourhood and street.

Make me a witness, Lord,
   With every talent given;
And let my treasure all be stored
   In deepest vaults of heaven.

Make me a witness, Lord,
   By gift, and prayer, and pen,
In native land and far abroad
   Telling Thy love to men.

Make me a witness, Lord,
   And use me in Thy way;
Though sacrifices we applaud,
   'Tis better to obey.

Make me a witness, Lord;
   Thou needest even me;
How strange that I can aid afford
   When captives Thou wouldst free.

Make me a witness, Lord;
   That souls on Thee may call,
And glorify Thy name adored,
   O Jesus, Lord of all!
                —G. Alexander

(Acts 1. 8)

1159. Witness.
A thirteen-year old girl left
her village and was travelling to another place.
On the road a priest met her. He asked her,
'Child, I think you are a Christian. Is it
because your father is a Christian that you have
become a Christian?'

To that she replied, 'No, a Christian Sadhu
came to our house and preached. I thought
about it again and again. Then from my own
experience I knew that Christ was the Saviour.
That is why I became a Christian.'

The lama burned with anger. He took her
and shut her in a dark room, giving her no food
or water. The man was amazed to hear her
singing with great gladness. After four days
he went to see her. What was it that he saw
there? He did not see that poor child singing.
She was speaking quietly to someone, and
with eyes closed. What was she saying? The
lama tried to understand. This is what he
heard from her:

'O Lord, I thank Thee that I have received
the privilege of suffering for Thee. Lord, have
mercy on this lama. Open the eyes of his heart
to see the light.'

Hearing this sincere prayer, the man broke
down and cried. He fell at her feet and before
very long he accepted her words as he would

the words of a Guru. That lama told everyone he saw about the wonderful strength of the girl; and not only that, he desired to receive that wonderful strength himself.

—Sadhu Sundar Singh

(2 Kings 5. 2, 3; Acts 1. 8; 5. 41)

1160. Witness—To the Bible. When the train came in my colleague, Robertson, was glad to find an empty compartment, and as he sped through the rich fields of the County Clare, he refreshed himself with the fruits of the richer fields of the Word of God.

After some time the train stopped at a station, and a priest came in. Directly it started he courteously said: 'What is that book you are reading?' 'The Word of God,' replied Robertson. He was not ashamed to call the Bible the Word of God, for so had his Master and the inspired writers named it (Mark 7. 13; John 10. 35; Rom. 10. 17; 2 Cor. 2. 17).

The priest, expecting to hear the word 'Bible', looked somewhat confused at this answer, but after a moment or two of hesitation asked: 'How do you know it is the Word of God?'

'I know what you want me to say.'

'What do I want you to say?'

'You want me to say that I know it is the Word of God because your Church says so.'

'Well, how do you know it is God's Word?'

'By a threefold witness—The first, external; the second, internal; the third, personal. The external evidence is: that the Old Testament was given to us by the Hebrew Church, and the New Testament by the Greek Church, after a most minute safeguarding and transcription of the original documents by these Churches. Your Church had nothing whatever to do with the matter. The internal evidence is prophecy. There are thousands of predictions —some of them thousands of years old—in the books. Many of these have been fulfilled, others are now in the course of fulfilment; and the remainder will most certainly be fulfilled. These predictions were impossible to the keenest of human foresight. For instance, it was foretold that the Messiah should be born in a certain village; that on a certain day in a certain year He would ride into the city of Jerusalem seated on a colt the foal of an ass; that He would be crucified, and buried; and after three days rise again. All this came to pass exactly as foretold centuries beforehand. The personal evidence is that this Book is the only book that revealed me to myself. I learned from it that I am totally corrupt; that my heart is a depthless source of all forms of sin known and unknown; that I am incapable of self-recovery; and that no Church has power to give me a new moral nature. But the Book made a further revelation to me—it revealed Christ to me. It told me how He loved me, and how He suffered on the Cross, beneath the wrath of God, the full penalty of my sins, and of my sinful nature; and it assured me that if I committed myself by faith to Him, He would make Himself known to me inwardly; would

remove from my conscience the sense of guilt and fear; would fill my heart with joy and peace, and flood my whole being with divine love. I found all this to be true. He did reveal Himself to my heart. I know Him—I love Him—He has saved me from the wrath to come; and I have the joyful consciousness, by His Holy Spirit, that He will save me from wrath; and that His promise is true that whoever trusts Him shall never perish; and that all who rest their sinful souls upon Him and upon His precious blood, and upon His divine promises, never shall be, and never can be, confounded. So I know by personal experience that this Book is the Word of God.'

The priest had evidently never heard such a triple testimony in his life. His face betrayed the surprise, the confusion, the darkness, and the awe, which he felt. Just at this moment the train stopped at his station. He rose and, with a bow, left the carriage.

—George Williams

(Isa. 41. 21-23; 1 John 5. 9, 10)

1161. Witness—to Christ the Saviour. 'Witnesses unto Me.' George Cutting the author of *Safety, Certainty and Enjoyment*, when cycling past a cottage in a Norfolk village, felt it right to shout: 'Behold the Lamb of God that taketh away the sin of the world!' The impulse came a second time, and again he shouted. Six months after, visiting from house to house in that village, he entered the cottage. Asking the good woman if she was saved, she replied, 'Oh yes! Six months ago I was in great distress of soul; and while pleading for God's help, a voice cried: "Behold the Lamb of God that taketh away the sin of the world"; and when I asked God to repeat what He had said, the voice came again.'

(John 1. 29; Acts 1. 8)

1162. Witness—to Christ the Saviour. Sophie —of *Sophie's Sermons* fame—was a converted scrub woman who said that she was called to scrub and preach. She was made fun of by someone who said she was seen talking of Christ in front of a cigar store to a wooden Indian. Sophie replied, 'Maybe I did; my eyesight is not good any more. But talking to a wooden Indian about Christ is not as bad as being a wooden Christian and never witnessing about Christ to anyone.'

During the 1859 revival in Ireland an ignorant man was converted. He could do nothing more than tell what the Lord had done for his soul. He went over to Scotland to work in some mills there, and in the factory where he worked 1300 hands were employed. So great was the impression made upon them by his simple testimony that no less than 600 were led to Christ.

(Ps. 66. 16; Acts 1. 8; 4. 33)

1163. Wits' End Corner.

Are you standing at 'Wits' End Corner',
Christian, with troubled brow?
Are you thinking of what is before you
And all you are bearing now?
Does all the world seem against you,
And you in battle alone?
Remember—at Wits' End corner
Is just where God's power is shown.

Are you standing at Wits' End Corner,
Blinded with wearying pain,
Feeling you cannot endure it,
You cannot bear the strain,
Bruised through the constant suffering,
Dizzy and dazed and numb?
Remember—to Wits' End Corner
Is where Jesus loves to come.

Are you standing at Wits' End Corner,
Your work before you spread,
All lying, begun, unfinished
And pressing on heart and head,
Longing for strength to do it,
Stretching out trembling hands?
Remember—at Wits' End Corner
The Burden Bearer stands.

Are you standing at Wits' End Corner,
Yearning for those you love,
Longing and praying and watching,
Pleading their cause above,
Trying to lead them to Jesus,
Wond'ring if you've been true?
He whispers—at Wits' End Corner—
'I'll win them as I won you.'

Are you standing at Wits' End Corner?
Then you're just in the very spot
To learn the wondrous resources
Of Him Who faileth not!
No doubt to a brighter pathway
Your footsteps will soon be moved,
But only at Wits' End Corner
Is the 'God Who is able' proved.

(Ps. 34. 19; 107. 27)

1164. Wonders of Old. The Seven Wonders of the ancient world were:

1. The Great Pyramid
2. The Colossus of Rhodes (overthrown by an earthquake)
3. The Hanging Gardens of Babylon
4. The Temple of Diana in Ephesus
5. The Statue of Jupiter in Athens
6. The Halicarnassus (Mausoleum)
7. The Pharos Lighthouse at Alexandria.

But God's Wonders of old far exceed any and all of these.

(Ps. 77. 11, 14; 105. 5; Dan. 4. 2, 3)

1165. Wonders of God's Works. Queen Elizabeth—known as Good Queen Bess—had as her motto, graven on some of her coins, the words in Latin, 'A Domino factum est istud et mirabile oculis noris'. The English translation is: 'This is the Lord's doing and it is marvellous in our eyes.'

When she was told that she had become Queen of England, these were the words she uttered.

(Ps. 118. 23; Rom. 15. 19; Heb. 2. 4)

1166. Wonders of God's Works. A Scottish botanist sallied forth to the moors one bright morning to study his favourite flowers. He plucked a heather bell and put it upon the glass of his microscope. Stretching himself on the ground, he began to scrutinize it through his microscope. Moment after moment passed, and still he remained there, entranced by the beauty of the simple flower. Suddenly a shadow fell on the ground beside him, and, looking up, he saw a tall weather-beaten shepherd gazing down with a smile of half-concealed amusement at the man who was spending his time looking through a glass at so common a thing as a heather bell. The botanist handed him the glass and bade him have a look.

The shepherd took the microscope and looked through it at the little flower, then rose with tears streaming down his weather-beaten face. 'Isn't it beautiful?' asked the botanist. 'It's beautiful beyond words,' replied the shepherd, 'but oh! the thousands of times I've trampled them under my feet.'

(Matt. 6. 28, 29)

1167. Words. The authority of words depends on the speaker. A proclamation in words made ex-king Edward king. His own written words deprived him of his kingdom.

One day, when the Emperor Napoleon was reviewing his troops, his horse attempted to bolt. A private soldier sprang forward quickly and stopped it. 'Thank you, Captain,' said the Emperor. 'Of what regiment, sire?' asked the soldier. 'Of my guards,' was the reply. Walking over to a group of officers, the soldier announced his rank and was laughed at. 'Who said it?' asked they. 'The Emperor,' he replied; and that was enough.

(Ps. 89. 34; John 10. 35; 1 Pet. 1. 25)

1168. Work. In the Concordance the order is—Word, Work, Worker, World. It is the Word—God's Word—for the whole world; but, between the two and indispensable, are work and worker. Often the true sequence is reversed. Christians feel the need of the world, look for a work to do, and then turn to the Word for their message.

(Isa. 55. 11; Mark 16. 15; 2 Tim. 4. 2)

1169. Work—Life's. Holman Hunt, painter of 'The Light of the World', started life in a London office. The firm with which he was employed was engaged in the cotton trade. He drew flies on the window so well that his employer thought them real. Had he remained in the office, he would have missed his vocation.

H. G. Wells was first a draper's assistant, then a science master, and after that he found his life's work in writing.

David Livingstone, who spent so many years and endured so many hardships as a missionary in Africa, found his life's work right away, and, like Isaiah, responded to the call of the Lord, 'Here am I: send me'.

(Jer. 1. 5; 1 Tim. 1. 12, 13)

1170. **Work—Life's.** Our life's work is a complete whole, yet it is made up of little things, good works. 'We are God's workmanship': and the word Paul uses is the Greek word from which we derive the English word 'Poem'.

In her book *Odd Patterns in the Weaving*—Mrs. Sonia E. Howe in her narration mentions something seen when she was still in her teens. A famous Russian academician was working at a Mosaic, a copy of an old oil painting which had been in a famous Cathedral. He was putting in tiny pieces of marble, one by one, to carry out the beautiful design. Sonia Howe approached him and said, 'Is not this fearfully dull, uninteresting work?'

'No, not at all,' the artist replied, 'for, you see, it is work for eternity.'

(1 Cor. 15. 58; Col. 1. 28, 29)

1171. **World—Man of the: converted.** It is now many years since my friend Kilner was one of the shining lights of London, as he had just been the leading counsel in a well-known society law case concerning a certain celebrated pearl necklace.

'I remember it was about this time that his mother came to me in great distress. She and her only daughter were devoted and prayerful Christians, and had succeeded in persuading my brilliant friend, who was far from the fold, to go one night to the Metropolitan Tabernacle to hear Mr. Moody, who was then holding services in it. He had gone, and thence he went on to his club, and at midnight he returned home and knocked at his mother's bedroom door and told her with great emphasis and in strong language that it was the last religious service he would attend. "Mother," he said, "I love you and Dora, and never hope to do anything else; but I beg of you never to ask me to go to a service. I can't stand the stuff; the world is good enough for me".'

With these words Dr. A. T. Schofield commences his story of 'The West-end Barrister'. The doctor remembered that Kilner had a lovely tenor voice. Dr. Schofield each night used to sit in the gallery at D. L. Moody's meetings singing tenor in the choir, but felt the tenor was very weak. After much prayer he ventured to put the suggestion to Kilner that he come and help to sing the tenor part in his choir.

'Certainly, certainly,' he said; 'I'll come with pleasure if I can be of any help; and if it's not too difficult.'

So they arranged to meet on the following Tuesday night at 8 p.m. on Westminster Bridge. At the appointed hour Dr. Schofield found his friend waiting for him.

When they got to the Tabernacle, Dr. Schofield said, 'We turn in here.' 'Why, that is the place I was in to hear that American preacher,' he said. 'I'm not going in there; not if I know it,' said Kilner.

The doctor persuaded the barrister to accompany him inside, telling him he must come and sing like a bird.

The great building was crammed to the roof, and the doctor knew that somewhere in the building two women were sitting crying to God in their agony for their only son and brother. When the singing began, the neighbouring members of the choir all turned round at the sound of the magnificent tenor voice they thought Dr. Schofield had developed, but soon discovered it was his friend Kilner who sang magnificently, for nothing is more easy to divorce than the heart and the voice. As the choir was composed of born-again Christians, the doctor realised that technically he had no right whatever to introduce Kilner.

When the singing was over, Kilner naturally wanted to go. He was glad to have been of help but he had an appointment.

'Look here, Kilner,' said Dr. Schofield, 'I know all about that appointment. What you are really afraid of is the sermon. Well, you needn't be. The fact is, we've another piece coming on at the end, and I'd dearly like you to stay for that.'

'All right, old man,' he said, 'you've got me here and intend to keep me. Anyhow, I'll see you through.' And so he stayed, and Moody began.

Schofield was in agony as he listened to Moody preach what he considered an impossible and hopeless sermon that consisted of a purely imaginary conversation between John the Baptist and Herod the Great on the topics of the day. The plan of salvation and the work of Christ were all introduced, but Schofield wanted the direct Gospel message which none could deliver like Moody. At last the sermon came to an end, and then Kilner's fine tenor was heard once more, and the service was over.

'Come along now,' said Kilner, 'we'll have supper at my club.' Then, seeing a crowd, he whispered, 'Hallo, where are all those people going to?'

'Oh!' said Schofield, 'they're going to the after-meeting.'

'Are you going?' Kilner asked.

'Well, I was,' said the doctor. 'At any rate, if you don't mind, you go on, and I'll follow you in half-an-hour.'

But the barrister would have none of that. So they walked together into the crowded hall, and he took a front seat opposite to D. L. Moody. Away in a corner the doctor caught sight of the pale faces of Kilner's mother and sister.

Then the real Moody shone forth. 'Well,' said he, leaning his arms on his desk, 'you've heard all about it. Won't you come? Won't you come? We're here for business and want to know which of you will close with the offer of salvation, and take Jesus Christ for his Saviour. Don't be afraid; He is waiting for you. Now, what man has courage to rise and take the Lord Jesus as his Saviour?'

Up got Kilner, the first of any one, and walked across the room to the evangelist. He held out his hand, and said, 'I'll take Him, Mr. Moody.'

So the man of the world, who had said, 'The world is good enough for me,' was brought to know and serve the Lord Jesus Christ Who said, 'Ye are not of the world, even as I am not of the world.' The depth, reality and Divine power of the gospel were afterwards demonstrated for many years by the Christian life of the Society Clubman, George Kilner. Dr. A. T. Schofield never had any idea as to what actually caused the miracle of Kilner's conversion. 'The wind bloweth where it listeth.'

(John 3. 8; 17. 16; Eph. 2. 2)

1172. World—or the Word? A rich lord in England who was a friend of Royalty years ago was converted. He lost his taste at once for the pleasures of the Court and the high society into which his state brought him. He retired from it all, and in the country district where he had his residence used to gather to break bread with a very few humble folk.

He began to love his Bible, and soon found that his gardener who had been a believer for years knew much more about it than he. Often he would walk out of his large mansion and search for his gardener. On finding him he would tell him to put down his tools for an hour and bring his Bible, and there they would talk over the Scriptures, the lord asking the questions and finding great joy in the new treasures he had discovered in the Word as shown to him by the humble gardener. An hour spent like this was far sweeter to him than an invitation to court. In fact the society of the world became painful to him, while the fellowship of believers was very precious.

—A. L. Goold (India)

(Rom. 12. 2; 1 John 2. 15-17)

1173. World. If you go to the banks of a little stream and watch the flies that come and bathe in it, you will notice that, while they plunge their bodies, they keep their wings high out of the water and fly away with their wings unwet. Now, that is the lesson for us. Here we are, immersed in the cares and business of the world, but let us keep the wings of our faith and love out of the world so that, with these unclogged, we may be ready to take our flight to heaven.

—Charles Inglis

The Christian is not ruined by living in the world, but by the world living in him.

(John 17. 16-19; Gal. 6. 14; 1 John 2. 15-17)

1174. World. The world is like an ocean. In the world we are boats. A boat is only useful in the water: if the boat is in the water, it is useful. If the water is in the boat, it will sink beneath the waves. Therefore bale out the water.

—Sadhu Sundar Singh

(John 17. 16-18; Rom. 12. 2; James 4. 4)

1175. World. A greatly-used minister of the Word of God who had a wide and accurate knowledge of the Scriptures was approached, after one of his addresses, by one of his audience who said, 'I'd give the world to know the Scriptures as you know them.' His immediate reply was—'And that's just what it cost me—the world.'

(Gal. 1. 4; Phil. 3. 19, 20)

1176. Worm—Helpless. When William Carey was suffering from a dangerous illness, he was asked, 'If this illness should prove fatal, what would you select as the text for your funeral sermon?' He replied, 'Oh! I feel that such a poor sinful creature is unworthy to have anything said about him; but if a funeral sermon must be preached, preach from the words, "Have mercy upon me".' He directed in his will that his tombstone should be inscribed:

WILLIAM CAREY.

Born—August 17, 1761. Died—
A wretched, poor and helpless worm,
On Thy kind arms I fall.

Dr. Jowett wrote, 'Could anything be in greater contrast than a worm and an instrument with teeth. The worm is bruised by a stone, crushed beneath a passing wheel. An instrument with teeth can break and not be broken. And the mighty God can convert one into another. The mighty God can make us stronger than our circumstances.'

(Gen. 18. 27; Isa. 41. 14, 15)

1177. Worry.
Worry! Why worry? what can worry do?
It never keeps a trouble from overtaking you.
It gives you indigestion and woeful hours at night,
And fills with gloom the passing days, however
*   fair and bright.*
It puts a frown upon your face and sharpness in
*   your tone;*
You're unfit to live with others and unfit to live
*   alone.*
Worry! Why worry? what can worry do?
It never keeps a trouble from overtaking you.

Pray! Why pray? What can praying do?
Praying really changes things, arranges life anew.
It's good for digestion, gives peaceful hours at
*   night,*
And fills the grayest, gloomiest days with rays of
*   glowing light.*
It puts a smile upon your face, and the love-note
*   in your tone,*
Makes you fit to live with others and fit to live
*   alone.*
Pray! Why pray? What can praying do?
It brings God's love and power from Heaven to
*   live and work with you.*

Praise! Why praise? What does praising do?
Praise satisfies the heart of God and brings new
joy to you,
Provides a tonic for the soul, and keeps you
always bright
With memories of blessings sent, and joyful
songs at night.
And when there's 'Thank you' on your face, and
the praise-note's in your tone,
Folks all will want to live with you: you'll never
be alone.
Praise! Why praise? What does praising do?
Praise always says that God is good: experience
proves it true.
(Phil. 4. 6-7)

1178. Worry. 'Worry,' we are told, is from
an Anglo-Saxon word which means 'harm' and
is another form of the word 'wolf'. It is something harmful and bites and tears as a wolf
which mangles a sheep. There are times, no
doubt, when we must feel anxious because of
harm suffered or anticipated by ourselves or
others, and this may be beneficial because it
rouses to necessary activity; but often worry
has the opposite effect, paralyses us and unfits
us for duty, and also distracts our thoughts
and obscures our vision.

An old story tells of an angel who met a
man carrying a heavy sack and enquired what
was in it. 'My worries,' said the man. 'Let me
see them,' asked the angel. When the sack was
opened, it was empty. The man was astonished
and said he had two great worries. One was
of yesterday which he now saw was past; the
other of tomorrow which had not yet arrived.
The angel told him he needed no sack, and the
man gladly threw it away.

                  —*Workers Together*
(Matt. 6. 25, 34; 1 Pet. 5. 7)

1179. Worry.

  Said the Robin to the Sparrow,
    'I should really like to know
  Why these anxious human beings
    Rush about and worry so.'
  Said the Sparrow to the Robin,
    'Friend, I think that it must be
  That they have no Heavenly Father
    Such as cares for you and me.'

The Born-again Human's Reply to the Sparrow

I believe I have a Heavenly Father,
  I believe He knows just what I need;
I believe He's able to relieve me,
  I believe He listens when I plead.

I am sure His Word can never fail me,
  I am sure He means just what He says,
I am sure He'll carry out His promise,
  I am sure He'll guide me all my days.

I can trust Him though I cannot trace Him,
  I can trust Him even in the dark;
I can trust Him for He is my Pilot,
  I can trust Him with my little barque.

I will wait until He sends the answer,
  I will wait until He opes the door;
I will wait until He lifts the burden,
  I will wait upon Him evermore.

I do praise Him, for He is my Saviour,
  I do praise Him, for He is my Lord,
I do praise Him for His grace and favour,
  I do praise Him for His holy Word.
                  —E. C. Adams
(Matt. 6. 31-33)

1180. Worry.

Well, I am done, my nerves are on the rack:
  I've laid it down today:
It was the last straw broke the camel's back—
  I've laid that down today.
And I'll not fume, nor fret, nor fuss, nor fight:
  I'll walk by faith a bit and not by sight.
I think the universe will work all right—
  I've laid it down today.

So here and now, the overweight, the worry—
  I'll lay it down today.
The all-too-anxious heart, the tearing hurry—
  I'll lay it down today.
O eager hands! O feet so prone to run!
  I think that He Who made the stars and sun
Can mind the things you've had to leave undone:
  Do lay them down today!
(Ps. 44. 22; 1 Pet. 5. 7)

1181. Worry. Bishop Taylor Smith used to
write the following in his autograph books:
  The worried cow would have lived till now
    If she had saved her breath;
  But she feared her hay wouldn't last all day,
    And she mooed herself to death.
(Luke 12. 29-32)

1182. Worry.

When you see the lilies spinning in distress,
Taking thought to manufacture loveliness;
When you see the little birds build barns for store,
That's the time for you to worry, not before.
(Luke 12. 27, 28)

1183. Worship.

To give God the service of the body and
not of the soul—is Hypocrisy:
To give God the service of the soul and not
of the body—is Sacrilege:
To give God neither is Atheism:
To give God both is Worship.
(Ps. 29. 2; 96. 9)

1184. Worship. The word 'Worship' is an
Anglo-Saxon word, and means 'worthship' or
'worthiness'. The word commonly translated
'worship' in the New Testament—though there
are several other Greek words—is 'Proskuneo',
to kiss the hand toward. This is thought to be
derived from the slave's manner of salutation
and homage when he entered the presence of
his master, the act being a mark of reverence
and respect, and also implying affection.
Hence, in ascriptions of worship, we have the
expression—'Thou art worthy'.

During one of the Crusades, Philip Auguste, king of France, before he went into one of his battles, removed his royal crown from his head and, setting it on a table with the inscription 'Au plus digne' (to the most worthy), he made his oration, as was the custom of leaders in those days. He asked his nobles, knights and men to forget that he was their king and commander, and to consider that the crown which he had laid aside for the battle would be the prize of the one who carried himself most worthily and bravely and contributed most to their victory. They entered the battle and returned victorious. All gathered round the table on which the crown had been placed. One of the nobles, stepping forward, took in his hands the royal crown and, advancing toward the monarch, placed it on his head, saying—'Tu, O roi, es le plus digne' (Thou, O king, art the most worthy).

(Rev. 4. 4; 5. 9, 10, 12)

1185. Worship. A distinguished explorer spent a couple of years among savages of the Upper Amazon. He attempted a forced march through the jungle at an extraordinary speed. All went well for two days. On the third morning all the natives were sitting on their haunches looking very solemn. The Chief explained: 'They're waiting for their souls to catch up with their bodies.'

—James Truslow Adams

(Num. 8. 24; 1 Chron. 6. 32; John 4. 24)

1186. Worship. When Charles Lamb was discussing with some associates the persons they would like to have seen, he added, 'There is one other person. If Shakespeare was to come into this room we should all rise to meet him, but if that person was to enter, we should fall down and try to kiss the hem of His garment.' He alone is worthy of the soul's most reverent and submissive attitude. To see Him is to come to the greatest experience, to see the greatest hour, and feel the intensest passion that any life can experience.

—John Macbeath

(Rev. 1. 17; 5. 6-10)

1187. Worship. It is often very blessed around the Lord's table to have the mind and heart directed, through suitable teaching and exhortation, to the death and resurrection of the Lord Jesus, and also to the practical godliness that such grace lays claim to in the lives of the children of God; and surely it commends itself to the spiritual judgement of all that what of ministry precedes the 'breaking of bread' should be in the way of concentrating the attention upon the Lord Jesus Himself and His great redemptive work. Other teachings, useful and necessary in their own place, might at such a time be an intrusion and a positive hindrance to spiritual worship.

The saints ought indeed to be in fit condition to worship. But are they so? Do not many come and surround the Lord's table weary, careworn, burdened, vexed with wandering thoughts, finding themselves often incapable of rising above themselves and their circumstances.

—J. R. Caldwell

(John 4. 23; 1 Cor. 11. 26)

1188. Worship.
My God, how wonderful Thou art, Thy majesty
   how bright!
How beautiful Thy mercy-seat in depths of
   burning light!
How dread are Thine eternal years, O everlasting
   Lord!
By prostrate spirits, day and night, incessantly
   adored.

How wonderful, how beautiful the sight of Thee
   must be,
Thine endless wisdom, boundless power and
   awful purity!

O how I fear Thee, living God, with deepest,
   tenderest fears,
And worship Thee with trembling hope and
   penitential tears!

Yet I may love Thee too, O Lord, Almighty as
   Thou art,
For Thou hast stooped to ask of me the love of my
   poor heart.

No earthly father loves like Thee; no mother, e'er
   so mild,
Bears and forbears as Thou hast done with me,
   Thy sinful child.

—F. W. Faber

(Ps. 96. 9; John 4. 23-25)

1189. Worship—and Worshippers.
Night-watchmen, vigilant, devout—
   Successors in the Shepherd line
Of martyrs, prophets, kings—were out
   Among the hills of Palestine.
Amazed, they saw Heav'n's sons of flame,
   And sought and found th'Incarnate Lord,
And Shepherd-Chief, of fairest Name;
   They watched Him, worshipped and adored.

Aged Simeon, with inward sight
   Illumined, and with power endowed,
Held in his arms the One Whose might
   Upheld all things. 'Fore Him there bowed
The hearts of all that remnant-race
   That feared the Lord, and oft made tryst
With one another. Now in grace
   Their gladdened eyes beheld the Christ.

And from the sunny East were drawn
   The sages by His magnet-love.
And Joseph's home with treasure shone,
   And worship rose to God above.
Their gifts they joyfully unveiled:
   Pure, burnished gold of Ophir's kind,
While frankincense and myrrh exhaled
   And incense sweet—'twas LOVE enshrined.

—A. Soutter

(Matt. 2. 1-11; Luke 2. 8-16; 28)

1190. Worship.

We adore Thee, Sinless One!
For the battle fought and won,
For the thorn-crown on Thy brow,
For the crown Thou wearest now;

For the hands nailed to the tree,
Hands that opened Heaven for me:
Sacred feet pierced through for sin,
Side that let the red spear in.

We adore Thee for the blood
Sprinkled by the Throne of God,
Blood that bathed a crimson tide—
Brow and hands and feet and side.

Blood that o'er my sins doth flow,
Making me as white as snow,
Shed for me when Jesus died.
We adore Thee, Crucified!

(Rev. 1. 5, 6; 5. 9, 10)

1191. Worth—How much?

Supposing today were your last day on earth,
The last mile of the journey you've trod,
After all of your struggles, how much are you
worth?
How much could you take home to God?

Don't count as possessions your silver and gold,
For tomorrow you leave them behind.
And all that is yours to have and to hold
Are the blessings you've given to mankind.

Just what have you done as you've journeyed
along,
That was really and truly worth while?
Do you feel you've done good and returned it for
wrong?
Could you look o'er your life with a smile?

(Gal. 6. 9)

1192. Wrath of God.

In the days of ancient Greece, Dionysius I illustrated the lot of princes by seating Damocles, the flatterer, who had enviously praised his master's princely state, at a sumptuous banquet with a sword suspended by a single hair.

The man of the world without Christ may enjoy the pleasures of sin and the treasures of this world, but if he has not obeyed the Son of God, 'the wrath of God abideth on him'.

(John 3. 36)

1193. Writing—by the Spirit.

Dr. John Owen said to King Charles II, 'Your Majesty, if I could write as does that tinker—John Bunyan —in Bedford, I would gladly lay down all my learning.'

In prison, where he wrote his *Pilgrim's Progress*, John Bunyan had only a Bible and a Concordance, but the Holy Spirit guided his pen as he wrote.

(Jer. 36. 2, 4; Heb. 2. 2; Philem. 19)

1194. Writing on the Wall.

Belshazzar there in the kingly hall
Is holding royal festival.

The vassals sat in glittering line,
And emptied the goblets of glowing wine.

The yelling laughter was hushed, and all
Was still as death in the royal hall.

And see! and see! on the white wall high
The form of a hand went slowly by;

And wrote, and wrote, on the broad wall white,
Letters of fire, and vanished in night.

Pale as death, with a steady stare,
And with trembling knees, the king sat there;

The horde of slaves sat shuddering chill;
No word they spoke but were deathlike still.

The Magicians came, but of them all,
None could read the flame-script on the wall.

But that same night in all his pride,
By the hands of his servants Belshazzar died.
—Heinrich Heine, trans. by C. G. Leland

(Dan. 5)

1195. Writing on the Wall.

During the Second World War, one of the German leaders, Rudolf Hess, a close associate of Adolf Hitler, flew to Britain and landed in a field in Scotland where he was made captive. He said he had come on a visit to the Duke of Hamilton, his friend. Remarking on the incident at the time, Lord Halifax said, 'He saw the writing on the wall', using an illustration from the Bible.

(Dan. 5. 5, 24-28)

1196. Yielding to God.

'Why am I not happy?' inquired a wealthy lady as she stood beside the missionary, Dr. Goforth of China, in her home.

'Have you surrendered all?' enquired the man of God, quietly.

'Yes, as far as I know, I have surrendered all,' responded the woman.

'Are you sure?' insisted Dr. Goforth, 'that your all is on the altar?'

'My all is on the altar, I believe,' answered the woman again.

'And you are willing for God to take your little girl here and send her to China?' asked the missionary, placing his hand on her head.

'God take my daughter and make her a missionary in China! I should say not. I want her with me,' exclaimed the mother.

'And yet you tell me you have yielded all, and you haven't even given your own child to God. How can you expect God's blessing and peace and joy? You stand as it were between God and His will for your daughter, and you say to Him, "Thus far shalt Thou come and no farther. You can have my home; You can have my money; You can have me, but—don't touch my daughter." Madam do you call that surrender?'

(Mark 12. 44; Rom. 6. 13; 12. 1; Phil. 3. 8)

1197. Youth

I took a piece of plastic clay
And idly fashioned it one day,
And as my fingers pressed it still,
It moved and yielded to my will.

I came again when days were past,
The bit of clay was hard at last;
The form I gave it still it bore,
But I could change that form no more.

I took a piece of living clay
And gently formed it day by day,
And moulded with my power and art
A young child's soft and yielding heart.

I came again when years were gone:
It was a man I looked upon;
He still that early impress wore,
And I could change him nevermore.

(Exod. 2. 9; Prov. 22. 6)

1198. Youth. The story is told of the poet Coleridge who had listened to quite a vehement argument by a visitor against religious instruction of the young. His caller had concluded with the statement of his determination not to prejudice his children in any form of religion, but to allow them at maturity to choose for themselves. Coleridge made no immediate comment, but shortly afterwards asked this same visitor if he would like to see his garden. Receiving a reply in the affirmative, he led his guest to a strip of lawn overgrown with weeds.

'Why, this is no garden. It is nothing but a weed-patch,' said the guest.

'Oh,' replied Coleridge, 'that is because it has not come to its age of discretion. The weeds you see have taken the opportunity to grow and I thought it unfair in me to prejudice the soil toward roses and strawberries.'

(Prov. 22. 6)

1199. Youth and Salvation. It has been calculated that—

after 25 years of age, only one in 1,000 is saved:

after 35 years of age, only one in 50,000 is saved:

after 45 years of age, only one in 200,000 is saved:

after 55 years of age, only one in 300,000 is saved:

after 75 years of age, only one in 700,000 is saved.

Dr. Wilbur Chapman once tested a meeting in which 4,500 were present. The result was:

400 of those present were saved under 10:

600 were saved between 10 and 14:

600 were saved between 14 and 16:

1000 were saved between 16 and 20:

24 only were saved after 36.

The number of unsaved present was 1,875.

All this goes to prove the importance of reaching the youth of any country with the gospel message, with a view to leading them to Christ.

(Eccles. 12. 1; Acts 7. 58; 9. 11-18)

1200. Youth and Salvation. Sir James Falshaw, formerly Chairman of the North British Railway Company, a personal friend of Queen Victoria, a shrewd financier, and a most successful business man, was asked, during the progress of a banquet given in his honour when he was eighty years of age, 'In the interests of the young men present, who are anxious to make the most of life, I wish to ask one question, Sir James. Is there anything in your life, any one factor, upon which you can lay your finger as the secret of your wonderful prosperity.'

The old man rose up, straight as a dart, and said, 'I can answer that question without much difficulty. Whatever prosperity, success and honour have attended my life, I attribute to the fact that when I was fifteen years of age, I gave my heart to God.'

(Eccles. 12. 1; Prov. 23. 26)

GENERAL INDEX

	Item
Happiness	519, 520, 521, 522, 523, 756
Harmony	524
Heart	525, 526
Heaven	527, 528, 529, 530, 531, 532, 547, 548, 751
„ Bliss of	108
„ Entrance to	110, 111
„ Home in	533, 534, 535
„ No Disappointment in	536
Hell	537, 538, 539
Help—in time of need	540
Hereafter	277, 278, 279, 280, 281
Hiding—place	541
High Priest	1055
„ Aaron and Christ	543, 544
„ Girdle of	449
„ Robes of	961
Hitherto—Henceforth	542
Holiness—of God	545
Holy Spirit	438, 439, 510, 511, 1034
Holy things	578
Home	546
„ Heavenly	533, 534, 535, 547, 548
Honesty	549
Hope—Coming of Christ	184
„ Purchase of	550
Horses	1125
Hosts—Lord of	623
Humility	551, 552, 553, 554, 555, 556, 557
Hymns	558
„ Writing of	747, 821, 937, 963, 1005

I

Idols	62
Illumination	559
Illustrations	560, 561
Image—Broken	562
„ the Lost	563
„ Nebuchadnezzar's	564
Imagination	565
Immanuel's Land	566
Immutability	1111, 1112
Imprecations	912
Impressions	567
Incarnation	569, 570, 571
Indifference	572
Infallibility	1113
Infidelity	573, 574
Infirmities	575
Influence	576
„ Spiritual	577
Iniquity—of the Holy things	578
Inside	568
Inspiration	579
Invitation	580, 581 582,
Iron—Man of	55
„ Nails of	583
Israel	584, 585
„ Guidance of	507
Ittai	586

J

	Item
Jacob	587
Jehovah	588
„ His People's Keeper	617
Jeremiah	600
Jesus—Love of	690, 691
„ Name of	771, 772, 773
Jews	589, 590, 591, 592, 593
„ their History	594
„ their Months	595
Job—Book of	596
John—the Apostle	597
Joined—to the Lord	598
Jordan	599
„ the Swellings of	600
Joseph—God's purpose for	601
Josephus	21, 152, 153
Joy—the Christian's	602, 603
„ in Presence of the Angels	604
Judas Iscariot	1082, 1083
Judge	14, 605
Judgement	606, 607, 608, 609, 610
Julius Caesar	33
Justice	611, 612
Justification	613, 614
Justified	615, 616

K

Keeper—Jehovah His People's	617
Kindness	176, 618
King—Christ the	619
„ Crowned with Thorns	620
„ Earthly and Heavenly	621
„ Eternal	622
„ Lord of Hosts	623
„ Love for the	624
„ Voice of the	625
„ and the King of Kings	626
Kings—Death of	285
Kingdom—Christ's	627, 628, 629
Kinsman—Christ our	630, 631
Kiss—Told in a Cross	632
Kneeling	633
Knowledge	634
„ of Bible	79, 80 ,81
„ of God	635, 636
„ of the Good Shepherd	637
„ of the Way of Salvation	638
Knox—John	348, 1020

L

Lamb of God	639
Laughter	640
Law	650
Laziness	641
Leading—the Lord's	642
Leaning—on the Lord	643, 644
Leaves—Nothing but	645
Leaving—All with Jesus	646
Lending—to the Lord	647
Leonardo da Vinci	157
Letter—writing	648
Liberality	451, 452, 453, 454, 455, 456, 457, 458, 459,
Liberty	649
„ or Licence	650
Licence—or Liberty	650

INDEX OF TEXTS

226